ORGANI ~~ZATIONAL~~
BEHAVIOR
READINGS AND EXERCISES

McGraw-Hill Series in Management

Fred Luthans and Keith Davis, *Consulting Editors*

ORGANIZATIONAL BEHAVIOR

READINGS AND EXERCISES

SEVENTH EDITION

Keith Davis, Ph.D.
Arizona State University

John W. Newstrom, Ph.D.
University of Minnesota, Duluth

McGRAW-HILL BOOK COMPANY
New York St. Louis San Francisco Auckland Bogotá
Hamburg Johannesburg London Madrid Mexico Montreal New Delhi
Panama Paris São Paulo Singapore Sydney Tokyo Toronto

This book was set in Times Roman by The Saybrook Press.
The editors were John R. Meyer and Joseph F. Murphy;
The production supervisor was Marietta Breitwieser.
The cover was designed by Robin Hessel.
New drawings were done by Fine Line Illustrations, Inc.
Halliday Lithograph Corporation was printer and binder.

ORGANIZATIONAL BEHAVIOR
Readings and Exercises

1 2 3 4 5 6 7 8 9 0 HALHAL 8 9 8 7 6 5 4

ISBN 0-07-015508-9

Library of Congress Cataloging in Publication Data
Main entry under title:

Organizational behavior.

(McGraw-Hill series in management)
Accompanies Human behavior at work / Keith Davis,
John W. Newstrom.
Includes bibliographies and indexes.
1. Organizational behavior. 2. Personnel management.
3. Industrial sociology. I. Davis, Keith, date
II. Newstrom, John W. III. Davis, Keith, date
Human Behavior at work. IV. Series.
HD58.7.07135   1985   658.3   84-17139
ISBN 0-07-015508-9

42,117

ABOUT THE AUTHORS

KEITH DAVIS is Professor Emeritus of Management at Arizona State University, College of Business Administration. He is the author of prominent books on management and a consulting editor for approximately eighty books in the McGraw-Hill Book Company's Series in Management. He is a fellow in both the Academy of Management and the International Academy of Management. Prior to entering the teaching field he was a personnel specialist in industry and a personnel manager in government.

Professor Davis received his Ph.D. from Ohio State University and has taught at the University of Texas and Indiana University. His fields of work are organizational behavior, personnel management, and social issues in management. He has been visiting professor at a number of universities, including the University of Western Australia and the University of Central Florida. He also has served as consultant to a number of organizations, including Mobil Oil Company, Texaco, the U.S. Internal Revenue Service, and the State of Hawaii.

Professor Davis is a former president of the Academy of Management, and he received the National Human Relations Award from the Society for Advancement of Management. He also has been a National Beta Gamma Sigma Distinguished Scholar. He is an Accredited Senior Professional in Human Resources in the American Society for Personnel Administration.

Two other popular books by Professor Davis are (with William B. Werther) *Personnel Management and Human Resources* (2d ed., 1985) and (with William C. Frederick) *Business and Society* (5th ed., 1984), both published by McGraw-Hill Book Company. He also has contributed chapters to over 100 other books, and he is the author of over 150 articles in journals such as *Harvard Business Review, Academy of Management Journal, Management International*, and *California Management Review*. Four of his books have been translated into other languages.

JOHN W. NEWSTROM is Professor of Management and Industrial Relations in the School of Business and Economics at the University of Minnesota, Duluth. He previously taught at Arizona State University after receiving his Ph.D. from the University of Minnesota. His fields of interest are management development, performance appraisal, alternative work schedules, management by objectives, and group dynamics.

Professor Newstrom is a former chairperson of the Management Education and Development Division of the Academy of Management, and is on the board of directors of the American Society for Training and Development. He has served on the editorial review boards of the *Academy of Management Review, Academy of Management Journal, Journal of Management Development,* and *Personnel Administrator.* He also has been a training consultant to numerous organizations, including the Bureau of Indian Affairs, Blandin Paper Company, Diamond Tool, and Minnesota Power.

Professor Newstrom is the coauthor (with Keith Davis) of *Organizational Behavior: Human Behavior at Work* (7th ed., 1985) and (with Edward E. Scannell) of *More Games Trainers Play* (1983). He also has prepared two other books published by McGraw-Hill Book Company, and is the author of over fifty articles in journals such as *Personnel Psychology, Journal of Management, Journal of Occupational Behaviour,* and *Academy of Management Journal.*

This book is dedicated,
with deep appreciation, to
Sue Davis
and
Diane, Scott, and Heidi Newstrom

CONTENTS

PREFACE

One of the greatest challenges to be faced during the remainder of this century is to use our resources productively. To meet this challenge, society must find ways to increase the effective use of its human resources in work organizations. This book can assist with that task. The text is designed to provide an overview of key topics for university courses such as organizational behavior, behavior in organizations, human relations, organizational psychology, or behavioral science for managers. It also may be used in business to stimulate discussion about the human element in organizations. This seventh edition of the book is fine-tuned from twenty-six years of classroom use in its former editions, so it should be helpful to student learning and be "user-friendly."

OBJECTIVE

The objective of this book is to present a comprehensive sampling of organizational behavior ideas that have their roots in various social science and behavioral science disciplines. Articles cover conceptual frameworks, research studies, and reports of ideas in action. Frameworks are necessary to intelligently observe, analyze, and compare behavior in organizations. Research studies represent the prime vehicle for advancing the state of the art. Applications also are essential because they are the critical test of effective organizational behavior.

Complete articles are included in most instances to provide the full scope of the author's ideas. In other cases, part of an article is sufficient to provide the flavor of the paper. (For these excerpts, three asterisks are used before, within, or after an article to indicate that other material has been deleted.) In every case, the entire reference has been shown so interested readers may explore the complete material if they wish.

SOURCES USED

Both classical authors of distinction and current writers are represented in the selections in this book. Their articles have been carefully selected from over thirty leading journals and other sources (see the Contents) to include conflicting viewpoints, established as well as newer concepts, and reports of both successes and failures. Collectively, they provide a fair portrait of the complex field of organizational behavior. Although readability was an important factor in the selection of articles, different levels of sophistication are represented throughout the book to provide an intellectual challenge to interested readers. To guide and stimulate the reader's response to each article, one or more discussion questions follow each item.

READINGS

The book is divided into two parts. The first part contains a set of seventy-two readings organized into twenty-one chapters. These topics reflect current subjects covered in organizational behavior textbooks, and the structure complements the plan followed in our basic textbook, *Human Behavior at Work: Organizational Behavior,* 7th ed. (New York: McGraw-Hill Book Company, 1985). New chapters in this edition of the readings and exercises book include Chapter 5 (Job Satisfaction and Organizational Variables), Chapter 7 (Power and Politics), Chapter 18 (Labor Relations and Conflict Resolution), and Chapter 20 (International Issues). Many contemporary topics such as socialization, mentoring, attributions, robotics, burnout, and Theory Z are introduced in this edition, which has approximately 75 percent new selections.

EXERCISES

The second part of the book contains a set of fourteen experiential exercises to help students learn behavioral ideas from classroom experiences. These classroom-tested activities typically give readers an opportunity to record some personal data, share the results with other group members, and then reflect on both the knowledge gained and their reaction to the experience. Consequently, these exercises create an active learning process that supplements the intellectual ideas gained from the readings. Each exercise is cross-referenced to the relevant chapters.

We are especially grateful for the cooperation of the authors and publishers who granted permission to use their materials. Our appreciation goes to the reviewers whose input helped shape this edition, and to the supportive staff at McGraw-Hill, including Kathi Benson, John Meyer, and Joe Murphy, who provided editorial guidance. We give special thanks to colleagues such as Jon Pierce and Steve Rubenfeld who provided their support and encouragement for the project. Finally, we wish to note that William G. Scott of the University of Washington was an editor of the first three editions of this book.

Keith Davis
John W. Newstrom

READINGS

CHAPTER 1

ORGANIZATIONAL BEHAVIOR FRAMEWORKS

READING 1

Evolving Models of Organizational Behavior

Keith Davis*

The affluent society of which John Kenneth Galbraith wrote some years ago has become even more affluent.[1] There are many reasons for this sustained improvement in productivity, and some of them are advancing technology, available resources, improved education, and a favorable economic and social system. There is, however, another reason of key significance to all of us. That reason is management, specifically the capacity of managers to develop organizational systems which respond productively to the changing conditions of society. In recent years this has meant more complex administrative systems in order to challenge and motivate employees toward better teamwork. Improvement has been made by working smarter, not harder. An increasingly sophisticated knowledge of human behavior is required; consequently, theoretical models of organizational behavior have had to grow to absorb this new knowledge. It is these evolving models of organizational behavior which I wish to discuss; then I shall draw some conclusions about their use.

The significant point about models of organizational behavior is that the model which a manager holds normally determines his perception of the organizational world about him. It leads to certain assumptions about people and certain interpretations of events he encounters. The underlying model serves as an unconscious guide to each manager's behavior. He acts as he thinks. Since his acts do affect the quality of human relations and productivity in his department, he needs to be fully aware of the trends that are occurring. If he holds to an outmoded model, his success will be limited and his job will be harder, because he will not be able to work with his people as he should.

Similarly, the model of organizational behavior which predominates among the management of an organization will affect the success of that whole organization. And at a national level the model which prevails within a country will influence the productivity and economic development of that nation. Models of organizational behavior are a significant variable in the life of all groups.

Many models of organizational behavior have appeared during the last 100 years, and four of them are significant and different enough to merit further discussion. These are the autocratic, custodial, supportive, and collegial models. In the order mentioned, the four models represent a historical evolution of management thought. The autocratic model predominated 75 years ago. In the 1920s and 1930s it yielded ground to the more successful custodial model. In this

---

*From *Academy of Management Journal,* March, 1968, pp. 27–38. Copyright 1967. Reprinted with permission.
[1]John Kenneth Galbraith, *The Affluent Society* (Boston, Mass.: Houghton Mifflin, 1958).

generation the supportive model is gaining approval. It predominates in many organizations, although the custodial model probably still prevails in the whole society. Meanwhile, a number of advanced organizations are experimenting with the collegial model.

The four models are not distinct in the sense that a manager or a firm uses one and only one of them. In a week—or even a day—a manager probably applies some of all four models. On the other hand, one model tends to predominate as his habitual way of working with his people, in such a way that it leads to a particular type of teamwork and behavioral climate among his group. Similarly, one model tends to dominate the life of a whole organization, but different parts therein may still be pursuing other models. The production department may take a custodial approach, while supportive ideas are being tried in the office, and collegial ideas are practiced in the research department. The point is that one model of organizational behavior is not an adequate label to describe all that happens in an organization, but it is a convenient way to distinguish one prevailing way of life from another. By comparing these four models, we can recognize certain important distinctions among them.

THE AUTOCRATIC MODEL

The autocratic model has its roots deep in history, and certainly it became the prevailing model early in the industrial revolution. As shown in Figure 1, this model depends on power. Those who are in command must have the power to demand, "You do this—or else," meaning that an employee will be penalized if he does not follow orders. This model takes a threatening approach, depending on negative motivation backed by power.

In an autocratic environment the managerial orientation is formal, official authority. Authority is the tool with which management works and the context in which it thinks, because it is the organizational means by which power is applied. This authority is delegated by right of command over the people to whom it applies. In this model, management implicitly assumes that it knows what is best and that it is the employee's obligation to follow orders without question or interpretation. Management assumes that employees are passive and even resistant to organizational needs. They have to be persuaded and pushed into performance, and this is management's task. Management does the thinking; the employees obey the orders. This is the "Theory X" popularized by Douglas McGregor as the conventional view of management.[2] It has its roots in history and was made explicit by Frederick W. Taylor's concepts of scientific management. Though Taylor's writings show that he had worker interests at heart, he saw those interests served best by a manager who scientifically determined what a worker

---

[2]Douglas McGregor, "The Human Side of Enterprise," in *Proceedings of the Fifth Anniversary Convocation of the School of Industrial Management* (Cambridge, Mass.: Massachusetts Institute of Technology, April 9, 1957). Theory X and Theory Y were later popularized in Douglas McGregor, *The Human Side of Enterprise* (New York: McGraw-Hill, 1960).

FIGURE 1
FOUR MODELS OF ORGANIZATIONAL BEHAVIOR

	Autocratic	Custodial	Supportive	Collegial
Depends on:	Power	Economic resources	Leadership	Mutual contribution
Managerial orientation:	Authority	Material rewards	Support	Integration and teamwork
Employee orientation:	Obedience	Security	Performance	Responsibility
Employee psychological result:	Personal dependency	Organizational dependency	Participation	Self-discipline
Employee needs met:	Subsistence	Maintenance	Higher-order	Self-realization
Performance result:	Minimum	Passive cooperation	Awakened drives	Enthusiasm
Morale measure:	Compliance	Satisfaction	Motivation	Commitment to task and team

Source: Adapted from Keith Davis, *Human Relations at Work: The Dynamics of Organizational Behavior* (3rd ed.; New York: McGraw-Hill, 1967), p. 480.

should do and then saw that he did it. The worker's role was to perform as he was ordered.

Under autocratic conditions an employee's orientation is obedience. He bends to the authority of a boss—not a manager. This role causes a psychological result which in this case is employee personal dependency on his boss whose power to hire, fire, and "perspire" him is almost absolute. The boss pays relatively low wages because he gets relatively less performance from the employee. Each employee must provide subsistence needs for himself and his family; so he reluctantly gives minimum performance, but he is not motivated to give much more than that. A few men give higher performance because of internal achievement drives, because they personally like their boss, because the boss is a "natural-born leader," or because of some other fortuitous reason; but most men give only minimum performance.

When an autocratic model of organizational behavior exists, the measure of an employee's morale is usually his compliance with rules and orders. Compliance is unprotesting assent without enthusiasm. The compliant employee takes his orders and does not talk back.

Although modern observers have an inherent tendency to condemn the autocratic model of organizational behavior, it is a useful way to accomplish work. It has been successfully applied by the empire builders of the 1800s, efficiency engineers, scientific managers, factory foremen, and others. It helped to build great railroad systems, operate giant steel mills, and produce a dynamic industrial civilization in the early 1900s.

Actually the autocratic model exists in all shades of gray, rather than the extreme black usually presented. It has been a reasonably effective way of management when there is a "benevolent autocrat" who has a genuine interest in his employees and when the role expectation of employees is autocratic leadership.[3] But these results are usually only moderate ones lacking the full potential that is available, and they are reached at considerable human costs. In addition, as explained earlier, conditions change to require new behavioral models in order to remain effective.

As managers and academicians became familiar with limitations of the autocratic model, they began to ask, "Is there a better way? Now that we have brought organizational conditions this far along, can we build on what we have in order to move one step higher on the ladder of progress?" Note that their thought was not to throw out power as undesirable, because power is needed to maintain internal unity in organizations. Rather, their thought was to build upon the foundation which existed: "Is there a better way?"

THE CUSTODIAL MODEL

Managers soon recognized that although a compliant employee did not talk back to his boss, he certainly "thought back!" There were many things he wanted to say to his boss, and sometimes he did say them when he quit or lost his temper. The employee inside was a seething mass of insecurity, frustrations, and aggressions toward his boss. Since he could not vent these feelings directly, sometimes he went home and vented them on his wife, family, and neighbors; so the community did not gain much out of this relationship either.

It seemed rather obvious to progressive employers that there ought to be some way to develop employee satisfactions and adjustment during production—and in fact this approach just might cause more productivity! If the employee's insecurities, frustrations, and aggressions could be dispelled, he might feel more like working. At any rate the employer could sleep better, because his conscience would be clearer.

Development of the custodial model was aided by psychologists, industrial relations specialists, and economists. Psychologists were interested in employee satisfaction and adjustment. They felt that a satisfied employee would be a better employee, and the feeling was so strong that "a happy employee" became a mild obsession in some personnel offices. The industrial relations specialists and economists favored the custodial model as a means of building employee security and stability in employment. They gave strong support to a variety of fringe benefits and group plans for security.

The custodial model originally developed in the form of employee welfare programs offered by a few progressive employers, and in its worst form it became known as employer paternalism. During the depression of the 1930s emphasis changed to economic and social security and then shortly moved toward various labor plans for security and control. During and after World War II, the main

---

[3]This viewpoint is competently presented in R. N. McMurry. "The Case for Benevolent Autocracy." *Harvard Business Review* (Jan.–Feb., 1958), pp. 82–90.

focus was on specific fringe benefits. Employers, labor unions, and government developed elaborate programs for overseeing the needs of workers.

A successful custodial approach depends on economic resources, as shown in Figure 1. An organization must have economic wealth to provide economic security, pensions, and other fringe benefits. The resulting managerial orientation is toward economic or material rewards, which are designed to make employees respond as economic men. A reciprocal employee orientation tends to develop emphasizing security.

The custodial approach gradually leads to an organizational dependency by the employee. Rather than being dependent on his boss for his weekly bread, he now depends on large organizations for his security and welfare. Perhaps more accurately stated, an organizational dependency is added atop a reduced personal dependency on his boss. This approach effectively serves an employee's maintenance needs, as presented in Herzberg's motivation-maintenance model, but it does not strongly motivate an employee.[4] The result is a passive cooperation by the employee. He is pleased to have his security; but as he grows psychologically, he also seeks more challenge and autonomy.

The natural measure of morale which developed from a custodial model was employee satisfaction. If the employee was happy, contented, and adjusted to the group, then all was well. The happiness-oriented morale survey became a popular measure of success in many organizations.

Limitations of the Custodial Model

Since the custodial model is the one which most employers are currently moving away from, its limitations will be further examined. As with the autocratic model, the custodial model exists in various shades of gray, which means that some practices are more successful than others. In most cases, however, it becomes obvious to all concerned that most employees under custodial conditions do not produce anywhere near their capacities, nor are they motivated to grow to the greater capacities of which they are capable. Though employees may be happy, most of them really do not feel fulfilled or self-actualized.

The custodial model emphasizes economic resources and the security those resources will buy, rather than emphasizing employee performance. The employee becomes psychologically preoccupied with maintaining his security and benefits, rather than with production. As a result, he does not produce much more vigorously than under the old autocratic approach. Security and contentment are necessary for a person, but they are not themselves very strong motivators.

In addition, the fringe benefits and other devices of the custodial model are mostly off-the-job. They are not directly connected with performance. The employee has to be too sick to work or too old to work in order to receive these benefits. The system becomes one of public and private paternalism in which an

[4]Frederick Herzberg, Bernard Mausner, and Barbara Snyderman, *The Motivation to Work* (New York: John Wiley and Sons, 1959).

employee sees little connection between his rewards and his job performance and personal growth; hence he is not motivated toward performance and growth. In fact, an overzealous effort to make the worker secure and happy leads to a brand of psychological paternalism no better than earlier economic paternalism. With the psychological variety, employee needs are dispensed from the personnel department, union hall, and government bureau, rather than the company store. but in either case dependency remains, and as Ray E. Brown observes, "Men grow stronger on workouts than on handouts. It is in the nature of people to wrestle with a challenge and rest on a crutch. . . . The great desire of man is to stand on his own, and his life is one great fight against dependency. Making the individual a ward of the organization will likely make him bitter instead of better."[5]

As viewed by William H. Whyte, the employee working under custodialism becomes an "organization man" who belongs to the organization and who has "left home, spiritually as well as physically, to take the vows of organizational life."[6]

As knowledge of human behavior advanced, deficiencies in the custodial model became quite evident, and people again started to ask, "Is there a better way?" The search for a better way is not a condemnation of the custodial model as a whole; however, it is a condemnation of the assumption that custodialism is "the final answer"—the one best way to work with people in organizations. An error in reasoning occurs when a person perceives that the custodial model is so desirable that there is no need to move beyond it to something better.

THE SUPPORTIVE MODEL

The supportive model of organizational behavior has gained currency during recent years as a result of a great deal of behavioral science research as well as favorable employer experience with it. The supportive model establishes a manager in the primary role of psychological support of his employees at work, rather than in a primary role of economic support (as in the custodial model) or "power over" (as in the autocratic model). A supportive approach was first suggested in the classical experiments of Mayo and Roethlisberger at Western Electric Company in the 1930s and 1940s. They showed that a small work group is more productive and satisfied when its members perceive that they are working in a supportive environment. This interpretation was expanded by the work of Edwin A. Fleishman with supervisory "consideration" in the 1940s[7] and that of Rensis Likert and his associates with the "employee-oriented supervisor" in the 1940s and 1950s.[8] In fact, the *coup de grace* to the custodial model's dominance was

---

[5]Ray E. Brown, *Judgment in Administration* (New York: McGraw-Hill, 1966), p. 75.
[6]William H. Whyte, Jr., *The Organization Man* (New York: Simon and Schuster, 1956), p. 3.
[7]An early report of this research is Edwin A. Fleishman, *"Leadership Climate" and Supervisory Behavior* (Columbus, Ohio: Personnel Research Board, Ohio State University, 1951).
[8]There have been many publications by the Likert group at the Survey Research Center, University of Michigan. An early basic one is Daniel Katz et al., *Productivity, Supervision and Morale in an Office Situation* (Ann Arbor, Mich.: The University of Michigan Press, 1950).

administered by Likert's research which showed that the happy employee is not necessarily the most productive employee.

Likert has expressed the supportive model as the "principle of supportive relationships" in the following words: *"The leadership and other processes of the organization must be such as to ensure a maximum probability that in all interactions and all relationships with the organization each member will, in the light of his background, values, and expectations, view the experience as supportive and one which builds and maintains his sense of personal worth and importance."*[9]

The supportive model, shown in Figure 1, depends on leadership instead of power or economic resources. Through leadership, management provides a behavioral climate to help each employee grow and accomplish in the interests of the organization the things of which he is capable. The leader assumes that workers are not by nature passive and resistant to organizational needs, but that they are made so by an inadequate supportive climate at work. They will take responsibility, develop a drive to contribute, and improve themselves, if management will give them half a chance. Management's orientation, therefore, is to support the employee's performance.

Since performance is supported, the employee's orientation is toward it instead of mere obedience and security. He is responding to intrinsic motivations in his job situation. His psychological result is a feeling of participation and task involvement in the organization. When referring to his organization, he may occasionally say "we," instead of always saying "they." Since his higher-order needs are better challenged, he works with more awakened drives than he did under earlier models.

The difference between custodial and supportive models is illustrated by the fact that the morale measure of supportive management is the employee's level of motivation. This measure is significantly different from the satisfaction and happiness emphasized by the custodial model. An employee who has a supportive leader is motivated to work toward organizational objectives as a means of achieving his own goals. This approach is similar to McGregor's popular "Theory Y."

The supportive model is just as applicable to the climate for managers as for operating employees. One study reports that supportive managers usually led to high motivation among their subordinate managers. Among those managers who were low in motivation, only 8 per cent had supportive managers. Their managers were mostly autocratic.[10]

It is not essential for managers to accept every assumption of the supportive model in order to move toward it, because as more is learned about it, views will change. What is essential is that modern managers in business, unions, and government do not become locked into the custodial model. They need to abandon any view that the custodial model is the final answer, so that they will be

---

[9]Rensis Likert, *New Patterns of Management* (New York: McGraw-Hill, 1961), pp. 102–103. (Italics in original.)

[10]M. Scott Myers, "Conditions for Manager Motivation," *Harvard Business Review* (Jan.–Feb., 1966), p. 61. This study covered 1,344 managers at Texas Instruments, Inc.

free to look ahead to improvements which are fitting to their organization in their environment.

The supportive model is only one step upward on the ladder of progress. Though it is just now coming into dominance, some firms which have the proper conditions and managerial competence are already using a collegial model of organizational behavior, which offers further opportunities for improvement.

THE COLLEGIAL MODEL

The collegial model is still evolving, but it is beginning to take shape. It has developed from recent behavioral science research, particularly that of Likert, Katz, Kahn, and others at the University of Michigan,[11] Herzberg with regard to maintenance and motivational factors,[12] and the work of a number of people in project management and matrix organization.[13] The collegial model readily adapts to the flexible, intellectual environment of scientific and professional organizations. Working in substantially unprogrammed activities which require effective teamwork, scientific and professional employees desire the autonomy which a collegial model permits, and they respond to it well.

The collegial model depends on management's building a feeling of mutual contribution among participants in the organization, as shown in Figure 1. Each employee feels that he is contributing something worthwhile and is needed and wanted. He feels that management and others are similarly contributing, so he accepts and respects their roles in the organization. Managers are seen as joint contributors rather than bosses.

The managerial orientation is toward teamwork which will provide an integration of all contributions. Management is more of an integrating power than a commanding power. The employee response to this situation is responsibility. He produces quality work not primarily because management tells him to do so or because the inspector will catch him if he does not, but because he feels inside himself the desire to do so for many reasons. The employee psychological result, therefore, is self-discipline. Feeling responsible, the employee disciplines himself for team performance in the same way that a football team member disciplines himself in training and in game performance.

In this kind of environment an employee normally should feel some degree of fulfillment and self-realization, although the amount will be modest in some situations. The result is job enthusiasm, because he finds in the job such Herzberg motivators as achievement, growth, intrinsic work fulfillment, and recognition. His morale will be measured by his commitment to his task and his team, because he will see these as instruments for his self-actualization.

---

[11]Likert describes a similar model as System 4 in Rensis Likert, *The Human Organization: Its Management and Value* (New York: McGraw-Hill, 1967), pp. 3–11.

[12]Herzberg *et al., op. cit.*

[13]For example, see Keith Davis, "Mutuality in Understanding of the Program Manager's Management Role," *IEEE Transactions on Engineering Management* (Dec. 1965), pp. 117–122.

SOME CONCLUSIONS ABOUT MODELS
OF ORGANIZATIONAL BEHAVIOR

The evolving nature of models of organizational behavior makes it evident that change is the normal condition of these models. As our understanding of human behavior increases or as new social conditions develop, our organizational behavior models are also likely to change. It is a grave mistake to assume that one particular model is a "best" model which will endure for the long run. This mistake was made by some old-time managers about the autocratic model and by some humanists about the custodial model, with the result that they became psychologically locked into these models and had difficulty altering their practices when conditions demanded it. Eventually the supportive model may also fall to limited use; and as further progress is made, even the collegial model is likely to be surpassed. There is no permanently "one best model" of organizational behavior, because what is best depends upon what is known about human behavior in whatever environment and priority of objectives exist at a particular time.

A second conclusion is that the models of organizational behavior which have developed seem to be sequentially related to man's psychological hierarchy of needs. As society has climbed higher on the need hierarchy, new models of organizational behavior have been developed to serve the higher-order needs that became paramount at the time. If Maslow's need hierarchy is used for comparison, the custodial model of organizational behavior is seen as an effort to serve man's second-level security needs.[14] It moved one step above the autocratic model which was reasonably serving man's subsistence needs, but was not effectively meeting his needs for security. Similarly the supportive model is an effort to meet employees' higher-level needs, such as affiliation and esteem, which the custodial model was unable to serve. The collegial model moves even higher toward service of man's need for self-actualization.

A number of persons have assumed that emphasis on one model of organizational behavior was an automatic rejection of other models, but the comparison with man's need hierarchy *suggests that each model is built upon the accomplishments of the other.* For example, adoption of a supportive approach does not mean abandonment of custodial practices which serve necessary employee security needs. What it does mean is that custodial practices are relegated to secondary emphasis, because employees have progressed up their need structure to a condition in which higher needs predominate. In other words, the supportive model is the appropriate model to use *because* subsistence and security needs are already reasonably met by a suitable power structure and security system. If a misdirected modern manager should abandon these basic organizational needs, the system would quickly revert to a quest for a workable power structure and security system in order to provide subsistence-maintenance needs for its people.

Each model of organizational behavior in a sense outmodes its predominance by gradually satisfying certain needs, thus opening up other needs which can be better served by a more advanced model. Thus each new model is built upon the

---

[14]A. H. Maslow, "A Theory of Human Motivation," *Psychological Review* (L, 1943), 370–396.

success of its predecessor. The new model simply represents a more sophisticated way of maintaining earlier need satisfactions, while opening up the probability of satisfying still higher needs.

A third conclusion suggests that the present tendency toward more democratic models of organizational behavior will continue for the longer run. This tendency seems to be required by both the nature of technology and the nature of the need structure. Harbison and Myers, in a classical study of management throughout the industrial world, conclude that advancing industrialization leads to more advanced models of organizational behavior. Specifically, authoritarian management gives way to more constitutional and democratic-participative models of management. These developments are inherent in the system; that is, the more democratic models tend to be necessary in order to manage productively an advanced industrial system.[15] Slater and Bennis also conclude that more participative and democratic models of organizational behavior inherently develop with advancing industrialization. They believe that "democracy is inevitable," because it is the only system which can successfully cope with changing demands of contemporary civilization in both business and government.[16]

Both sets of authors accurately point out that in modern, complex organizations a top manager cannot be authoritarian in the traditional sense and remain efficient, because he cannot know all that is happening in his organization. He must depend on other centers of power nearer to operating problems. In addition, educated workers are not readily motivated toward creative and intellectual duties by traditional authoritarian orders. They require high-order need satisfactions which newer models of organizational behavior provide. Thus there does appear to be some inherent necessity for more democratic forms of organization in advanced industrial systems.

A fourth and final conclusion is that, though one model may predominate as most appropriate for general use at any point in industrial history, some appropriate uses will remain for other models. Knowledge of human behavior and skills in applying that knowledge will vary among managers. Role expectations of employees will differ depending upon cultural history. Policies on ways of life will vary among organizations. Perhaps more important, task conditions will vary. Some jobs may require routine, low-skilled, highly programmed work which will be mostly determined by higher authority and provide mostly material rewards and security (autocratic and custodial conditions). Other jobs will be unprogrammed and intellectual, requiring teamwork and self-motivation, and responding best to supportive and collegial conditions. This use of different management practices with people according to the task they are performing is called "management according to task" by Leavitt.[17]

---

[15]Frederick Harbison and Charles A. Myers, *Management in the Industrial World: An International Analysis* (New York: McGraw-Hill, 1959), pp. 40–67. The authors also state on page 47, "The design of systems of authority is equally as important in the modern world as the development of technology."

[16]Philip E. Slater and Warren G. Bennis, "Democracy Is Inevitable," *Harvard Business Review* (March–April, 1964), pp. 51–59.

[17]Harold J. Leavitt, "Management According to Task: Organizational Differentiation," *Management International* (1962), No. 1, pp. 13–22.

In the final analysis, each manager's behavior will be determined by his underlying theory of organizational behavior, so it is essential for him to understand the different results achieved by different models of organizational behavior. The model used will vary with the total human and task conditions surrounding the work. The long-run tendency will be toward more supportive and collegial models because they better serve the higher-level needs of employees.

REVIEW QUESTIONS

1 Compare and contrast Davis's four models of organizational behavior.
2 Which model best describes how you would like to be treated? How you would likely treat other employees?
3 Why is it important to identify your personal model?

READING 2

The Human Side of Enterprise

Douglas McGregor*

It has become trite to say that the most significant developments of the next quarter century will take place not in the physical but in the social sciences, that industry—the economic organ of society—has the fundamental know-how to utilize physical science and technology for the material benefit of mankind, and that we must now learn how to utilize the social sciences to make our human organizations truly effective.

Many people agree in principle with such statements; but so far they represent a pious hope—and little else. Consider with me, if you will, something of what may be involved when we attempt to transform the hope into reality.

I

Let me begin with an analogy. A quarter century ago basic conceptions of the nature of matter and energy had changed profoundly from what they had been since Newton's time. The physical scientists were persuaded that under proper conditions new and hitherto unimagined sources of energy could be made available to mankind.

We know what has happened since then. First came the bomb. Then during the past decade, have come many other attempts to exploit these scientific discoveries—some successful, some not.

*From *Proceedings of the Fifth Anniversary Convocation of the School of Industrial Management, Massachusetts Institute of Technology*, Cambridge, Apr. 9, 1957. Reprinted with permission.

The point of my analogy, however, is that the application of theory in this field is a slow and costly matter. We expect it always to be thus. No one is impatient with the scientist because he cannot tell industry how to build a simple, cheap, all-purpose source of atomic energy today. That it will take at least another decade and the investment of billions of dollars to achieve results which are economically competitive with present sources of power is understood and accepted.

It is transparently pretentious to suggest any *similarity* between the developments in the physical sciences leading to the harnessing of atomic energy and potential developments in the social sciences. Nevertheless, the analogy is not as absurd as it might appear to be at first glance.

To a lesser degree, and in a much more tentative fashion, we are in a position in the social sciences today like that of the physical sciences with respect to atomic energy in the thirties. We know that past conceptions of the nature of man are inadequate and in many ways incorrect. We are becoming quite certain that, under proper conditions, unimagined resources of creative human energy could become available within the organizational setting.

We cannot tell industrial management how to apply this new knowledge in simple, economic ways. We know it will require years of exploration, much costly development research, and a substantial amount of creative imagination on the part of management to discover how to apply this growing knowledge to the organization of human effort in industry.

May I ask that you keep this analogy in mind—overdrawn and pretentious though it may be—as a framework for what I have to say this morning.

Management's Task: Conventional View

The conventional conception of management's task in harnessing human energy to organizational requirements can be stated broadly in terms of three propositions. In order to avoid the complications introduced by a label, I shall call this set of propositions "Theory X":

1 Management is responsible for organizing the elements of productive enterprise—money, materials, equipment, people—in the interest of economic ends.

2 With respect to people, this is a process of directing their efforts, motivating them, controlling their actions, modifying their behavior to fit the needs of the organization.

3 Without this active intervention by management, people would be passive—even resistant—to organizational needs. They must therefore be persuaded, rewarded, punished, controlled—their activities must be directed. This is management's task—in managing subordinate managers or workers. We often sum it up by saying that management consists of getting things done through other people.

Behind this conventional theory there are several additional beliefs—less explicit, but widespread:

4 The average man is by nature indolent—he works as little as possible.

5 He lacks ambition, dislikes responsibility, prefers to be led.

6 He is inherently self-centered, indifferent to organizational needs.

7 He is by nature resistant to change.

8 He is gullible, not very bright, the ready dupe of the charlatan and the demagogue.

The human side of economic enterprise today is fashioned from propositions and beliefs such as these. Conventional organization structures, managerial policies, practices, and programs reflect these assumptions.

In accomplishing its task—with these assumptions as guides—management has conceived of a range of possibilities between two extremes.

The Hard or the Soft Approach?

At one extreme, management can be "hard" or "strong." The methods for directing behavior involve coercion and threat (usually disguised), close supervision, tight controls over behavior. At the other extreme, management can be "soft" or "weak." The methods for directing behavior involve being permissive, satisfying people's demands, achieving harmony. Then they will be tractable, accept direction.

This range has been fairly completely explored during the past half century, and management has learned some things from the exploration. There are difficulties in the "hard" approach. Force breeds counterforces: restriction of output, antagonism, militant unionism, subtle but effective sabotage of management objectives. This approach is especially difficult during times of full employment.

There are also difficulties in the "soft" approach. It leads frequently to the abdication of management—to harmony, perhaps, but to indifferent performance. People take advantage of the soft approach. They continually expect more, but they give less and less.

Currently, the popular theme is "firm but fair." This is an attempt to gain the advantages of both the hard and the soft approaches. It is reminiscent of Teddy Roosevelt's "speak softly and carry a big stick."

Is the Conventional View Correct?

The findings which are beginning to emerge from the social sciences challenge this whole set of beliefs about man and human nature and about the task of management. The evidence is far from conclusive, certainly, but it is suggestive. It comes from the laboratory, the clinic, the schoolroom, the home, and even to a limited extent from industry itself.

The social scientist does not deny that human behavior in industrial organization today is approximately what management perceives it to be. He has, in fact, observed it and studied it fairly extensively. But he is pretty sure that this behavior is *not* a consequence of man's inherent nature. It is a consequence rather of the nature of industrial organizations, of management philosophy, policy, and practice. The conventional approach of Theory X is based on mistaken notions of what is cause and what is effect.

"Well," you ask, "what then is the *true* nature of man? What evidence leads the social scientist to deny what is obvious?" And, if I am not mistaken, you are also thinking, "Tell me—simply, and without a lot of scientific verbiage—what you think you know that is so unusual. Give me—without a lot of intellectual claptrap and theoretical nonsense—some practical ideas which will enable me to improve the situation in my organization. And remember, I'm faced with increasing costs and narrowing profit margins. I want proof that such ideas won't result simply in new and costly human relations frills. I want practical results, and I want them now."

If these are your wishes, you are going to be disappointed. Such requests can no more be met by the social scientist today than could comparable ones with respect to atomic energy be met by the physicist fifteen years ago. I can, however, indicate a few of the reasons for asserting that conventional assumptions about the human side of enterprise are inadequate. And I can suggest—tentatively—some of the propositions that will comprise a more adequate theory of the management of people. The magnitude of the task that confronts us will then, I think, be apparent.

II

Perhaps the best way to indicate why the conventional approach of management is inadequate is to consider the subject of motivation. In discussing this subject I will draw heavily on the work of my colleague, Abraham Maslow of Brandeis University. His is the most fruitful approach I know. Naturally, what I have to say will be overgeneralized and will ignore important qualifications. In the time at our disposal, this is inevitable.

Physiological and Safety Needs

Man is a wanting animal—as soon as one of his needs is satisfied, another appears in its place. This process is unending. It continues from birth to death.

Man's needs are organized in a series of levels—a hierarchy of importance. At the lowest level, but preeminent in importance when they are thwarted, are his physiological needs. Man lives by bread alone, when there is no bread. Unless the circumstances are unusual, his needs for love, for status, for recognition are inoperative when his stomach has been empty for a while. But when he eats regularly and adequately, hunger ceases to be an important need. The sated man has hunger only in the sense that a full bottle has emptiness. The same is true of the other physiological needs of man—for rest, exercise, shelter, protection from the elements.

A *satisfied need is not a motivator of behavior!* This is a fact of profound significance. It is a fact which is regularly ignored in the conventional approach to the management of people. I shall return to it later. For the moment, one example will make my point. Consider your own need for air. Except as you are deprived of it, it has no appreciable motivating effect upon your behavior.

When the physiological needs are reasonably satisfied, needs at the next higher level begin to dominate man's behavior—to motivate him. These are called safety needs. They are needs for protection against danger, threat, deprivation. Some people mistakenly refer to these as needs for security. However, unless man is in a dependent relationship where he fears arbitrary deprivation, he does not demand security. The need is for the "fairest possible break." When he is confident of this, he is more than willing to take risks. But when he feels threatened or dependent, his greatest need is for guarantees, for protection, for security.

The fact needs little emphasis that since every industrial employee is in a dependent relationship, safety needs may assume considerable importance. Arbitrary management actions, behavior which arouses uncertainty with respect to continued employment or which reflects favoritism or discrimination, unpredictable administration of policy—these can be powerful motivators of the safety needs in the employment relationship *at every level* from worker to vice president.

Social Needs

When man's physiological needs are satisfied and he is no longer fearful about his physical welfare, his social needs become important motivators of his behavior— for belonging, for association, for acceptance by his fellows, for giving and receiving friendship and love.

Management knows today of the existence of these needs, but it often assumes quite wrongly that they represent a threat to the organization. Many studies have demonstrated that the tightly knit, cohesive work group may, under proper conditions, be far more effective than an equal number of separate individuals in achieving organizational goals.

Yet management, fearing group hostility to its own objectives, often goes to considerable lengths to control and direct human efforts in ways that are inimical to the natural "groupiness" of human beings. When man's social needs—and perhaps his safety needs, too—are thus thwarted, he behaves in ways which tend to defeat organizational objectives. He becomes resistant, antagonistic, uncooperative. But his behavior is a consequence, not a cause.

Ego Needs

Above the social needs—in the sense that they do not become motivators until lower needs are reasonably satisfied—are the needs of greatest significance to management and to man himself. They are the egoistic needs, and they are of two kinds:

1 Those needs that relate to one's self-esteem—needs for self-confidence, for independence, for achievement, for competence, for knowledge.

2 Those needs that relate to one's reputation—needs for status, for recognition, for appreciation, for the deserved respect of one's fellows.

Unlike the lower needs, these are rarely satisfied; man seeks indefinitely for more satisfaction of these needs once they have become important to him. But they do not appear in any significant way until physiological, safety, and social needs are all reasonably satisfied.

The typical industrial organization offers few opportunities for the satisfaction of these egoistic needs to people at lower levels in the hierarchy. The conventional methods of organizing work, particularly in mass production industries, give little heed to these aspects of human motivation. If the practices of scientific management were deliberately calculated to thwart these needs—which, of course, they are not—they could hardly accomplish this purpose better than they do.

Self-Fulfillment Needs

Finally—a capstone, as it were, on the hierarchy of man's needs—there are what we may call the needs for self-fulfillment.These are the needs for realizing one's own potentialities, for continued self-development, for being creative in the broadest sense of that term.

It is clear that the conditions of modern life give only limited opportunity for these relatively weak needs to obtain expression. The deprivation most people experience with respect to other lower-level needs diverts their energies into the struggle to satisfy *those* needs, and the needs for self-fulfillment remain dormant.

III

Now, briefly, a few general comments about motivation:

We recognize readily enough that a man suffering from a severe dietary deficiency is sick. The deprivation of physiological needs has behavioral consequences. The same is true—although less well recognized—of deprivation of higher-level needs. The man whose needs for safety, association, independence, or status are thwarted is sick just as surely as is he who has rickets. And his sickness will have behavioral consequences. We will be mistaken if we attribute his resultant passivity, his hostility, his refusal to accept responsibility to his inherent "human nature." These forms of behavior are *symptoms* of illness—of deprivation of his social and egoistic needs.

The man whose lower-level needs are satisfied is not motivated to satisfy those needs any longer. For practical purposes they exist no longer. (Remember my point about your need for air.) Management often asks, "Why aren't people more productive? We pay good wages, provide good working conditions, have excellent fringe benefits and steady employment. Yet people do not seem to be willing to put forth more than minimum effort."

The fact that management has provided for these physiological and safety needs has shifted the motivational emphasis to the social and perhaps to the egoistic needs. Unless there are opportunities *at work* to satisfy these higher-level needs, people will be deprived; and their behavior will reflect this deprivation. Under such conditions, if management continues to focus its attention on physiological needs, its efforts are bound to be ineffective.

People *will* make insistent demands for more money under these conditions. It becomes more important than ever to buy the material goods and services which can provide limited satisfaction of the thwarted needs. Although money has only limited value in satisfying many higher-level needs, it can become the focus of interest if it is the *only* means available.

The Carrot and Stick Approach

The carrot and stick theory of motivation (like Newtonian physical theory) works reasonably well under certain circumstances. The *means* for satisfying man's physiological and (within limits) his safety needs can be provided or withheld by management. Employment itself is such a means, and so are wages, working conditions, and benefits. By these means the individual can be controlled so long as he is struggling for subsistence. Man lives for bread alone when there is no bread.

But the carrot and stick theory does not work at all once man has reached an adequate subsistence level and is motivated primarily by higher needs. Management cannot provide a man with self-respect, or with the respect of his fellows, or with the satisfaction of needs for self-fulfillment. It can create conditions such that he is encouraged and enabled to seek such satisfactions *for himself*, or it can thwart him by failing to create those conditions.

But this creation of conditions is not "control." It is not a good device for directing behavior. And so management finds itself in an old position. The high standard of living created by our modern technological know-how provides quite adequately for the satisfaction of physiological and safety needs. The only significant exception is where management practices have not created confidence in a "fair break"—and thus where safety needs are thwarted. But by making possible the satisfaction of low-level needs, management has deprived itself of the ability to use as motivators the devices on which conventional theory has taught it to rely—rewards, promises, incentives, or threats and other coercive devices.

Neither Hard nor Soft

The philosophy of management by direction and control—*regardless of whether it is hard or soft*—is inadequate to motivate because the human needs on which this approach relies are today unimportant motivators of behavior. Direction and control are essentially useless in motivating people whose important needs are social and egoistic. Both the hard and the soft approach fail today because they are simply irrelevant to the situation.

People, deprived of opportunities to satisfy at work the needs which are now important to them, behave exactly as we might predict—with indolence, passivity, resistance to change, lack of responsibility, willingness to follow the demagogue, unreasonable demands for economic benefits. It would seem that we are caught in a web of our own weaving.

In summary, then, of these comments about motivation:

Management by direction and control—whether implemented with the hard, the soft, or the firm but fair approach—fails under today's conditions to provide effective motivation of human effort toward organizational objectives. It fails because direction and control are useless methods of motivating people whose physiological and safety needs are reasonably satisfied and whose social, egoistic, and self-fulfillment needs are predominant.

IV

For these and many other reasons, we require a different theory of the task of managing people based on more adequate assumptions about human nature and human motivation. I am going to be so bold as to suggest the broad dimensions of such a theory. Call it "Theory Y," if you will.

1 Management is responsible for organizing the elements of productive enterprise—money, materials, equipment, people—in the interest of economic ends.

2 People are not by nature passive or resistant to organizational needs. They have become so as a result of experience in organizations.

3 The motivation, the potential for development, the capacity for assuming responsibility, the readiness to direct behavior toward organizational goals are all present in people. Management does not put them there. It is a responsibility of management to make it possible for people to recognize and develop these human characteristics for themselves.

4 The essential task of management is to arrange organizational conditions and methods of operation so that people can achieve their own goals *best* by directing *their own* efforts toward organizational objectives.

This is a process primarily of creating opportunities, releasing potential, removing obstacles, encouraging growth, providing guidance. It is what Peter Drucker has called "management by objectives" in contrast to "management by control."

And I hasten to add that it does *not* involve the abdication of management, the absence of leadership, the lowering of standards, or the other characteristics usually associated with the "soft" approach under Theory X. Much on the contrary. It is no more possible to create an organization today which will be a fully effective application of this theory than it was to build an atomic power plant in 1945. There are many formidable obstacles to overcome.

Some Difficulties

The conditions imposed by conventional organization theory and by the approach of scientific management for the past half century have tied men to limited jobs which do not utilize their capabilities, have discouraged the acceptance of responsibility, have encouraged passivity, have eliminated meaning from work. Man's habits, attitudes, expectations—his whole conception of membership in an industrial organization—have been conditioned by his experience under these circumstances. Change in the direction of Theory Y will be slow, and it will require extensive modification of the attitudes of management and workers alike.

People today are accustomed to being directed, manipulated, controlled in industrial organizations and to finding satisfaction for their social, egoistic, and self-fulfillment needs away from the job. This is true of much of management as well as of workers. Genuine "industrial citizenship"—to borrow again a term from Drucker—is a remote and unrealistic idea, the meaning of which has not even been considered by most members of industrial organizations.

Another way of saying this is that Theory X places exclusive reliance upon external control of human behavior, while Theory Y relies heavily on self-control and self-direction. It is worth noting that this difference is the difference between treating people as children and treating them as mature adults. After generations of the former, we cannot expect to shift to the latter overnight.

V

Before we are overwhelmed by the obstacles, let us remember that the application of theory is always slow. Progress is usually achieved in small steps.

Consider with me a few innovative ideas which are entirely consistent with Theory Y and which are today being applied with some success:

Decentralization and Delegation

These are ways of freeing people from the too-close control of conventional organization, giving them a degree of freedom to direct their own activities, to assume responsibility, and importantly, to satisfy their egoistic needs. In this connection, the flat organization of Sears, Roebuck and Company provides an interesting example. It forces "management by objectives" since it enlarges the number of people reporting to a manager until he cannot direct and control them in the conventional manner.

Job Enlargement

This concept, pioneered by I.B.M. and Detroit Edison, is quite consistent with Theory Y. It encourages the acceptance of responsibility at the bottom of the organization; it provides opportunities for satisfying social and egoistic needs. In fact, the reorganization of work at the factory level offers one of the more challenging opportunities for innovation consistent with Theory Y. The studies by A. T. M. Wilson and his associates of British coal mining and Indian textile manufacture have added appreciably to our understanding of work organization. Moreover, the economic and psychological results achieved by this work have been substantial.

Participation and Consultative Management

Under proper conditions these results provide encouragement to people to direct their creative energies toward organizational objectives, give them some voice in decisions that affect them, provide significant opportunities for the satisfaction of social and egoistic needs. I need only mention the Scanlon Plan as the outstanding embodiment of these ideas in practice.

The not infrequent failure of such ideas as these to work as well as expected is often attributable to the fact that a management has "bought the idea" but applied it within the framework of Theory X and its assumptions.

Delegation is not an effective way of exercising management by control. Participation becomes a farce when it is applied as a sales gimmick or a device for kidding people into thinking they are important. Only the management that has confidence in human capacities and is itself directed toward organizational objectives rather than toward the preservation of personal power can grasp the implications of this emerging theory. Such management will find and apply successfully other innovative ideas as we move slowly toward the full implementation of a theory like Y.

Performance Appraisal

Before I stop, let me mention one other practical application of Theory Y which—while still highly tentative—may well have important consequences. This has to do with performance appraisal within the ranks of management. Even a cursory examination of conventional programs of performance appraisal will reveal how completely consistent they are with Theory X. In fact, most such programs tend to treat the individual as though he were a product under inspection on the assembly line.

Take the typical plan: substitute "product" for "subordinate being appraised," substitute "inspector" for "superior making the appraisal," substitute "rework" for "training or development," and, except for the attributes being judged, the human appraisal process will be virtually indistinguishable from the product inspection process.

A few companies—among them General Mills, Ansul Chemical, and General Electric—have been experimenting with approaches which involve the individual in setting "targets" or objectives *for himself* and in a *self*-evaluation of performance semi-annually or annually. Of course, the superior plays an important leadership role in this process—one, in fact, which demands substantially more competence than the conventional approach. The role is, however, considerably more congenial to many managers than the role of "judge" or "inspector" which is forced upon them by conventional performance. Above all, the individual is encouraged to take a greater responsibility for planning and appraising his own contribution to organizational objectives; and the accompanying effects on egoistic and self-fulfillment needs are substantial. This approach to performance appraisal represents one more innovative idea being explored by a few managements who are moving toward the implementation of Theory Y.

VI

And now I am back where I began. I share the belief that we could realize substantial improvements in the effectiveness of industrial organizations during the next decade or two. Moreover, I believe the social sciences can contribute much to such developments. We are only beginning to grasp the implications of the growing body of knowledge in these fields. But if this conviction is to become a reality instead of a pious hope, we will need to view the process much as we view the process of releasing the energy of the atom for constructive human ends—as a slow, costly, sometimes discouraging approach toward a goal which would seem to many to be quite unrealistic.

The ingenuity and the perseverance of industrial management in the pursuit of economic ends have changed many scientific and technological dreams into commonplace realities. It is now becoming clear that the application of these same talents to the human side of enterprise will not only enhance substantially these materialistic achievements but will bring us one step closer to "the good society." Shall we get on with the job?

REVIEW QUESTIONS

1 In your own words, what do Theory X and Theory Y mean?
2 Relate Theory X and Y to Davis's four models of organizational behavior.
3 Think back over your work experiences. What has been your reaction to a Theory X or a Theory Y environment?

READING 3

The Principle of Supportive Relationships

Rensis Likert*

*   *   *

The principle of supportive relationships is a general principle which the members of an organization can use to guide their relationships with one another. The more fully this principle is applied throughout the organization, the greater will be the extent to which (1) the motivational forces arising from the noneconomic motives of members and from their economic needs will be harmonious and compatible and (2) the motivational forces within each individual will result in cooperative

---

*From *The Human Organization: Its Management and Value* (New York: McGraw-Hill Book Company, 1967), p. 47–48. Copyright 1967. Reprinted with permission.

behavior focused on achieving organizational goals. The principle is stated as follows:

> The leadership and other processes of the organization must be such as to ensure a maximum probability that in all interactions and in all relationships within the organization, each member, in the light of his background, values, desires, and expectations, will view the experience as supportive and one which builds and maintains his sense of personal worth and importance.[1]

In applying this principle, the relationship between the superior and subordinate is crucial. This relationship, as the principle specifies, should be one which is supportive and ego-building. The more often the superior's behavior is ego-building rather than ego-deflating, the better will be the effect of his behavior on organizational performance. In applying this principle, it is essential to keep in mind that the interactions between the leader and the subordinates must be viewed in the light of the subordinate's background, values, and expectations. The subordinate's perception of the situation, rather than the supervisor's, determines whether or not the experience is supportive. Both the behavior of the superior and the employee's perceptions of the situation must be such that the subordinate, in the light of his background, values, and expectations, sees the experience as one which contributes to his sense of personal worth and importance, one which increases and maintains his sense of significance and human dignity.

*   *   *

REVIEW QUESTION

1 Why does Likert define supportive relationships in terms of the *subordinate's* perceptions?

[1]R. Likert, *New Patterns of Management* (New York: McGraw-Hill Book Company, 1961), p. 103.

READING 4
Situational Theories of Behavior
Jay W. Lorsch*

* * *

Neither universal theories nor the resulting techniques have been the only behavioral science ideas available to managers. Another set of ideas is built on the premise that the organization can be viewed as a social system. This approach developed out of the Hawthorne studies by Elton Mayo, F. J. Roethlisberger, and William Dickson.[1]

In this well-known study, it was learned that worker behavior is the result of a complex system of forces including the personalities of the workers, the nature of their jobs, and the formal measurement and reward practices of the organization. Workers behave in ways that management does not intend, not because they are irresponsible or lazy but because they need to cope with their work situation in a way that is satisfying and meaningful to them. From this perspective, what is effective management behavior and action depends on the specifics in each situation.

Although many scholars, including Roethlisberger and Mayo themselves, elaborated on these ideas and taught them at many business schools, managers never gave them the attention they gave to the universal ideas. Interestingly enough, many saw the central significance of the Hawthorne studies as being either the *universal* importance of effective interpersonal communication between supervisors and workers or the so-called "Hawthorne Effect." The latter is the notion that any change in practice will *always* lead to positive results in the short run simply because of the novelty of the new practice.

In essence, this world-renowned study, which its authors saw as proving that human issues need to be viewed from a "social system," or situational perspective, was interpreted by others as a call for universal techniques of "good human relations." (For Roethlisberger's comments on this, see *The Elusive Phenomena*.)[2]

Of course, stating that one should *always* take a situational perspective could be seen as a universal prescription itself. My concern is not with universal ideas, such as this and others which I shall mention shortly, which seem to hold generally true. Rather, it is with techniques invented under a specific set of conditions,

---

*Reprinted by permission of the *Harvard Business Review*. "Making Behavioral Science More Useful," by Jay W. Lorsch, vol. 57, no. 2, pp. 173–174. Copyright © 1979 by the President and Fellows of Harvard College; all rights reserved.

[1]Elton Mayo, *The Human Problems of an Industrial Civilization* (New York: Viking Press, 1960); F. J. Roethlisberger and William Dickson, *Management and the Worker* (Cambridge, Mass.: Harvard University Press, 1939).

[2]F. J. Roethlisberger, *The Elusive Phenomena*, ed. George F. F. Lombard (Boston: Division of Research, Harvard Business School, 1977).

which have not been more widely tried but which their advocates argue have universal application.

Why these social-system concepts did not catch on is a matter of conjecture, but one reasonable explanation is that managers naturally prefer the simplest apparent approach to a problem. When faced with the choice between the complex and time-consuming analysis required to apply such situational ideas and the simpler, quicker prescriptions of universal theories and techniques, most managers seem to prefer the simpler universal approach. The human tendency to follow the fads and fashions also adds to the appeal of these techniques. If competitors are trying T-groups for management development, shouldn't we? If the company across the industrial park is using MBO, shouldn't we as well?

In spite of the rush to simple popular solutions in the last decade, some behavioral scientists have become aware that the universal theories and the techniques they spawned have failed in many situations where they were inappropriate. These scholars are trying to understand situational complexity and to provide managers with tools to analyze the complex issues in each specific situation and to decide on appropriate action. Examples of these efforts are listed in *Exhibit I.*

These behavioral scientists do not all agree on what variables are important to understand. At this stage, people conceptualize the issues and define the variables and the important relationships among them in many different ways. Also, the "theories" they have developed often throw light on a limited set of applications.

All these behavioral scientists focusing on situational theories, however, share two fundamental assumptions. First, the proper target of behavioral science knowledge is the complex interrelationships that shape the behavior with which all managers must deal. Harold J. Leavitt, in his well-known text *Managerial Psychology*, presents a diagram (see Exhibit II) that illustrates clearly the basic set of relationships.[3] Behavior in an organization results, he writes, from the interaction of people's needs, their task requirements, and the organization's characteristics. He uses two-headed arrows to both suggest this complex interdependence and indicate that behavior itself can influence the other forces over time.

Although Leavitt's was an early and, from today's perspective, a simplified view of the relationships involved, it captures the essential issues in situational theories and is very close to the Roethlisberger and Dickson conception.

The second assumption that behavioral scientists focusing on situational theories seem to share is that, at this juncture, they cannot hope to provide a grand and general theory of human behavior in organizations. Rather, what the behavioral sciences can, and should, provide are what L. J. Henderson called "walking sticks" to guide the managers along complex decision-making paths about human affairs.[4] In this case, by walking sticks I mean conceptual models for understanding the complexity of the human issues a manager faces.

[3]Harold J. Leavitt, *Managerial Psychology* (Chicago: University of Chicago Press, 1958), p. 286.
[4]L. J. Henderson, *On The Social System: Selected Writings* (Chicago, Ill.: University of Chicago Press, 1970).

EXHIBIT I
EXAMPLES OF SITUATIONAL FRAMEWORKS

Author	Publication	Major focus
Fred E. Fiedler	*A Theory of Leadership Effectiveness* (New York: McGraw-Hill, 1967).	Leadership of a work unit
John P. Kotter	*Organizational Dynamics* (Reading, Mass.: Addison-Wesley, 1978).	Organizational change
Edward E. Lawler	*Pay and Organizational Effectiveness: A Psychological View* (New York, McGraw-Hill, 1971).	Employee motivation
Paul R. Lawrence and Jay W. Lorsch	*Organization and Environment* (Division of Research, Harvard Business School, Harvard University, 1967).	Organizational arrangements to fit environmental requirements
Harry Levinson	*Men, Management and Mental Health* (Harvard University Press, 1962).	Employee motivation
Jay W. Lorsch and John Morse	*Organizations and Their Members* (New York: Harper and Row, 1975).	Organizational arrangements and leadership in functional units
Edgar H. Schein	*Career Dynamics: Matching Individual and Organizational Needs* (Reading, Mass.: Addison-Wesley, 1978).	Life stage careers, and organizational requirements
Robert Tannenbaum and Warren H. Schmidt	*"How To Choose A Leadership Pattern"* (HBR May–June 1973).	Leadership
Victor H. Vroom and Philip W. Yetton	*Leadership and Decision-Making* (University of Pittsburgh Press, 1973).	Leadership behavior for different types of decisions
Joan Woodward	*Industrial Organization: Theory and Practice* (Oxford University Press, 1965).	Organizational design

EXHIBIT II
Basic forces shaping behavior.

Such models represent the product these scholars have to offer managers. Universal prescriptions or techniques are like a mirage. Each situation is unique and the manager must use these conceptual models to diagnose it. With an understanding of the complex and interrelated causes of behavior in the organization, the manager can use his or her intellect and creative ability to invent a new solution or to judge what existing solutions might fit the situation.

*   *   *

REVIEW QUESTION

1 In your own words, state the meaning of the situational approach to organizational behavior.

READING 5

The American Productivity Crisis

C. Jackson Grayson, Jr.*

Q. Speaking of the crisis of productivity, you have said, "we must face the problem of producing competitively or sinking from the scene as did Greece and Rome." What justifies such a dramatic statement?

A. I know it may sound un-American, but I don't believe that we were born to be number one. America won't be number one forever as a genetic or historic right. We must work at it all the time. I think it entirely conceivable that the United States could lose its world economic leadership. It is no longer unthinkable that we could fade away. Remember that Britain kept saying that productivity stagnation was unacceptable even as her position steadily deteriorated. I think that unless this nation decides it is going to do something about the problems that have generated our productivity stagnation, we will fade away. As Toynbee said, "Civilizations die leisurely."

Q. The productivity conference report urges cooperation to achieve a goal of competitiveness. Do you see anything contradictory in these ideas?

A. It has been traditional in America to think that if people behave individually it means competition and that it will preclude cooperation. That's what our term "individualism" tends to mean. But I think the Japanese have shown us this is not necessarily the case. You can have people working together to improve themselves against a goal, such as overall quality, but not necessarily to best the person next to them. Cooperation means many people engaged in a common task, in many cases competitively against another firm or against another nation. I think cooperation in the organization includes having an active competitive spirit.

Q. What do you think of the criticism that it is unrealistic for the United States to adopt Japanese management methods because we aren't Japanese?

*From Patricia Galagan, "Staying Alive: Jack Grayson on the American Productivity Crisis," *Training and Development Journal*, January 1984, pp. 59–62. Reprinted with permission.

A. Absolute hogwash! There is no question that nations have histories and cultures that are different from one another. But there are common elements of Japanese management systems that are so similar to ours that they would travel extremely well. In fact, many of them travelled from here to Japan in the first place. The Japanese listened to our behavioral scientists, our industrial engineers, our management experts. Those ideas are just as movable back here.

People who say that Japanese management is endemic to Japanese culture haven't looked at some facts. In the 1940s, Japanese labor/management relations were not good. There were frequent strikes and a lot of resistance by management to the idea of employment security. They didn't have lifetime employment then. But the Japanese realized they weren't going to be competitive in the world unless they changed. There isn't any culture-bound identity that prevents us from doing as well or better than the Japanese. The need to be competitive is the need to survive. There's nothing like knowing that you have a strong competitor to force you to return to fundamentals about how you run a business.

Q. The report calls for a "fundamental shift in management." Would you describe the shift and explain why the impetus should come from management as the report suggests.

A. The traditional management attitude is a look down from the top at how to use resources and assign them. Business schools teach that the manager is the allocater and controller of these resources. They are almost always assumed to be passive: people, materials and energy. It's a one-way focus that assumes that the resources will behave in the way the manager wants them to. That hierarchical view will have to shift fundamentally and become more lateral and interactive.

Another important issue related to this question is socialization of membership— the need to feel that one is working for a common goal instead of there being a detached group at the top that has different values and goals than the group at the bottom. In some firms this is accomplished by what's called "management by walking around." It's managers letting themselves be seen as individuals, managers being real members of the organization.

Today's managers have lost contact with the most important parts of their operations—with productivity, with the way things are run. They've paid more attention to what I would regard as the less important variables—the well-known, external, short-term focus on financial or legal or public relations goals. There's nothing wrong with any of those, but if the focus shifts there entirely, you lose the thrust of how to run a business. There's a lack of attention to detail, a lack of attention to what it is to make a product.

Another fundamental shift needs to take place in the area of capital development. Our tax laws and our discussions of policy almost always concern physical capital investment, taking human capital for granted. But it's becoming clear that perhaps our human capital isn't what we thought it was. I think that the current public interest in education is a manifestation of this. To develop human capital, as human resource developers would like to do, requires programs and legislation, and these in turn require hard numbers. If you want to argue tax incentives for human capital development, for instance, right away you're going to be pushed for numbers.

I was trained at the Harvard Business School. I've taught at Stanford. I've been the dean of two business schools, and I can say that I was part of the group that helped to lead current managers into some of the ways we now manage. Now I'm trying to say we've all made a mistake.

I think the initiative for the shift that's needed must come from management because it still directs the decision-making and control apparatus. It is extremely difficult to change a situation from below. There are too many odds to overcome— too much inertia and too much power. I think that managers have the opportunity and the burden to make the shift. They still are the primary influence on the direction of an organization. Most firms bear the imprint of a CEO, and that person needs to be involved in such fundamental management shifts. If not, the other managers are going to find it difficult to make the kinds of changes that are needed.

Q. What action would you recommend to a human resource director who wanted to persuade a CEO to adopt participative management practices?

A. Try to get the CEO to go to Japan. I'd recommend sending managers at several levels in the organization as well as union representatives. It's an experience that often causes managers to take a new, urgent look at their practices and to develop a new attitude. My second recommendation to the HRD manager is to talk regularly with the CEO about participative management and to create opportunities for the CEO to discuss the topic with peers. If the CEO is not receptive, I'd recommend that the HRD manager work harder and longer. It's reasonable to expect the process of shifting a manager's viewpoint on such a fundamental issue to take several years.

*   *   *

Q. How important is sharing and giving up power in an attempt to gain cooperation?

A. The more power you give up, the more you gain, but it's a different kind of power. You might lose legitimate institutional power derived from the organizational structure, but you will gain the power to lead people to greater productivity and higher quality. It's the difference between how you lead people in a democracy and in a dictatorship. You have power in a democracy by persuasion, by example, by role modeling. When you give up institutional authority you gain in other dimensions personally.

Managers are often fearful of giving up authority because they fear a takeover by the worker. In employee involvement programs, I've never found any challenge to the need for management. Employees won't say to managers, "We don't need you any more." Employees want legitimate involvement in the decision-making process. Most don't even want the final decision-making power. They want consultation on the decisions. They want a high degree of input. They want to be heard. And when something is going to be different, they want to know why.

At the beginning of the conference I told participants that I recognized their fear of losing power. Such fears are realistic, although sometimes exaggerated, and management should be prepared for some difficult areas of discussion.

Q. The final report of the White House Conference on Productivity makes recommendations in seven areas: cooperation in the work place, health care, information workers/measurement, quality, reward systems and technology and training. You've expressed concern about the will to make the recommendations work. Where should that come from?

A. From the example of those who are having success. That's why it's important to spread success stories, especially American success stories. Then people can see they don't lose power and they gain higher quality through cooperation.

It's said that we have lost the work ethic, but I think that the loss of the work ethic among certain people is a symptom. There *are* people who have been so held down, so unrecognized and uninvolved that their outward manifestation has been a loss of the will to work. I think we are observing behavior that's reflecting the norms of the last 20 years.

A climate of cooperation exists in some organizations but not in the majority. I'd say it will take at least 10 years before there are widespread changes in culture, in ways of behaving, in reward systems.

Q. The conference report emphasizes the requirements of the whole nation rather than the individual requirements of corporations. This sounds more like Marx and Engels than a group of capitalists. Do you really mean that organizations should give up individual goals for a collective goal of productivity?

A. Only in the sense that the collective goal is to be a competitive nation, to be productive, to survive and to have high quality goods. That's a goal of Adam Smith. The idea is not to subjugate individual organizations to an overall collective goal. What participants did, through the computer conferences, was to share general ideas that cross without giving away confidential information or advantages. There is a tremendous amount that can be discussed among organizations without destroying anyone's competitive advantage. It is, after all, implementation of ideas that is the greatest problem, not the knowledge of them.

REVIEW QUESTIONS

1 Summarize the "fundamental shifts" that Grayson calls for.
2 Grayson suggests that a manager gains power by giving it up. Give an example illustrating this idea.
3 Relate Grayson's ideas to the evolving models of organizational behavior put forth by Davis. Are they compatible?

CHAPTER 2

HISTORICAL
FOUNDATIONS

READING 6

The Objective
of Scientific Management

Frederick W. Taylor*

*   *   *

"And I want to make it perfectly clear, because I do not think it *is* clear, that my interest, and I think the interest of any man who is in any way engaged in scientific management, in the introduction of the principles of scientific management must be first the welfare of the working men. That must be the object. It is inconceivable that a man should devote his time and his life to this sort of thing for the sake of making more money for a whole lot of manufacturers."

*   *   *

REVIEW QUESTION

1 Why do you suspect Taylor found it necessary to state his objective in this fashion?

*Testimony before Industrial Relations Commission, April 1914, quoted in Horace B. Drury, *Scientific Management*, Columbia University Studies in History, Economics, and Public Law, vol. LXV, no. 2 (New York: Longmans, Green & Co., Inc., New York, 1915), p. 204.

READING 7

An Industrial Organization as a Social System

F. J. Roethlisberger
William J. Dickson*

*   *   *

We shall now attempt to state more systematically than was possible in a chrono-logical account the results of the research and some of their implications for practice. . . . The point of view which gradually emerged from these studies is one from which an industrial organization is regarded as a social system. . . .

The study of the bank wiremen showed that their behavior at work could not be understood without considering the informal organization of the group and the relation of this informal organization to the total social organization of the company. The work activities of this group, together with their satisfactions and dissatisfactions, had to be viewed as manifestations of a complex pattern of interrelations. In short, the work situation of the bank wiring group had to be treated as a social system; moreover, the industrial organization of which this group was a part also had to be treated as a social system.

By "system" is meant something which must be considered as a whole because each part bears a relation of interdependence to every other part.[1]

*   *   *

REVIEW QUESTION

1 What are the dangers involved in *not* treating a group or organization as a social system?

*From *Management and the Worker* (Cambridge, Mass.: Harvard University Press, 1949), p. 551. Copyright © 1939, 1967 by the President and Fellows of Harvard College. Reprinted with permission.

[1]"The interdependence of the variables in a system is one of the widest inductions from experience that we possess; or we may alternatively regard it as the definition of a system." Henderson, L. J., *Pareto's General Sociology*, Harvard University Press, 1935, p. 86.

READING 8

The Hawthorne Studies: A Synopsis*

From 1924 to 1933, the Western Electric Company conducted at its Hawthorne Works a research program or series of experiments on the factors in the work situation which affect the morale and productive efficiency of workers. The first of these, the so-called "Illumination Experiments," was studied in cooperation with the National Research Council of the National Academy of Sciences. In the remainder of the studies, the company was aided and guided by the suggestions of Professor Elton Mayo and several of his associates from Harvard University. Because of the large part that Harvard played in the project, it is often referred to as the Hawthorne-Harvard experiments or studies.

ILLUMINATION EXPERIMENTS

The purpose of the Illumination Experiments (1924−27) was to determine the "relation of quality and quantity of illumination to efficiency in industry."

Three formal experiments were conducted with various groups of workers. The intensity of illumination was increased and decreased and the effect on output was observed. The effect was puzzling. Output bobbed up and down in some groups or increased continually in others, or increased and stayed level in still others. But in no case was the increase or decrease in proportion to the increase or decrease in illumination.

After many objective tests, it appeared to the Western Electric people involved that:

1 Light was only one factor (and apparently minor) among many which affect employees' output.

2 The attempt to measure the effect of the light factor had failed because the other factors had not been controlled, and studies in regular shop departments or large groups involved so many factors that it was hopeless to expect to isolate any one of them.

At this point, the National Research Council withdrew from the studies, but Western Electric continued them, and soon thereafter had the collaboration of people from Harvard University.

---

*From *Industrial Engineering*, November 1974, pp. 14−15. Copyright 1974. Reprinted with permission. This very brief summary was extracted from *The Hawthorne Studies 1924/1974: A Synopsis*, a booklet published by Western Electric Company in conjunction with the 50th anniversary of the beginning of the famous Hawthorne Studies.

RELAY ASSEMBLY TESTS

Inasmuch as it had appeared that some of the odd effects of the illuminating experiments resulted from the way workers felt about what they were doing (i.e., speeded up because they thought increased production was expected, or slowed down because they were suspicious of the investigator's motives), the investigators tried to set up a situation in which the employees' attitudes would remain constant and unaffected, and other variables might be eliminated.

Assembly of relays was selected for carefully structured tests of factors that might influence productivity. These tests were conducted over a five-year period, 1927–32. The operators were chosen selectively, and given periodic physical examinations as one means of eliminating variables. The experiments were precisely controlled; detailed results were recorded.

During this same period a second relay assembly group of five assemblers was formed. The objective was to test the possibility that change to a small wage incentive group was responsible for improved performance.

The Mica Splitting Test Room was selected for another experiment on the effect of wage incentives. Here, changes in working conditions were introduced without changing the wage incentive plan.

SOME CONCLUSIONS

The underlying premises of both the illumination and the test room experiments had been that a change in working conditions would result in a change in production. A "good" change produces a good result (i.e., an increase in production); a "bad" change produces a bad result (i.e., a decrease in production).

When the illumination experiments failed to substantiate this premise, it was assumed that extraneous factors had interfered, primarily the feelings and attitudes of the operators. Therefore the test room setup was devised with the idea of keeping the operators' attitudes constant while making other changes; there, presumably, the only reactions would be automatic physical reactions—the operators would work faster or slower.

But in their attempts to keep constant the attitudes of the girls in the test room, the investigators made many changes in the treatment of the girls which made their situation very untypical of workers in general. In the very attempt to prevent change, they introduced change.

More and more the investigators came to realize that the significant information they were acquiring had to do with the way people thought and felt—their attitudes. That is, change does not lead to a direct, automatic result; change affects the employee's attitude, *which in turn* affects the result.

So the chief result of the first two years of the Relay Assembly Test Room demonstrated the importance of employee attitude and preoccupations. All attempts to eliminate such considerations had been unsuccessful.

What practical consequences did these results have?

Management regarded these experiments as an attempt to compile a sound body of knowledge upon which to base executive policy and action. And although it was recognized that such research is a long-term proposition, management was ready to make use of any findings which seemed to have been sufficiently tested.

What impressed management most were the stores of latent energy and productive cooperation which could be obtained from people working under the right conditions. Among the factors making for these conditions the attitudes of the employees stood out as being predominant.

The conclusions led to further studies. The Interviewing Program, 1928–30, covering 21,000 employees, provided data of immediate value in improving working conditions, supervisory training, and other employee relations activities conducted by management. Of even more historical significance, it developed insights into methods of listening to and understanding an employee's view of his own personal situation. In short, this part of the program perfected the interviewing technique itself.

Later, the Bank Wiring Observation Room (1931–32) was set up to observe the worker in his work environment. It developed a method of studying group behavior that supplemented interviewing with actual on-the-job data on behavior patterns in the working group. Out of this phase came the concept of the informal organization and its influence on productivity, as well as other new information demonstrating the impact of social factors in the industrial setting.

REVIEW QUESTION

1 State three major contributions of the Hawthorne studies.

READING 9

The Hierarchy of Needs

A. H. Maslow*

*   *   *

1 There are at least five sets of goals which we may call basic needs. These are briefly physiological, safety, love, esteem, and self-actualization. In addition, we are motivated by the desire to achieve or maintain the various conditions upon which these basic satisfactions rest and by certain more intellectual desires.

2 These basic goals are related to each other, being arranged in a hierarchy of prepotency. This means that the most prepotent goal will monopolize conscious-

*From A. H. Maslow, "A Theory of Human Motivation," *Psychological Review*, vol. 50, 1943, pp. 394–395. © 1943 by the American Psychological Association. Reprinted with permission.

ness and will tend of itself to organize the recruitment of the various capacities of the organism. The less prepotent needs are minimized, even forgotten or denied. But when a need is fairly well satisfied, the next prepotent ("higher") need emerges, in turn to dominate the conscious life and to serve as the center of organization of behavior, since gratified needs are not active motivators.

Thus, man is a perpetually wanting animal. Ordinarily the satisfaction of these wants is not altogether mutually exclusive, but only tends to be. The average member of our society is most often partially satisfied and partially unsatisfied in all of his wants. The hierarchy principle is usually empirically observed in terms of increasing percentages of nonsatisfaction as we go up the hierarchy. Reversals of the hierarchy are sometimes observed. Also it has been observed that an individual may permanently lose the higher wants in the hierarchy under social conditions. There are not only ordinarily multiple motivations for usual behavior, but in addition many determinants other than motives.

3 Any thwarting or possibility of thwarting of these basic human goals, or danger to the defenses which protect them, or to the conditions upon which they rest, is considered to be a psychological threat. With a few exceptions, all psycho-pathology may be partially traced to such threats. A basically thwarted man may actually be defined as a "sick" man, if we wish.

*   *   *

REVIEW QUESTION

1 Maslow's hierarchy of needs is often interpreted too simplistically. What modifications of it did he imply (or can you infer)?

READING 10

Characteristics of Achievers
David D. McClelland*

*   *   *

Considerations like these focus attention on what there is about the job of being a business entrepreneur or executive that should make such a job peculiarly appropriate for a man with a high concern for achievement. Or, to put it the other way around, a person with high *n* Achievement has certain characteristics which enable him to work best in certain types of situations that are to his liking. An

*From "Business Drives and National Achievement," *Harvard Business Review*, July–August 1962, pp. 103–105. Copyright 1962. Reprinted with permission.

entrepreneurial job simply provides him with more opportunities for making use of his talents than do other jobs. Through careful empirical research we know a great deal by now about the man with high *n* Achievement, and his characteristics do seem to fit him unusually well for being a business executive. Specifically:

1 *To begin with, he likes situations in which he takes personal responsibility for finding solutions to problems.* The reason is obvious. Otherwise, he could get little personal achievement satisfaction from the successful outcome. No gambler, he does not relish situations where the outcome depends not on his abilities and efforts but on chance or other factors beyond his control. For example:

> Some business school students in one study played a game in which they had to choose between two options, in each of which they had only one chance in three of succeeding. For one option they rolled a die and if it came up, say, a 1 or a 3 (out of six possibilities), they won. For the other option they had to work on a difficult business problem which they knew only one out of three people had been able to solve in the time allotted.
>
> Under these conditions, the men with high *n* Achievement regularly chose to work on the business problem, even though they knew the odds of success were statistically the same as for rolling the dice.

To men strong in achievement concern, the idea of winning by chance simply does not produce the same achievement satisfaction as winning by their own personal efforts. Obviously, such a concern for taking personal responsibility is useful in a business executive. He may not be faced very often with the alternative of rolling dice to determine the outcome of a decision, but there are many other ways open to avoid personal responsibility, such as passing the buck, or trying to get someone else (or a committee) to take the responsibility for getting something done.

The famed self-confidence of a good executive (which actually is related to high achievement motivation) is also involved here. He thinks it can be done if *he* takes responsibility, and very often he is right because he has spent so much time thinking about how to do it that he does it better.

2 *Another characteristic of a man with a strong achievement concern is his tendency to set moderate achievement goals and to take "calculated risks."* Again his strategy is well suited to his needs, for only by taking on moderately difficult tasks is he likely to get the achievement satisfaction he wants. If he takes on an easy or routine problem, he will succeed but get very little satisfaction out of his success. If he takes on an extremely difficult problem, he is unlikely to get any satisfaction because he will not succeed. In between these two extremes, he stands the best chance of maximizing his sense of personal achievement.

The point can be made with the children's game of ring toss, some variant of which we have tried out at all ages to see how a person with high *n* Achievement approaches it. To illustrate:

> The child is told that he scores when he succeeds in throwing a ring over a peg on the floor, but that he can stand anywhere he pleases. Obviously, if he stands

next to the peg, he can score a ringer every time; but if he stands a long distance away, he will hardly ever get a ringer.

The curious fact is that the children with high concern for achievement quite consistently stand at moderate distances from the peg where they are most apt to get achievement satisfaction (or, to be more precise, where the decreasing probability-of-success curve crosses the increasing satisfaction-from-success curve). The ones with low n Achievement, on the other hand, distribute their choices of where to stand quite randomly over the entire distance. In other words, people with high n Achievement prefer a situation where there is a challenge, where there is some real risk of not succeeding, but not so great a risk that they might not overcome it by their own efforts.

Again, such a characteristic would seem to suit them unusually well for the role of business entrepreneur. The businessman is always in a position of taking calculated risks, of deciding how difficult a given decision will be to carry out. If he is too safe and conservative, and refuses to innovate, to invest enough in research or product development or advertising, he is likely to lose out to a more aggressive competitor. On the other hand, if he invests too much or overextends himself, he is also likely to lose out. Clearly, then, the business executive should be a man with a high concern for achievement who is used to setting moderate goals for himself and calculating carefully how much he can do successfully.

Therefore, we waste our time feeling sorry for the entrepreneur whose constant complaints are that he is overworking, that he has more problems than he knows how to deal with, that he is doomed to ulcers because of overwork, and so on. The bald truth is that if he has high n Achievement, he loves all those challenges he complains about. In fact, a careful study might well show that he creates most of them for himself. He may talk about quitting business and living on his investments, but if he did, he might then *really* get ulcers. The state of mind of being a little overextended is precisely the one he seeks, since overcoming difficulties gives him achievement satisfaction. His real problem is that of keeping the difficulties from getting too big for him, which explains in part why he talks so much about them because it is a nagging problem for him to keep them at a level he can handle.

3 *The man who has a strong concern for achievement also wants concrete feedback as to how well he is doing.* Otherwise how could he get any satisfaction out of what he had done? And business is almost unique in the amount of feedback it provides in the form of sales, cost, production, and profit figures. It is really no accident that the symbol of the businessman in popular cartoons is a wall chart with a line on it going up or down. The businessman sooner or later knows how well he is doing; salesmen will often know their success from day to day. Furthermore, there is a concreteness in the knowledge of results which is missing from the kind of feedback professionals get.

Take, for example, the teacher as a representative professional. His job is to transmit certain attitudes and certain kinds of information to his students. He does get some degree of feedback as to how well he has done his job, but results are fairly imprecise and hardly concrete. His students, colleagues, and even his college's administration may indicate that they like his teaching, but he still has no real evidence that his students have *learned* anything from him. Many of his students do well on examinations, but he knows from past experience that they will forget most of that in a year or two. If he has high *n* Achievement and is really concerned about whether he has done his job well, he must be satisfied with sketchy, occasional evidence that his former pupils did absorb some of his ideas and attitudes. More likely, however, he is not a person with high *n* Achievement and is quite satisfied with the affection and recognition that he gets for his work which gratify other needs that he has.

The case of the true entrepreneur is different. Suppose he is a book publisher. He gets a manuscript and together with his editors decides that it is worth publication. At time of issuance, everyone is satisfied that he is launching a worthwhile product. But then something devastatingly concrete happens— something far more definite than ever happens to a teacher—namely, those monthly sales figures.

Obviously not everyone likes to work in situations where the feedback is so concrete. It can prove him right, but it also can prove him wrong. Oddly enough, the person with high *n* Achievement has a compelling interest to know whether he was right or wrong. He thrives and is happier in this type of situation than he is in the professional situation.

Two further examples from our research may make the point clearer. Boys with high *n* Achievement tend to be good with their hands, to like working in a shop or with mechanical or electrical gadgets. What characterizes such play again is the concrete feedback it provides as to how well a person is doing. If he wires up an electric circuit and then throws the switch, the light either goes on or it does not. Knowledge of results is direct, immediate, and concrete. Boys with high *n* Achievement like this kind of situation, and while some may go on to become engineers, others often go into business where they can continue getting this kind of concrete feedback.

* * *

REVIEW QUESTION

1 Given your knowledge of achievement-oriented persons, list three specific ways that you might treat them to capitalize on that trait.

READING 11

Personality vs. Organization
Chris Argyris*

*   *   *

Approximately every seven years we develop the itch to review the relevant literature and research in personality and organization theory, to compare our own evolving theory and research with those of our peers—an exercise salutary, we trust, in confirmation and also confrontation. We're particularly concerned to measure our own explicit model of man with the complementary or conflicting models advanced by other thinkers. Without an explicit normative model, personality and organization theory (P. and O. theory) tends to settle for a generalized description of behavior as it is observed in existing institutions—at best, a process that embalms the status quo; at worst, a process that exalts it. Current behavior becomes the prescription for future actions.

By contrast, I contend that behavioral science research should be normative, that it is the mission of the behavioral scientist to intervene selectively in the organization whenever there seems a reasonable chance of improving the quality of life within the organization without imperiling its viability. Before surveying the P. and O. landscape, however, let's review the basic models of man and formal organization.

FUNDAMENTALS OF MAN AND ORGANIZATION

The following steps indicate how the worlds of man and formal organization have developed:

1 Organizations emerge when the goals they seek to achieve are too complex for any one man. The actions necessary to achieve the goals are divided into units manageable by individuals—the more complex the goals, other things being equal, the more people are required to meet them.

2 Individuals themselves are complex organizations with diverse needs. They contribute constructively to the organization only *if on balance*, the organization fulfills these needs and their sense of what is just.

3 What are the needs that individuals seek to fulfill? Each expert has his own list and no two lists duplicate priorities. We have tried to bypass this intellectual morass by focussing on some relatively reliable predispositions that remain valid irrespective of the situation. Under any circumstances individuals seek to fulfill these predispositions; at the same time, their exact nature, potency, and the

*Reprinted by permission from the publisher from *Organizational Dynamics*, Fall 1974, pp. 3–6.
© 1974, AMACOM, a division of American Management Associations.

degree to which they must be fulfilled are influenced by the organizational context—for example, the nature of the job. In their attempt to live, to grow in competence, and to achieve self-acceptance, men and women tend to program themselves along the lines of the continua depicted in Figure 1.

Together, these continua represent a developmental logic that people ignore or suppress with difficulty, the degree of difficulty depending on the culture and the context, as well as the individual's interactions with the key figures in his or her life. The model assumes that the thrust of this developmental program is from left to right, but nothing is assumed about the location of any given individuals along these continua.

A central theme of P. and O. theory has been the range of differences between individuals and how it is both necessary and possible to arrange a match between the particular set of needs an individual brings to the job situation and the requirements—technical and psychological—of the job itself, as well as the overall organizational climate.

We have written four studies that highlighted an individual's interrelationship with the work context. In each study, a separate analysis was made of each participant that included (1) the predispositions that he or she desired to express, (2) the potency of each predisposition, (3) the inferred probability that each would be expressed, and (4) a final score that indicated the degree to which the individual was able to express his or her predispositions.

A personal expression score enabled us to make specific predictions as to how individuals would react to the organization. We had expected individuals with low scores, for example, to state that they were frustrated and to have poorer attendance records and a higher quit rate—expectations that also showed how individual differences in predispositions were differentially rewarded in different types of departments. Bank employees with a need to distrust and control others, for example, instinctively opted for positions in the internal audit department of the bank.

So much for the model of man. Now to organizations, which have a life of their own, in the sense that they have goals that unfortunately may be independent of or antagonistic to individual needs. The next step was to determine if there was a genetic logic according to which organizations were programmed.

FIGURE 1
DEVELOPMENTAL CONTINUA

Infants begin as	Adults strive toward
1 being dependent and submissive to parents (or other significant adult)	1 relative independence, autonomy, relative control over their immediate world
2 having few abilities	2 developing many abilities
3 having skin-surfaced or shallow abilities	3 developing a few abilties in depth
4 having a short time perspective	4 developing a longer time perspective

FIGURE 2
CONTINUA OF ORGANIZATIONAL ACTIVITIES

low	Designing specialized and fractionalized work	high
low	Designing production rates and controlling speed of work	high
low	Giving orders	high
low	Evaluating performance	high
low	Rewarding and punishing	high
low	Perpetuating membership	high

Observation and reading combined to suggest that most organizations had pyramided structures of different sizes. The logic behind each of these pyramids—great or small—was first, to centralize information and power at the upper levels of the structure; second, to specialize work. According to this logic, enunciated most clearly by Frederick Winslow Taylor and Max Weber, management should be high on the six organizational activities summarized in Figure 2.

This model assumed that the closer an organization approached the right ends of the continua, the closer it approached the ideal of formal organization. The model assumed nothing, however, about where any given organization would be pinpointed along these continua.

PERSONALITY VS. ORGANIZATION

Given the dimensions of the two models, the possibilities of interaction are inevitable and varied; so is the likelihood of conflict between the needs of individuals and the structured configuration of the formal organization. The nature of the interaction between the individual and the organization and the probability of conflict vary according to the conditions depicted in Figure 3.

From this model, we can hypothesize that the more the organization approaches the model of the formal organization, the more individuals will be forced to behave at the infant ends of the continua. What if—still operating at the level of an intellectual exercise—the individuals aspired toward the adult end of the continua? What would the consequences be? Wherever there is an incongruence between the needs of individuals and the requirements of a formal organization, individuals will tend to experience frustration, psychological failure, short-time perspective, and conflict.

What factors determine the extent of the incongruence? The chief factors are: first, the lower the employee is positioned in the hierarchy, the less control he has over his working conditions and the less he is able to employ his abilities; second, the more directive the leadership, the more dependent the employee; and last, the more unilateral the managerial controls, the more dependent the employee will feel.

FIGURE 3
CONDITIONS OF INTERACTION

If the individual aspired toward	And the organization (through its jobs technology, controls, leadership, and so forth) required that the individual aspire toward
1 adulthood dimensions	1 infancy dimensions
2 infancy dimensions	2 adulthood dimensions
3 adulthood dimensions	3 adulthood dimensions
4 infancy dimensions	4 infancy dimensions

We have said that individuals find these needs difficult to ignore or suppress, and if they are suppressed, frustration and conflict result. These feelings, in turn, are experienced in several ways:

• The employee fights the organization and tries to gain more control—for example, he may join a union.
• The employee leaves the organization, temporarily or permanently.
• The employee leaves it psychologically, becoming a half-worker, uninvolved, apathetic, indifferent.
• The employee downgrades the intrinsic importance of work and substitutes higher pay as the reward for meaningless work. Barnard observed almost 40 years ago that organizations emphasized financial satisfactions because they were easiest to provide. He had a point—then and now.

We want to emphasize several aspects about these propositions. The personality model provides the base for predictions as to the impact of any organizational variable upon the individual, such as organizational structure, job content, leadership style, group norms, and so on. The literature has concentrated on employee frustration expressed in fighting the organization, because it's the commonest form of response, but we shouldn't ignore the other three responses.

In a study of two organizations in which technology, job content, leadership, and managerial controls confined lower-skilled employees to the infancy end of the continua, their response was condition three—no union, almost no turnover or absenteeism, but also apathy and indifference.

Last, we believe that the model holds regardless of differences in culture and political ideology. The fundamental relationships between individuals and organizations are the same in the United States, England, Sweden, Yugoslavia, Russia, or Cuba. A drastic statement but, we think, a true one.

* * *

REVIEW QUESTION

1 Summarize the essence of Argyris's "congruency" model of the fit between the employee's personality and the formal organization.

CHAPTER 3

UNDERSTANDING INDIVIDUAL BEHAVIOR IN ORGANIZATIONS

READING 12

The Work Ethic—
An Idea Whose Time Has *Gone*?

Alan L. Porter*

The economic problem, the struggle for subsistence, always has been hitherto the primary, most pressing problem of the human race. If the economic problem is solved, mankind will be deprived of its traditional purpose.

Will this be of a benefit? If one believes at all in the real values of life, the prospect at least opens up the possibility of benefit. Yet I think with dread of the readjustment of the habits and instincts of the ordinary man, bred into him for countless generations, which he may be asked to discard within a few decades . . . thus for the first time since his creation man will be faced with his real, his permanent problem—how to use his freedom from pressing economic cares, how to occupy his leisure, which science and compound interest will have won for him, to live wisely and agreeably and well.—John Maynard Keynes[1]

Work is something we take very seriously—as individuals and as a society. Just compare the warm, approving feeling we get from phrases like "a good worker," "a solid day's work," or "a steady job" with the negative, even frightening, associations of "out of work." Individuals who have lost jobs, particularly men, report a sense of failure, a loss of sexual identity, and a feeling of isolation in the absence of those 40 hours a week of contact with fellow workers. Retirement is a widely feared trauma: As one retiree put it, "I had no place to go, nothin' to do."[2] Lottery winners keep on working. Managers and employees, men and women, all share a virtually automatic approval for the notion of work. Our reactions on a societal level are analogous. We grow very concerned by stories of "hundreds idled in plant closing,"[3] "national productivity slipping," or "further movement toward the welfare state." There are automatic political points to be scored by decrying those evils and taking action to create jobs and produce more goods. Implicit in these concerns is a sense of moral duty associated with work—that is, the "work ethic."

For most of us, the work ethic is so obviously right that to question it seems foolish, if not downright sinful. Whether from religious belief, patriotic duty, or practical desire to better ourselves, is it not obvious that we must work? On scrutiny the evidence is not so clear. For instance, we have all heard enough (perhaps too much) about the "blue-collar blues," with hourly employees asking

*From "The Work Ethic—An Idea Whose Time Has *Gone*?" *Business*, January–February 1981, pp. 15–22. Reprinted with permission. Copyright 1981 by the College of Business Administration, Georgia State University, Atlanta.

more from their jobs than their paychecks. We are now starting to see distinct signs of a similar discontent growing among middle managers.[4] Nationally, other troublesome instances arise. The last few years have forced us to take a second look at the costs of increasing production and consumption. Pressures on energy and material supplies lead to difficult foreign-policy squeezes; environmental damages loom serious; and the stability of our economy is challenged. As a society, as well as individually, are we striking a sound bargain in our single-minded emphasis on productive work?

This article proposes that the answer to the question just posed may, in fact, be "no!"—at least in some cases, for some people. I suggest that the complex set of values and beliefs comprising the work ethic is a rather recent and ephemeral phenomenon in our historical understanding of work. On closer examination, the concept of work is itself complex. It seems useful to distinguish work from basic individual and societal needs, which can then be used as yardsticks to assess the true worth of work. Simply put, people work for at least three different reasons— extrinsic reward (a paycheck), intrinsic rewards (direct fulfillment of human needs through work itself), and societal good (much work that is not intrinsically very rewarding serves societal interests). The work ethic, however, adds a fourth factor—that one *ought* to work, regardless of how little one gets paid, how unpleasant the job is, or how little society is improved by the effort. It is the sense of "ought" that has passed its zenith and may become positively harmful as we move into post-industrial society. The work ethic is an idea whose time has come—and gone.

HISTORICAL PERSPECTIVE

On first impulse, work might seem to be a basic attribute held in constant value by everyone, at all times. Not so! The work ethic as we know it is essentially a phenomenon of the last century or so and has primarily developed in America and Protestant Europe.

Prehistoric man's life consisted almost solely of the work necessary to meet basic needs for survival. "Man was born, he worked, and he died."[5] Not until technological advance and the division of labor yielded a productive surplus did it generally make much sense to distinguish work from other human activities. Thereupon work became considered almost a curse, as by the ancient Hebrews and Greeks.[6] The Hebrews looked on work as painful drudgery and eyed the kingdom to come for blessed idleness.[7] Aristotle contrasted work to culture, finding little to applaud in physical labor.[8] The ancient world may not have regarded manual labor, per se, as degrading, but rather, the dependency created by working for others in return for payment.[9] The social subordination of the worker is epitomized in the form of slavery. The notion that work must in some way be irksome is a legacy from such roots. It is notable that "as late as 1789, Edmund Burke wrote that the occupation of a hairdresser or of a candlemaker could not be a matter of honor to any person—'to say nothing of a number of more servile employments.'"[10]

Then where did our high regard for the worker arise? Referring to the ethic of the worker, Simon succinctly summarizes:

"There can be no doubt that these notions and feelings represent one of the most interesting cultural trends in modern times. Their origin can be traced to the rising middle class which carried out the commercial and industrial revolutions between the sixteenth and nineteenth centuries, at which time these ideas and sentiments were eventually taken over in somewhat modified form by various labor movements. The belief that work is the highest value, the fullest and perhaps the only meaningful form of human activity appears to have been expressed most forcefully."[11] The industrialization of society thus elevated work to a preeminent place. Adam Smith asserted that labor was the source of wealth, and Marx underlined that. Bourgeoisie and proletariat, capitalist and communist, all focused on work as the basis of personal worth.

Kindred to the emerging work ethic was the "Protestant ethic," probably most pronounced in America. (The Protestants do not have a monopoly on the work ethic. The commercial success of the Iranian Baha'is, whose motto is "work is a prayer," may be attributed to their work ethic that has helped propel them into middleclass status.[12]) Without getting into which ethic—Protestant or work—led which, the emerging paradigm emphasized dedication to hard work with a strict repression of personal indulgence. This combination contains features that add up to a nasty paradox today.[13] For the Puritan, sloth was perhaps the deadliest of sins. (Passive contemplation, so highly regarded by the classicists such as Aristotle and by many Eastern philosophies of life, was rejected.) A compulsive thrust to be active toward industrious ends led to a boom in productivity. Productivity exerted pressure to consume the goods produced. Consumption, in turn, placed stress on the nonindulgent Protestant ethic that helped generate the productive surplus. Today one can observe a complex interplay between the promotion of consumption, the guilt associated with that consumption, and a fear that religious values are imperiled by a materialistic culture.

What are the implications of this historical progression? An important pattern can be inferred with respect to a society's stage of development and its attitudes toward work. In the most primitive situations, everyone must work nearly all of the time to eat, so work is a necessity. As agriculture and basic manufacturing emerge, society develops a bit of a surplus, so that some do not have to work continuously, and society places high esteem on that freedom from toil. As industrialization appears, there is a tremendous need for workers and a corresponding prestige for work. Post-industrial society requires fewer "productive" workers, allowing for a shift to service work—from making things for people to doing things for them.

As society's need for physical labor in the fields and factories decreases, the value placed on such work is apt to decline. Demands on the service sector depend on less concrete human needs and are liable to change (e.g., as self-reliance becomes a widely held social value). Furthermore, technological advances, such as computers and robotics, could reduce the requirement for human workers in the service sector. Where then would people work? What value would society place on work? The image of society with reduced work requirements is uncertain and frightening, but less so than that of a society clinging to a work ethic from an outmoded age of industrial development. As society grows beyond the industrial era, so must its norms with respect to work.

THE MEANING(S) OF WORK

I should make clear that in questioning the work ethic, I am not trying to advocate some opposite notion, such as a "play ethic" or an "idleness ethic." The key to the critique of the work ethic is its implied moral obligation to engage in a certain form of activity for its own sake rather than for intended effects on the individual and/or society. The key to the concept is the meaning of "work."

Rather than offer a single definition, it seems more sensible to explore a number of dimensions in which people have tried to distinguish work from other human activities. The box [below] lists seven such dimensions.

Let's take a quick look at each of these dimensions. The prototype of the worker is someone who does physical labor. Simon recounts that academics reacted strongly to his definition of work, which excludes intellectual activity per se. Nonetheless, he holds that those who turn materials to human use perform a more fundamental work than those who are not direct producers (e.g., government employees, managers). External orientation and social utility are character-

---

WHAT IS WORK?

The following dimensions have been used by some scholars (some of the time) to characterize work:

Work-like	Non-work-like
Action on physical nature (manual labor)	Action on people (priests, politicians)
Externally oriented action	Contemplation
Yields social utility	Yields individual utility
Legal obligation	Free human development
Serious, even irksome	Enjoyable
Paid	Unpaid
Means	Ends

istics that distinguish work from inner-directed actions (e.g., contemplation, whittling). It should be emphasized that Simon places value (possibly of a higher order) on many human activities, such as meditation, that rise above the mere utility of work.[14] He also notes the distinction between legal obligation (required, necessary) and free development (of one's own volition). The obligatory characteristic of work is an important element in this critique of the work ethic, as is the notion that it is in some way irksome. The words for "work" in various European languages share a common association with pain (as in "labor," also often linked to the pangs of birth). Other associations tie to burden, poverty, and even torture (the French *travailler*).[15] While "work" can be our most general word for doing something, it is predominantly used to mean paid employment.[16] The tie between work and pay is growing stronger—in 1875 less than 50% of the employed people worked for wages or salaries; in 1971, some 88% of the nonagricultural work force in the United States fell in this category.[17] (Feminist efforts to have housework considered as work illustrate one dissatisfaction with that usage.)

The last of the seven dimensions follows Simon's sense that work is inherently a means to some other ends. C. Wright Mills states this position strongly: "Neither love nor hatred of work is inherent in man, or inherent in any given line of work. For work has no intrinsic meaning."[18] (I note that some would disagree. For example, Dorothy Sayers has said, "Work is not primarily a thing one does to live, but the thing one lives to do."[19] Also, the Task Force on Work in America concluded that satisfying work is a basic human need.[20]) The distinction between means and ends with respect to work has been most developed by psychologists. Herzberg, for one, distinguished between satisfaction, tending to arise from the content of the work, and dissatisfaction, tending to result from the ancillary features of a job.[21] There can be no doubt that many workers attain great personal reward (beyond any payments received) from their work. However, work does not seem to be the end in itself. As Best puts it, "Work is purposeful *human* activity directed toward the satisfaction of *human* needs and desires."[22]

To summarize, work connotes a host of meanings. For present purposes, a simple composite image is suitable. Thus the "work" in work ethic should be taken as serious, paid labor performed for others (as opposed, say, to self-motivated activities done for their own interest). It is vital to note that this definition allows for a wealth of rewarding activities besides "work." Again, the challenge to the work ethic is not a call for idleness.

RELATIONSHIP TO HUMAN NEEDS

If work is not an end in itself, it is necessary to decide how it relates to individual and collective human ends. Maslow's framework will serve to consider individual need fulfillment; societal interests will be addressed in terms of certain critical issues.

The basic human needs identified and ordered by Maslow are *survival*, *security*, *belonging*, *esteem*, and *self-actualization*.[23] Both the intrinsic (psychological) and extrinsic (financial) rewards of work pertain. The financial returns translate into satisfying one's basic survival and security needs (e.g., through purchase of food and shelter), and, indirectly, the esteem needs (e.g., through prestige associated with the accouterments of income and consumption). Psychological returns may include job security, esteem, belongingness, and self-actualization. Thus work can play a prominent role in fulfilling the individual's needs.

What must be emphasized, however, is that there are other ways to achieve such fulfillment; work is not the only source. Indeed, phenomena such as American "leisure seizure" suggest that prevailing work arrangements are found wanting. Basic survival and security needs could be well-served by a guaranteed-income arrangement. Belonging and esteem needs might be better met by a system that allowed alternatives to paid work as a source of social status. Self-actualization would be more consistent with activities designed to provide direct fulfillment than through jobs designed for mass production or to make work. Schumacher shows that such an orientation is feasible in describing "Buddhist economics."[24] Release from the obligation to put in 40 hours at a paid job could open tremendous actualization potentials, were such freedom unaccompanied by social condemnation. If forecasts are right that the nation is moving toward greater emphasis on the higher needs, especially self-actualization, this may put further stress on traditional work patterns.[25] Alternative work schedules and part-time positions offer a first step to relieve such stress and enable individuals to better attain their personal ends.[26]

Determining social needs or national goals is even more daunting than consideration of individual needs. However, the following five national objectives provide a workable basis for consideration of work and the work ethic: Control *inflation*, improve social *equity*, enhance the *quality of life*, carefully manage energy and material *resources*, and preserve national *security*. (The attainment of full employment is also a national goal mandated by Congress since 1946.)[27]

Our national objectives are multiple in nature as we struggle with complex issues matched against pluralistic social values. A systems perspective warrants that we are unlikely to be successful in meeting multiple objectives if these are addressed one at a time. In particular, I am concerned by the trade-offs associated with the aim that everyone should have a job. Let me illustrate the point three ways.

One worry about our economy (with national-security overtones) is its inability to compete internationally, given its poor rate of productivity improvements. To encourage modernization we consider industrial-investment credits that often translate to reduced labor-intensiveness. Yet we cringe so at automation and layoffs that we guarantee featherbedding.

As a second instance, we try to control inflation by inflicting the miseries of unemployment on additional millions. Presumably this reduces consumption demand and puts pressure on the lower echelons of workers to moderate their wage demands because of the reserve army of unemployed eager for their jobs. Yet if the unemployed need be so for the economy to function better, shouldn't we acknowledge their social value and our social equity objective by providing for them adequately? But if unemployment were freed from hardship and stigma, wouldn't that undermine its effectiveness as an inflation fighter?

A third instance consists of the effort to increase employment (make work) by prompting additional consumption. For example, income tax credits are urged in the hope that the money will be used to consume more, in turn boosting production and inducing jobs. In place of conspicuous consumption for consumption's sake, we push consumption to make work. But such an endless loop of evergrowing production and consumption fuels inflation, puts pressures on energy and material supplies (in turn increasing our dependence on foreign sources), and increases the waste-disposal burdens on our environment. Furthermore, the attendant increases in the standard of living have been challenged as lowering the quality of life.

In sum, attempts to maintain high employment can run counter to other societal interests. In particular, creation of artificial jobs fueled by unneeded consumption in a world of limited resources and environmental resilience would seriously endanger societal survival. Returning to the premise that work is not an end in itself, work should be considered as but one alternative means to achievement of our more basic aims.

FUTURE PROSPECTS

The preceding arguments add up to a call for a change in the work ethic. The patterns of historical progression and the emerging individual and societal needs suggest forces acting to bring about such change. However, these forces are confronted by a religious fervor ready to defend the work ethic at any cost. The outcome of this clash is hard to predict, confounded as it is with uncertainties in related factors such as the future state of the economy, war or peace, possible technological breakthroughs, and so on. To get a better feel for what the options may be, I sketch two alternative futures—one dominated by the work ethic and one that essentially abandons it.

"Jobs for All"

The heading for this vignette on life in the United States in 2020 derives from a political campaign of the first decade of the 21st century. A succession of recessions and international crises coupled with continuing inflation had jolted the economic system. Unemployment levels rose and fell, but continuously drifted upward through each crest. What should be done to settle this economic situation became the dominant political issue. The Democrats responded by adopting a platform principle of provision for everyone's needs no matter whether they worked or not. Such a stance was too far "left" for the American voters, and they lined up behind the work-oriented, "jobs for all" position of the Republican majority.

The government still faces many difficulties. Resource constraints are severe. Energy shortages have strained transportation, electric-power generation, and industrial production in some sectors. Many types of materials (foods as well as minerals) are in increasingly short supply, inducing international tensions as these are power-brokered. Industrial production levels continue to rise, leading to a series of environmental crises related to healthful air and water supplies. New technologies have contributed greatly to keeping the world economy functional, with great advances in energy production, weaponry, information processing, and leisure products. Of course, these have raised fears for the environment, business competition, and protection of jobs.

Life is both similar to and different from that of 40 years ago. The basic human values held by most Americans are much like they were. Prominently emphasized in the values profile is the work ethic, held to be a keystone in America's efforts to meet international competition and to provide for its own. A key difference from the past is where people work. Fewer than 2% of the work force is employed in agriculture and only 7% in basic manufacturing (continuing longstanding trends).

The "service" and "knowledge" sectors dominate, with virtually half of the entire work force being government employees. Continual complaints are heard about the low productivity of the massive, and still growing, bureaucracies— governmental and private. Employment is generally for life; it essentially takes court action (a growth sector in its own right) to fire someone. Jobs are precious and society functions to preserve them.

Consumption is pressed to fuel the economy, but the system is increasingly fragile as shortages of a critical mineral can shut down an industry, say automobiles, thus threatening the whole edifice. "Defense" is a recourse, just as when oil and aluminum supplies were cut off in the 20th century. Luckily, the resulting defense actions have not yet caused a general nuclear conflict.

Some observations on life-styles and general conditions convey what life is like in the early 21st century. Wages are high because of the pressure to maintain a high standard of living despite rising prices. This creates an inflationary spiral that encourages consumption. Surprisingly, some technological advances are actively opposed. For instance, the government now demands a "work-impact statement" in conjunction with research and development activities to demonstrate that further jobs will not be threatened.

The "post-industrial" society has less inherent need for human work, leading to tremendous emphasis on educational activities (often not work-related, as plumbers pick up doctorates in sociology) and increased leisure. The average workweek is now 28 hours (four 7-hour days), with average retirement at age 57. Tensions have arisen between older people pursuing their individual rights to keep working and the need for jobs for younger people.

Despite growth in the GNP, people report that things are likely to get worse before they get better. Concerns center on security—people fear the economic instabilities, crime is not under control, and war is a real threat. People cling strongly to the available anchors of security, especially work. As the party platform states—

- Every man has a right to employment by virtue of his nature, dignity, and need for personal growth.
- Every man has the obligation to work.
- Production, distribution, and consumption of goods are not ends in themselves, but creative activities to permit the development of working life.[28]

Nonetheless, support for the opposition's notion of "to each according to his need" seems to be growing.

"Justice for All"

Many of the premises of the previous scenario hold true for life as it "really" is in the year 2020. The nation has progressed through a series of economic difficulties, and resources are severely constrained. However, international tensions are greatly reduced and technological developments have been focused on meeting the most pressing societal needs, especially energy and material conservation. Moreover, the outcome of the great political struggle actually went the other way— the Democrats with their platform of "justice for all" triumphed in the early days of the 21st century. The consequent national policy—that all Americans merit financial support above the poverty level, regardless of whether or not they are working—has changed the face of the nation.

National policy and long-range planning focus on attainment of an equitable, secure, sustainable, resource-conserving economy. Equity and financial security have been gradually dissociated from employment. The negative income tax enacted over the past 15 years has removed the financial need to work to provide the basics of human survival, health care, and educational opportunity.

National security has been enhanced largely through reduced dependence on foreign materials. Although the concept of equity has not been significantly extended to sharing with other nations, our world image and relations are more positive than in the past. The sustainable, resource-conserving perspective has reduced our consumption of worldwide resources.

In lieu of the drive to maximize GNP, we now pursue the maximization of quality of life through balanced production of goods and provision of services, striving for environmental protection. Indeed, the GNP (no longer an accepted indicator) equates to under $1 trillion in 1980 terms. The levels of economic activity and consumption have decreased.

The value systems of many Americans have shifted rather drastically from those of 40 years ago. Material values have declined. For instance, conspicuous consumption is a social taboo, resulting in some interesting quirks as those who still hunger for the "good life" camouflage their activities (e.g., a black market in small electrical appliances and travel under assumed identities). Indeed, long-life product design is now mandated by several laws, in striking contrast to the planned obsolescence of days gone by. Not needing to pump up the economy to provide work has allowed for better balancing of the national objectives.

The most prominent change in values is the diminution of the work ethic. The old notion that an individual without a (paid) job had no basis for self-esteem has largely passed. Today, people are motivated by a more diverse set of aims. Of course, the overwhelming majority of American households (91%) still have at least one paid "worker" engaged over 1,500 hours per year. Over half (57%) of the households with two or more adults have two or more engaged in paid activities. What is striking is that many "work" part-time, on an ad hoc basis, on nonroutine work schedules, as volunteers and/or on personal activities without serious prospect of monetary reward (such as painting).

In conjunction with the institution of the negative income tax came a demise of the regulations on working—the minimum-wage laws and hour limits—as well as the make-work programs. The "work" place has returned to a free-market arrangement over and above the guaranteed income floor. Nowadays, one negotiates on an individual basis to set an acceptable wage rate, work assignment, and pay rate for any job.

Besides the death of the unions, some interesting twists have resulted. For one, productivity has skyrocketed. Since people no longer feel compelled to stay at their jobs, they have a more positive orientation to them. Current average pay for less desirable jobs (not hard physical labor, which is much desired for health reasons) surpasses that for skilled work, for which supply outstrips demand (e.g., university professors, despite the boom in education).

Job security and its attendant inertia are gone—civil service and the need to show cause for firing an employee went out together when the Supreme Court ruled that there was no longer a basis for them, given the security of the national guaranteed-income system. One consequence was the dismemberment of many long-standing bureaucracies. Today, the "adhocracy" is alive and well.

Local, or even national, computer files provide a prospective employer with information on available individuals. It is not uncommon for someone to take a project job for six months, to vacation for three months, then return to a new job for a period thereafter. This has caused psychological difficulties for some who long for the old format that guaranteed a routine lifetime on the job. The new freedom for personal development has resulted in expanded religious, social, and aesthetic activities—both conventional and radical. Very few people would willingly contemplate a return to the old "9-to-5" lifetime grind. Americans are more optimistic about the future than ever before.

CONCLUDING OBSERVATIONS

The age-old premise "if one did not work, one did not eat" no longer fits the realities of our economy.[29] Simply put, the proportion of our potential work force required to produce food, shelter, and the other basics of human survival is small and shrinking. The continuing reduction in society's need for conventional, paid work is a force for change. One direction of change would be an increased commitment to the work ethic reflected in increasingly awkward struggles to make work. The opposite would be to recognize the evolving societal needs, to

correspondingly reduce our emphasis on paid work, and to begin to take fuller advantage of the potentials for human development thereby opened. I advocate the latter.

Certainly, any attempt to lessen the role of work in our society deserves careful consideration. However, recalling our consideration of the term "work," a critical point was that it has no intrinsic meaning; it is not an end in itself. Work provides one way to meet our needs, but not the only way. As Keynes suggest in the quote at the beginning of this article, freedom from work can be a marvelous opportunity, albeit a staggering one. The work ethic is too deeply held to be quickly sloughed off. Thus in the near term any changes must be gradual.

Measures such as alternative work schedules, part-time work, and increased welfare and unemployment benefits can ease the constraints of the 40-hour workweek. Reduction in the average hours worked could both lower unemployment and increase leisure time. However, this would do nothing to reduce the dichotomy between work as drudgery and enjoyment obtained elsewhere. More ideal would be movement to integrate work and play so that one set of activities could better serve human needs, including self-actualization. At the national level, we should immediately reconsider whether attempting to make work for everyone impedes attainment of our objectives of a secure, equitable economic system. To the extent that this is the case, changes are due.

In the longer term, more drastic reconsideration of the place of conventional, paid work is required. The "Justice for All" scenario is just one of many possibilities, but it does suggest important points. First, the notion of a guaranteed-income plan is certainly feasible for a society that only requires 10% of its potential work force to provide for its necessities of life. Such a scheme could effectively satisfy the basic survival needs of people but only if social approbation accompanied it. Second, the scenario implies drastic changes in the motivations and organizational structure associated with work. The implications of these need to be explored thoroughly. Morever, the extent of the changes appears so great that they could come about only in conjunction with a broad consensus for value change with respect to the work ethic—a most difficult proposition.

Is such change in the work ethic of American society plausible? Based on a historical perspective, the answer seems to go beyond "yes" to "inevitable." The work ethic has evolved over time to meet changing societal needs as the industrial revolution progressed. It helped propel individuals, groups, and nations to the economic forefront. But it will grow increasingly out of place in a post-industrial society whose concerns lean to moderated consumption in a resource-constrained world. In such a setting, it is utter folly to stimulate consumption to make work, because that costs too much in terms of resource diminishment, ecological stresses, foreign dependence, and general reduction of the resilience of the economic system.

We must set aside our thoughtless allegiance to the work ethic. While the prospect of unemployment is personally frightening, it need not be. A combination of economic and social changes could help loosen us from this constraint. On a societal level, this is not to decry productivity. Rather, the suggested directions for change could enhance productivity by eliminating the unhappy psychosocial baggage that has accumulated with the notion of work. The moral obligation to work exerts a counterproductive force in many ways, such as prompting regulations that tend to ossify and bureaucratize both the public and private sectors. The work ethic is dangerous ideology that threatens our society's ability to develop a sustainable, post-industrial economic system. It demands harsh questioning. And that implies a difficult dialogue that ought to begin now.

REFERENCES

1 Quoted by Fred Best, ed., *The Future of Work* (Englewood Cliffs, New Jersey, Prentice-Hall, 1973), p. iii.
2 Studs Terkel, *Working* (New York, Avon Books, 1975), p.562.
3 "Detroit: Hitting the Skids," *Newsweek*, April 28, 1980, p. 58.
4 George A. Steiner, "Can Business Survive Its New Environment?" *BUSINESS*, January–February 1980, pp. 13–19.
5 Melvin Kranzberg and Joseph Gies, *By the Sweat of Thy Brow* (New York, G. P. Putman's Sons, 1975), p. 3.
6 Lloyd H. Lofquist and Rene V. Dawis, *Adjustment to Work* (New York, Appleton-Century-Crofts, 1969).
7 C. Wright Mills, *White Collar: The American Middle Class* (New York, Oxford University Press, 1951), pp. 215–223.
8 Yves R. Simon, *Work, Society, and Culture* (New York, Fordham University Press, 1971), p. 145. Simon notes that interpretation of Aristotle's views requires care; Aristotle's distinction between a craft and a profession may approach Simon's.
9 Kranzberg and Gies, *By the Sweat of Thy Brow*, p. 28.
10 Simon, *Work, Society, and Culture*, p. 3.
11 Ibid., pp. 40–41.
12 "The Minority That Iran Persecutes," *Newsweek*, March 24, 1980, p. 61.
13 George W. Albee, "The Protestant Ethic, Sex and Psychology," *American Psychologist*, February 1977, pp. 150–161.
14 Simon, *Work, Society, and Culture*, p. 110.
15 Ibid., p. 18.
16 Raymond Williams, *Keywords* (New York, Oxford University Press, 1976), p. 282.
17 Paul Dickson, *The Future of the Workplace* (New York, Weybright and Talley, 1975), p. 315.
18 Mills, *White Collar*, p. 215.
19 Quoted in Dennis Clark, *Work and the Human Spirit* (New York, Sheed and Ward, 1967), p. 110.
20 Cited by Dickson, *Future of the Workplace*, p. 22.
21 Frederick Herzberg, "The Motivation-Hygiene Concept and Problems of Manpower," *Personnel Administration*, January–February 1964, pp. 3–7.
22 Best, *The Future of Work*, p. 2.
23 See Abraham Maslow, *Motivation and Personality* (New York, Harper & Row, 1970).
24 E. F. Schumacher, *Small Is Beautiful: Economics as if People Mattered* (New York, Harper Torchbooks, 1973).
25 D. Elgin and A. Mitchell, "Voluntary Simplicity," *The Co-Evolution Quarterly*, Summer 1977, pp. 4–19.

26 John D. Owen, *Alternative Work Schedules: A Technology Assessment* (Washington, D.C., National Technical Information Service, 1977).

27 Dennis Clark, *Work and the Human Spirit* (New York, Sheed and Ward, 1967), p. 80.

28 Clark, ibid., proposes these as some principles of a new work ethic.

29 Best, *The Future of Work*, p. 126.

REVIEW QUESTIONS

1 After your reading of Porter's article, what does the "work ethic" mean to you?

2 What evidence can you provide that the work ethic has *not* diminished among Americans?

3 Rate the strength of your work ethic on a scale from 1 = low to 10 = high. What factors have influenced its development?

READING 13

Organizational Socialization

Patricia Sanders
John M. Yanouzas*

Just as a supervisor can make or break a newcomer's job experiences, a trainer can make or break a new trainee's learning experiences. Part of the success of training depends upon the trainer's ability to orient or "socialize" trainees to the learning environment.

Broadly defined, the concept of socialization as related to organizations refers to the process by which "new members learn the value system, the norms and the required behavior patterns of the society, organization or group which they are entering,"[1] In the learning environment, socialization encompasses the process or method the trainer adopts to inform trainees of expectations. That is, trainees must be made aware of what is expected of them, of the role of the trainer and of the desired outcomes.

This article describes a model and method for socializing trainees into the learning environment. More specifically, it presents a model of organizational socialization; demonstrates how this model may be applied to training/learning environments; and offers some suggestions for socializing trainees into the learning environment.

The literature on organizational socialization is concerned primarily with orienting new members to the organization and to the work environment. Three distinct phases of socialization emerge from this literature.

*From "Socialization to Learning," *Training and Development Journal*, July 1983, pp. 14–16. Reprinted with permission.

Prearrival or Anticipatory Socialization[2,3,4]   This phase encompasses all the learning that occurs prior to membership in a new position. An individual arrives at an organization with an existing set of attitudes, values, behaviors and expectations. These predispositions may be congruent or incongruent with organizational expectations. In addition, an individual may have realistic or unrealistic expectations of the organization. The degree and extent of congruence or realism depends on the nature of previous learning and socializing experiences. The initial process of socialization involves relinquishing or realigning preexisting attitudes, values and dispositions.

Encounter[5,6,7]   Organizations, likewise have preexisting norms, goals, values and expectations. At the point of entry into the organization, an individual's existing dispositions encounter those of the organization. Sometimes this encounter results in a head-on collision. More typically, it involves a period of adaptation in which the new member sees what the new organization is like and in which there is an initial shifting of values and expectations. The success or failure in this initial shifting process depends on two factors which are not always under the organization's control.[8]

The first factor is the level of motivation of the new member to join the organization. If the level is high, the new member will be very tolerant of uncomfortable socializing experiences. If the level of motivation is low, however, socializing efforts will not succeed, and the new member eventually may leave the organization.

The second factor influencing the success of early socialization efforts is the degree to which the organization can hold the new member captive by offering incentives and reinforcers. These incentives, coupled with the entrant's level of realism about the organization, will influence the success of early socialization efforts.

The socialization process during the encounter phase includes orienting the new member to work tasks, to work-group norms and values and to role definition.[9] Initiation to the task involves the entrant's capabilities and feelings of competence in learning the new job. Initiation to the work group involves learning the norms and values of co-workers and being accepted and trusted by them. Role definition involves learning and clarifying job duties, responsibilities, priorities and allocation of time, as well as defining role and position within the work group.

Change and Acquisition   The final phase of socialization requires some change and the acquisition of new relationships, new values and new modes of behavior.[10,11,12] Before a new member can acquire fully the skills and abilities to perform successfully in the organization, the entrant must first go through an "unfreezing" process, wherein he or she discards incongruent values or unrealistic expectations.[13] Once this unfreezing is accomplished, and if socializing efforts have been successful, the new member most likely will change in the direction favored by the organization.

The final socialization phase results not only in changing some preexisting values and expectations, but also in the acquisition of a new self-image. Caplow notes that the "self-image of a fully socialized member mirrors the entire organization, although not always perfectly."[4] Finally, the goal of all socializing efforts should be the acquisition of a new set of behaviors needed for successful performance and survival in the organization.

While the foregoing three phases are distinctly defined, there is overlap between them.

*   *   *

REFERENCES

1 Schein, E. H. Organizational socialization and the profession of management. *Industrial Management Review*, 1968, *9*, 1–16.
2 Feldman, D. C. The multiple socialization of organization members. *Academy of Management Review*, 1981, *6*, 309–318.
3 Porter, L. W., Lawler, E. E. & Hackman, J. R. *Behavior in organizations*. New York: McGraw-Hill, 1975.
4 Van Maanen, J. Breaking in: A consideration of organizational socialization. In R. Dubin (Ed.), *Handbook of work, organization, and society*. Chicago: Rand-McNally, 1975.
5 Porter et al. *op cit.*
6 Van Maanen. *op cit.*
7 Caplow, T. *Principles of organization*. New York: Harcourt, Brace, & World, 1964.
8 Schein. *op cit.*
9 Feldman, D. C. A contingency theory of socialization. *Administrative Science Quarterly*, 1976, *21*, 433–452.
10 Feldman. *op cit.*
11 Porter et al. *op cit.*
12 Caplow. *op cit.*
13 Schein. *op cit.*
14 Caplow. *op cit.*

REVIEW QUESTION

1 Describe the ways in which you have experienced the three phases of socialization in your career as a student.

READING 14

Learned Helplessness

Mark J. Martinko
William L. Gardner*

Passive and maladaptive organizational behavior resulting from properties of the organization and its environment has been described by a number of organizational theorists. Argyris (1957), for example, argues that there is an incongruency between the needs of individuals to become healthy and mature and the properties of modern bureaucracies such as formalization, standardization, and rigid rules. Over time, he argues, employees become shaped by the organization and are unable to demonstrate creative and mature behavior even when it is desired and rewarded.

Blauner's (1974) research on alienation is closely related. Although Blauner expected to find alienation directly related to increasing levels of technology, he found that it was more a function of bureaucratization, centralization, and rigid rules. In general, he concluded that alienation was caused and characterized by a sense of powerlessness and lack of control over the production process. Like Argyris' worker victimized by the organization, the alienated worker was generally passive and could not be depended on to exercise initiative on the rare occasions when it was encouraged and rewarded.

In addition to the above descriptions, there are numerous other examples of passive maladaptive behavior in organizations that appear to be related to rigid organizational policies and structures coupled with the perception of lack of control. Cherniss (1980), for example, contends that staff "burnout" by health service professionals is produced by unpredictable work environments that cause workers to feel helpless and to withdraw. In a related but dissimilar example, Stedry and Kay (1966) found that people reduced their levels of productivity when they believed it was impossible to achieve imposed goals. Finally, Larwood and Wood (1977) suggest that cultural and organizational conditioning encourages passive behavior by women and thus reduces the probability of assertive and aggressive behavior when it is appropriate.

These examples demonstrate that there is a continuing concern and belief that characteristics and properties of organizations inadvertantly condition passive behavior in organizations. Up to the present, the theoretical explanations for this problem often have been oversimplified, circular, and even teleological. Blauner (1964), for example, explains alienation in terms of employees' perceptions of

*From "Learned Helplessness: An Alternative Explanation for Performance Deficits," *Academy of Management Review*, April 1982, pp. 195−204. Reprinted with permission.

The authors would like to acknowledge discussions with Steve West of Arizona State University and Margaret M. Clifford of the University of Iowa which were extremely helpful in the development of this manuscript.

lack of control over the methods for doing their jobs. Because alienation is at least partially defined as a perception of lack of control, this explanation is circular and adds little to the understanding of the process by which alienation occurs.

The purpose of the present review is to present an alternative explanation for passive behavior in organizations. Many previous explanations have focused on the characteristics of the environment and the organization as the primary explanation for passive behavior. Presented in this paper is an attributional perspective of learned helplessness (LH) that focuses on how individuals process information about their environment and the organization. Through emphasis on individual cognitions and attributions, another level of explanation for passive organizational behavior is developed from which strategies are generated for minimizing and alleviating organizationally induced helplessness (OIH).

RESEARCH FOUNDATIONS

Definition and Early Research

LH is the notion that after repeated punishment or failure, persons become passive and remain so even after environmental changes that make success possible. The concept of LH was developed by Overmier and Seligman (1967), who observed that dogs repeatedly exposed to inescapable electric shocks eventually discontinued their efforts to escape even after the situation was changed so that escape was possible. During the first set of trials in this experiment the dogs were completely immobilized in a harness and repeatedly shocked. Initially, they reacted very strongly, struggling to free themselves. However, after repeated trials the animals discontinued their escape attempts and passively accepted the shock. At this point, the experimenters removed the harnesses, making escape possible by moving to the other side of the grid. The pretreated animals, for the most part, did not attempt to escape. In contrast to dogs that did not receive prior exposure to inescapable shock, they continued their passive behavior despite the changed conditions. Overmier and Seligman (1967) suggested that the source of interference in the dogs' escape responses was a "learned helplessness." Their explanation for the dogs' passive behaviors was that they had learned that the shock was independent of their behavior and that this expectancy transferred to new situations, thus inhibiting escape responses and learning.

LH in Humans

Experiments designed to explore the LH hypothesis in humans quickly followed Overmier and Seligman's (1967) experiment. In early studies, escape avoidance training tasks similar to those used in the animal research documented performance deficits in humans that paralleled those found in the comparative literature (Hiroto, 1974; Krantz, Glass, & Snyder, 1974; Thorton & Jacobs, 1971). Later, researchers replaced the simple escape avoidance training procedures with more complex tasks such as anagram solutions (Gatchel & Proctor, 1976; Hiroto &

Seligman, 1975; Miller & Seligman, 1975) and cognitive problem solving tasks (Diener & Dweck, 1980; Dweck & Bush, 1976; Roth & Bootzin, 1974; Roth & Kubal, 1975). The range and variety of tasks with which these studies document LH in humans support Overmier and Seligman's (1967) original notion that LH is a fundamental type of learning. Thus, it seems reasonable to conclude that the basic principles and findings from these laboratory studies generalize to behavior in more open systems. Indeed, LH has been demonstrated to be a reasonable explanation for the behavior of clinically depressed mental patients (Kupier, 1975; Seligman, 1975), staff burnout in social service agencies (Cherniss, 1980), and motivational deficits in classrooms (Diener & Dweck, 1980; Dweck & Bush, 1976). As of yet, however, the notion of LH has not received attention in the organization literature despite its demonstrated effectiveness in explaining performance deficits in other settings.

A MODEL

A variety of models of LH have been developed (Abramson, Seligman, & Teasdale, 1978; Miller & Norman, 1979; Zuroff, 1980), and each provides valuable insight into the nature and process of LH. However, none of the existing models focuses specifically on organizations and those aspects of organizations that are most likely to induce LH. In order to fill this void, a model of OIH has been developed and is presented in Figure 1.

At the outset, it is emphasized that, although some of the relationships depicted in the model have not yet been described by others, the majority of the components are parts of existing and accepted theory. The overall framework for the model is the social learning theory approach recently suggested by Davis and Luthans (1980) and frequently referred to as the S-O-B-C paradigm. Within the S-B-O-C paradigm, the intrapersonal cognitive processes of the organism are emphasized with particular attention focusing on the person's attributions. Because this model builds on previous research and theory, it already has substantial support in the existing literature.

An overview of the OIH model will help clarify subsequent discussion. Basically, the model indicates that cues from the environment are coupled with the person's past outcome history in order to make causal attributions for performance. The processing of this information is moderated by individual differences such as sex, need for achievement, and locus of control, which influence the attributions that people make about their environment. People attribute performance outcomes to one of four causes: ability, effort, task difficulty, or luck/chance. This causal schema is from the original two dimensional matrix suggested by Heider (1958) and more fully explicated by Weiner, Frieze, Kukla, Reed, Rest, and Rosenbaum (1971). The first dimension, stability, indicates whether or not the cause changes over time. Both ability and task difficulty are stable causes that are relatively invariant over time, whereas luck/chance and effort are unstable, changing over time. The second major dimension of the matrix is locus of control, based on Rotter's (1966) work. As Figure 1 depicts, both ability and

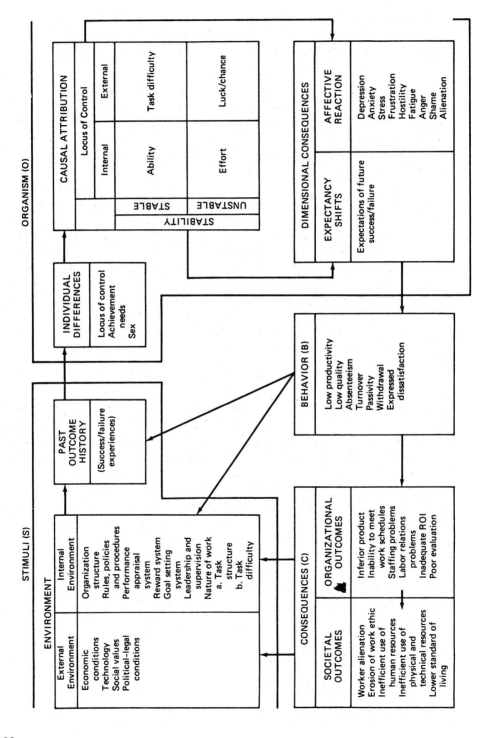

effort are internal causes because they lie "within" the person, whereas the task difficulty and luck/chance are classified as external causes controlled by the environment. It should be noted that although other attributional dimensions such as intentionality (Rosenbaum, 1972), specificity (Abramson et al., 1978), and controllability (Weiner, 1979) have been suggested, they have not received the same general empirical support as the Weiner et al. (1971) taxonomy and would unnecessarily complicate the model at this point.

Once an attribution is made, it influences the person's affective states and expectancies, which, in turn, influence behavior. For example, the literature suggests that if an employee attributes poor performance to the stable internal dimension of lack of ability, it is likely that the employee will become depressed, have lowered expectations for performance, and behave in a passive maladaptive way by failing to perform or withdrawing from the situation. On the other hand, if the employee attributes poor performance to lack of effort, it is more likely that the employee will not feel depressed, will expect that performance can be improved, and will behave in a productive way. Thus, within the present model, the attribution is a key component that drives the behavior and is responsible for organizational and societal outcomes.

Despite the absence of research specifically designed to test the LH hypothesis in organizations, a considerable amount of management literature can be interpreted as supportive of the OIH model. In the following sections, the management and the social psychology literature are integrated and the research that supports selected portions of the model is described.

The Environment

Both the internal and external organizational environment can function as cues for OIH. However, because of the macro nature of the external environment, very few studies have been able to offer convincing documentation and articulation as to its impact on behavior. Thus it is difficult to specify the exact influence of the external environment on OIH. Research by Burns and Stalker (1961), Woodward (1965), and Lawrence and Lorsch (1967) at least suggests that macroenvironmental variables affect individual behavior. In addition, work by Toffler (1970) provides evidence that rapidly changing external environments are associated with workers' feelings of alienation and helplessness.

Although the research on the external environment is limited, research on the internal environment suggests a variety of relationships between environmental variables and OIH.

Organizational Structure and Policies   Research by both Blauner (1964) and Aiken and Hage (1966) indicates that employees of relatively centralized, bureaucratic organizations that rely on formal rules and policies often experience feelings

---

FIGURE 1
A model of organizationally induced helplessness.

of alienation, frustration, and helplessness. An OIH interpretation of these findings consistent with Aiken and Hage's own explanation is that the workers' inabilities to determine their work methods resulted in perceptions of noncontingency between performance and efforts and/or abilities. These causal attributions then resulted in frustration, helplessness, and passive behavior. Finally, these passive attitudes produced a sort of self-fulfilling prophecy whereby the workers were unlikely to respond to opportunities, even when they became available. Thus, LH had been inadvertently induced.

Evaluation Systems   The validity of evaluations conducted by superiors has been seriously questioned (Anderson, Roush, & McClary, 1973; Kane & Lawler, 1979). Recently, Green and Mitchell (1979) have suggested that attribution theory is a useful vehicle for understanding the manner in which superiors evaluate subordinate performance. Furthermore, these authors suggest that attributional biases such as the actor-observer (Jones & Nisbett, 1972) and self-serving (Miller & Ross, 1975; Zuckerman, 1979) biases may distort superiors' attributions. In particular, the actor-observer bias suggests that superiors (observers) will favor internal subordinate attributions such as lack of ability or effort for poor performance, where as subordinates (actors) will favor external environmental explanations for poor performance. Studies by Mitchell and Wood (1980) and McFillen and New (1979) provide empirical evidence of attributional biases of supervisors. An OIH interpretation of these findings is that employees in evaluation situations often feel that their evaluations are unrelated to their performance. Within this "no win" situation, they may become passive, deciding that it is impossible to improve. Thus, because of built-in biases such as the actor-observer and self-serving biases, it appears that, within the context of evaluation, employees are predisposed toward LH.

Reward Systems   In a survey of over 600 managers, Lawler (1966) found that they perceived virtually no relationship between their pay and performance evaluations. In addition to pay, many other rewards such as promotions, fringe benefits, and vacations are seen as unrelated to performance. Specific examples of the noncontingent relationship between performance and organizational rewards are documented by Kerr (1975). To the extent that employees perceive these rewards as noncontingent, the OIH hypothesis suggests that the employees become passive and apathetic, failing to behave appropriately when contingencies can or may be reinforced.

Organization Goals   In Locke's classic paper on goal setting, he indicated that "people who do stop trying when confronted by a hard task are people who have decided the goal is impossible to reach and who are no longer trying for that goal" (1968, p. 168). A review of the goal setting literature (Latham & Yukl, 1975) and the research by Stedry and Kay (1966) already cited supports Locke's contention. Again, the Stedry and Kay (1966) study found that workers who perceived goals to be impossible reduced their levels of performance. Considering this study and

Locke's theory from an OIH perspective, Locke's notion of intention is moderated by perceptions of contingency. When persons perceive that a goal is difficult or impossible, as they did in the Stedry and Kay study, they fail to perceive a relationship between their behavior and outcomes. Thus helplessness is induced and they become passive with respect to goal achievement.

Leadership Although LH has not been specifically considered within the context of leadership, attributional interpretations of leadership—for example, Green and Mitchell (1979) and Mitchell and Wood (1980)—suggest a variety of interesting questions related to OIH. A study by Dweck and Bush (1976), for example, shows that subjects have different reactions to failure, reactions that are dependent on evaluator characteristics. Thus, particular styles of leadership may serve as cues for LH.

The actor-observer bias (Jones & Nisbett, 1972), already mentioned, also poses interesting questions for leadership research. If the actor-observer bias is operating, leaders should blame subordinates more frequently than is justified for poor performance. The study by Mitchell and Wood (1980) did find that leaders clearly preferred internal rather than external explanations for subordinates' poor performances. Thus, it appears likely that, over time, leader's misattributions might inadvertently induce LH.

Finally, the self-serving bias (Miller & Ross, 1975) is potentially related to OIH. If this bias is operating, leaders will take most of the credit for success and will blame failure on their subordinates. Over time, it is likely that subordinates no longer will see a relationship between success and their efforts or abilities and will experience the depression, anxiety, and feelings of helplessness associated with OIH.

Nature of Work The Hackman and Oldham (1976) job characteristics model of work motivation emphasizes the importance of core job characteristics on work motivation. A number of reviews and studies document the effect of job characteristics on work attitudes and motivation (Champoux, 1980; Hackman & Oldman, 1976; Pierce & Dunham, 1976). The majority of these reviews and research have emphasized that increased job scope leads to increased job satisfaction and motivation, but the reciprocal hypothesis also deserves some attention. That is, from the present perspective, the negative affective states and decreased levels of motivation associated with jobs that are deficient in scope suggest that OIH is occurring. Thus, the broad range of literature documenting the relationship among job characteristics, work satisfaction, and motivation may be interpreted as supportive of the OIH model.

Individual Differences

Some employees may be more vulnerable to OIH than others. The research indicates that locus of control, sex, and achievement needs are important individual differences related to LH. Pittman and Pittman (1980), for example, found that people with an internal locus of control were especially susceptible to LH. The relationship between achievement motivation and LH is documented by Krantz et al. (1974). They found that persons whose life style is characterized by high need achievement motivation are more resistant to LH than are persons with opposite life styles. Sex differences with respect to both the degree of LH experienced and later recovery were observed by Dweck and Bush (1976) and Dweck and Repucci (1973), respectively. In the latter study, it was found that males attributed outcomes to effort more frequently than did females and that these attributions resulted in smaller performance deficits. The importance of sex differences is documented further by Baucom and Danker-Brown (1979), who found that both masculine sex-typed and feminine sex-typed persons are particularly susceptible to LH, whereas those who cannot be clearly typed are more resistant.

The latter finding has significant implications. It suggests that women who fail to violate stereotypes are more prone to OIH. Koff and Handlon (1978) label one category of women in management as the "stay-put prone group." They describe these women as being passive, low risk takers with negative self-concepts. Although Koff and Handlon suggest that fear of failure and fear of success are useful explanatory concepts for the behavior of these women, the OIH hypothesis may be equally useful. Specifically, it is likely that women who are frustrated by discriminatory employment practices eventually become passive, displaying OIH. After reviewing the literature on the relationships between sex and employee evaluation, Nieva and Gutek concluded that "studies focusing on the evaluation of qualifications in selection and promotion situations and research on the perceived causes of performance show fairly consistent bias in favor of men" (1980, p. 273). Thus, sexual prejudice and attributional biases are likely to solidify the perceptions of many women that evaluations and organizational rewards are unrelated to performance and heighten their susceptibility to OIH.

The individual difference factors mentioned above are the ones that appear most salient at present. However, others also are likely to be important moderators of OIH. Racial minorities, like women, may be particularly prone to LH. Similarly, the individual differences that moderate the relationship between task characteristics and performance (Aldag & Brief, 1979; Kim, 1980; O'Reilly, Parlette, & Bloom, 1980) may be important predictors of susceptibility to OIH.

Affective Reactions

The affective states that typify LH have been well documented in the social psychology literature. In general, these affective reactions are a function of the locus of control dimension (Feather, 1967; Storms & Nisbert, 1970). The most frequent affective reaction observed in conjunction with LH is depression (Klein & Seligman, 1976; Seligman, 1975). Other feelings found to be associated with LH are anxiety, stress, frustration, hostility, resignation, apathy, fatigue, anger, and shame (Seligman, 1975; Weiner, 1979).

Affective reactions resulting from OIH have not been specifically investigated.

However, it is reasonable to assume that at least some of the affective reactions documented in the organizational literature may be associated with OIH. For example, Blauner's (1964) research on alienation and the research on stress as it relates to role conflict (Kahn, Wolfe, Quinn, Snoek, & Rosenthal, 1964) could be interpreted through an OIH framework.

Expectancy Shifts

The influence of expectancies on organizational behavior has been well documented. In the context of the model, OIH develops when a person experiencing repeated failure begins to expect future failures. Research on expectancies (McMahon, 1973; Rosenbaum 1972) indicates that individuals attributing success or failure to stable causes of ability or task difficulty have similar expectations for future performance. In contrast, individuals attributing success or failure to unstable causes such as effort or luck/chance often expect different levels of performance in the future, believing that their effort or luck may change. Thus, it appears that the attributional component of the OIH model has potential for enhancing the predictions derived from expectancy theory.

OIH Consequences

The consequences of OIH affect both the organization and society and are approximately the same as those resulting from any state of depressed worker motivation. The organization produces an inferior work product, has difficulty meeting production or service schedules, experiences difficulty in staffing and labor relations, and thus has an inadequate return on investment. From a societal perspective, workers become alienated, the work ethic is eroded, standards of living are reduced, and resources are wasted.

OIH probably is more frustrating for managers than are other types of motivational deficits. Workers have the skills, abilities, and opportunities for successful performance but fail to perform because of prior rather than present contingencies. Thus, the model of OIH presents a perspective of performance deficits in organizations which is self-perpetuating. Low levels of performance contribute to an outcome history of failure and solidify expectations of future failure, resulting in additional failures. The self-perpetuating nature of the OIH cycle is emphasized by the feedback loops illustrated in Figure 1.

MINIMIZING OIH

One of the features of the OIH perspective is that it offers another level of explanation for performance deficits. Each component of the model emphasizes a different aspect of the OIH process and is a potential key to reducing the debilitating effects of OIH. Certain strategies may be employed to immunize against OIH or alleviate it. At the outset, it is recognized that there still is controversy on the nature and causes of LH (Abramson et al., 1978; Miller &

Norman, 1979). These strategies thus are tentative, still subject to validation in organizational environments.

Immunization

Immunization strategies are pretreatment strategies designed to provide individuals with experiences that will reduce susceptibility to LH. Although the early studies suggested that high levels of success (100 percent) were effective immunization strategies (Seligman & Maier, 1967; Thorton & Powell, 1974), more recent research suggests that partial schedules are more effective. Jones, Nation, and Massad (1977), for example, found that a ratio of 50 percent success was effective, whereas 0 percent and 100 percent success ratios were not. Similar results were reported by Clifford (1978), who concluded that continuous success may be as potentially debilitating as failure.

Although much of the above research was conducted in educational settings, there are clear implications and applications for immunizing persons from OIH. Women, minorities, new workers, and others who may be vulnerable to OIH may be pretreated by designing jobs so that the employees will experience reasonable levels of success early in their careers. These strategies could be incorporated into training and/or orientation programs. Similarly, individuals expected to perform tasks that may have relatively low levels of success may be pretreated. MIS design personnel, for example, might be particularly careful to provide success experiences for users before challenging them with difficult operations.

Discrimination Training

These strategies are based on the assumption that people do not sufficiently assess environmental cues associated with their successes and failures. They often need periodic feedback to help identify important cues. Klein and Seligman (1976), for example, successfully alleviated LH by providing people with success experiences and feedback based on their performance.

Strategies for eliminating OIH based on discrimination training focus on helping employees recognize differences between prior and present situations. Thus, for example, management might carefully point out the differences between prior and current promotional policies or between a previous and a current MIS system.

Attributional Training

Attributional training is a strategy suggested by Abramson et al. (1978). It focuses on performance attributions and is oriented toward directing unrealistic attributions toward more realistic sources. Essentially, it is a type of counseling in which LH employees are convinced that their failures are due to specific, external, and unstable causes whereas their successes are dependent on internal, global, and stable causes. In an example provided by Abramson et al., an LH woman who has not been promoted is told, "The system minimized opportunities for women. It is not that you are incompetent" (external attribution); "The system is changing. Opportunities that you can snatch are opening at a great rate" (unstable attribution); "Marketing jobs are still relatively closed to women, but publishing jobs are not" (specific). On the other hand, a woman experiencing success might be told that her success is caused by her ability (internal, stable attribution) and that she would be successful anywhere (global attribution).

Perceptions of Contingency

Another treatment closely related to attributional training is the changing of expectancy from uncontrollability to controllability. This strategy is most appropriate when the employees do not recognize that a performance-reward relationship has changed from noncontingent to contingent. If employees possess the required skills but do not expect adequate performance to be rewarded, direct exposure to the performance-reward relationship is required. If employees do not possess adequate skills to perform at the levels required to receive the contingent rewards, training to develop these skills is also required.

Ego Defense

This strategy is based on Frankel and Snyder's (1978) self-esteem explanation of LH. According to their hypothesis, LH is experienced to the degree that failure threatens self-esteem. When self-esteem is threatened, individuals discontinue effort and protect their egos by explaining their behavior in terms of reduced effort, changing environmental conditions, or task difficulty. This hypothesis suggests that OIH can be avoided if managements are careful to respect and protect employee self-esteem when failures do occur. Thus, for example, feedback during appraisal or goal setting sessions that is specific and based on incidents of employee behavior probably will be more effective than will general feedback regarding attitudes, which may threaten self-esteem. Similarly, performance-related discussions should be more effective when they are oriented toward developing attributions for performance that are not ego-threatening and self-defeating.

Modeling

A final technique suggested in the literature is modeling. Research by DeVellis, DeVellis, and McCauley (1978) demonstrates that people can learn LH by observing a model. Thus, the reciprocal proposition that people can "unlearn" OIH vicariously appears reasonable. This method encourages organizations to develop programs to make successful employees more visible and to reward success through strategies such as social recognition. It should be noted that this strategy is consistent with recently suggested models of organizational behavior (Davis &

TABLE 1
MINIMIZATION STRATEGIES FOR ORGANIZATIONALLY
INDUCED HELPLESSNESS

Strategy	Description
1 Immunization	Pretreatment with specific levels of success
2 Discrimination training	Through reinforcement and cue management, emphasize the difference between prior and present conditions
3 Attribution training	Teach people to attribute inappropriate failure to specific, external, and unstable dimensions while teaching them to attribute inappropriate success to general, internal, and stable dimensions
4 Perceptions of contingency	Emphasize the relationships between appropriate behavior and rewards through direct demonstration or counseling
5 Ego defense	In performance related discussions, help employees develop attributions that do not threaten self-esteem. Avoid general feedback based on attitudes that may be interpreted as a threat to self-esteem.
6 Modeling	Make success in the organization visible through social reinforcement strategies.

Luthans, 1980; Manz & Sims, 1981) that propose that a large proportion of organizational behavior is learned vicariously.

The strategies discussed above have been summarized in Table 1.

CONCLUSION

As contrasted with prior explanations of passive organizational behavior, the OIH perspective offers a level of explanation not previously suggested. The model provides a thorough intrapersonal analysis of the passive performer's cognitive states and the environment that serves as a basis for interventions designed to immunize or alleviate OIH.

Although the OIH model has not been tested in an organizational setting, there appears to be enough research on the components of the model and the basic cognitive process represented to suggest that the model is valid. Without question, considerable research needs to be done in organizations for further validation of the model and to identify specific areas in which OIH is occurring.

Some words of caution on the application of the OIH model are warranted. First, not all performance deficits are OIH. Poor performance may be a function of lack of ability, lack of resources, or any number of other unrelated factors. Second, and most important, all examples of helplessness are not "learned" helplessness. As Kerr (1975) points out so well, employees often have rational and sound motivational reasons for poor performance. Organizations frequently fail to reward and they inadvertently punish productive behavior. It becomes OIH only when the situation and its contingencies have changed so that the prior behavior is no longer appropriate.

The development and presentation of this model has involved some rather large inferential leaps and some simplifying assumptions. If the reader takes exception to the assumptions and propositions presented and if that stimulates further research, the objective of this paper will have been accomplished.

REFERENCES

Abramson, L. Y., Seligman, M. E. P., & Teasdale, J. D. Learned helplessness in humans: Critique and reformulation. *Journal of Abnormal Psychology*, 1978, 87, 49–74.

Aiken, M., & Hage, J. Organizational alienation: A comparative analysis. *American Sociological Review*, 1966, 31, 497–507.

Aldag, R. J., & Brief, A. P. *Task design and employee motivation*. Glenview, Ill.: Scott Foresman, 1979.

Anderson, H. E., Roush, S. L., & McClary, J. E. Relationships among ratings, production efficiency, and the general aptitude test battery scales in an industrial setting. *Journal of Applied Psychology*, 1973, 58, 77–82.

Argyris, C. *Personality and organization*. New York: Harper, 1957.

Baucom, D. J., & Danker-Brown, P. Influence of sex roies on the development of learned helplessness. *Journal of Consulting and Clinical Psychology*, 1979, 47, 928–936.

Blauner, R. *Alienation and freedom: The factory worker and his industry*. Chicago: University of Chicago Press, 1964.

Burns, T., & Stalker, G. M. *The management of innovation*. London: Tavistock Publications, 1961.

Champoux, J. E. A three sample test of some extensions to the job characteristics model of work motivation. *Academy of Management Journal*, 1980, 23, 466–478.

Cherniss, C. *Staff burnout*. Beverly Hills: Sage Publications, 1980.

Clifford, M. M. Have we underestimated the facilitative effects of failure? *Canadian Journal of Behavioral Science*, 1978, 10, 308–316.

Davis, T. R. V. & Luthans, F. A social learning approach to organizational behavior. *Academy of Management of Review*, 1980, 5, 281–290.

DeVellis, R. F., DeVellis, B. M. & McCauley, C. Vicarious acquisition of learned helplessness. *Journal of Personality and Social Psychology*, 1978, 36, 894–899.

Diener, C. I. & Dweck, C. S. An analysis of learned helplessness: II. The processing of success. *Journal of Personality and Social Psychology*, 1980, 39, 940–952.

Dweck, C. S., & Bush, E. S. Sex differences in learned helplessness: I. Differential debilitation with peer and adult evaluators. *Developmental Psychology*, 1976, 12, 147–156.

Dweck, C. S., & Repucci, N. D. Learned helplessness and reinforcement responsibility in children. *Journal of Personality and Social Psychology*, 1973, 25, 109–116.

Feather, N. T. Variance of outcome and expectation of success in relation to task difficulty and perceived locus of control. *Journal of Personality and Social Psychology*, 1967, 7, 372–386.

Frankel, A., & Snyder, M. L. Poor performance following unsolvable problems; Learned helplessness or egotism? *Journal of Personality and Social Psychology*, 1978, 36, 1415–1423.

Gatchel, R. J., & Proctor, J. D. Physiological correlates of learned helplessness in man. *Journal of Abnormal Psychology*, 1976, 85, 27–34.

Green S. G., & Mitchell, T. R. Attributional processes of leaders in leader-member interactions. *Organizational Behavior and Human Performance*, 1979, 23, 429–458.

Hackman, J. R., & Oldham, G. R. Motivation through the design of work: Test of a theory. *Organizational Behavior and Human Performance*, 1976, 16, 250–279.

Heider, F. *The psychology of interpersonal relations*. New York: Wiley, 1958.

Hiroto, D. S. Locus of control and learned helplessness. *Journal of Experimental Psychology*, 1974, 102, 187–193.

Hiroto, D. S., & Seligman, M. E. P. Generality of learned helplessness in man. *Journal of Personality and Social Psychology*, 1975, 31, 311–327.

Jones, E. E., & Nisbett, R. E. The actor and the observer: Divergent perceptions of causes of behavior. In E. Jones, D. Kanouse, H. Kelly, R. Nisbett, S. Valins, & B. Weiner (Eds.), *Attribution: Perceiving the causes of behavior*. Morristown, N.J.: General Learning Press, 1972, 1–16.

Jones, S. L., Nation, J. R., & Massad, P. Immunization against learned helplessness in man. *Journal of Abnormal Psychology*, 1977, 86, 75–83.

Kahn, R., Wolfe, D., Quinn, R., Snoek, J., & Rosenthal, R. *Organizational stress: Studies in role conflict and ambiguity*. New York: Wiley, 1964.

Kane, J. S., & Lawler, E. E. Performance-appraisal effectiveness: Its assessment and determinants. In B. Staw (Ed.), *Research in organizational behavior* (Vol. 1). Greenwich, Conn.: JAI Press, 1979, 425–478.

Kerr. S. On the folly of rewarding A, while hoping for B. *Academy of Management Journal*, 1975, 18, 769–783.

Kim, J. S. Relationships of personality to perceptual and behavioral responses in stimulating and non-stimulating work tasks. *Academy of Management Journal*, 1980, 23, 307–319.

Klein, D. C., & Seligman, M. E. P. Reversal of performance deficits in learned helplessness and depression. *Journal of Abnormal Psychology*, 1976, 85, 11–26.

Koff, L. A., & Handlon, J. H. Women in management: Keys to success or failure. In B. A. Stead (Ed.), *Women in management*. Englewood Cliffs, N.J.: Prentice-Hall, 1978, 239–248.

Krantz, D. S., Glass, D. C., & Snyder, M. L. Helplessness, stress level, and the coronary-prone behavior pattern. *Journal of Experimental Social Psychology*, 1974, 10, 284–300.

Kupier, N. A. Depression and causal attribution for success and failure. *Journal of Personality and Social Psychology*, 1975, 31, 311–327.

Larwood, L., & Wood, M. M. *Women in management*. Lexington, Mass.: Lexington Books, 1977.

Latham, G.P., & Yukl, G. A. A review of research on the application of goal setting in organizations. *Academy of Management Journal*, 1975, 18, 824–845.

Lawler, E. E. The mythology of management compensation. *California Management Review*, 1966, 9, 11–22.

Lawrence, P. R., & Lorsch, J. W. *Organization and environment*. Boston: Harvard Business School, Division of Research, 1967.

Locke, E. A. Toward a theory of task motivation and incentives. *Organizational Behavior and Human Performance*, 1968, 3, 157−189.

Manz, C. C., & Sims, H. P. Vicarious Learning: The influence of modeling on organizational behavior. *Academy of Management Review*, 1981, 6, 105−114.

McFillen, J. M., & New, J. R. Situational determinants of supervisor attributions and behavior. *Academy of Management Journal*, 1979, 2, 793−809.

McMahon, I. D. Relationship between causal attributions and expectancy of success. *Journal of Personality and Social Psychology*, 1973, 28, 108−114.

Miller, D. T., & Ross, M. Self-serving bias in the attribution of causality, *Psychological Bulletin*, 1975, 85, 213−225.

Miller, I. W., & Norman, W. H. Learned helplessness in humans: A review and attribution theory model. *Psychological Bulletin*, 1979, 86, 93−118.

Miller, W. R., & Seligman, M. E. P. Learned helplessness, depression, and anxiety, *Journal of Nervous and Mental Disease*, 1975, 161, 347−357.

Mitchell, T. R., & Wood, R. E. Supervisor's responses to subordinate's poor performance: A test of an attribution model. *Organizational Behavior and Human Performance*, 1980 25, 123−138.

Nieva, V. F., & Gutek, B. A. Sex effects on evaluation. *Academy of Management Review*, 1980, 5, 267−276.

O'Reilly, C. A., III, Parlette, G. N., & Bloom, J. R. Perceptual measures of task characteristics: The biasing effects of differing frames of reference and job attitudes. *Academy of Management Journal*, 1980, 23, 118−131.

Overmier, J. B., & Seligman, M. E. P. Effects of inescapable shock upon subsequent escape and avoidance learning. *Journal of Comparative and Physiological Psychology*, 1967, 63, 28−33.

Pierce, J. L., & Dunham, R. B. Task design: A literature review. *Academy of Management Review*, 1976, 1 (4), 83−97.

Pittman, T. S., & Pittman, N. L. Deprivation of control and the attribution process. *Journal of Personality and Social Psychology*, 1980, 39, 377−389.

Rosenbaum, R. M. *A dimensional analysis of the perceived causes of success and failure.* Unpublished Ph.D. Dissertation, University of California, Los Angeles, 1972.

Roth, S., & Bootzin, R. R. The effects of experimentally induced expectancies of external control: An investigation of learned helplessness. *Journal of Personality and Social Psychology*, 1974, 29, 253−264.

Roth, S., & Kubal, L. Effects of noncontingent reinforcement on tasks of differing importance: Facilitation and learned helplessness. *Journal of Personality and Social Psychology*, 1975, 32, 680−691.

Rotter, J. B. Generalized expectations for internal versus external control of reinforcement. *Psychological Monographs*, 1966, 80, 1−28.

Seligman, M. E. P. *Helplessness: On depression, development and death.* San Francisco: Freeman, 1975.

Seligman, M. E. P. & Maier, S. F. Failure to escape traumatic shock. *Journal of Experimental Psychology*, 1967, 74, 1−9.

Stedry, A. C., & Kay, E. The effects of goal difficulty on performance. *Behavioral Science*, 1966, 11, 459−470.

Storms, M. D., & Nisbett, R. E. Insomnia and the attribution process. *Journal of Personality and Social Psychology*, 1970, 16, 319−328.

Thorton, J. W., & Jacobs, P. E. Learned helplessness in human subjects. *Journal of Experimental Psychology*, 1971, 87, 369−372.

Thorton, J. W., & Powell, G. D. Immunization to and alleviation of learned helplessness of man. *American Journal of Psychology*, 1974, 87, 351–367.

Toffler, A. *Future shock*. New York: Random House, 1970.

Weiner, B. A theory of motivation for some classroom experiences. *Journal of Educational Psychology*, 1979, 71, 3–25.

Weiner, B., Frieze, I., Kukla, A., Reed, L., Rest, S., & Rosenbaum, R. M. *Perceiving the causes of success and failure*. Morristown, N.J.: General Learning Press, 1971.

Woodward, J. *Industrial organization*. London: Oxford, 1965.

Zuckerman, M. Attributions of success and failure revisited, or: The motivational bias is alive and well in attribution theory. *Journal of Personality*, 1979, 47, 245–287.

Zuroff, D. C. Learned helplessness in humans: An analysis of learning processes and the roles of individuals and situational differences. *Journal of Personality and Social Psychology*, 1980, 39, 120–146.

REVIEW QUESTIONS

1 Can you believe that some employees would continue to exhibit learned helplessness even after environmental changes make success possible? Why?

2 How would an organization discover that its structure and policies are inducing people to become helpless?

3 Thinking back to Readings 2 and 3, what do you think McGregor and Likert would say about the prospects of learned helplessness in a Theory Y/supportive organization?

READING 15

Seeing Eye to Eye: Practical Problems of Perception

John Senger*

Byron Cartwright, Plant Superintendent, ran his fingers worriedly through his thick, greying hair. He had a tough decision on his hands. With Frank Bauer's retirement he was faced with the problem of selecting a new foreman for the machine shop. But instead of the usual problem of a dearth of qualified people to promote, Byron felt that he had two equally well qualified men to take over. Pete Petronia and Sam Johansen were both highly skilled machinists, conscientious workers, liked and respected by the other men in the department.

To help make up his mind, Byron called Pete and Sam into his office separately to talk to them about how they thought the shop should be run. He didn't actually say to either of them that he was considering them for the foremanship, but they knew why they were there. In fact the other men in the shop had been talking for

*From *Personnel Journal*, October 1974, pp. 744–751. Copyright 1974 by Personnel Journal, Inc. Reprinted with permission.

some time about which one of them would succeed "Mr. Bauer." Both Pete and Sam were aware of these discussions and their own obvious qualifications for the job.

Byron even felt that either man had so much potential talent that one of them could succeed him as superintendent some day. With the new equipment orders in, it looked like a bright future for the machine shop—a great opportunity for the man he selected. That's what was bothering him so much. Which man?

But this was Byron's perception of the matter: opportunity, advancement, achievement, getting-ahead. He didn't know what was going on inside Pete's head. Pete, as a matter of fact, was very upset by the prospect. He recognized the "opportunity" and the extra hundred bucks every month. A chance to get his wife, Marge, a car of her own and, additionally, put something away in the bank. But Pete just doesn't like to tell other people what to do; he doesn't want the responsibility for planning the shop's work and keeping everyone busy. He doesn't want to be involved in paperwork—he doesn't even do that at home. Marge pays all the bills and figures the taxes and does the family planning.

What Pete loves is being a machinist. He likes the odor of the hot metal as it curls, shining away from the cutting edge of the turning tool. He likes the "feel" of the calipers as he slips them over the surface of a finished part, checking dimensions. He likes the precision, the craftsmanship, the sense of productiveness of his occupation. Pete likes to use his long, strong fingers for something besides shuffling papers. He doesn't want to tell other guys what to do. He doesn't want the responsibility for somebody else's work.

Byron Cartwright finally does make the decision to promote Sam, and he feels guilty every time he passes Pete hunched over his lathe. But, boy, is Pete relieved! He tells Byron how pleased he is that Sam is going to be the new foreman. But Byron doesn't really believe him. Pete, however, could take a deep breath for the first time in weeks without the worried tightness across his chest. Marge, his wife, is a little disappointed. She thought he deserved the promotion—he'd been there longer than Sam. But she had also been aware of Pete's edginess the past several weeks, and his noticeable relief since the announcement.

People's actions, emotions, thoughts and feelings are triggered by their perceptions of their surrounding situations. In the instance above, Byron Cartwright perceived the shop foremanship situation in one way—as a reward, a chance to get ahead, an opportunity to exercise authority, an achievement. Pete Petroni perceived it in quite a different way—as a threat, taking responsibility for others' mistakes, forcing his will on others, being separated from his lathe. Pete, while friendly and well-liked, preferred doing his own thing—alone.

Pete's perception is somewhat unusual in our "achieving society," but by no means rare. Even at that, Pete would have probably accepted the promotion. He was expected to, and Pete is enough of a child of his culture not to question that it is important to accept promotions and "get ahead," much as he might dislike it. That, after all, was his conflict.

But the point here is not about attitudes toward achievement, but about kinds of perception. The same set of circumstances can result in widely divergent perceptions. And differences in perception between managers and their subordinates make managing a tougher job.

We sense that people do see things differently. But we are at times so much a captive of our own perceptual sets that it becomes virtually impossible to see things as others see them. Part of the difference in what people perceive can be explained by the fact that they do *see different* things. Some of what is there to be seen may be physically obscured or unavailable knowledge to one perceiver. After all, Pete had never supervised and couldn't really accurately assess the situation. It might not be as bad as he thinks. But the important thing is that this information was not available to him, and this affected his perception.

Even greater differences in perception are the result of selectivity. One's senses are so overwhelmed by the mass of stimuli vying for attention that in order to carry on any directed activity we must somehow decide what we want most to attend to and block out or sublimate perceptual inputs that aren't related to that activity. If we go too far with selectivity, however, we block out some useful information and make it much more difficult to understand, or even be aware of, another's perception. Cartwright is an achiever, and to be an achiever he has to block out and sublimate distracting non-achievement oriented stimuli. In the process, he blocks out a perception of how someone like Pete Petroni sees things.

ORGANIZATION OF PERCEPTION

Selectivity is an important means of handling the perceptual overload. We further attempt to handle the myriad of perceptual inputs by various manners of organizing perceptions. A group of German psychologists, identified with the organization of perceptions, called themselves Gestalt psychologists, and placed great emphasis upon the organization and interrelationship perceptions. No, Virginia, there was no one named Wolfgang Gestalt. Gestalt is a German word essentially meaning to organize.

Common methods of organizing perceptions include grouping, figure-ground and closure. These techniques which we unconsciously utilize in an effort to cope with the mass of stimuli were first identified in connection with visual perception, but they help explain nearly as well much of social perception, as will be seen in the following illustrations.

FIGURE-GROUND

When Doris Graham started to work as secretary to Myron Green in the accounting department, the whole place and the people in it were a kind of amorphous blur in her mind. Slowly, it seemed, features of her new environment began to emerge. At first she was only aware of chief accountant Myron Green's name and face, and employment manager Dave Briggs' name and face. As she began taking dictation and typing, she began to realize Mr. Portley was in important figure to Myron Green and, therefore, to her. Otto Kowalski seemed helpful and Bill Crandell nice, but she didn't really define them against the background of the rest of the accounting department at first. Then, after a couple weeks or so, they began to emerge as people as well as important contacts in her job as secretary.

Here we see the figure-ground phenomenon at work. Certain "figures," Myron Green, Dave Briggs, Mr. Portley, Otto Kowalski and Bill Crandell, emerge from the "ground" represented by the people and things that make up the rest of the accounting department and the company. Then, slowly, the entire department begins to emerge as a "figure" against the "ground" of the entire company. Dave Briggs was the person to emerge as a "figure." (She had memorized his name from the slip of paper given her at White Collar Employment Agency before she ever got out to the company.) He had made her feel comfortable and a little as if she belonged. But now, only several weeks later, because of lack of contact, he was fading into the general company "ground" as the accounting department became a more distinct entity. Here we see the phenomenon of figure-ground reversal, not unlike the visual eye trick which occurs when silhouetted designs can be seen to reverse themselves, so that when, for example, the design is looked at one way, a white vase (the figure) appears against a dark background, and when the white portion of the design is perceived as the ground, the dark portions appear to represent a new figure, two faces.

This reversal was also seen by Doris, back when she was identified by the rest of the office as attached to Mr. Green, and she herself identified with Myron Green more than she did with the others. As time went on, she and the rest of the office got to know one another better. Sometimes when she knew Mr. Green and Mr. Portley were going to be away from the office for a certain period of time, she would pass the information along to the gang and they could all relax a little. A mutual trust developed and the office group began to emerge as the figure, while Myron Green and Mr. Portley tended to become a part of the general company background.

Figure-ground, a phenomenon long known as a visual parlor stunt, is a useful means of organizing our perceptions. It is a helpful way to think about what we see and experience and why we happen to perceive some things the way we do.

GROUPING

Stan Menke eased the Mustang to a stop in one of the lines of traffic funneling out of the South Parking Lot, and half turned to address Allyn White in the back seat. "Whaddya think the raise is going to be this time, Allyn?" "Gee, I dunno," replied Allyn. But Allyn, by now, wasn't surprised that Stan should ask him about details of important company decisions. So did Pete Petroni and Juan Fernandez, the other guys in the pool. All were older and had been with the company much longer than Allyn. Stan was a foreman and Allyn just a clerk. Juan was active in the union and knew a lot about how the wage negotiations were going. But Stan asked Allyn. Why?

Because Allyn worked in the accounting department, and the accounting department was on the second floor with the executive offices. Allyn wore a coat and tie, as did Mr. Portley and the rest of the executives. So Allyn was being "grouped" with the seat of the power in the company and was thought to be privy to important information. The fact that this was not the case didn't prevent the grouping from taking place.

This tendency to group persons or things that appear to be similar in certain ways, but not in all, is a common means of organizing our perceptions. Because these persons and things are similar in certain ways, but not all, distortion of perception can take place, as was the case with Allyn. Grouping helps us learn, it helps us remember, it is a valuable cognitive device, but it does carry with it the not infrequent cost of perceptual distortion.

A common example of grouping in the organization: The design engineers, the industrial engineers, the production engineers, the cost people, the production control group, who may be every bit as realistic and shop-problem oriented as the people on the shop floor, are viewed by the shop as "unrealistic," "too theoretical," "head-in-the-clouds," "ivory tower" and generally unconcerned with the shop. Why? Because they operate out of the second floor, don't wear blue collars (though some wear sport shirts and no ties) and are educated differently. They are up there with the sales people, the administrative people, the office girls and others less involved with production. They are *grouped* with those less involved with the factory floor. Proximity and similarity contribute strongly to grouping. Some lack of awareness of shop problems among the engineers, cost accountants and production control people is perhaps justified, but certainly not to the degree the grouping indicates.

It should be re-emphasized, on the other hand, that *grouping*, like *figure-ground*, helps us organize and cope with our environment. Without such aids we would be overwhelmed by detail, forced to make too many decisions. When the guys in the shop see somebody wandering around in a coat and tie and assume he's somebody pretty important, they are *usually* right. It's just that more than occasionally such generalizations can be misleading if followed blindly.

CLOSURE

Otto Kowalski is big and broad shouldered. He has a thick neck and a jutting jaw. He never wears a coat in the office, and works with his sleeves rolled up, his tie pulled down and his collar open. He walks like a bear with a slight charley horse. His voice is very deep and coarse. He looks tough, although he's not tough at all. Otto is not a stevedore, but an accountant. On Saturday afternoons he listens to the symphony on FM, not the excited voice of a television sports announcer. Or he tends his roses. People who know Otto only casually find this all very confusing. Why? Because Otto's appearance, voice and bearing send out certain perceptual signals from which the observer begins building a perceptual image of Otto. Big, loud guys with rolling gaits are "jocks," right? Tough, right? Aggressive, insensitive, kinda dumb, right? Wrong. Otto isn't any of these things. He is sensitive, intelligent, not particularly athletic, and gentle. Then why is almost everyone wrong about Otto on first impression?

Because of the perceptual phenomenon of "closure." Big, muscular guys are frequently stereotyped as athletic, aggressive, tough, insensitive, and, often, not too smart. It doesn't make any difference if this is the case or not. It's common belief and when we meet someone who looks like Otto, we start with those parts of his apparent behavior we observe, and then fill in the gaps left by those parts we don't observe; that is, we "close." It is just like seeing a line that curves around until it almost meets itself. We see it as a circle with a gap in it, not a curved line. We meet someone and like several things about him. So we go right ahead and close and assume that we also like the many other characteristics of this person. The tendency to assume that because we like someone, almost everything about him is good, is referred to as a "halo effect," a special case of closure.

And then, there's Myron Green. He has a sallow complexion, round shoulders, a bald head, wears rimless glasses, terribly conservative clothes and a perpetual scowl. Myron Green is, therefore, cold, aloof, over-meticulous, inhibited, unathletic, has a "Friden for a brain," and is kind of sneaky, right? Right! You see we don't miss them all. But it's seductively easy to fill in an image based upon incomplete evidence and come up with the *wrong* answer.

Organization of our perceptions helps us cope with an overabundance of perceptual information, but it also misleads us sometimes, and we should be aware of this possibility, both in ourselves and others. We don't react equally to all stimuli that bombard us, but select or attend to certain of them.

ATTENTION: EXTERNAL FACTORS

Industrial engineer Eldon Peavey's clothes are not conservative. Some people refer to them as "far out," some say "flashy," some say "too much." But no one can really ignore them—or Eldon. And that's Eldon's intent. He wants to attract attention to himself, and we do find ourselves attending to guys like Eldon. The biggest, brightest, loudest things clamor for our attention. Over in accounting, Otto Kowalski attracts our attention because he is so big. Like six feet four, and two hundred and thirty-five. We therefore will perceive Otto and Eldon before we perceive others less large or more mousey. If two objects are competing for our attention at the same time we shall perceive the more intense first. The Safety Department was thinking about this when they painted the exposed moving parts of machines red, in contrast to the drab grey of the rest of the machine. Size and intensity are important attention-getters.

Why did the Peabody Company finally close a deal with Harry Balou, even though Harry's price on the pumps was higher than that of the competition? Largely because Harry kept beating away at them about the superiority of "his" pumps. Monthly, sometimes weekly visits. Brochures. Telephone calls, Personal letters. He constantly reiterated the advantage of the pumps. Peabody finally had to pay attention. *Repetition* has been known for a long time by salesmen, and particularly advertisers, as an excellent means of attracting attention. When the company was big on the "Zero Defects" campaign in an attempt to cut down on scrap costs and improve quality, the term was seen everywhere. Taped to machines, on every bulletin board, in the company magazine, under windshield wipers in the parking lot, on the sign board in front of the factory, over the loud speaker system, in the cafeteria. Repeated and repeated and repeated. And it did appear to have an effect on quality and scrap. Certainly everyone was aware of the campaign.

The noticeability of coats and ties in the shop was previously mentioned. And the men who go up to the office from the shop are just as noticeable because of their clothes. Contrast also attracts attention. Byron Cartwright is usually pretty subdued and quiet-spoken at the weekly foreman's meetings, so when he's upset about something and raises his voice a little, everyone snaps to. If he shouted all the time, his change of tone wouldn't be as effective. Contrast again. And it works the other way. Myron Green keeps a very close eye on everything and everyone in the accounting office, and when he steps into Mr. Portley's office or is preoccupied with someone or something else, his subordinates immediately sense it. The termination of a stimulus can be nearly as attention-provoking as its onset.

ATTENTION: INTERNAL FACTORS

"Bleeding us! Taking what rightfully belongs to us workers. How can Portley have that big fat smile on his face with his right hand stuffed so deep into my wallet? Look at this picture in the paper. Look at him! Proud that he's taking 18% profit out of the company. Bragging about it. Look at my hands. Look at your own hands. That's what makes the pumps—and the money—for this company! Not Portley sitting around on his big fat chair in his big fancy office! Not the stockholders. What have they ever done to turn out one single pump? Little old ladies doing nothing but pampering their dogs are the ones who get all that profit. Doing nothing. And their dogs eat better than I do!"

Sean O'Flaretty, fiery old unreconstructed Trotskyite, was very upset by Mr. Portley's announcement in the company paper that profits were up for the year. Holding forth to the luncheon crowd lounging on the castings pile outside the foundry, as orange peels, egg shells and "baggies" were gathered up and stuffed back onto lunch boxes. Sean continued, "I ask you guys, why is it we do all the work around here and Portley and the little old ladies take all the money out of the place? It's not fair, never been fair, and one of these days you guys will quit sitting around doing nothing and demand your rightful share."

Obviously Sean—and maybe several others—was upset by the increased profit announcement. Why? Because the word "profit" to Sean is like a red flag to a bull. The word to him is filtered through a set of values which perceive profits as money taken away from the workers. Mr. Portley doesn't see it that way at all. He has a different set of filters. And he sees profits as evidence of a healthy organization, a feedback as to how well he is running the company, a source of income to those persons who had risked their savings in his enterprise, the generation of new wealth which can cause the company to expand and flourish.

The values, interests, beliefs and motivations that people have tend to distort their perceptions. It is little wonder people have difficulty understanding one another when the values they hold cause them to perceive the same work quite differently. To Mr. Portley, "profit" is a very satisfying term; to Sean O'Flaretty, a threat.

Postman, Bruner and McGinnies tested people to find what their major value orientations were.Then for a brief millisecond they flashed the words representing these values on a screen. The time the word remained on the screen was gradually increased until it was there long enough to be recognized by all the participants in the experiment. It was found, for example, that those persons with a strong religious value orientation were able to see the word "religion" when it was on the screen for a very brief instant. Others, less religiously oriented, required that the word be on the screen for a longer period before they recognized it. Things that are important to us, those which we value, are the ones we perceive.

SET

Sam Johansen looked up from the schedule board to see Pete Petroni bending over his lathe, while beside him the tote pan for finished parts contained only a dozen of the counter-shafts Pete was making up for a special order, No. 5008. Sam stood beside Pete and watched for a while. "Say, Pete," he asked, "what's wrong with this job that it's taking you so long to get it out?" "Long?" from Pete, "I only got started on this job just this morning." "Well, then you oughta be half done. I only see twelve in the tote pan. Are the rest of them someplace else?" Sam wanted to know. "Ye gods, no, Sam," replied Pete, "whaddaya mean? It takes a little while to make all these double-oh-one cuts." ".001? Are you holding those things to a .001 tolerance?" blurts Sam. "Lemme see the print. Yeah, see here, it says .01. Right there. See?" "Oh, my pet cow!" grumbled Pete, "you mean all these little deals are only supposed to be held to .01. How could I have done that? I'll tell you how I did it. I haven't done anything to that loose a tolerance in five years. I just simply read another 'oh' in there. Oh, my pet cow!" "Yeah, that's probably it, Pete," replied Sam. "The new guys who normally do this kind of work were tied up on long runs, so I simply scheduled it over here." "I sure didn't see there was just one 'oh' behind that point. Well, yah got a dozen nice expensive countershafts, Sam. I'm awful sorry," said Pete dejectedly. Pete had a *preparatory set*, an expectancy, to see what he saw: one more order for highly skilled, close tolerance work of the kind he was accustomed to doing. We go through life having our perceptions influenced by such preparatory sets. Our previous experience prepares us to see something such as we have seen before, and it's not just a matter of past experience, either. What we need and want to see also causes a perceptual set.

We all have sets, as the result of previous experiences and as the result of personal needs and interests. What might simply look like an old letter to you or me may be an object of intense interest to a stamp collector. An automobile enthusiast may pick out the exhaust tone of a Ferrari which is lost in the cacophony of traffic noises, to someone else. To see Juan Fernandez take a couple of quick steps from his turret lathe to deposit a finished part in a tote pan and then move briskly back to start work on the next piece appears to be efficient performance, to most people. But the fellows in industrial engineering immediately identify the action as evidence of an inefficient job layout. The way they see it, *no* steps should be taken, and better yet, the part should come out of the chuck and drop immediately into a tote pan untouched by Juan. The industrial engineers have a set to perceive wasted motion, which most of us miss. We are set to perceive what we value, what we're interested in, what we are trained to see, and what we've seen before.

PROJECTION

Allyn White turned into the accounting office and was just about to close the door behind him when the tail of his eye caught a glimpse of Eldon Peavey coming down the hall behind him. He didn't close the door all the way, but left it slightly ajar. Now Eldon was quite obviously not coming into the accounting department, but was headed for his desk in the industrial engineering department two doors down. But Allyn just couldn't shut the door in his face. Why? Because Allyn felt that Eldon would perceive the act as a personal rejection. Eldon probably wouldn't even have noticed, and had he noticed, he wouldn't look upon a closing door as an act of rejection. You had to get a lot more blunt than that before Eldon felt rejected. But Allyn, in the same situation, would have felt rejected. So what Allyn was doing was *projecting* his own feelings.

We can misinterpret others' actions and motives rather markedly, as a result of projection. Our perceptions are distorted in the direction of our own needs and attitudes, which we tend to assume are needs and attitudes shared by others. If one tends to be insincere, he perceives others as being insincere. Sears and Frenkel-Brunswick found that to be true in experimentation with both American and Austrian students.

Myron Green tends to be a sneaky sort and, sure enough, he distrusts everyone else a good deal. We saw Byron Cartwright assuming that because he liked achieving, directing and taking responsibility, Pete Petroni did, too. Otto Kowalski likes to help people, and so assumes that nearly everyone else does, also, to his frequent disillusionment. Projection is a very common, internalized perception distorter. An acute form of perceptual distortion, through over-simplification, is stereotyping.

STEREOTYPE

Dave Briggs, employment manager, was working his way down through the pile of recently received application letters, when he came to a resume that caused him to emit a low whistle and reach for the telephone. Dialing quickly, Dave got Ed Yamamoto, chief engineer, on the phone. "Ed," enthused Dave, "I think I have the group leader for the bi-valve pump section." The bi-valve pump design had been getting along without a direct supervisor since last February, when Hal Coombs had left the company. Herb Borgfeldt, senior man in the section, had twice refused the job, saying he was a designer, not a straw boss, and no one among the rest of the men in the section was experienced enough to take over as supervisor. The job really needed an expert pump designer, preferably with some supervisory experience.

"Graduated from Cal Tech, honors, three years with Livermore Radiation Lab, seven years with Cleveland Pump, last two and a half as supervisor of the bi-valve section. Lessee, two patents in own name, paper in 'Hydraulic Occlusion' at last year's SME meeting—" "Wow!" from Ed. "—and her letter says she wants to relocate here to be close to her mother, and since we are the only pump manufacturer in town, I can't see why we can't get her."

"Wait one minute," Ed burst forth, "you said 'her'?" "Yeah," replied Dave, "Ann Farmer. She apparently grew up here. Lessee, went to Horace Mann High School, where she was salutatorian and editor of the yearbook." "A woman!" snorted Ed. "Look, I'm no male chauvinist, you understand, but this is no job for a girl! There's lots of pressure. She'll be too emotional to run things, too illogical to think through design problems, too absorbed with details to see the big picture, too—" "W-a-i-t," protested Dave. "I'm not insisting you hire this engineer, but you did sound enthusiastic when I read her qualifications." "Well, *sure*, who wouldn't be? Cal Tech, supervisory experience, patents, papers, honors. But you hadn't told me he's a her!"

Ed is going through a form of perceptual distortion known as *stereotyping*, a form of categorization. Categorization is, of course, an extremely useful cognitive device, permitting us to handle and understand large bodies of complex information. Used restrictively, however, it causes the observer to draw conclusions from too narrow a range of information, and to generalize too many other traits from this minimal data, usually relating to the categorization of people. The way it works is for the perceiver to have established several ready-made, oversimplified categories of people who he thinks possess a few distinctive characteristics. Then he classifies the people he meets into one of these categories. The classification is made on the basis of one or a very few characteristics. The person so classified is then assumed to have all the characteristics thought to represent the category. Ed classified Ann Farmer as a woman, not as an engineer. Under Ed's "woman" classification are the characteristics of emotionalism, illogic, detail-mindedness, etc. Ed's prejudiced, but then there are those who would stereotype Ed as an engineer, which to them would tend to mean that he is unemotional, socially inept and so on. Stereotypes are usually learned young and go unquestioned. The learning usually takes place out of intimate contact with those assigned to the stereotyped category; therefore, the resulting attributed characteristics cannot help but be distorted.

SELECTIVE PERCEPTION AND BEHAVIORAL REVERSAL

Mabel Lindsey, typing pool supervisor, is aware that the girls in the typing pool don't like the clatter and din of working together in one big, noisy room; she knows they prefer doing work for one or a few people rather than typing whatever is parceled out to them, that they dislike the lack of individuality being a member of the pool implies. She is aware that Charlotte Bettendorf's loudness and exhibitionism irritate the rest of the girls in the pool, and that her own perfectionism is often hard to live with. She is aware of all these irritants *at the subconscious level.* To protect her own sanity, she has sublimated her awareness of these irritants and does not really perceive them anymore at the conscious level. If she were to consciously perceive and be sensitive to all the needs of her girls, she wouldn't have time to do anything else. In order to get on with her work, she must selectively stifle those perceptions of disturbing stimuli which don't contribute to what she perceives as important to her job as typing pool supervisor. This phenomenon has been described by Harold Leavitt as a self-imposed psychological blindness which helps persons maintain their equilibrium as they pursue their goals.

If, on the other hand, all the same week, first Betty, and then Claudine and then Hope were to complain about the noise, the irritation might break through Mabel's selective defense. She might then immediately burst in upon office manager Clyde Ferguson and demand that the ceiling be insulated. Selective perception, with its blackout of mild disturbances, can suddenly change to acute perception when the irritant exceeds a certain threshold. At this point, the individual shifts his attention sharply and fully to the irritant. As Leavitt puts it, "The distant irritation increases to a point at which it becomes so real, so imminent, and so threatening that we reverse our course, discard the blindfold and preoccupy ourselves competely with the thing we previously ignored." The phenomenon is a complex one, because if things are threatening, they must be fended off, but in order to fend them off they must first be seen. Therefore, in order for one to protect himself from threat, he must first perceive that threat and then manage to deny to himself that he has seen it. This combination of selective perception and defensive behavior helps explain some actions on the part of others that would otherwise be extremely puzzling.

SELF-PERCEPTION

Bill Crandell, senior accountant, doesn't really think much of Bill Crandell. The company's personnel records show Bill's intelligence to be in the upper 98th percentile of the general population. He has clear-eyed good looks, with an open, ingenuous expression appealing to everyone. He moves with an easy grace. No one else can put others at their ease as readily as Bill does. His MBA is from a prestigious business school. He is vice president of the Midwestern division of the CPA Association. He has an adoring wife and two happy kids doing well in Lakeside Heights Elementary School. Everyone likes Bill. But Bill doesn't like himself very much.

He doesn't feel that he's doing nearly as well as he should, professionally. He doesn't feel that he is providing adequately for his family. He can't afford household help, nor the riding lessons his daughter wants so much, and he can only just manage to rent a place at the lake for the family during the summer.

If only he had the ability to concentrate like Otto Kowalski. If he only had

Myron Green's coldly efficient approach. If he could only speak in public like Eldon Peavey. If he could acquire Mr. Portley's ability to see the big picture.

So, bright, charming Bill Crandell sees himself as plodding, ineffectual Bill Crandell. He has a self-percept that is not all realistic, but realistic or not it's the one he has. It causes him to be depressed a lot of the time, and it seems to be developing into a self-fulfilling prophecy. Bill sees himself as pleasant but ineffectual, and as a result, he is becoming pleasant but ineffectual. He doesn't extend himself much anymore. He just takes orders from Myron Green. His intelligence and training permit him to do an adequate job, but he shows very little initiative. He loves being with people because it takes his mind off his own problems. But even this tends to be self-defeating. He spends more and more time talking, and less time working. A low self-percept is a difficult cross to bear.

Low self-percept? Not so with Gordon Green. Although no brighter than Bill Crandell and not nearly as charming, Gordon thinks of himself as a real winner. He chose industrial engineering in college because he figured this would be the place he could learn more about the operation of a company faster than from any other starting point. As he saw it, he could quickly move up to chief, then shift over into line management as superintendent, then VP of production and right on up. Gordon thinks he's good and he is, though probably not *that* good. But as a result, he probes every opportunity to see where he can make his impact. Gordon's self-percept is high, but not excessively high. He *may* accomplish many of his goals. In the case where one's perception is too high, the accompanying lack of realism can often cause a poor social adjustment. It can also result in a series of too-ambitious undertakings that can't end up anywhere but in failure. Still, society probably has more to gain from those with high self-percepts than from those with low ones. The high self-perceivers will at least *try* many things and some are bound to be successful.

REVIEW QUESTIONS

1 What are the positive ways in which organization of our perceptions helps us cope on our job?

2 Describe ways in which your perceptions have been distorted by a preparatory set, projection, and stereotypes.

3 How can managers act to make employee perceptions more congruent with "objective reality"?

CHAPTER 4

MOTIVATION

READING 16

The Concepts of Valence and Expectancy

Victor H. Vroom*

*   *   *

THE CONCEPT OF VALENCE

We shall begin with the simple assumption that, at any given point in time, a person has preferences among outcomes or states of nature. For any pair of outcomes, x and y, a person prefers x to y, prefers y to x, or is indifferent to whether he receives x or y. Preference, then, refers to a relationship between the strength of a person's desire for, or attraction toward, two outcomes.

Psychologists have used many different terms to refer to preferences. The terms, valence (Lewin, 1938; Tolman, 1959), incentive (Atkinson, 1956b), attitude (Peak, 1955), and expected utility (Edwards, 1954; Thrall, Coombs, and Davis, 1954; Davidson, Suppes, and Siegel, 1957) all refer to affective orientations toward outcomes. Other concepts like need (Maslow, 1954), motive (Atkinson, 1958b), value (Allport, Vernon, and Lindzey, 1951), and interest (Strong, 1958) are broader in nature and refer to the strength of desires or aversions for large classes of outcomes.

For the sake of consistency, we use the term valence throughout this book in referring to affective orientations toward particular outcomes. In our system, an outcome is positively valent when the person prefers attaining it to not attaining it (i.e., he prefers x to not x). An outcome has a valence of zero when the person is indifferent to attaining or not attaining it (i.e., he is indifferent to x or not x), and it is negatively valent when he prefers not attaining it to attaining it (i.e., he prefers not x to x). It is assumed that valence can take a wide range of both positive and negative values.

*   *   *

THE CONCEPT OF EXPECTANCY

The specific outcomes attained by a person are dependent not only on the choices that he makes but also on events which are beyond his control. For example, a person who elects to buy a ticket in a lottery is not certain of winning the desired prize. Whether or not he does so is a function of many chance events. Similarly, the student who enrolls in medical school is seldom certain that he will successfully complete the program of study; the person who seeks political office is seldom certain that he will win the election; and the worker who strives for a promotion is

*From Victor H. Vroom, *Work and Motivation* (New York: John Wiley & Sons, Inc. 1964), pp. 15 and 17. Copyright 1964 by John Wiley & Sons, Inc. Reprinted with permission.

seldom certain that he will triumph over other candidates. Most decision-making situations involve some element of risk in determining the choices that people do make.

Whenever an individual chooses between alternatives which involve uncertain outcomes, it seems clear that his behavior is affected not only by his preferences among these outcomes but also by the degree to which he believes these outcomes to be probable. Psychologists have referred to these beliefs as expectancies (Tolman, 1959; Rotter, 1955; Atkinson, 1958b) or subjective probabilities (Edwards, 1954; Davidson, Suppes, and Siegel, 1957). We use the former term throughout this book. An expectancy is defined as a momentary belief concerning the likelihood that a particular act will be followed by a particular outcome. Expectancies may be described in terms of their strength. Maximal strength is indicated by subjective certainty that the act *will* be followed by the outcome while minimal (or zero) strength is indicated by subjective certainty that the act *will not* be followed by the outcome.

*　　*　　*

REVIEW QUESTION

1 Differentiate between valence and expectancy.

READING 17

Low Productivity?
Try Improving the Social Environment

Keith Davis*

Advanced technology and the high quality of work life in the United States should encourage higher productivity; in fact, productivity has inched up rather slowly, and at times even declined, during the last two decades. Our productivity gains, compared with those of other advanced nations, are among the lowest. There are several major reasons for our low gains in productivity; I want to focus on an important—and usually neglected—one.

A major cause of low productivity is that society does not provide a rewarding environment *outside the company* for motivation within the company. Motivating employees by building better job environments and improving the quality of work life is important; but by focusing only on the job, we are focusing on only half of the motivational problem. We are overlooking the other half—the social environ-

*From "Low Productivity? Try Improving the Social Environment," *Business Horizons*, June 1980, p. 27–29. Reprinted with permission.

ment outside the company. We are putting all our efforts into the superstructure of motivation and ignoring the foundation.

There are two types of motivation. Micromotivation, which we will call Type A, relates to the conditions on the job and within a single company. Macromotivation, which we will call Type B, relates to conditions in the social environment outside the company that may influence motivation on the job.

In order to improve Type A motivation, managers have tried new incentive plans, supervisory training, quality assurance campaigns, organizational development, and other such programs. They have brought in experts in motivation, who also emphasize Type A motivation because they were employed to do so. These efforts usually bring about some improvement, but often the results are not as good as expected. Both management and the experts may walk away muttering to themselves, "Do we really understand motivation? I wonder if we are overlooking something."

Neither managers nor experts can be faulted for continuing to work on Type A motivation; it is beneficial and it is the type that management can do a good deal to control. But more attention needs to be paid to Type B motivation.

TYPE B MOTIVATION

Type B motivation is vital to job motivation because it strongly influences employee responses to both the job and its rewards. The employees' social environment determines their attitudes toward work, their feelings about working conditions, their response to incentives, their expectations about supervision, and most of their other job responses. This conditioning also determines whether or not the rewards that management offers will be perceived by employees as rewards. Without a suitable Type B environment, the chances for high job motivation are weak.

Some employees, for example, reject a promotion to a supervisory position because the rewards are not worth the necessary extra effort. Other employees refuse to work very diligently because they prefer leisure; they want to earn just enough to live on while they enjoy other pursuits. The social environment is weakening job motivation in these and other ways, none of which management can control. Examples are as follows:

• *A declining work ethic.* According to surveys, the work ethic has been declining for years in the United States. It is giving way to a leisure ethic and other alternatives, so that a number of today's employees come to work without the strong motivation that employees had in the past.

• *Lower status for work.* Some people who still operate under the work ethic are regarded favorably by the social system, but others, especially those in business, are likely to be condemned as grubby money chasers. Still others are labeled workaholics by their children and accused of being out of step with modern times. People with a strong work ethic are rarely our modern heroes.

• *Inflation.* Employees who still insist on hard work will find that their paychecks and savings are eaten away by inflation. The net reward for hard work is low, hardly worth the cost to employees and their families.

• *A tax system that penalizes hard work and success.* Those who work to improve themselves are taxed at a higher rate as they earn more pay. This clearly is a penalty for improved performance. And the progressive tax brackets are not indexed to inflation, so that even those workers who receive no increase in real income are being pushed steadily by inflation into higher tax brackets. This is a penalty for merely continuing to work.

• As a typical employee earns more, the payments made into social security increase faster than potential benefits. Again, a penalty exists.

• According to surveys, many employees work hard to build an estate for retirement and for their families after their deaths. But progressive income and estate taxes along with inflation leave many employees who have worked hard and saved for a comfortable retirement with only a subsistence living.

These are only six examples from a multitude of social penalties for hard work. These problems seem to have been overlooked or ignored by most politicians, intellectuals, motivation specialists, and managers. I have worked in the area of motivation for thirty years, and rarely have I heard Type B motivation even mentioned at professional meetings. Perhaps we need to change our priorities for managing motivation. Or perhaps we need to go back to the drawing board and build more of Type B motivation into our models. As long as the Type B foundation is weak, the Type A superstructure will remain shaky.

It is true that if job conditions are unrewarding, motivation is likely to be weak no matter how supportive the external environment is. However, the reverse also applies. If environmental conditions do not support better job performance, motivation tends to be weak, even when conditions on the job are favorable. Both Type A and Type B motivation need to be improved if productivity is to increase at a higher rate. But this is not a job management can do alone—social attitudes and the social environment must be changed too.

REVIEW QUESTIONS

1 What is the difference between Type A and Type B motivation?

2 Looking ahead to your employment in industry, discuss which type will be most important early in your career.

3 Type B motivation is clearly a macro concept. What can an organization do to create it?

READING 18

An Interview with Frederick Herzberg: Managers or Animal Trainers?*

MR: Maybe the best place to start is with the title of your Harvard Business Review *article, "One More Time: How Do You Motivate Employees?"*

Herzberg: Historically, we have to begin with a grant I received to investigate the whole area of job attitudes when I was at Psychological Services in Pittsburgh. This particular interest originated during my days in the Graduate School of Public Health. After I got my Ph.D., I went to Public Health School and received an M.P.H. in what's called Industrial Mental Health—it's never been properly defined. When I went to Psychological Services as research director, I was interested in aspects of mental health, which certainly included job attitudes. The first stage of this research program, obviously, was to review the literature. We had a bibliography of 3,000 books and articles. The result was a book called *Job Attitudes: Review of Research and Opinion*, a scholarly review of what was known on attitudes from 1900 to 1955.

However, when we had finished *Job Attitudes: Review of Research and Opinion* we could make no sense out of it. It seemed that the human being was forever debarred from rational understanding as to why he worked.

We looked again at some of the data describing what people wanted from their jobs and noticed that there was a hint that the things people said positively about their job experiences were not the opposite of what they said negatively about their job experiences; the reverse of the factors that seemed to make people happy in jobs did not make them unhappy. So what happens in science, when your research leads to ambiguity? You begin to suspect your premises. In my Public Health School days I had conceived the concept that mental health was not the opposite of mental illness; that mentally healthy people were just not the obverse of mentally sick people. So I took a stab on the basis of mental health not being the opposite of mental illness and came up with a new concept.

MR: That was your core insight?

Herzberg: That was the core insight. I said, perhaps we're talking about two different modalities. Job satisfaction, let's use that term, and job dissatisfaction are not opposites; they are completely separate continua, like hearing and vision. If this is true, if we recognize that they are separate continua, then they must be produced by different factors and have their own dynamics. That was the stab I made.

Then I said, O.K., let's test this idea. Obviously, what had to be done was to find out what made people happy separately from finding out what made people unhappy. And you couldn't just ask people, "What do you like about your job?"

*Reprinted by permission of the publisher from *Management Review*, July 1971, pp. 2–5. © 1971 by the American Management Association, Inc. The initials "MR" stand for *Management Review*, the interviewer.

That's like asking, "How do you feel?"—a nonsensical question. In fact, two questions must be asked: What makes you happy on the job? And, equally important, What makes you unhappy on the job?

MR: Your methodology was different, too, as I recall.

Herzberg: Yes, people respond for the sake of responding. And they tend to give the answers that will win the approval of the people asking the questions. You ask people a lot of questions in a public opinion poll and you get a lot of answers without any real feelings about them. Instead of asking people what makes them happy or unhappy, I thought it would be better to get at the kinds of experiences that produced satisfaction or dissatisfaction with a job. By doing these two things—by asking two questions where one was usually asked and by obtaining my data from analysis of the kinds of experiences people had rather than what they say makes them happy or unhappy—I found that the two systems existed.

With the appearance of the two systems, my thinking that what makes people happy and what makes people unhappy were not the same things was verified. In analyzing the commonalities among the factors that make people definitely unhappy or definitely happy, I found that the factors which make people happy all are related to what people did: the job content. Contrariwise, I found that what made people unhappy was related to the situation in which they did their job: job environment, job context—what I called hygiene factors. So now you have a finding that makes much more sense. What makes people happy is what they do or the way they're utilized, and what makes people unhappy is the way they're treated. That pretty much summarizes my second book, *The Motivation to Work.*

MR: Then in your third book, Work and the Nature of Man, *you searched for the psychological underpinnings for your theory.*

Herzberg: Why does job content make people happy? Yes. I had to ask that question. Further research and experience suggested what makes people unhappy is pain from the environment. We have this in common with all animals. We're all trying to adjust to the environment—to avoid pain. On the other hand, man is also different from an animal and what makes him different is that he is a determiner, whereas the animal is always determined. What man does determines his human characteristics—I cannot become psychologically taller unless I do things.

So I developed the Adam and Abraham concept, the two natures of man. As Adam, he's an animal, and as an animal he tries to avoid pain from the environment as all animals do. As Abraham, he's a human being, and as a human being he's not the opposite of an animal, he's qualitatively different. His dynamic is to manifest his talents, and the only way he can manifest his talents is by doing things that allow him to develop his potential. In short, *Work and the Nature of Man* provided the rationale for the finding of what motivated men to work.

In summary, you had a three-step sequence. First, what we knew about job attitudes from the past made no sense, so we had to look at the problem differently. Second, when the problem was redefined, a very different research result was obtained. Third, I had to explain the research results. Now I have a theory, documented with research and supported by an understanding of why the theory worked. You ask, how do you apply it? Now we come to "One More Time."

MR: How do you apply the theory? That was also the subject of the last chapter in Work and the Nature of Man.

Herzberg: "One More Time" does two things. First, it suggests that you can get people to do things as Adam, and you can get people to do things as human beings—but the ways you get them to do things are very different. To get people to do things as animals, you move them. When I respond as an animal because I want to avoid being hurt, that's movement. I called it KITA, for "kick in the ass." When a human being does something, he's motivated. The initiative comes from within. Further, I showed how the various techniques of human relations are just different forms of positive and negative KITA.

Second, I went on to demonstrate the difference between management by movement and management by motivation or job enrichment. How, by changing what people do, you motivate them to do better work. I described how job enrichment paid off handsomely in one company—AT&T, although it wasn't identified as such in the article. Since then, many other companies have applied job enrichment with equal success. That's what happened in the past.

Most of my work now consists of looking at the total problem of mankind living in society through motivation-hygiene theory. Not only must we reorient our management thinking in terms of how you motivate people for better P&L statement, but how we apply the same theory to develop a sane society. AT&T faces not only problems with dial tones and profits, but the central and more crucial problem of whether or not it can survive as a social institution in our society. Of course, the problem is not unique to AT&T. It faces every institution.

That pretty much summarizes motivation-hygiene theory, what it is, how it came to be, and where it is going.

*   *   *

REVIEW QUESTIONS

1 According to Herzberg, what makes employees happy? Unhappy?
2 Describe a situation in which you were motivated from within, and one in which you were moved by external forces.
3 The two-factor theory of Herzberg can be misinterpreted as implying an either/or approach for managers to choose from. Criticize (or defend) such an implication.

READING 19

O.B. Mod.: Meeting the Productivity Challenge with Human Resources Management

Fred Luthans
Walter S. Maciag
Stuart A. Rosenkrantz*

It is generally recognized that productivity in this country is in real trouble. About 15 years ago the U.S. productivity growth rate started to skid; now the United States has one of the lowest productivity growth rates among the industrialized countries of the world.

Many solutions to our productivity problems have been offered in recent years. For example, engineers suggest more modern facilities and equipment, computerization and robotics. Economists, on the other hand, suggest tax incentives, increased personal savings, and lower interest rates to stimulate investment and a more favorable balance of trade. Obviously, all these solutions and many others can affect productivity. But like most other problems facing modern society, in the final analysis the major solution to the productivity challenge probably gets down to people. The way in which human resources are managed has a, if not *the*, major impact on the productivity of all organizations.

The Japanese, in particular, have demonstrated the important role that human resources management plays in improving productivity. It is well known that the technology the Japanese use was largely copied from U.S. technology, but the Japanese have outstripped the United States in productivity by successfully using people to apply the technology in more efficient ways. The lesson here is not that the United States should merely copy the group-centered Japanese human resources management style (although we certainly should examine and try out some of their techniques), but rather that U.S. managers learn from the Japanese that the way in which human resources are managed can have a tremendous impact on the organization's overall, "bottom-line" productivity.

The authors are convinced that human resources management techniques can be developed and effectively applied in U.S. firms to increase their productivity. One such approach that we have spent considerable time developing and researching over the past decade is called organizational behavior modification. In this article, we plan to briefly describe this approach to human resources management and then report on the dramatic impact that it had on the productivity of one large firm in the Midwest.

WHAT IS O.B. MOD.?

Organizational behavior modification, or simply O.B. Mod., has its roots in modern behaviorist psychology and, in particular, the work of B. F. Skinner. His principles of operant conditioning (that is, behavior is a function of its consequences) combined with the classic Law of Effect (behavior followed by positive consequences will tend to be strengthened and repeat itself; behavior followed by negative consequences will tend to be weakened and repeat itself less frequently) provide the basis for the prediction and control of employee behavior. The background and implementation of O.B. Mod. were outlined in a *Personnel* article that was published in the July–August 1974 issue. To recapitulate briefly, the O.B. Mod approach assumes the following perspectives:

1 *Observable behavior is the unit of analysis.* In an O.B. Mod. approach, the focus is on critical performance behaviors that are observable and measurable. Thus employee attitudes, motives, or satisfaction are not of direct concern. Instead, the units of analysis are such behaviors as absenteeism, tardiness, and staying at the work station, or such "behavioral products" as the quantity and quality of work. Although it is recognized that equipment or technological processes, training, and ability may indeed affect the quantity and quality of work, in most cases of low productivity these causes can be ruled out—and, if they are, the problem becomes a behavioral one suitable for an O.B. Mod. approach.

2 *Emphasis is on systematic evaluation and "bottom-line" results.* In contrast to motivationally based approaches to human resources management (human relations training or job enrichment, for example), the O.B. Mod. approach emphasizes the systematic evaluation of the intervention's impact on performance improvement. Irritating behaviors, such as complaints or unusual work habits, are not targeted for change unless an empirical relationship can be demonstrated between these behaviors and measurable, "bottom-line" performance. This emphasis on evaluation and performance allows O.B. Mod. to meet the "accountability problem" facing all human resources management techniques today.

In addition to these two general perspectives, the steps by which O.B. Mod. is implemented can be briefly summarized as follows:

1 *Identify the critical performance behavior.* This is probably the most important step because, like any problem-solving model, everything else flows from it. Such critical behavior must be observable and measurable and usually affects quantity and/or quality of performance.

2 *Measure the behavior identified in the first step.* The quantity and/or quality of output and the frequency of specified behaviors are usually available through existing records (for example, industrial engineers have been gathering productivity figures for years and the computerized management information systems of most organizations store a variety of relevant data). The archival data may have to be "ferreted" out for use in the O.B. Mod. process, but it is usually there. If not, then a measurement scheme must be established. Once these data are obtained, they are put into graphical terms (frequency over time). It is interesting to note that this measurement step itself may become an intervention (that is , cause the behavior to change because it is now being measured) and, if it does have the desired impact on performance, this is fine. However, the intent of the O.B. Mod. process at this step is simply to determine how often the critical performance behavior is really occurring under existing conditions. When put to the test of measurement, the results (both good and bad) are often quite surprising.

3 *Analyze the behavior.* A functional analysis of the antecedents that cue the behavior or set the occasion for the behavior to occur and of the consequences that currently maintain the behavior is carried out in this third step of O.B. Mod. This A-B-C (antecedent-behavior-consequence) analysis provides important information for developing an effective intervention strategy. In some cases the critical behavior is not occurring because, on the antecedent side, the employee does not know what the goals are or does not have the proper training or equipment/information to behave properly. In most cases, however, the problem stems from the consequence side. Although the antecedents serve as a cue to trigger the behavior and therefore can control it, the behavior is still a function of its consequences. Thus the intervention strategies are concerned mainly with the behavior's consequences.

4 *Intervene to accelerate the desirable performance behaviors and decelerate the undesirable ones.* The major intervention strategy is to provide both feedback on the critical performance-related behavior and positive reinforcement for progress and attainment. The more immediate, objective, accurate, and positive this feedback is, the more effective it becomes an intervention for improving performance. The accompanying positive reinforcement can take many forms. Most often, simple attention ("They know that you know.") and recognition are more effective and longer lasting than "sugar-coated" praise. The key is that this reinforcement must be administered only when performance improves. Most pay plans do not meet the criteria of this type of contingent administration. (An exception would be commissioned sales and some simple piecework incentive systems), and thus they are not an effective reinforcement strategy for day-to-day performance behaviors. However, the feedback/attention intervention strategy that is recommended under the O.B. Mod. approach is not only contingent on performance but really costs the organization nothing.

5 *Evaluate the intervention to ensure that performance is indeed improving.* This evaluation utilizes the data that were initially gathered in step two and tries to be as sophisticated as possible. The remainder of the article describes such an evaluation of an O.B. Mod. program that was recently implemented.

APPLICATION OF O.B. MOD.

The O.B. Mod. approach briefly outlined above was recently applied to eleven major product areas of a very large, labor-intensive company. In total, 135 first-line production supervisors participated in a 12-hour course that taught them the background of and steps involved in the O.B. Mod. approach to human resources management. These trained supervisors were then charged with using this approach to increase productivity and/or quality in their areas of responsibility. Typically each supervisor had to (1) conduct an analysis/audit of the specific, observable, and measurable employee behaviors that contributed to quality and/or quantity of output (for example, performing a particular operation more efficiently or delivering a certain piece of material in a more timely manner); (2) measure and then chart the frequency of occurrence of this critical behavior; (3) analyze the antecedents and consequences of this critical behavior; (4) set up a feedback system; (5) provide social reinforcement for progress and attainment; and, (6) monitor the results to determine the exact impact on performance.

The supervisors who participated in this O.B. Mod. program were in charge of unionized, hourly production employees in two shifts at one large plant (called groups A and B hereafter) and one shift at another large plant (called group C hereafter). Historically, the productivity of these employees had been carefully measured by industrial engineers in terms of overall number of units produced per week or the number of units produced per employee per hour. Quality was measured by the percentage of defective units produced per week or by the percent of time that unit quality was at or above standard. The productivity and quality results of all product areas where O.B. Mod. was applied are in Figure 1.

As shown in this figure, dramatic improvements in performance occurred in all product areas. Upon casual inspection, however, only small percentage gains were recorded for products 2 and 6. Yet it is important to note that the 2 percent increase in product 2 represents an annual gain of nearly $900,000 for this company, and the 1.4 percent increase in product 6 represents an annual gain of $750,000. Projected annual value of the gains from other product areas are estimated as follows: product 1, + $259,000; product 3, + $510,000; product 4, + $371,000; and product 5, an impressive + $2,276,000. Data for computing

FIGURE 1
THE IMPACT OF O.B. MOD. ON PRODUCTIVITY
AND QUALITY IN A LARGE PRODUCTION OPERATION

Product	Group	Measure of performance	Results
1	B	Quality improvement	Up 50%
2	A	Productivity	Up 2%
3	A	Quality improvement	Up 15%
4	A	Quality improvement	Up 23%
	C	Quality improvement	Up 64%
5	A	Quality improvement	Up 35%
	C	Quality improvement	Up 51%
6	A	Productivity	Up 1.4%
7	B	Productivity	Up 15%
8	B	Productivity	Up 16%
9	B	Quality improvement	Up 42%
10	B	Quality improvement	Up 39%
11	B	Productivity	Up 52%

the actual dollar values of the improvements for products 7 through 11 were not available, but they would compare favorably with those already described. In addition to this tremendous impact on dollar value added (several million dollars for this company), it is important to realize that in no case did O.B. Mod. result in decreased performance.

Besides the dramatic improvement in productivity and quality, the approach seems also to have had a positive effect on reducing the variability of performance in these product areas. Low performance variability is essential to providing a stable base for planning and control. Figure 2 indicates the baseline (preintervention) and postintervention variance for quality and quantity of products 1 through 6 among the three work groups in the program. Of the eight product-work group combinations for which data were available, seven indicated performance consistency improvement of from 1.7 to 30 times (as measured by the proportion of baseline to intervention variance). Product 3 exhibited only half of its original production consistency after the intervention, but still increased in output by 15 percent after the O.B. Mod. program was implemented. The reduced variability for the other products can greatly remedy resource allocation and improve inventory control.

CAN THE RESULTS BE ATTRIBUTED TO O.B. MOD.?

A highly controlled experiment designed to show the causal impact of the O.B. Mod. program on performance was not possible in this case. Nevertheless, there is considerable evidence that the O.B. Mod. program was behind the improved performance, not some alternative. For instance, Figure 3 shows the effects of the O.B. Mod. program, implemented at different points in time, on productivity and quality of products. Although the amounts of change are not to scale, the performance changes following the staggered starting dates of the program support the conclusion that the effects were indeed caused by the program rather than some

---

FIGURE 2
PERFORMANCE VARIABILITY UNDER O.B. MOD.

Product	Group	Baseline variance	Post-intervention variance	Improvement factor
1	B	3.53	.20	18×
2	A	.012	.0004	30×
3	A	.28	.56	0.5×
4	A	1.99	.46	4×
	C	14.9	1.34	11×
5	A	6.42	.905	7×
	C	16.8	1.07	16×
6	A	.016	.0095	1.7×

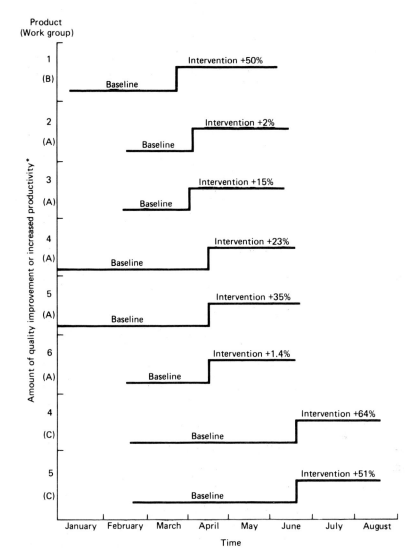

FIGURE 3
Effects of staggered O.B. Mod. interventions.

other factor. This is sometimes called a "multiple baseline technique" of evaluation, from which causal conclusions can be drawn. In every product area for which data were available, the start of the program was followed almost immediately by a dramatic change in worker behavior that resulted in performance improvement.

The change in behavior (and resulting performance) generally stabilized two to four weeks after the O.B. Mod. approach was applied. However, it was also clear

that this was not a "one-time" process with permanence assured. The approach
had to be pursued and followed up on a continuing basis. For example, Figure 4
depicts a chain of events that approximate an introduction, withdrawal, and
reintroduction of the approach. This "reversal technique" of evaluation provides
powerful evidence for attributing the results to the O.B. Mod. program. The
baseline for product 1, work group B was measured from January 10 through
March 21. The O.B. Mod. approach was initiated by a trained supervisor on
March 28—an event followed by a sharp decrease in measured defective product
(that is, improved quality) in his department. This improved quality continued for

FIGURE 4
A reversal analysis of the effect of O.B. Mod. on decreasing the number of defective products
(improving quality).

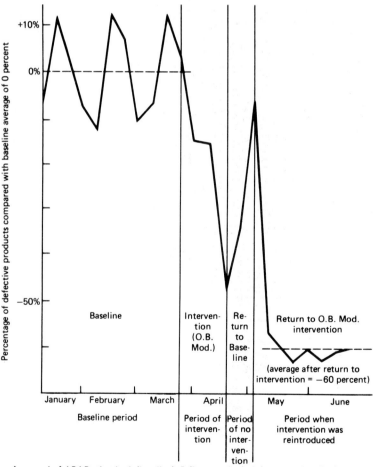

A reversal of ABAB—that is, A (baseline), B (intervention), A (return to baseline),
B (return to intervention) — analysis is commonly used in behavioral management to
assess the causal impact of the intervention.

three weeks. Then the supervisor was replaced by an untrained supervisor who did not use O.B. Mod. During this new supervisor's first two weeks (the weeks of April 18 and 25) the amount of defective product in this department clearly tended to return to the degree exhibited during the baseline condition. Then, after receiving O.B. Mod. training, this new supervisor reintroduced the approach, which resulted in the second dramatic improvement in quality that stabilized after two to three weeks. This reversal provides considerable evidence that O.B. Mod. caused the change in the quality performance.

Although the other products were evaluated only on a before-and-after basis, which by itself cannot lead to cause-and-effect conclusions, in combination with the reversal (Figure 4), considerable overall evidence gives the O.B. Mod. program credit for the dramatic improvement in productivity and quality in this company.

CONCLUSIONS

There is no question that all organizations in the United States today need to reassess the ways they manage their human resources. The challenge of increasing productivity requires new thinking and new techniques. One answer may be found in O.B. Mod. This five-step approach (identify, measure, analyze, intervene, and evaluate) is based on a sound theoretical and research foundation and certainly had a dramatic impact in the application described in this article. O.B. Mod. programs have had similar results in other manufacturing firms, hospitals, and service organizations. The point is that O.B. Mod. seems to have demonstrable results on performance outcomes. It is obviously not the only answer to the productivity challenge nor will it, without good training and a strong commitment, have the impact that it has demonstrated so far. But O.B. Mod. certainly represents the type of thinking and approach to human resources management that can get us back on the track of being the most productive and prosperous nation in the world.

REVIEW QUESTIONS

1 Briefly summarize the nature of organizational behavior modification.
2 Assuming that the quality and productivity improvements reported in this article are typical, why don't more firms use O.B. Mod.?
3 How does O.B. Mod. relate to Vroom's concepts of valence and expectancy?

READING 20

Why We Don't Reinforce: The Issues

Judi Komaki*

Have you ever wondered, as I have, why such an obviously beneficial strategy as positive reinforcement is so routinely avoided in work settings? It doesn't take an advanced degree to figure out its importance, and the principle on which it rests is fairly straightforward.

I asked participants at three professional forums to give me their sense of why reinforcement does not play a larger role in the workplace. A total of 60 persons replied, with mean age and experience levels of 37.4 and 7.9 years respectively. Approximately 20% held corporate staff positions and 5% worked in nonprofit organizations; the rest, either faculty or students, had academic affiliations. Virtually all had been trained in industrial/organizational psychology and had grappled with the problem of work motivation.

Cultural Factors

Speculation ranged widely as to why managers avoid providing reinforcement for performance. Cultural factors and their effects were cited by half of the respondents (51%) as the major reason (Table 1).

Noting that reinforcement was not part of the traditional work environment, many people cited the prevalence of the management by exception approach. One person, for instance, observed that "most of us were brought up to believe in aversive controls."

Another set noted the problem of reconciling the reinforcement of employees with what Ed Levine (1980) refers to as the "masculine managerial stereotype." One respondent admitted, "Giving and receiving praise can be embarrassing, it's not macho"; another mentioned the "fear of appearing to be a 'soft' boss.

The net result of these cultural assumptions is that few models exist of how to reinforce. Consequently, managers lack the appropriate skills: "Because one is rarely the subject of praise, praise is ineffectively administered to others." Several respondents specifically mentioned their own uneasiness, acknowledging, as one put it, that "giving praise makes me uncomfortable."

The other reasons given for avoiding the use of positive reinforcement focused on the person receiving the recognition rather than the deliverer. Just as managers have a difficult time providing recognition, employees have trouble accepting it gracefully: "Employees don't know how to respond to a compliment. When employees respond with something like 'I was just trying to do my job,' the manager feels that the recognition was not appreciated." Another frequently

*Reprinted by permission from *Journal of Organizational Behavior Management*, vol. 4, nos. 3/4, Fall/Winter 1982. © 1982 by The Haworth Press, Inc. All rights reserved.

TABLE 1
REASONS FOR AVOIDING THE USE OF POSITIVE
REINFORCEMENT

Cultural factors		51%
Management by exception	20%	
Masculine stereotype	5%	
Lack of skills or models	11%	
Deliverer's discomfort	6%	
Subordinates' reactions	9%	
Personality factors		15%
Environmental factors		12%
Time pressures	7%	
Poor appraisal instruments	5%	
Doubt benefits or lack knowledge		11%
Other reasons		11%

mentioned reason was the fear that employees would be suspicious ("Wonder what you have up your sleeve") or would make unreasonable demands ("If I'm doing such a great job, why don't you promote me?") A counter-argument was offered by one respondent, however, who pointed out that "Managers will give up this excuse when they reflect on their own reaction to receiving a pat on the back. They know they don't ask for anything and generally they accept that their employees are not different."

Personality Factors

The next largest group of reasons (15%) dealt with the predispositions of those in the position of providing reinforcement. The implication of many of the responses in this category was that managers were willfully neglectful: "Too much trouble," "Just don't want to bother."

Environmental Factors

Another sizeable number of respondents (12%) listed environmental factors as reasons for avoiding the use of positive reinforcement. The assumption here is that managers are willing but not able, given the present circumstances. Several noted time pressures and having too many things to do. Others pointed out that they do not reinforce their employees because standards are seldom clear.

Other Reasons

Only 11% stated that they or other persons in their work setting were unaware of or doubted the potential benefits of positive reinforcement. The remaining 11% fell within the miscellaneous category. One person, for instance, questioned the basis for providing recognition: "People in my organization seldom do things worth recognizing." Another respondent recommended that enrolling in EST training was the answer.

Now What?

The results target several significant questions that must be addressed before positive reinforcement will become a firmly established part of the work environment:

• How can the long-term benefits of reinforcement be made to take precedence over the more immediate but potentially damaging effects of the management by exception approach?

• How can the opinion that successful managers rarely reinforce be countered?

• How can persons be convinced that reinforcement is not limited to delivering praise but also involves providing feedback about one's performance and the contingent use of organizational reinforcers such as training opportunities and travel?

• How can managerial repertoires be expanded so that managers will not only have the skills to deal with different situations but will be able to serve as reinforcement models to their employees?

• How can work environments be set up to be conducive to evaluating and reinforcing performance?

• How can the principle of reinforcement best be adapted to fit into busy managerial schedules?

• What are the best ways to clarify performance standards and make better performance appraisals?

Progress on these issues would put us well on our way to a more extensive and productive use of reinforcement in the workplace.

REFERENCE

Levine, E. L. Let's talk: Effectively communicating praise. *Supervisory Management*, September, 1980, pp. 17–25.

REVIEW QUESTIONS

1 Examine the reasons for avoiding the use of positive reinforcement that Komaki presents in Table 1. Which of these appear to be legitimate, and which are mostly based on emotions?

2 Assume that you are working for a manager who seldom gives you positive reinforcement? What could you do to change his or her behavior?

3 Explore Komaki's concept of the "male managerial stereotype" as a barrier to reinforcement. Do you agree that it is pervasive? Is there a comparable factor among females?

CHAPTER 5

JOB SATISFACTION AND ORGANIZATIONAL VARIABLES

READING 21

Job Satisfaction:
A Misunderstood Variable*

Interest in the concept of *job satisfaction*, the idea that the way people feel about their jobs has a relationship to job performance, is a 20th century phenomenon. It all began in the 1920s with the classic Hawthorne studies, conducted by Elton Mayo and Fritz Roethlisberger of the Harvard Business School, at the Hawthorne plant of Western Electric Co., near Cicero, IL.

Over 12 years, the Hawthorne studies unearthed the first hints that social factors at work influence productivity. From that "Aha!" was born the human relations school of management and the first real industrial psychology. In the ensuing half century, research into job satisfaction and its relatives, employee satisfaction and organizational climate measurement, has dominated much of the industrial psychology literature, resulting in well over 4,000 job-satisfaction studies. But despite this flood of investigation, we still don't quite understand the relationship between work, worker and satisfaction.

Some would argue that only marginal progress has been made since 1935, when Robert Hoppock of New York University did the first in-depth study of job satisfaction. Hoppock's work, a model of in-depth fact-finding and investigation, also marks the debut of the job satisfaction survey onto the scene.

Hoppock interviewed the working population of an entire town, using structured interviews, survey techniques and psychological test procedures. He also did intensive research on selected samples of employed and unemployed workers and satisfied and dissatisfied teachers. His use of such a wide range of methods yielded a robust information base for understanding the logic and limits of the worker attitudes and spurred many others on to further research.

The importance of measuring and worrying over job satisfaction is related to what social science critic David Bell calls "moo-cow sociology." Early occupational sociologists were convinced that job satisfaction was a worthy end in itself.

But early 20th century industrialists weren't terribly impressed by or much interested in such arguments. So the questers took another tack, arguing that job satisfaction isn't just an important dependent variable but an important independent variable—or causal factor—in the productivity formula.

In short, the work researchers and theorists of the '20s and '30s evolved the argument that "just as contented cows give more milk, contented milkmaids milk more cows." The theorem obviously hit pay dirt.

Is the formula true? According to Yale University's Victor Vroom, a motivation and satisfaction theorist, the jury is still out. In a review of all studies attempting to correlate high satisfaction with high productivity, Vroom found the

---

*Reprinted with permission from an article by Ron Zemke in the May 1982 issue of *Training: The Magazine of Human Resources Development*, pp. 87–88. Copyright 1982 Lakewood Publications, Minneapolis, Minn. All rights reserved.

average or mean relationship to be .14. (On a scale of 0 to 1.0, that's pretty low.) Although many studies *suggest* that job satisfaction is probably important in the work = attendance = turnover = effort formula of productivity, the extent of that importance, and the way we can affect it, is less clear.

The difference between job satisfaction and worker attitudes toward X, Y, or Z often gets blurred. We often hear, "Since 78% of the employees were very positive toward benefits, salary and working hours, we can conclude that job satisfaction at Worldwide Widget, Inc., is at an all-time high."

It ain't necessarily so. When people are asked, "How do you feel about benefits or working hours or parking lot assignments?" they tend to tell you just that. The theory of "summative effect"—that satisfaction with benefits + satisfaction with hours + satisfaction with parking = overall job satisfaction—has never been acceptably demonstrated.

Frederick Herzberg's two-factor theory of job satisfaction is the most recent attempt to reconcile differences in the "attitude toward _____" and job satisfaction concepts. Most famous of his findings was that "I am paid too little" may be an attitude leading to overall dissatisfaction. But "I am paid the right amount" does not automatically lead to overall satisfaction. Researchers, however, have been hard-pressed to reproduce the findings that led to this so-called "motivator/ hygiene theory" of job satisfaction.

WORKER ATTITUDES

Though researchers have been disappointed in their quest to understand job satisfaction, they have unearthed some interesting and significant information:

• Measures of job satisfaction are related, but only indirectly, to withdrawal from the job. Studies of job satisfaction versus tardiness, absenteeism and poor work quality show consistent correlation between the variables.

• Attempts to associate job satisfaction and dissatisfaction with specific behaviors generally fail. Since job satisfaction is an attitude, or at least measured as an attitude, it suffers the same fate as most attempts to directly correlate behaviors and attitudes—disappointment.

• Claims that job satisfaction ratings of the American work force are on a downhill slide should be examined carefully since not all polls agree with this assessment. Gallup poll data on job satisfaction collected in 1963 and 1973 varied from 87% to 92% positive and the question "Are you satisfied with your pay?" remained a constant 65% "yes" over the same period.

• Young people tend to be less satisfied than older people. Changes in work-force demographics may account for some of the reports of decreasing job satisfaction in the work force as a whole.

• Job satisfaction ratings vary by occupation. Most- to least-satisfied occupational groups are professional and scientific, managerial/proprietary, sales, crafts, service, clerical, assembly line/unskilled.

• Sex and job satisfaction don't correlate except in two situations. Working women with preschool children tend to be more satisfied. People in traditional sex role jobs were more satisfied than those in nontraditional sex role jobs. A third exception is that some studies show that when *pay* was balanced statistically—and absences and time in rank were equalized—women were more satisfied than men in the same position.

• Position in the organization and job satisfaction are related: The higher up the organization ladder one is, the greater the job satisfaction.

Despite some fairly clear and persuasive research to the contrary, most people believe there is a simple and powerful relationship between job satisfaction and productivity. An article in a recent in-flight magazine typifies.

Attempting to explain organizational development to his seat-belt-bound readers, the author proclaims that, "a growing number of American corporations are investing heavily in their employees" because "trite as it may sound, a happy, content, frustration-free staffer, whether on the assembly line, in the executive suite or someplace in between, is simply more productive." Trite is right! And terribly misleading as well.

As Michael M. Gruneberg, editor of *Job Satisfaction* (John Wiley, 1976) summarizes, "The relationship between job satisfaction and productivity is a complex one, and even though there is likely to be a relationship between certain aspects of job satisfaction and productivity, the older view of a major and direct relationship has had to be abandoned."

Or to put it another way, for every complex problem there is a simple solution. And that simple solution is usually wrong. Job satisfaction has never been a simple problem. Pretending it is won't make understanding it any easier. It will only make it wrong.

REVIEW QUESTIONS

1 Describe the nature of the relationship between satisfaction and productivity.
2 What types of employees tend to be the most satisfied?
3 Examine the current level of your "job satisfaction" in your role as a student. What factors contribute to it, and what detracts from it?

READING 22

Directions in Job Satisfaction Research

Vida Scarpello
John P. Campbell*

* * *

The present data poses numerous questions for future job satisfaction research. Some of the more important ones may be the following. To what extent does the working environment (e.g., functional unit) influence the types of variables the individual considers when evaluating his/her overall job satisfaction? Does the working environment influence the "meaning" respondents attach to items measured by job satisfaction questionnaires? What are the variables which influence both job satisfaction and life satisfaction off the job? What is the directional relationship between specific job facets and life and job satisfactions? Given that job satisfaction data are used for many purposes, should different overall measures be used when the intent is to determine changes in job satisfaction for societal policy decisions as opposed to organizational policy decisions? Lastly, is the job satisfaction construct so broad that identification of the major determinants of overall job satisfaction a futile task? Instead of measuring job satisfaction should we focus our efforts on more restrictive organizationally relevant outcomes (e.g., propensity to turnover, satisfaction with pay, satisfaction with supervision) and relate these outcomes to particular job facets?

REVIEW QUESTION

1 Scarpello and Campbell imply (in their last statement) that we should pay more attention to outcomes than satisfaction itself. What do you think would be most important if you were a manager?

*From Vida Scarpello and John P. Campbell, "Job Satisfaction: Are All the Parts There?" *Personnel Psychology*, Autumn 1983, p. 599. Reprinted with permission.

READING 23

Turnover Overstated: The Functional Taxonomy

Dan R. Dalton
William D. Todor
David M. Krackhardt*

The dysfunctional aspects of employee turnover on the organization have been variously described as "axiomatic" (Dalton & Todor, 1979) and as the "sine qua non" (Muchinsky & Tuttle, 1979) of the withdrawal literature. Given this view, it is not surprising that employee turnover continues to be of interest to organizational theorists and practitioners alike. It has been estimated, for example, that there are well over 1,000 relevant citations in the literature addressing employee turnover (Muchinsky & Morrow, 1980; Steers & Mowday, 1981). Staw (1980) suggests that the implicit assumption underlying these efforts has been that turnover is an important organizational problem that is costly and should be reduced. It is notable, and arguably presumptive evidence, that nearly all previous research has correlated (or otherwise associated) independent variables with measures of turnover and tested for significant differences from zero (Staw & Oldham, 1978).

Although it is true that turnover traditionally has been thought of as dysfunctional to the organization, there is some discussion that suggests otherwise (Dalton, 1981; Dalton & Todor, 1979; Dalton & Todor, in press; Muchinsky & Morrow, 1980; Muchinsky & Tuttle, 1979; Staw, 1980; Staw & Oldham, 1978). It has been argued that turnover may actually benefit both the individual and the organization (Dalton & Todor, 1979; Dalton & Todor, in press; Muchinsky & Tuttle, 1979).

Although somewhat anecdotal, Staw and Oldham (1978) report descriptive notes that are thought provoking. As shown in a 1973 national survey (Department of Labor, 1975), job tenure in the railroad industry was 19.6 years as compared to 5.7 years in durable goods manufacturing and 5.3 years in nondurable goods. Railroad employee tenure is some seven times that of wholesale and retail trade (2.6 years). Job tenure in the postal service (10.3 years) also is relatively higher than most other sectors of the economy. To suggest that the performance of the United States' railroad industry and the Postal Service, in general terms, is not popularly respected is something of an understatement.

It may be, then, that the stated dysfunctional aspects of turnover, although not in error, are overstated. Aside from the issue of the costs of turnover versus the value of its benefits, there is another factor that may lead to a systematic overstatement of the impact of turnover: its measurement and reporting.

*From *Academy of Management Review*, January 1982, pp. 117–123. Reprinted with permission.

MEASUREMENT AND REPORTING

Traditionally, turnover is separated into two categories: voluntary and involuntary (Price, 1977). Attempts to reduce turnover focus on voluntary turnover as the dependent variable (Graen & Ginsburgh, 1977; Krackhardt, McKenna, Porter, & Steers, 1981; Mowday, Porter, & Stone, 1978; Mowday, Stone, & Porter, 1979). The classification of turnover in this manner, although subject to some methodological difficulties (Price, 1977), seems sound. Price (1977) outlined several reasons for this concentration on voluntary turnover: the majority of turnover is voluntary, theory formation is eased by homogeneity, voluntary and involuntary turnover probably have different determinants, and voluntary turnover is more subject to control by organizations. It is suggested that this dichotomy of turnover is necessary, but insufficient for an accurate examination of organizational turnover.

AN EXPANDED TAXONOMY

A comparison of the graphics in Figure 1 illustrates a fundamental difference in the interpretation of turnover in the organization. Graphic 1 is representative of the traditional approach to measuring and reporting turnover. Each cell represents a condition of the employment relation between an employee and the organization.

1 Cell a illustrates a condition in which the organization is positively disposed toward the individual and the individual is similarly disposed toward the organization. In this condition, both parties are content to maintain the employment relation.

2 In cell b the individual would like to maintain the employment relation. However, the organization is not so inclined. In this situation, the organization will terminate (fire) the employee.

3 Cell c illustrates the condition in which the employee, for whatever reasons, does not wish to continue the employment relation. The employee quits. Importantly, this cell represents "voluntary" turnover.

The second graphic is like the first except that in this case the voluntary turnover sector is divided further into two cells: c and d (????). This, however, is a fundamental and, arguably, very important distinction.

The bottom sections of both graphics represent voluntary turnover, and the numerical count of individuals in this category in both cases would be identical. In other words, the reported level of turnover would be the same. It is irrelevant for these purposes (although certainly not as a methodological issue) which of many means of calculating turnover is used. In both cases (graphics 1 & 2) the reported level of voluntary turnover will be the same.

The impact of that turnover on the organization, however, is not identical and, in fact, may not be remotely related. Notice in Figure 1 (graphic 2) that cell c represents the condition wherein the employee wants to terminate the employment relation but the employer has a positive evaluation of the employee. In this

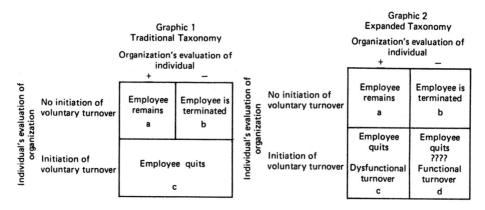

FIGURE 1
A comparison of turnover taxonomies.

case, it may well be that this voluntary turnover is dysfunctional to the organization. Simply stated, in this condition, employees are leaving when the organization would prefer that they remain.

In cell d, there is an entirely different situation. Here is the case of an individual leaving the organization when the organization has a negative evaluation of the employee. To include those individuals who can be categorized as cell d in the measurement and reporting of turnover would seem to overstate the dysfunctional aspects. It is hard to argue that individuals in cell d represent dysfunctional turnover; indeed, it can be argued that they represent functional turnover. Such turnover may be a decided benefit to the organization.

This raises an interesting question. Why wouldn't such people be dismissed by the organization if, in fact, their departure would benefit the organization? There probably are a variety of reasons that marginal (or worse) employees are not terminated. Turnover can adversely affect the social dynamics of the work organization (Muchinsky & Tuttle, 1979). It may be that qualitative factors such as organizational climate and group cohesion, for instance, may suffer as a consequence of turnover. Steers and Mowday (1981), although restricting their discussion to voluntary turnover, posit that turnover has consequences for those who remain in the organization. Turnover, in this case, may be interpreted by co-workers of an individual who leaves the workplace as an implicit, if not explicit, recognition that better employment opportunities exist elsewhere. This may lead remaining co-workers to reevaluate their condition.

Probably the most prevalent reason for maintaining marginal employees is the institutionalization of employment security, widespread in both the private and the public sectors. Labor unions, employee associations, administrative appeal boards, and their equivalents, for example, routinely provide a mechanism whereby employees who might be in cell d cannot be terminated.

University tenure is a classic example. In most institutions there may be faculty members with institutionalized job security (tenure) whose leaving could hardly be classified as dysfunctional to their various departments. Job security, as a function of collective bargaining agreements, may operate similarly to maintain the employment of individuals whose leaving would be no cause for consternation. Such individuals may never actually commit (or omit) behaviors that likely would be sufficient to fire them. This, however, need not be interpreted to mean that they are indispensable to the organization or even valued by it.

The fundamental point is that the summation of cases in cells c and d in graphic 2 to determine turnover in the organization serves to overstate the gravity of turnover in the organization. In the measurement and reporting of turnover, however, no attempt is made traditionally to identify the distinction between the cells. Cell d is referred to as "????" because there is not, in the field, a term to describe this condition. Perhaps functional turnover—turnover that actually is beneficial to the organization—is appropriate.

HOW MUCH FUNCTIONAL TURNOVER?

Naturally, the extent of functional turnover is unknown. Presumably, it would vary depending on the nature of the organization. Organizations marked by institutionalized job security, for example, may have relatively less functional turnover. Arguably, organizations that are not subject to harsh review on employee terminations would have fewer persons in cell d because such persons would long since have been dismissed.

It is suspected that the number of people who could be categorized in cell d is substantial, perhaps half or more of total voluntary turnover. Again, this remains to be determined. However, noting a certain lack of methodological rigor, one might look around at co-workers and ask, "How much damage would be done if those persons left?" A guess, and it is a guess, is that many people would be in this category.

This does not suggest that turnover in the functional cell is without cost to the organization in absolute terms. Sundry recruitment, training costs, and some portion of administrative overhead undoubtedly will be incurred and must be defrayed by the organization. In the balance, however, it could be argued that such turnover, despite its cost, is not dysfunctional to the organization.

IDENTIFYING FUNCTIONAL TURNOVER

The individual's assessment of the organization can be inferred quite simply from graphic 2 of Figure 1. With respect to cells a and b if the employee remains or is fired, it can be assumed that the individual had felt a positive regard for the organization at least with respect to membership.

This, of course, is a relatively simplistic analysis, a snapshot actually of the turnover process from the individual's perspective. Clearly, not all employees who are negatively disposed toward their employer will quit; not all employees who are positively disposed will remain. There may be external events (such as the transfer of a spouse) that may "force" employees to leave an organization even though they are (were) positively disposed. Also, an alternate employment opportunity may arise that may "force" an employee's movement although she or he remains positive with respect to the organization. Even so, employees who leave under these and similar circumstances are no longer members of cell a; they become members of cell c. They initiate the movement themselves. If they are valued employees, they represent dysfunctional turnover; if not, they represent functional turnover.

A comprehensive model of the turnover process must include opportunity among other factors. Indeed recent models do so (Mobley, 1977; Price, 1977; Steers & Mowday, 1981). For purposes of measurement and reporting of turnover, however, distinctions such as opportunity and other external forces are unnecessary. But they are essential to the discussion of managerial control in a later section.

MEASUREMENT OF FUNCTIONAL TURNOVER

Rehire?

The critical issue here is identifying the organization's assessment of the employee. In some organizations, this can be accomplished rather easily. Many organizations (usually larger ones) have formal separation documents for their employee files. When an employee leaves the organization voluntarily (for any reason) or is fired, these papers are completed and sent to the personnel department. Among other items, the reason for leaving or the dismissal is outlined, and the official date of separation, vacation time remaining, pension rights, and so on are noted. Frequently, the first level supervisor is asked on the form if the separating employee "is recommended for rehire."

This relatively simple recommendation may serve as a valid indicator of functional turnover. Presumably, individuals who are not recommended for rehire (for any reason) are functional separations. It may be true that the organization would not act (or has not acted) to dismiss such employees for any number of reasons, but the lack of rehire recommendation may be valid testimony of the organization's evaluation of the departing employee.

It is true, of course, that any such judgment is subjective. A rehire appraisal by the first level supervisor may be suspect. There may be some encouragement in the requirement that ordinarily the second level supervisor must sustain the judgment of the employee's direct supervisor (first level). Presumably, if an employee is not recommended for rehire, the first level supervisor would be asked to justify that assessment.

Another, perhaps creative, approach would be to obtain rehire appraisals of departing employees from co-workers. A disadvantage is that this information ordinarily would not be available as a matter of organizational policy. It does, however, suggest a fascinating research topic: the comparison of dysfunctional/functional turnover assessments by supervision and rank and file employees.

Quality and Replaceability

When rehire recommendations do not exist as a matter of policy in an organization, there may be other metrics that may serve to identify the organization's assessment of the employee: quality and replaceability.

Presumably the departure of high quality employees is more likely to be dysfunctional to organizations than that of low quality. The quality of employees, once again, is a subjective judgment. This could be accomplished by supervisory ratings (validated by multiple judging) or peer ratings. Obviously, where available, "hard" measures of quality are superior and more indicative of bottom line performance than are "softer" measures (Dalton, Todor, Spendolini, Fielding, & Porter 1980). Supervisory appraisals, self-perceptions, and similar measures are soft and should be relied on less heavily than such measures as productivity, sales, commissions, and services rendered, which arguably are harder measures (Dalton et. al., 1980).

The quality and replaceability measures may be orthogonal. These factors may be essential to the firm, but under different circumstances. For example, it is quite possible for a truly stellar (very high quality) employee to leave the work unit; yet, because of the nature of the work or the work force, many equally or even better qualified people are available to replace him/her. Such turnover is not a threat to the organization even though it involves high quality performers. In the market condition as described, these people are easily replaced.Correspondingly, a relatively poor performer may be better than none. If no replacements are available for such persons, their departure may be a genuine cause of concern for the organization.

Both quality of employee and replaceability may be sound metrics to determine functional turnover. The more preferred of the two may depend on the nature of the organization. Both measures have the advantage of being able to be applied retrospectively. Employment records of departed employees can be reviewed with the appropriate first and second level supervisors, or peer groups, and a fair estimation of functional turnover can be determined. With this information of the ratio between functional and dysfunctional turnover, a more responsible estimate of the gravity of turnover on the organization can be assessed.

Organizational Control

Earlier it was noted that voluntary turnover is thought to be more subject to control by organizations. Reviews of the turnover phenomenon demonstrate rather clearly that the preponderance of research has been dedicated to determining its antecedents or determinants (Mobley, Griffeth, Hand, & Meglino, 1979; Muchinsky & Tuttle, 1979; Porter & Steers, 1979; Price, 1977). This may be interpreted as presumptive evidence of an interest to reduce the incidence of turnover in the organization. If it is to be reduced, then voluntary turnover must be under organizational control. Any portion of voluntary turnover that is not under the control of the organization and cannot be reduced tends to overstate numerically the impact of turnover.

It has been argued that only cell c represents turnover that is truly dysfunctional to the organization. Even in cell c, however, there are cases that, although upsetting to the organization, are not avoidable. In other words, the total number of employees in cell c does not necessarily represent turnover over which the organization has control. Employees who voluntarily leave the organization for education, family commitment (spouses being transferred, etc.), retirements, and health matters, among others, are not normally under organizational control. Employee deaths, less frequent, also belong in this category. If an aim of the organization is to reduce turnover, the inclusion of these people in its statistics is misleading. From a research perspective, including these cases to determine the antecedents and/or determinants of turnover is questionable as well. It is very hard to argue that these quits are homogeneous with the remainder of cell c separations.

It has been suggested that some portion of employee turnover is unavoidable. This may be somewhat shortsighted. In theory, with the obvious exception of employee death, no turnover is unavoidable. Organizations probably have the wherewithal to persuade most members not to quit if they choose to use their resources in this manner. However, as a practical matter, the categories described here are essentially unavoidable. As Dalton and Todor have noted, "It may be far less expensive to cope with turnover than to prevent it" (1979, p. 226). This may be such an occasion.

SUMMARY

The notion that turnover is dysfunctional to the organization recently has been subject to criticism (Dalton, 1981; Dalton & Todor, 1979; Dalton & Todor, in press; Muchinsky & Morrow, 1980; Muchinsky & Tuttle, 1979; Staw, 1980; Staw & Oldham, 1978). Whether or not one is inclined to view employee turnover as largely dysfunctional or otherwise may be a function of its measurement. The traditional dichotomy separating turnover into its voluntary and involuntary segments for purposes of research and practice may be necessary, but insufficient.

By separating turnover further into dysfunctional and functional categories and considering that certain turnover, for all practical purposes, is unavoidable, one might be able to obtain a more responsible estimate of the impact of turnover. Figure 2 is an illustration of the possible effects of considering these factors in the measurement and reporting of turnover and its dysfunctional consequences on the organization.

The essential point represented in Figure 2 is that the category voluntary turnover has a clear tendency to overstate the gravity of turnover on the organization. By dividing voluntary into its functional and dysfunctional components, one might be able to make a somewhat more meaningful examination of a balance that may exist among the consequences of turnover on the organization. For most organizations, Figure 2 is presumed to represent this stepdown phenomenon. Clearly, dysfunctional turnover (by percentage) is less than total voluntary turnover. The percentages on Figure 2 are strictly hypothetical to illustrate the point.

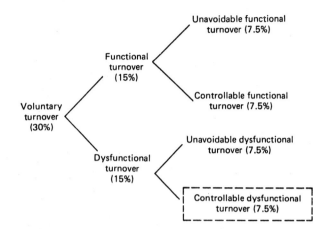

FIGURE 2
Dysfunctional/functional taxonomy with unavoidable separations. (All values are
hypothetical.)

Given a 30 percent voluntary turnover rate with an assumption of an equal distribution of functional and dysfunctional components, "bad" turnover is reduced by
half, to 15 percent. Here again, the reliance on the voluntary turnover rate (30
percent) with its accompanying dysfunctional prejudices would seem to overstate
the gravity of turnover. From this hypothetical treatment in Figure 2, dysfunctional turnover is reduced by half. There is no reason, of course to discount the
remaining 15 percent. Indeed, this portion of turnover is actually beneficial to
the organization.

Similarly, by considering whether the resulting dysfunctional turnover is reasonably subject to managerial control, a further step down is evident. If any
employee turnover is considered to be unavoidable, that is, no reasonable management intervention could have prevented it, such turnover is less a concern.
Attempts to reduce any portion of voluntary turnover that is not under the control
of the organization tends to focus organizational resources in vain. Arguably,
resources dedicated in this manner are not wisely used. Again, given the assumption that half of voluntary turnover, irrespective of its categorization, is essentially
unavoidable, dysfunctional turnover subject to managerial control is reduced to
7.5 percent.

The highlighted section of Figure 2, then, represents dysfunctional turnover
that is potentially controllable by the organization. For the practitioner, this
expanded taxonomy provides a more realistic portrayal of the impact of turnover
on the organization. It also provides a guideline for the responsible expenditure of
organizational funds for reducing turnover. The hypothetical 7.5 percent of turnover is not trivial; it is, however, less onerous and certainly more responsibly
reported than is the original 30 percent voluntary rate. Succinctly, the reporting of
the 30 percent rate at least implicitly tends to overstate the dysfunctional, controllable effects of voluntary turnover on the organization.

For the organizational researcher, this expansion may provide a rationale for
relatively low associations between turnover and its suspected antecedents or
determinants. Perhaps, when using voluntary turnover as a dependent variable,

researchers were not dealing with a homogeneous subset. This is especially bothersome because, as noted, Price (1977) suggested that one of the primary reasons why researchers have used the voluntary/involuntary dichotomy is to assure homogeneity. It is not clear that the same antecedents, correlates, or determinants are shared between individuals who are characterized as functional and those characterized as dysfunctional.

If associated variables (whatever they may be) are dissimilar, organizations may be able to minimize dysfunctional turnover without artificially suppressing functional turnover. In fact, it is not inconceivable that organizations might endeavor to encourage functional turnover.

Whether there are substantive levels of functional turnover and whether differences exist in the antecedents and determinants of turnover for these employees remains an empirical question. The effects of functional versus dysfunctional turnover on the organization could hardly be overstated. These may be questions worthy of future inquiry.

REFERENCES

Dalton, D.R. Turnover and absenteeism: Measures of personnel effectiveness. In R. S. Schuler, J. M. McFillan, & D. R. Dalton (Eds.), *Applied readings in personnel and human resource management*. St. Paul, Minn.: West Publishing Company, 1981, 20−38.

Dalton, D. R., & Todor, W. D. Turnover turned over: An expanded and positive perspective. *Academy of Management Review*, 1979, 4, 225−236.

Dalton, D. R., & Todor, W. D. Turnover: A lucrative hard dollar phenomenon. *Academy of Management Review*, in press.

Dalton, D. R., Todor, W. D., Spendolini, M. J., Fielding, G. J., & Porter, L. W. Organizational structure and performance: A critical review. *Academy of Management Journal*, 1980, 8, 49−64.

Department of Labor. Employment and training report of the President. Washington: Government Printing Office, 1975.

Graen, F., & Ginsburgh, S. Job resignation as a function of role orientation and leader acceptance: A longitudinal investigation of organizational assimilation. *Organizational Behavior and Human Performance*, 1977, 19, 1−17.

Krackhardt, D. M., McKenna, J., Porter, L. W., & Steers, R. M. Supervisory behavior and employee turnover: A field experiment. *Academy of Management Journal*, 1981, 24, 249−259.

Mobley, W. H. Intermediate linkages in the relationship between job satisfaction and employee turnover. *Journal of Applied Psychology*, 1977, 62, 237−240.

Mobley, W. H., Griffeth, R. W., Hand, H. H., & Meglino, B. M. Review and conceptual analysis of the employee turnover process. *Psychological Bulletin*, 1979, 86, 493−522.

Mowday, R., Porter, L. W., & Stone, E. F. Employee characteristics as predictors of turnover among female clerical employees in two organizations. *Journal of Vocational Behavior*, 1978, 12, 321−332.

Mowday, R. T., Stone, E. F., & Porter, L. W. The interaction of personality and job scope in predicting turnover. *Journal of Vocational Behavior*, 1979, 15, 78−89.

Muchinsky, P. M., & Morrow, P. C. A multidisciplinary model of voluntary employee turnover. *Journal of Vocational Behavior*, 1980, 17, 263−290.

Muchinsky, P. M. & Tuttle, M. L. Employee turnover: An empirical and methodological assessment. *Journal of Vocational Behavior*, 1979, 14, 43–77.

Porter, L. W., & Steers, R. M. Organizational, work, and personal factors in employee turnover and absenteeism. *Psychological Bulletin*, 1973, 80, 151–176.

Price, J. L. *The study of turnover*. Ames, Iowa: The Iowa State University Press, 1977.

Staw, B. M. The consequences of turnover. *Journal of Occupational Behavior*, 1980, 1, 253–273.

Staw, B. M., & Oldham, R. R. Reconsidering our dependent variables: A critique and empirical study. *Academy of Management Journal*, 1978, 21, 539–559.

Steers, R. M., & Mowday, R. T. Employee turnover and post-decision accommodation processes. In L. L. Cummings & B. M. Staw (Eds.), *Research in organizational behavior (Vol. 3)*. Greenwich, Conn.: JAI Press, 1981, 3, 235–282.

REVIEW QUESTIONS

1 What could a manager do to increase functional turnover? To decrease dysfunctional turnover?

2 Should a manager be held accountable for turnover? Why?

3 Why might an employee quit even though the organization's evaluation is positive?

CHAPTER 6

INTERPERSONAL RELATIONS

READING 24

Phases of the Mentor Relationship

Kathy E. Kram*

* * *

RELATIONSHIP PHASES

A mentor relationship has the potential to enhance career development and psychosocial development of both individuals. Through career functions, including sponsorship, coaching, protection, exposure-and-visibility, and challenging work assignments, a young manager is assisted in learning the ropes of organizational life and in preparing for advancement opportunities. Through psychosocial functions including role modeling, acceptance-and-confirmation, counseling, and friendship, a young manager is supported in developing a sense of competence, confidence, and effectiveness in the managerial role (see Exhibit 1). In providing a range of developmental functions, a senior manager gains recognition and respect from peers and superiors for contributing to the development of young managerial talent, receives confirmation and support from the young manager who seeks counsel, and experiences internal satisfaction in actively enabling a less experienced adult to learn how to navigate successfully in the world of work.

Examination of the phases of a mentor relationship highlights the psychological and organizational factors that influence which career and psychosocial functions are provided, and it shows how each manager experiences the relationship at any given point in time. Although developmental relationships vary in length (average length of five years in the research sample), they generally proceed

EXHIBIT 1
MENTORING FUNCTIONS

Career functions[a]	Psychosocial functions[b]
Sponsorship	Role modeling
Exposure-and-visibility	Acceptance-and-confirmation
Coaching	Counseling
Protection	Friendship
Challenging assignments	

[a]Career functions are those aspects of the relationship that primarily enhance career advancement.

[b]Psychosocial functions are those aspects of the relationship that primarily enhance sense of competence, clarity of identity, and effectiveness in the managerial role.

*From *Academy of Management Journal*, December 1983, pp. 613−614 and 621−625. Reprinted with permission.

through four predictable, yet not entirely distinct, phases: an *initiation* phase, during which time the relationship is started; a *cultivation* phase, during which time the range of functions provided expands to maximum; a *separation* phase, during which time the established nature of the relationship is substantially altered by structural changes in the organizational context and/or by psychological changes within one or both individuals; and a *redefinition* phase, during which time the relationship evolves a new form that is significantly different from the past, or the relationship ends entirely.

*   *   *

IMPLICATIONS

This phase model illustrates how a mentor relationship moves through the phases of initiation, cultivation, separation, and redefinition (see Exhibit 2). Each phase is characterized by particular affective experiences, developmental functions, and interaction patterns that are shaped by individuals' needs and surrounding organizational circumstances.

This dynamic perspective delineates how a mentor relationship can enhance both individuals' development as it unfolds. When primary tasks are complementary, a mentor relationship is likely to reach the cultivation phase and to provide a range of career and psychosocial functions that enable the young adult to meet the challenges of initiation into the world of work, and the senior adult to meet the challenges of reappraisal at midlife. When, however, the young adult begins to feel established and more autonomous, s/he no longer will look toward the senior adult for the same kind of guidance and support. If the senior adult has other avenues for creative expression of generative needs and can accept continued growth and advancement in the younger adult, then the relationship will follow its course through separation and redefinition.

Under certain conditions, a mentor relationship can become destructive for one or both individuals (Kram, 1980). For example, a young manager may feel undermined and held back by his or her mentor, or a senior mentor may feel threatened by his or her protégé's continued success and opportunity for advancement. Either is likely to occur when a senior adult enters a difficult midlife transition and/or a young adult encounters organizational barriers to advancement. Continued research in a variety of organizational contexts will further illuminate the factors that contribute to these dysfunctional dynamics as well as the range of organizational circumstances that facilitate movement through the phases of a mentor relationship in a manner that maximizes benefits to both individuals.

The research data from which the relationship phases were delineated indicated significant limitations in cross-sex relationships. The lack of an adequate role model in a male mentor caused young female managers to seek support and guidance from other female peers (Shapiro, Haseltine, & Rowe, 1978). Collusion in stereotypical behaviors encouraged women to maintain feelings of dependency

EXHIBIT 2
PHASES OF THE MENTOR RELATIONSHIP

Phase	Definition	Turning points[a]
Initiation	A period of six months to a year during which time the relationship gets started and begins to have importance for both managers.	Fantasies become concrete expectations. Expectations are met; senior manager provides coaching, challenging work, visibility; junior manager provides technical assistance, respect, and desire to be coached. There are opportunities for interaction around work tasks.
Cultivation	A period of two to five years during which time the range of career and psychosocial functions provided expand to a maximum.	Both individuals continue to benefit from the relationship. Opportunities for meaningful and more frequent interaction increase. Emotional bond deepens and intimacy increases.
Separation	A period of six months to two years after a significant change in the structural role relationship and/or in the emotional experience of the relationship.	Junior manager no longer wants guidance but rather the opportunity to work more autonomously. Senior manager faces midlife crisis and is less available to provide mentoring functions. Job rotation or promotion limits opportunities for continued interaction; career and psychosocial functions can no longer be provided. Blocked opportunity creates resentment and hostility that disrupts positive interaction.
Redefinition	An indefinite period after the separation phase, during which time the relationship is ended or takes on significantly different characteristics, making it a more peer-like friendship.	Stresses of separation diminish, and new relationships are formed. The mentor relationship is no longer needed in its previous form. Resentment and anger diminish; gratitude and appreciation increase. Peer status is achieved.

[a]Examples of the most frequently observed psychological and organizational factors that cause movement into the current relationship phase.

and incompetence when they were attempting to become independent contributors (Kanter, 1977; Sheehy, 1976). Concerns about increasing intimacy and concerns about the public image of the relationship caused both individuals to avoid interaction that had the potential to provide a wide range of career and psychosocial functions. Similar complexities are likely to exist in cross-race relationships. There is a need to study further the unique attributes of cross-sex and cross-race relationships to determine whether observed relationship limitations can be alleviated.

Given that such developmental relationships are limited in value and time duration as a result of changing individual needs and organizational circumstances, it is likely that an individual will have, over the course of an organizational career, several developmental relationships that provide a range of critical career and psychosocial functions at each life/career stage. The wish to find one senior manager who will carry an individual through his or her career, and who will continue to be responsive to individual concerns, is one that is likely to generate considerable disappointment and disillusionment.

It would be fruitful, therefore, to investigate the patterns of relationships that individuals have at successive career stages in order to illuminate other developmental relationships as alternatives to the primary mentor relationship. Not only is the mentor relationship limited in value and duration, but it may not be readily available to all individuals in the early stage of a career because of organizational conditions and/or limited individual capacities to form enhancing relationships. Peer relationships appear to offer a valuable alternative to the mentor relationship; they can provide some career and psychosocial functions, they offer the opportunity for greater mutuality and sense of equality, and they are more available in numbers. Future research efforts designed to clarify the role of peer relationships in early and midcareers would offer insight into the range of developmental relationships that are possible at each career stage.

Because relationships are shaped by both individual needs and organizational circumstances, interventions designed to enhance relationship-building skills and to create organizational conditions that foster developmental relationships in a work setting should be explored. In preparation for this applied work, however, it is necessary to delineate further the characteristics of individuals who seek out and benefit from relationships with mentors, as well as the characteristics of organizations that facilitate or hinder initiation and cultivation of enhancing relationships. It is essential that next steps in research be conducted in a variety of settings so that the relevant organizational factors can be identified.

REFERENCES

Berlew, D. E., & Hall, D. T. The socialization of managers: Effects of expectations on performance. *Administrative Science Quarterly*, 1966, 11, 207–223.

Bray, D., Campbell, R., & Grant, D. *Formative years in business: A long-term study of managerial lives*. New York: Wiley, 1974.

Clawson, J. *Superior-subordinate relationships for managerial development*. Doctoral dissertation, Harvard Business School, 1979.

Clawson, J. Mentoring in managerial careers. In C. B. Derr (Ed.), *Work, family, and the career*. New York: Praeger, 1980, 144–165.

Dalton, G., Thompson, P., & Price, R. The four stages of professional careers—A new look at performance by professionals. *Organizational Dynamics*, 1977, 6(1), 19–42.

Dalton, M. *Men who manage*. New York: Wiley, 1959.

Davis, R. L., Garrison, P. A. Mentoring: In search of a taxonomy. Masters thesis, MIT Sloan School of Business, 1979.

Erikson, E. *Childhood and society*. New York: Norton, 1963.

Erikson, E. *Identity, youth and crisis*. New York: Norton, 1968.

Erikson, E. (Ed.). *Adulthood*. New York: Norton, 1978.

Filstead, W. *Qualitative methodology*. Chicago: Markham, 1970.

Glaser, B. G., & Strauss, A. L. *The discovery of grounded theory: Strategies for qualitative research*. Chicago: Aldine, 1967.

Gould, R. The phases of adult life: A study in developmental psychology. *The American Journal of Psychiatry*, 1972, 129, 521–531.

Gould, R. *Transformations: Growth and change in adult life*. New York: Simon & Schuster, 1978.

Hall, D. T. *Careers in organizations*. Glenview, Ill.: Scott, Foresman, 1976.

Hall, D. T., & Kram, K. E. Development in midcareer. In D. Montross & C. Shinkerman (Eds.), *Career development in the 80's*. Springfield, Ill.: Charles C. Thomas, 1981, 406–423.

Jacques, E. Death and the mid-life crises. *International Journal of Psychoanalysis*, 1965, 46, 502–514.

Jung, C. *Modern man in search of a soul*. New York: Harcourt, 1933.

Kanter, R. M. *Men and women of the corporation*. New York: Basic Books, 1977.

Kram, K. E. *Mentoring processes at work: Developmental relationships in managerial careers*. Doctoral dissertation, Yale University, 1980.

Levinson, D. J., Darrow, C. N., Klein, E. B., Levinson, M. A., & McKee, B. *Seasons of a man's life*. New York: Knopf, 1978.

Levinson, H. *Psychological man*. Cambridge, Mass.: Levinson Institute, 1976.

Missirian, A. K. *The corporate connection: Why executive women need mentors to reach the top*. Englewood Cliffs, N.J.: Prentice-Hall, 1982.

Neugarten, B. *Middle age and aging: A reader in social psychology*. Chicago: University of Chicago Press, 1968.

Osherson, S. *Holding on or letting go*. New York: The Free Press, 1980.

Philips, L. L. *Mentors and proteges: A study of the career development of women managers and executives in business and industry*. Doctoral dissertation, UCLA, 1977, University Microfilms International No. 78-6517.

Reinharz, S. *On becoming a social scientist*. San Francisco, Cal.: Jossey-Bass, 1979.

Schein, E. H. *Career dynamics: Matching individual and organizational needs*. Reading, Mass.: Addison-Wesley, 1978.

Schein, E. H., & Van Maanen, J. Career development. In J. R. Hackman & J. L. Suttle (Eds.), *Improving life at work*. Glenview, Ill.: Scott, Foresman, 1977, 30–95.

Shapiro, E., Haseltine, F., & Rowe, M. Moving up: Role models, mentors, and the "patron system." *Sloan Management Review*, 1978, 19(3), 51–58.

Sheehy, G. The mentor connection. *New York Magazine*, April 5, 1976, 30–39.

Sofer, C. *Men in mid-career*. London: Cambridge University Press, 1970.

Super, E. E. *The psychology of careers*. New York: Harper and Row, 1957.

Vaillant, G. *Adaptation to life*. Boston: Little, Brown, 1977.

Webber, R. Career problems of young managers. *California Management Review*, 1976, 18(4), 19–33.

REVIEW QUESTION

1 Think of a time when someone has been a mentor to you. Give examples of what happened at each of the four phases of the relationship.

READING 25

Effective Subordinancy

Cal W. Downs
Charles Conrad*

After he had worked one year for his company, a recent MBA graduate was asked by a consultant, "How are things going?" He replied, "Well, it's been a hard year. When I was working on my MBA, everybody taught me how to be a good leader; nobody ever talked to me about how to be a good subordinate." He had hit upon a most interesting point, one that should merit some attention.

There has been much research on this incredibly complex relationship between supervisors and their subordinates, but nearly all of it has focused primarily on the supervisors. In his excellent review of this literature, Jablin (1978) divided the studies into the following categories: 1) interaction patterns and related attitudes, 2) openness in communication, 3) upward distortion, 4) upward influence, 5) semantic distance, 6) effective vs. ineffective superiors, 7) feedback, and 8) personal characteristics. In most of these studies, the real aim is to understand supervision; subordinancy is peripheral. On the other hand, there have been several attempts to investigate and understand "effective subordinancy."

First, one of the most developed is Zaleznik's (1965) neo-Freudian psycho-analysis of subordinate types. He explains superior-subordinate conflicts in terms of the subordinates' tendencies to be impulsive, compulsive, masochistic, or with-drawn. His treatment is highly theoretical and suffers from the limitations of all generalized psychoanalysis.

Second, effective subordinates have sometimes been defined implicitly by models of effective supervision. Focusing on traits like "intelligence" or "inter-personal skill," these models construct what effective subordinates should be, but they do not discover what effective subordinates actually are.

Third, some researchers investigate subordinate satisfaction apparently on the assumption that high morale directly influences effective performance (Burke and Wilcox, 1969). This approach not only fails to provide a behavioral definition of subordinate effectiveness, but the basic assumption also has been empirically challenged (Downs, 1977).

Fourth, Wernimont (1971) demonstrated a relationship between accuracy of role expectations and subordinate satisfaction. His most important contribution was to assess behavioral indices of subordinancy. Notably, his respondents were asked to list their expectations of all subordinates, not just the effective ones. Even though his results did include specific behaviors, the final data summary also developed clusters around traits of loyalty, industriousness, and initiative. This happened because respondents answered in terms of traits or personal charac-

*From *Journal of Business Communication*, Spring 1982, pp. 27–37. Reprinted with permission.

teristics despite the fact that his questions were oriented toward behaviors. Finally, his research focused on surbordinancy in general but did not investigate what distinguishes "effective" subordinates from the rest.

In summary, research has focused primarily on supervisors, and descriptions of subordinates have emphasized traits over behaviors. Therefore, determining what an effective subordinate does has been difficult.

PURPOSE

The purpose of this research is to assess the specific communication behaviors that comprise the general effective subordinate. It attempts 1) to identify those behaviors which are perceived as being most important, and then 2) to determine whether or not the respondent's frame of reference as either superior or subordinate substantially alters these assessments.

METHOD

Data was collected from 700 middle managers from private industry and government agencies over a period of seven years. All respondents, participants in management training seminars, were asked to look at subordinancy a) from the point of view of themselves as the superior relating to a subordinate and b) from the point of view of themselves as subordinates relating to their supervisors. Both perspectives are natural for the subjects, since their positions require them to be both superiors and subordinates. The research goal was to discover how they felt about effective subordinancy in a completely unstructured way. Therefore, open questions and critical incidents were used.

Questionnaire

First, they were asked a question from the point of view of themselves as managers. "Think of an effective subordinate. What are three things about his/her communication that make him/her an effective subordinate?" Responses (N = 1372) were grouped into categories, inductively established from the responses themselves and defined with the terms used by the subjects. These responses were tabulated in order of frequency and percentage and the results are included in Table 1.

Second, they responded to a similar question from the subject-as-subordinate perspective. "As a manager, you are also subordinate to someone. Describe three communication characteristics of you which make you an effective subordinate." These responses (N = 1496) were analyzed according to the procedures described above, and Table 1 identified 18 specific communication behavioral categories which were mentioned. These categories are not completely mutually exclusive, but every attempt was made to use the respondents' own words in deriving the clusters.

Not shown in Table 1 were numerous responses which described traits or

TABLE 1
CHARACTERISTICS OF SUBORDINATES

Specific communication behaviors	Manager as superior N = 1370 percent	Manager as subordinate N = 1496 percent
1 Encodes *clear* messages—articulate; explicit, uses illustrations, writes and speaks clearly.	16.0	12.0
2 Provide feedback—confirms understanding; responds freely; expesses feelings.	8.3	11.8
3 Communication timely—on time; prompt; current; up-to-date.	7.7	4.0
4 Is brief—succinct, gets to the point; does not waste time; concise.	7.7	7.0
5 Listens—pays attention; listens carefully.	7.5	13.2
6 Is factual and thorough—researches topic; adequate detail; does not confuse inferences with observations; "red flags" critical information; does not filter bad news.	7.0	11.8
7 Asks questions—requests details; seeks clarification.	5.3	5.4
8 Checks perception: Paraphrases—restates discussion in own words; repeats back assignments.	4.8	4.2
9 Anticipates superior's needs—gives me no surprises; informs me to prevent problems; does not bother me with trivia.	3.8	2.9
10 Follows instruction—takes guidance and direction; carries out orders; follows through.	3.7	3.8
11 Volunteers substantive input—acts as sounding board; provides new ideas and relations; recommends; willing to approach me; keeps channels open by volunteering upward communicaton; discusses plan of action; attempts to solve problems.	4.2	4.2
12 Confronts—verifies; candid; not afraid to disagree; expresses disagreement.	2.9	2.6
13 Initiates communication—willingness to start communication, do not have to drag things out of him; eager to contribute ideas, seeks direction.	3.1	2.1
14 Prepares—Investigates and plans; prepares well; sets goals; defines problems; sets agendas.	.2	.7
15 Follows structure—uses chain of command.	.1	1.1
16 Organizes well.	1.0	—
17 Takes notes—writes summaries that I initial; keeps records.	.5	1.2
18 Liaison; relays to other shifts; is a link in indirect corporate lines of communication; effective intermediacy; uses proper channels.	1.5	2.0

outcomes. Just as had happened in the Wernimont study, many responses described personality characteristics of honesty, openness, enthusiasm, confidence, or flexibility. Another cluster described productivity and job competencies. A final cluster revolved around relationships. Included in this group were "being loyal" and "relating well to others." These categories comprised only 16 percent of the responses and were not included because they do not relate specifically to behavior.

Critical Incidents

Critical incidents were obtained from the sample from both the subject-as-manager and subject-as-subordinate perspectives. In each perspective they were asked to "describe an actual communication between you and (your superior or subordinate). Specify what occurred, when, and the immediate results. Classify the incident as either effective or ineffective." The incidents were filled out at their leisure and were handed in on a questionnaire form.

Critical incident methodology, originated by John C. Flanagan (1954), has two primary advantages. First, critical incidents are self-reported by people who actually experienced the situations. Consequently, they stress what these people assess as having high priorities. Second, the reports deal primarily with incidents which have a significant impact upon the success or failure of an operation. "The fundamental difference in the procedure, from the trait analysis technique . . ., was that this new approach dealt only with critical requirements—those factors which made a difference." (Mackintosh, 1973, p. 65)

A total of 457 critical incidents were collected for the subject-as-manager perspective, and 294 were collected from the subject-as-subordinate perspective. Three basic steps were involved in analyzing the data. First, *ad hoc* categories for classification were derived from the incidents themselves through a process of content analysis. These fit the listing of categories listed by the open-end questions. Second, the reliability of the categories was checked among four independent coders. Correlations among the coders ranged from .86 to .94. Third, the incidents were tabulated in terms of frequency; the results are introduced in Tables 2 and 3. For each category, they were classified as either "effective" or "ineffective," to permit comparisons.

CONCLUSIONS

Perhaps the most obvious result of this study is the simple compilation of the behavioral characteristics of subordinates which are deemed most important to their being effective in communicating with supervisors. The components which were listed most frequently also tend to be the ones into which most of the critical incidents were classified. We can conclude, therefore, that the most important communicative behaviors for subordinates are the following:

TABLE 2

CRITICAL INCIDENTS OF MANAGER AS SUBORDINATE

Communication behaviors	Effective (53.7%) N = 158	Ineffective (46.2%) N = 136	Critical incident totals N = 294
1 Clear	11	29	40
2 Feedback	16	10	26
3 Timely	3	1	4
4 Is brief	5	1	6
5 Listens	5	6	7
6 Factual	29	25	54
7 Asks questions	1	1	2
8 Checks perception	3	13	16
9 Anticipates	3	2	5
10 Follows instructions	11	2	3
11 Volunteers input	14	4	18
12 Confronts	21	4	25
13 Initiates	1	0	1
14 Prepares	—	—	—
15 Follows structure	6	7	13
16 Organizes well	—	—	—
17 Takes notes	—	—	—

TABLE 3

CRITICAL INCIDENTS OF MANAGER AS SUPERIOR

Communication behaviors	Effective (39.17%) N = 179	Ineffective (60.8%) N = 278	Critical incident totals N = 457
1 Clear	12	57	69
2 Feedback	16	19	35
3 Timely	5	3	8
4 Is brief	4	2	6
5 Listens	7	25	32
6 Factual	15	30	45
7 Asks questions	5	8	13
8 Checks perception	7	14	21
9 Anticipates	6	1	7
10 Follows instructions	19	13	32
11 Volunteers input	21	4	25
12 Confronts	22	7	29
13 Initiates	—	—	—
14 Prepares	—	—	—
15 Follows structure	8	17	25
16 Organizes well	—	—	—
17 Takes notes	—	—	—

1 Encode clear messages.
2 Provide feedback.
3 Communicate in a timely manner.
4 Be brief and concise.
5 Listen.
6 Be factual and thorough.
7 Ask questions.
8 Check perceptions.
9 Anticipate superior's needs.
10 Volunteer input.
11 Follow instructions.

Finally, this data suggests that specific behaviors, as opposed to internal states or external factors, distinguished *effective* from *ineffective* subordinates in their communication.

Although two-way communication was reinforced, by listing both sending and receiving skills, it is noteworthy that upward communication received the heaviest emphasis. And some of the factors emphasized not only the ability to communicate upward but also the willingness to do so. One way to document the emphasis on upward communication is to examine the data from critical incidents. Because they can be classified as effective or ineffective, the critical incident data allows an added insight into what distinguishes some subordinates as being more effective than others. The *problems* most often identified in each frame of reference are listed in order:

1 Lack of clarity.
2 Failure to listen.
3 Failure to be factual/thorough.
4 Failure to give feedback.
5 Failure to paraphrase.

On the other hand, the effective incidents conveyed importance to a somewhat different set of behaviors.

1 Confront.
2 Volunteer input.
3 Follow instructions.
4 Give feedback.
5 Be factual/thorough.

Only two of the items—giving feedback and being factual—occur in both lists; and 8 out of the 10 factors mentioned on these lists relate to upward communication. The nature of upward communication in this data takes two forms.

First, the most effective subordinates are apparently the ones who will risk confrontation. Emphasized under both perspectives, confrontation is listed significantly more times as being effective (13 percent) than as being ineffective (3 percent). This is perhaps one of the most significant findings in the study. Since confrontation generally connotes challenging or giving unwanted information, the folk wisdom is that ambitious subordinates will not take the risk. Furthermore, several studies suggest subordinates are willing to send positive information upward, but they are less willing to send negative or unfavorable information upward (Jablin, 1978). Perhaps subordinates in general do not, but this study indicates that *effective* subordinates do—and they avoid some communication problems by doing so.

However, there was a subtle difference between those incidents that were effective and those that were not. In the effective cases, subordinates employed one of two strategies. Some would include thoroughly researched supporting evidence; and we have already noted that "being factual and thorough" is one dimension of "good" communication. Others used an internal or external expert to lend credibility to their ideas; they did not rely only on their own resources. In these circumstances the managers reported that they were glad that their subordinates had been willing to be confrontive.

Second, effective subordinates volunteer input; they take the initiative to give unsolicited recommendations and keep the superior informed. One important aspect of this involves protecting superiors. Effective subordinates are able to anticipate superiors' needs and keep them informed so they will not be caught ignorant of things they ought to know.

In addition to following instruction and responding well to downward communication, effective subordinates are the ones who respond in ways that permit them to check their perceptions and thereby reduce misunderstandings and/or mistakes. Three of the most frequently mentioned behaviors were: 1) providing feedback, 2) asking questions, and 3) paraphrasing. Furthermore, the failures to do these are listed as the causes of the most frequent problems found in the critical incidents.

While it is important to note that supervisors expect subordinates to volunteer feedback and check perceptions, previous research gives a clear implication that the extent to which subordinates do this depends upon the kind of climate that the supervisor sets. For example, Brenner and Sigband (1973) found that feedback increased when supervisors told subordinates what to do with completed assignments and when the subordinates felt that the supervisor would actually give clarifications if asked. While supervisors have a general expectation that subordinates will provide feedback, Redding's extensive review of the literature suggests feedback is facilitated or inhibited by certain kinds of supervisory actions (1972). In other words, supervisors behave in ways that determine whether or not their expectation will be met.

Clarity is not only the most frequently mentioned communication behavior but the lack of clarity is the most frequently mentioned problem in the critical incidents. Therefore, it is given tremendous importance. These facts pinpoint once again the existence of semantic/information distance between superiors and subordinates. Yet, effective subordinates are the ones who somehow overcome this gap. Since the judgment about "clarity' is more a dimension of the superior's understanding than a characteristic of a message, effective subordinates are those who can adapt their messages to the understanding patterns of their superiors. Whereas this study did not examine specific topics on which there are semantic gaps, other research has developed quite an array of topics where there is considerable variance in both information and understanding between subordinates and superiors (Jablin, 1978). These differences apparently lead inevitably to feelings that the other person is not communicating clearly. And further research ought to try to probe more what managers mean when they say that subordinates fail to be clear.

The views of subordinancy tend to be very similar between the two perspectives of the manager-as-superior and the manager-as-subordinate. The same items are listed as strengths and problems in both frames of reference. There are, however, two major differences. First, in terms of specific behaviors managers emphasize listening (13 to 7.5 percent) and being factual and thorough (11.8 to 6.7 percent) as being more characteristic of themselves as subordinates than is characteristic of their own good subordinates. Second, the managers listed more effective critical incidents when considering themselves as subordinates than they did in considering their own subordinates' communication; the comparison was 51 percent to 40 percent. The most frequently identified problems on critical incidents are similar to the ones listed on the questionnaire.

IMPLICATIONS AND APPLICATIONS

The purpose of this research is to identify common expectancies about subordinates. The results are compiled across many people and do not, therefore, guarantee that they are expected by each individual manager. Nevertheless, such results could have important implications for the training of subordinates.

First, in their training, supervisors need to be confronted with their own expectations of subordinates. They could then explore their own behaviors which could facilitate more effective performance by the subordinates. For example, supervisors can be trained to provide subordinates incentives for desired behaviors. They can be trained to *ask* for feedback or to ask questions themselves if messages are unclear or detail is inadequate. In other words, supervisors need to assess their own role in generating effective communication by subordinates.

Second, training programs for subordinates can similarly focus on effectiveness-enhancing behaviors. Training by the author on effective subordinancy is now included in one company's orientation program. In some cases, training that is common for supervisors evidently would be profitable for subordinates, also. Notable examples are report writing, active listening, and perception checking. Incentives for expected behaviors should also be clearly identified. The goal is to create subordinate expectations that specific behaviors are both desired and rewarded.

Third, a study like this provides an interesting perspective in looking at the same person as both supervisor and subordinate. Although we focused on effective subordinancy, respondents were confronted with the fact that they were neither just supervisor or just subordinate. Most were both. Therefore, being a good manager involved being a good subordinate, and this perspective is an important dimension of the study. Perhaps, more research should focus on the way that peoples' roles as subordinates affect how they manage their own subordinates.

BIBLIOGRAPHY

Brenner, M. H. and Sigband, N. B. "Organizational Communication—An Analysis Based on Empirical Data." *Academy of Management Journal.* 16 (1973), 323–325.

Burke, R. J. and Wilcox, D. S. "Effects of Different Patterns and Degrees of Openness in Superior-Subordinate Communication on Subordinate Job Satisfaction." *Academy of Management Journal,* 12 (1969), 319–326.

Downs, Cal W. "The Relationship Between Communication and Job Satisfaction" in *Readings in Interpersonal and Organizational Communication,* edited by Richard C. Huseman, Boston: Holbrook Press, 1977.

Flanagan, J. C. "The Critical Incident Technique." *Psychological Bulletin,* 51 (July, 1954), 327–358.

Jablin, Fredric M. "Superior-Subordinate Communication: The State of the Art." International Communication Association Convention, Chicago, 1978.

Mackintosh, Hartley B. *A Critical Incident Study of the Communication Factors Utilized by Prison Guards,* M.A. thesis, University of Kansas, 1973.

Read, William C. "Upward Communication in Industrial Hierarchies." *Human Relations,* 15 (1962), 3–15.

Redding, W. C. *Communication Within the Organization.* New York: Industrial Communication Council, 1972.

Wernimont, Paul "What Supervisors and Subordinates Expect of Each Other." *Personnel Journal* (March, 1971).

Zaleznik, Abraham. "Dynamics of Subordinancy." *Harvard Business Review,* 43 (May, 1965), 119–131.

REVIEW QUESTIONS

1 What are the pros and cons of providing employees with training in "effective subordinancy"?

2 Examine the various characteristics listed in Table 1. Which of those listed there could also be included in a list of effective *managerial* behaviors?

3 To what extent do you think that subordinancy and managerial behaviors are compensatory—that is, if one party exhibits those behaviors, the other party has much less need to do so?

READING 26

Attributions and Actions:
A Note of Caution

Terence R. Mitchell*

Attribution theory is concerned with how people make inferences about the causes of their own and other people's behavior. The research literature in social and organizational psychology over the last five years has demonstrated an expanding interest in the area. Pepitone (1981) went so far as to say that "Now in the 1980's, attribution theory is probably the most prominent and active area in social psychology" (p. 979).

The reasons for its popularity are numerous. Attributional processes clearly fall into the general "information processing" or cognitive type of psychology, which is currently in vogue. But attributions also seem to have important functions: they help in the categorization process, reduce ambiguity, increase our understanding of our actions, and help us understand the actions of others.

It is this last point on which I wish to focus in this paper. More specifically, one of the major functions of attributions about other people is that such attributions are helpful in guiding our actions toward other people. That is, our assessment of why people do the things they do influences how we behave toward them.

The critical point is that attributions are important for action. The interpersonal exchange is seen as a two-step process. First, we diagnose why people do things (make attributions) and second, we select or choose some response. This latter choice is seen as being, in part, determined by attributions.

However, the major portion of attributional research has focused on the first step in the process. A great percentage of the published papers in the area deal with the causes of attributions and the various errors associated with this process, such as the actor-observer error or self-serving biases (Ross, 1977; Kelley & Michela, 1980).

Recently, there has been a slight shift in this emphasis. Some researchers are showing concern for how attributions are affecting actions—such as physical abuse (Frieze, Bar-Tal & Carroll, 1979; Richardson & Campbell, 1980), delinquent behavior (Wells, 1980) and helping behavior (Ickes & Kidd, 1976). In the areas of organizational behavior and industrial psychology we find papers on how attributions are related to discrimination (Pettigrew, 1979), selection (Haefner, 1977; Phillips & Lord, 1981; Staw & Ross, 1980), performance appraisal (Baserman & Atkin, 1978; and Feldman, 1981), use of social power (Kipnis, 1976), and supervisor treatment of poor performers (Green & Mitchell, 1979; Mitchell, Green & Wood, 1981; and Kipnis, 1972, 1976).

*From *Journal of Management*, Spring 1982, pp. 65–74. © 1982 by the Southern Management Association. Reprinted with permission of the publisher, Southern Management Association, and the author.

These attempts to relate attributions to actions have resulted in only moderate success. The research on helping behavior and delinquent behavior seems to indicate that these behaviors are partly determined by the social context (who and how many people are around). Wells' (1980) research, for example, suggests that delinquent behavior is more often caused by social pressure (e.g., who is present and what they want to do) than by attributions about internal traits or motivations. Selection decisions may be influenced by social pressure. For example, both Tucker & Rowe (1979) and Haefner (1977) show that the information present in letters of reference has significant effects on selection decisions as does the credibility of the source of information (Beach, Mitchell, Daton & Prothero, 1978). Leadership ratings and performance appraisal may also be more a result of general cognitive maps or models or external factors like the rating instrument or use of the rating than attributions. For example, Phillips & Lord (1981) show that ratings of leaders are predicted better from knowledge of the leader's salience (intrusiveness in the action) than the rater's attributions about the leader's behavior. A study by Ilgen & Knowlton (1980) demonstrated that performance appraisal ratings were significantly affected by whether the ratee was going to see the ratings or not. In short, attributions seem to be only moderately related to action.

The purpose of the present paper is to make this point clearly and explicitly with regard to one area: the treatment of poorly performing subordinates by their supervisor. In giving a brief summary of what we have found over a whole series of studies, I hope to show what sorts of factors besides attributions are important and to perhaps increase people's interest in and research about these other factors. The model we have used will be briefly discussed, the research describing the relationship between attributions and actions will be reviewed and the implications of these findings will be discussed.

THE RESEARCH MODEL

The model that has guided our work is presented in Figure 1. Basically, the model involves a two-step process. First, the supervisor engages in a diagnosis of the cause of the problem. Central to this process are the factors that contribute to what is called an internal attribution (i.e., something internal to the subordinate, like his or her effort or ability) or an external attribution (i.e., something external to the subordinate, such as a difficult task or bad luck). Various rational factors such as the subordinate's past work history or the supervisor's job experience as well as some errors or biases are seen as influencing this judgment.

The second step in the process involves the choice of a response to the poor performer. If an internal attribution is made then a response focusing on the subordinate is seen as more likely (e.g., reprimands or dismissal if effort is the perceived cause, training or transfer if ability is seen as the problem). If an external attribution is made then a response directed at the environment should occur (e.g., job enrichment or job restructuring if the task is the problem or extra support if other people were the cause). Various other social and situational

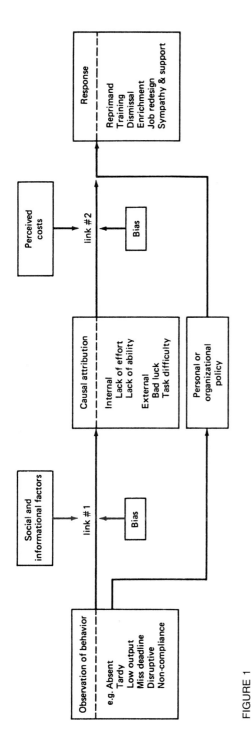

FIGURE 1
An attributional model of a leader's response to a subordinate's poor performance.

143

factors may influence this choice of behavior. I will describe these factors more fully in a moment.

RESEARCH ON STEP 1

The first few years of our research focused on the first step of the model: the causes of attributions. As expected, we found that the past performance and the performance of others influenced the judgment, as did the experience of the supervisor. The poorer the past performance of the focal subordinate and the better the performance of others, the more internal the attribution. The greater the experience, the more external the attribution.

We also found that certain other processes influenced the judgments. Supervisors gave more internal attributions than did the subordinates (an actor-observer difference) and supervisors were influenced by the outcomes of the poor performance—a factor over which the subordinate frequently had little control. Also, the more salient the internal or external information cues the more they were used. Reviews of this work are available elsewhere (Mitchell, Green & Wood, 1981; Mitchell & Kalb, 1982).

RESEARCH ON STEP 2

The last few years' work has concentrated on predicting the supervisor's response to the poorly performing subordinate. The research has been conducted using laboratory studies, job simulations and field studies; the dependent variables include such things as feedback given to the subordinate, recommendations for future actions, performance appraisals, and the docking of pay or the use of bonuses. Thus, a wide variety of research strategies and actions have been investigated.

The first few studies that we did demonstrated clearly that attributions were related to responses as predicted (e. g., Knowlton & Mitchell, 1980; Mitchell & Wood, 1980). However, the variance accounted for in the responses, while significant, was often less than we had expected or was potentially confounded by halo or rating errors. In the series of studies described below we attempted to look at other variables that might influence action and in some cases we crossed these variables with attributions so that we could assess the independent contribution of these variables to action.

Outcome Valence

One variable that seems to influence the supervisor's response is the outcome of the poor performance. For example, in Mitchell & Wood (1980) we demonstrated that nurse supervisors were more punitive toward a poor performer when bad outcomes occurred (e.g., the patient had a setback) than when benign outcomes occurred (e.g., the patient continued to recover). Since the outcome of the behavior (e.g., whether a patient falls out of bed when the bed railing is left down) is often out of the subordinate's control, differential treatment for the same behavior may result—a condition that leads to feelings of inequity and conflict.

We should note that the first study described in Mitchell & Wood (1980) demonstrated that the seriousness of outcome had only a marginal effect on attributions but a strong effect on actions. In the second study reported in the paper, attributions (internal/external) were crossed with outcome valence (serious/benign). Outcome valence still had a significant main effect on responses: more serious outcomes led to more serious punishment, independent of attributions.

Apologies

In two subsequent studies with nurse supervisors (Wood & Mitchell, 1981) we crossed the account given by the subordinate (internal/external) with apologies given by the subordinate (present/absent). In the first study the stimulus materials were in the form of critical incidents while in the second study a film was used showing an interaction between a nurse supervisor and her subordinate. In both studies apologies were not related to attributions while accounts were. More internal attributions were made when the subordinate account was internal (i.e., admitting that she was the cause) than when the subordinate account was external (e.g., the environment was presented as the cause). Of more importance for the current paper was that apologies, while unrelated to attributions, were significantly related to actions. The supervisor was more lenient and less punitive toward the subordinate who apologized. Note again that the apology manipulation was independent of the account manipulation.

Social Context

Another study had business students playing the role of a supervisor rating the performance of a group of subordinates that was charged with the development of an affirmative action program (Mitchell & Liden, 1982). The information given to the supervisors was constructed such that one person performed poorly while the other two performed well. The variables manipulated were the social attractiveness of the poor performer (liked or not liked by the other two group members) and the leadership skills of the poor performer (rated as high or low on leadership skills by the other two group members). The dependent variables were performance ratings, a financial bonus (or decrease in pay) and recommendations for action (e.g., promote, monitor closely, transfer, give important assignments).

The results showed that the poor performer was rated higher when the supervisor felt the poor performer was liked and had leadership potential than when the reverse was true. This occurred even though the performance was exactly the same. Of perhaps more importance was the fact that when the poor performer was liked and had high leadership skills the *two other group members* were rated lower on the dependent variables than when the poor performer was disliked and did not have leadership skills. Since the performance and group ratings of these other two members were constant in all conditions these data suggest strongly that the actions taken by the supervisor were influenced by the social context—the relative standing of all the group members on variables that were social in nature.

Interdependence

In a study by Ilgen, Mitchell & Fredrickson (1981) we had people working on a coding task. Again, the supervisor was confronted with one poor and two good performers and the poor performer was either interdependent with the supervisor (i.e., the supervisor's pay was partly a function of the subordinate's performance) or not interdependent with the supervisor (i.e., the supervisor was paid independently). The dependent variables were the performance evaluations, feedback, and suggested changes in pay (bonus, docking).

As expected the performance manipulation had a major effect on all of the dependent variables. The results indicated, in fact, that the effect of performance on the attributions was less strong than the effect on the performance ratings, feedback, and pay changes. Interdependence also was significantly related to the dependent variables. When the supervisor was dependent on the poor performing subordinate the ratings of his performance were higher than when he was not dependent on him. The effects of the interdependence manipulation seemed to be about equally strong on attributions and responses.

Costs/Benefits of Responses

In a recent series of studies we developed a film of an administrative assistant who is performing poorly at her job. Then, using a training program of supplementing the film with other information we have demonstrated that we can train people to attend to either internal cues (e.g., laziness, sloppiness) or external cues (e.g., a disruptive environment, an unclear job assignment) as causes of this person's poor performance (Heerwagen, 1982).

In a second study we crossed this training (internal/external) with costs of using various responses. That is, responses directed at the subordinate (such as reprimands or training) were made to appear as difficult or easy to implement as were responses directed at the environment such as providing another assistant or restructuring the job (Heerwagen, 1982).

In the first experiment, where we simply trained people and looked at their attribution and suggested responses, the training was highly related to attributions and attributions were related to responses (e.g., accounting for 20–30% of the variance in responses). When the film and training was crossed with the costs and benefits of the responses (Study 2) we got a very different picture. The costs and benefits accounted for 62% of the variance in responses while attributions accounted for only 5–10% of the variance. The costs and benefits of various actions clearly outweighed the attributions as to the cause of the problem.

Policies

Finally, if one refers back to Figure 1, one can see that there is a line that bypasses the whole attributional process. In some cases either personal or organizational policies dictate the response and attributions simply are not used. In one study by Green & Liden (1980) a role-playing exercise was used in which students played the subordinate and supervisor roles in a discussion of an incident of poor performance. The treatment by the supervisor was shown to be a joint function of the organizational policy and the supervisor's attribution.

In another study that we recently conducted (Liden & Mitchell, 1982) we interviewed faculty members in three different departments of a large university. These interviews indicated that in 92% of the undergraduate classes the faculty employed a grading policy when dealing with a student who performed poorly on an exam. These policies treated all the students the same by either 1) letting the grade stand and offering (or not offering) help on subsequent tests, or 2) letting everyone have the same treatment or option for remedial or make-up work (e.g., book report, paper, drop the worst test, etc.). These data suggest that, at least in these departments and for these courses, very little attributional work went on.

DISCUSSION

The overwhelming conclusion we have drawn is that attributions are only part of the picture. Clearly a number of interpersonal (e.g., apologies), task (e.g., outcomes), context (e.g., interdependence, subordinate's role in group) and situational (e.g., costs/benefits) factors influence responses. Both our results suggest that we need to go even one step further. Not only are attributions only one contributor to action—a conclusion with which most people would agree—according to our findings attributions play a *minor* role. That is, there are many settings where action may be simply determined by personal, social or organizational policies. Attributions would be completely bypassed. In many other settings it appears that contextual, task, social and cost/benefit type factors are as important or more important than attributions. Therefore, in many settings attributions may be weakly related to action at best.

This word of caution needs to be made very explicit because presently it does not seem to be widely recognized. While, as we mentioned in the introduction, there is some shift to using behavior as the dependent variable in attribution studies it is still not done very often. For example, the Kelley & Michela (1980) review devotes twenty pages to the antecedents of attributions and eight to their consequences. And of the studies cited in the consequences section, most of the dependent variables are feelings, attitudes and expectations, not behavior.

This continued focus on attributions rather than actions as a dependent variable has occurred for a variety of reasons. First, attributions may have many functions other than influencing behavior. Clarification of expectations, attitudes and feelings are important phenomena themselves. Some researchers may simply be interested more in these other topics than in action.

A second reason is that the laboratory methodology or questionnaires that have been used for most of this research lend themselves easily to the use of evaluation, attitudes and attributions as dependent variables. It is, in many ways, a more difficult methodology to manipulate attributions and look at actual behavior, especially in the field setting. But we should not be fooling ourselves that this emphasis on attitudes or simpler methodology substitutes for predictions of actions.

On a more general level our conclusion about the attribution-action link seems to be similar to that of other authors looking at other areas or more encompassing questions. Pepitone (1981) for example suggests that the whole field of social psychology should pay more attention to social, task and situational causes of behavior. Salancik & Pfeffer (1977, 1978) have argued that the research on topics such as motivation or job attitudes would benefit greatly from a better understanding of the social context. O'Reilly & Weitz (1980) have made a similar argument for the area of leadership and recent work by Peters (Peters & O'Connor, 1981; Peters, O'Connor & Rudolf, 1980) has demonstrated how task and situational variables are important for predicting job performance. Thus, the results presented here fit into a somewhat expanding recognition of the importance of these social and situational factors for understanding various types of behavior important for management.

At the more specific level of leadership research the results suggest that supervisor actions toward subordinates are influenced by numerous factors other than the subordinate's performance level and what the supervisor sees as the cause of that level. As Landy & Farr (1980) have argued, we need to understand the total context in which such evaluations and actions take place. To date our emphasis has clearly been more on the cognitive processes taking place. Perhaps it is time for a shift with greater research effort being placed on social, situational and context factors.

One such approach that does take recognition of these social factors is the substitutes for leadership theory suggested by Kerr & Jermier (1978). These authors demonstrate that characteristics of the subordinate (e.g., indifference, ability), of the task (e.g., routine, provides own feedback) or the organization (e.g., formalization, inflexibility, spatial distances) often take precedence over leader behavior in terms of influencing subordinate behavior.

In our model we are concerned with the impact of these variables on the leader's behavior (not the subordinate's). In retrospect, it is clear that Link 2 in Figure 1 is more complex than we originally believed. Besides the factors we mentioned (perceived costs and biases) other variables need to be taken into account. Characteristics of the situation (e.g., group cohesiveness, norm clarity) and the organization (e.g., formality, flexibility, plant layout) may clearly intervene between attributions and action. What is needed now is a better understanding of those situations in which attributions contribute directly and strongly to action and where they do not.

We have known for a long time that behavior is a function of the person and the environment. In that respect what we are saying is not new or novel. However, it is equally clear that the overwhelming emphasis has been to study the person—his/her personality traits, abilities, and cognitive processes. What is suggested here is that the social context and physical environment are perhaps equally or more important predictors of behavior and that more research is badly needed in this area.

REFERENCES

Baserman, M. H., & Atkins, R. S. Performance appraisal: An information-processing and attributional perspective. (Working paper no. 25-78-79.) Pittsburgh: Carnegie-Mellon University, Graduate School of Industrial Administration, 1978.

Beach, L. R., Mitchell, T. R., Deaton, M. D., & Prothero, J. Information relevance, content, and source credibility in the revision of opinions. *Organizational Behavior and Human Performance*, 1978, *21*, 1–16.

Calder, B. J. An attribution theory of leadership. In B. M. Staw & G. R. Salancik (eds.), *New Directions in Organizational Behavior*. Chicago: St. Clair Press, 1977.

Feldman, J. M. Beyond attribution theory: Cognitive processes in performance appraisal. *Journal of Applied Psychology*, 1981, *66*, 127–148.

Frieze, I. H., Bar-Tal, D., & Carroll, J. S. *New Approaches to Social Problems: Applications of Attribution Theory*. San Francisco: Jossey-Bass, 1979.

Green, S. G., & Liden, R. C. Contextual and attributional influences on control decisions. *Journal of Applied Psychology*, 1980, *65*, 453–458.

Green, S. G., & Mitchell, T. R. Attributional processes of leaders in leader-member interactions. *Organizational Behavior and Human Performance*, 1979, *23*, 429–458.

Haefner, J. E. Race, age, sex and competence factors in employment selection of the disadvantaged. *Journal of Applied Psychology*, 1977, *62*, 199–202.

Heerwagen, J. Supervisors' responses to poor performance: The effects of attributional training and the analysis of costs of actions. Unpublished doctoral dissertation. Department of Psychology, University of Washington, Seattle, 1982.

Ickes, W. J. & Kidd, R. F. An attributional analysis of helping behavior. In J. H. Harvey, W. J. Ickes and R. F. Kidd (eds.), *New Directions in Attribution Research* (vol. 1). Hillsdale, N.J.: Lawrence Erlbaum Assn., 1976, 311–334.

Ilgen, D. R., & Knowlton, W. A., Jr. Performance attributional effects on feedback from superiors. *Organizational Behavior and Human Performance*, 1980, *25*, 441–456.

Ilgen, D. R., Mitchell, T. R., & Fredrickson, J. W. Poor performers: Supervisors' and subordinates' responses. *Organizational Behavior and Human Performance*, 1981, *27*, 386–410.

Kane, J. S., & Lawler, E. E. III. Performance appraisal effectiveness: Its assessment and determinants. In B. Staw (ed.), *Research in Organizational Behavior*, (vol. 1), Greenwich, Conn.: JAI Press, 1979.

Kelley, H., & Michela, J. Attribution theory and research. In M. Rosenzweig and L. Porter (eds.), *Annual Review of Psychology*. Palo Alto: Annual Reviews, 1980.

Kerr, S., & Jermier, J. M. Substitutes for leadership: their meaning and measurement. *Organizational Behavior and Human Performance*, 1978, *22*, 375–403.

Kipnis, D. Does power corrupt? *Journal of Personality and Social Psychology*, 1972, *24*, 33–41.

Kipnis, D. *The Powerholders*. Chicago: University of Chicago Press, 1976.

Knowlton, W. A., Jr., and Mitchell, T. R. Effects of causal attributions on a supervisor's evaluation of subordinates' performance. *Journal of Applied Psychology*, 1980, *65*, 459–466.

Landy, F. J., & Farr, J. L. Performance rating. *Psychological Bulletin*, 1980, *87*, 72–107.

Liden, R. C., & Mitchell, T. R. The use of personal policies in responding to student poor performance. Working paper. Seattle: School of Business, University of Washington, 1982.

Mitchell, T. R., Green, S. G., & Wood, R. E. An attributional model of leadership and the poor performing subordinate: Development and validation. In B. Staw and L. L. Cummings (eds.), *Research in Organizational Behavior*. Greenwich, Conn.: JAI Press, 1981.

Mitchell, T. R., & Kalb, L. S. The effects of job experience on supervisor attributions for a subordinate's poor performance. *Journal of Applied Psychology*, 1982, *67*, 181–188.

Mitchell, T. R., & Liden, R. C. The effects of the social context on performance evaluations. *Organizational Behavior and Human Performance*, 1982, *29*, 241–246.

Mitchell, T. R., & Wood, R. E. Supervisor's responses to subordinate poor performance: A test of an attributional model. *Organizational Behavior and Human Performance*, 1980, *25*, 123–138.

O'Reilly, C., & Weitz, B. Managing marginal employees: The use of warnings and dismissals. *Administrative Science Quarterly*, 1980, *25*, 467–484.

Pepitone, A. Lessons from the history of social psychology. *American Psychologist*, 1981, *36*, 972–985.

Peters, L. J., & O'Connor, E. J. Situational constraints and work outcomes: The influence of a frequently overlooked construct. *Academy of Management Review*, 1981, *5*, 391–398.

Peters, L. J., O'Connor, E. F., & Rudolf, C. J. The behavioral and affective consequences of situational variables relevant to perfomance settings. *Organizational Behavior and Human Performance*, 1980, *25*, 79–96.

Pettigrew, T. F. The ultimate attribution error: Extending Allport's cognitive analysis of prejudice. *Personality and Social Psychology Bulletin*, 1979, *5*, 461–476.

Phillips, J. S., & Lord, R. G. Causal attributions and perceptions of leadership. *Organizational Behavior and Human Performance*, 1981, *28*, 143–163.

Richardson, D. C., & Campbell, J. L. Alcohol and wife abuse: The effect of alcohol on attributions of blame for wife abuse. *Personality and Social Psychology Bulletin*, 1980, *6*, 51–56.

Ross, L. The intuitive psychologist and his shortcomings: Distortions in the attribution process. In L. Berkowitz (ed.), *Advances in Experimental Social Psychology* (vol. 10). New York: Academic Press, 1977.

Salancik, G. R., & Pfeffer, J. An examination of need satisfaction models of job attitudes. *Administrative Science Quarterly*, 1977, *22*, 427–456, 1978.

Salancik, G. R., & Pfeffer, J. A social information processing approach to job attitudes and task design. *Administrative Science Quarterly*, 1978, *23*, 224–263.

Staw, B. M., & Ross, J. Commitment in an experimenting society. A study of the attribution of leadership from administrative scenarios. *Journal of Applied Psychology*, 1980, *65*, 249–260.

Tucker, D. H., & Rowe, P. M. Relationship between expectancy, causal attributions and final hiring decisions in the employment interview. *Journal of Applied Psychology*, 1979, *64*, 27–34.

Wells, K. Adolescents' attributions for delinquent behavior. *Personality and Social Psychology Bulletin*, 1980, *6*, 63–67.

Wood, R. E., & Mitchell, T. R. Manager behavior in a social context: The impact of impression management on attributions and disciplinary actions. *Organizational Behavior and Human Performance*, 1981, *28*, 356–378.

REVIEW QUESTIONS

1 A student fails an examination. Give examples of the two internal attributions the professor might provide, and the two external attributions the student is likely to offer.

2 Summarize Mitchell's argument that factors other than attributions are important predictors of behavior. What are they?

3 Given our knowledge of the attributional process, suggest several guidelines for managerial behavior in dealing with poorly performing subordinates.

CHAPTER 7

POWER AND POLITICS

READING 27

The Effective Use of Managerial Power

Gary Yukl
Tom Taber*

Influence over the attitudes and behavior of subordinates is the essence of competent leadership. It is impossible to be an effective manager without influencing subordinates. Despite its obvious importance, however, the way in which managers exert their power has not been subjected to much research. There have been only a small number of studies on the relationship between leader power and effectiveness. In most of these studies, power was classified in terms of the taxonomy developed by J. R. P. French Jr. and B. Raven in 1959. This taxonomy identifies five distinct types of power:

- *Authority* (legitimate power): the legitimate right of the leader to make certain kinds of requests.
- *Reward power*: the leader's control over rewards valued by subordinates.
- *Coercive power*: the leader's control over punishments.
- *Expert power*: the leader's task-relevant knowledge and competence, as perceived by subordinates.
- *Referent power*: subordinate loyalty to the leader and desire to please him or her.

The research revealed that effective leaders rely most on expert and referent power to influence subordinates. The use of expert and referent power was positively correlated with subordinate performance or satisfaction in most of the studies. Use of legitimate and coercive power tended to be negatively correlated with effectiveness, or to be uncorrelated with it. Results for reward power were mixed, with no clear trend across studies. The results from this research seem plausible, even though the correlations were not strong or consistent.

THE USE OF POWER AND SUBORDINATE REACTION

To understand how a leader's use of power can affect subordinate performance, it is necessary to consider such intervening processes as subordinate motivation and effort. The motivational outcome of an influence attempt by the leader can be classified according to whether it produces commitment, compliance, or resistance in the subordinate.

*Reprinted by permission of the publisher from "The Effective Use of Managerial Power," by Gary Yukl and Tom Taber, in *Personnel*, March–April 1983, © 1983 by AMACOM, a division of American Management Associations, pp. 37–44. All rights reserved.

When subordinates are committed, they are enthusiastic about carrying out the leader's requests and make a maximum effort to do so. Committed employees accept the leader's goals and exert maximum effort to accomplish them. Simple compliance, on the other hand, is only a partially successful outcome of leader influence. Subordinates go along with the leader's requests without necessarily accepting the leader's goals. They are not enthusiastic and may make only the minimal acceptable effort in carrying out such requests. Resistance, as most managers know, is a clearly unsuccessful outcome. Subordinates reject the leader's goals and may pretend to comply, but, instead, intentionally delay or sabotage the task. Unfortunately, only a few studies have considered subordinate motivation as an intervening variable. From the limited evidence available, we can piece together a picture of the likely causal relationships between leader power bases and subordinate motivation.

As Figure 1 illustrates, expert and referent power tend to result in subordinate commitment, authority and reward power tend to result in compliance, and coercion tends to result in resistance. Because group performance is usually better when subordinates are highly motivated to do the task, the use of expert and referent power usually leads to a higher level of performance.

The problem with most of the power research is that it overlooks the leader's skill in exercising power. The outcome of a particular attempt to influence subordinates will depend as much on the leader's skill as on the type of power used. It is quite possible that expert and referent power could result merely in compliance or even in resistance if not used skillfully. By the same token, authority and reward power could result in subordinate commitment when used in an appropriate situation by a very skilled leader. Coercion does not necessarily have to result in resistance; it may result in subordinate compliance if used skillfully.

Thus the power studies yield somewhat misleading findings. One gets the false impression that an effective leader uses only expert and referent power—with no need at all to use authority, rewards, or coercion. However, this impression is at odds with findings from motivation research that indicate that rewards can be very effective in increasing subordinate effort and performance in some situations. Motivation research also provides evidence that punishment is sometimes effective in getting subordinates to comply with rules and regulations. And various

---

FIGURE 1
OUTCOMES THAT RESULT FROM DIFFERENT TYPES OF POWER

Power source	Commitment	Compliance	Resistance
Authority	Possible	LIKELY	Possible
Reward power	Possible	LIKELY	Possible
Coercive power	Unlikely	Possible	LIKELY
Expert power	LIKELY	Possible	Possible
Referent power	LIKELY	Possible	Possible

kinds of evidence indicate that exercising authority with a legitimate request is the most common approach used for influencing subordinates, and one that is quite important in the day-to-day operations of a work unit. Thus it is likely that effective leaders use all five types of power at one time or another. Leader effectiveness stems from knowing the appropriate type of power to use in each situation and how to exercise this power skillfully to maximize subordinate commitment.

THE LEADERSHIP MODEL

Figure 2 shows a model that depicts the relationship between power and leader effectiveness. The model differs in some important respects from traditional thinking about leader power. First, the model holds that mere possession of power by itself has no consistent effects on subordinate motivation; power merely acts as a moderator variable to condition the effects of a leader's influence attempts. Second, the model clearly distinguishes between having power and using it. The successful use of power requires the leader to have relevant skill and a desire to exercise power, as well as the power resources themselves. Finally, the feedback loops in the model, indicated by dash lines, recognize that power relationships are reciprocal and historical. A leader's behavior over time can increase or diminish his or her power, and the leader's behavior is itself influenced by subordinate behavior and performance.

In the process of accumulating power and exercising it, leaders are confronted with an interesting paradox. Any increase in power gives a leader greater potential for influencing subordinates, but a power differential also increases the propensity for resistance. The existence of a power differential is generally disturbing to the person who has lower power and status. Subordinates are aware that a powerful leader has the potential to cause them great harm or inconvenience. For this reason, even a benevolent leader's subordinates tend to be very sensitive to the leader's behavior, including subtle indications of approval or

FIGURE 2
A model of leader power and effectiveness.

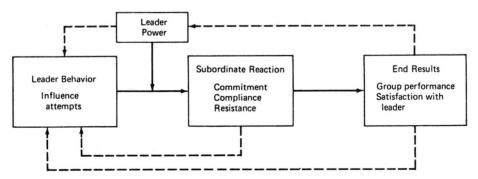

disapproval. Involuntary dependence on the whims of a powerful authority figure can cause resentment as well as anxiety, particularly for subordinates with strong needs for esteem and independence. A leader who treats subordinates as somehow inferior— who acts arrogant, bossy, and manipulative—will quickly elicit resistance to requests and commands.

Thus successful use of power requires influence attempts that do not threaten the subordinates' self-esteem. A number of other factors contribute to the success of an influence attempt, such as clarity of communication, timing, and appropriateness of requests as well as the leader's ability to relate requests to subordinates' needs and concerns. Previous leadership research does not tell us much about the way to exercise power successfully. However, some useful insights are provided by studies of motivation, attitude change, counseling, and conflict resolution. From this research, we have learned we ought to offer some tentative guidelines on how to use and maintain each of the five types of power.

GUIDELINES FOR USING AUTHORITY

Subordinates generally accept their boss's right to make requests and tell them what work to do. However, they do not like to be given orders in a way that implies they are not as good as the leader—people don't want to be treated like slaves. Thus effective leaders exercise authority by making polite requests, not by making arrogant demands.

Legitimate requests should be made in clear, simple language, and the leader should check to make sure subordinates understand what is required, especially if there is any indication that subordinates are confused. Whenever appropriate, the reason for the request should be explained so that subordinates understand why it is necessary. If anyone is likely to raise a question about the legitimacy of the leader's request, subordinates must be made to understand that it is indeed within the scope of the leader's formal authority to make such a request. Finally, the leader should follow up to verify that subordinates have complied with such requests. Subordinates who are reluctant to do something requested by the leader may wait to see if he or she is serious enough to insist on compliance. If the leader doesn't, subordinates may assume it is safe just to forget about it.

GUIDELINES FOR USING REWARDS

A common use of reward power is to offer specific incentives for doing what the leader wants. Incentive plans are usually very mechanical; subordinates automatically earn a bonus or commission for each item they make or sell. This type of mechanical incentive may be appropriate when there is a repetitive, tedious task with an objective output measure. But for more complex jobs, mechanical incentives are not the best way to exercise reward power. One danger in emphasizing explicit incentives is that subordinates quickly define their relationship to the leader in purely economic terms, and they come to expect special rewards every time the leader wants them to do something new or unusual. A much better relationship between leader and subordinate is one based on mutual loyalty and teamwork rather than an impersonal exchange of benefits.

There are other dangers in offering specific incentives. One is that they tend to make the leader appear manipulative—something subordinates may resent. Another limitation of incentives is that they are unlikely to result in commitment, even under the best of conditions. The typical response to specific incentives is to do only what is needed to earn the reward and no more. Subordinates may be tempted to neglect the less visible aspects of the task so they can complete it quickly.

Thus, in most situations, it is better to use rewards not as a bribe for doing what the leader wants, but rather to reinforce desirable behavior after it has already occurred. Tangible rewards can be used in conjunction with praise and recognition to communicate the message that the leader appreciates subordinates who are competent and committed. The size of the reward should be based on an evaluation of the subordinate's total performance, rather than on just some narrow aspect of it, as tends to be the case with incentives. The reward need not be limited to money. An effective leader will discover what other things subordinates value and use these as rewards also. It may be more time off, a better work schedule, or more desirable work assignments—but regardless of what type of reward is used, it is imperative to avoid the appearance of manipulation.

GUIDELINES FOR USING COERCION

Effective leaders generally avoid the use of coercive power except when absolutely necessary, because coercion is likely to create resentment and undermine their referent power. Coercion is most appropriately used to deter behavior that is very detrimental to the organization, such as violation of safety rules, reckless behavior endangering lives or valuable assets, and direct disobedience of legitimate requests. Skillfully used, coercion stands a reasonably good chance of getting subordinates to comply with rules, regulations, and orders.

Before criticizing or disciplining a subordinate, the leader should try to find out whether the subordinate is really at fault. A hasty reprimand that turns out to be unjustified can prove very embarrassing and seriously impair relations with subordinates. If a warning or punishment is needed, the leader should impose discipline promptly and consistently without showing any favoritism. Warnings should be stated in a way that avoids the appearance of personal hostility toward the subordinate. The leader should remain calm and convey a sincere desire to help the subordinate comply with rules and requirements to avoid the necessity for punishment. The subordinate should be invited to share in assuming responsibility for correcting disciplinary problems, including the setting of improvement goals and development of improvement plans. For all but the most serious of infractions, one or more warnings should be given before punishment is meted out. However, to protect the credibility of their coercive power, leaders should avoid issuing idle or exaggerated warning that they are not prepared to carry out. Finally, when it is necessary to use punishment, the magnitude of the punishment should fit the seriousness of the infraction.

GUIDELINES FOR USING EXPERT POWER

Expert power depends on the subordinates' perception that the leader knows the best course of action in a given situation. A leader's expert power increases when he or she suggests a course of action that turns out to be highly successful. Expert power is decreased when the leader shows faulty judgment or makes decisions that lead to failure by the group. Thus, to accumulate expert power, a leader should foster an image of experience and competence. It is essential to preserve credibility by avoiding careless statements and rash decisions. The leader should keep informed about technical matters and outside developments that affect the group's work. In a crisis, it is essential to remain calm and act confident and decisive. A leader who appears confused, who vacillates or, even worse, is obviously panicked, will quickly lose expert power.

Like authority, expert power involves a risk of highlighting status differences between leader and subordinates. Leaders who act arrogant and talk down to subordinates encounter resistance to their direction. Comments that threaten subordinates' self-esteem are strictly taboo. Even leaders who are more knowledgeable than subordinates in a particular matter should show respect for subordinates' ideas and suggestions and try to incorporate these into plans whenever feasible. If subordinates have serious concerns about the leader's planned course of action, the leader should recognize these concerns and try to deal with them instead of simply dismissing them with such comments as, "Don't be ridiculous, you have nothing to worry about." The leader should carefully explain why the proposed plan of action is the best one possible and what steps will be taken to minimize any risk to subordinates.

GUIDELINES FOR USING REFERENT POWER

Referent power, like expert power, increases or decreases over the course of successive interactions between leader and subordinates. Referent power is increased by being considerate toward subordinates, showing concern for their needs and feelings, treating them fairly, and defending their interests when dealing with superiors and outsiders. Referent power is diminished when a leader expresses hostility, distrust, rejection, or indifference toward subordinates, or when the leader fails to defend subordinates' interests with superiors. Over time, actions speak louder than words, and a leader who tries to appear friendly but who takes advantage of subordinates or fails to stick up for them will eventually find that his or her referent power has eroded away.

One effective way to use referent power is to make a personal appeal that evokes subordinate feelings of loyalty. The leader should indicate that the request is personally very important and that he or she is counting on subordinates for their support and cooperation. The leader should be careful not to use personal appeals too often or to ask for more than is reasonable, given the nature of the relationship. There are limits to what can be asked in the name of loyalty and friendliness. If the request appears unreasonable to subordinates, the leader can end up with reduced referent power as well as resistance to the request.

A more indirect way to use referent power is through role modeling. Here the leader sets an example by behaving the way that subordinates should behave. Subordinates will tend to imitate a leader whom they admire, because they want to please him or her and because they want to be more like him or her. Thus a leader with considerable referent power can influence subordinates in a positive way without even making explicit requests.

A CALL FOR FURTHER RESEARCH

These guidelines for using each type of power are tentative, most require further confirmation and elaboration. Much basic research remains to be done on how leaders use or should use power effectively. Past research has not explored the subject deeply enough to reveal many of the subtle nuances and nonverbal behaviors involved in influencing subordinates. Nor has previous research examined the complex interaction among the various forms of influence. In addition to taking the usual questionnaire approach, more observational studies are needed.

Researchers should also examine a broader range of influence behavior. It is now evident that the French and Raven taxonomy fails to include some forms of influence that can be very important to leaders or managers, such as inspirational appeals, informational control, situational engineering (including job design), and use of participation. Finally, as mentioned earlier, the dynamic nature of influence processes requires more longitudinal research to examine the evolution of influence relationships between leader and followers over time. Research on how to use power effectively offers tremendous benefits to practicing managers, and it is now time to start taking this kind of research more seriously.

REVIEW QUESTIONS

1 Consider the five types of power. Which of these does your instructor have available? Make use of?
2 The authors identify a classic paradox: an increase in leader power increases both influence and propensity to resist. How do you reconcile the two products of the use of power?
3 Someone once suggested that "no one ever gives you power, you have to take it by yourself." How does this relate to each of the five power bases?

READING 28

Patterns of Political Behavior in Organizations

Dan Farrell
James C. Petersen*

Now that organizational scholars have discovered and explored the environment, the new growth stock appears to be organizational politics. A host of recent works (Bacharach & Lawler, 1980; Gandz & Murray, 1980; Mayes & Allen, 1977; Pfeffer, 1978, 1981; Tushman, 1977) have attempted to remedy the neglect of power and politics that scholars such as Mowday (1978) and Madison, Allen, Porter, Renwick, & Mayes (1980) have seen as characteristic of the organizational literature. Despite this upsurge of attention to politics, some aspects of political phenomena continue to be neglected in the organizational literature. This paper argues for the theoretical importance of individual political behavior, proposes three key dimensions of political behavior, and suggests a typology derived from these dimensions. Also, variables useful for predicting the form of individual political actions are suggested.

The current wave of literature on organizational power and politics may be viewed best as a "rediscovery" of politics in organizations. Issues of power and politics within organizations were central to classic organizational writers such as Weber and Michels. The development of scientific management and human relations schools, with their managerial perspectives, diverted attention to motivation and productivity. Only rarely did organizational scholars return to the issues of power and politics—for example, March (1962), and Mechanic (1962)—until the renaissance of such literature in the late 1970s.

It is difficult to account for the timing of this rediscovery. The authors do not share a single paradigm and many of the papers are, in fact, largely descriptive rather than explicitly theoretical. It is suspected, however, that among the factors behind the revival of interest in organizational power and politics is the penetration of organizations by employees socialized into politics during the protests of the 1960s. Further, political behavior in organizations recently has been highlighted against a societal background of decreasing trust in authority and by an increase in journalistic revelations of wrongdoing. Within the scholarly literature there has been an increase in Marxist and conflict theories of organizations (see the special issue of *Sociological Quarterly*, Winter, 1977). Pfeffer, for example, has observed that the dominant managerial perspective within organizational studies has neglected "one of the most important issues and activities—the conflict in preferences among organizational participants and the resulting contest over the organization" (1978, p. 29). Also, the various attacks—for example,

*From *Academy of Management Review*, July 1982, pp. 403–412. Reprinted with permission.

March and Olsen (1976) and Weick (1979)—on the goal approach and the general rational model of organizations may have made political models of organizations seem more relevant.

The new wave of interest in organizational politics and organizational power is composed of several distinct types of work. First, a number of authors (Butler, Hickson, Wilson, & Axelson, 1977–78; Mayes & Allen, 1977; Tushman, 1977) have simply urged that organizations be viewed as political arenas or have provided a conceptual framework to permit such an approach. These calls for political analysis of organizations are an essential starting point. Dachler and Wilpert (1978), although not explicitly concerned with politics, provided a conceptual framework for participation in organizations. The implications of participation for democratization and the diffusion of decision making suggest that this might also be seen as a call for political analysis.

Second, the theme of power in organizations is receiving substantial attention. Although organizational theorists generally have treated power as distinct from organizational politics, the two concepts are linked theoretically and empirically. Madison et al. reported that among their sample of managers "the successful practice of organizational politics is perceived to lead to a higher level of power, and once a high level of power is attained, there is more opportunity to engage in political behavior" (1980, p. 94). Contemporary writers, in returning to the Weberian interests of power and authority, are focusing on bases of power (Salancik & Pfeffer, 1974), loci of power (Madison et al., 1980), influence processes (Mowday, 1978), and the measurement of power. Power typically is explained by linking it to environmental uncertainty and resource control. A limitation of this literature is that it provides only a partial view, focusing on either the upward or downward flow of power. The organizational literature on power would benefit from Gamson's (1968) widely acclaimed synthesis of the social control and influence literatures on power. Incorporating Gamson's work would ensure that future discussion of power would be more comprehensive and would permit greater integration of structure, authority, power, and politics.

Among the recent works on organizational politics, actual studies of political behavior are, in fact, quite rare. There are, however, studies of attributions of politicization and perceived organizational politics (Gandz & Murray, 1980; Madison et al., 1980). There also are studies of group behavior, especially interorganizational power relations—for example, Salancik and Pfeffer (1974)—and coalitions—for example, Bacharach and Lawler (1980). Work on political behavior by individuals is scarce although recent research on the filing of grievances (Dalton & Todor, 1979; Muchinsky & Maassarani, 1980) provides a good example.

The relative neglect of individual political behavior in the current wave of interest in organizational research seems strange. Dominant American values stress individualism and American social science typically reflects this with a heavy stress on individual behavior. Furthermore, several early articles on organizational politics (Burns, 1962; Mechanic, 1962; Strauss, 1963) dealt with political actions by individual organizational members. But these early leads have not been followed with much vigor. It is believed that the neglect of individual political behavior has three principle sources: (1) failure to distinguish required job behavior from discretionary political behavior, (2) failure to distinguish calculated from accidental political behavior, and (3) failure to distinguish clearly between macro and micro levels of analysis. Political behavior has been described as providing the "non-rational influence on decision making" (Miles, 1980, p. 154) and as existing as a "backstage" activity (Burns, 1962, p. 260). However, current definitions of organizational politics that focus on the exercise of power (Miles, 1980), the manipulation of influence (Madison et al., 1980), or the mobilization of resources in competition (Burns, 1962) do not clearly distinguish political behaviors from those actions required while filling organizational positions. The present authors agree with Mayes and Allen that "a suitable definition of organization politics must allow exclusion of routine job performance from consideration" (1977, p. 674). Porter, Allen, and Angle (1981) also exclude behaviors that are required or expected from their discussion of organizational politics, treating political behavior as discretionary. The present authors believe that political behavior resides in informal structures and relates to the promotion of self and group interests rather than being part of those formal roles regulated by organizational norms and goals. Further, examinations of political behaviors in organizations should focus on intended or overt actions by members while recognizing that unintended actions or even personal idiosyncrasies may have political consequences. Friendships and romantic associations occasionally may have indirect consequences for organizational politics, but they should not be a first focus of attention. Finally, existing analyses of organizational politics blur the distinction among different units of analysis by talking about the power of individuals, units, and interorganizational networks in the same discussion. By combining macro and micro levels of analysis at the initial stage of discussion, organizational scholars fail to consider the critical issues of the distinctiveness or similarity of correlates of politics for each level of analysis as well as the linkages between different levels.

INDIVIDUAL POLITICAL BEHAVIOR

In order to focus attention on individuals, it is suggested that the term political behavior be reserved for political activities by individual organization members. Political behavior in organizations may be defined as those activities that are not required as part of one's organizational role but that influence, or attempt to influence, the distribution of advantages and disadvantages within the organization. This definition draws on Froman's (1962) resource conceptualization of politics. It provides a definition of individual political behavior general enough to encompass such diverse examples of organizational politics as whistleblowing, filing of grievances, using symbolic protest gestures, spreading rumors, leaking information to the media, and filing lawsuits.

These political behaviors within organizations, although widely recognized by organization members, have not been integrated into organizational theory. Development of an organizational analogue to political participation in societies promises to have important implications for theory development. A brilliant example of an organizational analogy drawn from another social unit is Albert Hirschman's (1970) seminal work, *Exit, Voice and Loyalty: Responses to Decline in Firms, Organizations, and State*. Political scientists and political sociologists have long recognized that one of the most basic political acts is the "personalized contact" (Verba, Nie, & Kim, 1971) in search of either a social or an individualized outcome. Hirschman (1970) referred to this type of interest articulation as "voice" and demonstrated that it could be applied with equal utility in various social groups. In a recent exposition, Kolarska and Aldrich (1980) refined voice by distinguishing between indirect and direct voice. Direct voice refers to appeals to authorities within the focal organization; indirect voice refers to appeals to outside authorities or agents. In subtle ways voting is an essential part of many organizations. Zaleznik (1970) argues that the flow of capital funds and subordinate enthusiasm for manager's projects constitute referenda. Further, the process of leadership selection and control of authority in business and other organizations can resemble, under some conditions, the campaign and election procedures of other political communities (Lipset, Trow, & Coleman, 1956). When problems arise with internal processes, proxy fights and boardroom showdowns often are the organizational counterparts to recalls and ethics committee investigations. The incorporation of these and similar groups of behaviors not only supplements the rational model but also links organizational theory to a rich empirical tradition.

PATTERNS OF POLITICAL BEHAVIOR

Given the great variety of political behavior within organizations and the substantial amount of work remaining to be done in mapping its diversity, it is premature to propose an exhaustive set of dimensions of political behavior. Instead, proposed here is the consideration of three key dimensions of political behavior that are clearly useful in classifying political activities in organizations: the internal-external dimension, the vertical-lateral dimension, and the legitimate-illegitimate dimension. These dimensions represent distinct continuua along which political activities may be ordered. They reflect tactical choices that organizational members make in seeking resources or mobilizing available resources to influence the distribution of advantages and disadvantages within the organization.

The internal-external dimension of political behavior is concerned with the focus of resources sought by those engaging in political behavior in organizations. In cases such as whistleblowing, lawsuits, leaking information to the media, or forming alliances with persons outside the focal organization, organization members attempt to expand the resources available for mobilization by going outside the boundaries of the organization and attempting to involve "outsiders." Internal political behaviors, on the other hand, employ resources already within the organization, as in the exchange of favors, trading agreements, reprisals, obstructionism, symbolic protest gestures, "touching bases," forming alliances with other organization members and, in coercive organizations, riots and mutinies. It seems likely that organizational members may progress from internal to external activities as they come to believe that success is possible only if resources outside the organization can be mobilized. As Kolarska and Aldrich note, however, appeals to outside authorities or interest groups (indirect voice) may be resorted to for a variety of reasons:

> People may use indirect voice after direct voice fails, when they are afraid of using direct voice, when they do not believe in the effectiveness of direct voice or when they do not know how to use direct voice [1980, p. 44].

It is contended here that external political behavior will be attempted more often by lower participants in organizations or by those with lower levels of power because they are most likely to expect defeat if conflicts are resolved without introducing outside resources. As Weinstein has observed, whistleblowing may be seen as "attempts to change a bureaucracy by those who work within the organization but do not have any authority" (1979, p. 2).

Hierarchy is a dominant feature of most organizations and the vertical-lateral dimension of political behavior recognizes the difference between influence processes relating superiors to subordinates and those relating equals. Such political activities as complaining to a supervisor, bypassing the chain of command, apple polishing, and mentor-protege activities are best seen as vertical political behavior. Mechanic's (1962) discussion of sources of power of lower organizational participants points out that implicit trading agreements often develop between physicians and ward attendants in situations in which attendants relieve the M.D.s of many obligations and duties in return for increased power over patients.

Lateral political behaviors have received less systematic attention but would include exchange of favors, offering help, coalition organizing, and talking to an occupational peer outside the organization. Some examples also can be found in the leadership literature under discussion of lateral relations (Hunt & Osborn, 1981; Osborn & Hunt, 1974; Sayle, 1964)

> These "exchanges" between a leader and those at or near his own organizational level, outside his own chain of command, are quite often important but often neglected. While we call this aspect of leadership "lateral relations," perhaps a more common term is "politics." Regardless of the label used, these exchanges can build discretion by providing a more consistent flow of varied resources, reducing uncertainty and/or increasing independence or autonomy [Hunt & Osborn, 1980, p. 57].

Dalton's (1959) classic study of managers recognized the importance of discretionary lateral political behaviors. Employees of the Milo Company were quickly socialized regarding the importance of Masonic and Yacht Club memberships. When executives are appraised for promotion, political skills are considered in addition to formal competence because of the need to "utilize and aid necessary cliques, and control dangerous ones" (Dalton, 1959, p. 181). In his discussion of lateral relations among purchasing agents, Strauss observed that "to some extent agents operate on the principle of 'reward your friends, punish your enemies,' and are involved in a network of exchange of favors—and sometimes even reprisals" (1963, p. 174). Lateral political actions may occur at all levels of organizations although it seems likely that those at lower levels, lacking substantial resources, may be highly motivated to increase their power by joining forces with peers. In large pyramidal organizations, middle level management would seem to have the most opportunities to engage in vertical political behaviors.

The final dimension, legitimate-illegitimate, acknowledges that in organizations, as in states, distinctions are made between normal everyday politics and extreme political behavior that violates the "rules of the game." Though unofficial and unauthorized, organizational politics is widely recognized as a reality by organizational participants, especially those who like to feel they are "playing hardball." The rules of the game that develop in organizations typically rule out certain kinds of actions as too dangerous or threatening to the organizations. Kolarska and Aldrich report, for example, that research in Poland "uncovered the existence of a set of moral norms regulating interorganizational exchange. One norm concerned the impropriety of using forms of voice such as lawsuits, press leaks, and appeals to supervising organizations (indirect voice)" (1980, p. 52). Such norms, of course, change and evolve, and one would hardly expect a young executive to respond to a symbolic office protest with quite the horror of the stereotypical gray flannel-suited manager. Political behaviors widely accepted as legitimate would certainly include exchanging favors, "touching bases," forming coalitions, and seeking sponsors at upper levels. Less legitimate behaviors would include whistleblowing, revolutionary coalitions, threats, and sabotage. During the Vietnam War, another illegitimate activity received considerable publicity—the killing of officers in military units ("fragging"). Legitimate politics typically is expected to be engaged in by those at upper levels of organizations and by those who are strongly committed to the organization. Illegitimate political behavior is likely to be action taken by alienated members and by those who feel they have little to lose.

A TYPOLOGY OF POLITICAL BEHAVIOR

A cross-tabulation of the three dimensions of political behavior (internal-external, vertical-lateral, and legitimate-illegitimate) permits the development of a multidimensional typology of political behavior in organizations. Cross-classifying these three dichotomized dimensions yields an 8-celled collocation. Despite the renewed interest in organizational power and politics, no other system has emerged that explored the variety and interrelationships of these behaviors. The typology offered by Mayes and Allen (1977) organized organizational politics relative to normal job behaviors, but it did not deal with specific political behaviors. The examples provided in Figure 1 are not exhaustive of all political actions in organizations, but they include those forms of political behavior that have received scholarly and journalistic attention. In addition, the three dimensions are sufficiently general to make the typology inclusive of all forms of organizational political behavior.

| | LEGITIMATE | | | ILLEGITIMATE | |
	VERTICAL	LATERAL		VERTICAL	LATERAL
INTERNAL	I Direct voice Complain to supervisor Bypassing chain of command Obstructionism	II Coalition forming Exchanging favors Reprisals	**INTERNAL**	V Sabotage Symbolic protests Mutinies Riots	VI Threat
EXTERNAL	III Lawsuits	IV Talk with counter- part from another organization Outside professional activity	**EXTERNAL**	VII Whistleblowing	VIII Organizational duplicity Defections

FIGURE 1
A typology of political behavior in organizations.

It is contended that the four types of political behavior included in the "legitimate" category include the vast majority of all organizational political actions. Cell I behaviors, which are normal internal political behaviors, would, it seems, be most frequent in organizations with large differences in rewards, in tall organizations, and in those in which participation in decisions is limited. Under such conditions obstructionism is a common tactic by which lower participants resist organizational policies and decisions through inaction or excessive adherence to rules. Lateral political behaviors, such as those described in Cell II, can be expected to increase under loose supervision, if there is more equal positional power, and in nonline-and-staff organizations (Cleland, 1967).

External-vertical behaviors such as lawsuits or indirect voice (Cell III) generally occur in areas in which the legitimacy of conflict is well established. The growth of work related regulatory agencies such as N.L.R.B., E.E.O.C., and O.S.H.A. is an indication of increasing social recognition of the need to provide institutionalized means for resolving recurring disputes. Through occupational and informal contacts with those outside the focal organization (Cell IV), organizational members frequently gain access to information and other power resources. Such contacts, though not required, are accepted behavior for higher participants.

Unlike legitimate political behaviors, illegitimate actions pose the very real risk of loss of membership or extreme sanctions. Mutinies and riots are the most dramatic examples of vertical-internal illegitimate behavior (Cell V). Related but frequently overlooked are symbolic protests by organizational members. Unorthodox dress, button wearing, and "blue flu" may be miniature forms of organizational revolt. A form of illegitimate behavior that, in contrast, has attracted great journalistic attention is whistleblowing (Cell VII). This action, which also has been called "internal muckraking" (Peters & Branch, 1972), occurs when organizational members go public and release to the media details of organizational misconduct, neglect, or irresponsibility that jeopardize the public interest. Organizational defections (Cell VIII) occur when executives move to a competitor or begin their own firms, abandoning loyalty to the first firm. In cases of organizational duplicity, however, there is dual membership and uncertain loyalties. A classic example is the dedicated journalist who dons "bunny ears" to write a good story.

PREDICTING TYPES OF POLITICAL BEHAVIOR

Empirical studies of the process by which individuals select the types of political behavior in which they engage have not been conducted. An exchange framework, however, permits certain predictions about such choices. An exchange approach is especially appropriate to the study of political behavior because exchange theory emphasizes the person-organization relationship and also stresses the distribution of scarce resources (advantages and disadvantages). The use of four abstract concepts allows one to describe, from the perspective of the organizational actor, the context of the political exchange. Furthermore, these four abstract variables permit the incorporation of a substantial amount of previous research.

Investments

Investments encompass those resources that organizational participants commit to a relationship in the expectation of increased future benefit (Farrell & Rusbult, 1981). Typically, workers become invested in a firm as they acquire nonportable training, friendship, and seniority. These "side-bets," as Becker (1960) calls them, decrease an individual's propensity to leave an organization by increasing the cost of exit. The present authors believe that investments also lessen the likelihood of an individual engaging in illegitimate political behavior because such behavior places the investments at risk and there exist expectations of better outcomes in the future. Those with low investments, on the other hand, have little to lose by illegitimate political behavior. In some cases investments can be induced. Kolarska and Aldrich cite the action of authorities who attempt "to socialize the dissidents into the special organizational knowledge of the inner professional circle" (1980, p. 51).

Investments may have other effects in directing political behavior. Vertical behavior may be increased, Mechanic (1962) argues, because investments in specialized skills and knowledge produce dependence; in this manner upper level participants lose power to technical staff. The likelihood of internal or external political behavior also can be shaped by the extent of investments. When investments are high and portable as in professions or what Thompson (1967) calls "late-ceiling" occupations, employees seek advantage by going outside the organization. In early-ceiling occupations, however, individuals "seek leverage in the negotiation process through collective action" (Thompson, 1967, p. 113).

Alternatives

Alternatives are readily available opportunities to obtain rewards from other associations. The quality of an individual's alternatives is improved when there is a favorable labor market, when the person has acquired scarce skills or knowledge, and when the individual makes an extensive search for alternatives. In some organizations, however, alternatives may not exist or may be extremely limited. Prisons virtually eliminate alternatives for specified periods of time, as do most military units, especially ships at sea. Employees in isolated company towns may be captives of their employer. In general, poor alternatives prevent members from leaving the organization and thus increase the likelihood of internal protest. Hirschman has argued that "the voice option is the only way in which dissatisfied customers or members can react whenever the exit option is unavailable" (1970, p. 33).

As alternatives are unrealized associations, subjective perceptions play a key role in the absence of objective data. Classic organizational cosmopolitans frequently exercise disproportionate influence within the focal organization because it is difficult for other members to assess precisely the magnitude of external power bases. Another perceptual distortion occurs when alternatives are limited: "a lack of alternatives raises people's perceived investments in an organization and increases the potential payoff of voice" (Kolarska & Aldrich, 1980, p. 53). Even perceived increases in investments should result in more structured low-risk political behaviors.

When the available alternatives are very different types of associations offering nonparallel sets of rewards, as when an individual exchanges corporate membership for the risks and challenge of independent entrepreneurship (Perrucci, Anderson, Schendel, & Trachtman, 1980; Wright, 1980); illegitimate external behaviors may become more likely.

> So far only a few journalistic and legal studies have been reported that describe cases of individuals in business firms and government agencies who regarded the public interest as overriding the interest of the organization they served and decided to "blow the whistle"—to inform public or legal authorities that their organization was involved in corrupt, socially harmful, or illegal activity. . . . While there were unique features in every case, the whistle-blowers seem to have had in common a strong sense of professional standards, a high level of personal self-esteem, and social support from a spouse or close friend, which enabled them to overcome both subtle pressures from respective organizations to remain "team players" and unsubtle threats of blacklisting, social ostracism, and dismissal [Janis & Mann, 1977, p. 273].

Trust

Trust refers to the perceived necessity for influence (Gamson, 1968). When lower participants hold high levels of trust, they express the belief that authorities will produce desired outcomes without the participants taking any action. Those with low trust, however, hold no expectation of receiving such desired outcomes. The trust concept, prominent in discussion of society and the state (Gamson, 1971; Miller, 1974), also can be applied to political behavior within organizations. The salience of politics is associated with the level of trust of organizational members: "If there is an extraordinarily high degree of trust, such as participants assuming that each is acting in each other's interests, then there need be little concern with issues of control and governance" (Pfeffer, 1978, p. 38). Trust is very closely related to perception of organizational dependability (Alutto & Belasco, 1972; Buchanan, 1974; Spencer & Steers, 1980).

In addition to helping predict the overall level of political behavior, trust helps dictate the form of such behavior. High levels of trust should be associated with the exercise of legitimate political behavior because to do otherwise is to risk backlash from authorities expected to produce desired outcomes. In contrast, those with low levels of trust experience few restraints to extreme actions. Thus Gamson observes that an appeal to the disaffected that they are hurting their cause by illegitimate behaviors will fall on deaf ears: "to point out to poor negroes in urban ghettos that riots are resented is rather irrelevant communication to a group which feels there is little likelihood of obtaining favorable actions from authorities in the absence of such riots" (1968, p.169). Beyond suppressing the level of political behavior in general and inhibiting illegitimate actions in particular, high trust should reduce vertical political behaviors. To the extent that trust is directed at higher authorities, there is little reason for those who already expect desired outcomes to expend resources in attempting vertical influence. Lack of leader control over some advantages, zero-sum conditions, or organizational retrenchment may produce lateral political behaviors even in high trust environments.

Efficacy

Efficacy is generally treated as the perceived ability to influence (Gamson, 1968). Thus it refers not to the need to engage in political behavior, but rather to the expectation that one's political actions will yield desired outcomes and thus be worth the costs of action. Those who perceive their efficacy within the organization to be low will, in the long run, engage in little political behavior. It may be that new organizational members (or those who have changed units within the organization) and those who experience low levels of efficacy will respond by intensified efforts to gain political influence. Unless such actions result in increased levels of perceived ability to influence, however, the level of political behavior would be expected to decline as members come to define their actions as futile.

External political behaviors frequently are pursued when it is impossible to engage in internal political behavior or when there is little expectation of success through internal actions (Kolarska & Aldrich, 1980). Individuals with low internal efficacy may go outside the organization either to seek additional resources or simply to leave the organization. Hirschman observed that "the decision whether to exit will often be taken in light of the prospects for the effective use of voice" (1970, p. 37). In his view, exit may serve as a "last resort after voice has failed." In addition to shaping the internal-external flow of political activity, efficacy affects the selection of legitimate or illegitimate forms of political behaviors. It is believed that those organizational members with high levels of efficacy will tend to engage in legitimate political behaviors as they have a vested interest in maintaining the organization and thus they will play within the rules and avoid threatening the organization

IMPLICATIONS

In calling for a focus on individual political behavior in organizations, a supplement to the rational model of organizations is suggested. Those organizational theories that draw on the rational model, although they provide a useful simplification of organizational reality, inevitably explain only a portion of the behavior that occurs. Organizational life involves contradictions because it encompasses two organizational realities: the rational and the political (Miles, 1980). Although these two realities may involve contradictions, they frequently complement one another. Burns has observed that "members of a corporation are at one and the same time cooperators in a common enterprise and rivals for the material and intangible rewards of successful competition with each other" (1962, p. 258).

Identifying the internal-external, vertical-lateral, and legitimate-illegitimate dimensions of political behavior provides added insight to the current understanding of organizational behavior, and it offers options for future research. It now appears that research in the rational tradition seems to focus almost exclusively on internal legitimate political behaviors. As the typology presented here indicates, however, this hardly exhausts the range of political activity that may occur in organizations. The handful of existing studies that have looked at such phenomena as whistleblowing (Parmerlee, Near, & Jensen, 1980; Perrucci et al., 1980), organizational dissent (Stanley, 1981), and organizational protest (Lipset, 1971), now may be more clearly related to the full range of political behavior in organizations. Illegitimate political behaviors, though uncommon, provide a rich site for future research. Not only are they of interest in themselves, but they provide insight into organizational norms and values.

The integration of a focus on political behavior in organizations with the rational model can enrich the understanding of such key organizational problems as effectiveness. The rational view always has assumed that efficient means-ends chains are the route to organizational effectiveness. The present authors believe that successful management of political activity in organizations is equally necessary for producing organizational effectiveness. In some instances, political activity is a precondition of rational administrative behavior. Bargaining has been shown to maintain organizational structure (Burns, 1962), and successful coalition formation within the executive structure, Zaleznik (1970) argues, helps avoid paralysis in decision making. Political tactics also may serve as a direct managerial tool, as in Mowday's (1978) finding that selective filtering of information and exchanging favors were associated with high effectiveness among elementary school principals. In light of such findings, to attempt to explain organizational effectiveness without incorporating political variables is to guarantee no more than partial success.

REFERENCES

Alutto, J. A., & Belasco, J. A. A typology for participation in organizational decision making. *Administrative Science Quarterly*, 1972, 17, 117–125.

Bacharach, S. B., & Lawler, E. J. *Power and politics in organizations*. San Francisco, Cal.: Jossey-Bass Publishing, 1980.

Becker, H. S. Notes on the concept of commitment. *American Journal of Sociology*, 1960, 66, 32–40.

Buchanan, B. Building organizational commitment: The socialization of managers in work organizations. *Administrative Science Quarterly*, 1974, 19, 533–546.

Burns, T. Micropolitics: Mechanisms of organizational change. *Administrative Science Quarterly*, 1962, 6, 257–281.

Butler, R. J., Hickson, D. J., Wilson, D. C., & Axelson, R. Organizational power, politicking and paralysis. *Organization and Administrative Science*, 1977–78, 8 (4), 45–49.

Cleland, D. I. Understanding project authority. *Business Horizons*, 1967, 10 (1), 63–70.

Dachler, H. P., & Wilpert, B. Conceptual dimensions and boundaries of participation in organizations: A critical evaluation. *Administrative Science Quarterly*, 1978, 23, 1–39.

Dalton, M. *Men who manage*. New York: Wiley, 1959.

Dalton, D., & Todor, W. D. Manifest needs of stewards: Propensity to file a grievance. *Journal of Applied Psychology*, 1979, 64, 654–659.

Farrell, D. J., & Rusbult, C. E. Exchange variables as predictors of job satisfaction, job commitment, and turnover: The effects of rewards, costs, alternatives, and investments. *Organizational Behavior and Human Performance*, 1981, 28, 78–95.

Froman, L. A. *People and politics*. Englewood Cliffs, N.J.: Prentice Hall, 1962.

Gamson, W. A. *Power and discontent*. Homewood, Ill.: Dorsey, 1968.

Gamson, W. A. Political trust and its ramifications. In G. Abcarian & J. Soule (Eds.), *Social psychology and political behavior*. Columbus, Ohio: Merrill, 1971, 40–55.

Gandz, J., & Murray V. V. The experience of workplace politics. *Academy of Management Journal*, 1980, 23, 237–251.

Hirschman, A. O. *Exit, voice and loyalty: Responses to decline in firms, organizations, and states*. Cambridge, Mass.: Harvard University Press, 1970.

Hunt, J. G., & Osborn, R. N. A multiple-influence approach to leadership for managers. In P. Hersey & J. Stinson (Eds.), *Perspectives in leadership effectiveness*. Athens, Ohio: Ohio University Press, 1980, 47–62.

Hunt, J. G., & Osborn, R. N. Towards a macro-oriented model of leadership: An odyssey. In J. G. Hunt, H. Sekaran, & C. A. Schriesheim (Eds.), *Leadership: Beyond establishment views*. Carbondale, Ill.: Southern Illinois University Press, 1981, 196–221.

Janis, I. L., & Mann, L. *Decision making*. New York: Free Press, 1977.

Kolarska, L., & Aldrich, H. Exit, voice, and silence: Consumers' and managers' responses to organizational decline. *Organization studies*, 1980, 1, 41–58.

Lipset, S. M. *Rebellion in the university*. Boston: Little, Brown & Co., 1971.

Lipset, S. M., Trow, M., & Coleman, J. *Union democracy*. Glencoe, Ill.: The Free Press, 1956.

Madison, D. L., Allen, R. W., Porter, L. W., Renwick, P. A., & Mayes, B. T. Organizational politics: An exploration of managers perceptions. *Human Relations*, 1980, 33, 79–100.

March, J. G. The business firm as a political coalition. *Journal of Politics*, 1962, 24, 662–678.

March, J. G., & Olsen, J. P. *Ambiguity and choice in organizations.* Bergen, Norway: Universitetsforlaget, 1976.

Martin, N. H., & Sims, J. H. Power tactics. In D. A. Klog, I. M. Rubin, & J. M. McIntyre (Eds.), *Organizational psychology.* 2nd ed. Englewood Cliffs, N.J.: Prentice-Hall, 1974.

Mayes, B. T., & Allen, R. W. Toward a definition of organizational politics. *Academy of Management Review,* 1977, 2, 672–678.

Mechanic, D. Sources of power of lower participants in complex organizations. *Administrative Science Quarterly,* 1962, 7, 349–364.

Miles, R. H. *Macro organizational behavior.* Santa Monica, Cal.: Goodyear Publishing, 1980.

Miller, A. H. Political issues and trust in government. *American Political Science Review,* 1974, 68, 951–972.

Mowday, R. T. The exercise of upward influence in organizations. *Administrative Science Quarterly,* 1978, 23, 137–156.

Muchinsky, P. M., & Maassarani, M. A. Work environment effects on public sector grievances. *Personnel Psychology,* 1980, 33, 403–414.

Osborn, R. N., & Hunt, J. G. Environment and organizational effectiveness. *Administrative Science Quarterly,* 1974, 19, 231–246.

Parmerlee, M. A., Near, J. P., & Jensen, T. C. Correlates of whistle blowers' perceptions of organizational reprisal. Working paper, Indiana University, 1980.

Perrucci, R., Anderson, R. M., Schendel, D. E., & Trachtman, L. E. Whistle-blowing: Professionals' resistance to organizational authority. *Social Problems,* 1980, 28, 149–164.

Peters, C., & Branch, T. *Blowing the whistle.* New York: Praeger, 1972.

Pfeffer, J. The micropolitics of organizations. In Marshall Meyer & Associates (Eds.), *Environments and organizations.* San Francisco: Jossey-Bass, 1978, 29–50.

Pfeffer, J. *Power in organizations.* Boston, Mass.: Pitman Publishing, 1981.

Porter, L. W., Allen, R. W., & Angle, H. L. The politics of upward influence in organizations. In L. L. Cummings & B. M. Staw (Eds.), *Research in organizational behavior* (Vol 3). Greenwich, Conn.: JAI Press, 1981.

Salancik, G. R., & Pfeffer, J. The cases and uses of power in organizational decision making: The case of a university. *Administrative Science Quarterly,* 1974, 19, 453–473.

Sayles, L. R. *Managerial behavior.* New York: McGraw-Hill, 1964.

Spencer, D. G., & Steers, R. M. The influence of personal factors and perceived work experiences on employee turnover and absenteeism. *Academy of Management Journal,* 1980, 23, 567–572.

Stanley, J. E. Dissent in organizations. *Academy of Management Review,* 1981, 6, 13–19.

Strauss, G. Tactics of lateral relationship: The purchasing agent. *Administrative Science Quarterly,* 1963, 1, 161–185.

Thompson, J. D. *Organizations in action.* New York: McGraw-Hill, 1967.

Tushman, M. L. A political approach to organizations: A review and rationale. *Academy of Management Review,* 1977, 2, 206–216.

Verba, S., Nie, N. H., & Kim, J. O. *The modes of democratic participation: A cross-national comparison.* Beverly Hills, Cal.: Sage Publications, 1971.

Weick, K. E. *The social psychology of organizing.* 2nd ed. Reading, Mass.: Addison-Wesley Publishing Co., 1979.

Weinstein, D. *Bureaucratic opposition.* New York: Pergamon Press, 1979.

Wright, J. P. *On a clear day you can see General Motors: John Z. DeLorean's look inside the automotive giant*. Ossining, New York: Carolina House, 1980.

Zaleznik, A. Power and politics in organizational life. *Harvard Business Review*, 1970, 48 (3), 47–60.

REVIEW QUESTIONS

1 How do the authors define political behavior? How does this discussion differ from the discussion of power offered by Yukl and Taber?

2 Give at least four distinct examples of the different ways you have exhibited political behavior, and classify each of them as one of the eight types shown in Figure 1.

3 How can a manager prevent, or at least minimize, the use of political behavior by subordinates?

READING 29

Upward Influence in Organizations

Warren K. Schilit
Edwin A. Locke*

An enormous literature exists on the methods used by managers to attain compliance from their subordinates (downward influence). However, research on the strategies used by subordinates to influence their supervisors (upward influence) is relatively sparse.

*   *   *

The present study provides a comprehensive set of categories and supporting data for analyzing the upward-influence process in organizations. The results indicate that subordinates and supervisors report similar agents and methods of influence regardless of whether they are describing successful or unsuccessful attempts; similar outcomes of influence attempts; and similar causes of success in upward-influence attempts.

According to the present study, both subordinates and supervisors agree that subordinates use logical presentations more than any other tactic in upward-influence attempts. The results tend to be more supportive of Kipnis, Schmidt, and Wilkinson (1980), than of Porter, Allen, and Angle (1981), or of Weinstein (1979), who reported that indirect tactics are the most commonly used methods of upward political influence. It is still unclear why a specific method is used by a

*From "A Study of Upward Influence in Organizations," *Administrative Science Quarterly*, June 1982, pp. 304, 314–316. © 1982 by Cornell University. Reprinted with permission.

subordinate. Do subordinates utilize a specific technique in their attempts to equalize power with their supervisors (Mulder, 1977)? Do they select a method because of its rewards or costs (Thibaut and Kelley, 1959)? Are subordinates necessarily rational in their selection of a method? Future research should address these issues.

In general, subordinates and supervisors claimed that outcomes of unsuccessful attempts were neutral, for both the organization and the subordinate, rather than negative. They also agreed that successful attempts resulted in positive outcomes for both the subordinate and the organization.

*   *   *

REFERENCES

Kipnis, David, Stuart M. Schmidt, and Ian Wilkinson: 1980, "Intraorganizational influence tactics: Explorations in getting one's way." Journal of Applied Psychology, 65: 440–452

Mulder, Mauk: 1977, The Daily Power Game. Leiden, the Netherlands: Martinus Nijhoff, Social Sciences Division.

Porter, Lyman W., Robert W. Allen, and Harold L. Angle: 1981, "The politics of upward influence in organizations." In B. Staw and L. Cummings (eds.), Research in Organizational Behavior, 3. Greenwich, CT: JAI Press.

Thibaut, J., and H. Kelley: 1959, The Social Psychology of Groups. New York: Wiley.

Vroom, Victor: 1964, Work and Motivation. New York: Wiley.

Weinstein, Deena: 1979, Bureaucratic Opposition: Challenging Abuses of the Workplace. New York: Pergamon Press.

REVIEW QUESTION

1 Compare the idea of upward influence with effective subordinancy, which was introduced in Reading 25.

CHAPTER 8

LEADERSHIP

READING 30

Applying the Contingency Model of Leadership

Fred E. Fiedler*

*   *   *

In sum, if we want to improve leadership performance, we can either change the leader by training, or we can change his leadership situation. Common sense suggests that it is much easier to change various aspects of a man's job than to change the man. When we talk about leadership behavior, we are talking about fairly deeply ingrained personality factors and habits of interacting with others. These cannot be changed easily, either in a few hours or in a few days. In fact, as we have seen, not even four years of military academy and 5 to 17 years of subsequent experience enable a leader to perform significantly better on different tasks than someone that has had neither training nor experience.

We have seen that a leader's performance depends not only on his personality, but also on the organizational factors that determine the leader's control and influence, that is, the "situational favorableness." As we have shown, appropriate training and experience improve situational favorableness. Whether or not they improve performance depends upon the match between the leader's motivational pattern and the favorableness of the situation. This means that a training program that improves the leader's control and influence may benefit the relationship-motivated managers, but it will be detrimental to the task-motivated managers, or vice versa, depending upon the situation.

The idea that we can improve a leader's performance by increasing the favorableness of his situation is, of course, far from new. A poorly performing manager may be given more authority, more explicit instructions, more congenial coworkers in the hope that it will help him do a better job. Moreover, decreasing the favorableness of the situation in order to improve a manager's performance is also not quite as unusual as it might appear at first blush. If a man becomes bored, stale, or disinterested in his job, a frequent remedy is to transfer him to a more challenging job. As it turns out, "challenging" is just another way of saying that the job is less structured, has less position power, or requires working with difficult people. It is certainly well known that some men perform best under pressure and that they get into difficulty when life is too calm. These are the trouble shooters who are dispatched to branch offices or departments that need to be bailed out.

*Reprinted by permission of the publisher from "How Do You Make Leaders More Effective? New Answers to an Old Puzzle," *Organizational Dynamics*, Autumn 1972, pp. 3–18. © 1972 by AMACOM, a division of American Management Associations, Inc.

What, then, can an organization do to increase managerial performance? As a first step, it is necessary to determine which of the managers are task- and which are relationship-motivated. This can be accomplished by means of a short scale. Second, the organization needs to categorize carefully the situational favorableness of its managerial jobs. (Scales are available in Fiedler, F. E., *A Theory of Leadership Effectiveness*, McGraw-Hill, 1967.) Third, the organization can decide on a number of options in its management of executive personnel.

The least expensive and probably most efficient method is to develop a careful program of managerial rotation that moves some individuals from one job to another at a faster rate than it moves others. For example, it will be recalled that the relationship-motivated elementary school principals on the average became less effective after two years on the job. Moving these men to new jobs probably would have made them more effective than leaving them at the same school for many more years. Likewise, moving the task-motivated secondary school principals after two years probably would have increased their performance. In the case of the consumer cooperatives, it took 15 to 20 years in the organization (as employee and assistant manager, as well as manager) before the relationship-motivated managers began to go stale. How long a man should stay on a particular job must, or course, be determined empirically in each organization.

A second major option is management training. The problem here is whether to train only some people or all those who are eligible: training a task-motivated manager who is accepted by his group and has a structured task is likely to improve his performance; training a relationship-motivated manager for the same job is likely to make him less effective. The organization would, therefore, be better off if it simply did not train relationship-motivated managers for these particular jobs. On the other hand, the relationship-motivated but not the task-motivated managers should be trained for jobs in which the situational favorableness is intermediate.

Leadership training should devote more effort to teaching leaders how to modify their environment and their own job so that they fit their style of leadership. We must get rid of the implicit assumption that the environment and the organization, or a particular leadership position, are constant and unchanging. In addition to changes which occur as the leaders gain experience, they also continuously modify their leadership positions. They often speak of showing their men who is boss, presumably to assert their position power or of "being one of the boys" to deemphasize it; they speak of getting to know their men, presumably to establish better relations with them; they speak of different approaches to their work; they look for certain types of assistants who complement their abilities; they demand more authority, or they play down the authority they already have; they ask for certain types of assignments and try to avoid others. The theory that has here been described merely provides a basis for more rational modification of the leadership job.

How can we train leaders to determine the conditions under which they are most likely to succeed or fail, and how can they learn to modify their own leadership situation? The frequently negative relationship between leadership experience and leader performance undoubtedly stems in part from the difficulties in obtaining feedback about one's own leadership effectiveness. As research has shown, unless the group fails utterly in its task, most leaders are unable to say with any degree of accuracy how well their group performed in comparison with other groups.

Leadership training away from the organization should provide the prospective leader with a wide range of leadership situations in which he can get immediate feedback on how well he has performed. On the basis of these experiences, he must learn to recognize which situations fit his particular style of leadership and how he can best modify situations so that they will enable him to perform effectively. This may involve the development of six to eight leadership tasks and situations, or adequately measured organizational tasks, in which each trainee is required to lead. He must then be given an objective appraisal of how well his group's performance compared with the performance of others under the same conditions.

The closest approximation to the all-around good leader is likely to be the individual who intuitively or through training knows how to manage his environment so that the leadership situation best matches his leadership style.

It may be desirable for various reasons to train all managers of a certain level, especially since being sent to executive training programs has in many organizations become a symbol of success. Men are sent to these training programs not because they need to learn, but because they need to be rewarded. If this is the case, the organization might do well to place the manager who completes the training program into a position that matches his leadership motivation pattern. For example, in the consumer cooperative companies, the relationship motivated managers might have been given staff jobs, or jobs with troubled companies at the conclusion of an extensive training program.

CONCLUSION

As a consequence of our research, we have both discredited some old myths and learned some new lessons.

The old myths:

• That there is one best leadership style, or that there are leaders who excel under all circumstances.
• That some men are born leaders, and that neither training, experience, or conditions can materially affect leadership skills.

The lessons, while more pedestrian and less dogmatic, are more useful. We know that people differ in how they respond to management situations. Furthermore, we know that almost every manager in an organization can perform effectively, providing that we place him in a situation that matches his personality, providing we know how to match his training and experience to the available jobs—and providing that we take the trouble.

REVIEW QUESTION

1 Summarize the options that organizations have available to them for matching their managers with favorable situations.

READING 31

Path-Goal Theory of Leadership

Robert J. House
Terence R. Mitchell*

An integrated body of conjecture by students of leadership, referred to as the "Path-Goal Theory of Leadership," is currently emerging. According to this theory, leaders are effective because of their impact on subordinates' motivation, ability to perform effectively and satisfactions. The theory is called Path-Goal, because its major concern is how the leader influences the subordinates' perceptions of their work goals, personal goals and paths to goal attainment. The theory suggests that a leader's behavior is motivating or satisfying to the degree that the behavior increases subordinate goal attainment and clarifies the paths to these goals.

HISTORICAL FOUNDATIONS

The path-goal approach has its roots in a more general motivational theory called expectancy theory.[1] Briefly, expectancy theory states that an individual's attitudes (e.g., satisfaction with supervision or job satisfaction) or behavior (e.g., leader behavior or job effort) can be predicted from: (1) the degree to which the job, or behavior, is seen as leading to the various outcomes (expectancy) and (2) the evaluation of these outcomes (valences). Thus, people are satisfied with their job if they think it leads to things highly valued, and they work hard if they believe that effort leads to things that are highly valued. This type of theoretical rationale can be used to predict a variety of phenomena related to leadership, such as why leaders behave the way they do, or how leader behavior influences subordinate motivation.[2]

This latter approach is the primary concern of this article. The implication for leadership is that subordinates are motivated by leader behavior to the extent that this behavior influences expectancies, e. g., goal paths, and valences, e.g., goal attractiveness.

*Reprinted with permission of the *Journal of Contemporary Business*, Autumn 1974, pp. 81–97. Copyright 1974.

Several writers have advanced specific hypotheses concerning how the leader affects the paths and the goals of subordinates.[3] These writers focused on two issues: (1) how the leader affects subordinates' expectations that effort will lead to effective performance and valued rewards, and (2) how this expectation affects motivation to work hard and perform well.

While the state of theorizing about leadership in terms of subordinates' paths and goals is in its infancy, we believe it is promising for two reasons. First, it suggests effects of leader behavior that have not yet been investigated but which appear to be fruitful areas of inquiry. And, second, it suggests with some precision the situational factors on which the effects of leader behavior are contingent.

The initial theoretical work by Evans asserts that leaders will be effective by making rewards available to subordinates and by making rewards contingent on the subordinate's accomplishment of specific goals.[4] Evans argued that one of the strategic functions of the leader is to clarify for subordinates the kind of behavior that leads to goal accomplishment and valued rewards. This function might be referred to as path clarification. Evans also argued that the leader increases the rewards available to subordinates by being supportive toward subordinates, i. e. by being concerned about their status, welfare and comfort. Leader supportiveness is in itself a reward that the leader has at his or her disposal, and the judicious use of this reward increases the motivation of subordinates.

Evans studied the relationship between the behavior of leaders and the subordinates' expectations that effort leads to rewards and also studied the resulting impact on ratings of the subordinates' performance. He found that when subordinates viewed leaders as being supportive (considerate of their needs) and when these superiors provided directions and guidance to the subordinates, there was a positive relationship between leader behavior and subordinates' performance ratings.

However, leader behavior was only related to subordinates' performance when leaders' behavior also was related to the subordinates' expectations that their effort would result in desired rewards. Thus, Evans' findings suggest that the major impact of a leader on the performance of subordinates is clarifying the path to desired rewards and making such rewards contingent on effective performance.

Stimulated by this line of reasoning, House, and House and Dessler advanced a more complex theory of the effects of leader behavior on the motivation of subordinates.[5] The theory intends to explain the effects of four specific kinds of leader behavior on the following three subordinate attitudes or expectations: (1) the satisfaction of subordinates, (2) the subordinates' acceptance of the leader and (3) the expectations of subordinates that effort will result in effective performance and that effective performance is the path to rewards. The four kinds of leader behavior included in the theory are: (1) directive leadership, (2) supportive leadership, (3) participative leadership and (4) achievement-oriented leadership. Directive leadership is characterized by a leader who lets subordinates know what is expected of them, gives specific guidance as to what should be done and how it should be done, makes his or her part in the group understood, schedules work to be done, maintains definite standards of performance and asks that group members follow standard rules and regulations. Supportive leadership is characterized by a friendly and approachable leader who shows concern for the status, well-being and needs of subordinates. Such a leader does little things to make the work more pleasant, treats members as equals and is friendly and approachable. Participative leadership is characterized by a leader who consults with subordinates, solicits their suggestions and takes these suggestions seriously into consideration before making a decision. An achievement-oriented leader sets challenging goals, expects subordinates to perform at their highest level, continuously seeks improvement in performance *and* shows a high degree of confidence that the subordinates will assume responsibility, put forth effort and accomplish challenging goals. This kind of leader constantly emphasizes excellence in performance and simultaneously displays confidence that subordinates will meet high standards of excellence.

A number of studies suggest that these different leadership styles can be shown by the same leader in various situations.[6] For example, a leader may show directiveness toward subordinates in some instances and be participative or supportive in other instances.[7] Thus, the traditional method of characterizing a leader as either highly participative and supportive *or* highly directive is invalid; rather, it can be concluded that leaders vary in the particular fashion employed for supervising their subordinates. Also, the theory, in its present stage, is a tentative explanation of the effects of leader behavior—it is incomplete because it does not explain other kinds of leader behavior and does not explain the effects of the leader on factors other than subordinate acceptance, satisfaction and expectations. However, the theory is stated so that additional variables may be included in it as new knowledge is made available.

PATH-GOAL THEORY

General Propositions

The first proposition of path-goal theory is that leader behavior is acceptable and satisfying to subordinates to the extent that the subordinates see such behavior as either an immediate source of satisfaction or as instrumental to future satisfaction.

The second propositon of this theory is that the leader's behavior will be motivational, i.e., increase effort, to the extent that (1) such behavior makes satisfaction of subordinates' needs contingent on effective performance and (2) such behavior complements the environment of subordinates by providing the coaching, guidance, support and rewards necessary for effective performance.

These two propositions suggest that the leader's strategic functions are to enhance subordinates' motivation to perform, satisfaction with the job and acceptance of the leader. From previous research on expectancy theory of motivation, it can be inferred that the strategic functions of the leader consist of: (1) recognizing and/or arousing subordinates' needs for outcomes over which the leader has some control, (2) increasing personal payoffs to subordinates for work-goal attainment, (3) making the path to those payoffs easier to travel by coaching and direction, (4) helping subordinates clarify expectancies, (5) reducing frustrating barriers and (6) increasing the opportunities for personal satisfaction contingent on effective performance.

Stated less formally, the motivational functions of the leader consist of increasing the number and kinds of personal payoffs to subordinates for work-goal attainment and making paths to these payoffs easier to travel by clarifying the paths, reducing road blocks and pitfalls and increasing the opportunities for personal satisfaction en route.

Contingency Factors

Two classes of situational variables are asserted to be contingency factors. A contingency factor is a variable which moderates the relationship between two other variables such as leader behavior and subordinate satisfaction. For example, we might suggest that the degree of structure in the task moderates the relationship between leaders' directive behavior and subordinates' job satisfaction. Figure I shows how such a relationship might look. Thus, subordinates are satisfied with directive behavior in an unstructured task and are satisfied with nondirective behavior in a structured task. Therefore, we say that the relationship between leader directiveness and subordinate satisfaction is contingent upon the structure of the task.

The two contingency variables are (a) personal characteristics of the subordinates and (b) the environmental pressures and demands with which subordinates must cope in order to accomplish the work goals and to satisfy their needs. While other situational factors also may operate to determine the effects of leader behavior, they are not presently known.

With respect to the first class of contingency factors, the characteristics of subordinates, path-goal theory asserts that leader behavior will be acceptable to subordinates to the extent that the subordinates see such behavior as either an immediate source of satisfaction or as instrumental to future satisfaction. Subor-

FIGURE I
Hypothetical relationship between directive leadership and subordinate satisfaction with task structure as a contingency factor.

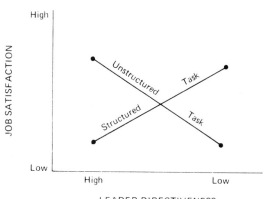

dinates' characteristics are hypothesized to partially determine this perception. For example, Runyon[8] and Mitchell[9] show that the subordinate's score on a measure called Locus of Control moderates the relationship between participative leadership style and subordinate satisfaction. The Locus-of-Control measure reflects the degree to which an individual sees the environment as systematically responding to his or her behavior. People who believe that what happens to them occurs because of their behavior are called internals; people who believe that what happens to them occurs because of luck or chance are called externals. Mitchell's findings suggest that internals are more satisfied with a participative leadership style and externals are more satisfied with a directive style.

A second characteristic of subordinates on which the effects of leader behavior are contingent is subordinates' perception of their own ability with respect to their assigned tasks. The higher the degree of perceived ability relative to task demands, the less the subordinate will view leader directiveness and coaching behavior as acceptable. Where the subordinate's perceived ability is high, such behavior is likely to have little positive effect on the motivation of the subordinate and to be perceived as excessively close control. Thus, the acceptability of the leader's behavior is determined in part by the characteristics of the subordinates.

The second aspect of the situation, the environment of the subordinate, consists of those factors that are not within the control of the subordinate but which are important to need satisfaction or to ability to perform effectively. The theory asserts that effects of the leader's behavior on the psychological states of subordinates are contingent on other parts of the subordinate's environment that are relevant to subordinate motivation. Three broad classifications of contingency factors in the environment are:

- The subordinate's tasks
- The formal authority system of the organization
- The primary work group

Assessment of the environmental conditions makes it possible to predict the kind and amount of influence that specific leader behaviors will have on the motivation of subordinates. Any of the three environmental factors could act upon the subordinate in any of three ways: first, to serve as stimuli that motivate and direct the subordinate to perform necessary task operations; second, to constrain variability in behavior. Constraints may help the subordinate by clarifying expectancies that effort leads to rewards or by preventing the subordinate from experiencing conflict and confusion. Constraints also may be counterproductive to the extent that they restrict initiative or prevent increases in effort from being associated positively with rewards. Third, environmental factors may serve as rewards for achieving desired performance, e.g., it is possible for the subordinate to receive the necessary cues to do the job and the needed rewards for satisfaction from sources other than the leader, e.g., coworkers in the primary work group. Thus, the effect of the leader on subordinates' motivation will be a function of how deficient the environment is with respect to motivational stimuli, constraints or rewards.

With respect to the environment, path-goal theory asserts that when goals and paths to desired goals are apparent because of the routine nature of the task, clear group norms or objective controls of the formal authority systems, attempts by the leader to clarify paths and goals will be both redundant and seen by subordinates as imposing unnecessary, close control. Although such control may increase performance by preventing soldiering or malingering, it also will result in decreased satisfaction (see Figure I). Also with respect to the work environment, the theory asserts that the more dissatisfying the task, the more the subordinates will resent leader behavior directed at increasing productivity or enforcing compliance to organizational rules and procedures.

Finally, with respect to environmental variables the theory states that leader behavior will be motivational to the extent that it helps subordinates cope with environmental uncertainties, threats from others or sources of frustration. Such leader behavior is predicted to increase subordinates' satisfaction with the job context and to be motivational to the extent that it increases the subordinates' expectations that their effort will lead to valued rewards.

These propositions and specification of situational contingencies provide a heuristic framework on which to base future research. Hopefully, this will lead to a more fully developed, explicitly formal theory of leadership.

Figure II presents a summary of the theory. It is hoped that these propositions, while admittedly tentative, will provide managers with some insights concerning the effects of their own leader behavior and that of others.

FOOTNOTES

1 T. R. Mitchell, "Expectancy Model of Job Satisfaction, Occupational Preference and Effort: A Theoretical, Methodological and Empirical Appraisal," *Psychological Bulletin* (1974, in press).

2 D. M. Nebeker and T. R. Mitchell, "Leader Behavior: An Expectancy Theory Approach," *Organizational Behavior and Human Performance*, 11 (1974), pp. 355–367.

3 M. G. Evans, "The Effects of Supervisory Behavior on the Path-Goal Relationship," *Organizational Behavior and Human Performance*, 55 (1970), pp. 277–298; T. H. Hammer and H. T. Dachler, "The Process of Supervision in the Context of Motivation Theory," Research Report No. 3 (University of Maryland, 1973); F. Dansereau, Jr., J. Cashman and G. Graen, "Instrumentality Theory and Equity Theory as Complementary Approaches in Predicting the Relationship of Leadership and Turnover among Managers," *Organizational Behavior and Human Performance*, 10 (1973), pp. 184–200; R. J. House, "A Path-Goal Theory of Leader Effectiveness," *Administrative Science Quarterly*, 16, 3 (September 1971), pp. 321–338; T. R. Mitchell, "Motivation and Participation: An Integration," *Academy of Management Journal*, 16, 4 (1973), pp. 160–179; G. Graen, F. Dansereau, Jr. and T. Minami, "Dysfunctional Leadership Styles," *Organizational Behavior and Human Performance*, 7 (1972), pp. 216–236;———, "An Empirical Test of the Man-in-the-Middle Hypothesis among Executives in a Hierarchical Organization Employing a Unit Analysis," *Organizational Behavior and Human Performance*, 8 (1972), pp. 262–285; R. J. House and G. Dessler, "The Path-Goal Theory of Leadership: Some Post Hoc and A Priori Tests," to appear in J. G. Hunt, ed., *Con-*

FIGURE II
SUMMARY OF PATH-GOAL RELATIONSHIPS

Leader behavior	and	Contingency factors		Cause	Subordinate attitudes and behavior
1 Directive		1 Subordinate characteristics		Personal perceptions	1 Job satisfaction Job→Rewards
2 Supportive		Authoritarianism			
		Locus of control	*influence*		2 Acceptance of leader Leader→Rewards
3 Achievement-oriented		Ability			
		2 Environmental factors		Motivational stimuli	3 Motivational behavior
4 Participative		The task	*influence*	Constraints	Effort→Performance
		Formal authority system		Rewards	Performance→Rewards
		Primary work group			

tingency Approaches to Leadership (Carbondale, Ill.: Southern Illinois University Press, 1974).

4 M. G. Evans, "Effects of Supervisory Behavior";———, "Extensions of a Path-Goal Theory of Motivation," *Journal of Applied Psychology*, 59 (1974), pp. 172–178.

5 R. J. House, "A Path-Goal Theory"; R. J. House and G. Dessler, "Path-Goal Theory of Leadership."

6 R. J. House and G. Dessler, "Path-Goal Theory of Leadership"; R. M. Stogdill, *Managers, Employees, Organization* (Ohio State University, Bureau of Business Research, 1965); R. J. House, A. Valency and R. Van der Krabben, "Some Tests and Extensions of the Path-Goal Theory of Leadership" (in preparation).

7 W. A. Hill and D. Hughes, "Variations in Leader Behavior as a Function of Task Type," *Organizational Behavior and Human Performance* (1974, in press).

8 K. E. Runyon, "Some Interactions between Personality Variables and Management Styles," *Journal of Applied Psychology*, 57, 3 (1973), pp. 288–294; T. R. Mitchell, C. R. Smyser and S. E. Weed, "Locus of Control: Supervision and Work Satisfaction," *Academy of Management Journal* (in press).

9 T. R. Mitchell, "Locus of Control."

REVIEW QUESTION

1 Present three examples of ways that managers can manipulate the environment to facilitate an employee's path toward goal attainment.

READING 32

Substitutes for Leadership

Jon P. Howell
Peter W. Dorfman*

Several writers have recently pointed out an apparent assumption in all current theories of leadership—that some form of hierarchical leadership is always important in influencing subordinate attitudes and/or performance (Kerr, 1977; Kerr & Jermier, 1978). Although theories vary somewhat in their prescriptions regarding the appropriateness of different leader behaviors in a given situation, all assume that the effective leader provides some type of guidance and/or positive feelings for subordinates as they carry out their job tasks. For example, the highly researched path-goal theory of leadership predicts that a leader's behavior will be motivating and/or satisfying to subordinates when the behavior clarifies paths to goal attainment, clarifies contingent rewards, and increases subordinates' ex-

*From "Substitutes for Leadership: Test of a Construct," *Academy of Management Journal*, December 1981, pp. 714–716, 728. Reprinted with permission.

pected and actual attainment of goals and rewards (House & Mitchell, 1974). Another popular theoretical approach, the transactional or interaction approach makes the explicit assumption that "the *quality* of leadership does matter" (Hollander, 1978, p. 1). Continual leader-subordinate interaction is emphasized with this approach. The leader directs subordinates toward mutually desired results; subordinates reciprocate by providing increased status, esteem, and support for the leader. Notwithstanding the inherent logic and empirical support for these leadership paradigms, leadership variables continue to account for only a small portion of the criterion variance in most empirical studies.

Kerr (1977) has suggested the concept of *substitutes for leadership* to help explain the occasional successes and frequent failures of leadership predictions. Leadership substitutes replace or "act in place of" a specific leader behavior. They also may act as moderator or suppressor variables by influencing the relationship between leader behavior and subordinate attitudes and/or performance. However, by acting in place of a specific leader behavior, substitutes can play a much more important role than simply as a moderator variable. Kerr suggests that substitutes render hierarchical leadership both unnecessary and impossible in terms of the potential impact of leadership on important subordinate outcomes.

Kerr and Slocum describe professional orientation as an example of a leadership substitute. "Professionals' expertise . . . reduces their need for task-related information, and both expertise and claims for autonomy reduce their receptivity toward efforts by leaders to provide such information. Preference for collegial maintenance of standards can also impair leaders' efforts to control [professional] subordinates' performance" (1981, p. 35). Jermier and Berkes (1979) have described other possible examples of leadership substitutes in a police organization. The reliance on closely-knit, cohesive work groups (two-man patrol units) during the evening shift was seen as preventing and replacing the impact of hierarchical leadership on subordinate morale. Jermier and Berkes also suggest that the existence of intrinsically satisfying work tasks may substitute for a leader's supportive behavior. In each of these cases a characteristic of the organization, the subordinate, or the subordinates' job task may substitute for the hierarchical leader by impacting on important subordinate outcomes and also preventing the hierarchical leaders' behavior from having an impact.

Several variables that characterize professionals working in organizations have been suggested as potential substitutes for hierarchical leadership. These include: the degree of professionalism of organizational participants; their ability, experience, training, and knowledge; task-provided feedback concerning accomplishment; the degree of intrinsic satisfaction derived from task accomplishment; and the presence of a closely knit cohesive work group (Kerr, 1977).

In preliminary validation studies, Kerr and Jermier (1978) obtained findings indicating that two additional variables also may be important leadership substitutes. These are the degree of organizational formalization that is present (e.g., clear written job goals, objectives, and responsibilities; written performance appraisals and work schedules) and the existence of unambiguous, routine, and methodologically invariant tasks. Other findings by Miles and Petty (1977) have been interpreted as support for organizational formalization as a possible substitute. Clearly, these organizational and task characteristics may have the potential to provide the necessary task guidance and direction for subordinates' behavior that is often provided by a hierarchical superior.

Although there is a clear rationale for the concept of substitutes for leadership, research in this area has been minimal and the empirical data are not strong.

* * *

REFERENCES

1 Georgopoulos, B. A. *Hospital organization research: Review and source book*. Philadelphia, Pa.: W. B. Saunders Company, 1975.

2 Hollander, E. P. *Leadership dynamics: A practical guide to effective relationships*. New York: Free Press, 1978.

3 House, R. J., & Mitchell, T. R. The path goal theory of leadership. *Journal of Contemporary Business*, 1974, 3, 81−97.

4 House, R. J., Rizzo, J. R., & Lirtzman, S. I. Role conflict and ambiguity in complex organizations. *Administrative Science Quarterly*, 1970, 15 (2), 150−163.

5 Jermier, J., & Berkes, L. Leader behavior in a police command bureaucracy: A closer look at the quasi-military model. *Administrative Science Quarterly*, 1979, 24 (1), 1−23.

6 Kerlinger, F. N., & Pedhazur, E. J. *Multiple regression in behavioral research*. New York: Holt, Rinehart & Winston, 1973.

7 Kerr, S. Substitutes for leadership: Some implications for organizational design. *Organization and Administrative Sciences*, 1977, 8 (1), 135−403.

8 Kerr, S., & Jermier, J. Substitutes for leadership: Their meaning and measurement. *Organizational Behavior and Human Performance*, 1978, 22 (4), 375−403.

9 Kerr, S., & Slocum, J. W., Jr. Controlling the performances of people in organizations. In P. C. Nystrom and W. H. Starbuck (Eds.), *Handbook of organizational design* (Vol. 2). New York: Oxford University Press, 1981, 116−134.

10 Miles, R. H., & Petty, M. M. Leader effectiveness in small bureaucracies. *Academy of Management Journal*, 1977, 20, 238−250.

11 Mowday, R. T., Steers, R. M., & Porter, L. W. *The measurement of organizational commitment: A progress report* (Tech. Report No. 15). Eugene, Ore.: University of Oregon, 1978.

12 Porter, L. W., & Smith, F. J. *The etiology of organizational commitment*. Unpublished manuscript, University of California-Irvine, 1970.

13 Schriesheim, C. A. *Development, validation, and application of new leader behavior and expectancy research instruments*. Unpublished doctoral dissertation, Ohio State University, 1978.

14 Schuler, R. S., Aldag, R. J., & Brief, A. P. Role conflict and ambiguity: A scale analysis. *Organizational Behavior and Human Performance*, 1977, 20 (1), 111−128.

15 Szilagyi, A. D., & Sims, H. P. An exploration of the path-goal theory of leadership in a health care environment. *Academy of Management Journal*, 1974, 17, 622−635.

16 Weiss, D. J., Dawis, R. V., England, G. W., & Lofquist, L. H. *Manual for the Minnesota Satisfaction Questionnaire*. Minneapolis, Minn.: University of Minnesota, 1967.

REVIEW QUESTION

1 Describe a situation in which you have personally experienced one or more substitutes for leadership.

READING 33

Self-Management as a Substitute for Leadership: A Social Learning Theory Perspective

Charles C. Manz
Henry P. Sims, Jr.*

Within organizations, leadership can be described as a process through which the supervisor structures reinforcement contingencies that modify the behavior of subordinates [Sims, 1977]. It is important to note, however, that a work environment entails many important contingencies of reinforcement that the supervisor does not directly control. The primary purpose of this paper is to focus on a generally neglected substitute for leadership: the capability of the subordinate to exercise self-management. The concept of self-management will be described and evaluated, primarily from a social learning theory perspective [Bandura, 1977], and the role of the organizational leader in the development of subordinate self-management will be discussed.

Kerr [1976] and Kerr and Jermier [1978] have suggested that, when task demands are well known, then this task-related knowledge, whatever the source, can be regarded as "a substitute for leadership." They have suggested further that when substitutes for leadership are salient, then the causal link between leader behavior and subordinate performance would be weak. In essence, subordinate performance would be primarily influenced by the substitutes for leadership rather than by any direct action or behavior on the part of the leader.

A social learning theory view of employee behavior recognizes the influence of reinforcement contingencies on the behavior of employees within organizations. A reinforcement contingency refers to the environmental cues that precede employee behavior (i.e., discriminative stimuli), and to the rewards that subsequently reinforce employee behavior. When initiated from nonleader sources, the contingencies can be regarded as substitutes for leadership. If an individual is instrumental in specifying contingencies of self-reinforcement, this self-influence might well be regarded as a substitute for leadership.

The focus of our paper is the role of the individual in managing his or her own behavior. Our goal is to shed light on the what, why, how, and when of self-

*From *Academy of Management Review*, July 1980, pp. 361–367. Reprinted with permission.

management, or, more specifically, *what* self-management is, *why* it might be a desirable pursuit for organizations, and *how* and *when* the leader might trigger effective self-management in individuals.

WHAT IS SELF-MANAGEMENT?

Definition and Description

Self-management, more often called self-control, has been defined as follows: "A person displays self-control when in the relative absence of immediate external constraints, he engages in behavior whose previous probability has been less than that of alternatively available behaviors" [Thoresen & Mahoney, 1974, p. 12]. Self-control can be said to include the following major characteristics: the existence of two or more response alternatives; different consequences for the alternatives; and , usually, the maintenance of self-controlling actions by longer-term external consequences [Thoresen & Mahoney, 1974].

The administration of consequences plays an important role in both self-management and the management of others. However, the question of who actually administers the consequences is perhaps less important than the determination of who evaluates whether the response requirements for reinforcement have been met. Goldiamond reminds us of Skinner's suggestion that all reinforcement could be described as self-administered because it is the person's response that produces the reinforcement. Thus, an important consideration is the issue of who has the evaluative control in determining if responses have met the criteria for reinforcement [Goldiamond, 1976; Bass, 1972].

In summary, several aspects of self-management are potentially important. It can be described as a process whereby a person is faced with immediate response alternatives involving different consequences and the person chooses an apparent low-probability response. Self-management behavior may include personal goals, self-instructions toward achieving goals, self-administered consequences, and plans for one's behavior patterns [Mischel, 1973]. The self-management process may be encouraged and maintained by desirable long-term consequences. Finally, its true effects will be mediated by whoever evaluates responses against existing criteria.

The Natural Occurrence of Self-Management

We all exercise self-control over our own behaviors to some degree. Typically we set certain behavior standards and reward or punish ourselves according to judgments we make of our performance in relation to these standards [Bandura, 1969]. Bandura indicates that we typically set standards in comparison to three referents: past performance, the observed performance of others, and socially acquired performance criteria [Mahoney, 1974, p. 155]. The difficulty of these self-imposed standards is determined by what we see in highly observable models and by our socialization history [Mischel, 1973].

Furthermore, the topography of self-control behavior is itself a function of the resulting consequences. This suggests the existence of two levels of consequences: those directly involved in the self-controlling process, and those resulting from the outcomes of self-controlling behavior. Consider the example of a long-distance runner. Imagine that this individual praises herself for each mile run during training. Then, if she goes on to win a gold medal in a marathon, she has received an external consequence contingent on her performance. Self-praise served as an internal consequence and was part of the self-control process that helped to manage the training behavior. The winning of a gold medal was an external consequence resulting from the effective training that should serve to reinforce such self-controlling behavior in the future. In the absence of long-term external reinforcement, such self-controlling behavior is not likely to be continued [Thoresen & Mahoney, 1974]. Furthermore, intermediate or sustaining achievements, such as learning and physical conditioning, would aid progress toward winning a gold medal.

In summary, a certain degree of self-control is present even in situations with extremely strong external contingencies. Conversely, in situations where a high degree of self-control is present, long-term external consequences may be critical for maintaining the self-controlling behavior.

The Role of Covert Processes

Social learning theory proposes that an integration of cognitive and environmental determinants yields a more adequate explanation of human behavior than does focus on strictly environmental determinants [Bandura, 1977; Mahoney, 1977]. This perspective inspires a new focus on the self-regulatory behaviors of individuals in conjunction with the external consequences that now receive major attention. Thoreson and Mahoney point out that covert self-instructions, self-evaluations, and self-reactions are invariably involved wherever an individual alters the consequences of his own behavior [1974, p. 107].

Furthermore, some have argued that covert activity may be governed by the same basic principles as overt behavior. For example, Thoresen and Mahoney have described what is called "covert behavior modification," which suggests that internal phenomena (i.e., thought(s)) can be considered as internal behavior responses similar to those of external behavior.

When one considers the possibility that covert events are capable of the same basic three functions as overt events (antecedents, target behaviors, and consequences), several complex interactions between the overt and covert level are possible. Thoresen and Mahoney conclude that the most successful covert self-control methods typically involve some interaction with external control. All this suggests that careful scrutiny be made of *both* covert and overt forces, and the possible interaction of the two.

WHY SELF-MANAGEMENT?

Effective self-management appears to offer potential benefits to individual employees and organizations. For example, a primary assumption of attribution theory is that the way we respond to others is dependent on the attributes (reasons) we assign for others' behavior [Jones, 1976]. One common tendency of individuals is explaining others' behavior by internal personal dispositions, while explaining their own behavior in terms of the external situation. This tendency has been called "over attribution" [Jones, 1976; Jones & Nisbett, 1972; Mischel, 1973]. A manager, for example, may attribute poor performance to internal attributes of the subordinate ("He has a bad attitude") rather than to inadequacies in the structure of external reinforcement contingencies that support desirable employee behavior. If an employee takes responsibility for his own behavior, on the other hand, some observer biases may be limited. A person would not be likely to attribute a decrease in his own performance to a character flaw, when it has, in fact, been caused by situational constraints. Ineffective self-management, however, may result if an individual attributes failures to the situation when they could in fact be prevented with one's own initiative.

Furthermore, from a cost/benefit perspective, self-management can be considered a desirable objective because it involves less expense to the organization, in terms of dollars and time, than having someone else serve as a manager [Luthans & Kreitner, 1975]. Furthermore, the employee's manager is free to address longer-term problems and issues that need attention.

Finally, because all individuals appear to engage in some sort of self-controlling behavior, it is too important for organizations to ignore. Indeed, many individuals may engage in *dysfunctional* self-management. For example, a person who sets unrealistically high goals may become frustrated rather than motivated to achieve them [Thoresen & Mahoney, 1974, p. 45].

HOW TO DEVELOP SELF-MANAGEMENT

In this section, we will describe strategies and procedures for developing self-management behavior in subordinates. Thoresen and Mahoney suggest two general strategies: environmental planning and behavioral programming. Environmental planning involves changing situational factors before the performance of target behaviors. An employee who is making an effort to cut down on time spent chatting with others might rearrange the office furniture so that the desk does not face the door. Behavioral programming includes the self-administration of consequences contingent on the performance of target responses. An example might be rewarding oneself with a steak dinner and bottle of expensive wine after a sale.

Two important elements of self-management can be delineated in these strategies. First, before a target behavior, environmental cues and personal goals or standards are important. Second, after a target behavior, the consequences of one's performance are important. Following are some specific procedures to implement these strategies.

Self-Management Procedures

Self-observation involves systematic data gathering about one's own behavior, thus establishing the basis for self-evaluation, which in turn provides information on which to base self-reinforcement. The individual who desires to reduce informal conversations might record the number of such conversations in each day and the conditions that existed at that time. Thus a basis is established for self-evaluation and reinforcement as well as possible insight regarding the causes of one's behavior. A long-distance runner, on the other hand, could time her daily practice runs.

Specifying goals is another technique of effective self-management. Latham and Yukl [1975] have reviewed research which concludes that specific goals result in improved performance. Furthermore, goal attainment seems to possess strong reinforcing properties, subsequently leading to further goals in the pursuit of organizational objectives. Indeed, Mahoney and Arnkoff [1979] suggest that goal setting might be a sufficient self-regulatory stategy in itself. They point out that goals may be more effective if they are publicly stated, focus on behavior change, and are short range instead of distant. The long-distance runner, for example, can set distance and time goals as a part of her training.

Cueing strategies (stimulus control) can be described as the gradual limiting of discriminative stimuli that precede maladaptive behavior while simultaneously increasing exposure to stimuli evoking more desirable behavior [Mahoney & Arnkoff, 1979]. Bandura [1969] has suggested that the aim is to regulate the frequency of certain behaviors by altering stimulus conditions. For the individual seeking to reduce informal conversation behavior, rearranging the office removes the visual cue (i.e., viewing of people passing in the hall) that tends to stimulate the undesired behavior (i.e., initiating an informal conversation with colleagues who go by the door). Another cueing strategy might be to close the door. Luthans and Davis [1979] provide several examples of successful applications of cueing strategies.

Incentive modification can be divided into self-reinforcement and self-punishment, both of which are based on self-evaluation. There are several factors that apparently influence the execution of self-reinforcement. Bandura indicates that individuals who gain self-control over administration of reinforcers are likely to reinforce themselves in a manner similar to the way that they were initially externally reinforced by socialization agents [1969, pp. 32–33]. An individual who has been liberally reinforced externally for mediocre performance, for example, is likely to continue with internal reinforcement in similar circumstances. Furthermore, Speidel points out that special conditions may mediate the effect of self-reinforcement: the self-control behavior already in an individual's repertoire, the level of aversiveness of the task, and the level of attractiveness of the reward itself [1974, p. 530]. There is substantial support for the notion that self-reinforcement can be effective for self-management. Mahoney and Arnkoff [1978] concluded that self-reinforcement has consistently yielded positive outcomes. In reviewing experimental evidence, Scott and Rosentiel [1975] found covert positive reinforcement to be successful in modifying wide varieties of behaviors.

The apparent effectiveness of self-reinforcement does not seem to be shared by self-punishment, which attempts to reduce undesired behavior by self-administering *aversive* consequences. Because the aversive consequence for undesired behavior is self-administered, it can be freely avoided [Thoresen & Mahoney, 1974]. Successful use of self-punishment requires the consequence to be sufficiently aversive to suppress undesired behavior yet not so aversive that it won't be used [Mahoney & Arnkoff, 1978].

Rehearsal is the systematic practice of a desired performance [Mahoney & Arnkoff, 1979]. Rehearsal can occur either overtly or covertly (i.e., imagined performance of desired behavior). Kazdin [1974], for example, found that covert rehearsal was effective in producing assertive behavior. Mahoney and Arnkoff [1978] point out that covert rehearsal allows an individual to rehearse a desired performance before an attempt at actual overt performance. In addition, Kazdin [1974, 1976] suggests that the effects of rehearsal may be mediated by the consequences following imagined performance of behavior. In other words, rehearsal might be paired with imagined or actual consequences, or both. A salesperson, for example, could rehearse a sales presentation both covertly and overtly and thereby refine it. Then, through intentionally imagining the desirable consequences of a successful sale, feelings of confidence could be reinforced.

Encouraging Self-Management for Subordinates

How can a leader encourage subordinates to engage in self-management? First, the importance of modeling should not be underestimated. Bandura suggests that individuals who effectively use self-management procedures can serve as models for others to learn self-management [1969, p. 33]. Persons will adopt the standards for self-reinforcement that they observe in exemplary models and then evaluate their own performance according to these standards. In addition, if a leader reinforces self-management in one subordinate, a self-management model is available for other subordinates. Above all, whether intentional or not, the leader's own self-management behavior inevitably serves as a model to subordinates. Consequently, overdependence by the leader on the behaviors of superiors would provide a poor self-management model.

A more directed procedure (originally offered by Meichenbaum [1973]) is described by Thoresen and Mahoney [1974]: "initial modeling, guided participation, and gradual development of covert self-control." These procedures might be adapted to the "leader-subordinate" situation. For example, in the guided participation phase, the verbal behavior of the leader is critical. The leader attempts to evoke subordinate self-management through a series of directed questions. First, self-observation: "Do you know how well you are doing right now?" "How about keeping a record of how many times that happens?" Second, self-goal setting: "How many will you shoot for?" "When do you want to have it finished?" "What will your target be?" Then, self-evaluation leading to self-reinforcement: "How do you think you did?" "Are you pleased with the way it went?" Finally, rehearsals: "Why don't we try it out?" "Let's practice that." The aim, of course, is to give the employee practice in self-management behaviors.

It is also important that social reinforcement be applied when these self-management behaviors do occur. Unfortunately, some social reinforcement may detract from the development of effective self-management capabilities (i.e., reinforcement by peers that encourages over-conformity). Note the elements that seem to be of particular importance: the evaluative and reinforcement functions are gradually shifted from external sources to the individual; the progress made in self-regulatory behavior is reinforced; and a shift is made from external material rewards to self-administered covert consequences [Bandura, 1969; Thoresen & Mahoney, 1974; Mahoney & Arnkoff, 1979].

Finally, the most important requirement is that reinforcing functions and patterns of the leader change as the subordinate becomes more and more capable of self-management. Initially, the leader reinforces specific performance-related behaviors by the subordinate. As time goes by, the reinforcement shifts from the performance-related behaviors to the process of self-management. That is, the primary function of the leader becomes that of encouraging and reinforcing processes such as goal setting and self-reinforcement rather than *directly* reinforcing subordinate performance. Some supervisors may resist this shift because it involves less direct control over subordinates. Over the long run, however, this decrease of direct control is desirable because overall subordinate effectiveness should be improved as a result of increased self-management capability.

A note of caution is important. Bandura points out that self-management attempts can fail because of vague self-instructions that have no immediate implications for behavior [1969, p. 255]. Furthermore, self-control behavior may be difficult to sustain without some form of "self-reinforcing operations" for support [p. 256]. Finally, once self-management procedures are established, an individual is faced with both external and self-administered consequences, which at times may conflict [p. 27]. Therefore, care must be taken in developing self-management in subordinates.

WHEN SHOULD MANAGERS ENCOURAGE EMPLOYEE SELF-MANAGEMENT?

Overall, we have taken the position that moving employees toward self-management is advantageous to the organization. Nevertheless, it is naive to assume that self-management is *always* appropriate. Indeed, external managerial control will always play an important role in any organization. Also, it is incorrect to assume that self-management and external control are mutually exclusive. Even in the most intensive external control situations, employees always exercise some degree of self-management. Conversely, even when self-management is deliberately encouraged, some external control by management, primarily focused on output measures, or at the task boundary, is commonly found and is typically wanted by employees. In addition, external reinforcement of the self-control process will be necessary to make it work. There are several important situational factors that will likely influence the appropriateness of attempts to develop self-management in subordinates. These include the nature of the task, the nature of the problem, the availability of time, and the importance of subordinate development.

The nature of the task itself has some connection with the potential applicability of self-management. Cummings [1978] and Slocum and Sims [1980] have attempted to link concepts of technology/task with self-regulation types of control systems. In addition, a managerial decision to "enrich" a job is typically concerned directly with the issue of self-management. It seems clear that when a task is largely creative, analytical, or intellectual in nature, greater self-management would be appropriate [House, 1979].

Self-management might be viewed as falling on a participative decision continuum [Manz, 1979]. Managers must make decisions as to how much self-management to encourage in subordinate employees, and some criteria are available to help enlighten this decision [Maier, 1970; Vroom & Yetton, 1973]. In general, more participative decision methods are appropriate when (1) the problem is not highly structured; (2) information is needed from subordinates, (3) solutions must be accepted by subordinates to ensure implementation, and (4) subordinates share organizational goals.

The time available for decision making or problem solving is another element that has bearing on whether self-management should be encouraged. In crisis situations, the time may simply not be available to develop self-management. However, if crisis situations are *likely* to occur in the absence of a leader, then self-management training would be appropriate.

At the extremes are the "development" mode versus the "short-term efficiency" mode. In the latter, self-management will be de-emphasized, except as required by the immediate task, in order to speedily carry out the task. In the development mode, subordinate self-management will be emphasized and encouraged and will be regarded as an investment for the future. One might term this mode as "leader investment behavior" from which a return in later time periods is expected. Most managers will operate in some zone between these two extreme modes of encouraging employee self-management. In the end, each manager must evaluate the specific situation. Such factors as individual employees' eagerness, desire, and present capacity for self-management are important. House [1979] has even suggested that an individual's Need Achievement [McClelland, 1961] "may well be a measure of an individual's orientation/predisposition toward self-management." Furthermore, it would be naive to argue that the self-administration of external rewards such as one's pay would not lead to organizational problems. Many other reinforcers could be tapped, however. (See Luthans and Kreitner [1975], for example, regarding nonmonetary organizational incentives.)

SUMMARY

We have presented definitions and descriptions of self-management (a critical element of social learning theory), as well as examples of specific self-management techniques that can be used by organizational employees. The role of the leader as one who can encourage and develop self-managed subordinates has been discussed. Overall, we have taken the position that self-management by individual employees can be instrumental in achieving organizational goals, and that it is a useful and legitimate role of the supervisor to develop and encourage self-management capabilities. Subordinate self-management can reduce the need for close supervision because it can indeed be a "substitute for leadership."

REFERENCES

Bandura, A. *Principles of behavior modification*. New York: Holt, Rinehart & Winston, 1969.

Bandura, A. *Social learning theory*. Englewood Cliffs, N.J.: Prentice-Hall, 1977.

Cummings, T. Self-regulating work groups: A sociotechnical synthesis. *Academy of Management Review*. 1978, *3*, 625−634.

Goldiamond, I. Self-reinforcement. *Journal of Applied Behavior Analysis*, 1976, *9*, 509−514.

House, R. J. Personal communication, 1979.

Jones, E. E. How do people perceive the causes of behavior? *American Scientist*, 1976, *64*, 300−305.

Jones, E. E.; & Nisbett, R. E. The actor and the observer: Divergent perceptions of the causes of behavior. In E. E. Jones et al. (Eds.), *Attribution: Perceiving the causes of behavior*. Morristown, N.J.: General Learning Press, 1972.

Kazdin, A. E. Effects of covert modeling and model reinforcement on assertive behavior. *Journal of Abnormal Psychology*, 1974, *83*, 240−252.

Kazdin, A. E. Effects of covert modeling, multiple models, and model reinforcement on assertive behavior. *Behavior Therapy*, 1976, *7*, 211−222.

Kerr, S. Substitutes for leadership. *Proceedings of the American Institute for Decision Sciences*, 1976.

Kerr, S.; & Jermier, J. Substitutes for leadership: Their meaning and measurement. *Organizational Behavior & Human Performance*, 1978, *22*, 375−403.

Latham, Gary P.; & Yukl, Gary A., A review of research on the application of goal setting in organizations. *Academy of Management Journal*, 1975, *18*, 824−845.

Luthans F.; & Davis, T. Behavioral self-management (BSM): The missing link in managerial effectiveness. *Organizational Dynamics*, 1979, *8*, 42−60.

Luthans, F.; & Kreitner, R. *Organizational behavior modification*. Glenview, Ill: Scott-Foresman, 1975.

Mahoney, M. J. *Cognition and behavior modification*. Cambridge: Ballinger Publishing, 1974.

Mahoney, M. J. Cognitive therapy and research: A question of questions. *Cognitive Therapy & Research*, 1977. *1*, 5−16.

Mahoney, M. J.; & Arnkoff, D. B. Cognitive and self-control therapies. In S. L. Garfield & A. E. Borgin (Eds.), *Handbook of psychotherapy and behavior change*. New York: Wiley, 1978, pp. 689−722.

Mahoney, M. J.; & Arnhoff, D. B. Self-management: Theory, research, and application. In J. P. Brady & D. Pomerleau (Eds.), *Behavioral medicine: Theory and practice*. Baltimore: Williams & Williams, 1979, pp. 75−96.

Maier, N. R. F. *Problem solving and creativity in individuals and groups*. Belmont, Calif.: Brooks-Cole 1970.

Manz, C. C. Sources of control: A behavior modification perspective. *Proceedings of the Eastern Academy of Management*, 1979.

McClelland, D. *The achieving society*. Princeton: Van Nostrand-Reinhold, 1961.

Meichenbaum, D. H. Cognitive factors in behavior modification: Modifying what clients say to themselves. *Annual Review of Behavior Therapy Theory & Practice*, 1973, *1*, 416–431.

Mischel, W. Toward a cognitive social learning reconceptualization of personality. *Psychological Review*, 1973, *80*, 252–283.

Scott, D. S.; & Rosentiel, A. K. Covert positive reinforcement studies: Review, critique, and guidelines. *Psychotherapy Theory, Research, & Practice*, 1975, *12*, 374–384.

Sims, H. P. The leader as a manager of reinforcement contingencies: An empirical example and a model. In J. G. Hunt & L. L. Larson (Eds.), *Leadership: The cutting edge*. Carbondale.: Southern Illinois University Press, 1977, pp. 121–137.

Slocum, J. W.; & Sims, H. P. A typology for integrating technology, organization, and job redesign. *Human Relations*, 1980, *33* (3), 193–212.

Speidel, G. E. Motivating effect of contingent self-reward. *Journal of Experimental Psychology*, 1974, *102*, 528–530.

Thoresen, E. E.; & Mahoney, M. J. *Behavior self-control*. New York: Holt, Rinehart & Winston, 1974.

Vroom, V. H.; & Yetton, P. W. *Leadership and decision making*. Pittsburgh: University of Pittsburgh Press, 1973.

REVIEW QUESTIONS

1 Explain the relationship between social learning theory, substitutes for leadership, and self-management.
2 Give some examples of ways that you have engaged in self-management. Why did you do so?
3 Is the idea of self-management a realistic one for many managers in light of trends regarding the work ethic? (You might wish to review the Porter article.)

CHAPTER 9

PARTICIPATIVE MANAGEMENT

READING 34

Participative Management: The State of the Art

Peter Brownell*

Over the past several decades, a great deal of research has explored the impact of participative systems of management. The effects of participation on a wide variety of areas within organizations have been examined. The results of this line of inquiry, however, have often tended to conflict with one another. Some research studies have shown that employee attitudes, job satisfaction, morale, and even performance will benefit from a high level of participation. Other studies have flatly contradicted these, especially in the area of performance.

What is the manager to conclude on the basis of the evidence from research thus far? Participation works? Participation doesn't work? Participation works sometimes?

The last of these is most true. Yet, by itself, it doesn't say much. It is the type of statement that causes managers to smile when the subject of academic research comes up. It does, however, point the direction in which both academic researchers and practicing managers ought to be moving. If participation works sometimes, the next step is to try to determine when and under what circumstances it works.

A communications gap clearly exists between the academic and managerial communities, for while academics have been keen to pursue new and different perspectives and situations within which to study participation, they have been remiss in effectively integrating and juxtaposing the mass of previous results, usually leaving the practicing community befuddled as to the state of our knowledge in this area. In reviewing the significant work done in the past, and pointing out some of the conditional factors affecting the prospects for participation, I hope to link the research efforts of the academic community with the practical needs of managers confronted with the problem of implementing and managing a participative decision-making program.

My own work, and much of that cited here, has focused on participation in the budget process. However, the results are applicable to the range of decisions facing management in the area of participation within the organization. Four major groups of variables systematically influence the relationship between participation and its consequences for the organization and its employees. They are *cultural, organizational, interpersonal,* and *individual* variables.

Cultural Variables. An important factor in influencing the consequences of participative schemes of management is the broad social and political environment in which they are attempted. Culture has a substantial impact on the

*From *The Wharton Magazine*, Fall 1982, pp. 38–43. Reprinted with permission.

likelihood of the success or failure of participation. Cultural variables may be divided into *national, political,* and *social* factors.

A pair of studies done in 1948 and 1960, respectively, provide particularly useful evidence of the effects of differences connected to *nationality.*

In 1948, L. Coch and J. R. P. French, Jr., studied an "in-house" experiment conducted at the Harwood Manufacturing Company, in which management tested three schemes of employee involvement in decisions related to the production budget: 1) all employees affected were actively involved in budget decisions, 2) selected employee representatives participated in meetings with top management, and 3) the usual company procedure of simply informing employees of the final decision was followed.

The results graphically revealed the relative desirability of the three schemes. Members of the third group experienced 17 percent resignations—typical when budget changes had been made in the past—and significant deteriorations in productivity. Among the second group, who were partially involved in the decisions affecting them, nobody resigned, and there was a slow improvement in productivity. The greatest improvement in productivity was made by members of the first group, who were fully consulted during the decision process. As in the second group, there were no resignations.

However, when French, J. Israel, and D. As repeated the experiment in 1960 at a footwear factory in Norway, an increase in productivity *did not* follow from greater direct participation. Most likely, this was due to the strong union ties among Norwegian workers, which may have promoted an attitude that representation through unions was preferable to a more direct method.

IDEOLOGICAL INFLUENCES

Various participation systems have been directly inspired by *political* or *social* ideologies, such as the Workers' Councils of the socialist world and the kibbutz system in the state of Israel.

In Yugoslavia, for example, Workers' Councils provide a formidable measure of joint management. Introduced in 1950, such councils afford all employees of an enterprise ultimate authority with regard to the basic policy, personnel, and technical issues facing a firm. The difference in control exercised at the top and bottom levels of an organization in Yugoslavia is significantly less than among comparable Western organizations, and studies have shown that the Yugoslav industrial system has proven itself in terms of national productivity.

An even more extreme level of participation is exhibited by the kibbutz of Israel, which has expanded well beyond its traditional agricultural context to include a wide range of manufacturing activities. Organization structure in the kibbutz contains many participative features. For instance, officers from first-line supervisors on up are elected by the workers, and their tenure is limited to between three and five years. Also, a Management Board, consisting of the plant manager, production manager, and workers' representatives, is responsible for a wide range of organizational decisions. A study of Israeli kibbutz plants showed that they were more efficient than comparable non-kibbutz plants, and that labor-management conflict was virtually nonexistent.

Cross-cultural generalizations concerning the probable impact of participation should be carefully guarded against. Perhaps the most dangerous generalization is from Western culture to Eastern, and vice versa, but there are important distinctions to be drawn between the industrial climates of Europe and the United States as well.

Organizational Variables. The nature of the organization itself has a substantial bearing on the comparative usefulness of systems of participation. Four major factors are involved in this area in deciding the extent to which it is appropriate for an organization to build participative features into its management strategy: *environmental stability, technology, task uncertainty,* and *organizational structure.*

A 1967 study attempted to determine what kind of organization was most effective in dealing with various environmental, economic, and market conditions. P. R. Lawrence and J. W. Lorsch studied firms in three industries: plastics, food processing, and containers. These industries were seen as being on a continuum of *environmental stability,* with plastics facing the most turbulent and dynamic environment and containers the most stable.

Successful firms in the plastics industry exhibited a low degree of formal structure, fewer levels in the organizational hierarchy, less frequent performance evaluation, and fewer objective performance criteria. The flow of information was primarily lateral rather than vertical—exchanges between relative equals rather than upward to superiors. Broad decision-making authority—and the high degree of knowledge necessary for it—resided at comparatively low levels of the organization. However, even within a single plastics firm, influence in decision making varied according to the level of environmental turbulence faced by particular divisions. A much broader base of authority was found in a division such as marketing, which is substantially exposed to the external environment, than in production, for instance, which is relatively buffered from external forces.

In contrast, successful firms in the container and food processing industries, facing more or less unchanging environments, were characterized by a greater level of formal structure and hierarchy, with authority and information restricted to the upper levels of the organization. Employees in the worst performing container firms actually felt they had considerably more influence in decision making compared with those employed in firms that performed at a higher level!

Another major factor affecting participation at the organizational level is *technology.* In a study of British companies performed in 1961, T. Burns and G. M. Stalker found that where the rate of technical innovation was low, successful firms were managed by "mechanistic" systems characterized by functional specialization and detailed definitions of duties and responsibilities, while rapid technical change was associated with more "organic" systems of management, with comparatively flexible organizational arrangements, more consultation and participation, and less rigorously specified tasks. This same basic result has emerged from most examinations of the impact of technology on different organizational responses. For repetitive, easily-programmable production activities, a more hierarchical structure with upward information flows and downward authority flows appears appropriate. Nonrepetitive, short production run, custom-type production activities are not so amenable to programmed controls and are probably better managed by individual supervision with small spans of authority.

As an organization becomes more complex and faces a greater need for information, *task uncertainty* may become a concern. Task uncertainty has been defined by J. Galbraith as the difference between the amount of information required and the amount possessed by the organization. Faced with this discrepancy between what is needed and what is available, an organization may either reduce its need through such devices as the creation of self-contained tasks, or increase the availability of information through the use of vertical information systems, and by creating lateral relations. The latter of these information handling strategies is particularly relevant in the context of participation. Galbraith, when referring to lateral relations, has in mind the idea of reducing the number of decisions referred upward in the organization and bringing the "decision point" down to the "action point" where the information exists. In other words, increased influence of lower-level organization members in decision making is one key strategy used to deal with uncertainty and the attending level of information handling capacity.

The role of *organizational structure* as a factor influencing the impact of participation was examined by W. J. Bruns and J. H. Waterhouse in 1975. They confirmed that managers in decentralized organizations perceive themselves as having more influence, participating more in budget planning, and being satisfied with budget-related activities. On the other hand, managers in centralized organizations are granted less responsibility, report less involvement in budget planning, experience superior-initiated pressure, and see budgets as being less useful and limiting their flexibility. A review of the evidence in this area leads to the conclusion that different structures create the need for different control mechanisms, with centralized organizations relying more on procedure specification, and decentralized organizations on budgetary systems which provide for more managerial discretion.

Interpersonal Variables. A number of studies has focused on the effects of leadership style on performance, attempting to gauge the circumstances in which more flexible, considerate styles of leadership, as opposed to more rigid, structured styles, are appropriate. While the results have often been mixed, one consistent finding has been that the exclusive use of *any* single style in all situations is inappropriate. The view more recently taken has been that leader behavior should be *situationally* consistent only, countering previous opinion that consistency is desirable because it allows subordinates to predict their superior's behavior and adapt to it.

STYLES OF LEADERSHIP

Three distinct classes have been shown to affect the impact of leadership style at the interpersonal level. These are *task characteristics, group characteristics*, and *situational characteristics*.

A variety of *task characteristics* has been examined. For instance, a study of military platoons revealed that in low-pressure situations such as training, members preferred a more relaxed, considerate style of leadership, while in stressful environments such as combat, a highly structured style was more satisfactory. It has been suggested that the source of task pressure was the critical variable here. Where pressure is seen as external to the group, structure is appropriate; when the tension comes from within the group, a more flexible approach is preferable.

The level of intrinsic interest in a given task is also important. Structured styles of leadership are less likely to be successful when work is not satisfying in itself. In general, results indicate that for straightforward, routine tasks, a considerate leadership style is best. On the other hand, poorly specified tasks may require more structured supervisory behavior.

Group characteristics such as group composition and structure are important moderating effects on leadership style. Small work groups may be better managed by supervisors who act as technical specialists and exhibit supportive, considerate behavior. An emphasis on administrative functions and a greater reliance on structured behavior is necessary with larger groups, for the most part.

The importance of the average skill level of group members in comparison to that of their supervisor was suggested by F. A. Heller, who found that a more directive style of leadership appears appropriate where there is a substantial discrepancy between the two. He further concluded that the amount of training necessary to elevate subordinates to the level of their superior is positively related to the need for structuring behavior. And, in all cases, supervision will necessarily be more directive when subordinates disagree over the solution to a problem or task, than when all are in agreement.

Situational characteristics, as, for instance, an individual's position in the hierarchy of an organization, also seem to relate to his or her reaction to various leadership styles. Lower-level members are more amenable to, and may actually prefer, more structured leadership, while the same structure causes resentment among more highly placed members.

Different styles of leadership may be necessary when responding to different individuals, even when they are performing the same tasks. Participative styles appear more appropriate when subordinates with a strong need for growth engage in ambiguous, wide-ranging tasks. However, when the same tasks are attempted by individuals with less ambition, a more directive style may be preferable. Other variables that have been shown to influence the effectiveness of various leadership styles include the quality of the relationship between leaders and subordinates, the degree of trust exhibited by the superior, the need for a speedy decision, and the existence of formal communication channels.

Through their leadership style, managers condition the perceptions of their subordinates concerning the extent of their involvement and influence in issues relating to the organization. The effectiveness of a given style has been seen to depend on a variety of task, group, and situational characteristics. In general, the evidence indicates that large groups of differently skilled subordinates involved in ambiguous, relatively unspecified tasks will require close, directive supervision. Smaller groups of highly skilled workers involved in more routine, straightforward tasks appear to respond poorly to excessively structured supervision from their superiors.

An extremely important caveat is necessary here. Almost without exception, the research in this area has been produced through the use of survey techniques. This raises a question regarding the causal direction of the results. J. B. Ritchie has cogently articulated this question: "Does democratic supervision cause high performance, or is democratic behavior a luxury permitted only supervisors whose subordinates are already highly productive?"

Individual Variables. The final group of variables influencing the effects of participation are individual variables, which may be divided into *individual characteristics, personality variables,* and *individual perceptions.*

Individual characteristics are differences among people apart from their various personality traits. The effects of participation are subject to some of these variables. Age, for example, may significantly affect the impact of participation. Precisely how is far from settled, however. In one study, older managers appeared far more content than their younger counterparts with moderate levels of participation. Another study related this effect to tenure within the organization, a finding that the first study specifically rejected.

Numerous *personality variables* have been shown to influence the effects of participation. A classic study conducted by V. H. Vroom in 1960 revealed that individuals who tended to accept formal authority easily and were more comfortable in an autocratic situation (high authoritarians) preferred less participation in budgetary and other decision making than did those who found it more difficult to contend with a highly rigid hierarchy (low authoritarians).

A recent study of my own concerned the different reactions to participation among internally and externally focused individuals. Internally focused people attribute the outcomes of their actions to themselves, while those who are externally focused tend to credit outcomes to chance, fate, or luck. The results of the study showed that internals preferred, and performed better, under high participation conditions, while the opposite was true among externals.

The way *individuals perceive* situations may influence the effects of participation in a number of ways. One example would be different reactions to participation in different areas. For instance, the participation of foremen in the technical standards component of budget preparation has been found to be significantly correlated to job satisfaction. On the other hand, participation in the development of more aggregate, financial objectives within the budget seems to elicit little positive effect. Participation, therefore, is most satisfying where individuals perceive that they have a valid contribution to make based on their on-the-job experience.

Another influential effect is the perception of sources of reward and reinforcement. The perception of reward structure held by those involved has a major impact on the relationship between participation and job satisfaction. A laboratory study of participative budgeting divided subjects into groups, one of which had a high degree of influence in developing a budget, while another was given little opportunity to participate. Those in the high participation group reported greatest job satisfaction when rewards were based, at least in part, on achieving the budget, while a much lower level of satisfaction resulted from rewards based solely on output. Those in the imposed budget group, who, not having participated in making the budget, had little personal stake in it, showed a clear preference for rewards connected with output only.

A BASIS FOR EVALUATION

I discovered a similar effect in a study of the perceived emphasis placed by superiors on budget-related results in subordinate performance evaluation. The results indicated that participation will be ineffective unless the resulting budget is perceived to provide the major basis for evaluation of the performance of subordinates involved in setting the budget.

In 1975, J. Rosen and J. L. Livingstone introduced the *expectancy model* of motivation to provide support for the view that unless participation is perceived by subordinates as instrumental in their achieving desired outcomes, it will be ineffective. The expectancy model posits that individuals will exert effort towards achieving a goal only to the extent that 1) such effort has a reasonable probability of being instrumental in achieving the goal, and 2) that achieving the goal is associated with positive expectations of reward.

While the expectancy theory framework has generated numerous studies of budget system design and operation, none of the work done thus far focused specifically on the potential impact of participation. However, it is useful to consider some propositions which may be deduced from the model. For example, participation, by enhancing commitment to the budget by subordinates, may improve the intrinsic value to the individual of achieving the budget, and at the same time enhance the probability that goal-directed behavior will be successful. By contrast, the failure to base rewards on budget achievement can impair the effectiveness of participation by reducing the probability that the accomplishment of budget-related goals will lead to extrinsic rewards.

Research on the effects of participation in budgetary and other matters affecting the organization has been extensive and wide-ranging, which I hope this review has sufficiently suggested. The results have at times been conflicting. Still, it is possible to devise a model of the interactive effects of participation which places cultural, organizational, interpersonal, and individual variables within a single, unifying framework. From this, the reader may get an idea of what the "state of the art" is in this area, and what the implications are for management policy and practice in the future.

The first two sets of variables, cultural and organizational, we may call "antecedent moderators"—preconditions which might *dictate* the need for (or the need to avoid!) participation. Interpersonal and individual variables, on the other hand, are "consequence moderators." They influence the *effects* of participation.

Antecedent moderators concern the context within which organizational design issues, such as the level of participation, are considered. In establishing their objectives, organizations more or less submit themselves to a particular set of environmental, technological, and, possibly, cultural considerations. The organization is then designed in such a way as to manage these contextual circumstances as effectively as possible. The choice of an appropriate system of participation— or non-participation—would typically be accommodated within this process, and, therefore, may not be wholly at the discretion of management. The effects of the level of participation chosen will then be conditioned by the consequence moderators.

The policy implications of these two sets of moderators are quite different. Once management has assessed the appropriate level of participation for its particular organizational setting, the question becomes one of contending with the effects arising from that decision. In other words, even when management makes an appropriate response to its organizational and cultural environment, there is still no assurance that the response will be effective. Personnel management still faces the task of ensuring that appropriate types of individuals are "fitted" to organizational roles involving various levels of participation, and management development and training activities within the organization must focus on the leadership qualities required for effective supervision.

It is in the area of consequence moderators that research has tended to place emphasis, examining the effects *of* participation without exhibiting a similar degree of concern with the initial environmental prospects for its success or failure. This comparatively one-sided view is unfortunate, for the practical considerations that govern the antecedent and consequence moderators are very different. Yet they are equally important in determining the effectiveness of participation.

The introduction of participative schemes of management, then, is essentially a two-step process. First, managers should carefully consider the organizational and cultural settings in which they find themselves and fashion a design for the firm that adequately deals with its setting. Following that, the responsibility for ensuring the effectiveness of a participative system rests with the management of a vast range of functional areas within the organization. A failure on the part of management to make a concerted effort to accomplish both parts of this task is bound to jeopardize the potential for participation.

SUGGESTED READING

Peter Brownell, "Participation in the Budgeting Process—When It Works and When It Doesn't," *Journal of Accounting Literature*, Spring 1982. The paper on which this article is based. Provides a more detailed description of the literature, and an extensive bibliography.

Peter Brownell, "Participation in Budgeting, Locus of Control and Organizational Effectiveness," *The Accounting Review*, October 1981. Explores the effect of a personality variable, internal-external locus of control, on the relationship between budgetary participation and performance.

REVIEW QUESTIONS

1 Brownell states that effective participation is a function of four situational groups of variables. Describe their impact.

2 Differentiate between antecedent moderators and consequence moderators of participation. What do they imply for managers considering the adoption of participative methods?

READING 35

Going in Circles with Quality Circles? Management Development Implications

William B. Werther, Jr.*

IBM, General Motors, RCA, Westinghouse, Control Data, Union Carbide, Tektronics, Lockheed, Northrup Aircraft, Babcock and Wilcox, Waters Associates, Solar Turbines, and American Express are operating effective quality circle efforts. Companies like Motorola, Champion International, TRW, and others use different forms of team building that are closely related to the quality circle concept. As a result, the print and electronic media are creating waves of favourable publicity about the idea. These "success stories" are leading a number of executives to consider quality circles for their company. Unfortunately, publicity releases and press reports seldom alert top management to potential problems.

The pitfalls that are emerging from corporate programmes do not mark the demise of quality circles. Their success establishes them as a useful management tool. Quality circles work; they are unlikely to be a fad. The problems discussed here are not fatal flaws in the concept but may be fatal to company programmes that ignore them. Certainly, for those who seek reasons to avoid quality circles, ample ammunition follows. However, a variety of businesses operate successful quality circle efforts—and these efforts may be a path through the productivity crisis that faces other companies.

HOW QUALITY CIRCLES OPERATE

Exhibit I outlines the most common aspect of quality circles (QC). It defines quality circles and indicates their organisation, training, and process requirements. Although each user may vary the specifics of the reporting relationships,

*From *Journal of Management Development*, 2:1, 1983, pp. 3–18. Reprinted with permission.

EXHIBIT I
AN OVERVIEW OF QUALITY CIRCLES: THEIR ORGANISATION, TRAINING AND PROCESS

QC Definition
A quality circle is a group of workers and their supervisor who voluntarily meet to identify and solve job-related problems.

QC Organisation
Quality circle efforts rely extensively on the existing line structure in the organisation. To train and support the quality circle teams, a coordinator (or facilitator) position is established. This full-time person usually reports to a high level line manager, such as a plant, division, manufacturing, or other executive officer. The facilitator's role includes the design of the programme and training materials, introduction of the concept to potential circle members, training of members, liaison among the circles and other departments, coaching circles, and keeping the steering committee informed of circle activities.

The steering committee is composed of representatives from groups affected by circle actions. The committee members are usually the heads of the staff and line departments at the location where the programme is operating. Thus, a plant-wide programme finds the committee members consist of the plant manager's direct reports. If the programme is on a divisional or corporate basis, the committee will include the direct reports of the divisional or corporate executive.

QC Training
1 *Employees*—although each firm adjusts its training according to the needs of circle members, most companies give workers eight hours of training, usually in one session. The training includes an explanation of quality circles and decision making techniques. Normally the techniques taught are brainstorming, cause-and-effect (or "fishbone") diagrams, graphing approaches including Pareto analysis, basic quality control sampling and charting methods, and presentation skills.

2 *Supervisors*—again, the training varies from firm to firm, but usually includes all the topics taught to employees. In addition, the supervisors receive training about group dynamics, human behaviour, leadership, quality of work life, and committee skills. This training usually lasts two days.

3 *Facilitators*—training for facilitators includes the same materials taught to supervisors. Topics such as individual behaviour, group dynamics, committee skills, leadership, and quality of work life, however, are covered in more detail. Facilitators also receive training in teaching skills since they usually serve as in-house trainers. Training programmes for facilitators by the American Productivity Center or the International Association of Quality Circles last five days.

4 *Steering Committee*—members of the steering committee are often given a one-half to full-day seminar. The seminar describes quality circles, their structure, and their training needs. The seminar also explains the benefits and commitments associated with quality circles.

The Quality Circle Process
Once managers, supervisors and employees are trained, the process usually begins with a brainstorming session to identify likely problems the group can address. Through discussion a consensus is reached by the members as to which problem should be tackled. The problem is defined. Likely causes are then identified, usually through a cause-and-effect diagram. Data may be needed to identify specific causes. This information is obtained through the workers' use of observation and check sheets or by securing needed data from the facilitator. Data are arrayed usually graphically in a Pareto Chart to isolate most common causes.

Once a solution is agreed upon, the members present their analysis and recommendations to the appropriate manager or the steering committee. Feedback is received from management, and another problem is identified and the process repeats.

Usually meetings are in company time and last one hour per week. When continuous process production or other demands preclude meeting during regular hours, workers meet on an overtime basis before or after work.

the composition of the steering committee, or the training content, all pro-grammes make extensive use of facilitators and training.

Perhaps the most important feature of quality circles is their potential impact. When fully deployed throughout a plant or company, circles may transform the organisation's culture into one which facilitates constructive change. The circle process identifies and evaluates areas of needed change. Employee ideas are encouraged. Success with the process moves the organisation toward more open communications, trust, and involvement of employees in the decision making process. At first glance, quality circles appear to demand an instant transforma-tion of the corporate culture. However, implementation generally proceeds slow-ly so that the organisation can evolve gradually into the new culture.

Although substantial research into the benefits of quality circles is lacking, extensive case studies reveal important advantages of this management tool. Of these gains, executives and productivity administrators emphasise a few as being most significant. Access to employee ideas usually heads the list.

For an organisation to more fully reap the benefits of its employees' ideas requires the development of a highly trained cadre of managers—managers who are self-confident enough to seek and use the good ideas of employees. Managers, who by their day-to-day behaviour encourage those around them to share in the excitement of meaningful accomplishments, however measured.

Quality circles, by themselves, will not transform an organisation's culture into this ideal state. However, the training in group dynamics, consultation skills, and decision making help develop circle participants. On-going coaching from the facilitator furthers the developmental process. And, the voluntary nature of circles serves as a check on autocratic excesses by supervisors or managers, since members can resign if the circle process is not satisfying to them. If the process is initially successful and top management continues its *active* interest and support, the benefits in Exhibit II spread through the organisation. In time, these atti-tudinal changes are reflected in the behaviour of management and non-manage-ment employees. Continued long enough in the presence of a far sighted top management, the very culture of the organisation evolves to one more conducive to high productivity and quality of work life. How long circles serve up these benefits parallels the length of management's on-going commitment to develop-ing its people. When top management forgets circles are primarily a development tool, it courts "cost savings reports" and detailed productivity measures that may communicate only limited interest in the development of human resources. Inter-est by all is then likely to wane.

Quality circles yield well-reasoned and substantiated ideas. It is from employee ideas that the benefits of quality circles accrue to the employer and workers. By design, these ideas are aimed at workplace obstacles that prevent higher pro-ductivity and lower the employees' quality of work life. Often these ideas initially seem trivial. For example, employees on the F-5 assembly line at Northrup Aircraft had long complained of dull drill bits. The usual response was, "Get a new bit." When one of the circles studied this problem, they found that some bits would break before drilling one hole, while other bits efficiently drilled hundreds

EXHIBIT II
SOME BENEFITS OF QUALITY CIRCLES

Awareness	• Increases management's awareness of employee ideas • Increases employee awareness of management's desire for ideas • Increases employee awareness of the need for innovation
Commitment	• Creates an employee commitment to the organisation, its product/service quality, and co-workers • Creates a commitment by the organisation to employee ideas
Communications	• Improves supervisory/employee communication • Facilitates upward communications
Competitiveness	• Allows the firm to become more competitive through improved costs, quality, and/or commitment to QWL • Improves recruiting and retention of quality employees that enhances competiveness
Development	• Develops supervisors into better leaders and decision makers by providing them with new tools • Develops employees to think as managers and gives them new decision making tools
Innovation	• Encourages innovation through receptivity to employee ideas
Respect	• Shows management's respect for the needs and ideas of employees • Allows the supervisor to earn the respect of employees
Satisfaction	• Enhances employee satisfaction through participation in decision making • Enhances supervisory satisfaction by improving communication • Reduces employee and supervisory dissatisfaction caused by resistance to change
Teamwork	• Requires teamwork for successful QC meetings • Furthers teamwork outside the QC meetings

of holes before they needed to be reworked. Circle members recommended tightening rework tolerances on used bits and management agreed. The result was several thousand dollars saved in that one department, increased productivity per hour, and improved quality of work life for employees. What often surprises management is not just the dollar savings but the sophistication and thoroughness of the employees' analysis.

Another frequently mentioned benefit is the "carry-over effect." Employees usually spend one hour per week in circle meetings, but their effort does not stop there. Employees often are overheard discussing the problem on breaks or seen working on displays during lunch hours. This carry-over effect also extends to employee-supervisory cooperation outside the circle meeting. Supervisors are seen as more receptive to employees which leads to improved communications, satisfaction, organisational loyalty, teamwork, and an air of mutual respect. The result is a free-flow of productivity improvement ideas.

Observation of circle meetings and presentations also helps management identify potential leaders. Self-confidence, communication skills, and other leadership traits stand out during circle activities. In fact, many Japanese managers consider the development and identification of potential leaders to be a major benefit of quality circles.

Dollar savings are another obvious benefit. However, for a variety of reasons, many companies deliberately do not trace the total costs and financial returns on quality circle efforts. As a result, the dollar returns are seldom quantified— although facilitators and executives usually estimate direct returns in the 200 to 400 per cent range. One exception is Solar Turbines. When its programme began, it was a subsidiary of International Harvester and it tracked financial costs and benefits closely. During the 18 month start-up period, its total outlays were $79,000. At the end of that period, circle ideas had contributed $90,000 in first year savings! These figures understate the true return to Solar in several ways. The $79,000 figure included all start-up costs, facilitator salaries, and costs of developing training materials. The $90,000 figure was the *first year's net savings*, after the costs of implementing the ideas were subtracted. Since many of those ideas will generate savings in subsequent years, the actual discount cash savings from those ideas is undoubtedly two or three times higher. Finally, the savings do not include any estimate of the carry-over effects, such as improved communications, loyalty, absenteeism, turnover, or morale. After the start-up period, Solar has consistently posted a return on its quality circle programme of 400 per cent, which is in line with similar programmes at other firms. On the other hand, those companies that use circles primarily to emphasise quality of work life seldom trace the return on their quality circle investment.

Although many other benefits are discussed in Exhibit II, the most important gains may be intangible. Circles create a more open atmosphere in the organisation. Innovation is encouraged. Participation in problem solving enhances feelings of teamwork and satisfaction. Progress is part of everyone's job, not something imposed from on high.

Since most companies have been successful without quality circles, many top managers do not sense an urgent need to use this management tool. Their reasoning is often a variant of the following: "We have been successful with our traditional 'top-down' approach. Why risk future success on a relatively new technique?" Perhaps the best way to respond to this reasoning is to review the origins of quality circles.

Origins of Quality Circles

Following World War II, the Japanese faced staggering problems. With half the population of the United States living in an area about the size of Montana, Japanese leaders quickly realised that national prosperity rested with exporting. To export successfully, resource-poor Japan had to import natural resources, add value, and export quality products. But in the immediate post-war era, "made in Japan" meant "cheap junk." To avoid becoming an economic colony of the United States and to overcome their image of poor quality, Japanese industry focused on producing quality products.

Quality circles were born out of necessity. The only significant resource the

Japanese had was an educated and diligent workforce. Japanese management provided workers with training in quality control and decision making concepts. Then company time was allowed for workplace meetings to solve quality problems. Today, eight million Japanese workers are in circles formally registered with the Japanese Union of Scientists and Engineers.

When non-registered circles and variations on this concept are considered, estimates range to more than 25 million circle participants—or about half of the Japanese workforce.

OPPORTUNITIES AND ROADBLOCKS

To tap this nearly limitless resource, more and more companies are turning to quality circles or other variations of employee involvement. However, this emerging trend—limited mostly to multi-billion corporations—is a major undertaking. It demands new management attitudes and behaviours, which change slowly and with great difficulty. Those managements that adhere to traditional attitudes and behaviours may find themselves unable to respond to competitors who have attained greater employee dedication to productivity and quality.

The following pages outline the fundamental changes required to make quality circles work. Where these changes do not occur, problems with quality circles will arise. How top management deals with these challenges to past attitudes and behaviours will determine the success of individual quality circle efforts. For, in the final analysis, quality circles are not merely the application of a new technique, but a basic change in how management manages.

Top-Down Commitment

Quality circles change the culture of the organisation. To succeed, management must be receptive to the ideas of employees—particularly at the hourly and supervisory level. In the circle meetings, supervisors serve as discussion leaders. If they seek to impose their will on the group, the selection of problems and solutions is not arrived at by consensus. Since the employees do not feel a sense of ownership in the process or its outcomes, resistance to change is likely to remain and the effectiveness of the quality circle process is severely damaged. In extreme cases of supervisory dominance, the group disbands since membership is voluntary.

Although supervisory training helps avoid this pitfall, no amount of training makes supervisors receptive to the process without a strong commitment from upper management. For example, supervisors are usually under pressure to produce results—whether those results are higher production or fast solutions to workplace problems. If middle management expresses disdain for the circle process or if they express contempt for the "slow pace" of decision making, the supervisor may dominate circle meetings.

The implications for top management are twofold: First, quality circles must be explained even to middle managers who are not directly involved in conducting meetings. It is unreasonable to expect middle management support when these managers do not understand the process. Second, the top manager and other members of the steering committee must exhibit their commitment to quality circles. Speeches, directives, and articles in the house organ help. Attendance at circle meetings helps even more. But top management must evaluate middle managers on the effectiveness of the circles under their jurisdiction. If middle managers are rated on the success of quality circles, they are more likely to understand and support the concept.

A final note of caution about commitment concerns top management's view of quality circles. If they are seen as merely a quick-fix or a programme to be layered on top of the existing organisation culture, management's commitment is actually little more than permission—permission for someone to try circles in some remote enclave of the organisation. Facilitators, middle managers, supervisors, and employees will sense this low-level of commitment. When production problems or other pet programmes conflict with circle activities, the circles will likely get "back-burner" treatment. Some circles may survive, but long-term and widespread successes are unlikely. The lack of commitment is most common when a new middle or plant manager begins to supervise those with circles. Circles are seen as someone else's programme; the need for patience and meeting time is not understood. Support is withdrawn and the circles fade away. Lockheed's pioneering effort in quality circles met this fate when key managers were changed.

Bottom-Up Receptivity

Most western organisations rely on downward communications. New ideas are initiated by managers and "imposed" on the organisation from the top. This approach has several flaws. It assumes that those further down the hierarchy have little to contribute other than their labour. However, productivity improvement starts with those actually creating the company's products or services; they are the true experts.

The top-down communication of ideas is damaging in other ways. When a new idea is imposed on a work group, they have little invested in its success or failure. It's not their idea. Resistance to change is likely. Resistance is even more likely when employees have other ideas they deem to be better. Fundamentally, the top-down approach is resented by those upon whom management relies for success because it does not acknowledge that employees have good ideas, too.

Many managers react to these observations with defensive statements like: "But, we want and use the good ideas of employees." Yet, most attitude surveys in those same firms show hourly employees find little opportunity for creativity. Why the disparity?

The disparity between management's desire for ideas and the paucity of creativity in most hourly-paid jobs arises from low levels of receptivity to employee ideas. What really happens when a new employee has a usable idea? The employee discusses it with the supervisor. The experienced supervisor knows the middle manager will look for flaws in the idea. To ensure that the idea is practical, the supervisor will likely grill the employee, who often has not thoroughly thought through the idea. Some flaw usually is uncovered and the idea dies. It dies because every idea carries the potential for disruption if not failure. To implement the idea is to risk disruption or error. What incentive does the supervisor have to try the idea? The safest course of action is to kill the idea in its infancy. After one or two more tries with other ideas, the employee soon learns that management (in the form of the supervisor) does not want new ideas. The flow of ideas from hourly workers slows. Since new ideas are necessary for productivity improvement and organisational survival, they must come from the top with all its attendant problems and resistance.

Resistance to employee ideas stems from an informal cost/benefit analysis. The supervisor (and higher levels of management) evaluate the cost of employee ideas. The costs include not only the direct expenses but also the indirect ones such as lost-time to sell the idea, overcoming the boss's resistance to change, new controls, and the resulting disruption to present production. Since many of these costs cannot be quantified, they loom large in the eyes of decision makers. As a result, many ideas are rejected. (Of course, those ideas that originate further up the hierarchy may not factor in these costs so more of these ideas seem feasible to their originators.)

More employee ideas would be implemented if supervisors and their managers adopted a "no harm/implement philosophy." This approach assumes all employee ideas are sound and are to be implemented unless a demonstrated harm is shown. Here, the burden is on experienced managers to *use* employee ideas. Of course, ideas that are illegal, impair the quality of work life of others, or have direct costs that exceed benefits are rejected. If management cannot point to specific shortcomings, the idea is implemented. Even when ideas only break even financially, benefits accrue. The employee learns that management genuinely wants ideas. The next time an employee has an idea, it is more likely to be presented to management. Even when ideas are rejected under the no harm/ implement philosophy, the employee is given specific reasons for rejection, not broad platitudes about infeasibility or company policy. Ideas that are rejected for cause are less likely to dam the flow of new ideas than the grilling and disinterest many workers now encounter.

Quality circles help get employee ideas accepted. Not only does management expect ideas as the return on its investment in a quality circles undertaking, but the process assures that ideas are researched and cost/benefit justified. When the process is truly a consensus, decision makers sense the group's commitment to successful implementation. This commitment lessens management's fears of intangible costs such as work disruption and resistance to change. As a result, most companies implement over 80 per cent of quality circle ideas.

For circles to succeed, they must occur in a setting receptive to employee ideas. The receptive setting should precede the implementation of circles. Managers who think a mandated circle effort will automatically change the corporate culture are likely to find quality circles do not work well. If implementation is not accompanied by top management's *active commitment*—rather than mere permission—quality circles are not likely to work at all.

Purpose, Name and Location

What is the purpose of the company's quality circle programme? Is it to improve quality? Productivity? Quality of work life? Profits? Costs? All of these? The answer to these questions will establish a theme and direction for the programme.

No one approach is inherently superior. If the major impediment to organisational success is product quality, worker commitment, costs, or the like, the company's purpose for quality circles is clear. For example, the Japanese recognised that their firms had a poor quality image in the 1950s and 1960s. Circles were started specifically to address product quality. As quality became less of an issue, the theme in many Japanese programmes became costs. Today many Japanese managers view circles as a quality of work life and employee/supervisory development programme.

Nevertheless, the initial theme selected by top management does hold significant implications. At Control Data, for example, quality circles are viewed as a vehicle for quality of work life improvement. As a result of that perspective, Control Data does not maintain detailed records or perform detailed audits of savings that result from team suggestions. Cost savings and quality improvement are by-products of their programme. At Solar Turbines, the focus was quality. Their customers are more concerned with quality and reliability of turbine powered compressors and power generation platforms than cost. As a result, Solar's programme seeks quality improvements and cost reduction; quality of work life improvements are a by-product of their circles.

The purpose of the circle effort carries implications for the name of the programme and its organisational location. At Solar Turbines and in most Japanese companies, for example, the quality circle name is used. Since quality was their primary focus, the term, quality circles, was appropriate. At Control Data, Tektronics, and Union Carbide's Y-12 plant, different themes led to different names: Control Data has *Involvement Teams*; Tektronics has *Tekcircles*; and Union Carbide has *Employee Pride Circles*, which stands for *Productivity through Recognition, Involvement and Development of Employees*. These companies and many others sought to avoid the term quality circles because they did not want the connotation that circles were aimed solely or primarily at quality.

Another implication of the programme's purpose is the reporting relationship for the chief facilitator or administrator. Little agreement has emerged as to whom the circle effort should report. Many programmes are located in the manufacturing hierarchy with the administrator reporting to the plant, divisional, or corporate manufacturing director. Tektronics and Control Data are examples. Plant-wide programmes often report to the plant manager or the steering committee. A few programmes are housed in the human resource department, as is done at the western regional offices of American Express. Although all of these approaches work, they have a common element: Each administrator reports to an executive (or group of executives) with clout. Access to top management indicates their commitment and earns the administrator the attention of middle managers.

Speed, Consultants and Failure

Once committed to the quality circle concept, top management seeks action—often quickly. But, beginning too quickly may spell failure. Quality circles usually represent a change in the culture of the organisation. Changing the corporate culture is analogous to changing an individual's personality: It can be done but only slowly and with great effort. Virtually every successful circle programme has six months to a year of staff work behind it *before* the first group of workers is trained. Time is needed to find and train a facilitator, design training materials, educate the steering committee, and solicit interest from supervisors and workers.

Consultants can help speed up implementation. Many have packages of training material that can be painlessly adapted to the company's needs. They may be able to help recruit, evaluate, and train facilitators. And, they can help top management understand and evaluate the quality circle process. However, the risk is that the programme becomes dependent upon the consultant's availability. It is the "consultant's" programme, not top management's. The presence of the consultant may lull management into a low level of commitment. Many successful programmes at companies like Tektronics, Union Carbide, and American Express used consultants in the planning and design phases. However, these firms and others quickly shift responsibility to in-house staff to make the programme succeed.

Growth and Success

Not only do successful circle approaches require careful planning, they grow slowly. The most common start-up involves two to five circles, usually started at the rate of one per month.

During the planning phase, the facilitator learns which middle managers are likely to be supportive. In conversations with these managers, the facilitator seeks to identify the best first-line supervisors. "Best" is defined as supervisors who have a good rapport with their employees, who are open to employee ideas, and who are participative in their approach to leadership. Also, these supervisors usually are selected from line departments that are already successful. Line departments often are selected because productivity measures are likely to be available. Since the programme starts small and uses line departments, productivity and quality of work life improvements can be compared with groups that were not involved with circles. These comparisons, along with the measured savings from the circles' ideas, give top management data on the effectiveness of the quality circle process.

Once preparations are complete and middle managers advised of the circle process, likely supervisors are identified. These supervisors then are invited to a brief in-house presentation that describes the quality circle concept. Volunteers are sought, since participation is voluntary for all involved. A meeting with these supervisors and their employees is held to explain the concept and seek volunteers among the supervisors' employees. Supervisory and employee training follows—

usually in a one-day, off-site session for employees after the supervisors receive their two days of training.

The pilot circles often operate for three months to a year. If an assessment of the programme is positive, additional circles are usually added at the rate of one or two per month thereafter. Here again, top management's zeal may cause damage. Once favourable results are achieved, top management may seek a very rapid expansion of the quality circle effort. "If a few circles are good, many more circles would be better" seems to be the logic. This logic, however, fails for several reasons. The initial circles were "hand selected." Other circles may not have the same high-quality leadership. Another problem is that existing circles must be serviced. A facilitator does not merely train people, attend the first couple of sessions, and abandon the circle to start more of them. Advice, assistance, information, and other demands are made on the facilitator's time by existing circles. As one facilitator commented, "It is easier to start circles than to service them." When circles are still in their first year, a facilitator can handle about ten of them. After the circles gain a year's experience, the facilitator can seldom assist more than twenty circles.

These mathematics lead to the problem of insufficient facilitators, which serves as a brake on the growth of circles. Most facilitators come from within the organisation since there are few to be found by recruiting. As a result, in-house facilitators must be trained—usually through a process of external training programmes and internal apprenticeships.

Admittedly, some companies have started scores of quality circles within the first year. But companies like Tektronics and Reynolds Metals Company are exceptions. Tektronics added over 250 circles in a little more than a year. But it already had made extensive use of the workplace teams before starting quality circles. Furthermore, the culture of the organisation was receptive to quality circles and experienced facilitators were available. Reynolds' approach to rapid growth relies on decentralisation. A corporate team—after considerable planning— began installing circle programmes on a plant-by-plant basis. The local plant management and facilitators then were responsible for the growth at their site. In Reynolds' case, their strategy was to start multiple circle programmes rather than using a circle-by-circle approach.

Grass Roots Fanfare and Expectations

As with many new programmes, there is an almost irresistible urge for fanfare. The tendency is to have kick-off articles in the company newspaper, mass meetings with speeches from top management, posters, banners, and other hoopla. All this is done in the name of "communicating with the employees."

The problem with fanfare is the expectations it creates among workers. Even a quick expansion of circles throughout the company is unlikely to involve more than a small fraction of the employees during the first year. At Tektronics, for example, less than 3,000 employees were in circles after the first 18 months. Although an impressive number, that still leaves 19,000 employees not in circles.

What happens to the expectations of those not reached by quality circles? If corporate-wide fanfare is used, many (if not most) employees will view circles as another "programme-of-the-month."

Virtually every successful circle effort begins quietly. A small group of supervisors and workers are involved after their middle management people are briefed on it. When other employees see members leave their job for a meeting, curiosity and the grapevine will publicise what is happening. Interest of non-members will be a function of employee comments—a more powerful endorsement than meetings, banners, or speeches would ever generate. However, since the effort is both experimental at first and completely voluntary, the grapevine should produce few anxieties. A supervisor whose employees express interest is more likely to be receptive to circles because employee eagerness is substituted for resistance. In fact, the most common problem with the use of grass roots fanfare is that facilitators often find more interest for new circles than they can accommodate.

Long-Term Viability

Experience in Japan suggests that circles continue in a supportive environment for as long as work place problems exist. Although US firms do not have the length of experience of the Japanese, circles have been in continuous use in some companies for six years.

Besides a drop in management's commitment to circles, several other factors can destroy the on-going success of circles. The most obvious is a lack of employment stability within the circle. High turnover among circle members can ruin the group's cohesion. It matters little whether this turnover is caused by layoffs, transfers, quits, promotion, or reorganisations. Particularly damaging is to replace the supervisor—especially with someone who is not familiar with the circle process. Companies like Control Data try to train supervisors and employees who transfer into a work group whose members are in an active circle.

Another potentially damaging problem is non-joiners. Since circle membership is voluntary, some employees may not join. Most companies train these employees along with those who elect to join so at least non-joiners understand the process. Tektronics goes a step further and posts minutes of the circle meetings in the work area for all to review.

Since circles are usually limited to ten employees, several strategies have been developed when more than that number want to join. If the supervisor has a broad span of control, two circles may be formed with each group working on different problems. When two circles are not used, participants are usually rotated. After each problem is solved, some members are rotated out of the circle to make room for others. Usually half or less of the members are affected in any one rotation in order to provide continuity.

Risk and Failure

Many managers are more comfortable buying a new piece of technology or even acquiring another company than beginning quality circles. Purchases of equipment are subject to detailed analysis with estimatable payoffs. Quality circles—like most other human resource undertakings—are not precisely predictable nor measurable. Even for human resource managers to propose quality circles carries high risks. Success or failure of quality circles is largely outside the control of those who are responsible for their implementation. A distrustful organisational culture, lack of commitment by any level of management, budget cutbacks, or other changes can seal the fate of even a well-conceived circle effort.

Thus, why have so many companies committed themselves to this idea? The answer seems to be in two parts: Competition and benefits. As more and more competitors benefit from innovative approaches to management, laggards risk losing key employees and even their competitive position. Although attributing Japan's success solely to quality circles would be a crass exaggeration, few can doubt that circles have helped them build a productive and committed workforce. Corporate benefits are another consideration since successful quality circles repeatedly yield returns of 200, 300, or even 400 per cent. Few companies face investment opportunities even one-fourth as attractive. And the *major* corporate benefits may come from improved employee commitment to their jobs and productivity in ways that are not measurable as a return on investment.

Even if quality circles fail, what has been lost? Virtually every dollar spent on circles is directed at training people to be better leaders and decision makers. Although dividends from training are difficult to measure, the monies spent on employees are never totally lost.

Moving beyond competition and benefits, one comes to humanitarian considerations. What makes a job enjoyable? For many management and staff people, it is being involved in decisions that matter. It is being where the action is! The people in hourly jobs are no different—in any fundamental way—from top managers. They may lack degrees, experience, mentors, and luck. But, they too seek satisfaction from their jobs. They too seek to be involved in the decisions that directly affect them. Technology and efficiency may dictate repetitive, mundane work. But, to deprive hourly workers of the opportunity to use their creativity, deprives them of job satisfaction and commitment to their employer. From a bottom-line perspective, it deprives the company of the good ideas that employees can offer. Simply put, quality circles offer hourly paid employees a chance to use their creativity—a chance to improve their jobs and the company's productivity.

TOWARD BETTER ORGANISATIONS

Quality circles are not an academic pipe dream. They have worked in Japan for decades and have been successful in the United States for several years. From the experiences of executives, facilitators, and consultants in these organisations, a pattern for success is emerging. Although there is no one best way to make a quality circle effort work, there is growing agreement among these experienced people about the most common problems and pitfalls.

Avoiding the danger points outlined here does not guarantee success; other roadblocks exist that are unique to individual organisations. The biggest danger, however, is a long-standing reluctance to form a partnership between management and workers that allows participation in the decision making process. In the name of efficient decision making and accountability, employee participation is limited. This limitation on involvement creates a more damaging barrier to corporate success: Resistance to change by the very people who produce the company's goods and services.

There is little question that quality circles work. In less than a decade, a sprinkling of leading corporations have begun successful efforts. These pioneers stand as proof of both the feasibility and usefulness of quality circles. Too many of these companies find significant benefits from quality circles to dismiss this idea as either fad or folly. What remains to be seen is whether the widespread use of quality circles in these companies will lead to decisive, competitive advantages. If improvements in quality of work life and productivity yield a significant advantage, those without quality circles may be unable to apply this "people technology" fast enough to catch up. If they launch quality circles on a crash basis, failure is likely because of the need for a radical change in corporate culture. If they wait too long to begin a circle effort, a methodical introduction may be too little, too late. In the final analysis, the major challenge confronting executives in coming years may be the need for organisations that tap the creativity of all their people.

In the long run, the major pitfall may simply be the initial success of quality circles. Many productivity administrators suffer a nagging concern that once a circle effort is established and no longer a novelty, top management will lose interest. As one vice president commented in reference to his company's president, "I wonder if quality circles can survive their own success or economic prosperity?" The verdict is still out. However, if top management's attention begins to focus on summary reports about the number of solutions implemented quarterly or the firm's annual return on its "investment" in quality circles, other levels of management will forget that. Quality circles are primarily a management development programme. Neglect by top management is likely to be an early clue to declining interest by middle and lower level managers. The programme will wane. Task forces will be appointed to revitalise circles and management will be "going in circles with quality circles."

REVIEW QUESTIONS

1 Werther suggests that quality circles are basically a management development program. What does he mean?
2 The author provided a positive overview of quality circles. What possible weaknesses of the idea can you see?
3 Under what conditions are quality circles most likely to be successful? Are Brownell's criteria for effective participation applicable here?

READING 36

The Myths of Industrial Democracy

Richard G. Nehrbass*

Several years ago, when concern over the quality of worklife seemed to be at a higher pitch than today, there was a flurry of public interest in "industrial democracy," especially German-style Mitbestimmung or codetermination.

Today, the public debate has waned, but not the movement to introduce industrial democracy in American firms. In fact, spurred on by misinformation and myths concerning the processes, industrial democracy is stronger than ever and promises to become one of the major areas of concern for management in the decade ahead.

The basics of industrial democracy are already familiar to most American managers. In its most common form it means permitting workers a voice in a firm's policy and decision-making by setting aside a certain number of seats on the board of directors for worker representatives. In its more extended form (in Germany, for instance), it also provides for "works councils": worker-elected boards with varying degrees of influence over day-to-day management decisions (layoffs, work scheduling, promotions, and so forth).

The rationale for all of this, of course, is summed up by the emotive term "democracy." Since we have long recognized the value of democracy in other spheres of our life—to labor unions, politics, school boards, and so forth—why not in the business firm also? The firm will benefit by direct communications with the people who actually do the work and by the new sense of community that will exist between management and labor. And, of course, workers will benefit by finally being able to influence the decisions that affect their lives.

HOW DEMOCRACY HAS FARED

This, at least, is the theory. For years the proponents of industrial democracy have pointed with pride to the concept's birthplace—West Germany in 1951—as an example of what it could accomplish, and there's no denying the country's remarkable economic growth in the past 30 years.

Germany, of course, was only the first country to mandate industrial democracy. In the '60s and '70s the concept spread rapidly—in one form or another—to most of the rest of Europe: Sweden, Denmark, the Netherlands, Luxembourg, Austria, Norway, as well as a number of non-European countries. (Great Britain is currently in a "holding pattern," with a new law proposed but not yet accepted.)

In America, industrial democracy has generally been greeted with suspicion even by labor leaders, most of whom reject the notion that they become involved in management decisions—"a junior partner in success and a senior partner in failure," in the words of Tom Donahue of the AFL-CIO. William Winpisinger of the International Association of Machinists agrees, adding that "you must be on one side or the other," a succinct summation of the traditional labor view that management of the firm is the responsibility and privilege of "management."

CHANGING ATTITUDES

Times change, however, and this traditional union antipathy to a labor-management "partnership" is beginning to weaken as a new generation of labor leaders assumes power. Many of these leaders are looking at industrial democracy with renewed interest. Douglas Fraser and the United Auto Workers, of course, have already shown the way by winning a seat on the boards of Chrysler and American Motors after surprisingly little opposition from the firms involved. Now a number of other labor leaders, government officials and social activists have joined in with demands for greater "democratization" of the workplace or worker representation on boards, or both.

Perhaps the most obvious manifestation of the concept's renewed political attractiveness is the Corporate Democracy Act, backed by Ralph Nader and first introduced in Congress in 1980, and the recent Papal encyclical, *Laborem Exercen*, with its call for greater worker involvement in management. Surprisingly, even a major industry group has endorsed the idea of worker-directors, albeit as an inducement to the work force to reject unionization (a rather dubious notion at best).

But before American firms rush headlong into this fundamental departure from the traditional and decades' old separation of powers, it would be wise to take a close and unemotional look at industrial democracy and the foundation of myths that underpins its acceptability.

THAT OLD MYSTIQUE

No doubt much of the interest in industrial democracy results from the aura of the terms involved. There is something rather sinister, after all, in the notion of Americans opposing "democracy." But how democratic is industrial democracy in practice?

The answer—although it varies by country—is not much. Most laws have been written in such a way that access to company boards is either severely limited for typical workers or totally restricted to union leaders or their designees. The sense of democracy—of equal participation by all constituencies in the governance of the firm—does not exist except as a slogan: it is the union, and not the workers, that comes into the board room. Of course, this same process of restricting board members to the union leadership is being duplicated in this country if the UAW agreements are any indication.

WORKER APATHY

Study after study of industrial democracy in European countries indicates that while most workers claim to support the concept, relatively few are actually sufficiently interested or motivated to become involved in the process. According to Kenneth F. Walker of the European Institute of Business Administration, only an "active minority" takes advantage of the opportunity to participate in their own newly formed councils or vote in elections.[1]

Apathy is so widespread, according to another observer, that many German workers do not even know the names of their representatives on the board.[2] Indeed, most researchers feel that workers are seldom interested in policy-level decisions, but they are vitally interested in the workplace issues (tasks, responsibilities, authority, etc.) not addressed by the concept.

NOT A CURE-ALL

In Germany, where we have three decades of experience to draw upon, it appears that many workers view the entire process with a healthy cynicism or as completely ineffective window dressing. In fact, industrial democracy may actually increase dissatisfaction with management by providing more opportunities for conflict and placing another level of bureaucracy (the works councils) between workers and management.[3]

Access to the boards is, as we have seen, usually restricted to union officials, many of whom haven't been on the shop-floor in years. Even where access is open to all employees, top management contact is limited to contact with a handful of employees, and not necessarily the most knowledgeable.

If management is truly concerned about tapping the vast wealth of knowledge that exists in the workplace, it would be better to provide formal procedures (e.g., quality circles or other participative techniques) in which all interested workers can be involved, rather than the militant and angry few.

THE FUTURE?

Worker participation in the policy decisions of the firm is likely to become the most controversial issue that personnel specialists are going to have to deal with in the '80s. Depsite growing evidence that industrial democracy falls far short of its claims, there is every likelihood that demands for some sort of "democracy" will continue to escalate in this country as well as overseas.

In addition to the expected calls by union leaders and social activists, there has been increased interest in the concept from government officials, academics, religious and even business groups. The personnel professional should tread lightly, however, and make certain that the firm's policy makers understand the ramifications of industrial democracy, and that alternative forms of worker participation can involve far more workers and be much more democratic.

REFERENCES

1 Walker, Kenneth. "Toward the Participatory Enterprise: A European Trend," *The Annals of the Academy of Political and Social Science*, Vol. 431 (May 1977), p. 9.
2 Sturmthal, Adolf F. "Unions and Industrial Democracy," *The Annals of the Academy of Political and Social Science*, Vol. 431 (May 1977), p. 18.
3 Walker, p. 6.

REVIEW QUESTION

1 The author contends that European workers are apathetic toward industrial democracy. What do you predict would be the reaction of American workers toward the practice?

CHAPTER 10

QUALITY OF WORK LIFE

READING 37

Job Enrichment Lessons from AT&T

Robert N. Ford*

There is a mounting problem in the land, the concern of employed persons with their work life. Blue-collar workers are increasingly expressing unhappiness over the monotony of the production line. White-collar workers want to barter less of their life for bread. More professional groups are unionizing to fight back at somebody.

The annual reports of many companies frequently proclaim, "Our employees are our most important resource." Is this a statement of conviction or is it mere rhetoric? If it represents conviction, then I think it is only fair to conclude that many business organizations are unwittingly squandering their resources.

The enormous economic gains that sprang from the thinking of the scientific management school of the early 1900's—the time-and-motion study analysts, the creators of production lines—may have ended insofar as they depend on utilizing human beings more efficiently. Without discarding these older insights, we need to consider more recent evidence showing that the tasks themselves can be changed to give workers a feeling of accomplishment.

The growing pressure for a four-day workweek is not necessarily evidence that people do not care about their work; they may be rejecting their work in the form that confronts them. To ask employees to repeat one small task all day, at higher and higher rates of speed, is no way to reduce the pressure for a shorter work-week, nor is it any longer a key to rising productivity in America. Work need not be so frequently a betrayal of one's education and ability.

From 1965 to 1968 a group of researchers at AT&T conducted 19 formal field experiments in job enrichment. The success of these studies has led to many company projects since then. From this work and the studies of others, we have learned that the "lifesaving" portion of many jobs can be expanded. Conversely, the boring and unchallenging aspects can be reduced—not to say eliminated.

Furthermore, the "nesting" of related, already enriched jobs—a new concept—may constitute another big step toward better utilization of "our most important resource."

First in this article I shall break down the job enrichment strategy into three steps. Then I shall demonstrate what we at AT&T have been doing for seven years in organizing the work beyond enrichment of individual jobs. In the course of my

*From *Harvard Business Review*, January–February, 1973, pp. 96–106. © 1973 by the President and Fellows of Harvard College; all rights reserved. Used with permission.

Author's note: I wish to acknowledge the collaboration of Malcolm B. Gillette of AT&T and Bruce H. Duffany of Drake-Beam & Associates in the formulation of the job enrichment strategy discussed in this article.

discussion, I shall use no illustrations that were not clearly successful from the viewpoint of both employees and the company.

While obviously the functions described in the illustrations differ superficially from those in most other companies, they are still similar enough to production and service tasks in other organizations to permit meaningful comparison. It is important to examine the nature of the work itself, rather than the external aspects of the functions.

Moreover, in considering ways to enrich jobs, I am not talking about those elements that serve only to "maintain" employees: wages, fringe benefits, clean restrooms, a pleasant atmosphere, and so on. Any organization must meet the market in these respects or its employees will go elsewhere.

No, employees are saying more than "treat me well." They are also saying "use me well." The former is the maintenance side of the coin; the latter is the work motivation side.

ANATOMY OF ENRICHMENT

In talking about job enrichment, it is necessary to go beyond such high-level concepts as "self-actualization," "need for achievement," and "psychological growth." It is necessary to specify the steps to be taken. The strategy can be broken down into these aspects—improving work through systematic changes in (a) the module of work, (b) control of the module, and (c) the feedback signaling whether something has been accomplished. I shall discuss each of these aspects in turn.

Work Module

Through changing the work modules, Indiana Bell Telephone Company scored a striking success in job enrichment within the space of two years. In Indianapolis, 33 employees, most of them at the lowest clerical wage level, compiled all telephone directories for the state. The processing from clerk to clerk was laid out in 21 steps, many of which were merely for verification. The steps included manuscript reception, manuscript verification, keypunch, key punch verification, ad copy reception, ad copy verification, and so on—a production line as real as any in Detroit. Each book is issued yearly to the customers named in it, and the printing schedule calls for the appearance of about one different directory per week.

In 1968, the year previous to the start of our study, 28 new hires were required to keep the clerical force at the 33-employee level. Obviously, such turnover had bad consequences. From every operating angle, management was dissatisfied.

In a workshop, the supervisors concluded that the lengthy verification routine, calling for confirmation of one's work by other clerks, was not solving the basic problem, which was employee indifference toward the tasks. Traditional "solutions" were ineffective. They included retraining, supervisor complaints to the employees, and "communicating" with them on the importance to customers of error-free listing of their names and places of business in the directories. As any employee smart enough to be hired knows, an incorrect listing will remain monumentally wrong for a whole year.

The supervisors came up with many ideas for enriching the job. The first step was to identify the most competent employees, and then ask them, one by one, if they felt they could do error-free work, so that having others check the work would be pointless. Would they check their own work if no one else did?

Yes, they said they could do error-free work. With this simple step the module dropped from 21 slices of clerical work to 14.

Next the supervisory family decided to take a really big step. In the case of the thinner books, they asked certain employees whether they would like to "own" their own books and perform all 14 remaining steps with no verification unless they themselves arranged it with other clerks—as good stenographers do when in doubt about a difficult piece of paperwork. Now the module included every step (except keytape, a minor one).

Then the supervisors turned their attention to a thick book, the Indianapolis directory, which requires many hands and heads. They simply assigned letters of the alphabet to individuals and let them complete all 14 steps for each block of letters.

In the past, new entries to all directories had moved from clerk to clerk; now all paperwork connected with an entry belonging to a clerk stayed with that clerk. For example, the clerk prepared the daily addenda and issued them to the information or directory assistance operators. The system became so efficient that most of the clerks who handled the smaller directories had charge of more than one.

Delimiting the Module   In an interview one of the clerks said, "It's a book of my own." That is the way they felt about the books. Although not all modules are physically so distinct, the idea for a good module is usually there. Ideally, it is a slice of work that gives an employee a "thing of my own." At AT&T I have heard good modules described with pride in various ways:

- "A piece of turf" (especially a geographic responsibility).
- "My real estate" (by engineers responsible for a group of central offices).
- "Our cradle-to-grave modem line" (vastly improved Western Electric switching-device production line).
- "Our mission impossible team" (a framemen's team, Long Lines Department).

The trouble with so much work processing is that no one is clearly responsible for a total unit that fails. In Indianapolis, by contrast, when a name in a directory is misspelled or omitted, the clerk knows where the responsibility lies.

Delimiting the module is not usually difficult when the tasks are in production, or at least physically defined. It is more difficult in service tasks, such as handling a telephone call. But modules make sense here, too, if the employee has been prepared for the work so that nobody else need be involved—in other words, when it is not necessary to say to the caller, "Let me connect you with my supervisor about that, please" or "May I give you our billing department please?"

It is not always true that any one employee can handle a complete service. But our studies show that we consistently erred in forming the module; we tended to "underwhelm" employees. Eventually we learned that the worker can do more, especially as his or her experience builds. We do not have even one example from our business where job enrichment resulted in a *smaller* slice of work.

In defining modules that give each employee a natural area of responsibility, we try to accumulate horizontal slices of work until we have created (or recreated) one of these three entities for him or her:

1 A customer (usually someone outside the business).

2 A client (usually someone inside the business, helping the employee serve the customer).

3 A task (in the manufacturing end of the business, for example, where, ideally, individual employees produce complete items).

Any one of these three can make a meaningful slice of work. (In actuality, they are not separated; obviously, an employee can be working on a task for a *customer*.) Modules more difficult to differentiate are those in which the "wholeness" of the job is less clear—that is, control is not complete. They include cases where—

- the employee is merely one of many engaged in providing the ultimate service or item;
- the employee's customer is really the boss (or, worse yet, the boss's boss) who tells him what to do;
- the job is to help someone who tells the employee what is to be done.

While jobs like these are harder to enrich, it is worth trying.

Control of the Module

As an employee gains experience, the supervisor should continue to turn over responsibility until the employee is handling the work completely. The reader may infer that supervisors are treating employees unequally. But it is not so; ultimately, they may all have the complete job if they can handle it. In the directory-compilation case cited—which was a typical assembly-line procedure, although the capital investment was low—the supervisors found that they could safely permit the employee to say when sales of advertisements in the yellow pages must stop if the ads were to reach the printer on time.

Employees of South Central Bell Telephone Company, who set their own cutoff dates for the New Orleans, Monroeville, and Shreveport phone books, consistently gave themselves less time than management had previously allowed. As a result, the sale of space in the yellow pages one year continued for three additional weeks, producing more than $100,000 in extra revenue.

But that was only one element in the total module and its control. The directory clerks talked *directly* to salesmen, to the printer, to supervisors in other departments about production problems, to service representatives, and to each other as the books moved through the production stages.

There are obvious risks on the supervisor's side as they give their jobs away, piece by piece, to selected employees. We have been through it enough to advise, "Don't worry." Be assured that supervisors who try it will say, as many in the Bell System have said, "Now, at last, I feel like a manager. Before I was merely chief clerk around here."

In other studies we have made, control has been handed by the supervisor to a person when the employee is given the authority to perform such tasks as these:

- Set credit ratings for customers.
- Ask for, and determine the size of, a deposit.
- Cut off service for nonpayment.
- Make his or her own budget, subject to negotiation.
- Perform work other than that on the order sheet after negotiating it with the customer.
- Reject a run or supply of material because of poor quality.
- Make free use of small tools or supplies within a budget negotiated with the supervisor.
- Talk to anyone at any organizational level when the employee's work is concerned.
- Call directly and negotiate for outside repairmen or suppliers (within the budget) to remedy a condition handicapping the employee's performance.

Feedback

Definition of the module and control of it are futile unless the results of the employee's effort are discernible. Moreover, knowledge of the results should go directly to where it will nurture motivation—that is, to the employee. People have a great capacity for mid-flight correction when they know where they stand.

One control responsibility given to excellent employees in AT&T studies is self-monitoring; it lets them record their own "qualities and quantities." For example, one employee who had only a grade-school education was taught to keep a quality control chart in which the two identical parts of a dry-reed switch were not to vary more that .005 from an ideal dimension. She found that for some reason too many switches were failing.

She proved that the trouble occurred when one reed that was off by .005 met another reed that was off by .005. The sum, .010, was too much in the combined component and it failed. On her own initiative, she recommended and saw to it that the machine dies were changed when the reeds being stamped out started to vary by .003 from the ideal. A total variance of .006 would not be too much, she reasoned. Thus the feedback she got showed her she was doing well at her job.

This example shows all three factors at work—the module, its control, and feedback. She and two men, a die maker and a machine operator had the complete responsibility for producing each day more than 100,000 of these tiny parts, which are not unlike two paper matches, but much smaller. How can one make a life out of this? Well, they did. The six stamping machines and expensive photometric test equipment were "theirs." A forklift truck had been dedicated to them (no waiting for someone else to bring or remove supplies). They ordered rolls of wire for stamping machines when they estimated they would need it. They would ship a roll back when they had difficulty controlling it.

Compared with workers at a plant organized along traditional lines, with batches of the reeds moving from shop to shop, these three employees were producing at a fourfold rate. Such a minigroup, where each person plays a complementary part, is radically different psychologically from the traditional group of workers, where each is doing what the others do.

(In the future, when now undreamed-of computer capacities have been reached, management must improve its techniques of feeding performance results directly to the employee responsible. And preferably it should be done *before* the boss knows about it.)

IMPROVING THE SYSTEM

When a certain job in the Bell System is being enriched, we ask the supervisory family, "Who or what is the customer/client/task in this job?" Also, "How often can the module be improved?" And then, "How often can control or feedback be improved? Can we improve all three at once?"

These are good questions to ask in general. My comments at this stage of our knowledge must be impressionistic.

The modules of most jobs can be improved, we have concluded. Responsibilities or tasks that exist elsewhere in the shop or in some other shop or department need to be combined with the job under review. This horizontal loading is necessary until the base of the job is right. However, I have not yet seen a job whose base was too broad.

At levels higher than entrance grade, and especially in management positions, many responsibilities can be moved to lower grade levels, usually to the advantage of every job involved. This vertical loading is especially important in mature organizations.

In the Indianapolis directory office, 21 piecemeal tasks were combined into a single, meaningful, natural task. There are counterparts in other industries, such as the assembly of an entire dashboard of an automobile by two workers.

We have evidence that two jobs—such as the telephone installer's job and the telephone repairman's job—often can make one excellent "combinationman's" job. But there are some jobs in which the work module is already a good one. One of these is the service respresentative, the highly trained clerk to whom a customer speaks when he wants to have a telephone installed, moved, or disconnected, or when he questions his telephone bill. This is sometimes a high-turnover job, and when a service representative quits because of work or task dissatisfaction, there goes $3,450 in training. In fact, much of the impetus for job enrichment came through efforts to reduce these costs.

In this instance the slice of work was well enough conceived; nevertheless, we obtained excellent results from the procedures of job enrichment. Improvements in the turnover situation were as great as 50%. Why? Because we could improve the control and feedback.

It should be recognized that moving the work module to a lower level is not the same as moving the control down. If the supervisor decides that a customer's account is too long overdue and tells the service representative what to do, then both the module and the control rest with the supervisor. When, under job enrichment procedures, the service repesentative makes the decision that a customer must be contacted, but checks it first with the supervisor, control remains in the supervisor's hands. Under full job enrichment, however, the service representative has control.

Exhibit I shows in schematic form the steps to be taken when improving a job. To increase control, responsibility must be obtained from higher levels; I have yet to see an instance where control is moved upward to enrich a job. It must be acknowledged, however, that not every employee is ready to handle more control. That is especially true of new employees.

Moreover, changing the control of a job is more threatening to supervisors than is changing the module. In rejecting a job enrichment proposal, one department head said to us, "When you have this thing proved 100%, let me know and we'll try it."

As far as feedback is concerned, it is usually improvable, but not until the module and control of it are in top condition. If the supervisory family cannot come up with good ways for telling the employee how he or she is doing, the problem lies almost surely in a bad module. That is, the employee's work is submerged in a total unit and he or she has no distinct customer/client/task.

EXHIBIT I
Steps in improving a job.

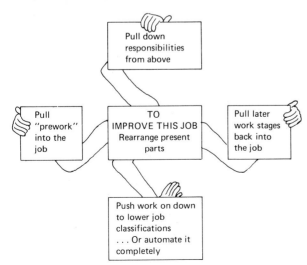

When the module is right, you get feedback "for free"; it comes directly from the customer/client/task. During the learning period, however, the supervisor or teacher should provide the feedback.

When supervisors use the performance of all employees as a goad to individual employees, they thwart the internalization of motivation that job enrichment strives for. An exception is the small group of mutually supporting, complementary workers, but even in this case each individual needs knowledge of his or her own results.

These generalizations cannot be said to be based on an unbiased sample of all jobs in all locations. Usually, the study or project locations were not in deep trouble, nor were they the best operating units. The units in deep trouble cannot stand still long enough to figure out what is wrong, and the top performers need no help. Therefore, the hard-nosed, scientifically trained manager can rightfully say that the jury is still out as to whether job enrichment can help in all work situations. But it has helped repeatedly and consistently on many jobs in the Bell System.

JOB 'NESTING'

Having established to its satisfaction that job enrichment works, management at AT&T is studying ways to go beyond the enriching of individual jobs. A technique that offers great promise is that of "nesting" several jobs to improve morale and upgrade performance.

By way of illustration I shall describe how a family of supervisors of service representatives in a unit of Southwestern Bell Telephone Company improved its service indexes, productivity, collection of overdue bills, and virtually every other index of performance. In two years they moved their Ferguson District (adjacent to St. Louis) from near the bottom to near the top in results among all districts in the St. Louis area.

Before the job enrichment effort started, the service representatives' office was laid out as it appears in *Exhibit II*. The exhibit shows their desks in the standard, in-line arrangement fronted by the desks of their supervisors, who exercised close control of the employees.

As part of the total job enrichment effort, each service rep group was given a geographical locality of its own, with a set of customers to take care of, rather than just "the next customer who calls in" from anywhere in the district. Some service reps—most of them more experienced—were detached to form a unit handling only the businesses in the district.

Then the service representatives and their business office supervisors (BOS) were moved to form a "wagon train" layout. As *Exhibit III* shows, they were gathered into a more-or-less circular shape and were no longer directly facing the desks of the business office supervisors and unit managers. (The office of the district manager was further removed too.)

Now all was going well with the service representatives' job, but another function in the room was in trouble. This was the entry-level job of service order

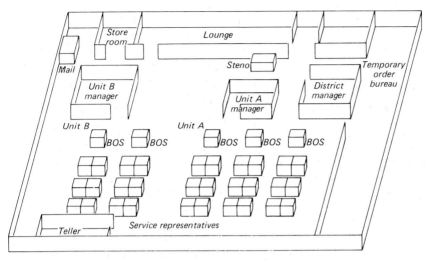

BOS — Business office supervisor

EXHIBIT II
Ferguson District service representatives' office layout before job enrichment.

EXHIBIT III
Service representatives' office layout after job enrichment program was implemented.

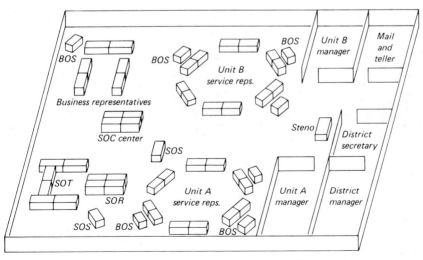

SOS — Service order supervisor
SOC — Service order control
SOR — Service order reviewers
SOT — Service order typists

typist. These typists transmit the order to the telephone installers and the billing and other departments. They and the service order reviewers—a higher-classification job—had been located previously in a separate room that was sound-proofed and air-conditioned because the TWX machines they used were noisy and hot. When its equipment was converted to the silent, computer-operated cathode ray tubes (CRTs), the unit was moved to a corner of the service reps' room (see *Exhibit III*).

But six of the eight typists quit in a matter of months after the move. Meanwhile, the percentage of service orders typed "on time" fell below 50%, then below 40%.

The reasons given by the six typists who quit were varied, but all appeared to be rationalizations. The managers who looked at the situation, and at the $25,000 investment in the layout, could see that the feeling of physical isolation and the feeling of having no "thing" of their own were doubtless the real prime factors. As the arrangement existed, any service order typist could be called on to type an order for any service representative. On its face, this seems logical; but we have learned that an employee who belongs to everybody belongs to nobody.

An instantly acceptable idea was broached: assign certain typists to each service rep team serving a locality. "And while we're at it," someone said, "why not move the CRTs right into the group? Let's have a wagon train with the women and kids in the middle." This was done (over the protest of the budget control officer, I should add).

The new layout appears in *Exhibit IV*. Three persons are located in the station in the middle of each unit. The distinction between service order typist and service

EXHIBIT IV
Office layout after service order typists were "nested."

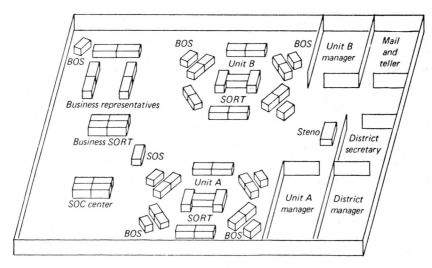

SORT — Service order review and typing

order reviewer has been abolished, with the former upgraded to the scale of the latter. (Lack of space has precluded arranging the business customer unit in the same wagon-train fashion. But that unit's service order review and typing desks are close to the representatives' desks.)

Before the changes were started, processing a service request involved ten steps—and sometimes as many persons—not counting implementation of the order in the Plant Department. Now the procedure is thought of in terms of people, and only three touch a service order on its way through the office. (See *Exhibit V*.) At this writing, the Ferguson managers hope to eliminate even the service order completion clerk as a specialized position.

Has the new arrangement worked? Just before the typists moved into the wagon train, they were issuing only 27% of the orders on time. Half a year later, in one particular month, the figure even reached 100%.

These results were obtained with a 21% jump in work load—comparing a typical quarter after "nesting" with one before—being performed with a net drop of 22 worker-weeks during the quarter. On a yearly basis it is entirely reasonable to expect the elimination of 88 weeks of unnecessary work (conservatively, 1½ full-time employees). Unneeded messenger service has been dispensed with, and one of two service order supervisor positions has been eliminated. The entire cost has been recovered already.

The service order accuracy measurement, so important in computerization, has already attained the stringent objectives set by the employees themselves, which exceeded the level supervisors would have set. Why are there fewer errors? Because now employees can lean across the area and talk to each other about a service order with a problem or handwriting that is unclear. During the course of a year this will probably eliminate the hand preparation of a thousand "query" slips, with a thousand written replies, in this one district.

EXHIBIT V
Old and new processing procedures in request for service department.

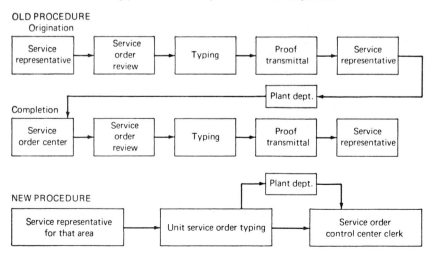

OLD PROCEDURE

Origination

Service representative → Service order review → Typing → Proof transmittal → Service representative → Plant dept.

Completion

Service order center → Service order review → Typing → Proof transmittal → Service representative → Plant dept.

NEW PROCEDURE

Service representative for that area → Unit service order typing → Plant dept. → Service order control center clerk

And what of the human situation? When on-time order issuance was at its ebb, a supervisor suggested having a picnic for the service representatives and the typists. They did, but not a single typist showed up. Later, when the on-time order rate had climbed over 90%, I remarked, "Now's the time for another picnic." To which the supervisor replied facetiously, "Now we don't need a picnic!"

The turnover among typists for job reasons has virtually ceased. Some are asking now for the job of service representative, which is more demanding, more skilled, and better paid. Now, when the CRTs or the computer is shut down for some reason, or if the service order typist runs out of work, supervisors report that typists voluntarily help the service reps with filing and other matters. They are soaking up information about the higher-rated jobs. These occurrences did not happen when the typists were 100 feet away; then they just sat doing nothing when the work flow ceased. (Because of this two-way flow of information, incidentally, training time for the job of service representative may drop as much as 50%.)

As the state general manager remarked when the results were first reported, "This is a fantastic performance. It's not enough to enrich just one job in a situation. We must learn how to put them together."

Different Configuration

While the Ferguson District supervisory family was making a minigroup out of the service reps and their CRT typists, a strikingly different minigroup was in formation in the Northern Virginia Area of the Chesapeake and Potomac Telephone Company. There the family hit on the idea of funneling to selected order typists only those orders connected with a given central office, such as the Lewinsville frame. Soon the typists and the framemen—those who actually make the changes as a result of service orders—became acquainted. The typists even visited "their" framerooms. Now some questions could be quickly resolved that previously called for formal interdepartmental interrogations through supervisors.

At the end of the first eight months of 1972, these 9 CRT typists were producing service order pages at a rate one third higher than the 51 service order typists in the comparison group. The absence rate in the experimental unit was 0.6%, compared with 2.5% for the others, and the errors per 100 orders amounted to 2.0 as against 4.6 in the comparison group.

The flow of service orders is from (a) service rep to (b) service order typist to (c) the frameroom. The Ferguson District enjoyed success when it linked (a) and (b), while productivity for the Lewinsville frame improved when (b) and (c) were linked. Obviously, the next step is to link (a), (b), and (c). We are now selecting trial locations to test this larger nesting approach.

LESSONS LEARNED

In summary fashion, at the end of seven years of effort to improve the work itself, it is fair to say:

• Enriching existing jobs pays off. To give an extreme example, consider the fact that Illinois Bell Telephone Company's directory compilation effort reduced the work force from 120 persons to 74. Enriching the job started a series of moves; it was not the only ingredient, but it was the precipitating one.

• Job enrichment requires a big change in managerial style. It calls for increasing modules, moving control downward, and dreaming up new feedback ideas. There is nothing easy about a successful job enrichment effort.

• The nesting or configuring of related tasks—we call it "work organization" —may be the next big step forward after the enrichment of single jobs in the proper utilization of human beings.

It seems to produce a multiplier effect rather than merely a simple sum. In the Ferguson District case the job modules were not changed; the service representatives were not asked to type their own orders on the cathode ray tubes, nor were the typists asked to take over the duties of the service representatives. The results came from enriching other aspects (control and feedback) and, more important, from laying out the work area differently to facilitate interaction among responsible people.

• While continuing job enrichment efforts, it is important not to neglect "maintenance" factors. In extending our work with job nesting, for example, we plan to experiment with "office landscaping," so called. The furniture, dividers, planters, and acoustical treatment, all must add to the feeling of work dedication. By this I mean we will dedicate site, equipment, and jobs to the employees, with the expectation that they will find it easier to dedicate themselves to customer/client/task. Especially in new installations, this total work environmental approach seems a good idea for experimentation. We will not be doing it merely to offset pain or boredom in work. The aim is to facilitate work.

• A "pool" of employees with one job (typing pool, reproduction pool, calculating pool and so on) is at the opposite extreme from the team or "minigroup" which I have described. A minigroup is a set of mutually supporting employees, each of whom has a meaningful module or part in meeting the needs of customer/client/task. What is "meaningful" is, like a love affair, in the eye of the beholder; at this stage, we have difficulty in describing it further.

A minigroup can have several service representatives or typists; one of each is not basic to the idea. The purpose is to set up a group of employees so that a natural, mutual dependence can grow in providing a service or finishing a task. It marks the end of processing from person to person or group to group, in separate locations of departments and with many different supervisors.

The minigroup concept, however, still leaves room for specialists. In certain Scandinavian auto plants, for example, one or two specialists fabricate the entire assembly of the exhaust pollution control system or the electrical system. Eventually, a group of workers may turn out a whole engine. In the United States, Chrysler has given similar trial efforts a high priority. The idea is to fix authority at the lowest level possible.

• Experience to date indicates that unions welcome the kind of effort described in our studies. Trouble can be expected, of course, if the economics of increases in productivity are not shared equitably. In the majority of cases, the economics can be handled even under existing contracts, since they usually permit establishment of new jobs and appropriate wage grades between dates of contract negotiation.

An employee who takes the entire responsibility for preparing a whole telephone directory, for example, ought to be paid more, although a new clerical rating must be established. Job enrichment is not in lieu of cash; good jobs and good maintenance are two sides of the same coin.

• New technology, such as the cathode ray tube, should enable us to break free of old work arrangements. When the Ferguson District service order typists were using the TWX machines, nesting their jobs was impractical because the equipment would have driven everybody to distraction. Installation of the high-technology CRTs gave the planners the opportunity to move together those employees whose modules of work were naturally related. This opportunity was at first overlooked.

Everyone accepts the obvious notion that new technology can and must eliminate dumb-dumb jobs. However, it probably creates more, rather than fewer, fragments of work. Managers should observe the new module and the work organization of the modules. This effort calls for new knowledge and skills, such as laying out work so attractively that the average employee will stay longer and work more effectively than under the previous arrangement.

Moreover, technology tends to make human beings adjuncts of machines. As we move toward computerized production of all listings in the white pages of the phone books, for example, the risk of an employee's losing "his" or "her" own directories is very great indeed. (Two AT&T companies, South Central Bell and Pacific Northwest Bell, are at this stage, and we must be certain the planned changes do not undermine jobs.) Making sure that machines remain the adjunct of human beings is a frontier problem which few managers have yet grappled with.

• Managers in mature organizations are likely to have difficulty convincing another department to make pilot runs of any new kind of work organization, especially one that will cause the department to lose people, budget, or size. Individual job enrichment does not often get into interdepartmental tangles, but the nesting of jobs will almost surely create problems of autonomy. This will call for real leadership.

• When the work is right, employee attitudes are right. That is the job enrichment strategy—get the work right.

REVIEW QUESTIONS

1 What is job enrichment? Why does it work?
2 Would you prefer to work on an enriched job or a simple task? Explain.
3 Why do you think that some employees might resist having their jobs enriched?

READING 38

Quality of Work Life: Perspectives and Directions

David A. Nadler
Edward E. Lawler, III*

More than a decade has passed since the phrase "quality of work life" (QWL) was first introduced. During this period, QWL has been the subject of many academic papers, experiments in different settings and, recently, increased interest among managers and the popular press. At the same time, we have witnessed increasing confusion about what QWL means and what its implications for action are. It now appears that QWL may become another victim of the managerial fadism syndrome that strikes down so many workplace innovations; this year's innovation quickly becomes passé as it ceases to be new and loses the attention of the press and of managers who have been told to use it. We feel it would be a major mistake to repeat this pattern with QWL because its demise could result in the loss of important concepts and valid approaches.

One antidote to fadism, in this case, would be a clear assessment and definition of QWL—that is, a sober realization of what it is, what can be done, what can be expected, and under what conditions one might truly expect QWL efforts to succeed. This article attempts to provide such a perspective. We will discuss the origins of QWL as a concern, as well as its various definitions. We will provide our own working definition of QWL, with the goal of focusing the discussion. Then we will raise certain issues and concerns about the current state of the art and, finally, discuss factors that our research indicates predict the success of QWL projects.

ORIGINS OF THE QWL MOVEMENT

Over the past 10 to 15 years, two distinct phases of QWL activity stand out. The original one occurred during the period 1969 to 1974, when a broad group of researchers, scholars, union leaders, and government figures became interested in how to influence the quality of an individual's on-the-job experiences. There are several reasons why this concern emerged at that time. In the larger, generally affluent U.S. society, there were growing concerns about the effects of employment on the health and well-being of employees and about job satisfaction. And we were also hearing about a number of European innovations with autonomous work groups.

A series of national attitude surveys conducted at the University of Michigan in

*Reprinted by permission of the publisher from "Quality of Work Life: Perspectives and Directions," by David A. Nadler and Edward E. Lawler, III, in *Organizational Dynamics*, Winter 1983. © 1983 by AMACOM, a division of American Management Associations, pp. 20–30. All rights reserved.

1969 and 1973 helped draw attention to what was called "the quality of employ-ment," or the sum total of the effects of job experiences on the individual. The Department of Health, Education, and Welfare sponsored an investigation of this issue that resulted in the widely publicized book *Work in America* (MIT Press, 1973). At the same time, the pressures of inflation prompted the government to address some of the same issues. It created a federal productivity commission, which in turn sponsored a series of labor-management QWL experiments that were jointly managed by the University of Michigan Quality of Work Program and the newly formed National Quality of Work Center.

This initial excitement and activity continued through the mid-1970s and then experienced a lull during the late 1970s as other issues, primarily inflation and energy costs, diverted national attention. Starting in 1979 and continuing to this day, a second cycle of interest in QWL emerged. What created this interest? The most important factor was probably international competition. The United States faced increasing competition in international markets—and in domestic ones from foreign-made goods. Previously, it had been easy to dismiss these foreign goods as the product of government subsidies or low-cost labor. But we began to recognize that perhaps other countries were doing something different manage-rially that might have something to do with their effectiveness. The Japanese stand out as the prime example of this phenomenon.

We became fascinated with the notion of alternative management styles and the prospect that other countries had developed management (once viewed as a U.S. preserve) to a higher level. At the same time, many quality of work life projects that were started during the early 1970s had matured and begun to bear fruit. In particular, certain high-visibility initiatives, such as those by General Motors, began to catch the public eye. Coinciding with the increasing national concern over productivity as a major issue, these initiatives produced a critical mass of QWL projects in the United States. Therefore, by the early 1980s quality of work life had once again become a major concern, and people were trying to understand exactly what it was and how they might use its concepts to improve their organizations.

THE MANY FACES OF QWL

It would be an understatement to say that there has been, and continues to be, confusion about what the term *quality of work life* means. It has been used to refer to a wide range of concerns and projects, and it has been defined differently by its most articulate champions. Indeed, some of its staying power may be chalked up to its ambiguity because it can be, and has been, redefined as times have changed and as different people have used it. One way of thinking about this term and the movement is to review the definitions that have evolved during the last 10 to 15 years; what we see is six potential definitions of QWL.

The first definition that emerged during the period 1959 to 1972 was *QWL as a variable*. In the original discussions, conferences, and studies, many of us working in this area saw quality of work life as an individual's reaction to work or the personal consequences of the work experience. So we talked about an individual's quality of work life or how to improve QWL for an individual. What was unique at that time about the QWL perspective was that it focused on such individual outcomes as job satisfaction or mental health, with an emphasis on the impact of the work on the individual and with the suggestion that organizations should be evaluated on the quality of work life they provide for individuals.

During the period 1969 to 1974, a number of projects were initiated with the primary aim of getting labor and management to work collaboratively to improve the quality of work life. These included the General Motors/United Automobile Workers (UAW) project at Tarrytown and the Harmon Industries/UAW project at Bolivar, Tennessee. Because of these projects and their subsequent publicity, the term *quality of work life* became synonymous with certain approaches. Thus a second definition, *QWL as an approach*, emerged. As in the earlier definition, the focus was on the individual rather than organizational outcomes, but at the same time QWL tended to be seen as meaning joint labor-management cooperative projects, particularly those aimed at improving outcomes for both the individual and the organization.

During the same period another definition emerged, stemming from some nonunion experiments that were using different innovations. In particular, the highly publicized project in the Topeka General Foods plant and similar projects in Procter and Gamble drew attention to specific ways of changing the workplace and its impact on individuals. These projects led to the third definition, *QWL as methods*. People using this definition talked of QWL as a set of methods, approaches, or technologies for enhancing the work environment and making it both more productive and more satisfying. In fact QWL was seen as being synonymous with such concepts as autonomous work groups, job enrichment, or the design of new plants as integrated social and technical systems.

As we have mentioned before, the late 1970s was a period during which QWL activity decreased. Many of us felt that interest in the subject had waned with the onslaught of economic problems and the energy problem. During this time, a number of people were concerned about maintaining the momentum that had been created, and they decided to identify a coalition of interests that would support the continuation of QWL activities. Meetings were held among people doing experiments to identify that broad coalition of people or groups who might be interested in continuing QWL projects. Organizations were formed to further the ideology of QWL. Out of these activities emerged the fourth definition, *QWL as a movement*.

QWL was seen as more of an ideological statement about the nature of work and the worker's relationship to the organization. The terms *participative management* and *industrial democracy* were frequently invoked as ideals of the QWL movement. In particular, effort was spent differentiating QWL from other approaches to organization development. The development of QWL as a movement, in retrospect, may have caused some division between those who use the QWL label and those who might have used other labels to describe their work to enhance an organization's health and effectiveness. A certain amount of stereotyping is at work here: With movements, all too often one is either part of them or "against" them; there are no other possibilities.

As we mentioned before, the late 1970s and early 1980s brought renewed interest in QWL. It was during this time that the fifth definition appeared. This definition is best described by the following scenario, which is based upon what we have witnessed in several large companies:

The chairman of the board of a large company is an enlightened and thoughtful individual concerned about the future of his organization. He attends some seminars or talks with some people at a cocktail party, or has a discussion with a consultant, and becomes aware of this thing called QWL. He may read about experiments at a particular company or about some things that were done overseas. Coincident with this, internal surveys in his own organization indicate that people are feeling less satisfied with their work, more uncertain about the future, and more alienated from management and the ideals of the company.

So the chairman decides that there is a need to improve QWL; he sends out memos or makes speeches discussing this concern. While everyone agrees, no one is sure exactly what it means, and typically there is some passive resistance from senior management, who are uncertain about this new development. Finally, the chairman decides that the firm will have a QWL program and sends out instructions to implement one or puts QWL into the objectives of senior management. Senior managers turn to managers in the next level down and say, "We need some QWL." In turn, those folks turn to their subordinates and convey the same message, until a human resources manager is told by his operating manager, "We need QWL. They're very interested in it upstairs. Get me some."

Faced with this situation, the human resources manager has several choices. One is to go out and buy some. (Indeed, there are an array of vendors willing to sell "QWL packages"—witness the current quality circle fad.) Another approach is for the human resources manager to survey the various activities that are going on, including organization development work, internal consulting, organizational effectiveness, and so forth, and then go back to his supervisor and say, "Boss, we already got some. We just didn't know we had it."

Out of this emerges the fifth definition, *QWL equals everything*.

In this scenario, all organization development or organizational effectiveness efforts become labeled as part and parcel of QWL. QWL is seen as a global concept and is frequently perceived as a panacea for coping with foreign competition, grievance problems quality problems low-productivity rates, and just about everything else. Clearly, the problem with this definition is that no innovation can deliver on all of these promises. In addition, this expansion of the QWL definition takes the concept to the point where managers become very concerned and confused about "what it is."

Because of the expectations being created by the QWL-equals-everything definition, a possible sixth definition may appear in the near future: *QWL equals nothing*. We are concerned that the inevitable failure of some QWL projects (to be expected in any innovation) and QWL's inability to deliver on some of the promises made will make the skeptics who went along with it only grudgingly turn against the concept. Finally, we will find that in many organizations the phrase *QWL* will become a forbidden term, along with *job enrichment, MBO,* and *organization development*. Our view is that it would be a real loss if this happened because the important substance of many QWL efforts might be lost in such a period of disillusionment.

Figure 1 summarizes the definitions of quality of working life presented so far. We will focus further on the issue of defining QWL after briefly highlighting our concerns with the current state of QWL practice and theory.

ISSUES AND CONCERNS

Our major concerns focus on how the concept of quality of work life has evolved and the state of its application today. The issues that concern us include the vagueness of the concept, fadism/religious experience vs. scientific/pragmatic perspective, the focus on low-level employees, naïve views of causes of individual behavior, naïve views of organizational behavior, and quality of work life and productivity.

• *Vagueness of the concept*. QWL has not been firmly and clearly defined. In fact, some proponents of QWL have talked explicitly about not developing specific definitions. We believe this has led to continued misunderstanding and puzzlement on the part of many managers, and it is no surprise that concern over the fuzziness of the concept has hindered its implementation and development.

• *Fadism/religiosity vs. science*. Many of those who have discussed or advocated QWL refer to it as a cure-all, as something that will work wonders as if by some mystical process. In the extreme, it's viewed as some sort of religious/sexual experience—that is, when you've got it, or when you've had it, you'll know what it

FIGURE 1
DEFINITIONS OF QUALITY OF WORKING LIFE

First Definition: QWL = Variable
(1969–1972)

Second Definition: QWL = Approach
(1969–1975)

Third Definition: QWL = Methods
(1972–1975)

Fourth Definition: QWL = Movement
(1975–1980)

Fifth Definition: QWL = Everything
(1979–1982)

Sixth Definition: QWL = Nothing

is. This contrasts with the scientific or pragmatic perspective that describes QWL as a couple of concepts and tools that might be useful and that might work in certain situations. Again, the problem is that ideologists alienate those who haven't bought into the ideological content of the definition, which, they feel, can create unreasonable expectations.

• *Focus on low-level employees.* Much QWL emphasis has been on first-level or line-operative employees. QWL has been described as something the top tells the middle to do to the bottom in organizations. This creates problems in two ways: First, employees at the bottom are frequently being asked to do things that the top is unwilling to do; specifically, to use participative decision making. This inconsistency or "Do what I say, not what I do" approach clearly has some inherent drawbacks. Middle managers or technical personnel have just as severe QWL problems as those of line-operative employees. To assume that only the person on the assembly line is concerned with QWL ignores other large groups of people who are entitled to the same level of consideration.

• *Naïve views of individual behavior.* Recently, those who have talked about QWL in some organizations have proposed that it will lead to greater effectiveness because it will make workers "happy"—and that, being more satisfied, they will produce more. Research on organizations has demonstrated consistently for the last 25 years that satisfaction does not necessarily lead to higher levels of performance although it may lead to decreases in turnover and absences. Again, the expectation that happy workers will be productive workers is misleading and therefore may be setting up unreasonable expectations.

• *Naïve views of organizational behavior.* A good many of those experts who have proposed QWL activities have described a process whereby pilot projects may be run and good ideas, having seen the light of day, will naturally spread throughout the organization and be institutionalized or made permanent. They also assume that projects at the lowest levels will succeed even if the environment within the larger organization is unfavorable to them. What we know about the systemic nature of organizations leads us to be very skeptical about the degree of potential for highly participative processes that are instituted at low organizational levels in authoritarian top-down organizations. The lessons of the job-enrichment movement in the late 1960s showed this again and again. Similarly, to expect that pilot projects will somehow spread throughout the organization ignores the reality that, in general, pilot projects tend to be encapsulated and do not get disseminated even when they are successful.

• *Quality of work life and productivity.* The actual relationship between quality of work life efforts and productivity is often ignored. Some assume that QWL activities will inevitably lead to increased productivity. In many cases, this is simply not true. Such activities may lead to higher levels of commitment, lower levels of turnover, and higher quality, but not necessarily to higher productivity. The important thing to keep in mind is that QWL and such individual outcomes as satisfaction and productivity can be addressed by some of the same kinds of actions, but they aren't in a direct cause-and-effect relationship. Careful analysis of each activity is needed to determine what effect it is likely to have. It is naïve to assume that merely doing something related to QWL will lead to higher productivity.

In summary, we have major concerns about QWL. If we were totally skeptical about the concept, we could end this article here with a warning to all to beware of QWL. However, we are not universally skeptical and we prefer to see a realistic discussion and pragmatic application of QWL concepts. We will, therefore, try to provide a working definition of the concept and share some of our observations on what conditions may lead to successful QWL activities.

A WORKING DEFINITION

We will begin by providing what we think is a concise working definition—that is, quality of work life is a way of thinking about people, work, and organzations. Its distinctive elements are (1) a concern about the impact of work on people as well as on organizational effectiveness, and (2) the idea of participation in organizational problem solving and decision making.

It is important to reflect on this definition. Specifically, there are two things that are important to keep in mind. First, the focus of QWL efforts is not only on how people can do work better, but on how work may cause people to do better. It is a concern that is different from other productivity or organizational enhancement efforts because of its focus on the outcomes for the individual. Second, a major distinctive aspect of QWL is participation in the process of making major organizational decisions, as differentiated from full "participative management." We are not saying that all decisions are made in a participative manner, but rather that people are involved in the process of making some important organizational decisions that affect them.

Another way of defining QWL is operationally, by illustrating some activities that one might perceive as representative of QWL efforts. While these include a broad range of activities, a few stand out. First is the idea of participative problem solving, involving organizational members at various levels. This may come about in many different ways—for example, in quality circles, which involve people at the work-group level in understanding, analyzing, and solving problems. Also, there are various participative organizational diagnosis designs and different types of labor-management cooperative problem-solving groups.

A second concern of QWL activity is restructuring the basic nature of the work that individuals do, and the work systems that surround them, to make those working arrangements more consistent with individual needs and with the social structures in the work setting. Work restructuring may include such things as job enrichment, the use of autonomous work groups, or the design of complete technical systems and sets of jobs and procedures—particularly in the development of new high-involvement plants.

A third type of activity involves rewards. We have long known that rewards are a major determinant of motivation, effort, and performance. In a number of experiments, the emphasis has been on creating innovative reward systems that will promote a different climate in the organization. Major examples of these are variations of the Scanlon plan, which divide the benefits of cost-saving innovations among workers.

A fourth type of activity involves improvements in the work environment. The emphasis here is on physical work and tangible conditions surrounding the individual. This may include changes in working hours, conditions, rules, or the physical environment. These changes, while visible and important in themselves, are typically limited in their impact, unless they occur in combination with other kinds of activities.

Thus the types of QWL activities can be listed as follows:

1 Participative problem solving.
2 Work restructuring.
3 Innovative rewards systems.
4 Improving the work environment.

This list is not intended to be inclusive, but it provides some idea of specific activities that fit our definition of QWL, and in our opinion, describe the vast majority of activities that are called QWL.

FACTORS THAT PREDICT SUCCESS

Having defined QWL, we turn next to determining which factors predict why some quality-of-work-life efforts are more successful than others. We will draw on several sources of experience and research with which we have been involved.

In recent years, we have observed, researched, and been involved with a variety of QWL projects that included union-management QWL projects, new high-involvement plants, gainsharing programs, work-redesign efforts, and problem-solving group programs. Our work on these has led us to identify six factors that predict success in QWL projects. These are as follows:

1 Perception of need.
2 Problem focus that is salient to organization.
3 Structure for problem identification and solving: theory/model-process-training and participants.
4 Rewards designed both for processes and for outcome.
5 Multiple systems affected.
6 Organization-wide involvement.

The first is a perception of need. QWL projects seem to succeed when all involved parties truly perceive that there is a problem or opportunity. This need may arise from a variety of factors, such as financial pressures or competitive issues. When there is no perception of need—when QWL is initiated purely through the instigation of an outside consultant, a messianic manager, or a fad-inspired executive—projects are unlikely to be successful.

Second, the need has to be one that is salient to the organization. QWL projects are more likely to succeed when the various parties are willing to make a significant commitment in terms of resources, consultative help, time, and effort. Obviously, this is more likely when QWL activities are perceived to be aimed at issues that are critical to the fundamental competitive issues of the organization, rather than at issues that are perceived as peripheral or of primarily cosmetic value.

Probably the most critical factor determining the success, viability, and long-term impact of QWL efforts is the structure of the participative processes that are created. Again, there are several key factors: The first is the need for an underlying theory or roadmap to help participants examine and understand issues. This roadmap might be a general diagnostic model of organizations, a model for looking at quality, or a model for considering the design of work. The specific model is not critical. The point is that it is crucial to have some underlying theory for the participants to use in dealing and looking at the issues that they will consider.

Second, it is important to have a process structured for problem solving—that is, a series of steps with appropriate kinds of support, tools, and instruments. To assume that people will be able to solve new problems, in new settings, in new relationships in a completely new and unstructured way, is simply naïve. Those places that have been most successful have provided participants with an orderly and systematic process for working on problems. This avoids putting them in the situation where new unstructured problems have to be approached with new unstructured methods.

Third, both of these factors imply the need for training participants. While it is exciting to think about the "noble working man or woman" and his or her innate intelligence and ability to solve problems, the fact is that many people in work settings do not necessarily have the skills to work successfully in groups doing complex problem solving. This is not to say those skills cannot be developed, rather, it is to say that they are not common—most people have not been trained in how to solve problems in groups. Therefore, most successful projects have tended to involve some significant element of training, both in the theory and models involved in the problem-solving process and in some of the elements of working together in teams. At the core of this is a sense that a QWL project, like any other project, requires some degree of competence and tools to work. To just throw people together in a room—be they labor, management, senior management, or lower management—and tell them to "solve problems" or "make decisions" and expect them to produce significant results, is wholly unreasonable.

Fourth, rewards must be built into both the processes and the outcome of QWL activities. Rewards may be internal; that is, people may feel that there is a reward in just being able to participate and having one's ideas listened to. Ultimately, in our experience, however, if a project is successful, the individual participants who see the organization gaining from their ideas will ask the question, "What's in it for me?" Therefore, in structuring projects, one needs to consider how the potential gains of the project can be shared with the participants, both as an equitable distribution of the gains and as a device for motivating people to continue to participate in the process.

On the other hand, the gains may not come quickly, and the concern may be how to motivate people early on. Here, the particular concern is with management—middle management, in particular—that may hesitate to become involved in QWL activities because of the perception that it requires an investment of time, effort, energy, money, and a loss of control with little measurable personal benefit.

Frequently, we have found that organizations tell managers to manage or create QWL projects while implicitly punishing them for doing so because of a concurrent emphasis on expense control, and so forth. In any case, it is important to build rewards into a project's early phases to recognize the participant's effort in implementing the project. In addition, it is important to change those aspects of the reward system that implicitly punish people for undertaking QWL initiatives.

Finally, it is important that QWL activities not be limited to certain groups in the organization. When only certain levels in the organization or certain groups of employees are involved, projects often fail because a "we/they" relationship develops. When lower-level employees are involved but management isn't, middle management often resists and blocks changes that are initiated by these groups. When some work groups or workers are involved and others at the same organization level are not, counterproductive intergroup rivalry often appears, and it becomes difficult to transfer the new structures and learnings to the rest of the organization. Even though it may be difficult to start everywhere in an organization at once, it is possible and important to put structures in place at startup that will quickly allow everyone to be involved, that will communicate what is occurring and that will show a commitment to implementing the new practices organizationwide.

CONCLUSIONS

Our discussion so far suggests that there are three major components of QWL efforts that must be managed well for a program to be successful. One factor is the development of projects at different levels—concerted, structured efforts to engage in organizational problem solving or the improvement of the organizational environment, the rewards system, or the structure of work through participative means. Projects of the types we've mentioned and those concerted efforts are important. It is not enough to say that we are now going to manage in a "QWL" manner. There must be tangible, specific, and observable actions aimed at changing the way in which work is done.

The second area of activity involves changes in management systems and organizational arrangements. They are necessary for two reasons. First, it may be necessary to change various types of structures, measures, goal systems, and so forth, to encourage and support QWL projects. Secondly, it may be important to look at those various changes in themselves as factors that are critical for QWL; for example, changes in rewards systems to build in gain sharing, changes in measurement to promote participation and problem solving.

Third, changes in senior management behavior are needed. As with any major change, the activities of the organization's leadership become critical in determining the ultimate viability of the change. If senior management takes a stance of, "Do what I say—not what I do," credibility is lost, and in the long term, it is doubtful whether changes will take place, or be institutionalized. Thus, for a QWL to be credible to all members of the organization, the senior management group must have some specific, tangible part in it.

Most important, our experience indicates that all three of these elements are important for the success of a major QWL change within an organization. The elements are interdependent and ideally support each other. Failures seem to be guaranteed when activities are limited to only one or two of these areas.

Overall, we are pleased and gratified by the increasing attention that is being paid to the nature-of-work organizations, to the quality-of-management practices, and to the impact that those factors have on individuals. This focus on organizations, the nature of organizational life, the quality of organizational behavior, and the fundamental health of our organizations is a very positive focus and one that has great potential for enhancing both organizational performance and the quality of work life that individuals experience. We end by expressing the hope that whatever happens to the term *QWL*, nothing happens to cause us to lose this focus.

SELECTED BIBLIOGRAPHY

For an early introduction to quality of work life, see L. E. Davis and A. B. Cherns's (eds.), *The Quality of Working Life*, Vols. I and II (Free Press, 1975) and *Work in America* (MIT Press, 1973).

Other important readings include J. Richard Hackman and Lloyd Suttle's *Improving Life at Work: Behavioral Science Approaches to Organizational Change* (Goodyear Publishing Co., 1977), Edward E. Lawler's "The New Plant Revolution" (*Organizational Dynamics*, Winter 1978), and Lawler's "Strategies for Improving the Quality of Work Life" (*American Psychologist*, May 1982).

REVIEW QUESTIONS

1 After your study of the Nadler-Lawler article, what does QWL mean to you?
2 On what bases could you defend the implementation of a QWL program in an organization? By contrast, what are the risks?
3 Predict the status of QWL programs in the year 2000, and explain why you feel that way.

READING 39

Why Quality of Work Life Doesn't Always Mean Quality

Deborah Shaw Cohen*

The New York Times has called it "the new gospel of worker participation." Recent cover stories in *Business Week* and *Fortune* announce "The New Industrial Relations." *Theory Z* and *The Art of Japanese Management*, books promoting what Americans can learn from the Japanese about "the human side of enterprise," are marching up the best seller lists—right next to *The Beverly Hills Diet* and *Dr. Atkins' Nutrition Breakthrough*.

We may not be in the midst of what *Fortune* has said could be "a new day for American industry," but after 30 years of behavioral science treatises on "participatory management," human resource issues have suddenly captured the attention of executive and line management. Some 200 companies have instituted Quality Control (QC) Circles, a device intended to elicit worker participation in solving production problems. The extent to which last year's behavioral science humanism is this year's bottom-line solution is perhaps best represented by the fact that Motorola has begun a corporate advertising campaign (the kind designed to make investors feel good) with full-page ads proclaiming "quality and productivity through employee participation in management."

In the great American tradition of self-help and fast food, we're going to solve our productivity problems and solve them now—with a little help from our friends the Japanese, and those folks over in the training and organization development department.

But, as the publishers of those lucrative diet books love to report, nobody stays thin from crash dieting. You have to permanently change your eating habits. Employee participation is no fad solution. The message from the "organization doctors" at Harvard, Wharton, MIT et al. is *yes*, employee participation and improving the quality of work life (QWL) can make organizations more effective. The evidence is inescapable and solid. But *no*, they warn with a paternalistic frown, it isn't easy, it's not fast, don't rush into it . . . see your doctor first.

Clinical data from 10 years of testing is in. The prescription for improving productivity through employee participation: a change in the way work gets done, a change in the values and management philosophy of your organization. The warning on the label: If you're going to do it, do it right!

Apple-Pie Virtues?

Techniques being promoted under the "quality of work life" rubric include QCs, horizontal business teams, labor/management committees, productivity gains sharing, autonomous work groups and the like. Comprehensive efforts have been labeled participatory management, open systems management, work restructuring or the more mysterious "Theory Z." The idea is that the bureaucratic, hierarchical principles underlying most American organizations are in need of updating; that the people doing the work often have the best ideas about how to do it better; that apple-pie virtues like openness, collaboration, equity, dignity and trust in work places *do* influence organizational effectiveness.

The goal of QWL programs is to involve employees in improving work and work life: remove some controls, give them information and problem-solving skills. Participation and influence aren't the only things important to employees: due process, pay tied to performance, time flexibility and leisure options all contribute to the quality of work life. Most QWL improvement efforts result in changes in all of these areas. But, the theory is, by using participatory processes, rather than top-down imposition and rigid structures, you can create a more people-oriented, collaborative organization, better able to respond to change and marshal its human resources.

Participatory techniques grow out of 30 years of investigation into how to design work and improve organizations. But as Malcolm Shaw, QWL consultant and director of The Center for Action Learning in Washington, DC, says, "We aren't just talking about making people feel good; QWL occurs at the operating level—affecting how decisions are made and work gets done. The bottom line is a genuine sharing of power."

'Charging Elephant'

An aging GM automobile assembly plant in Tarrytown, NY houses perhaps the most famous QWL experiment of them all. *Harvard Business Review* told the story of how a young, dissatisfied work force of several thousand was trained in participatory problem solving, taught about plant management, operations and products. When the plant switched to producing the 1980 X model, hourly workers got together with engineers and managers to plan the transition: evaluating assembly processes, work stations and job assignments. Over a period of years the plant went from one of the worst to one of the best in the system. The increased efficiency and improved climate saved GM millions of dollars.

These days, as *Newsweek* describes: "Like an elephant full charge, GM bellows the virtues of its QWL programs." GM has asked all 100,000 salaried employees to complete a quality of work life assessment questionnaire. They have projects in dozens of locations and have designed new plants from top to bottom to incorporate participatory techniques. They describe dramatic results: defect rates from 19,000 to 35 in three months, a drop in grievances from 3,000 to less than 70, absenteeism reduced by 90%.

In an effort to move decision-making down the hierarchy, GM has restructured even at the top management level. When a corporate giant invests millions in making life better for employees, you can be sure it's not just humanistically motivated. GM vice president George Morris describes what Jerome Rosow, director of the Work In America Institute, calls the double payoff: "It has been our experience that people-involvement activities result in two significant developments. One is improved operating effectiveness, measured in terms of lower absenteeism rates, reduced costs, improved product quality . . . Increased involvement also is reflected in higher morale and greater job satisfaction."

Other participation efforts are less dramatic.But names like AT&T, Ford, Eaton, Honeywell, TRW, Cummins, as well as several cities and government agencies, show up on the lists of organizations with QWL projects supported by the dozen or so university-based consultant groups and advocacy centers. Impressive successes have been documented across the country.

Change Comes Slowly

In 1973 management professor James O'Toole was the primary author of an HEW report that became a widely read book entitled *Work In America*—an optimistic argument for work reform and attention to quality of work life issues. Seven years later, O'Toole pessimistically wrote: "The general pattern in more than 100 plants [with experiments to restructure work environments] is one of a brief leap forward followed by prolonged backsliding."

It does seem that a review of the literature reveals more experiments that have floundered than have persevered and grown. Some argue that this proves employee participation is just another example of the "Hawthorne Effect." But a closer examination reveals that it's not that simple.

Item: At a manufacturing company, worker/management groups got involved in extensive educational programs, autonomous work groups, setting quality guidelines and improving work flow. The workers became more active in the union as a result of this involvement. The projects despite beginning successes, were pushed out by the established union, which felt threatened.

Item: At the Rushton Mining Company in Pennsylvania, an experimental group improved its productivity, skill levels and safety record. Other workers saw the young volunteers doing things "differently" and getting top pay, and voted not to join the experiment, remaining wary of the program.

Item: At General Foods' innovative Topeka pet foods plant, participatory programs were extremely successful and much publicized. But the plant remained an isolated oddity, resented by other management groups.

Item: At a food company, plant management went ahead and designed a new production line without mentioning it to their labor/management committees. Meanwhile, they asked committees to stick with employee-related issues like graffiti in the bathrooms.

A consultant to a number of QWL efforts describes one of the problems: "People think QWL can be instituted as a project. It can't. It's an organizational change . . . a tricky process of building trust, providing information, dealing with power issues."

Guidelines for Success

The Northeastern Labor Management Center, a Boston-based group that has facilitated a number of participatory projects, states in its latest newsletter: "An avalanche of companies are launching QC programs . . . Unfortunately some impatient companies . . . are rushing into 'installing' QC Circles without adequate study, planning and preparation. There are already cases of disappointment and disillusionment . . . More are coming!"

As the failures demonstrate, a lot can go wrong with efforts to improve working life. A lot can go right, too. It's not for every organization. When it works, it's because there is commitment, planning and intervention skill. You can't buy that stuff off-the-shelf.

Perhaps the best way to find out how to do it right is to talk with people who have "been there." The innovators have already made just about every mistake possible. Some of them, like GM, have seen it work. Harvard's Richard Walton, who has studied dozens of projects, cautions that you can't lift someone else's techniques. You have to begin with an understanding of where *your* organization is and tailor-make a program. But managers, employees and unions who have been through participation efforts can outline the problems and possibilities.

The "how tos," the caveats, the secrets for success with participation are beginning to fill books and week-long seminars. But a few ground rules seem to be apparent:

1 Make sure management really believes in QWL and is committed to seeing it through. QWL takes time and money. Management can't impose QCs by fiat and expect an improvement in morale. The first step is to educate management about participation—through seminars, consultants, meetings with other companies. QWL is not a motivation or productivity device; it requires a genuine and demonstrated belief in the value and rights of people. In a trusting partnership, job security is protected; employees usually share in cost savings. While management retains control over the business, the big payoffs come from allowing substantive participation. Employees will become involved in major issues—pay systems, technology, personnel choices. It's important that management be ready to let that happen.

2 Use strategic planning and political savvy. The Center for Action Learning advocates developing what theorist Richard Beckhard calls "transition management" strategies and structures. Practitioners suggest feasibility studies and diagnostic surveys to get a picture of where the organization is and what is possible before jumping in. As James J. Renier, president of Honeywell's control systems business says: "You can't just put out a memo saying 'You will be participative, you jerks.'" And, you can't just drop participation down in the middle of a competitive, hierarchical "culture" and expect it to get very far. Everyone has to know what's in it for them. Trust has to be built. Successful projects identify and involve key people, design a management structure, establish clear goals and build consensus. Harvard's Walton says managers need to find out what is already known about planned change. Too many companies start experimenting without drawing on state-of-the-art OD strategies.

3 Train everybody and train them again. Near the top of every list of reasons for failure is inadequate training. Training in participative problem solving and communications is critical. GM spent $1.6 million on training and other costs in their first big push at Tarrytown and they are now involved in an extensive retraining effort. Supervisors especially need preparation for new roles. Workers require education in quality control analysis, operations and new job skills.

4 Plan for diffusion and institutionalization from the onset. Isolation or gradual deterioration of experiments are typical problems. But Richard Ault, senior consultant with the American Productivity Center in Houston and architect of many of GM's activities, says you can prevent "encapsulation" if you start out right. He suggests beginning with small pilot programs and strategically building support. It takes groundwork, but the goal is to make participatory values integral to the system —incorporated into the company business plan and bonus program, for example.

If QWL projects, despite the difficulty, continue to spread in the '80s, and many people think they will, the challenge to human resources development (HRD) professionals is clear. As one consultant comments: "I'm using every OD skill I've got and it's not enough."

The management trend represented by the new interest in employee participation is of particular importance to HRD professionals. A company that genuinely tries to fulfill human needs at work, an organization looking to tap workers' ideas for improvement, is putting top priority on developing its human resources. Education and training are the indispensable fuels that make participative organizations run.

If companies do continue to turn to Quality Circles and Z techniques, it will be operating managers and HRD professionals *working together* that make them succeed.

REVIEW QUESTION

1 Cohen suggests that QWL programs must instill participative values into the system. How likely is this to happen in some of our bureaucratic organizations?

CHAPTER 11

REWARD SYSTEMS

READING 40

Labor-Management Cooperation—
The Scanlon Plan at Work

Judith Ramquist*

The Scanlon Plan is named for Joseph Scanlon, a labor-management consultant who came out of the depression in the 1930s with some radically new ideas. He believed that if the adversarial relationship between management and labor could be changed to one of cooperation, every member of an organization could be productive and make a contribution to the success of the business. His ideas were not intended to be a formula for success or a pat solution to problems; rather, they formed a philosophy for organizations founded on the principles of communication.

Because Joseph Scanlon never had a specific plan for how every company should proceed to set up this cooperative effort, it is somewhat surprising that we refer to the implementation of his ideas as the Scanlon Plan. It might also be misleading, because companies that use his philosophy seem to do so in various ways. There are, however, four principles that a number of Scanlon companies agree upon. The principles are identity, participation and accountability, equity, and managerial competence.

• *Identity*: the idea that employees contribute and participate to the extent that they are meaningfully informed about the organization's history, competition, customers, and business objectives.

• *Participation and accountability*: the idea that employees have an *opportunity* and a *responsibility* to influence the decision process in the organization, to be accurately informed and responsible within their areas of competence, and to be held accountable for their own performance in their jobs.

• *Equity*: the idea that all employees deserve a fair return on the investments of their time and talents and that they can expect to share in the results that come from their efforts.

• *Managerial competence*: the inescapable necessity for managers to be increasingly professional and competent as leaders within any organization. Without such competence and a *commitment* to the philosophy and process of participative management, a Scanlon process is not workable.

*Reprinted from "Labor-Management Cooperation—The Scanlon Plan at Work," by Judith Ramquist, *Sloan Management Review*, pp. 49–55, by permission of the publisher. Copyright © 1982 by the Sloan Management Review Association. All rights reserved.

A CASE STUDY

Herman Miller has used the Scanlon Plan since 1950. Through experience, we know that it works for us. We have learned how to use it effectively even though we have not always done that. We have had both good and difficult times during the thirty-two years we have used the plan, and I would like to share our experience with you.

Herman Miller was founded in 1905 as the Michigan Star Furniture Company, a manufacturer of traditional and period reproduction home furniture located in Zeeland, Michigan. Like many other furniture companies in the area, it began as a nonunion company and has remained so for seventy-seven years.

In 1922 D. J. De Pree (an employee of the company) bought the company with financial backing from his father-in-law (Herman Miller), and changed its name to Herman Miller. The company began to put new emphasis on quality and design, i.e., on better *copying* since almost every piece was a reproduction from some period.

By 1929 the company was on the verge of bankruptcy as a result of the depression and southern competition. At that point the company embarked on a new course through the visionary leadership of D. J. De Pree and the beginning of an association with an unknown designer, Gilbert Rhode. Rhode believed that it was time for a new kind of home furniture that would be appropriate for modern living in smaller houses which had lower ceilings, fewer rooms, and a simpler style. Because De Pree was willing to listen to these new ideas and take the risk, and because the risk is not that great when a company is on the brink of bankruptcy, Herman Miller began manufacturing modern furniture. The risk paid off. Between 1946 and 1968, the market for modern furniture was growing, and the company became recognized as a design leader and producer of high quality, innovatively designed products.

As a result of research on working environments (particularly in offices and health care facilities), the company began to develop systems products, creating two distinct product lines introduced in 1968 and 1972:

- *Action Office*: a system of components, panels, work surfaces, files, and tables that can be used to set up office work spaces without walls and to accomodate more people in less space, in more pleasant, private, and productive environments.
- *Co/Struc*: a materials handling system for hospitals with components including wall-hung lockers, work surfaces, tables and drawers, and carts that can move materials about easily and more efficiently.

Like the earlier decision to produce modern furniture, the development of systems products represented another major change in direction for the company, and Herman Miller had entered two new markets.

Today Herman Miller's sales volume is approaching $300 million; it has over 2,500 employees in the U.S. with manufacturing facilities in Michigan, California, and Georgia and sales facilities in all major U.S. cities. Its international operation includes licensees and subsidiaries throughout the world. The company distributes products through its own field sales and authorized dealers.

The Original Plan

In 1950 Herman Miller's sales volume was less than $2 million annually. It had about 120 employees; 90 percent were in direct production work. Workers were on piece rates; some of the rates were too high, while others were too low. There was fierce competition between the highly skilled and the not-so-skilled employees. Some people were on day work with no premium opportunity, and dissatisfaction was high. There was a suggestion system, but it was inadequate. No fair way had been devised to reward individuals for their ideas.

Management became interested in the Scanlon Plan after reading a 1950 *Fortune* article that described the Scanlon Plan at LaPointe Machine Tool Company. Dr. Carl Frost, who had worked with Joe Scanlon at M.I.T. and at LaPointe, was invited to Herman Miller to discuss the Scanlon Plan. To management's surprise, Frost did not proceed to "install the plan"; rather, he asked a number of questions:

- Was management ready?
- Was management willing to provide people with more information than ever before to enable them to be productive?
- Was management willing to relinquish certain prerogatives?

Management was also surprised to learn that Frost was not sure that management was ready to make a commitment to the plan.

However, a number of meetings were held with management and the employees, and the plan was begun in May 1950. It consisted of three basic elements: a participation structure, a bonus system (which replaced piece rates), and a communications process.

The participation structure included production committees and a screening committee. The production committees were composed of elected representatives from each department and an appointed member (usually a department head). They reviewed all suggestions from employees in the areas they represented and acted upon those that did not require the consent of other departments or more than $100 to implement. The screening committee was composed of elected representatives from twelve zones in the production area and seven appointed management members. Its primary function was to review, analyze, evaluate, and make recommendations concerning the total production performance of the company; this included all employee recommendations made to the committee.

The bonus system was based on labor productivity. The entire difference between labor earned and the actual payroll was paid to participating employees in a monthly bonus. *Labor earned* was based on direct and indirect labor allowances on each product. *Total payroll* was the sum of wages and salaries paid to employees, including overtime and an allowance for vacation and holidays. *Bonus earned* was the difference between the labor earned and the actual payroll per day. Each employee's bonus was in direct proportion to his or her base pay. Indirect employees in all areas except field sales were included in the bonus payout.

The third part of the process was the communications system which was set up as a series of monthly meetings to review performance. At the beginning of each month on Scanlon Day (as it was referred to), the screening committee met briefly to review the results of the previous month. This was followed by a meeting to brief supervisors, who then conducted departmental meetings to disseminate the information. The following day the bonus checks were distributed along with a Scanlon results memo that explained the bonus calculation and summarized the highlights of the month. Between the monthly meetings, charts and graphs distributed throughout the plant kept employees aware of how their performance was going during the month.

Almost all of the communications, as well as the measurements, were directed to the production employees. Because the Scanlon Plan had been started when 90 percent of all employees were in direct labor jobs, the so-called knowledge worker was not nearly so involved in this process. Although more indirect employees had been hired over the years since 1950, few adjustments had been made to accommodate them.

The structure, the bonus system, and the communications system are standard components of any Scanlon Plan, and for most of the first twenty-seven years of its operation, the plan worked well at Herman Miller (see Table 1). The best bonus results were in 1974 when the bonus averaged 22.83 percent. In no year did the bonus average go below zero for the year, although occasionally a month's performance produced a negative result.

A Challenge to the Plan

In 1978, however, things began to change very quickly at Herman Miller. Two years before, in part as a result of cost-savings suggestions from employees, the company had taken an unprecedented step in the office systems market and reduced the price across the board on its Action Office systems products. The 10 percent reduction came when most major competitors were raising their prices,

TABLE 1
BONUSES UNDER THE ORIGINAL SCANLON PLAN

Year	Employees	Bonus
1950	170	8.93%
1974	565	22.83
1977	1,202	13.51

and the price advantage this gave the company set off a dramatic increase in sales that significantly exceeded what had been planned.

The results, although not disastrous, were bad enough. Production capacity could not meet the increased demand. The lead time on some products was extended to twenty weeks; twelve weeks was standard for the industry, and most customers wanted eight weeks. It was difficult to make some shipments because critical parts were missing. Excessive inventories for certain materials became a significant problem. Clearly, the Scanlon Plan was not working. Bonuses dropped well below the historical 10 percent monthly average, and the company had a negative bonus result after fifty-six consecutive monthly bonuses. The bonus average for the year was only 4.39 percent.

The company was faced with a new situation:

• The 1950 structure, process, and bonus formula had been developed for a work force that was predominantly composed of hourly employees.

• The plan had continued almost unchanged for twenty-seven years.

• By 1977 almost half of Herman Miller's people were employed in *indirect* positions in data processing, marketing, sales, purchasing, finance, and production control. They had little participation in the suggestion system, and were unsure of how they contributed to the bonus. As one employee remarked, "I was one among this group of employees who received a bonus check each month without knowing exactly how I had made a contribution. Like other so-called knowledge workers, I never turned back a bonus check, but I was always aware that it had been earned by measuring the work of the people in direct jobs."

We also had many new employees (one-half had been with the company for less than two years). There were many managers who did not understand their role in a Scanlon organization: to keep employees continually informed, to assist them in their efforts to increase productivity, and to communicate the results of those efforts. Some managers even seemed openly resistant to participative management.

Herman Miller was not using the full potential of the Scanlon Plan to manage its explosive growth, and the results confirmed this. Competition from other companies was growing. Customers were demanding better service, and investors were concerned about their return.

Development of a New Plan

In the spring of 1978, Glenn Walters, then executive vice president of U.S. operations (and currently company president), decided that all employees should be alerted to the realities of Herman Miller's business situation. He and Frost held two-hour meetings with small groups of employees; eventually they met with all 2,300 U.S. employees. In these meetings Walters and Frost offered the employees their information, and the employees in turn provided them with some facts of their own. A secret vote was then taken on four questions. The questions and results follow:

1 Is there a need for the organization to change? 98 percent voted yes.
2 Is there potential for improvement? 98 percent said there was.
3 What's in it for you? 33 percent said job security; 25 percent said more money.
4 Will you be a part of the change process? 96 percent volunteered to be involved in the process.

This process involved talking personally to every employee in the company, and is an example of the responsibility of management in the implementation and ongoing maintenance of a Scanlon Plan. Unless managers are committed and willing to involve employees meaningfully in the management process, they cannot assume that employees will be willing to help solve company problems.

After the vote, Herman Miller set up an ad hoc committee of fifty-four elected employees from all areas and levels in the company. Several key managers were appointed to work with the committee. The committee consisted of managers and nonmanagers, salespeople and factory workers, supervisors and clerks, and representatives from all U.S. facilities. The committee's job was to assess the relevance of the Scanlon Plan to the new situation and propose changes that would meet both current and future problems. The work of this committee is one of the best examples of the Scanlon principle of *participation* that I have ever seen. It gave responsible people the opportunity to influence the management process within their areas of competence.

The committee members agreed very early that the Scanlon Plan was not just a bonus incentive, but rather a way of managing the entire company. The group met in three sub-committees (education and communications, rules and regulations, and equity) for nearly ten months.

At the beginning of the committee work, many members thought that the old Scanlon Plan could somehow be "fixed up." That idea was quickly discarded as the committee began to understand the complexity of the problems. The members soon agreed on one major decision: *the old plan was no longer a viable option.* A new plan had to be developed that would provide the following:

1 *Specific planning procedures* beginning with a statement by top management that would define exactly what Herman Miller's business is.
2 *Annual commitments* from every employee that would be used to measure performance.
3 *A new participation structure* that would include indirect, direct, and field sales employees from all areas of the company and that would provide a way to define and solve problems.
4 *A sophisticated monitoring system* to track performance.
5 *An expanded bonus formula* to reflect more accurately Herman Miller's performance as an organization.

The new participation structure replaced the old production committees and screening committee. The new structure is composed of a basic unit called the work team, a peer group called a caucus, and a combined group called a council. This same structure is set up in every area throughout the organization.

The work team, consisting of a supervisor or manager and the people who report to him or her, is the basic management unit in the company. This group first deals with all suggestions, questions, or problems that need to be resolved. The work team meets every month to review the plans and goals of the group and its performance to meet those goals.

The caucus is a peer group composed of people at the same level or with similar jobs in the same area or department. The caucus provides employees with a secondary channel to discuss problems or suggestions not resolved to their satisfaction in the work team. It gives employees a place to share ideas and an opportunity to gather support. The caucus elects representatives to an area council which is led by a director or an officer. The caucus meets regularly (usually once a month) prior to council meetings.

A council is formed in each major department and division throughout the company. It is led by a director or vice president, and includes the leader's work team and elected representatives from lower levels in the line structure. Its primary responsibility is to review suggestions from its area and, if necessary, to forward them to other areas for answers. The council leader must also ensure that any suggestions referred to his or her area by another are answered in an appropriate and timely manner. In order to ensure accountability, the ad hoc committee insisted that the responsibility for dealing with suggestions be handled by line management. The committee also wanted to avoid setting up a dual structure, and so the Scanlon and the line structures are the same.

The primary reason for setting up work teams, caucuses, and councils is *communications*. This is critical to making a participative management system work: to communicate to every employee the information needed to do his or her job and, if possible, to make a contribution to the total productivity of the organization. Both work teams and councils have responsibility for communicating to employees the goals and objectives of their group, how well performance meets these goals, and what is being done to resolve outstanding problems.

There is a well-defined set of subjects appropriate for caucus and council discussions. These include: productivity, customer service, work methods, cost savings, quality, safety, products, and the operation of the Scanlon Plan. Employment relationship issues (such as pay, benefits, promotion, performance appraisal, and discipline) are not discussed in caucuses or councils; instead, they are dealt with exclusively through line management. There is an appeals policy covering these issues that is administered directly by line management, rather than by representative channels.

The ad hoc committee also recommended that a new bonus measurement system be implemented. The Equity Subcommittee stated in its proposal that in order to ensure equity neither employees, customers, nor investors should receive benefits at the expense of the other two. This means that profitability should not decrease while employees' bonuses increase, and that bonuses should not suffer while investors benefit from productivity increases. The committee also stated that bonuses should only be paid when they are earned through increased productivity. The new bonus formula reflects the complexity of Herman Miller's business. It measures performance against the annual business plan in four key areas: customer service, effective use of human resources, effective use of materials, and effective use of money. Targets are set in each of these areas. When these targets are exceeded, the bonus which is shared among all employees is augmented. In addition to the four performance categories, cost savings is also measured against an annual goal.

The ad hoc committee's proposal was sixty pages long; it was distributed to all 2,300 U.S. employees for their study and questions. This was followed by a thorough training and education effort that began with the Executive Committee of the Board; it eventually included all employees in departmental groups.

The committee decided that it would require the approval of 90 percent of the employees before implementing the new plan. A company-wide vote was held on January 26, 1979, and Scanlon '79 (as it was called) was overwhelmingly approved by 95.9 percent of all employees.

Performance under the New Plan

For the last three years, Herman Miller has been working to implement the new plan. It is probably too early to claim success or to predict how well the company will be able to apply the Scanlon philosophy as it continues to grow. But there are some encouraging results.

Over the past three years, improvements that can be measured have provided better customer service and have made Herman Miller more effective as an organization. Monthly bonuses have averaged over 15 percent. The lead time on most products is now about eight weeks—the best the company has ever achieved. Mistakes in customer shipments have been minimized. Inventory investments have dropped steadily over the past three years. There is better control over expenses, and accounts receivable are being collected faster than ever before.

CONCLUSION

At Herman Miller interest in and support of the Scanlon Plan is high, and employees at all levels are enthusiastic about the changes that have been made. Participation of indirect employees is particularly encouraging. Suggestions are coming from employees who have never submitted suggestions before. A few weeks ago a vice president asked me for a suggestion form, because he had discovered a significant cost savings in his area and wanted to submit it himself. He had been with the company for a long time, so I asked him whether he had ever submitted a suggestion before. He smiled and said, "First one in twenty years."

What does all this mean for Herman Miller today? Clearly, we cannot be complacent. We have learned that a participative management process like the

Scanlon Plan may become ineffective if left to evolve unattended. We know that employees can become disillusioned and discouraged unless there is a commitment from top management, constant communication, and the opportunity to review regularly the process for relevancy. We know that productivity increases do not occur simply because management decides they should. We have learned about the ongoing responsibility for training and educating employees so that they can understand their jobs and the business of the organization. If we attend to these issues, productivity will improve.

REVIEW QUESTIONS

1 What is a Scanlon plan?
2 "The Scanlon plan is more a system of participative management than of economic rewards." Take a position (pro or con) and defend your view on this issue.
3 Summarize the major changes that were introduced in Herman Miller's "Scanlon '79" plan.

READING 41

More Is Not Better: Two Failures of Incentive Theory

Abraham K. Korman
Albert S. Glickman
Robert L. Frey, Jr.*

The use of incentives is a time-honored strategy for increasing work motivation. The rationale is straightforward: People offered the opportunity to accomplish specific valued purposes alter their behavior to attain these ends. Behavior is, therefore, "shaped" by the person controlling reward allocations. Yet, despite this logic, evidence has been accumulating that the theoretical support for commonly used incentives leaves something to be desired (Korman, Greenhaus, & Badin, 1977).

For explanations for this lack of support, we may look to the assumptions common to the use of incentives. One such assumption is that "more is better." That is, if the opportunity to attain valued ends is expected to effect a given behavioral outcome, then the more "value opportunity" provided (i.e., incen-

*From "More Is Not Better: Two Failures of Incentive Theory," *Journal of Applied Psychology*, April 1981, 66:2, pp. 255–259. Copyright 1981 by the American Psychological Association. Reprinted by permission of the publisher and author.

tives of greater magnitude, or more of them), the greater the likelihood that behavior will be changed.

This assumption generally obtains when we refer to extrinsic incentives (cf. Vroom, 1964) or intrinsic incentives (cf. Deci, 1972) separately. But, as Deci (1972) indicates, the assumption may not hold if we combine extrinsic and intrinsic motivations, for then one set of incentives could offset the other. This prediction has received considerable support (cf. Notz, 1975). Some equity theorists also note that rewards that exceed perceived value can have counterproductive effects (Adams, 1965; Lawler, 1973).

The research reported here represents a further test of the "more is better" assumption. We sought to determine whether civilian youths would be more favorably disposed toward enlistment in the Navy if (a) the number of incentives presented in a "package" was increased and (b) if the absolute magnitude of incentives was increased.

METHOD

Two studies were made of the impact of various recruiting incentives on enlistment motivation. In one, experimental incentives (not then in effect) were varied in absolute magnitude. In the other, the number of incentives made available to a prospect was varied.

Sample

The vehicle for administration of the experimental incentives was the national cluster sampling conducted by Gilbert Youth Research as part of a quarterly Omnibus Youth Survey. The sample was drawn from a population stratified within geographic regions according to age and school status. Race and socioeconomic background data were available for analyses, reported elsewhere (Frey, Glickman, Korman, Goodstadt, & Romanczuk, 1974).

Respondents in this research consisted of a nationwide representation of civilian males, ages 16–22 years. In the first study, 860 males were interviewed; in the second, 854. Both studies were conducted in 1973.

Procedure

The initial list of incentive statements was derived from earlier stages of this research (Glickman, Goodstadt, Korman, & Romanczuk, 1973; Korman, Goodstadt, Glickman, & Romanczuk, 1973). These were redefined and reduced by review processes including discussion with Navy people to ensure that the incentives to be presented would be viable in the Navy setting and trial runs to ensure that instructions and content would be understandable. The final list of statements was read by the interviewer as part of individual interviews. Respondents, on a 5-point scale, had to "Indicate what effect these changes would have on your interest in the Navy." (1 = "I would think *less favorably* of the Navy . . ."; 5 = "I would think *more favorably.* . . .")

In the first study, 17 experimental incentives were evaluated utilizing a special sampling designed to determine the effects of these incentives singly, as well as in combination with one another. Practical limitations ruled out use of all possible combinations. The total sample was subdivided on a random basis into seven subsamples, A—G (see Table 1). Each subsample responded to five (or six) sets of incentive statements. A set could contain a single statement or a combination of two or three statements. Identifying numbers in Table 1 refer to incentive statements. Table 2 lists the incentive statements used.

Except for Items 16 and 17 (discussed later), the incentives fit into five categories (rows in Table 1): (a) vocational and financial satisfaction, (b) integration of military and civilian life, (c) self-determination or fate control in vocational life, (d) reduction of perceived inequities, and (e) self-determination and vocational/financial satisfaction.

In Study 2, the 5 highest rated single incentives from Study 1 were used plus 10 new incentives.

RESULTS

Table 3 gives the means and standard deviations for responses to each item set in Study 1.

Effects of Increasing the Number of Incentives: Study 1

The first analysis investigated the more is better assumption when the number of incentives offered was varied. Within each category (row), the best single (identified from Table 3), double, and triple incentive packages were compared by analyses of variance. In no instance was there a significant difference. To eliminate any differential effects of educational status, age, family income, and race on response to incentives, all statistical tests were made after partialing out these variables (Overall & Spiegel, 1969).

Effects of Increasing Absolute Magnitude: Study 1

Two pairs of single incentives were used to see whether increases in absolute magnitude would enhance attractiveness of the Navy. Attractiveness of a $1,000 enlistment bonus was compared with a $3,000 bonus (Item 17 vs. Item 1). Two years of college was compared with 4 years after 4 years of active duty (Item 15 vs. Item 16). The mean attractiveness of the $1,000 bonus fell just short of being significantly greater than the $3,000 bonus ($p < .10$). However, when counts were made of the number choosing the most favorable alternative to the $1,000 and $3,000 bonuses, the percentages were 27% and 8%; an overwhelmingly signifi-

TABLE 1
SAMPLING DESIGN: STUDY 1

Subsamples						
A	B	C	D	E	F	G
1	2	3	1+ 2	2+ 3	1+ 3	1+ 2+ 3
4	5	6	4+ 5	5+ 6	4+ 6	4+ 5+ 6
7	8	9	7+ 8	8+ 9	7+ 9	7+ 8+ 9
10	11	12	10+11	11+12	10+12	10+11+12
13	14	15	13+14	14+15	13+15	13+14+15
16	17	—	—	—	—	—

Note: Numbers indicate incentive items to which subsamples responded. (See Table 2 for explanation of these items.)

TABLE 2
INTERVIEW INCENTIVE STATEMENTS: STUDY 1

Item no.	Statement
1	The Navy would give a person a bonus of $3,000 for enlisting.
2	The Navy would offer special job training after a person completed active duty, to help him get started in civilian life.
3	A person could enlist in the Navy for two years, instead of three or four years.
4	A person would be allowed to retire from the Navy and receive half pay after fifteen years instead of twenty years of service.
5	The pay and benefits for Navy jobs would be made about the same as pay and benefits for similar civilian jobs.
6	After twenty years of service, a person would be allowed to retire from the Navy and receive three-fourths pay instead of half-pay.
7	For each year of Navy service, a person could accumulate two months of educational leave with pay.
8	After the first two years of duty, the Navy would guarantee a person his choice of a home port for at least one year.
9	After one year in the Navy, a person could change his job specialty.
10	The Navy would assign women to duty aboard most ships.
11	In the Navy, a person could receive a yearly bonus of up to 25% of his base pay for exceptionally good performances.
12	The Navy would make pay for sea duty substantially higher than for shore duty.
13	A person who was not satisfied could get out of the Navy after three months, with no strings attached.
14	The Navy would reduce the educational requirement for officer training programs from four years to two years of college.
15	Enlisted men would be paid by the government for four years of college, including living expenses at the school of their choice, after completing four years of active duty in the Navy.
16	Enlisted men would be paid by the government for two years of college, including living expenses at the school of their choice, after completing four years of active duty in the Navy.
17	The Navy would give a person a bonus of $1000 for enlisting.

TABLE 3
MEANS AND STANDARD DEVIATIONS FOR INCENTIVE ITEM SUBSAMPLES A—G

Item	M	SD	Item	M	SD
	A($n = 142$)			D($n = 102$)	
1	2.81	1.03	1+2	2.89	1.01
4	2.60	1.05	4+5	2.82	.93
7	2.88	1.02	7+8	2.88	.95
10	2.93	1.13	10+11	2.94	1.07
13	3.29	1.22	13+14	3.30	1.11
16	3.06	1.14			
	B($n = 129$)			E($n = 133$)	
2	2.95	1.16	2+3	2.62	.80
5	2.76	1.12	5+6	2.65	.86
8	3.03	1.13	8+9	2.57	.85
11	3.12	1.24	11+12	2.54	.93
14	2.71	1.31	14+15	2.60	1.02
17	3.21	1.37			
	C($n = 160$)			F($n = 107$)	
3	2.88	1.09	1+3	2.93	1.07
6	2.93	1.06	4+6	2.79	1.02
9	2.76	1.04	7+9	3.07	1.05
12	2.70	1.03	10+12	3.22	1.18
15	3.03	1.14	13+15	3.51	1.18
				G($n = 87$)	
			1+ 2 +3	2.94	.89
			4+ 5 +6	2.72	.92
			7+ 8 +9	2.83	.87
			10+11+12	3.12	.90
			13+14+15	3.21	1.08

Note: See Table 2 for item statements.

cant difference (X^2 Yates' correction $= 16.7$, $p < .001$). No significant difference was found in attractiveness between the offers of 2 and 4 years of college expenses. In neither case is the more is better assumption warranted when either the number or magnitude of incentives is at issue.

Effects of Increasing the Number of Incentives: Study 2

Analyses parallel to Study 1 were carried out with Study 2 data. Here we found that one best double incentive package was significantly more attractive than *both* the best single incentive ($p < .03$) and the triple incentive package ($p < .05$). Considering that 30 significance tests were made, this exception to our findings offers little to a more is better generalization.

Effects of Increasing Absolute Magnitude: Study 2

In study 1, different subgroups (equivalent through randomization) rated each item of the pair; in Study 2, we had the same people rating items. Thus, Study 1 constitutes a between-groups test; Study 2 a within-groups test. Despite the potential for "demand" effects (since the differences were obvious to Study 2 respondents), there was no difference in attractiveness between a one-time $1,000 enlistment bonus and a bonus of $1,000 a year for 3 years. On the other hand, an offer of a bonus for good performance of 10% of base pay was significantly *more* attractive than a bonus of 25% ($p < .02$). Again, "more is not better" but "can be worse."

DISCUSSION

Though our interpretations must be tempered by the "as if" nature of the response mode—the incentives were not then in actual effect—the more is better assumption that prevails in organizational contexts gets little support from these studies. Indeed, it appears that "more is sometimes worse." Why is this? Several explanations are possible.

Too large an incentive may lead to distrust. ("It must be pretty bad if they are willing to pay such a big bonus. It is a trick.") There may be a perceived threat to freedom, or "reactance" (Brehm, 1966), coupled with anger at the institution. ("What are they trying to do? Take away my freedom of action? I can't be bought!") A violation of perceived equity norms (Adams, 1965) or guilt (Lawler, 1973) may be involved. ("You shouldn't get so much money just for joining the Navy.") Finally, because most teenage youths have had little real experience in handling or making decisions involving large sums, it may be that beyond a certain threshold level perceived as "a lot" (e.g. $1,000), additional incentive quantity (e.g., $3,000) has no meaning or weight.

Our research did not allow us to test the viability of these explanations (they are not mutually exclusive). Regardless of which of these might prove most fruitful, or others we have not thought of, the implications for organizations seem clear. Management cannot glibly assume that to attract good employees or to motivate better performance, it is only necessary to determine at what price the offer "cannot be refused." There may be no effect except cost increases, and possible boomerang effects cannot be ignored.

Likewise, our results, like Deci's (1972), raise questions about theoretical constructs that do not carefully discriminate between effects of intrinsic and extrinsic factors and do not attend to their interactions but that allow the convenience of manipulating tangible extrinsics to obscure the more subtle intrinsics. That is where more is better fallacies most often abide.

REFERENCES

Adams, J. S. Inequity in social exchange. In C. Berkowitz (Ed.), *Advances in experimental social psychology* (Vol. 2). New York: Academic Press, 1965.

Brehm, J. *A theory of psychological reactance.* New York: Academic Press, 1966.

Deci, E. L. The effects of contingent and non-contingent rewards and controls on intrinsic motivation. *Organizational Behavior and Human Performance*, 1972, *8*, 217–229.

Frey, R. L., Jr., Glickman, A. S., Korman, A. K., Goodstadt, B. E., & Romanczuk, A. P. *A study of experimental incentives as an influence on enlistment intention: more is not better.* Washington, D.C.: American Institutes for Research, 1974.

Glickman, A. S., Goodstadt, B. E., Korman, A. K., & Romanczuk, A. P. *Research and development for Navy career motivation programs in an all-volunteer condition: I. A cognitive map of career motivation.* Washington, D.C.: American Institutes for Research, 1973.

Korman, A.K., Goodstadt, B. E., Glickman, A. S. & Romanczuk, A. P. *An exploratory study of enlistment incentives among junior college students.* Washington, D.C.: American Institutes of Research, 1973.

Korman, A. K., Greenhaus, J., & Badin, I. Personnel attitudes and motivation. *Annual Review of Psychology*, 1977, *28*, 175–196.

Lawler, E. E., III. *Motivation in work organizations.* Monterey, Calif.: Brooks/Cole, 1973.

Notz, W. W. Work motivation and the negative effects of extrinsic rewards. *American Psychologist*, 1975, *30*, 884–891.

Overall, J. E., & Spiegel, D. K. Concerning least squares analysis of experimental data. *Psychological Bulletin*, 1969, *72*, 311–322.

Vroom, V. *Work and motivation.* New York: Wiley, 1964.

REVIEW QUESTIONS

1 Why is it that "more is not (necessarily) better"?

2 Are there other variables in organizational behavior that may not follow the "more is better" guideline? What are they?

3 What implications does this reading have for managers offering economic rewards to employees?

READING 42

Trade-0ff Analysis Finds the Best Reward Combinations

Lawrence B. Chonko
Ricky W. Griffin*

When a personnel manager makes a decision on how to improve employee satisfaction, that decision is often made on the basis of historical data or the manager's personal, subjective opinion. But there is a technique that allows us to find out what a particular group of employees wants most from the organization.

The technique, known as trade-off analysis, enables the manager to obtain from employees utility values that indicate preferences for forms of reward.

The underlying assumption of trade-off analysis is that by providing respondents with alternatives from which they must choose, inferences can be made concerning their value systems.

For example, suppose each employee was free to structure his job within organizational constraints. The employee would be forced to make relative judgments about the value of each job attribute. Undoubtedly, the employee would be choosing from a series of imperfect options. Since no job can possess the highest level of all job elements, it becomes important to determine the extent to which employees are willing to forego a higher level of one attribute to obtain a higher level of another. The proposed method, trade-off analysis, is based on employee decision behavior regarding several alternatives.

Conjoint measurement, of which trade-off analysis is a part, is based on the notion that the importance of various objects in an individual's environment can be determined relative to the value of other objects, when the value of the one object might be unmeasureable alone. Although the technique requires only rank-order data, it produces measurements that are stronger than rank order. Hence, conjoint measurement is similar in some respects to non-metric scaling (Johnson, 1974).

A primary criticism of conjoint measurement in its pure form is that data collection is rather cumbersome, usually involving the use of orthogonal arrays. Johnson (1974) approached the problem of data collection complexity by suggesting the use of trade-off matrices (hence the term "trade-off analysis"). The rows and columns of each matrix represent alternative levels of two different attributes (i.e., pay or vacation time). The respondent is presented with several of these matrices, the total number of which is determined by the number of attributes. Each attribute must be compared, pair-wise, with every other attribute. An example trade-off matrix is presented in Figure 1.

*From *Personnel Administrator*, May 1983, pp. 45ff. Copyright 1983. Reprinted with permission of The American Society for Personnel Administration, Alexandria, Va.

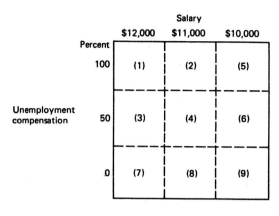

FIGURE 1
Sample trade-off matrix.

MAKING THE CHOICES

Levels of one attribute are listed across the top of each matrix, while levels of another attribute are listed along one side of the matrix. The respondent puts a "1" in the cell that represents his most desired combination of the two attributes, a "2" in the cell which represents the second most desired combination and so forth. Analysis of such matrices results in the computation of a utility function for each attribute, from which inferences can be made concerning individual preferences.

Analysis of this one matrix presented in Figure 1 yields significant information about this hypothetical employee. As might be expected, the employee's first choice is maximum salary ($12,000) and maximum unemployment compensation (100 percent). The choice behavior is more useful at the second and third levels, however, This individual is willing to "trade-off" $1,000 of salary to retain the security of 100 percent unemployment compensation. At the next level, preferences shift back to salary at the expense of reduced unemployment compensation. Such individual analysis is tedious, however, so a more practical approach is through aggregate analysis.

After the data has been collected, mean values for each cell are computed. Since this data is only at the rank order level, standard regression techniques are inappropriate. Monotone regression, however, can be properly utilized, A dummy variable coefficient matrix, consisting of zeros and ones, is used to indicate the presence or absence in an object of each level of each attribute.

This matrix has a row for each job dimension and a column for each attribute level (high, medium and low). The pair-wise regression algorithm developed by Johnson (1975) can be used to compute pair-wise utility values. This algorithm seeks a set of weights, one for each column, such that the weighted row sums of the coefficient matrix are monotonic with the respondent's rank order of preferences among the job elements described by that matrix. These weights, or utility values, can be interpreted as the importance of each attribute level for the total sample.

The practical usefulness of trade-off analysis has been primarily developed in the area of consumer research (Johnson, 1974; Fiedler, 1972). Other forms of the technique have also been used in analyzing preferences for hypothetical job offers differing in salary, city and type of work (Fischer, 1976) and in selecting preferred college applicants differing in intellectual ability, emotional stability and social facility (Tversky, 1969).

JOB DIMENSIONS EXPLORED

In a study conducted by the authors (Griffin & Chonko, 1977), the relative importance of four job dimensions—variety, autonomy, identity and feedback— was explored. As can be seen in Figure 2, trade-off analysis provides a utility function for each level of each factor.

To find the utility for jobs possessing combinations of these attributes, the utilities for each job dimension level are read from Figure 2. For example, a job possessing high levels of feedback and autonomy and low levels of identity and variety, has a total utility of 2.23 ($U_1 = .92 + U_2 = .97 + U_3 = .10 + U_4 = .24 = 2.23$), the sum of the four separate utilities.

The job that possesses the highest utility is the one which consists of high levels of feedback, autonomy, variety and medium levels of identity. Its total utility is

FIGURE 2
Utilities for four job dimensions.

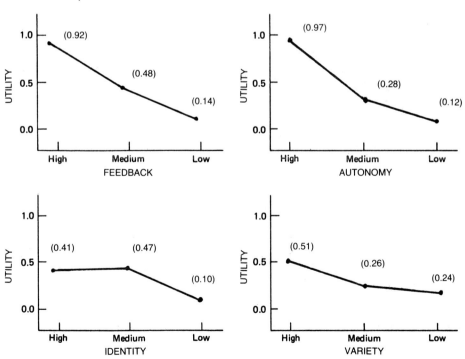

2.77 (.92 + .97 + .51 + .47 = 2.77). This procedure can be followed for all job design combinations.

High autonomy displays the highest utility, according to Figure 2. But how important is autonomy in relation to the other job dimensions? Since all of the utility scales are expressed in a common unit of measurement, utility ranges can be compared to get an idea of their relative importance. In the case of the job design data, the utility ranges are the following:

Feedback	(.92−.14) =	.78
Identity	(.47−.10) =	.37
Variety	(.51−.24) =	.27
Autonomy	(.97−.12) =	.85

Figure 3 depicts the relative sizes of the utility ranges. Job autonomy is the most important factor in job design, followed closely by feedback. These account for about 71 percent of the total utility range.

DESIGNING PACKAGES

Trade-off analysis has a number of possible applications by the personnel and/or wage and salary administrator. Traditionally, salary and benefit packages have been arbitrarily designed by management or by management and union negotiators. This approach is administratively efficient, since all employees receive the same benefit package. But it also suffers for this very reason. That is, it is universally applied within the firm, with little allowance for individual preferences.

At the other extreme is the new approach of the "cafeteria benefits plan," whereby each individual employee chooses the particular package of benefits and

FIGURE 3
Relative importance of four job dimensions.

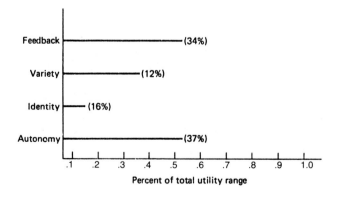

Percent of total utility range

salary appropriate for his/her own situation. This approach is popular among employees, but is administratively costly.

Trade-off analysis offers the alternative of a mid-range strategy. That is, personnel can take into account employee preferences at the group level without the administrative complexity of individualized plans.

The pair-wise task is a relatively simple one, capable of being used productively with employees from a wide range of socio-economic levels. In addition, trade-off analysis provides the researcher with robust predictions derived from simple rank order data. The personnel administrator has at his disposal a large variety of potential rewards that employees want. It is unlikely, however, that these are all of equal importance. The pair-wise approach possesses the advantage that the number of attributes to be studied is limited only by length of interview and respondent endurance considerations.

REVIEW QUESTIONS

1 Some motivational theories have attempted to identify the needs present in broad groups of employees. How is trade-off analysis different in its approach?

2 From a practical standpoint, trade-off analysis may assume that each employee's needs are relatively constant. How safe is this assumption?

3 In addition to job design factors and economic rewards, what other applications are there for trade-off analysis?

READING 43

The Design of Flexible Work Schedules and Employee Responses: Relationships and Process

Jon L. Pierce
John W. Newstrom*

*   *   *

A large body of literature extols the value of flexible working hours as a means of increasing employee job satisfaction and organizational attendance, strengthening organizational commitment, occasionally increasing performance, and decreasing experienced symptoms of stress. This literature also illustrates a wide

*Reprinted from Jon L. Pierce and John W. Newstrom, "The Design of Flexible Work Schedules and Employee Responses: Relationships and Process," *Journal of Occupational Behaviour*, October 1983, pp. 258–262. © 1983. Reprinted with permission of John Wiley & Sons, Ltd.

variation in the nature of flexible working hour programmes (e.g. staggered start, staggered week, flexitime, variable hours, and the variations within each) that have been devised and implemented. However, our conceptual understanding of the flexible hour–employee response relationship is still at an embryonic level. Empirically we have observed attitude and behaviour changes following a shift from fixed to flexible working hour arrangements. Previous studies have failed to explore which flexible working hour features are salient to employee attitudes and behaviours, or the process through which this association occurs. This study has attempted to examine empirically the relationship between a number of employee attitude and behaviour variables with different design features of flexible working hour arrangements. This study also examined one process by which flexible working hour systems influence employee attitudes and behaviours. Employee perceptions of time autonomy (i.e., experienced work scheduling flexibility) were examined as an intervening variable in the work schedule–employee response relationship.

STUDY OBSERVATIONS

In sharp contrast to almost all the previous literature, one of the most startling observations emerging from this investigation is the absence of a significant relationship between the flexible work schedule variables and employee job satisfaction. With regard to the other employee attitudes, the data suggest that the flexible work schedule variables may have an association with the level of employee commitment to the employing organization. In addition, experienced symptoms of psychological stress may be less under a flexible working hour arrangement.

The weakness of the relationships observed between the flexible working hour design features and the attitude variables may be a function of the process through which this association occurs. It was proposed that as work schedules become increasingly flexible employees will experience increased work schedule flexibility (time autonomy). As employees experience increased time autonomy, they will become increasingly job satisfied, organizationally committed, and they will experience fewer symptoms of psychological stress. Thus, it was posited that perceived time autonomy acts as an intervening variable in the flexible work schedule–employee response relationship.

In the process of testing the intervening variable relationship it was observed that the flexibility of the work schedule (especially flexibility stemming from schedule variability, schedule flexibility, the freedom to schedule work time without supervisory approval, and a small set of core times) was positively associated with employee perceptions of time autonomy. Time autonomy was also significantly associated with job satisfaction, organizational commitment, and experienced symptoms of psychological stress, while not related to either behavioural variable. Testing the full intervening variable model provided consistent and strong evidence that time autonomy mediates the flexible work schedule−employee attitude relationship. The employees who experienced increased time autonomy were increasingly job satisfied, organizationally committed, and experienced fewer symptoms of psychological stress.

Results from the study suggest that perceived time autonomy does not mediate the flexible work system−employee behaviour relationship. It is noted that a significant main effect for schedule flexibility exists for absenteeism and performance. Both of the behavioural variables have a positive association with the work schedule variables, suggesting increases in performance and absenteeism with increasingly flexible working hour arrangements. A detailed understanding of these main effects awaits further inquiry.

MANAGERIAL IMPLICATIONS

The results from this investigation have important implications for the design or modification of flexible working hour systems. These implications centre around the value of flexible hour systems, their multidimensionality, the critical design features to be included, and the necessity to ensure employee perceptions of time autonomy. The conclusions are offered here under the assumption that prevailing organizational conditions permit their implementation.

First, these results support the continued use of flexible working hour arrangements. This continues the line of support for the non-traditional approach to work scheduling as summarized by Glueck (1979), Golembiewski and Proehl (1978), Cohen and Gadon (1978), Pierce and Newstrom (1980), and Ronen (1981). Second, the designer of a flexible working hour system must be aware that flexible working hour arrangements are multidimensional systems. As a consequence the designer must not only consider the signals being sent to the employee from the total system, but consideration must also be given to the independent messages being transmitted from each of its component parts. (That is, are consistent messages being transmitted to the employee, or are some features giving autonomy while others restrict this autonomy?). Third, four design features appear to be particularly salient for favourable employee attitudes (i.e. job satisfaction, organizational commitment, and experienced symptoms of psychological stress) and behaviours (i.e. performance and absenteeism). The results suggest that *the flexible schedule should be designed with a relatively narrow set of core hours and multiple bands of flexible time, coupled with the option of changing frequently the pattern of hours worked without the necessity of obtaining prior supervisory approval.* Fourth, the flexible working hour system should be designed and implemented so as to provide maximum assurance that employees will *understand* its component parts and the totality, *identify* the degree of autonomy that the system provides, and *experience* the inherent flexibility. These results may be achieved by involving all employees in the design of a work schedule that is conducive to the coordination of work, that is in harmony with one's personal rhythms (i.e. social, personal, and circadian rhythms), and that encourages the employee to continually use the flexibility provided by the system.

LIMITATIONS OF THE STUDY AND RESEARCH NEEDS

This study has a number of methodological limitations that need to be recognized. The design of this study attempted to control for effects attributable to a single organization, organization type, size, and core technology. As a consequence the external validity of the study is limited by the fact that all eight samples derive from organizations operating in this same industry. Controlling for job classification gives rise to another and possibly more significant external validity problem. The sample is not only small, but it is exclusively clerical in nature. The control for certain threats to internal validity raises concern about whether the results are a function of other organizational, individual, or community-based factors which were not identified or accounted for by the design of the study. Future research should constructively replicate this study so as to extend its internal and external validity.

Time autonomy conceptually and empirically plays a central role in this investigation. It is important to note that this scale is still in its developmental stage. It is not known, for example, whether the full domain of this construct is being assessed, nor do we know whether there is contamination of this measure by other elements of autonomy provided by the work environment. Clearly, additional validation research for this scale is warranted.

The formal flexible working hour system was operationalized in this investigation. Future research needs to consider whether the employee is experiencing the formal flexible working hour arrangement, or whether some informal system is actually operating. This difference may account for some of the variance from this investigation.

As previously noted very little work has been directed toward the identification of design features for a flexible working hour arrangement. It is clear that more conceptual and experimental work is needed in this area. Future research should experimentally manipulate various design features so as to assess the independent and interactive role played by various design features.

A REVISED CONCEPTUAL PERSPECTIVE

The evidence from this investigation supports the conceptual position taken by Cohen and Gadon (1978), Pierce and Newstrom (1980), and Ronen (1981). In each case it was argued that flexible working hours provide the employee with flexibility, and flexibility becomes the central force generating favourable employee attitudes and behaviours.

The search for an understanding of the flexible work schedule–employee response relationship, however, is not complete. The results from this investigation suggest that two different approaches should be pursued in an attempt to understand this complex relationship.

From an attitudinal perspective there is evidence suggesting that there is a psychological process operating. It is believed that perceptions of time autonomy (i.e. experienced flexibility) impact employee attitudes through need fulfilment.

It has been argued (Pierce and Newstrom, 1980; Ronen, 1981) that many employees possess the need for autonomy and responsibility, the need for a harmonization between work and personal time demands, and a desire to participate in decisions. Flexible working hour arrangements provide for the fulfillment of these needs, thereby impacting cognitive and affective states (e.g., organizational commitment, job satisfaction).

The behavioural effects are less clearly understood. We speculate that there is an interaction going on between a psychological and behavioural process that mediates the flexible hour–behaviour relationship. Pierce and Newstrom (1980) argued that a flexible working hour arrangement can be associated with performance under the following conditions: through the reduction of stress, by adopting a work schedule that is in harmony with one's circadian rhythms, and through the avoidance/reduction of tardiness and absenteeism. If employees manage their work–non-work time so as to harmonize conflicting demands upon their time, to take advantage of their circadian rhythms, and to avoid absenteeism and tardiness we would expect to witness favourable behavioural reactions to a flexible working hour arrangement. In conclusion, we are proposing that not only must the employee *experience* the autonomy provided by a flexible schedule, but this autonomy must be behaviourally *managed*.

REFERENCES

Allenspach, I. (1972). 'Flexible working time: Its development and applications in Switzerland,' *Occupational Psychology*, **46**, 209–215.

Allport, G. W. (1947). 'The psychology of participation,' *Psychological Review*, **52**, 177–132.

Baum, S. and Young, W. M. (1974). *A Practical Guide to Flexible Working Hours*, Noyes Data Corporation, Park Ridge, N.J.

Cohen, J. (1970). 'Multiple regression as a general data-analytic system,' *Psychological Bulletin*, **6**, 426–443.

Cohen, A. R. and Gadon, H. (1978). *Alternative Work Schedules: Integrating Individual and Organizational Need*, Addison-Wesley, Reading MA.

Dawis, R. V., England, G. W. and Lofquist, L. H. (1968). 'A theory of work adjustment,' *Minnesota Studies in Vocational Rehabilitation* XXIII, Bulletin 67, University of Minnesota.

Fields, C. J. (1974). 'Variable work hours—It's MONY experience,' *Personnel Journal*, **53** (9) 675–678.

Gleuck, W. F. (1979). 'Changing hours of work: A review and analysis of the research,' *The Personnel Administrator*, **24**(3), 44–67.

Golembiewski, R. T. and Proehl, C. W., Jr. (1978). 'A survey of the empirical literature on flexible workhours: Character and consequences of a major innovation,' *Academy of Management Review*, **3**, 837–853.

Gordon, J. R. M. and Elbing, A. O. (1971). 'The flexible hour work week—European trend is growing,' *The Business Quarterly*, 66–72.

Harvey, B. H. and Luthans, F. (1979). 'Flexitime: An empirical analysis of its real meaning and impact', *Business Horizons*, **27**(3), 31–36.

Kim, J. S. and Campagna, A. F. (1981). 'Effects of flexitime on employee attendance and performance: A field experiment,' *Academy of Management Journal*, **24**, 729–741.

Nollen, S. D. and Martin, V. H. (1978). *Alternative Work Schedules, Part I: Flexitime*, American Management Association Survey Report: AMACOM.

Oldham, G. R. and Hackman, J. R. (1981). 'Relationships between organizational structure and employee reactions: Comparing alternative frameworks,' *Administrative Science Quarterly*, **25**, 66–83.

Orpin, C. (1981). 'Effects of flexible working hours on employee satisfaction and performance: A field experiment,' *Journal of Applied Psychology*, **66**, 113–115.

Patchen, M. (1970). *Participation, Achievement, and Involvement on the Job*. Prentice-Hall, Englewood Cliffs, N.J.

Pierce, J. L. and J. W. Newstrom (1980). 'Toward a conceptual clarification of employee responses to flexible working hours: A work adjustment approach,' *Journal of Management* **6**, 117–134.,

Porter, L. W., Steers, R. M., Mowday, R. T. and Boulain, P. V. (1974). 'Organizational commitment, job satisfaction, and turnover among psychiatric technicians,' *Journal of Applied Psychology*, **59**, 603–609.

Ronen, S. (1981). *Flexible Working Hours*, McGraw-Hill, New York.

Rousseau, D. M. (1978). 'Measures of technology as predictors of employee attitudes,' *Journal of Applied Psychology*, **63**, 213–218.

Schein, V. E., Mauner, E. H. and Novak, J. R. (1977). 'Impact of flexible working hours on productivity,' *Journal of Applied Psychology*, **62**, 463–465.

Steers, R. M. (1977). 'Antecedents and outcomes of organizational commitment,' *Administrative Science Quarterly*, **22**, 46–56.

Steers, R. M. and Rhodes, S. R. (1978). 'Major influences on employee attendance: A process model,' *Journal of Applied Psychology*, **63**, 391–407.

Swart, J. C. (1974). 'What time shall I go to work today?', *Business Horizons*, **17**(5), 19–26.

Weiss, D. J. Dawis, R. V., England, G. W. and Lofquist, L. H. (1967). *Manual for the Minnesota Satisfaction Questionnaire*, University of Minnesota, Industrial Relations Center, Work Adjustment Project, Minneapolis.

REVIEW QUESTIONS

1 Flexible work schedules are multidimensional, and complex. Why do they seem to result in desirable employee responses?

2 Describe the role of perceived time autonomy in affecting employee attitudes resulting from flexible work schedules. How does this relate to the Chonko-Griffin finding that autonomy has the highest utility?

3 Pierce and Newstrom suggest that time autonomy must be both experienced and managed by employees. What actions can a manager take to increase the likelihood of these two processes?

CHAPTER 12

ORGANIZATIONAL AND JOB DESIGN

READING 44

Trends in Organizational Design

Keith Davis*

From time to time it is appropriate to back away from a current situation in order to examine it in broader perspective. In this manner we can get a better understanding of the significance of events around us. The following discussion has that purpose. It seeks to understand the directions in which organizational design is moving. As used in this discussion the term "organizational design" refers both to the design of the job, such as the number of work elements performed, and the design of the organizational environment itself, such as rigidity of structure, communication systems, and amount of control.

CLASSICAL ORGANIZATIONAL DESIGN

Classical organizational design dominated management thinking for the first half of the twentieth century. It had its origins in the ideas of Adam Smith, who in 1776 in the *Wealth of Nations* [18] presented a discussion of pinmakers to show how division of labor could improve productivity a hundredfold or more. However, it was not until the early 1900's that the full philosophy of classical design was presented by Frederick W. Taylor [19] and Henri Fayol [5]. As it evolved from Taylor and Fayol, classical design used full division of labor, rigid hierarchy, and standardization of labor to reach its objectives. The idea was to lower costs by using unskilled repetitive labor that could be trained easily to do a small part of a job. Job performance was tightly controlled by a large hierarchy that strictly enforced *the one best way of work*.

In spite of our tendency occasionally to think otherwise, the classical design did gain substantial improvements. There were remarkable increases in economic productivity, something which was sorely needed by an impoverished world. *The difficulty was that these gains were achieved at considerable human costs.* There was excessive division of labor and overdependence on rules, procedures, and hierarchy. The worker became isolated from fellow workers. The result was higher turnover and absenteeism. Quality declined, and workers became alienated. Conflict arose as workers tried to improve their lot. Management's response to this situation was to tighten the controls, to increase the supervision, and to organize more rigidly. These actions were calculated to improve the situation, but they only made it worse. Management made a common error by treating the *symptoms* rather than the causes of the problems. The job itself simply was not satisfying.

*Adapted from Dennis F. Ray and Thad B. Green (eds.), *Academy of Management Proceedings*, 1973 (Mississippi State, Miss.: Academy of Management, 1974), pp. 1–16. © 1974 by Academy of Management. Reprinted with permission.

It took management—and academicians—some time to recognize the nature and severity of the problem. In 1939 Roethlisberger and Dickson published their powerful behavioral interpretation of management [17]. Then in 1949 Douglas McGregor in his insightful way warned, "Practically all the means of need-satisfaction which workers today obtain from their employment can be utilized *only after they leave their jobs*" [16, p. 117, italics in original]. He pointed out that all of the popular personnel devices of the time, such as vacations and insurance benefits, were satisfactions received off the job.

A few years later in 1957 Chris Argyris charged that poor organizational design established a basic incongruence between formal organizations and the workers' drives for self-actualization. Organizations tend to ignore the potential of people, he claimed. They fail to encourage self-development in areas that are meaningful to each individual. They do not encourage responsibility and innovation.They do not develop and employ the whole person. At lower levels the workers become alienated, frustrated, and unproductive, and they fight the company with a certain sense of social justice. The problem is also severe at management levels, because the situation lacks trust, openness, and risk-taking. The frustrated manager often abdicates his independence, becoming a servile "organization man" in the words of William H. Whyte [23].

Another straw in the wind for change was the famous need hierarchy presented by A. H. Maslow [15, pp. 370−396]. His hierarchy suggested that as society made social and economic progress, new needs of employees would arise. In turn, these new needs require new forms of job and organizational design. The problem was not so much that the work itself had changed for the worse, but rather *the employees were changing*. Design of jobs and organizations had failed to keep up with widespread changes in worker aspirations and attitudes. Employers now had two reasons for redesigning jobs and organizations.

1 Classical design originally gave inadequate attention to human factors.
2 The needs and aspirations of employees themselves were changing.

HUMANISTIC ORGANIZATIONAL DESIGN

In taking corrective action the most obvious direction for management to go was to swing the pendulum away from mechanistic classical design toward a more behavioral, participative, humanistic design, also called organic design by Burns and Stalker [4]. The new design furnished a wide variety of humanistic options, such as the following:

Classical design	Humanistic design
Closed system	Open system
Job specialization	Job enlargement
Centralization	Decentralization
Authority	Consensus

(Continued)

Classical design	Humanistic design
Tight hierarchy	Lose project organization
Technical emphasis	Human emphasis
Rigid procedures	Flexible procedures
Command	Consultation
Vertical communication	Multidirectonal communication
Negative environment	Positive environment
Maintenance needs	Motivational needs
Tight control	Management by objectives
Autocratic approach	Democratic approach

The objective was to make the job environment supportive rather than threatening to employees. The job should be a place that stimulates their drives and aspirations and helps them to grow as whole persons. Work should be psychologically rewarding as well as economically rewarding. By the 1950s organizations were moving gradually in this direction.

In addition to Maslow, McGregor, Argyris, and Roethlisberger already mentioned, the following persons made significant contributions to humanistic organizational design. Rensis Likert [14] emphasized organizational development and offered four categories called Systems 1, 2, 3, and 4, to describe the move from authoritarian management (System 1) to participative management (System 4). Organizational development was used to help organizations gradually move toward System 4, which was considered the ideal system.

Blake and Mouton [3] offered organizational development in the form of a managerial grid which emphasized leadership style. It was perceived that the leader set the environmental structure and climate for the work group; consequently, the most effective way to move toward humanistic design is through the leadership structure of the organization. By using the grid various managerial styles may be identified in order to discuss both existing styles which need correction and more idealized styles.

Herzberg [10] took an unusual and controversial approach by emphasizing a difference between maintenance and motivational factors. Herzberg identified some job conditions that operate primarily to dissatisfy employees when the conditions are absent, but their presence does not motivate employees in a strong way. These are dissatisfiers or maintenance factors, because they maintain the employee ready for effective motivation. These maintenance factors arise primarily from the "job context" or environment, such as pension, vacations, wages and interpersonal relations. Another set of conditions operates primarily to build strong motivation and high job satisfaction, but their absence rarely proves dissatisfying. These are satisfiers or motivational factors. They arise primarily from the job content itself, such as achievement, growth, and responsibility. The Herzberg model provoked much controversy about its correctness, but regardless it has been an effective vehicle to convince managers of significant distinctions in types of rewards offered by management.

Bennis [2] presented the fundamental ideal of humanistic democracy and insisted that in the work place "democracy is inevitable." According to this line of reasoning, democracy is inevitable because it is the only form which provides the flexibility and decentralization which large, complex organizations require. In the complex organization the top executive cannot know enough about all functions of the organization to make effective decisions. The executive must depend on extensive horizontal communication and functional expertise for guidance. Democratic, humanistic organizational systems are the most effective for this situation. They are a decision-making necessity and also a behavioral necessity, because they provide the optimal environment for today's knowledge workers.

Without question, humanistic designs were an improvement; however, a funny thing happened on the way to this proposed utopia. Just as classical design generated excesses, so did humanistic design. The model builders forgot that the behavioral system in an organization is part of several larger systems, such as the technological system and the economic system. If decisions are made in terms of only the behavioral system, the situation becomes unbalanced and the same kinds of rigidities develop that the classicists caused.

A prime example of the descent from humanistic utopia to worldly reality is the experience of Non-Linear Systems, Inc., of San Diego. In the 1960s it changed its organizational design to the behavioral model, entirely eliminating assembly lines and time cards. As the company grew, it was hailed as the harbinger of the future. One behavioral scientist commented about his associates. "There was so much excitement it was almost seductive." The excitement died when the company met a business slump and the new system was unable to endure adversity. Sales dropped nearly fifty percent and profits disappeared. In order to restore profitability the president took a more controlling, classical role. He commented, "I may have lost sight of the purpose of business, which is not to develop new theories of management." And he added a comment about the rigidities of the humanistic model, "We didn't take into account the varied emotional and mental capacities of our employees when we changed the assembly line." [21, pp. 99–100]

CONTINGENCY ORGANIZATIONAL DESIGN

The move toward a more system-wide way of thinking about organizations is producing a swing toward contingency or situational designs in the future. This is clearly the appropriate emphasis because it escapes narrow perspectives that have restricted earlier approaches. It is still strongly humanistic, but it is more complete than that, because it includes all situational factors including the technology and economic environment. *Contingency organization design* means that different environments require different organizational relationships for optimum effectiveness [9, p. 59]. No longer is there a "one best way" whether it is classical or behavioral.

Contingency management, for example, means that job enrichment should be applied with the realization that some employees do not want their jobs enriched. Some prefer easier and more routine work. Some are troubled by a challenge.

Others prefer a friendly situation and are not much concerned about job content. Each person and situation is different. Many organizations have policies and procedures that reflect a single value system based on the belief that all employees want the same work environment and fringe benefits; consequently, these firms are not able to adjust situationally to different conditions [1, pp. 8−23].

Early research evidence of contingency design was provided by Woodward in 1965 [24]. She studied 100 firms in England to determine what structural variables were related to economic success. Firms were classified according to three types of production technology: unit, mass, and continuous process production. Research disclosed that the effective form of organization varied according to the firm's technology. Mass production was more successful with classical design, while unit and process production were more successful when they used humanistic designs.

Fiedler probably provided the name for the contingency approach, with his studies of leadership published in 1967 [6]. He showed that an effective leadership pattern is dependent on the interaction of a number of variables including task structure and leadership position power. Generally a more classical approach is effective when conditions are substantially favorable or unfavorable for the leader, but a more behavioral approach is better in the intermediate zone of favorability. The intermediate conditions are the ones most commonly found in organizations.

Lawrence and Lorsch [13] popularized the contingency approach with their study of organizations in stable and changing environments in 1967. They showed that in certain stable environments the classical forms tend to be more effective. In changing environments the opposite is true. More humanistic forms are required to permit organizations to respond effectively to their unstable environment.

Since contingency design deals with a large number of variables, it is not easy to apply, but some experimental applications have produced excellent results. For example, in the Treasury Department of American Telephone and Telegraph Company, educated and intelligent employees handle correspondence with stockholders. Originally they worked in a highly structured environment under close supervision in order to assure a suitable standard of correspondence. Under these conditions, quality of work was low and turnover was high. The job design was too routine and lacking in challenge.

Using a control group and a test group, the jobs of the test group were enriched as follows: (1) the employees were permitted to sign their own names to the letters they prepared; (2) the employees were held responsible for the quality of their work; (3) they were encouraged to become experts in the kinds of problems that appealed to them; and (4) subject matter experts were provided for consultation regarding problems.

The control group remained unchanged after six months, but the test group improved by all measurements used. The measures included turnover, productivity, absences, promotions from the group, and costs. The quality measurement index climbed from the thirties to the nineties.

American Telephone and Telegraph Company also has achieved excellent results in other job enrichment efforts. In the directory-compilation function, name omissions dropped from 2 to 1 percent. In frame wiring, errors declined from 13 to 0.5 percent, and the number of frames wired increased from 700 to over 1,200 [7; 8].

Equally successful results have been achieved at Emery Air Freight using the behavioral modification ideas of B. F. Skinner. The company made design changes in the communication system in order to provide positive reinforcement for workers. In this situation the company had been using large containers to reduce handling costs for forwarding small packages. The company has a standard of 90 percent use of the containers for small packages, but research showed that actual utilization was only 45 percent.

The communications system was redesigned to give workers daily feedback on how near they came to the 90 percent goal. Furthermore, supervisors provided positive verbal reinforcement. The result was that when the new communications design was applied, *in a single day* use of large containers increased to 95 percent. As this design was applied to other facilities throughout the nation, use of large containers at these facilities also rose to 95 percent in a single day. The high performance level was maintained for three years following the new design [22, pp. 64–6].

A more complete effort was the organizational design of a new General Foods Corporation pet food plant to incorporate appropriate behavioral and system ideas. The new plant offered a completely different way of work compared with a traditional pet food plant. Work is performed by autonomous teams of 7–14 persons. Most support functions are integrated within the teams, meaning that very little staff is provided. Job design is used to enlarge jobs to increase the challenge in them. Decision making is decentralized, and group leaders encourage team members to make as many decisions as possible. Full feedback about performance is given to all members [20, pp. 70–81].

The result compared with other plants is that absenteeism and turnover are reduced and productivity has increased. Furthermore, rework of faulty quality material has been reduced 90 percent. The plant definitely shows superior results compared with conventionally designed plants, although it is too new to be sure whether these results will last indefinitely [12, p. 54].

Although experimental contingency design efforts have had remarkable success, they do not signal a quick coming of utopia at work. Classical design and strict behavioral design gave easy answers, but contingency design is difficult to apply. Much about the workplace is still unknown. We also know relatively little about people and the social systems in which they interact. The road ahead is going to be a rocky one. If predictions are appropriate at this point, my opinion is that progress in organizational design will be slower than most experts think. It is easy to theorize about how to redesign organizations and jobs, but actual practice is much more difficult. Furthermore, changes in design assume certain changes in the way managers think, and we all know that attitudes and frameworks change very slowly. Traditional ways of work and organizational design have been entrenched for centuries, and they will not change easily.

Meanwhile, workers are changing, and the resulting psychological dissonance between them and their jobs is likely to grow worse before it becomes better. There will be many conflicts as society wrestles with whether organizational design can be restructured to increase productivity and employee fulfillment. In all this turmoil, however, the important point to remember is that we are making progress. We are moving toward more contingency design with enriched jobs and open organizational systems.

REFERENCES

1 Argyris, Chris, *Personality and Organization: The Conflict between the System and the Individual* (New York: Harper & Row, Publishers, Inc., 1957).

2 Bennis, Waren G., *Changing Organizations: Essays on the Development and Evolution of Human Organization* (New York: McGraw-Hill Book Company, 1966).

3 Blake, Robert R., and Jane S. Mouton, *The Managerial Grid* (Houston: Gulf Publishing Company, 1964).

4 Burns, Tom, and G. M. Stalker, *The Management of Innovation* (London: Tavistock Publications, 1961).

5 Fayol, Henri, *General and Industrial Management* (1916) trans. by Constance Storrs (New York: Pitman Publishing Corporation, 1949).

6 Fiedler, Fred E., *A Theory of Leadership Effectiveness* (New York: McGraw-Hill Book Company, 1967).

7 Ford, Robert N., *Motivation through the Work Itself* (New York: American Management Association, 1969).

8 Gellette, Malcolm B., "Work Itself as a Motivator," speech at annual meeting, Western Division, Academy of Management, Salt Lake City, Utah (March 20, 1970).

9 Hellriegel, Don, and John W. Slocum, Jr., "Organizational Design: A Contingency Approach," *Business Horizons,* Vol XVI, No. 2 (April, 1973), pp. 59–68.

10 Herzberg, Frederick, Bernard Mausner, and Barbara Snyderman, *The Motivation to Work* (New York: John Wiley & Sons, Inc., 1959).

11 Hughes, Charles L., and Vincent S. Flowers, "Shaping Personnel Strategies to Disparate Value Systems," *Personnel,* Vol. 50, No 2 (March–April, 1973), pp. 8–23.

12 "Latest Moves to Fight Boredom on the Job," *U.S. News & World Report* (December 25, 1972), pp. 52–54.

13 Lawrence, Paul R., and Jay W. Lorsch, *Organization and Environment: Managing Differentiation and Integration* (Boston: Harvard Graduate School of Business Administration, 1967).

14 Likert, Rensis, *The Human Organization: Its Management and Value* (New York: McGraw-Hill Book Company, 1967).

15 Maslow, A. H., "A Theory of Human Motivation," *Psychological Review,* Vol. 50 (1943), pp. 370–396.

16 McGregor, Douglas, "Toward a Theory of Organized Human Effort in Industry," in Arthur Kornhauser, editor, *Psychology of Labor-Management Relations* (Champaign, Ill.: Industrial Relations Research Association, 1949), pp. 111–122.

17 Roethlisberger, F. J., and W. J. Dickson, *Management and the Worker* (Cambridge, Mass.: Harvard University Press, 1939).

18 Smith, Adam, *An Inquiry into the Nature and Causes of the Wealth of Nations* (1776) (New York: Modern Library, Inc., 1937).

19 Taylor, Frederick W., *The Principles of Scientific Management* (New York: Harper & Brothers, 1911).

20 Walton, Richard E., "How to Counter Alienation in the Plant," *Harvard Business Review*, Vol. 50, No. 6 (November–December, 1972), pp. 70–81.

21 "Where Being Nice to Workers Didn't Work," *Business Week* (January 20, 1973), pp. 99–100.

22 "Where Skinner's Theories Work," *Business Week* (December 2, 1972), pp. 64–65.

23 Whyte, William H., Jr., *The Organization Man* (New York: Simon and Schuster, Inc., 1956).

24 Woodward, Joan, *Industrial Organization: Theory and Practice* (London: Oxford University Press, 1965).

REVIEW QUESTIONS

1 Briefly contrast classical, humanistic, and contingency organizational design.

2 Based on your life experiences and the prior readings in this book, are you optimistic or pessimistic about the prospects for more enriched jobs and open organizational systems? Explain.

READING 45

Can Organizational Design Make Up for Motivational Decline?

John B. Miner
Norman R. Smith*

America may be running short of the kind of people it will need for top management roles in the near future. The heart of the problem is not numbers but motivation; test results suggest that, compared to the students of two decades ago, today's business students have values and attitudes that make them far less suited to run the typical hierarchical American corporation.

For our large business firms—and government agencies—this finding poses a substantial threat. Without some kind of active intervention there will soon simply not be enough good managers to go around. The intervention can take several forms which will be explored, but the need for action should already be apparent. If, as the test data indicate, the motivational problem started to become acute among the 20 year olds of some 15 years ago, then many companies should already have begun to experience the first effects of a talent shortage at the lower managerial levels.

*From *The Wharton Magazine*, Summer 1981, pp. 29–35. Reprinted with permission.

Such a shortage was forecast in a 1974 book by John B. Miner entitled *The Human Constraint*, which presented data for the period 1960–1973 on students' "motivation to manage." As will be seen, data for the rest of the 1970's indicate no significant increase among business students in the attitudes, or motivations, that correlate with managerial success.

What are these motivations? Before enumerating them, we should say a word about the theory underlying Miner's research: essentially, that for any given type of organization certain roles can be identified that the organization's members must play if it is to function effectively; further, these people must have certain underlying motivations that will induce them to play the appropriate roles. In the hierarchical organizations characteristic of American business today, the actions and motivations of managers are especially critical, since it is these people who must elicit (through positive or negative sanctions) productive contributions from lower-level employees. The roles successful managers must play and the motivations that will lead them to play these roles can be, we believe, described as follows (the importance of each role is also briefly explained):

Role Maintaining positive relations with higher-level management.
Motivational Base A favorable attitude toward people in positions of authority.
Importance In a hierarchical system, there must be communication and interaction with superiors; a manager must be able to represent his group upward in the organization and obtain support for his activities of higher level.

Role Competing with one's peers in the organization.
Motivational Base A desire to compete.
Importance In a hierarchy, rewards such as promotion to the highest levels and the largest salaries are unequally distributed; it therefore becomes necessary to distinguish oneself from one's peers.

Role Imposing one's will over subordinates.
Motivational Base A desire to exercise power over others.
Importance In a hierarchy, manipulation of sanctions and downward supervision are required: Managers must direct the behavior of subordinates so as to further their own objectives and the organization's; to the extent such activities yield satisfactions, they are more likely to be performed.

Role Playing a quasi-parental part in relations with subordinates.
Motivational Base A desire to assert oneself and guide others.
Importance In a hierarchy, the managerial role is, in many respects, modeled on a traditional parental role in the family, and accordingly, a degree of assertiveness (a "take charge" attitude) congruent with a parental role is required.

Role Standing out from the group.
Motivational Base A desire to be distinctive.

Importance   In a hierarchy, managers must assume a highly visible position, one clearly differentiated from the relative homogeneity of their subordinates.

Role   Handling routine administrative tasks.
Motivational Base   A desire to perform routine duties in a responsible manner.
Importance   In a hierarchy, it is essential that various routine decision-making and communication tasks be carried out; therefore, appropriate motivation and a sense of responsibility for such matters are required.

The degree to which people possess the motivations just enumerated can be measured by a paper-and-pencil test called the Miner Sentence Completion Scale (MSCS). It consists of forty open-ended statements such as "Members of Congress . . ."; "If I had to give a speech . . ."; "Doing paperwork . . ."; or "Playing tennis. . . ." (These are not actual questions.) Scores are obtained for overall motivation to manage and for each of the six attitudes described above that together constitute managerial motivation.

Evidence of the MSCS's validity for the purpose for which it was devised has now been obtained in more than 25 different samples. It does indeed appear to measure certain characteristics that make "a good manager." On the other hand, it has been consistently found to have practically no usefulness in predicting success in other contexts, such as in professional, entrepreneurial, or unstructured groups.

Miner's research with college students, using the MSCS, extends back to 1960 and now includes samples from the University of Oregon, the University of Maryland, Portland State University, Western Michigan University, the University of South Florida, Georgia State University, and Cleveland State University. In most cases, the samples were obtained in required undergraduate business administration courses, so that the students (mostly juniors) would represent a cross section of business majors, not just, say, marketing or accounting majors. At a number of schools, multiple samples were collected, and at some, data were collected for graduate business students as well.

The results of these two decades of testing are best illustrated using the data, presented in the accompanying table, obtained from undergraduate business students at the University of Oregon, where in 1960–1961 a total of 287 students were tested; in 1967–1968, 129 students; in 1972–1973, 86 students; and in 1980, 124 students. The average age of the students remained stable in the four samples (in the low twenties), but the proportion of women tripled between 1960–1961 and 1980, when it reached 43 percent of the sample.

As the table indicates, the proportion of the Oregon testees with high managerial motivation dropped from nearly two-thirds in 1960–1961 to only about a quarter in 1980. The figures in parentheses in the table refer to the number of testees showing high or low motivation. Looking at the components of motivation to manage, one sees that major decreases showed up in the extent of

TABLE 1
MOTIVATON TO MANAGE AMONG BUSINESS ADMINISTRATION STUDENTS
AT THE UNIVERSITY OF OREGON, 1960–1980

	1960–1961	1967–1968	1972–1973	1980
	Overall motivation to manage			
High motivation	64% (184)	39% (50)	23% (20)	26% (32)
Low motivation	36% (103)	61% (79)	77% (66)	74% (92)
	Favorable attitude toward authority figures			
High motivation	70% (200)	53% (69)	41% (35)	40% (50)
Low motivation	30% (87)	47% (60)	59% (51)	60% (74)
	Competitiveness			
High motivation	50% (143)	36% (46)	22% (19)	25% (31)
Low motivation	50% (144)	64% (83)	78% (67)	75% (93)
	Assertiveness			
High motivation	69% (197)	62% (80)	44% (38)	35% (43)
Low motivation	31% (90)	38% (49)	56% (48)	65% (81)
	Desire to exercise power			
High motivation	43% (123)	46% (59)	42% (36)	44% (54)
Low motivation	57% (164)	54% (70)	58% (50)	56% (70)
	Desire for a distinctive position			
High motivation	47% (136)	43% (56)	43% (37)	44% (54)
Low motivation	53% (151)	57% (73)	57% (49)	56% (70)
	Sense of responsibility			
High motivation	53% (151)	37% (48)	27% (23)	27% (33)
Low motivation	47% (136)	63% (81)	73% (63)	73% (91)

favorable attitudes toward authority figures, in competitiveness, in assertiveness, and in the desire to perform routine duties responsibly. The desires to exercise power and to assume a distinctive role, on the other hand, did not fluctuate in any meaningful fashion over the twenty-year period. Comparisons by Miner with the results from other schools show the Oregon data to be reasonably typical throughout the two decades.

These overall findings do need qualification in several respects. First, it appears that motivation began to decline in 1962 or 1963 (the date is impossible to pinpoint), continued to decline for approximately ten years, and then leveled off. The figures for 1980 are very close to those for 1972–1973. In fact, between 1972–1973 and 1980 the percent of students showing high motivation fluctuated by three points or less for all indexes except the assertiveness measure, where there was a nine percentage point drop. It would appear, then, that through the middle and late 1970's we were on a plateau. From this point, the figures could just as easily stay the same, plunge downward once again, or rise to their former generally positive levels.

A second qualification relates to the scores of men and women testees. In the early 1960's the females scored significantly below the males in overall managerial motivation and on a number of subscales, including those dealing with competitiveness, assertiveness, and desire for power. Although in some early samples female students exhibited more favorable attitudes toward authority and more administrative responsibility than males, the general pattern of MSCS results among business administration students in the early 1960's distinctly favored the males.

However, the pattern of decline since then has not been the same for both sexes. The females' scores have dropped less on overall motivation to manage, only about 60 percent as much as the males' scores. The women's decreases in favorable attitudes toward authority, competitiveness, and assertiveness, are all much less than those for the men, and on the two indexes that showed little change over the twenty years—those dealing with desire for power and assuming a distinctive role—the women's scores actually increased slightly (while the men's decreased). Only in the desire to perform administrative duties in a responsible manner is this pattern reversed, with the males' scores dropping less—69 percent of the female decline. The overall consequence of these changes is that in 1980 male and female business students were indistinguishable in terms of their managerial motivation. Among both groups, it was equally low.

How might companies cope with this managerial talent shortage as it hits them and expands at an accelerating rate through the organization? There are two basic types of approaches. One involves trying to upgrade managerial quality to fit the organization's demands. The other involves changing the structure of the organization itself to fit what might be the new motivations of its personnel.

The first approach includes such strategies as more rigorous selection procedures, the utilization of new sources of talent, and the use of role-motivation training to develop the requisite motives in managers. More rigorous selection means, among other things, starting with a larger pool of recruits, carefully assessing their motivation to manage, and offering highly attractive salaries and benefits to lure the best candidates. It may work for some organizations (largely at the expense of the competition) but becomes increasingly difficult as the overall talent pool shrinks. Similarly, drawing managers from previously neglected segments of the labor force (whether liberal arts rather than business majors, minority group members, or women) may well bring in new talent but may also prove to be of limited value. Whatever a person's background, that person will be a good manager only if he or she has, in addition to general intelligence, relevant knowledge to succeed in the job and, of course, motivation to manage.

Trying to give existing personnel greater motivation to manage, through managerial role-motivation courses, has produced positive results. These 20–30 hour lecture-discussion courses are aimed at helping managers deal with problems with subordinates and, at the same time, developing motivation to manage. Motivation has been shown to increase among both managers and business students completing such courses, although not everyone benefits equally; those who are less passive and more independent to start with seem to gain the most.

NEW ORGANIZATIONAL STRUCTURES

Of much greater current interest than these strategies for upgrading the managerial skills needed in a hierarchy are some of the newer organizational structures. These structures represent alternatives to hierarchy and therefore offer the possibility of substantially reducing the *need* for the kinds of people who function well as managers of hierarchically structured bureaucratic systems. Such alternatives include autonomous work groups, venture teams, and various methods of organizing the work of professionals.

To the extent that managers are actually displaced by these approaches, there will, of course, be less need for people with managerial motivation. At least in the case of autonomous work groups, it appears likely that managers will be displaced. The other approaches have not always yielded this result, but they appear to offer the opportunity to reduce managerial manpower if desired.

In autonomous work groups, hierarchical inducements are replaced by group pressure and rewards. In venture teams, aspects of the task itself, including a feeling of achievement, substitute for managerial actions. In professional units and organizations, the norms and sanctions of the profession become alternatives to managerial instructions and sanctioning.

To this point, then, the possibility of achieving a substantial reduction in the need for managerial manpower by creating nonbureaucratic structures appears feasible. However, there are two additional factors that must be considered. One is that the new nonbureaucratic structures, when applied to large organizations, typically operate at the lowest levels only. Almost without exception, large organizations become hierarchical once again above what would normally be considered the first level of supervision. In fact, we do not appear as yet to have a method of organizing the work of large numbers of individuals that is not, at some point, hierarchical in nature. Yet, substituting the new forms for even the first level of supervision would seem to offer all the managerial-manpower saving needed.

This may be true, but it is unlikely. For one thing, first-level supervisors have consistently been found to possess the lowest levels of motivation to manage. Thus, substituting for these positions may replace a large number of managers, but it will have practically no impact on the need for high levels of managerial motivation of the kind corporate officers typically possess. The impact on the total demand for motivated managers will not even approximate the reduction in number of managerial positions, because only low-managerial-motivation positions are being eliminated.

Furthermore, we are finding in our studies of plants organized into autonomous work groups that although the number of managers is down and productivity up in contrast with the traditional, hierarchical plants, these results are achieved in a context of *higher* levels of motivation to manage among those managers who do remain. The higher average motivation level probably is caused in part by the elimination of low-managerial-motivation, first-line supervisors in the autonomous-work-group plants, but it may also reflect a need for greater managerial motivation among those who remain in order to effectively manage the new boundary between hierarchical and autonomous-group systems.

What has been said is, of course, predicated on the assumption that methods of organizing large enterprises will not change dramatically in years to come. It is entirely possible that new forms will be found to replace the overarching bureaucratic umbrella that currently appears to be a necessity, regardless of the organizational form used at lower levels. Should this happen, the *managerial* talent shortage will unquestionably prove to have been a phantom.

But whatever happens with regard to the need for managerial motivation, there is no basis for assuming that talent shortages *per se* will not occur. The various alternatives to hierarchy all call for their own behavior and motivational patterns. As was said at the outset, in any type of organization there are certain identifiable roles the members must willingly play if the organization is to function effectively. It does not necessarily follow that because motivation to manage has declined, other motivational patterns that would make for the successful operation of other organizational forms have increased. In fact, it is entirely possible that all such patterns have decreased along with managerial motivation—in which case, we might well speak of a generalized decline in work motivation.

Unfortunately, in assessing motivational patterns unrelated to hierarchies, tools such as the Miner Sentence Completion Scale are, as has been noted, of virtually no help. The MSCS is simply not a predictor of effectiveness within the various alternatives to hierarchy.

Nevertheless, the roles and motives that would make such systems operate successfully can be at least tentatively identified and explained. For example, for one type of alternative, the group-based systems characteristic of autonomous work groups or voluntary organizations, the necessary roles and motives of members might be summarized as follows:

Role Interacting with other group members.

Motivational Base A desire for effective contact with people.

Importance In a group system, the members must spend considerable time working with each other in order to make and implement decisions; it is thus necessary that they enjoy affiliative relationships and the use of social skills to exert influence and minimize nonproductive conflict.

Role Maintaining group acceptance.

Motivational Base A desire for continuing group membership.

Importance In a group system, it is necessary that members identify with the group, both to facilitate participation in group processes and to make them responsive to group-administered sanctions, including the threat of expulsion; accordingly, a desire for acceptance and a sense of belonging in the group become necessary.

Role Having positive relations with peers.

Motivational Base A favorable attitude toward co-workers.

Importance Just as, in a hierarchy, favorable attitudes upward are required to facilitate communication, in a group system, favorable attitudes toward group members, or potential group members, are required to further the group's goals; these positive attitudes should take such forms as belief in others, trust, consideration, and mutual respect.

Role Cooperating with the group.

Motivational Base A desire to work with others in a cooperative fashion.

Importance In a group system, competition among members can disrupt communication and lead to withholding of needed information, even to group disintegration; for the group to work successfully, members must eschew competition in favor of cooperation and gain satisfaction from doing so.

Role Following democratic procedures.

Motivational Base A desire to participate in democratic group processes.

Importance In a group system, the major method of getting things done is some variant of the power-equalized, democratic process, in which there is open expression of views and decisions are reached by vote or some similar procedure; for these processes to function effectively, members must be favorably disposed toward them and desire to contribute to their effective operation.

In the absence of effective measuring instruments and the data they produce, it is difficult to guess whether the motivations needed for self-managing work groups to function well have become more or less common over the past twenty years. We do know from the MSCS findings that all motivational components need not follow the same patterns. Probably, the extent of favorable attitudes toward peers and desire for cooperative relationships has at least remained stable, but it is entirely possible that the desires for interaction, for group membership, and for participation in democratic processes have declined. Our point is that there is no basis for necessarily assuming an overall increase consonant with the decrease in hierarchical motivation. For lack of hard data, it is just as logical to assume a decline.

A second type of alternative to hierarchy is a task based or work-itself based system, such as operates in entrepreneurial firms and venture teams and among manufacturer's representatives, commission sales personnel, holders of enriched jobs, and the like. What might be the roles suited to such a structure?

Role Seeking individual achievement.

Motivational Base A desire to achieve results through one's own efforts and to be able to clearly attribute any success to those efforts.

Importance In a task-based system, individuals must be able to function independently; what will make them do so is an intrinsic desire to achieve through their own efforts and ability and to experience the enhanced self-esteem that such achievement permits—to be sure they did it themselves.

Role   Identifying the results of one's performance.
Motivational Base   A desire for some clear index of one's level of performance.
Importance   In a task-based system, where workers act independently, they must be able to gauge for themselves whether their way of operating is successful and appropriate; consequently, they must be motivated to actively seek out results-oriented feedback, expressed in terms of profitability, productive output, wastage, course grades, or the like.

Role   Being innovative.
Motivational Base   A desire to introduce novel or creative solutions.
Importance   In a task-based system, as has been noted, the lure of individual achievement works only to the extent that the individual can attribute it to his or her own efforts; since original or creative approaches have a distinctive quality that makes it easier to identify them as one's own and to take personal credit for them, a desire to introduce such approaches is more likely to make task inducement function properly.

Role   Taking risks.
Motivational Base   A desire to take moderate tasks which can be handled through one's own efforts.
Importance   In a task-based system, successful individuals must face considerable challenge and the prospect of being overextended, however briefly; tasks which they consider easy and already know how to deal with have little interest because there is no sense of achievement to be had in accomplishing them. On the other hand, desires to take high risks or to take risks related entirely to luck or fate (where one cannot ultimately reduce the risk through ones' own efforts) are not functional; in neither case can a sense of individual achievement be anticipated.

Role   Planning and setting goals.
Motivational Base   A desire to think about the future and anticipate future possibilities.
Importance   In a task-based system, the individual must be attracted to his or her work by the prospect of anticipated future rewards and, therefore, must approach life with a strong future orientation. There must be a desire to plan, to set personal goals that will signify success, and to plot paths to those goals.

What is called for in a task-based system can be summed up in the phrase achievement motivation. Although data bearing on the specific motivational patterns enumerated above are limited, there is substantial evidence that achievement motivation overall has been declining in the United States since the turn of the century. Certainly, there is no reason to conclude that simply because hierarchical motivation has decreased over the past twenty years, task motivation has increased.

Finally, certain new organizational structures are outgrowths of the knowledge explosion and the accelerated need for specialized expertise: professional units, project teams, group practices, and the like. For such structures, the following might be identified as the requisite roles, motives, and rationales:

Role   Acquiring further knowledge.
Motivational Base   A desire to be learning continually.
Importance   In a professional system, ongoing development, sharing, and use in the service of clients of technical expertise and knowledge are absolutely essential; accordingly, a professional must want to continually acquire the knowledge that permits providing an expert service.

Role   Abiding by professional behavior standards.
Motivational Base   A desire to identify with the profession.
Importance   In a professional system, there must be a strong tie to a profession, which keeps members responsive to its ethical norms.

Role   Accepting status.
Motivational Base   A desire to acquire status in the eyes of others.
Importance   In a professional system, the provision of service to clients is predicated on client recognition of the professional's expert status; unless professionals accept the status the profession carries and behave accordingly, their services will go unutilized.

Role   Providing assistance.
Motivational Base   A desire to help others achieve their best interests.
Importance   In a professional system, the professional is expected to assist the client in achieving desired goals or, in some instances, to do that which is specified by the profession as being in the client's best interest, even if not consciously desired; to function effectively, a professional must want to help others.

Role   Taking independent action.
Motivational Base   A desire to act on one's own.
Importance   In a professional system, the individual has a private and personally responsible relationship with each client that often requires independent action based on one's own best professional judgment; to meet this requirement the professional must be comfortable acting independently of others.

Although measurement of professional motivation is in its infancy, preliminary studies indicate that hierarchical motivation and professional motivation may be positively correlated, and that certain aspects of professional motivation, professional commitment in particular, but also the desires to acquire status and to provide help to others, may be positively related to age. All of these findings run counter to the idea that the decline in hierarchical motivation has been matched by an increase in professional motivation. Again, we find little basis for assuming that a shortage of managerial talent will mean an abundance of professional talent.

Our aim is not to sound an overpowering note of pessimism; the data are incomplete at best. It is important, however, to emphasize the not-entirely-obvious point that the decline in managerial motivation does not *ipso facto* mean an increase in every other kind of motivation. We can create new group, task, and professional structures and find them just as difficult to staff effectively as the old hierarchical structures. This is no reason not to experiment with the new and to diversify our organizations. It is reason to remain realistic and not be led into expectations that, when dashed upon the hard rocks of fact, leave us helpless to deal with the overwhelming problem of our time—that of human motivation.

REVIEW QUESTIONS

1 Summarize the nature of the newer organizational designs that Miner and Smith are referring to.

2 Assuming that students' motivation to manage has declined over a twenty-year period, what implications does this have for contemporary organizations?

3 Review the motivational bases for the various roles discussed by the authors. Which three are strongest for you? Weakest?

READING 46

Job Design in Perspective

Jon L. Pierce*

* * *

Job design has emerged as an issue of importance to both the practitioner and organization scholar. The evidence to date suggests that employee attitudes are strongly associated with job design characteristics. Some evidence suggests that the job is a more important attitude influence than organization and technology characteristics. Employee behavioral (e.g., performance, absenteeism, and turn-over) responses have not been as strongly nor as consistently related to job design variables. This may be attributed to environmental pressures or constraints which have a negating influence on employee behaviors.

While the literature suggests that design and redesign efforts should add versus subtract variety, autonomy, identity, significance, and feedback, a number of cautionary notes were discussed that should be attended to during job engineer-

*From *Personnel Administrator*, December 1980, pp. 67–76. Copyright 1980 by the American Society for Personnel Administration, Alexandria, Va.

ing efforts. It is clear that we cannot approach job design and redesign without considering the physical and psychological context in which the job is embedded.

As can be readily seen the good news is that many questions pertaining to the job design–employee response relationship have been answered and the bad news is that the number of unanswered questions has grown simultaneously. The bad news is that the science of discovery is slow and we have a long way to go before good operational guidelines can be provided for practitioners. The good news is that the study of job design is one of the most popular areas of inquiry in organizational behavior today.

*   *   *

REVIEW QUESTION

1 If you wanted to design an ideal job for someone, what dimensions could you manipulate?

CHAPTER 13

ORGANIZATIONAL CULTURE, DEVELOPMENT, AND CHANGE

READING 47

The Role of the Founder in Creating Organizational Culture

Edgar H. Schein*

How do the entrepreneur/founders of organizations create organizational cultures? And how can such cultures be analyzed? These questions are central to this article. First I will examine what organizational culture is, how the founder creates and embeds cultural elements, why it is likely that first-generation companies develop distinctive cultures, and what the implications are in making the transition from founders or owning families to "professional" managers.

The level of confusion over the term *organizational culture* requires some definitions of terms at the outset. An organizational culture depends for its existence on a definable organization, in the sense of a number of people interacting with each other for the purpose of accomplishing some goal in their defined environment. An organization's founder simultaneously creates such a group and, by force of his or her personality, begins to shape the group's culture. But that new group's culture does not develop until it has overcome various crises of growth and survival, and has worked out solutions for coping with its external problems of adaptation and its internal problems of creating a workable set of relationship rules.

Organizational culture, then, is the pattern of basic assumptions that a given group has invented, discovered, or developed in learning to cope with its problems of external adaptation and internal integration—a pattern of assumptions that has worked well enough to be considered valid and, therefore, to be taught to new members as the correct way to perceive, think, and feel in relation to those problems.

In terms of external survival problems, for example, I have heard these kinds of assumptions in first-generation companies:

The way to decide on what products we will build is to see whether we ourselves like the product; if *we* like it, our customers will like it.

The only way to build a successful business is to invest no more than 5 percent of your own money in it.

The customer is the key to our success, so we must be totally dedicated to total customer service.

In terms of problems of internal integration the following examples apply:

Ideas can come from anywhere in this organization, so we must maintain a climate of total openness.

*Reprinted by permission of the publisher from "The Role of the Founder in Creating Organizational Culture," by Edgar H. Schein, in *Organizational Dynamics*, Summer 1983. © 1983 by AMACOM, a division of American Management Associations, pp. 13–16. All rights reserved.

The only way to manage a growing business is to supervise every detail on a daily basis.

The only way to manage a growing business is to hire good people, give them clear responsibility, tell them how they will be measured, and then leave them alone.

Several points should be noted about the definition and the examples. First, culture is not the overt behavior or visible artifacts one might observe on a visit to the company. It is not even the philosophy or value system that the founder may articulate or write down in various "charters." Rather, it is the assumptions that underlie the values and determine not only behavior patterns, but also such visible artifacts as architecture, office layout, dress codes, and so on. This distinction is important because founders bring many of these assumptions with them when the organization begins; their problem is how to articulate, teach, embed, and in other ways get their own assumptions across and working in the system.

Founders often start with a theory of how to succeed; they have a cultural paradigm in their heads, based on their experience in the culture in which they grew up. In the case of a founding *group*, the theory and paradigm arise from the way that group reaches consensus on their assumptions about how to view things. Here, the evolution of the culture is a multi-stage process reflecting the several stages of group formation. The ultimate organizational culture will always reflect the complex interaction between (1) the assumptions and theories that founders bring to the group initially and (2) what the group learns subsequently from its own experiences.

WHAT IS ORGANIZATIONAL CULTURE ABOUT?

Any new group has the problem of developing shared assumptions about the nature of the world in which it exists, how to survive in it, and how to manage and integrate internal relationships so that it can operate effectively and make life livable and comfortable for its members. These external and internal problems can be categorized as shown in Figure 1.

The external and internal problems are always intertwined and acting simultaneously. A group cannot solve its external survival problem without being integrated to some degree to permit concerted action, and it cannot integrate itself without some successful task accomplishment vis-à-vis its survival problem or primary task.

The model of organizational culture that then emerges is one of shared solutions to problems which work well enough to begin to be taken for granted—to the point where they drop out of awareness, become unconscious assumptions, and are taught to new members as a reality and as the correct way to view things. If one wants to identify the elements of a given culture, one can go down the list of issues and ask how the group views itself in relation to each of them: What does it see to be its core mission, its goals, the way to accomplish those goals, the measurement systems and procedures it uses, the way it remedies actions, its particular jargon

FIGURE 1
EXTERNAL AND INTERNAL PROBLEMS

Problems of external adaptation and survival

1 Developing consensus on the *primary task, core mission, or manifest and latent functions of the group*—for example, strategy.

2 Consensus on *goals*, such goals being the concrete reflection of the core mission.

3 Developing consensus on the *means to be used* in accomplishing the goals—for example, division of labor, organization structure, reward system, and so forth.

4 Developing consensus on the *criteria to be used in measuring how well the group is doing against its goals and targets*—for example, information and control systems.

5 Developing consensus on *remedial or repair strategies* as needed when the group is not accomplishing its goals.

Problems of internal integration

1 *Common language and conceptual categories.* If members cannot communicate with and understand each other, a group is impossible by definition.

2 Consensus on *group boundaries and criteria for inclusion and exclusion.* One of the most important areas of culture is the shared consensus on who is in, who is out, and by what criteria one determines membership.

3 Consensus on *criteria for the allocation of power and status.* Every organization must work out its pecking order and its rules for how one gets, maintains, and loses power. This area of consensus is crucial in helping members manage their own feelings of aggression.

4 Consensus on *criteria for intimacy, friendship, and love.* Every organization must work out its rules of the game for peer relationships, for relationships between the sexes, and for the manner in which openness and intimacy are to be handled in the context of managing the organization's tasks.

5 Consensus on *criteria for allocation of rewards and punishments.* Every group must know what its heroic and sinful behaviors are; what gets rewarded with property, status, and power; and what gets punished through the withdrawal of rewards and, ultimately, excommunication.

6 Consensus on *ideology and "religion."* Every organization, like every society, faces unexplainable events that must be given meaning so that members can respond to them and avoid the anxiety of dealing with the unexplainable and uncontrollable.

and meaning system, the authority system, peer system, reward system, and ideology? One will find, when one does this, that there is in most cultures a deeper level of assumptions which ties together the various solutions to the various problems, and this deeper level deals with more ultimate questions. The real cultural essence, then, is what members of the organization assume about the issues shown in Figure 2.

In a fairly "mature" culture—that is, in a group that has a long and rich history—one will find that these assumptions are patterned and interrelated into a "cultural paradigm" that is the key to understanding how members of the group view the world. In an organization that is in the process of formation, the paradigm is more likely to be found only in the founder's head, but it is important to try to decipher it in order to understand the biases or directions in which the founder "pushes" or "pulls" the organization.

FIGURE 2
BASIC UNDERLYING ASSUMPTIONS AROUND WHICH CULTURAL PARADIGMS FORM

1 *The organization's relationship to its environment.* Reflecting even more basic assumptions about the relationship of humanity to nature, one can assess whether the key members of the organization view the relationship as one of dominance, submission, harmonizing, finding an appropriate niche, and so on.

2 *The nature of reality and truth.* Here are the linguistic and behavioral rules that define what is real and what is not, what is a "fact," how truth is ultimately to be determined, and whether truth is "revealed" or "discovered"; basic concepts of time as linear or cyclical, monochronic or polychronic; basic concepts such as space as limited or infinite and property as communal or individual; and so forth.

3 *The nature of human nature.* What does it mean to be "human," and what attributes are considered intrinsic or ultimate? Is human nature good, evil, or neutral? Are human beings perfectible or not? Which is better, Theory X or Theory Y?

4 *The nature of human activity.* What is the "right" thing for human beings to do, on the basis of the above assumptions about reality, the environment, and human nature: to be active, passive, self-developmental, fatalistic, or what? What is work and what is play?

5 *The nature of human relationships.* What is considered to be the "right" way for people to relate to each other, to distribute power and love? Is life cooperative or competitive; individualistic, group collaborative, or communal; based on traditional lineal authority, law, or charisma; or what?

*   *   *

REVIEW QUESTION

1 In your own words, summarize the meaning of "organizational culture."

READING 48

Q. What in the Name of OD Do We Do? A. Change

W. Warner Burke
Lynda McDermott
Jan Margolis*

Hurley: In his book, Organization Development: Principles and Practices, *(Little Brown, 1982) Warner Burke defines organization development as "a planned process of change in an organization's culture through the utilization of behavioral science technology, research and theory." How much agreement is there among you?*

*From interview conducted by Patricia Hurley, in *Training and Development Journal*, April 1983, pp. 42–48. Reprinted with permission.

Burke: Some people disagree with the part of the definition that mentions cultural change. Some people in the field say that organization development is just making improvements. Solving problems by using behavioral science techniques does not necessarily mean there's a system change.

McDermott: I wouldn't call that OD. I have a broader definition of organization development that focuses on planned, systematic change and isn't limited just to the techniques or the principles of behavioral science. So, while I have a more general definition, it is focused on culture and management systems and structures and processes.

Burke: My definition is limited in what I did not put into it. It doesn't include the fact that a consultant is involved—a third party. Usually in a consulting situation, you've got a manager and the people who report to him or her and the OD practitioner or consultant, so the definition should also include the words "by way of a consultant."

Margolis: Warner's definition calls for a consultant who becomes the agent for making change happen. I disagree. To the extent that the organization is dependent on a consultant, it's not institutionalizing cultural change or building in those adaptive processes that help it stay healthy. I think the primary responsibility for organization development is with the senior management function and that translates through to every level of management. I would prefer an organization that didn't need a consultant to do its organization development, internal or external.

McDermott: I think the benefit a consultant adds, on the other hand, is to keep the client honest by providing that third-party perspective, but I would agree with Jan that my ultimate goals would be to have the client bring about change. I question Warner's definition.

Burke: The answer goes back to the institutionalization process. That comes about through internal people, but not line managers. It happens through OD practitioners—internal consultants. Ideally, the external consultant is trying to work himself or herself out of a job by turning more and more of the consulting process over to the internal people who are in a staff, not a line role. Another reason the consultant is an absolute necessity is that it is impossible for the person who is the recipient of the change to be, at the same time, aware of all that is going on in his or her own unit. Where I have a vested interest, it's impossible for me to be objective.

Margolis: There are several parts of that I agree with and several parts I disagree with, but I don't think we are that far apart. A consultant is necessary in many organizations to get things started, to act as an educator, to act as a model, to act as a handholder and, if necessary, to act as a confronter. During the early stages of organization development, an internal or external consultant is very helpful, especially for credibility reasons. A consultant can say that the emperor indeed has no clothes and get away with it. That's a valuable, helpful role.

I think there are stages of maturity that organizations go through in their development. The leader—the CEO or the chairman—has a vested interest in shaping the culture according to his or her value systems or the culture or values that have been inherited. So in part you want the vested interest to protect those values, those aspects of the culture that have worked, that have made the company uniquely good at something. You want to tinker only with those things that are getting in the way of a change in strategy that may be required by the competitive environment.

Hurley: Would you comment on the role of power and politics in relation to the effort of the OD consultant or practitioner to bring about change.

McDermott: Those are two areas I immediately want to get information on when I go into an organization, because that will influence the strategy that I choose. That has nothing to do with colluding with the power and the politics. If I go in with a strategy that is counter to the political environment, then I really reduce my chances of success.

Margolis: I see power and politics as different from one another. Political behavior is a manifestation of how to get things done. You need to know the implicit, unstated ways of getting things done. Power is either formal or informal. It's formal in terms of your position or role in the organization or it's informal in terms of the chips you've collected, the information you can access or your adeptness at politics. I think it's important to know where the formal power is, but it's more important to understand the political nuances. Those are elements of culture.

Burke: Change will not occur in an organization unless power is exercised by somebody, so the OD consultant has got to be aware of where the power is in an organization because it represents the major lever for change. I agree that there's a distinction between power and politics, but it's important to know whether they relate—whether the political system reflects who really has power in an informal way rather than through position. It's critical because you don't change any organization without some exercise of power.

Hurley: What can the consultant do when there is resistance to change?

Burke: I don't think in general that people resist change. Getting a raise in pay is a change, and I've yet to resist that. I think what people resist is the imposition of change. When people don't feel like they've got any choice, there's where you've got resistance. What you want to determine, through interviews, questionnaires, whatever, is where they feel they have no choice. In the OD process, the consultant helps the manager clarify where the choices are for those who resist the change.

In most organizations, more often than not, the content of change is almost always a given. It comes sweeping and cascading from the top . . ."we are going to change, and this is the new structure." Where management really has an opportunity to provide people with choice is in how the change is going to be brought about. So it must be made clear what is a given and what are the boundaries within which a person can do some things and make some decisions. If you provide that, then resistance is a myth.

Margolis: I think the psychological process behind people's resistance to change has to do with loss. For example, you have a department that suddenly must start using word processing. That's a change. What do people lose? They lose their comfort level with their current skills. The skills they worked for 20 or 30 years to develop aren't valid any more, and new ones are required. There might, because of computerization, be a work force reduction in their area, and they might lose friends or have to work alone. They're going to lose things that are familiar, and perhaps they fear the unknown or fear being out of control. There are lots of things a manager can do in the face of change: communicate that the change is occurring and get early input; familiarize people with new equipment well before they have to use it; run old and new systems in tandem.

I think consultants often overlook the fundamental issue of loss, of the emotional response to loss.

Burke: It's worthwhile spending some time mourning a change because of that loss, although I've nearly been hooted out of the room by managers when I suggest that.

McDermott: I think it helps if you focus on how things will be better and different for those involved. My experience of organization change is that typically the focus is on what's in it for the organization, but to counter resistance to change, there has to be a focus, for some period of time, on what's in it for the individual.

Hurley: You have all recommended a participative approach to change. What about the OD practitioner or consultant working in a situation where this isn't acceptable or possible?

Burke: One thing you can do is present evidence from other sources about the effectiveness of participation. Try to explain the principle of involvement and remember that managers fear that if they allow participation, they're going to lose some of their own power. I try to make the argument that just the opposite can occur. If you get more people involved, you've got more clout in the overall system because people are behind you. So the first thing you try to do is persuade. The second thing you do is collect some data through interviews to show the gap between what is espoused, what bosses and subordinates say they want—and what is real. If you can present differences like that—between what people want and what is actually going on—psychology says there's some built-in motivation for change.

McDermott: When you mention participation these days to managers, they're likely to say, "Oh, that's Japanese management," and immediately begin to tell you why it won't work in the United States. There is a definitional problem for managers about what is meant by participation. What do you give up when you enter into a participatory style? What do you buy?

Margolis: A strong selling point for participation is that it's often very narrow. People don't want the whole department, they just want to participate in decisions about their job, what kind of desk they will have, where they will sit, that kind of thing.

Hurley: Warner Burke has written "Our expectations that the values of humanization and egalitarianism would promote organizational change—change in the direction of more humanism, a higher quality or work life, and a greater decentralization of power—have been naive and inappropriate." What methods of promot-

ing organizational change—that are unique to organizational development—have not proved naive and inappropriate and have withstood the test of time?

Margolis: If you look at the history of OD, you realize that it grew up during a period of great social upheaval and change. People were talking a lot about egalitarianism and participation, and so of course the culture of the time colored the values of the field. So I don't think those concerns were naive at the time. They proved unrealistic, but they were very much in sync with what was happening in the culture and the society.

McDermott: Process skills have survived. Viewing organizations and their various pieces from a systems perspective is a very critical skill/knowledge area that has survived.

Burke: If you want to define the field very narrowly, then you would say that the only skills that OD practitioners have that other types of consultants don't have are process skills—that is, how to identify what is occurring in a manager's team in terms of the communication process, the implicit norms, what people are not saying, how they are colluding and things like that. OD practitioners are supposed to be expert at understanding the process of interpersonal relationships. A lot of things OD consultants do are also done by other kinds of management consultants. Process skills have survived, and they had better continue to survive. I still believe what I once wrote in jest—"Process is our most important product."

McDermott: As for the current skills that are required for the OD professional to have impact on the organization, it's my bias that in addition to the process skills, the OD consultant needs to have some general business skills in order to have credibility with managers. I'm not suggesting that you have to become an accountant or a data systems specialist, but a least know what those functions are and know the concerns of the people who perform them.

Margolis: I'd even take it a step further. You have to understand the strategy of an organization and whether it's focused on the numbers for the quarter or on long-term goals. Secondly, you need to have a generalist's understanding of various functions and how the processes of selection, criticism, rewards and performance contribute to the enhancement of individual performance and reflect strategy, culture and values.

Hurley: Organization development is more appropriate in organic systems, but few of these exist. Bureaucracies, on the other hand, are abundant. Herb Shepperd has suggested that the only difference between an organization and a conspiracy is that the latter is dedicated to change, while an organization, as a bureaucracy, is built to resist change. What's an appropriate role for OD in a bureaucratic setting?

McDermott: I would argue against the idea that an organization, because it is bureaucratic, is not changing or is resistant to change. Organizations are constantly changing, even though there is resistance. A real challenge for someone who wants to move an organization toward more effectiveness is to tie into where the organization is naturally going to change, and to alter how the organization proceeds through that change. That might be the conspiratorial nature of change.

Burke: The conspiratorial factor is that the change is planned rather than haphazard. I don't think that size is necessarily equated with bureaucracy. Reading the Peters and Waterman book, *In Search of Excellence*, I didn't think the big organizations they described sounded like bureaucracies.

Margolis: Let's take a concrete example. There's been a move toward national chains in mass merchandising. Merchandisers who sell through those chains of distribution have had to undergo significant changes in their marketing and sales functions. It's required changing selection criteria for entry-level sales managers, changing selection criteria for managerial people in marketing. It's required changing the compensation and incentive mix because you don't compensate top managers like you do salespeople. It's required redesign of jobs for merchandisers. It's required greater communication between marketing, market research and sales. All these are interactive processes—that call for the skill of the OD person—and if they aren't done well, the change won't occur and the organization won't make the appropriate adaptation to the new market environment.

McDermott: Another value we bring to the organization is to focus attention on all those piecemeal qualities and on the effect that change in one part of the organization will have on other parts.

Burke: General systems theory of course predicts that. It becomes concrete in a recent paper by Rosabeth Kanter that shows that the pride and ownership that comes from team building can have detrimental effects on other units.

Hurley: Deal and Kennedy state in Corporate Cultures *that "the corporation may be among the last institutions in America that can effectively take on the role of shaping values." If there is a role for the OD practitioner in this task, what are some concrete, specific approaches?*

Burke: Values are the culture. To make a distinction doesn't compute for me. The role of the OD consultant in this domain is to surface the difference between stated values and behavior. Here's where top management really is key because the chief executive officer, more than anybody else, represents the central values of the organization and is supposed to be managing those values. Peters and Waterman make it clear that in successful organizations, the CEO was consciously aware of that role.

Margolis: After helping differentiate between espoused values and behaviors, the next step is to translate them into the human resource management system, to institutionalize them. What, for example, is the corporate posture on layoffs or work reductions, on unions, on development activities? How are values reflected in the appraisal system and the way we compensate people? Reflecting those values in the human resource management system is the internal OD person's task. Articulating the values is just the tip of the iceberg.

Hurley: What changes, challenges and opportunities will face the OD practitioner in the next few years?

McDermott: The nature of business in the United States is becoming more service oriented, and that's where our work will come in. I think also that OD consultants, in addition to having strong process skills, have to realize that the change process for many organizations is going to be around technology. Efforts to assist that kind of change will be seen as more relevant to the organization than efforts to improve the quality of work life or to make people feel good.

Margolis: I think the future challenges for the OD person are the same challenges that top management faces. A more subtle change than technology comes from the effect of an environment in which sales are down, profits are down and competition is so much more intense. A big question for the OD person and for the top manager is how do you squeeze from internal operating efficiencies, funds to support new product development, acquisitions or increased advertising? You're not going to get it from profits. Things are just too lean. You're going to get it from inside the organization, and that means organizations get meaner and demand more of people. There's more attention to productivity. I've noticed on my train commute, that the people who used to take the 8:05, and I was one of them, have in the past two years backed up to the 7:26 and the 7:00. We've kidded about it on the train, but everybody feels there's more work to do.

Burke: What you're both saying is that in the future the OD practitioner has got to be a step ahead of understanding the changing values of the society and the impact they will have on the organization. The "me generation" that Tom Wolfe, the novelist, identified and Yankelovich described with data is over because of the tightness that Jan was talking about. We're going to see some changes around the nuclear family, too. I don't know how to predict what 1988 will look like with respect to societal values, but the OD practitioner had better be attentive to them. One way is to be sensitive to changing habit patterns of the kind Jan mentioned. Another way is to be sensitive to differences between one part of the United States and another. Changes are often signaled in cities such as New York, Washington or San Francisco. What's happening there eventually reaches other places—even my home town of Gadsden, Alabama.

REVIEW QUESTIONS

1 What are the major similarities and differences among the authors in their definitions of organization development?
2 What role can consultants play in changing the culture of an organization?
3 "People, and organizations, resist change." How would the authors of this reading respond to that contention?

READING 49

Dealing with Resistance to Change

Joseph Stanislao
Bettie C. Stanislao*

Change is inevitable if an organization is to survive in a world of developing technology and new consumer and employee demands. Maintaining the status quo is likely to stifle success, so managers at all levels must develop skills in changing people, procedures, methods, and machinery. But even with adequate planning, the manager is likely to encounter resistance to change in employees. Such resistance stems from fear; this fear is easier to prevent than it is to remove once it has developed.

According to Certo, the major factors when changing an organization are determining what should be changed, what type of change needs to be made, who will be affected by the change, and who will be the change agent. These factors and their interaction collectively determine whether the change will be successful.[1]

Since major technological changes are few relative to the number of day-to-day changes in product, process, and procedures, the following discussion devotes attention to these day-to-day changes.

When considering the people to be affected, it is useful to distinguish between the individual who has authority to accept or reject a change and the individual who has no voice in acceptance or rejection of the proposed change. If the latter is affected, he or she must cooperate in order for the change to be successful; both groups deserve separate analysis.

Resistance to Change by a Person Having Veto Power

Any person with the authority to accept or reject a proposal may reject it for any one of the reasons outlined below.

Inertia An innate desire to retain the status quo exists, even when the current situation is inferior. Inertia is the tendency to want to do things in the accustomed manner. Thus, a supervisor will oppose the new method merely because it is different from the accustomed one. This person will not "get around to doing" anything differently unless impressed with necessity.

Uncertainty or Fear of the Unknown Regardless of how bad the existing method might be, at least how well it functions is known. Any deviation from the

*From *Business Horizons*, July–August 1983, pp. 74–78. Reprinted with permission.

[1]Samuel C. Certo, *Principles of Modern Management: Functions and Systems* (Dubuque, Iowa: Wm. C. Brown Company, 1980), p. 265.

known procedure involves risk, and the proposed method offers no guarantee of better results. In this case, supervisors are unwilling to trade inferiority of which they are certain, for superiority of which they are uncertain. This fear or uncertainty can be eliminated by training programs in the new methods.

Insecurity and Fear of Failure   The individual who is to accept the new idea may see no need for any change and may resist because of the fear of possible failure. In this case, implementing the change on a trial basis may reassure the supervisor that success is possible. Change on a trial basis should reduce the fear of personal loss and will give the people involved an opportunity to get more facts about the change.

Ignorance   Even when individuals are not directly involved, their failure to understand the new system will produce cautiousness and resentment. Properly prepare the employees for change by providing as much information as possible about the change. Lack of knowledge may lead to imaginary problems in addition to the real problems of change. Do not underestimate the grapevine as a source of information to employees, and do not underestimate the grapevine's capability of providing misinformation if given nothing better.

Obsolescence   People are afraid of having a skill which is considered obsolete. One who has invested years of experience in building up a high level of skill, knowledge, and judgment for a specific activity may resist any new proposal. A fear of not being or not becoming proficient in the new system may cause apprehension and a resistance to change.

Personality   Personality conflicts between the proposer and the proposee can produce resistance to change. Maintaining a friendly relationship with and showing respect for everyone helps in eliminating personality conflicts.

Outside Consultants   Reliance on outside help can cause resentment. A change developed by outsiders may not be accepted by insiders. The implication, as the insiders see it, is that insiders cannot handle their own problems. Make limited use of outside consultants in dealing with employees.

Resentment of Criticism   Criticism may erupt from the person who originated the present method, since changing the present method may be a threat to that person's security. Noncritical statements are sometimes construed as criticism, so beware of critical statements and of ones that might be taken as such. In reality, the resentment of criticism is probably more responsible for failure of change programs than is resistance to change itself.

Participation   When a change is proposed, staff members may be embarrassed at not having conceived an idea which, with hindsight, appears obvious. The importance of participation by all staff members from the start should not be underestimated. Student refers to "influence" as the focal element in any successful change process.[2] Having some influence as the change is being proposed will strengthen the support of people affected by the change. People are more likely to support what they help to create.

Tact Sometimes a few right words can make the difference between acceptance or resistance to change. The manner of presenting the proposal should be friendly, and words should be chosen to show personal regard for the persons affected. Encourage full participation of supervisors in helping employees accept change.

Confidence If the person who is to carry out the change doesn't perceive adequate experience and expertise in the person who proposed it, he or she will resist the change and think it is doomed to fail. The person selected to be the change agent should be someone who inspires confidence.

Timing Timing of the proposal is essential. Many good ideas are rejected because people are emotionally or physically upset, or unusually busy, or because business is in a temporary slump or labor relations are strained. Select a time when the receiver is in a receptive mood.

Resistance to Change by a Person Having No Veto Power

Resistance to change reactions may come from individuals who have no direct voice in the acceptance or rejection of the proposal, but who are directly affected by it, for any of the reasons given below.

Surprise Employees tend to resist change, especially when the change is unexpected, sudden, or radical in their view. People need time to evaluate change before it occurs. Those affected should be informed well in advance.

Lack of Information about How the Change Will Affect the Employee's Job Uncertainty will bring resistance even if the current situation is not satisfactory. The desire to resist is greater when risk of unemployment is involved in the change, particularly when those affected don't know how the idea was formulated. The worker may feel that any change is a move toward replacing him or her.

Lack of Training Failure to understand the new method or policy arouses suspicion or an insecure feeling rapidly, but feelings are hidden from immediate supervisors or other management personnel. Training programs to teach employees necessary skills should be started well before the change.

Lack of Real Understanding Ignorance is a major reason why workers resist

---

[2]Kurt R. Student, "Managing Change: A Psychologist's Perspective," *Business Horizons*, December 1978, pp. 28–33.

change. Too often little or no explanation is given to the workers, sometimes with the attitude that this is none of their business. The employees' parts in the program should be explained thoroughly, and changes planned with their help.

Loss of Job Status   Reduction in the skill required, or the importance of the job, or the responsibility of the worker involved may arouse resistance of the worker to a new idea. Such reduction in status of the employee will lead to insecurity. To prevent this, the worker should be reassured of his or her worth to the organization. Questions related to power, prestige, responsibility, skills required, and hours of work should be answered honestly.

Peer Pressure   The work group often resists new ideas even though the individual workers may not feel as strongly against the new ideas as their group actions would indicate. Every work group has certain ingrained policies, some expressed and others implied, which can resist new ideas. A person's reaction to change is usually influenced by what he or she knows or anticipates that the group wants. Being accepted by the group may motivate the employee to participate in resistance to change. Obtaining group support of the proposed change would eliminate resistance due to peer pressure.

Loss of Security   Fear of economic insecurity can cause an immediate resistance to new concepts, particularly if workers fear a reduction in earnings. Resistance to change may arise as a result of a reduction in job classification, a tightening of a time standard as a result of the change in question, or an inability to master the new method or to reach the level of proficiency that the worker had attained under the replaced method. Here again, reassuring the workers of their worth will be beneficial.

Loss of Known Work Group   Alteration of social relationships, coupled with the fear that a closely knit work group will be replaced or eliminated, may cause resistance. Workers need reassurance that they will not be expected to betray friends.

Personality Conflicts   Antagonism toward the person introducing the change may be a personal antagonism, or may be an antagonism toward the person's function, or may be toward management in general. Such hostility causes individuals and groups to resist almost any change that comes from management, referred to as resistance on general principles. The change agent, or person who tries to effect change, should be able to use behavioral science tools to influence the employees before and during the change. To be successful, the change agent must determine how much change the employees can withstand and should limit change to that amount. Changes must be made in such a way that employees who must change their behavior are given the opportunity to become ready to learn the new behavior, to try the new behavior, to make the new behavior useful, and to accept the new behavior as part of themselves. Lewin refers to these stages in the change process as unfreezing, changing, and refreezing.[3] The change agent must give ideas or innovations time to become acceptable.

Timing Poor timing may cause maximum resistance to change. If the business has slack periods, changes should be made during these periods to minimize confusion. The proposed change should wait until all employees who will be affected by it have received accurate information about how the change will affect them and their jobs. If possible, they should participate in change-related decisions.

Recommendations

The following recommendations should be considered in planning the introduction of an idea and in modifying the idea to make it more saleable and palatable. First, one should convincingly *explain* the need for change to receivers, particularly the workers. Use straightforward, clear, well-organized language to assure that they understand the method or policy. Do not take for granted the importance of this understanding. Tailor the communication format to suit the particular receiver. Many change programs have failed because of the lack of mutual understanding about what the program is trying to accomplish.

Facilitate participation, or at least the feeling of participation, in the formulation of the proposal. In general, people are concerned about making their own ideas and recommendations succeed. The feeling of participation may be imparted by consulting with the workers, and by seeking their information, opinions, and suggestions. Above all, show real interest in what these people have to say. Seeking their advice will encourage their participation in the change. Whenever possible, include the worthwhile suggestions of others in the final report and give credit to the appropriate individuals.

Use a tactful approach in introducing the change proposal. Watch wording and mannerisms and avoid implying criticism. In attempting to gain adoption of an idea, avoid making the proposal when the recipient is upset or busy. Allow sufficient time for the recipient to think it over. Also, avoid introducing certain changes when labor relations are abnormally strained.

In the case of major changes, try to design the proposal to *introduce the change in stages*. The mere magnitude of some proposals or ideas may frighten people and arouse objections. Capitalize on the features which provide the most personal benefits.

A procedure of *planting the idea* in the recipient's mind is usually effective if it can be properly executed. The difficulty with this planting concept is that it is not easily done, nor are people generally willing to allow others to get credit for their ideas.

Management should *show that it supports* the proposed change. Publicize the

---

[3]Kurt Lewin, "Frontiers in Group Dynamics: Concept, Method, and Reality of Social Sciences: Social Equilibria and Social Change," *Human Relations*, June 1947, pp. 5–14.

benefits of completed changes which are of interest to employees. Share the benefits of changes with the employees.

The foregoing measures, concerning the minimization of resistance to a specific change, are no substitute for a long-range plan for change. These measures should be supplemented by a long-term effort to prepare personnel for changes in general. Such a conditioning process will involve both technical and psychological preparation. Before the change is introduced and when considering long-term effort, plan for technical training, so that personnel will feel capable of mastering the new ideas and managerial techniques. Education on the importance of change, the consequences of change, the role of competition, and the need for change is emphasized through the psychological phase of minimizing resistance to change. Maintaining a policy of fair treatment of employees affected by change concerning job retention, job replacement and job content is also part of the psychological phase.

In general, an effective long-term measure in minimizing resistance to change is the very awareness of the phenomenon itself. Then if employees are aware of the causes, manifestations, and frequency of this reaction, the employee or supervisor will be less inclined to resist change.

REVIEW QUESTIONS

1 Examine the authors' recommendations for preventing/overcoming resistance to change. Which of the reasons listed on the preceding pages do you feel they have *not* addressed?

2 At least twenty-two reasons for resisting change are briefly described in this reading. Categorize these as being basically technical, rational, and objective, or as primarily emotional in nature.

3 Think of a time when you resisted a change. What tactics could have been useful in reducing or preventing that resistance?

CHAPTER 14

INFORMAL ORGANIZATIONS
AND GROUP BEHAVIOR

READING 50

The Development and Enforcement of Group Norms

Daniel C. Feldman*

Group norms are the informal rules that groups adopt to regulate and regularize group members' behavior. Although these norms are infrequently written down or openly discussed, they often have a powerful, and consistent, influence on group members' behavior (Hackman, 1976).

Most of the theoretical work on group norms has focused on identifying the types of group norms (March, 1954) or on describing their structural characteristics (Jackson, 1966). Empirically, most of the focus has been on examining the impact that norms have on other social phenomena. For example, Seashore (1954) and Schachter, Ellertson, McBride, and Gregory (1951) use the concept of group norms to discuss group cohesiveness; Trist and Bamforth (1951) and Whyte (1955a) use norms to examine production restriction; Janis (1972) and Longley and Puritt (1980) use norms to illuminate group decision making; and Asch (1951) and Sherif (1936) use norms to examine conformity.

This paper focuses on two frequently overlooked aspects of the group norms literature. First, it examines *why* group norms are enforced. Why do groups desire conformity to these informal rules? Second, it examines *how* group norms develop. Why do some norms develop in one group but not in another? Much of what is known about group norms comes from post hoc examination of their impact on outcome variables; much less has been written about how these norms actually develop and why they regulate behavior so strongly.

Understanding how group norms develop and why they are enforced is important for two reasons. First, group norms can play a large role in determining whether the group will be productive or not. If the work group feels that management is supportive, group norms will develop that facilitate—in fact, enhance—group productivity. In contrast, if the work group feels that management is antagonistic, group norms that inhibit and impair group performance are much more likely to develop. Second, managers can play a major role in setting and changing group norms. They can use their influence to set task-facilitative norms; they can monitor whether the group's norms are functional; they can explicitly address counterproductive norms with subordinates. By understanding how norms develop and why norms are enforced, managers can better diagnose the underlying tensions and problems their groups are facing, and they can help the group develop more effective behavior patterns.

*From the *Academy of Management Review*, January 1984, pp. 47–53. Reprinted with permission.

WHY NORMS ARE ENFORCED

As Shaw (1981) suggests, a group does not establish or enforce norms about every conceivable situation. Norms are formed and enforced only with respect to behaviors that have some significance for the group. The frequent distinction between task maintenance duties and social maintenance duties helps explain why groups bring selected behaviors under normative control.

Groups, like individuals, try to operate in such a way that they maximize their chances for task success and minimize their chances of task failure. First of all, a group will enforce norms that facilitate its very survival. It will try to protect itself from interference from groups external to the organization or harassment from groups internal to the organization. Second, the group will want to increase the predictability of group members' behaviors. Norms provide a basis for predicting the behavior of others, thus enabling group members to anticipate each other's actions and to prepare quick and appropriate responses (Shaw, 1981; Kiesler & Kiesler, 1970).

In addition, groups want to ensure the satisfaction of their members and prevent as much interpersonal discomfort as possible. Thus, groups also will enforce norms that help the group avoid embarrassing interpersonal problems. Certain topics of conversation might be sanctioned, and certain types of social interaction might be openly discouraged. Moreover, norms serve an expressive function for groups (Katz & Kahn, 1978). Enforcing group norms gives group members a chance to express what their central values are, and to clarify what is distinctive about the group and central to its identity (Hackman, 1976).

Each of these four conditions under which group norms are most likely to be enforced is discussed in more detail below.

(1) *Norms are likely to be enforced if they facilitate group survival.* A group will enforce norms that protect it from interference or harassment by members of other groups. For instance, a group might develop a norm not to discuss its salaries with members of other groups in the organization, so that attention will not be brought to pay inequities in its favor. Groups might also have norms about not discussing internal problems with members of other units. Such discussions might boomerang at a later date if other groups use the information to develop a better competitive strategy against the group.

Enforcing group norms also makes clear what the "boundaries" of the group are. As a result of observation of deviant behavior and the consequences that ensue, other group members are reminded of the *range* of behavior that is acceptable to the group (Dentler & Erikson, 1959). The norms about productivity that frequently develop among piecerate workers are illustrative here. By observing a series of incidents (a person produces 50 widgets and is praised; a person produces 60 widgets and receives sharp teasing; a person produces 70 widgets and is ostracized), group members learn the limits of the group's patience: "This far, and no further." The group is less likely to be "successful" (i.e., continue to sustain the low productivity expectations of management) if it allows its jobs to be reevaluated.

The literature on conformity and deviance is consistent with this observation. The group is more likely to reject the person who violates group norms when the deviant has not been a "good" group member previously (Hollander, 1958, 1964). Individuals can generate "idiosyncrasy credits" with other group members by contributing effectively to the attainment of group goals. Individuals expend these credits when they perform poorly or dysfunctionally at work. When a group-member no longer has a positive "balance" of credits to draw on when he or she deviates, the group is much more likely to reject that deviant (Hollander, 1961).

Moreover, the group is more likely to reject the deviant when the group is failing in meeting its goals successfully. When the group is successful, it can afford to be charitable or tolerant towards deviant behavior. The group may disapprove, but it has some margin for error. When the group is faced with failure, the deviance is much more sharply punished. Any behavior that negatively influences the success of the group becomes much more salient and threatening to group members (Alvarez, 1968; Wiggins, Dill, & Schwartz, 1965).

(2) *Norms are likely to be enforced if they simplify, or make predictable, what behavior is expected of group members.* If each member of the group had to decide individually how to behave in each interaction, much time would be lost performing routine activities. Moreover, individuals would have more trouble predicting the behaviors of others and responding correctly. Norms enable group members to anticipate each other's actions and to prepare the most appropriate response in the most timely manner (Hackman, 1976; Shaw, 1981).

For instance, when attending group meetings in which proposals are presented and suggestions are requested, do the presenters really want feedback or are they simply going through the motions? Groups may develop norms that reduce this uncertainty and provide a clearer course of action, for example, make suggestions in small, informal meetings but not in large, formal meetings.

Another example comes from norms that regulate social behavior. For instance, when colleagues go out for lunch together, there can be some awkwardness about how to split the bill at the end of the meal. A group may develop a norm that gives some highly predictable or simple way of behaving, for example, split evenly, take turns picking up the tab, or pay for what each ordered.

Norms also may reinforce specific individual members' roles. A number of different roles might emerge in groups. These roles are simply expectations that are shared by group members regarding who is to carry out what types of activities under what circumstances (Bales & Slater, 1955). Although groups obviously create pressure toward uniformity among members, there also is a tendency for groups to create and maintain *diversity* among members (Hackman, 1976). For instance, a group might have one person whom others expect to break the tension when tempers become too hot. Another group member might be expected to keep track of what is going on in other parts of the organization. A third member might be expected to take care of the "creature" needs of the group—making the coffee, making dinner reservations, and so on. A fourth member might be expected by others to take notes, keep minutes, or maintain files.

None of these roles are *formal* duties, but they are activities that the group needs accomplished and has somehow parcelled out among members. If the role expectations are not met, some important jobs might not get done, or other group members might have to take on additional responsibilities. Moreover, such role assignments reduce individual members' ambiguities about what is expected specifically of them. It is important to note, though, that who takes what role in a group also is highly influenced by individuals' personal needs. The person with a high need for structure often wants to be in the note-taking role to control the structuring activity in the group; the person who breaks the tension might dislike conflict and uses the role to circumvent it.

(3) *Norms are likely to be enforced if they help the group avoid embarrassing interpersonal problems.* Goffman's work on "facework" gives some insight on this point. Goffman (1955) argues that each person in a group has a "face" he or she presents to other members of a group. This "face" is analogous to what one will call "self-image," the person's perceptions of himself or herself and how he or she would like to be seen by others. Groups want to insure that no one's self-image is damaged, called into question, or embarrassed. Consequently, the group will establish norms that discourage topics of conversation or situations in which face is too likely to be inadvertently broken. For instance, groups might develop norms about not discussing romantic involvements (so that differences in moral values do not become salient) or about not getting together socially in people's homes (so that differences in taste or income do not become salient).

A good illustration of Goffman's facework occurs in the classroom. There is always palpable tension in a room when either a class is totally unprepared to discuss a case or a professor is totally unprepared to lecture or lead the discussion. One part of the awkwardness stems from the inability of the other partner in the interaction to behave as he or she is prepared to or would like to behave. The professor cannot teach if the students are not prepared, and the students cannot learn if the professors are not teaching. Another part of the awkwardness, though, stems from self-images being called into question. Although faculty are aware that not all students are serious scholars, the situation is difficult to handle if the class as a group does not even show a pretense of wanting to learn. Although students are aware that many faculty are mainly interested in research and consulting, there is a problem if the professor does not even show a pretense of caring to teach. Norms almost always develop between professor and students about what level of preparation and interest is expected by the other because both parties want to avoid awkward confrontations.

(4) *Norms are likely to be enforced if they express the central values of the group and clarify what is distinctive about the group's identity.* Norms can provide the social justification for group activities to its members (Katz & Kahn, 1978). When the production group labels rate-busting deviant, it says: "We care more about maximizing group security than about individual profits." Group norms also convey what is distinctive about the group to outsiders. When an advertising agency labels unstylish clothes deviant, it says: "We think of ourselves, personally and professionally, as trend-setters, and being fashionably dressed conveys that to our clients and our public."

One of the key expressive functions of group norms is to define and legitimate the power of the group itself over individual members (Katz & Kahn, 1978). When groups punish norm infraction, they reinforce in the minds of group members the authority of the group. Here, too, the literature on group deviance sheds some light on the issue at hand.

It has been noted frequently that the amount of deviance in a group is rather small (Erikson, 1966; Schur, 1965). The group uses norm enforcement to show the *strength* of the group. However, if a behavior becomes so widespread that it becomes impossible to control, then the labeling of the widespread behavior as deviance becomes problematic. It simply reminds members of the *weakness* of the group. At this point, the group will redefine what is deviant more narrowly, or it will define its job as that of keeping deviants *within bounds* rather than that of obliterating it altogether. For example, though drug use is and always has been illegal, the widespread use of drugs has led to changes in law enforcement over time. A greater distinction now is made between "hard" drugs and other controlled substances; less penalty is given to those apprehended with small amounts than large amounts; greater attention is focused on capturing large scale smugglers and traffickers than the occasional user. A group, unconsciously if not consciously, learns how much behavior it is capable of labeling deviant and punishing effectively.

Finally, this expressive function of group norms can be seen nicely in circumstances in which there is an inconsistency between what group members *say* is the group norm and how people actually *behave*. For instance, sometimes groups will engage in a lot of rhetoric about how much independence its managers are allowed and how much it values entrepreneurial effort; yet the harder data suggest that the more conservative, deferring, or dependent managers get rewarded. Such an inconsistency can reflect conflicts among the group's expressed values. First, the group can be ambivalent about independence; the group knows it needs to encourage more entrepreneurial efforts to flourish, but such efforts create competition and threaten the status quo. Second, the inconsistency can reveal major subgroup differences. Some people may value and encourage entrepreneurial behavior, but others do not—and the latter may control the group's rewards. Third, the inconsistency can reveal a source of the group's self-consciousness, a dichotomy between what the group is really like and how it would like to be perceived. The group may realize that it is too conservative, yet be unable or too frightened to address its problem. The expressed group norm allows the group members a chance to present a "face" to each other and to outsiders that is more socially desirable than reality.

HOW GROUP NORMS DEVELOP

Norms usually develop gradually and informally as group members learn what behaviors are necessary for the group to function more effectively. However, it also is possible for the norm development process to be short-cut by a critical event in the group or by conscious group decision (Hackman, 1976).

Most norms develop in one or more of the following four ways: explicit statements by supervisors or co-workers; critical events in the group's history; primacy; and carry-over behaviors from past situations.

(1) *Explicit statements by supervisors or co-workers.* Norms that facilitate group survival or task success often are set by the leader of the group of powerful members (Whyte, 1955b). For instance, a group leader might explicitly set norms about not drinking at lunch because subordinates who have been drinking are more likely to have problems dealing competently with clients and top management or they are more likely to have accidents at work. The group leader might also set norms about lateness, personal phone calls, and long coffee breaks if too much productivity is lost as a result of time away from the work place.

Explicit statements by supervisors also can increase the predictability of group members' behavior. For instance, supervisors might have particular preferences for a way of analyzing problems or presenting reports. Strong norms will be set to ensure compliance with these preferences. Consequently, supervisors will have increased certainty about receiving work in the format requested, so they can plan accordingly; workers will have increased certainty about what is expected, so they will not have to outguess their boss or redo their projects.

Managers or important group members also can define the specific role expectations of individual group members. For instance, a supervisor or a co-worker might go up to a new recruit after a meeting to give the proverbial advice: "New recruits should be seen and not heard." The senior group member might be trying to prevent the new recruit from appearing brash or incompetent or from embarrassing other group members. Such interventions set specific role expectations for the new group member.

Norms that cater to supervisor preferences also are frequently established even if they are not objectively necessary to task accomplishment. For example, although organizational norms may be very democratic in terms of everybody calling each other by their first names, some managers have strong preferences about being called Mr., Ms., or Mrs. Although the form of address used in the work group does not influence group effectiveness, complying with the norm bears little cost to the group member, whereas noncompliance could cause daily friction with the supervisor. Such norms help group members avoid embarrassing interpersonal interactions with their managers.

Fourth, norms set explicitly by the supervisor frequently express the central values of the group. For instance, a dean can set very strong norms about faculty keeping office hours and being on campus daily. Such norms reaffirm to members of the academic community their teaching and service obligations, and they send signals to individuals outside the college about what is valued in faculty behavior or distinctive about the school. A dean also could set norms that allow faculty to consult or do executive development two or three days a week. Such norms, too, legitimate other types of faculty behavior and send signals to both insiders and outsiders about some central values of the college.

(2) *Critical events in the group's history.* At times there is a critical event in the group's history that established an important precedent. For instance, a group

member might have discussed hiring plans with members of other units in the organization, and as a result new positions were lost or there was increased competition for good applicants. Such indiscretion can substantially hinder the survival and task success of the group; very likely the offender will be either formally censured or informally rebuked. As a result of such an incident, norms about secrecy might develop that will protect the group in similar situations in the future.

An example from Janis's *Victims of Groupthink* (1972) also illustrates this point nicely. One of President Kennedy's closest advisors, Arthur Schlesinger, Jr., had serious reservations about the Bay of Pigs invasion and presented his strong objections to the Bay of Pigs plan in a memorandum to Kennedy and Secretary of State Dean Rusk. However, Schlesinger was pressured by the President's brother, Attorney General Robert Kennedy, to keep his objections to himself. Remarked Robert Kennedy to Schlesinger: "You may be right or you may be wrong, but the President has made his mind up. Don't push it any further. Now is the time for everyone to help him all they can." Such critical events led group members to silence their views and set up group norms about the bounds of disagreeing with the President.

Sometimes group norms can be set by a conscious decision of a group after a particularly good or bad experience the group has had. To illustrate, a group might have had a particularly constructive meeting and be very pleased with how much it accomplished. Several people might say, "I think the reason we got so much accomplished today is that we met really early in the morning before the rest of the staff showed up and the phone started ringing. Let's try to continue to meet at 7:30 A.M." Others might agree, and the norm is set. On the other hand, if a group notices it accomplished way too little in a meeting, it might openly discuss setting norms to cut down on ineffective behavior (e.g., having an agenda, not interrupting others while they are talking). Such norms develop to facilitate task success and to reduce uncertainty about what is expected for each individual in the group.

Critical events also can identify awkward interpersonal situations that need to be avoided in the future. For instance, a divorce between two people working in the same group might have caused a lot of acrimony and hard feeling in a unit, not only between the husband and wife but also among various other group members who got involved in the marital problems. After the unpleasant divorce, a group might develop a norm about not hiring spouses to avoid having to deal with such interpersonal problems in the future.

Finally, critical events also can give rise to norms that express the central, or distinctive, values of the group. When a peer review panel finds a physician or lawyer guilty of malpractice or malfeasance, first it establishes (or reaffirms) the rights of professionals to evaluate and criticize the professional behavior of their colleagues. Moreover, it clarifies what behaviors are inconsistent with the group's self-image or its values. When a faculty committee votes on a candidate's tenure, it, too, asserts the legitimacy of influence of senior faculty over junior faculty. In addition, it sends (hopefully) clear messages to junior faculty about its values in terms of quality of research, teaching, and service. There are important "announcement effects" of peer reviews; internal group members carefully reexamine the group's values, and outsiders draw inferences about the character of the group from such critical decisions.

(3) *Primacy*. The first behavior pattern that emerges in a group often sets group expectations. If the first group meeting is marked by very formal interaction between supervisors and subordinates, then the group often expects future meetings to be conducted in the same way. Where people sit in meetings or rooms frequently is developed through primacy. People generally continue to sit in the same seats they sat in at their first meeting, even though those original seats are not assigned and people could change where they sit at every meeting. Most friendship groups of students develop their own "turf" in a lecture hall and are surprised/dismayed when an interloper takes "their" seats.

Norms that develop through primacy often do so to simplify, or make predictable, what behavior is expected of group members. There may be very little task impact from where people sit in meetings or how formal interactions are. However, norms develop about such behaviors to make life much more routine and predictable. Every time a group member enters a room, he or she does not have to "decide" where to sit or how formally to behave. Moreover, he or she also is much more certain about how other group members will behave.

(4) *Carry-over behaviors from past situations*. Many group norms in organizations emerge because individual group members bring set expectations with them from other work groups in other organizations. Lawyers expect to behave towards clients in Organization I (e.g., confidentiality, setting fees) as they behaved towards those in Organization II. Doctors expect to behave toward patients in Hospital I (e.g., "bedside manner," professional distance) as they behaved in Hospital II. Accountants expect to behave towards colleagues at Firm I (e.g., dress code, adherence to statutes) as they behaved towards those at Firm II. In fact, much of what goes on in professional schools is giving new members of the profession the same standards and norms of behavior that practitioners in the field hold.

Such carry-over of individual behaviors from past situations can increase the predictability of group members' behaviors in new settings and facilitate task accomplishment. For instance, students and professors bring with them fairly constant sets of expectations from class to class. As a result, students do not have to relearn continually their roles from class to class; they know, for instance, if they come in late to take a seat quietly at the back of the room without being told. Professors also do not have to relearn continually their roles; they know, for instance, not to mumble, scribble in small print on the black board, or be vague when making course assignments. In addition, presumably the most task-successful norms will be the ones carried over from organization to organization.

Moreover, such carry-over norms help avoid embarrassing interpersonal situations. Individuals are more likely to know which conversations and actions provoke annoyance, irritation, or embarrassment to their colleagues. Finally, when groups carry over norms from one organization to another, they also clarify what is distinctive about the occupational or professional role. When lawyers maintain strict rules of confidentiality, when doctors maintain a consistent professional distance with patients, when accountants present a very formal physical appearance, they all assert: "These are the standards we sustain *independent* of what we could 'get away with' in this organization. This is *our* self-concept."

SUMMARY

Norms generally are enforced only for behaviors that are viewed as important by most group members. Groups do not have the time or energy to regulate each and every action of individual members. Only those behaviors that ensure group survival, facilitate task accomplishment, contribute to group morale, or express the group's central values are likely to be brought under normative control. Norms that reflect these group needs will develop through explicit statements of supervisors, critical events in the group's history, primacy, or carry-over behaviors from past situations.

Empirical research on norm development and enforcement has substantially lagged descriptive and theoretical work. In large part, this may be due to the methodological problems of measuring norms and getting enough data points either across time or across groups. Until such time as empirical work progresses, however, the usefulness of group norms as a predictive concept, rather than as a post hoc explanatory device, will be severely limited. Moreover, until it is known more concretely why norms develop and why they are strongly enforced, attempts to *change* group norms will remain haphazard and difficult to accomplish.

REFERENCES

Alvarez, R. Informal reactions to deviance in simulated work organizations: A laboratory experiment. *American Sociological Review*, 1968, 33, 895–912.

Asch, S. Effects of group pressure upon the modification and distortion of judgment . In M. H. Guetzkow (Ed.), *Groups, leadership, and men*. Pittsburgh: Carnegie, 1951, 117–190.

Bales, R. F., & Slater, P. E. Role differentiation in small groups. In T. Parsons, R. F. Bales, J. Olds, M. Zelditch, & P. E. Slater (Eds.), *Family, socialization, and interaction process*. Glencoe, Ill.: Free Press, 1955, 35–131.

Dentler, R. A., & Erikson, K. T. The functions of deviance in groups. *Social Problems*, 1959, 7, 98–107.

Erikson, K. T. *Wayward Puritans*. New York: Wiley, 1966.

Goffman, E. On face-work: An analysis of ritual elements in social interaction. *Psychiatry*, 1955, 18, 213–231.

Hackman, J. R. Group influences on individuals. In M. Dunnette (Ed.), *Handbook of industrial and organizational psychology*. Chicago: Rand McNally, 1976, 1455–1525.

Hollander, E. P. Conformity, status, and idiosyncrasy credit. *Psychological Review*, 1958, 65, 117–127.

Hollander, E. P. Some effects of perceived status on responses to innovative behavior. *Journal of Abnormal and Social Psychology*, 1961, 63, 247–250.

Hollander, E. P. *Leaders, groups, and influence*. New York: Oxford University Press, 1964.

Jackson, J. A conceptual and measurement mode for norms and roles. *Pacific Sociological Review*, 1966, 9, 35–47.

Janis, I. *Victims of groupthink: A psychological study of foreign-policy decisions and fiascos*. New York: Houghton-Mifflin, 1972.

Katz, D., & Kahn, R. L. *The social psychology of organizations*. 2nd ed. New York: Wiley, 1978.

Kiesler, C. A., & Kiesler, S. B. *Conformity*. Reading, Mass.: Addison-Wesley, 1970.

Longley, J., & Pruitt D. C. Groupthink: A critique of Janis' theory. In Ladd Wheeler (Ed.), *Review of personality and social psychology*. Beverly Hills: Sage, 1980, 74–93.

March, J. Group norms and the active minority. *American Sociological Review*, 1954, 19, 733–741.

Schachter, S., Ellertson, N., McBride, D., & Gregory, D. An experimental study of cohesiveness and productivity. *Human Relations*, 1951, 4, 229–238.

Schur, E. M. *Crimes without victims*. Englewood Cliffs, N.J.: Prentice-Hall, 1965.

Seashore, S. *Group cohesiveness in the industrial work group*. Ann Arbor: Institute for Social Research, University of Michigan, 1954.

Shaw, M. *Group dynamics*. 3rd ed. New York: Harper, 1936.

Trist, E. L., & Bamforth, K. W. Some social and psychological consequences of the longwall method of coal-getting. *Human Relations*, 1951, 4, 1–38.

Whyte, W. F. *Money and motivation*. New York: Harper, 1955a.

Whyte, W. F. *Street corner society*. Chicago: University of Chicago Press, 1955b.

Wiggins, J. A., Dill, F., & Schwartz, R. D. On status-liability. *Sociometry*, 1965, 28, 197–209.

REVIEW QUESTIONS

1 Give three examples of group norms that you have encountered.
2 Under what conditions are groups likely to enforce their norms?
3 Examine the reasons why group norms develop. Which of these could supervisors possibly control to some degree?

READING 51

The Potential for "Groupthink" in Autonomous Work Groups

Charles C. Manz
Henry P. Sims, Jr.*

INTRODUCTION

The importance of organizations in our society as well as their shortcomings in terms of quantity and quality of production, work satisfaction, turnover and absenteeism, counterproductive behavior, etc., has been pointed out elsewhere (Cummings & Malloy, 1977). Furthermore, the emergence of a new type of environment ("turbulent field") in which organizations must function has been

*From *Human Relations*, September 1982, pp. 773–784. Reprinted with permission.

identified as a force necessitating new organizational approaches to deal with increasing interdependence, complexity, and uncertainty (Trist, 1977). As a result of current problems facing modern organizations, a number of strategies have been implemented to try to make improvements. Among the multitude of methods that have been tried, a general concept which has become increasingly recognized is what is referred to as "quality of work life." Quality of work life has been defined as a "process by which an organization attempts to unlock the creative potential of its people by involving them in decisions affecting their work lives" (Guest, 1979, p.76). Furthermore, Guest has indicated that "quality of work life" is a generic phrase that includes a person's feelings about every dimension of work, such as economic rewards and benefits, work conditions, organizational and interpersonal relationships, etc.

Susman (1976) has suggested that the work group is an appropriate unit to use in attempting to improve the quality of working life. Among the reasons he offers are that the work unit is small enough to include sufficient tasks for completion of products valued by members and the organization; to require sufficient variety, complexity, and uncertainty to allow challenging decision-making; and to allow individuals to exercise interpersonal skills for problem solving, conflict resolution, etc. Finally, he indicates that increased possibilities for innovative restructuring of tasks and relationships are possible at the work-group level as opposed to the individual job level. In particular, autonomous (i.e., self-managing) work groups have been used quite extensively in attempts to improve the quality of work life and to deal generally with many of the problems modern organizations are faced with.

AUTONOMOUS WORK GROUPS

The utilization of autonomous work groups has largely emerged from the application of the sociotechnical systems perspective (Cummings, 1978; Emery & Trist, 1969; Susman, 1976). The sociotechnical systems perspective emphasizes the social as well as the technical aspects of the work system. The intention is to design a work structure that is appropriate for the social and the psychological needs of the employees as well as the task requirements of the existing technology (Cummings, 1978). Consequently, this approach contrasts with both the more traditional engineering approach to work design that tends to ignore the psychological needs of employees and the psychological approaches that tend to underemphasize technological and environmental factors (Hackman, 1977).

The use of autonomous groups involves a shift in focus from individual methods of performing work to group methods. The rationale for making this shift in focus has been described as resulting from "the proposition that a group can more effectively allocate its resources when and where required to deal with its total variance in work conditions, than can an aggregate of individuals each of whom is assigned part of the variance" (Susman, 1976, p. 183). As a consequence of implementation of a self-managing group approach, group members tend to define their work role in terms of their value as contributors to the group's primary task rather than in relation to one specific job.

Many examples of the implementation of a self-managing work group type of work system do exist. They include work contexts such as a dog food plant (Walton, 1977), coal mines (Trist, Susman, and Brown, 1977), and a paint manufacturing plant (Poza & Markus, 1980). For a review of many of the projects that have been undertaken, see Cummings and Malloy (1977, pp. 38–49).

Utilization of autonomous work groups, in the contexts mentioned above and others, has been credited with various benefits including increased productivity and enhancement of the quality of work life. This paper, however, will explore a potential problem that can emerge within autonomous work groups and that can detract from their effectiveness. This problem can be referred to as "groupthink" (Janis, 1972). The notion of "groupthink" will be described and specific cases, observed in an autonomous work group system, revealing symptoms of "groupthink" will be presented. Finally, implications of this analysis will be discussed.

GROUPTHINK

What Is Groupthink?

Janis (1972) has described groupthink as "a mode of thinking that people engage in when they are deeply involved in a cohesive in group . . . members' striving for unanimity override their motivation to realistically appraise alternative courses of action . . . a deterioration of mental efficiency, reality testing, and moral judgment that results from in-group pressures" (p. 9). Furthermore, Janis (1971) has pointed out that when groupthink exists there are many indications that group norms are developed which bolster morale at the expense of critical thinking. Indeed, the concept of groupthink suggests that within groups presenting a positive outward appearance of high cohesiveness and a strong "team" orientation (as many autonomous work groups do) defective decision-making processes may be present.

A simple diagram of an interpretation of the process is presented in Fig. 1. The notion is that when a group entails both high cohesiveness (a strong commitment to the group and a desire to continue to belong to it on the part of group members) and high conformity (a strong desire on the part of group members to be in agreement with other group members), the potential for groupthink exists. Fur-

FIGURE 1
An interpretation of the groupthink process.

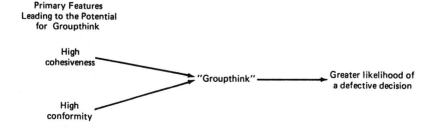

thermore, when groupthink does exist, decisions are more likely to be defective. The concept of groupthink can be more clearly understood by examining the symptoms that indicate its presence.

Symptoms of Groupthink

Janis (1971, 1972) has suggested that eight specific symptoms of groupthink can be identified. Each is listed and briefly described below.

1 *Illusion of Invulnerability*—group members display excessive optimism and tend to take extreme risks.

2 *Collective Rationalization*—group members collectively construct rationalizations that allow them to discount negative information concerning the assumptions upon which they base their decisions.

3 *Illusion of Morality*—group members display an unquestioned belief in the inherent morality of the group.

4 *Shared Stereotypes*—shared stereotyped views of opposing groups (particularly of their leaders) are held by group members (e.g., they are evil or weak).

5 *Direct Pressure*—direct pressure to conform is placed on group members who express doubts in, or question the validity of, beliefs held by the group.

6 *Self-Censorship*—avoidance of expression of views that are not consistent with the apparent group consensus, or avoidance of expression of doubts about that consensus, by individual group members.

7 *Illusion of Unanimity*—an illusion shared by group members that all are in agreement within the group (a belief that silence on the part of any group members indicates that they are in agreement with what is being expressed).

8 *Self-Appointed Mindguards*—group members take it upon themselves to screen out adverse information (from outsiders) to the group's general views that might break the complacency of the group.

Why Groupthink?

The groupthink framework offers the potential to make some interesting contributions to our understanding of autonomous work group decision process, and to the functioning and effective implementation of autonomous work groups. First, it offers considerable potential to be used as an observational behavioral category system. The use of an observational category approach to studying groups is not new (see Bales, 1950, for an example of the use of such an approach). More recently, Campbell (1977), however, expressed concern regarding over-reliance on self-report questionnaire measures and a need to focus more on the observation of behavior in one area of organizational behavior (i.e., leadership). His comments support the notion that focusing on actual ongoing behavior offers a number of advantages for conducting research. The symptoms of groupthink suggested by Janis could be used as categories from which to interpret ongoing autonomous workgroup behavior.

Furthermore, autonomous work groups would seem to be prime candidates for the phenomenon of groupthink. In autonomous workgroups, group members are largely responsible for managing the activities of their own group (e.g., problem solving, technical adjustments). Group members, consequently, are likely to experience a high level of interaction and support from other members in order to make necessary decisions and perform required tasks that the group is confronted with . Indeed, the potential for a high level of cohesiveness is likely to be high. Furthermore, in a self-managing group situation a tendency on the part of group members to conform with the general views of the group does not seem unlikely. Group members work as a unit on a daily basis and depend on each other for effective completion of group tasks. Consequently, the attractiveness of conforming in order to be accepted by the group is likely to be high. The point is that autonomous work groups are vulnerable to groupthink. Therefore, this potential threat to optimum group functioning is an important issue to address.

Finally, Janis (1971, 1972) has applied the groupthink framework to analyze defective decision processes in situations that are in many ways analogous to situations in work organizations. His analysis of defects in decision-making leading to the undetected invasion of Pearl Harbor by the Japanese provides an example. He explains that naval commanders in Hawaii perceived Pearl Harbor to be impregnable (illusion of invulnerability) and believed Japan was an inferior nation that would not dare to attempt such an attack (shared stereotypes). The same symptoms could be attributed to a marketing staff group in a company that believes its market share for a particular product is secure (illusion of invulnerability) and that a smaller competitor would not dare to enter the market (shared stereotypes).

In the following section specific cases observed in an actual work context using autonomous work groups will be presented. Then each case will be analyzed using the groupthink framework. The intention is to provide actual examples that suggest the relevance and potential usefulness of the groupthink framework for improving our understanding of autonomous work group decision processes.

CASES

Description of the Organizational Context

The cases to be presented are based on observations made in a nonunionized battery assembly plant in the southern United States. It is owned by a large corporation and employs approximately 320 employees. The technology used in the plant can be described as small parts production or assembly and it is sequentially interdependent.

The organization structure includes three distinct hierarchical levels: upper plant management, external work group leaders, and the work groups themselves. The size of the work groups varies from approximately 3–19 members. Each work group includes an elected within group team leader who is a member of the group but who has increased responsibilities and receives a higher level of pay than other group members.

An autonomous work group system is used in the plant. Consequently, work groups are assigned rather untraditional responsibilities. These include preparing an annual budget, making within group job assignments, recording quality control statistics (subject to audit), participating in the assessment of job performance of fellow group members, and scheduling the times during which the work group will perform its work. In addition, the work groups engage in various problem-solving activities that include dealing with production problems and group member problem behavior such as absenteeism.

Each work group has weekly team meetings that serve as the problem-solving forum in which such issues are addressed. Various conference rooms are used for these meetings as well as upper plant management offices when they are available. Often, the group's elected team leader will organize and conduct the meeting. Group problems are usually raised for open discussion, and group members are provided with the opportunity to voice their views of the issues. The work group's external team leader (next higher hierarchical level) or members of upper plant management are sometimes invited to work with a team during a meeting addressing a specific problem or issue.

The cases presented in this paper are based on observations made during various weekly team meetings of several groups. The size of the groups involved ranged from approximately six to twelve individuals. Three specific cases were selected that appear particularly useful for applying the groupthink framework to decision-making processes in autonomous work groups.

Case One

During one weekly group meeting of a production group in the plant (approximately 12 people were present), a group member raised the issue of changing group working shift hours. Several other group members responded quickly with reasons why changing shift hours was a poor idea. (One group member expressed the view that anybody wanting to come to work "that early" is "crazy." The proposed change involved starting the shift much earlier than usual so that workers could get out earlier in the afternoons.) Furthermore, it was stated that a vote is the "best way" of deciding and that the group had previously voted against such a change. The within group leader then pointed out that this subject was brought up at the last meeting and that "nobody" said that they disagreed with keeping the shift at the usual time, so he assumed that all were in agreement.

After listening to comments made by the individual who raised the issue, it became clear that the proposed change had been voted down by one vote in a previous meeting. He added, "It doesn't seem fair because almost half of us want to switch." He also proposed that the shift time be alternated every week (or month) so that all group members could have their preferences satisfied some of the time. He did not receive much aid from other employees, however, and with pressure from the team leader and opposing group members the subject was finally dropped. Observation of the nonverbal behavior of a number of the persons present indicated that they were not satisfied with the outcome but that they were not expressing their views.

Several of the behaviors observed during this meeting fit quite well under the various symptoms of group think as described below.

Direct Pressure. When the subject was first brought up, and after each additional argument for the shift change, various group members, including the team leader, applied direct pressure to the "deviant." The few comments made by supporting group members received a similar response.

Illusion of Unanimity. The group leader expressed the view that since no one argued against keeping the same shift time in the previous meeting, he assumed all were in agreement.

Self-Censorship. Although a previous vote for the change had lost by only one vote, very few comments were made to argue for the change during this meeting. Several nonverbal cues (e.g., frowns, tense movements, gestures suggesting anger) indicated that although several group members were not satisfied with the outcome, they did not express their views.

Case Two

One group meeting observed consisted of approximately six individuals who worked in a quality-control laboratory. The group's primary work involved checking battery materials for defects. During the meeting one member brought to the attention of the others that their group had been the target of an excessive number of complaints recently. The discussion that followed revealed that a particular work group of production workers had been dissatisfied with excessive "down time" that they blamed on the laboratory workers. They felt that production was suffering when potential defects were discovered because tests for materials defects were taking too long while production operations were shut down to avoid scrap.

A series of comments were made by various group members that supported the position of the laboratory staff. Statements that exemplified the views expressed included "they (the production workers) expect us to drop everything," and "they don't understand how long the tests take." Ultimately the subject was dropped, with no real alternative solutions to the problem being expressed. Group members seemed to be satisfied that they were in the "right" and that the complaints received were unreasonable and unjustified.

This second case illustrates behaviors that fall under different symptoms of groupthink than those highlighted by case one. These symptoms are discussed below.

Collective Rationalization. Group members expressed views, and provided support for views expressed by others, which allowed them to discount the importance of the negative information that had been received. The group avoided the critical thinking necessary to objectively examine the problem by emphasizing the unreasonableness of the complaints (i.e., collectively rationalizing their position).

Shared Stereotypes. Group members voiced common stereotyped views of the production workers. Statements that were made indicating that the production workers expected them "to drop everything" to work on a problem and that the production workers "don't understand how long the tests take" exemplify this symptom.

Case Three

The final case involved a production group of approximately eight individuals. The discussion concerned a quality control problem with battery casings. A unique feature of this case was that, unlike the situation in the first two cases, the external group leader was present at the meeting (the person who occupies the next higher formal level of the hierarchy; see earlier section on description of the organizational context). Participation in the problem-solving discussion was quite even, and group members appeared to be speaking freely. After a few minutes, however, the external group leader spoke up and with the statement "this is what I think you should do" took charge of the remainder of the meeting. Group members' participation was very limited from that point on. The external group leader presented the steps he wanted the group to take and the meeting ended with essentially a one-way flow of communication. Group members' nonverbal behavior (e.g., facial expressions) indicated that although members would comply with the leader's instructions, they did not feel they had contributed to the solution, nor did they agree with it.

A discussion of the most salient symptoms of groupthink revealed in the case follows.

Self-Censorship. Although the nonverbal behavior of group members indicated that they did not agree with the leader's views, their disagreement was not expressed. From the time that the leader spoke up and took charge of the meeting, group members' participation was practically nonexistent. (This is in sharp contrast to the earlier part of the meeting, the observation of which indicated that the workers not only had strong views on the problem but wanted to express these views.)

Illusion of Unanimity. The lack of participation on the part of group members appeared to convince the external group leader that little if any disagreement existed. The group leader seemed satisfied that a "group" decision had been made which all were in agreement with.

Case Implications

The three cases presented above represent a sampling of numerous observations made of autonomous work group meetings. The qualitative evidence they entail suggests that "groupthink" offers an insightful framework from which to study autonomous work group decision processes.

In addition to the qualitative approach used in this paper, the groupthink framework offers the potential for quantitative analysis. For example, recent leadership research has used video tape technology to capture ongoing organizational behavior (see Sims & Manz, 1980). The video tapes were subsequently coded by counting the number of verbal behaviors falling within a priori categories, thus providing the basis for quantitative analysis. The cases presented above provide evidence that related procedures might be used to capture and analyze ongoing autonomous work group decision processes. Overall, they suggest that "groupthink" is a relevant phenomenon that could potentially hinder the effectiveness of autonomous work groups and that its symptoms provide categories for studying and potentially quantifying decision processes within these groups.

CONCLUSIONS

Several conclusions can be drawn from this paper.

1 Autonomous work groups are likely to be vulnerable to the weaknesses inherent in group decision-making identified in the "groupthink" framework.

2 There is a need for more research on the potential threats posed by "groupthink" to effective group decision-making in autonomous work groups (and the research could be based on a more rigorous quantitative base through the use of the groupthink symptoms as behavioral categories for observational coding of behavior).

3 As our knowledge and understanding of autonomous work group decision-making expands, steps can be taken to avoid the pitfalls of groupthink. These include: *(a)* training of work group members aimed at increasing their decision-making skills and knowledge of the potential hazards involved; *(b)* training of work group leaders (both internal and external) aimed at increasing their knowledge of group decision processes and their leadership skills for facilitating these processes (e.g., nondirective leadership skills and methods for creating an atmosphere of critical evaluation); and *(c)* education of upper management concerning the unique needs and potential dangers of decision-making processes in autonomous work groups.

Numerous autonomous work group team meetings were observed, some revealing "groupthink" symptoms and some not. The authors are optimistic that the "groupthink" syndrome can be avoided if proper precautions are taken to enhance decision-making processes in autonomous work groups.

REFERENCES

Bales, R. A set of categories for the analysis of small group interaction. *American Sociological Review*, 1950, *15*, 257–263.

Campbell, J. C. The cutting edge of leadership: An overview. In J. C. Hunt and L. L. Larson (Eds.), *Leadership: The cutting edge.* Carbondale, Ill.: Southern Illinois University Press, 1977.

Cummings, T. Self-regulating work groups: A socio-technical synthesis. *Academy of Management Review*, 1978, *3*, 625–634.

Cummings T., & Malloy, E. S. *Improving productivity and the quality of work life.* New York: Praeger, 1977.

Emery, F. E., & Trist, E. L. Socio-technical systems. In F. E. Emery (Ed.), *Systems thinking*, London: Penguin Books, 1969.

Guest, R. H. Quality of work life: Learning from Tarrytown. *Harvard Business Review*, July–August 1979, 76–87.

Hackman, J. R. Work design. In J. Hackman and J. Suttle (Eds.), *Improving life at work*, Santa Monica, Calif.: Goodyear Publishing, 1977.

Janis, I. L. Groupthink, *Psychology Today*, November 1971, 43–46, 74–76.

Janis, I. L. *Victims of groupthink: A psychological study of foreign policy decisions and fiascos*. Boston: Houghton Mifflin, 1972.

Poza, E. J., & Markus, L. Success story: The team approach to work restructuring. *Organizational Dynamics*. Winter 1980, 3–25.

Sims, H. P., & Manz, C. C. *Categories of observed leader communication behaviors*. Proceedings of the Southwest Academy of Management, San Antonio, Texas, March 1980.

Susman, G. I. *Autonomy at work: A socio-technical analysis of participative management*. New York: Praeger 1976.

Trist, E. Collaboration in work settings: A personal perspective. *The Journal of Applied Behavioral Science*, 1977, *13*, 268–278.

Trist, E. L., Susman, G. I., & Brown, G. R. An experiment in autonomous working in an American underground coal mine. *Human Relations*, 1977, *30*, 201–236.

Walton, R. E. Work innovations at Topeka: After six years. *The Journal of Applied Behavioral Science*, 1977, *13*, 422–433.

REVIEW QUESTIONS

1 Reflect on the idea of "groupthink." Give an example of a time when you observed or experienced it.
2 Why do the authors suggest that autonomous work groups are prime candidates for "groupthink"?
3 Generate some recommendations for preventing or overcoming the phenomenon of "groupthink."

READING 52

Effects of Social Context on Consensus and Majority Vote Decision Making

Dean Tjosvold
Richard H. G. Field*

Because several persons can combine ideas, correct errors, and stimulate thinking to create and evaluate solutions, groups are thought to have great potential for decision making. Considerable research suggests that groups typically make decisions superior to those made by individuals (Kelley & Thibaut, 1968; Nichols

*From the *Academy of Management Journal*, September 1983, pp. 500–506. Reprinted with permission.

& Day, 1982) and induce greater acceptance of the decision (Maier, 1970) and more understanding of the problem (Laughlin, 1978). But not all groups are effective. Janis's (1972) work on groupthink dramatically illustrates that members sometimes conform, stifle discussion, and make unreasonable decisions. Researchers have identified several approaches to structure group interaction to improve decision making (Herbert & Yost, 1979; Van de Ven & Delbecq, 1974; White, Dittrich, & Lang, 1980). Consensus decision making, compared to majority vote, has long been thought to be effective because the views and ideas of all group members are considered and not hastily dismissed as unimportant minority opinion (Hall, 1971; Maier, 1970). The social context may affect the usefulness of consensus and majority vote. In particular, this study investigates the consequences of consensus and majority vote approaches to group decision making in a cooperative and competitive social context on the quality of commitment to the decision, individual understanding of the problem, time needed to make the decision, and attitudes toward the group.

Consensus and majority vote stipulate the rule that groups are to use to make their decisions. In consensus decision making, all group members express their opinions, discuss the issue, and then choose an alternative they all can agree to, or at least in part. Majority vote selects the alternative that more than half the group members think should be accepted. The cooperative and competitive context may affect the success of consensus and majority vote approaches. Cooperation occurs when persons perceive that their goals are positively linked: one's goal attainment helps others reach their goals (Deutsch, 1949, 1973). In competition, persons believe that their goals are negatively linked: one's goal attainment interferes with others' goals. The emphasis in competition is on winning and outdoing others; in cooperation, it is on working together for joint benefit.

Consensus is thought to contribute substantially to decision making. Hall (1971) argued that in consensus, opposing opinions are addressed directly, as all persons are encouraged to express their own views, and this open controversy results in a thorough exploration of the problem, understanding among group members, and the creation of high quality solutions to which members are committed. Groups that discuss controversy openly have been shown to be effective decision makers (Janis, 1972; Maier, 1970; Maier & Hoffman, 1964). Yet it is the skillfully managed, constructive controversy that promotes decision making. Considerable research supports Deutsch's (1973) argument that social context affects the course and outcomes of conflict and that cooperation results in constructive conflict. Group members who discuss their controversy in a cooperative context have been found to understand and incorporate each other's ideas into an effective decision. In competition, they were closed minded to using each other's ideas to make their decisions (Tjosvold, 1982; Tjosvold & Deemer, 1980). *It is hypothesized,* therefore, *that groups using consensus decision making are more effective under cooperative conditions than under competitive conditions.*

Majority vote may be useful when persons are in competition. Competitors express their own views to try to win and show that their ideas are better than others. They may be less interested in understanding, responding, and incorporating each other's ideas. Because they are not likely to compromise easily, they may welcome a majority vote rule as a way to end their conflicts, whereas consensus only prolongs them. *It is hypothesized that in competition, groups using majority vote, compared to consensus, use less time and have more positive attitudes toward their group.*

METHOD

Subjects

The participants were 114 undergraduates from Simon Fraser University, who were randomly assigned to 4 conditions and placed in groups of 5 with 1 group of 4. There were five groups in competitive-consensus and six groups in the other conditions. Subjects were given course credits for their participation in the study.

Procedures

The experiment had three phases. In phase 1, all subjects individually made their decisions on the rank order of importance of 15 items that may help persons return to the mother ship in the "Lost on the Moon" exercise (Hall, 1971). In phase 2, they were placed in groups and read the instructions that included the experimental inductions. They then discussed the issue and made their group decisions. In the last phase, the subjects individually indicated their decision and completed a questionnaire on their attitudes toward their group.

The experimental inductions were introduced when the subjects first formed their groups. In the cooperative conditions, subjects read that they were to work together for mutual benefit and not to try to win or outdo others. They were to search for a solution that was good for all. In the competitive conditions, subjects were told they were to try to win and show that their own ideas were superior to others. Subjects also were told that they were to make their decision through consensus or majority vote. Subjects in the consensus condition read that they were to reach decisions that everyone could agree to, at least in part. They were not to rely just on majority rule, but the decisions should be acceptable to all. In the voting condition, groups were told that the majority vote would determine the group's decisions. The experimenter answered questions and checked to make sure that all subjects understood the instructions. The groups had up to 60 minutes to complete the task.

Dependent Measures

The dependent variables were: quality of the group decision, individual commitment to the decision, understanding of the problem, time needed, and attitudes toward the group. To measure the quality of the group's decision, the absolute difference between the group's ranking and the correct one was computed. A similar procedure was used to measure individual understanding of the problem: the individual's post group discussion ranking was compared to the correct one.

To measure individual commitment to the group decisions, individual subjects' post discussion ranking was compared to their group's ranking. The lower the score, the more adequate the group's decision, the more individual understanding of the problem, and the greater the commitment to the group's decision.

After the discussion the subjects indicated on a questionnaire their attitudes toward their group: specifically, their beliefs about how effective their group was and their desire to work again with this same group. They used a 7-point scale with 7 labeled "a great deal" and 1 labeled "a very little" to indicate the extent to which they believed their group was effective overall and the extent to which they wanted to work again with this group.

Intercorrelations among the dependent measures were computed (Table 1). Individual understanding of the problem was related to decision quality and commitment to the decision. Individuals who learned in the discussion appear not only to have helped the group make a high quality decision, but also to become committed to that decision. Perhaps they also learned by being convinced of the group's arguments and decisions. Time was negatively related to decision quality, largely because subjects in the competitive-consensus condition took considerable time to make low quality decisions. Perceived effectiveness was moderately but negatively related to group decision quality but was related to willingness to work again with the group. Subjects appear to have based their desire to work with the group on their perception of effectiveness rather than on actual group effectiveness.

RESULTS

All subjects individually made the decision before they formed groups. No significant or nearly significant findings were obtained among conditions on this prediscussion individual decision. The means for the conditions are 48.97 for cooperative consensus, 47 for cooperative voting, 44.17 for competitive consensus, and 48.40 for competitive voting. The lack of statistically significant findings indicates that, as expected, general understanding of the problem was roughly equally distributed across experimental conditions.

TABLE 1
INTERCORRELATIONS AMONG DEPENDENT MEASURES

	Decision quality	Decision commitment	Understanding	Time	Perceived effectiveness of group
Commitment	.10				
Understanding	.56***	.47***			
Time	−.21**	−.09	−.09		
Effectiveness	−.14*	−.01	−.05	−.03	
Willingness to work again	−.07	−.05	−.01	−.01	.46***

*$p < .10$
**$p < .05$
***$p < .01$

Two items were included on the postdiscussion questionnaire to measure the effectiveness of the inductions. Subjects were asked to describe their relationships in their group on a 7-point scale with 1 labeled "very competitive," 4 as "neither competitive nor cooperative," and 7 as "very cooperative." As expected, subjects in the cooperative condition ($M = 5.34$) indicated that their relationship was more cooperative than did subjects in the competitive condition ($M = 3.21$), $[F(1, 112) = 21.87, p < .01]$. Subjects also described how their group made its decisions by checking either "decided by voting" or "we all tried to agree on the decisions." To compare, the voting option was scored as 1 and consensus as 2. The analysis indicated that, as expected, subjects in the voting condition ($M = 1.33$) indicated that they made decisions by voting, versus subjects in the consensus condition ($M = 1.96$), $[F(1,112) = 22.26, p < .01]$. These results indicate that the conditions necessary to test the hypothesis were created.

Contrary to expectations, groups from the different conditions did not differ significantly in the quality of their decisions (Table 2). However, subjects in the consensus condition revealed that they were more committed to their own group's decision than did subjects in the voting condition. In addition, subjects in the cooperative condition showed more individual understanding of the problem by making more accurate decisions than did those in the competitive condition.

The analysis of time to make the decision yielded both a main effect for social context and a two-way interaction. Overall, the cooperative subjects completed their decision more quickly than did competitive subjects. The significant interaction suggests that the method of decision had quite a different impact, depending

TABLE 2
COMPARISONS AMONG DEPENDENT MEASURES[a]

	Cooperation		Competition		
	Consensus	Voting	Consensus	Voting	F
Decision quality	35.33	29.33	33.40	37.67	
Decision commitment	10.87	14.63	6.70	18.10	Consensus vs. voting, 8.21***
Understanding	35.93	32.57	35.50	38.93	Cooperative vs. competitive 4.56**
Time	29.17	39.33	55.20	37.67	Cooperative vs. competitive 10.29*** Interaction, 14.83***
Perceived effectiveness of group	5.34	4.97	5.09	5.43	Interaction, 3.27*
Willingness to work again	5.07	4.50	4.61	5.10	Interaction, 3.09*

[a]The higher the score, the lower the decision quality, decision commitment, and understanding. Time is in minutes. Th higher the score, the greater the perceived effectiveness of the group and willingness to work again with the group.
*$p < .10$
**$p < .05$
***$p < .01$

on the social context. Consensus seemed to facilitate quick decisions under the cooperative condition, whereas voting facilitated speed under the competitive condition.

The social context and decision making method may have interacted to affect attitudes toward the group. However, the interactions were only marginally significant ($p < .10$) and suggestive. Overall, these results suggest that in a cooperative context, consensus facilitates perception of the group as effective and a group with which one would want to work again. In a competitive context the voting method seems to have induced more favorable attitudes.

DISCUSSION

Groups have been thought to promote acceptance of a decision and understanding of the problem (Laughlin, 1978; Maier, 1970; Vroom & Yetton, 1973). Results of this study, although limited by the type of task, the size and number in its sample, and other aspects of its operations, suggest the conditions that affect these outcomes of group decision making. Consensus appears to facilitate acceptance of the group's decision. Subjects' own personal decisions were closer to those of their group when their group used consensus rather than majority vote to make the decision. Perhaps persons in consensus both can influence their group decision to be close to their own and are more open to changing their ideas to support their group's decision than are persons who vote to make decisions. Results of this study also suggest that a cooperative context encourages learning. Group members in cooperation appear to have exchanged ideas and understood each other to learn about the problem, whereas those in competition were more closed minded to each other's perspectives and learned less.

Results provide some support for the idea that the success of consensus and majority vote decision making depends on the social context. Groups in cooperation made their consensus decisions more quickly than did those in competition; however, in competition the majority vote groups made decisions more quickly than did consensus ones. Indeed, the competitive-consensus group used nearly all the time allowed to make the decision. Also, subjects in cooperation tended to believe that their consensus group was more effective and desirable than the voting group; subjects in competition thought their majority vote group was more effective and desirable than the consensus groups. Taken together, these results suggest that the complaint that consensus decision making is time consuming and frustrating holds more when persons try to compete and outdo each other than when they work for mutual benefits.

Consensus-cooperative groups were expected to exchange information, correct errors, and stimulate thinking through constructive discussion of opposing views to arrive at high quality decisions. However, the analysis yielded no significant differences on the measure of decision quality. The task may not have lent itself to effective group consideration. Laughlin (1978) and Laughlin and Adamopoulous (1980) found that groups are successful problem solvers on intellective rather than judgmental tasks. Intellective tasks have a clearly demonstrable, correct answer. The task for this study is structured in that there is a correct answer (Herbert & Yost, 1979), but it is not a fully intellective one, because persons with the correct answers cannot always persuade even reasonable others. Future research could investigate the effects of consensus and majority vote decision making in different social contexts on intellective and judgmental tasks.

Researchers have tried to identify the conditions that facilitate group decision making on quality and acceptance of the decision and understanding of the problem. Training in human relations skills and experience in the group have been found to aid group decision making (Hall, 1971; Hall & Williams, 1970). The Delphi method and nominal group technique can provide a structure for groups without such training and experience (Van de Ven & Delbecq, 1974). The results of this study suggest that consensus decision making can induce commitment to the decision in that the individual's and group's decisions are congruent. A cooperative context was found to facilitate learning about the problem under discussion and to help consensus decision making groups use their time efficiently. Results also suggest that when persons feel competitive toward each other, a majority vote rule may be a reasonable way to reduce the controversy and the time needed for group decision making.

REFERENCES

Deutsch, M. A theory of cooperation and competition. *Human Relations*, 1949, 2, 129–152.
Deutsch, M. *The resolution of conflict*. New Haven, Conn.: Yale, 1973.
Hall, J. Decisions, decisions, decisions. *Psychology Today*, November 1971, 51–54, 86, 88.
Hall, J., & Williams, M. Group dynamics training and improved decision making. *Journal of Applied Behavioral Science*, 1970, 6, 39–68.
Herbert, T. T., & Yost, E. B. A comparison of decision quality under nominal and interaction consensus group formats: The case of the structured problem. *Decision Sciences*, 1979, 10, 358–370.
Janis, I. L. *Victims of groupthink*. Boston: Houghton, Mifflin, 1972.
Kelley, H. H., & Thibaut, J. W. Group problem solving. In G. Lindzey & E. Aronson (Eds.), *Handbook of social psychology* (Vol. 4). Reading, Mass.: Addison-Wesley, 1968, 1–101.
Laughlin, P. R. Ability and group problem solving. *Journal of Research and Development in Education*, 1978, 12, 114–120.
Laughlin, P. R., & Adamopoulous, J. Social combination processes and individual learning for six-person cooperative groups on an intellective task. *Journal of Personality and Social Psychology*, 1980, 38, 941–947.
Maier, N. R. F. *Problem-solving and creativity in individuals and groups*. Belmont, Cal.: Brooks/Cole, 1970.
Maier, N., & Hoffman, L. Financial incentives and group decision in motivating change. *Journal of Social Psychology*, 1964, 64, 369–378.
Nichols, M. L., & Day, V. E. A comparison of moral reasoning of groups and individuals on the "defining issues test." *Academy of Management Journal*, 1982, 25, 201–208.
Tjosvold, D. Effects of approach to controversy on superiors' incorporation of subordinates' information on decision making. *Journal of Applied Psychology*, 1982, 67, 189–193.

Tjosvold, D., & Deemer, D. K. Effects of controversy within a cooperative or competitive context on organizational decision making. *Journal of Applied Psychology*, 1980, 65, 590–595.

Van de Ven, A. H., & Delbecq, A. L. The effectiveness of nominal, Delphi, and interacting group decision making processes. *Academy of Management Journal*, 1974, 17, 605–621.

Vroom, V. H., & Yetton, P. W. *Leadership and decision-making*. Pittsburgh: University of Pittsburgh Press, 1973.

White, S. E., Dittrich, J. L., & Lang, J. R. The effects of group decision making processes and problem-situation complexity on implementation attempts. *Administrative Science Quarterly*, 1980, 25, 428–440.

REVIEW QUESTIONS

1 What are some of the positive consequences of the consensus-cooperative decision process?

2 Are there any reasons to support the use of a competitive social context for decision making?

3 Review the five dependent variables used in this study. From your perspective, rank them in order from most to least important.

CHAPTER 15

SOCIOTECHNICAL SYSTEMS

READING 53

Characteristics of an Organization

Douglas McGregor*

*   *   *

An industrial organization is an *open* system. It engages in transactions with a larger system: society. There are inputs in the form of people, materials and money and in the form of political and economic forces arising in the larger system. There are outputs in the form of products, services, and rewards to its members. Similarly, the subsystems within the organization down to the individual are open systems.

An industrial organization is an *organic* system. It is adaptive in the sense that it changes its nature as a result of changes in the external system around it. The adaptation, however, is not passive; the system affects the larger system as well as being affected by it. It copes with its environment as the individual human being copes with his. It is dynamic in the sense that it undergoes constant change as a result of interaction among the subsystems and with the larger environmental system.

Finally, an industrial organization is a *sociotechnical* system. It is not a mere assembly of buildings, manpower, money, machines, and processes.

The system consists in the *organization* of people around various technologies. This means, among other things, that human relations are not an optional feature of an organization—they are a built-in property. The system exists by virtue of the motivated behavior of people. Their relationships and behavior determine the inputs, the transformations, and the outputs of the system.

CONCLUSIONS

Thinking about an industrial organization as an open, organic, sociotechnical system has several advantages. One of the major ones is that it can represent reality more fully and more adequately than the conventional picture of the formal organization. It provides a better basis for understanding what does go on rather than what ought to go on. It brings the activities of the informal organization into the framework without excluding those of the formal organization. It enlarges and enriches the possibility of understanding the many complex cause-effect relationships constituting an organization. Thus it promises better prediction and better control.

*   *   *

*From *The Professional Manager* (New York: McGraw-Hill Book Company, 1967), pp. 40–41.

REVIEW QUESTION

1 What does it mean to you to describe an organization as an open, organic, sociotechnical system?

READING 54

Technology as a Tool for Organization Renewal

Pehr Gyllenhammar*

*   *   *

To give people the flexibility to reorganize themselves, Volvo's production technology had to be changed. The purpose was to make the working situation more satisfactory and productive, but the initial thrust at Kalmar, and later at our other plants, has simply been to make the technical systems work. Kalmar involved a great deal of innovation and thus a great deal of risk. The carriers gave us minor problems at first. Another minor but irksome problem concerned the conductive tapes in the floors. Tidy people involved in the layout invented a machine that made little grooves in the floor so the tape was hidden under a thin layer of hard plastic. This gave the impression that it couldn't be altered without tearing up the floor—a psychological barrier to the flexibility we wanted. Eventually we got the little bugs out of the carriers and eliminated the resistance to regrooving, but it took time and attention.

People often ask why we concentrated so much on the technical systems, and so little on the people for whose convenience they were designed, especially at first. The answer is fairly simple. If we failed with these technical systems, the chances of changing the work organization would drop drastically. If we succeed with the technical systems, we gain a visible, economic success, which is the prerequisite for acceptable overall performance. We could not "succeed" with the people themselves until we succeeded with the technology for people. As a result, we hope people will be motivated to reorganize their own work still further to suit themselves—and they will do a better and more dynamic job for us in the process.

Technology can strangle people. On the other hand, if it is designed for people, technology can also be a liberator. My hope was and is that the Kalmar solution would really be a tool for the employees, and that once its credibility was established, they would like to use it.

The best we can hope for, in Kalmar and our other plants, is to achieve a situation in which technology does not limit the freedom of the men and women who work there. Then we may experience a dynamic kind of organization development that comes not from management but from the work force itself. An organization that develops and changes at the instigation of its members rather than its managers has a better chance of renewing itself all the time, evolving to fit the true situation of its people.

*   *   *

REVIEW QUESTION

1 Why did Volvo focus on technology as a way to introduce organizational renewal?

READING 55

The Human Side of Robotics: How Workers React to a Robot

Linda Argote
Paul S. Goodman
David Schkade*

Robots are being used in increasing numbers in offices and factories throughout the world. However, little is known about how robots affect either individual workers or the structure, functioning, and effectiveness of organizations. This article focuses on workers' reactions to the introduction of a robot in a factory. We examine how workers react to the robot itself, as well as how the firm's strategy for introducing the robot affects these reactions. This knowledge should enable managers to make better decisions about the use of robots in their organizations.

In general, robots can be thought of as machines that can sense, think, and act in repeatable cycles. However, given the current state of robotic technology, the sensing and learning functions are not well developed. Thus, we will view robots as (electromechanical) devices with multiple task capability and programmability. The current functions of most robots in U.S. factories are to transfer material and to do certain processes, such as welding.

Currently, industrial robots are in limited use; it is estimated that from 3,500 to 5,000 robots were used in the U.S. in 1980.[1] There are, however, many reasons

*Reprinted from "The Human Side of Robotics: How Workers React to a Robot," by Linda Argote, Paul S. Goodman, and David Schkade, *Sloan Management Review*, Spring 1983, pp. 31–41, by permission of the publisher. Copyright © 1983 by the Sloan Management Review Association. All rights reserved.

that an increasing number of robots will be used in this country, including high labor costs, the current emphasis on productivity, and technological improvements in capabilities and costs of robots.[2]

As the use of robots increases, there is growing interest in the social impact of robotics. How will the use of robots affect employment levels?[3] Which jobs can be performed by robots?[4] What types of educational and training programs are needed for workers whose jobs are affected by robots?[5]

This study differs from other work on the social impact of robotics by examining how individual workers react to the introduction of a robot at their factory. Our focus is on understanding workers' psychological reactions (e.g., their attitudes and motivations) to the robot and to the manner in which the robot was introduced. The more positive workers' reactions to robots are, the more likely organizations will experience positive economic consequences, such as increased productivity through the use of robots.

While this study appears to be one of the first to examine the effects on individual workers of introducing a robot in a factory, there is literature on the impact of technological change on individuals and organizations. Several themes emerge from that literature which should help our understanding of the effects of robots in the workplace. One theme emphasizes the need to take into account the compatibility between an organization's technology, its structure, and its members.[6] Failure to consider these factors often results in unintended negative consequences, including increased absenteeism, higher accident rates, and decreased productivity.

Another theme from studies of technological change is that changes in technology often lead to changes in the job activities of individual workers. Whyte found that automation increased the extent to which jobs were mentally demanding.[7] Elizur and Mann and Hoffman reported that workers in automated organizations felt a greater sense of control and responsibility than their counterparts in less automated organizations.[8] Workers in automated organizations often experienced a greater sense of pressure than workers in less automated organizations.[9]

Technological change also affects social interaction patterns at work. Whyte found that increased automation decreased the opportunities workers had to interact with their coworkers.[10] Williams and Williams noted that new technologies often created new demands on support personnel and required more coordination activities between support and production personnel.[11]

Another theme from the organizational change literature is that worker involvement in the design of change affects worker acceptance of and commitment to the change.[12] In their classic study, Coch and French found that worker participation in the design of change was associated with higher productivity, lower turnover, and fewer acts of aggression against the company.[13] Similarly, Greiner and Crockett both stressed that a change attempt was more likely to be successful if everyone affected by the change was involved in its design and implementation.[14]

While this review is not exhaustive, it indicates that workers can resist technological change, that the opportunity to participate in a change may reduce resistance, and that technological change can affect social interaction patterns on the job. A decrease in the opportunity to interact with others is generally associated with increases in worker alienation, stress, and absenteeism. This review also suggests that new technologies can change work activities. If the change decreases variety, autonomy, and challenge in jobs, or if it introduces activities that are incompatible with the workers' abilities and preferences, workers' attitudes will probably become more negative and their motivational levels are likely to fall.

While robots may be viewed as another advance in automation, we believe that workers may view robots as qualitatively different from other forms of automation. Workers have been exposed to robots with glorified capabilities on television and in the movies. In addition, a robot often directly takes the place of a worker. We think these factors combine to make the introduction of a robot a very salient and possibly threatening event for workers.

RESEARCH SITE AND METHODOLOGY

To understand how workers react to the introduction of a robot, data were collected at a manufacturing plant that was installing its first robot. The plant, which had been in operation for approximately ten years, was involved in the forging and machining of various metal alloys. The work force, which numbered about 1,000, was nonunion, predominantly blue collar, and fairly stable. The average length of service for employees in the department where the robot was introduced was eight years. Relationships between labor and management appeared to be good; no walkouts or other examples of industrial strife had occurred at the plant in recent years.

The company had used a fairly comprehensive set of strategies to introduce the robot into the plant, including an open house to demonstrate the operation of the robot, talks by the plant manager, discussions with first-line supervisors, and notices posted in the cafeteria. The company had informed employees about a year in advance that a robot was going to be introduced at the plant.

The robot was introduced in a department that handled the milling and grinding of bar stock; this involved approximately ten different operations. The department had forty employees who worked in three shifts. Each person operated one or more of the milling and grinding machines, which were arranged in a horseshoe-like configuration.

The work flow in the department was primarily sequential. Workers moved products from one operation to another by hand. There was some flexibility in the order in which products went through the various operations. Although the majority of the products went through most of the operations, not every product went through every operation. There were some buffer inventories between operations.

The robot, which was placed at the beginning of the work flow in the department, loaded and unloaded two milling machines. One person operated the robot on each shift.

We interviewed production workers on each shift in the department before and after the robot was put on-line. These production workers were our primary sample. Interviews were conducted during two separate visits to the plant in 1981, about 2½ months before and 2½ months after the introduction of the robot. We interviewed the same individuals during both our first and second visits; however, some workers were not available during the second visit because of such factors as vacations and illness. During the first visit, thirty-seven employees were interviewed; during the second, twenty-five were interviewed. Our sample at time 2 appears to have been representative of our population at Time 1 with respect to such characteristics as tenure, job grades, and shifts.[15]

In addition to interviews with members of our primary sample, approximately thirty supplemental interviews were conducted with first- and second-line supervisors and managers; production workers in an adjacent department; individuals from engineering, maintenance, and personnel relations; and other plant staff. Each interview lasted about thirty minutes and contained both structured response and open-ended questions concerning the robot and the circumstances surrounding its introduction. We also observed the work force during the introduction of the robot and administered a satisfaction questionnaire to production workers.

RESULTS

We will first discuss the results of our study in terms of the effect the robot had on workers' beliefs, activities, and interactions. We will then examine how the organization was affected by the introduction of the robot.

Workers' Beliefs

Beliefs about the Robot   We were curious about how workers in our sample think about robots, so we asked the respondents an open-ended question: How would you describe a robot to a friend? Table 1 lists the phrases used to describe a robot. The major concepts seem to be: mechanical man, preprogrammed machine, something that loads machines, something that increases productivity, or something that reduces manual work. This list of descriptions falls into three categories: general descriptions (mechanical man), functions (loads machines), and consequences (reduces manual work). The general types of categories used by workers to describe robots show no significant changes between Time 1 and Time 2.[16] However, we found a significant increase in the number of concepts mentioned by each individual over time, which is consistent with the idea that more experience should lead to a more differentiated view of robots.[17]

As a follow-up to the first question, we asked workers how they learned about robots. The movie *Star Wars* and television shows depicting humanlike robots were frequently mentioned. These humanlike robots in the media probably contributed to the tendency of workers to anthropomorphize the robot: workers on each shift named the robot and endowed it with human qualities. This tendency was evident both in the interviews and in observations of people in the workplace.

Beliefs about the Effects of Robots   Table 2 presents workers' beliefs about robots in general at Time 2. Seven questions or statements were read to the

TABLE 1
WORKERS' DESCRIPTIONS OF ROBOTS

	Percent of total mentions	
	Time 1	Time 2
Mechanical man	15%	9%
Hydraulic arm	2	9
Computer	6	0
Preprogrammed machine	15	16
TV image	10	7
Moves material	4	9
Loads machine	12	14
Better productivity	15	5
Reduces manual work	15	23
Works continuously	6	8
	100%	100%

TABLE 2
WORKERS' BELIEFS ABOUT ROBOTS IN GENERAL AT TIME 2

	Percent of workers agreeing/strongly agreeing[a]
Robots will:	
Make U.S. more competitive	87%
Be capable of doing my job	29
Be capable of doing clerical jobs	8
Be capable of doing management jobs	17
Displace workers	50
Create less desirable jobs	21
Require more job retraining	87

[a]Questions were asked in this order.

workers, who responded by strongly agreeing, agreeing, slightly agreeing, slightly disagreeing, disagreeing, or strongly disagreeing. The results indicate that workers in our sample had positive attitudes toward robots. The workers felt that robots will help the United States remain competitive. There is some indication that workers believed that robots will displace other workers but not themselves, and will be limited to certain types of jobs. Workers perceived that the use of robots will require additional education and skill training for workers.

Table 3 focuses on workers' perceptions of the effects of the robot in their department, rather than on their general beliefs about robots. The respondents were presented with an outcome and asked at Time 1 whether the robot would increase, decrease, or have no effect on that outcome. Respondents were asked at Time 2 whether the robot had actually increased, decreased, or had no effect on the outcome. For example, let us consider one outcome: the chances for an accident.

355

TABLE 3
PERCEPTIONS OF THE EFFECT OF A ROBOT IN A PRODUCTION DEPARTMENT

	Percent of respondents who said robot had effect on:[a]									
	Productivity		Accidents		Costs		Quality		Number of people employed	
Effect	Time 1	Time 2	Time 1	Time 2	Time 1	Time 2	Time 1	Time 2	Time 1	Time 2
Increase	81%	67%	11%	29%	10%	33%	51%	17%	6	0
No effect	8	12	32	46	7	4	30	54	44	83
Decrease	3	12	41	21	55	42	3	21	44	17
Coefficient of time variable in probit model[b]	0.607		-0.687^d		-0.760^c		1.167^e		-0.533	

[a]The percent of respondents who said "Don't know" is not included in this table; hence, percentages for some outcomes will total less than 100%.
[b]A positive coefficient indicates that respondents were more likely at Time 2 than at Time 1 to move in the direction of saying the particular outcome decreased; a negative coefficient indicates that respondents were more likely at Time 2 than at Time 1 to move in the direction of saying the outcome increased.
[c]Statistically significant at 90% level.
[d]Statistically significant at 95% level.
[e]Statistically significant at 99% level.

Table 3 indicates that 11 percent of our respondents at Time 1 thought the robot would increase the chances of an accident; this had increased to 29 percent at Time 2. At Time 1, 41 percent thought the robot would decrease the chances of an accident; 21 percent of our Time 2 respondents thought the robot had decreased the chances of an accident.

The results of the probit analyses which tested whether there were significant changes in respondents' answers from Time 1 to Time 2 are also presented in Table 3.[18] For example, the results of the probit analysis on the chances of an accident outcome reveal that the coefficient of the time variable for accidents was -0.687. Thus, respondents were more likely at Time 2 than at Time 1 to say that the introduction of the robot increases the chances of an accident.

Table 3 indicates that a majority of the workers at Time 2 felt that robots increased productivity, but did not have much effect on the quality of output or the number of people who work in the department. The results of the probit analyses indicate that workers were significantly more likely at Time 2 than at Time 1 to say that the robot increased the chances of an accident, increased costs, and lowered the quality of the output. In short, Table 3 suggests that workers in the department where the robot was introduced became less optimistic over time about the effects of the robot.

We also asked respondents about the effect of the robot on jobs of individual workers. A majority of the workers at Time 2 believed that the robot had decreased the number of boring jobs and had reduced fatigue on the job. A majority of the workers also reported that robots required workers to learn greater skills, which is consistent with the information in Table 2.

We also asked these questions of production workers in a department adjacent to the one in which the robot was introduced in order to understand how perceptions of workers in other departments were affected by the introduction of the robot. Workers in this adjacent department had access to some of the same sources of information about the robot (e.g., the demonstration, the plant manager's talk, and the notices) as did workers in the department with the robot. Workers in the adjacent department were also able to watch the robot operate. The pattern of results obtained from workers in the adjacent department was similar to that described for our primary sample.[19] There was some evidence that workers in the adjacent department were more optimistic about the effects of the robot at Time 2 than were their counterparts in the department with the robot. For example, workers in both departments were more likely at Time 2 than at Time 1 to say that the chances for an accident increased and that costs increased; however, workers in the adjacent unit thought that the chances for an accident and costs increased to a smaller extent than did workers in the department with the robot.

Beliefs about Introducing Change In order to understand how workers learned about the robot, we asked the employees at Time 1 whether they learned about the robot from a particular source and about the extent to which the source increased their understanding of the robot. As Table 4 indicates, the most frequently mentioned source of information about robots was the weekly workplace meeting between supervisors and workers. However, these meetings increased workers' understanding of robots only to a small extent. Written communication and the demonstration at the open house were the most effective sources of information about the robot. However, less than half of our respondents attended the open house, and only 16 percent reported that they received a written communication. Thus, the various communication sources do not seem to have been very helpful in increasing workers' understanding of the robot.

In addition, we asked workers how much influence or involvement they *actually had* on decisions about: (1) whether the robot would be introduced in their department, (2) where it would be placed, and (3) who would run it. We also asked them how much influence they *should* have had. The workers reported that they had no influence on any of these decisions. They said they should have had a little influence on decisions about whether the robot would be introduced and who should run it. However, workers did not think they should be involved in decisions about where the robot was placed.

Activities

Our analysis thus far has focused on workers' beliefs; we will now address the question of how the robot introduction affected workers' activities. For this analysis our sample is composed of the individual on each shift who operated the robot. Special interview schedules were developed to measure the activities, work cycle, and interaction patterns of the operators' jobs before and after the robot was introduced.

TABLE 4
EFFECTIVENESS OF COMMUNICATION ABOUT THE ROBOT AT TIME 1

Communication source	Percent of workers who reported they received communication	Average extent communication increased workers' understanding[a]
Written communication	16%	2.6
Workplace meetings	89	4
Communication from supervisor	46	4.1
Movies or audiovisual presentations	13	3
Demonstrations	42	2.7
Informal sources, including the grapevine	37	4

[a]Questions were asked in this order. The response alternatives were: (1) to a very great extent, (2) to a great extent, (3) to a fair extent, (4) to a little extent, (5) not at all.

When the robot was introduced, a manufacturing cell (i.e., a set of interdependent machines operated by a worker) was created. The robot provided material handling functions for two milling machines. An operator was then responsible for the two milling machines and the robot. The introduction of the robot removed the materials from the operator's job and added a new activity—robot operator.

Before the robot's introduction, approximately twelve different products were passed through both milling machines to begin the work flow sequence for this production department. The work cycle for each machine included set-up activities and then relatively short milling times (one to two minutes) during a product run. Work was done to fine tolerances, and it was possible for the operator to determine, through some measurement procedures, whether the parts were milled correctly. The major quality control activity, however, was at the end of all the machine operations.

After the change, the number of products remained the same. The two milling machines were still located at the beginning of the work cycle where the bar stock went through the first two milling operations. The other machine operations were unchanged, and quality control activities were still at the end of all the machine operations.

The major change in activities in the new manufacturing cell came in the material handling activities. In the old system, the operator would pick up the stock, place it on machine one, clamp it in, start the machine, and then the milling machine would perform its work. The operator would then stop the machine, unclamp the stock, place it on the second machine, and the cycle would repeat. Each new stock would follow this cycle. When we asked the operators about the differences between their jobs before and after the robot introduction, they said:

- Now it's mainly watching . . . walking around the machines to be sure everything is running.
- We do more activities. Now you have to set up all three machines.
- There are also more functions . . . you need to program the robot.

The operators also reported that they were doing more activities and that the total work cycle had increased. They attributed the increased work cycle to more setups and delays in getting the new robot operational.

The change in activities was related to a change in skill requirements. The operators said:

- The job now requires more skills. . . . You have to learn how to program the robot and run it. . . . With more skills, of course, comes more responsibility.
- Operating the robot requires more skills . . . the job is more sophisticated.

If we combine the ideas in these quotations with those in the preceding ones, it is clear that the new skills are in observing and detecting problems in the interface between the three machines and in programming and operating the robot.

What are some of the consequences for the worker of these changes in activities? The literature on the relationship between job activities and individual characteristics indicates that improving the fit between the new job activities and the personal characteristics of the worker can lead to more positive attitudes and higher motivation. Conversely, introducing activities that are incompatible with a worker's abilities and preferences is likely to generate stress, negative attitudes, and lower motivation. Because we are examining the introduction of a single robot and are dealing with only three operators, it is difficult to identify statistically significant changes in our study. However, some trends are evident. The operators in our study experienced more stress or pressure. Two of the operators said:

> • There is more stress now. . . . We have more responsibility. . . . They want the robot to run and we have to keep it going. . . . That's hard because it is still relatively new.
> • It's nerve racking . . . there are lots of details . . . it's an expensive piece of equipment.

This stress stems partly from the new tasks and responsibilities of the operators and partly from operating a new costly piece of equipment. There was also a more subtle source of stress when workers compared themselves to the robot. There was much speculation during our first visit to the plant about whether an operator who was particularly quick would be able to beat the robot. By our second visit, workers seemed resigned to the fact that the robot would always be able to outproduce a human worker. The reason was simple: robots do not take breaks or go to lunch! Although objectively the operators controlled the robot and the two milling machines, they subjectively felt that there was competition between them and the machine. Operators reported that the robot could load and unload the two milling machines faster than they could when they operated the machines manually.

One of the operators in our sample said that although he found observing and monitoring more boring than manual activities, he was currently satisfied with his job because it still included many manual set-up activities. He commented, however, that without these set-up activities, the current job would be more boring than his previous job. We suspect that this incompatibility between activities required by the job and preferences of the worker was another source of potential stress.

We do not want to create a picture of unhappy operators. All these individuals voluntarily accepted the job of operating the manufacturing cell, and all received considerable recognition because of the "newness" of the robot. All operators acknowledged that the use of the robot eliminated the prior heavy and fatiguing work, and they reported approximately the same degree of satisfaction with most aspects of their job before and after the robot was introduced.

At the same time, however, workers experienced more stress than they had in their prior job. It would be premature at this point to speculate about whether this increased stress was good or bad for the individual or for the organization. Studies have shown that increased stress is associated with increased turnover and absenteeism, and that stress can lead to either increments or decrements in performance.[20]

Since the introduction of the robot could affect support personnel as well as operators, we interviewed people in engineering, maintenance, quality control, and scheduling. Engineering and maintenance were responsible for getting the machine up and running. Changes in the functioning of the machine could affect quality control and scheduling. Several themes emerged from our discussions with support personnel. First, some felt that the use of the robot had changed their job activities. Since the robot represented a new generation of technology, new knowledge and new job activities were necessary. Second, there were some feelings of frustration since not all support personnel were involved in planning for the robot and yet their job activities were affected by the robot. Third, there were positive feelings created by the recognition the workers received and by their personal pride in the successful operation of the robot.

Interactions

The formal and informal interactions that develop around job activities are important in the workplace. The introduction of a robot can change these interaction patterns, which in turn may have psychological and behavioral consequences. For example, if the new technology breaks up existing social interactions and isolates the worker, we would expect increases in feelings of alienation and more resistance to the new technology.

The operators reported at Time 2 that they had less opportunity to talk with people on the job than they had before the robot was introduced. Two of the operators said:

> • I haven't been able to talk as much. . . . I'm too involved with the robot. . . . You really have to concentrate.
> • I don't have time to talk with anyone . . . I don't want them breaking my concentration. . . . I'm isolated now.

The decreased opportunity to interact with others seemed to come mainly from the increased mental demands of the job. Because workers had to concentrate more, they did not have time to talk with their coworkers.

The introduction of the robot did not change the work flow in the department. All the workers, including the robot operator, were located in the same area and participated in the same part of the work flow. Thus, while our operators reported less opportunity to interact with others in the department, the set of people they interacted with in the department remained roughly the same. This might have provided built-in support mechanisms to buffer the workers from some of the effects of the change.

The major changes in interactions occurred between support personnel from the engineering and maintenance departments and the operators of the manufacturing cell. There was more frequent contact between engineering and maintenance personnel and the operators. Perhaps because the robot was new and represented the first major installation in the plant, support personnel as well as the operators were highly motivated to get the robot up and running, and they cooperated with each other. If many robots were being placed on-line and the support personnel had great demands on their time, then we might find more conflict between support personnel and the operators.

Organizational Unit

Our discussion thus far has focused exclusively on the effects of the robot on the individual. The introduction of this new technology also affected the department, requiring a reevaluation and reclassification of the operator's job. Some of the operator's job activities were eliminated and others were added. Given the net change, should the job retain the same grade or be upgraded? Although management upgraded the job, the workers felt that the new grade and associated pay for the operator's job were still too low.

We also examined whether the introduction of the robot affected other department policies, procedures, or formal coordination mechanisms. There was no evidence of any effect other than the changes in the pay system.

CONCLUSION

The purpose of this article is to focus attention on the consequences for the worker of introducing robots into the factory. Workers in our sample held positive beliefs about robots in general. When we asked them about the effect of the robot on their department, they initially reported that the robot would increase productivity, reduce costs, increase quality, make the job easier and less boring, and increase skill requirements. As workers acquired more experience with the robot, their beliefs about robots became more complex and somewhat more pessimistic (greater chances for accidents, cost increases, quality decreases).

We think this study has several major strengths. To our knowledge, it is the first systematic evaluation of the effect on workers of introducing a robot. The study used a variety of methods, including interviews, questionnaires, and observations. We collected data before and after the change to get some base line to study the effects of the robot introduction over time. In addition, we used a broad sample perspective to identify both individuals directly affected by the change and individuals indirectly affected (e.g., support personnel).

The study, of course, has certain limitations. Data were collected from only one organization. There was only one robot installation, and it was the first robot installation. The change also took place in a nonunion organization, and there were positive relations between labor and management. While interview data on the effects of the robot on such various outcomes as productivity were collected, company records data on these outcomes were not collected. Future research is needed involving multiple organizations and including records or archival data and interview data collected over several points in time (e.g., before, shortly after, and a year or so after the robot introduction).

What can we learn from this study that will help in new installations of robotics in factories? Despite the small sample size and the difficulty of systematically testing certain relationships, a number of findings have emerged from this study. These findings *combined with* findings from other studies of increased automation suggest some recommendations for managers introducing new technologies.

1 Before introducing the robot, important questions need to be resolved. For example, workers are likely to be most concerned about job security and pay.

Failure to resolve such questions before introducing the robot is likely to reduce the effectiveness of the introduction.

2 It is critical to analyze the organization before introducing change. What effects will the technological change have on the activities, interactions, and beliefs of workers? Managers must anticipate potential problems that the change may bring—both obvious problems (such as job loss) and subtle ones (e.g., new job activities).

3 Management must develop a strategy for worker involvement in introducing the new technology. There is a wide variety of possible strategies. In our study management provided virtually no opportunities for worker involvement in the robot introduction. The workers wanted some level of involvement in certain decisions but not in others. Some involvement is likely to increase understanding about the robot and may perhaps lead to greater commitment to the change process.

4 Certain communication techniques seem more effective than others in introducing robots. Demonstrations that illustrate the operations of a robot seem to be a powerful technique.

5 Some feedback mechanism to monitor communication effectiveness in introducing this technology is necessary. Our study showed a discrepancy between what management was trying to communicate to workers and what the workers actually received.

6 It is vital that first-line supervisors be given information about the robot and support from upper management in dealing with workers' reactions to the robot. In times of change workers are likely to go to their supervisors more frequently for information and advice. The attitudes and behaviors of supervisors are likely to have a big effect on the success of the robot introduction.

7 The robot will create new job activities. It is very important to do a careful analysis of the new job and to maximize the fit between job characteristics and the personal characteristics of the worker. The literature indicates that if there is a poor fit between a job and a particular worker, this may have a dysfunctional effect on both the individual and the organization. The question is not just whether the worker can do the new activities, but whether the worker *can do* and *prefers* these activites. If there is a poor fit between the job and the worker, management must consider alternatives in job redesign or in the selection procedures.

8 If the change in activities is from "doing" to "observing," workers may experience more boredom on the job. If this occurs, some mechanism to alleviate boredom, such as job rotation, may be helpful. Job rotation would increase task variety and build up a backlog of skills for future expansion of robotics.

9 It is important to train backup operators of the robot. In our study only one person per shift was initially trained to operate the robot. This led to disruptions in the work process when one of the operators was absent. Training backup operators would provide the organization with more flexibility and individual workers with more job variety.

10 The introduction of robots can affect the nature of social interaction patterns at work. Prior research shows that attempts to change these patterns can generate resistance to change. If analysis indicates that the change will break up existing social relationships, alternative strategies should be developed. For example, involving the worker in this part of the change may generate new work arrangements that will facilitate acceptance of the change.

11 A successful introduction of robots requires the cooperation of support personnel. Our study showed that not all support personnel were involved in planning for the introduction of the robot, and this created some stress. Involvement of support personnel and operators early in the change process should facilitate the introduction process.

REFERENCES

1 See: "Robots Join the Labor Force," *Business Week*, 9 June 1980; A. Salpukas, "Manufacturing Using Robots," *New York Times*, 23 October 1980.

2 See J. Engelberger, *Robotics in Practice* (New York: AMACOM, 1980).

3 See R. U. Ayres, "The Future of Robotics: A Meta Review" (prepared for The UNESCO/11 ASA Symposium on Scientific Forecasting and Human Needs: Methods, Trends, and Messages, Tbilisi, USSR, December 1981).

4 See R. U. Ayres and S. M. Miller, "Preparing for the Growth of Industrial Robots" (unpublished paper, Carnegie-Mellon University, 1981).

5 See "Technology Assessment: The Impact of Robotics" (Technical Report EC/2405801-FR-1, Eikonix Corporation, 1979).

6 See F. E. Emery and E. L. Trist, "Socio-technical Systems, in *Organizational Systems: General Systems Approaches to Complex Organizations*, F. Baker, ed. (Homewood, IL: Richard D. Irwin, 1973).

7 See W. F. Whyte, *Men at Work* (Homewood, IL: Richard D. Irwin, 1961).

8 See: D. Elizur, *Adapting to Innovation* (Jerusalem: Jerusalem Academic Press, 1970); F. C. Mann and L. R. Hoffman, *Automation and the Worker* (New York: Holt, 1960).

9 See E. Mumford and D. Banks, *The Computer and the Clerk* (London: Routledge and Kegan Paul, 1967).

10 See Whyte (1961).

11 See L. K. Williams and C. B. Williams, "The Impact of Numerically Controlled Equipment on Factory Organization," *California Management Review*, Winter 1964, pp. 25–34.

12 See M. Beer, *Organization Change and Development* (Santa Monica, CA: Goodyear, 1980).

13 See L. Coch and J. R. P. French, "Overcoming Resistance to Change," *Human Relations*, August 1948, pp. 512–532.

14 See: L. E. Greiner, "Patterns of Organization Change," *Harvard Business Review*, May–June 1967, pp. 119–128; W. Crockett, "Introducing Change to a Government Agency," in *Failures in Organization Development and Change*, P. H. Mirvis and D. N. Berg, eds. (New York: John Wiley & Sons, 1977).

15 Our Time 2 sample was drawn without replacement from the population of employees we interviewed at Time 1. Therefore, we used the hypergeometric distribution to construct a likelihood ratio test to investigate whether our Time 2 sample was representative of our Time 1 population on characteristics such as tenure, job grades, and shifts. The χ^2 values computed from the likelihood ratio statistic were not large enough to reject at more than moderate levels of significance ($p < .25$) the hypothesis that our Time 2 sample was a random sample drawn without replacement from the population of employees we interviewed at Time 1. Results of these analyses are available on request from the authors.

16 To test whether the frequency of mentions in various categories changed from Time 1 to Time 2, we pooled the frequency of mentions in each category at Time 1 and Time 2 to arrive at the frequency of mentions in the population. Using the hypergeometric distribution, we then tested whether the distribution of mentions at Times 1 and 2 were random samples drawn without replacement from our population. There was no evidence for rejecting the hypothesis that our Time 1 distribution was a random sample from the population, $\chi^2(2) = 1.04$, $p < .75$, or for rejecting the hypothesis that our Time 2 distribution was a random sample from the population, $\chi^2(2) = 0.82$, $p < .75$.

17 The significance level is $t(24) = 1.89$, $p < .10$.

18 The N-Chotomous probit model requires independence of the error terms. This requirement might be violated if, for example, observations for the same individual at different points in time were correlated. In using the probit model, we have assumed that this dependence, if it exists, is weak.

19 The probit analyses on the outcomes discussed above were run separately for each department with time (Time 1 vs. Time 2) as the predictor of the outcomes. The probit analyses were also performed on the data from both departments combined, with both time and deparment (department with the robot, adjacent department) as predictors of the outcomes. A similar pattern of results was obtained from the different analyses.

20 See: L. W. Porter and R. M. Steers, "Organizational, Work, and Personal Factors in Employee Turnover and Absenteeism," *Psychological Bulletin*, 1973, pp. 151–176; W. E. Scott, "Activation Theory and Task Design," *Organizational Behavior and Human Performance*, 1977, pp. 111–128.

REVIEW QUESTIONS

1 Examine Table 2 again. What general conclusions can you reach regarding workers' beliefs about robots?

2 What are your feelings about having a coworker replaced with a robot? What reactions would you likely have?

3 Assuming that social needs are important to many workers, how can these needs still be met when robots are introduced to the workplace?

READING 56

Humanizing the Robot

Fred K. Foulkes
Jeffrey L. Hirsch*

* * *

Regularly, in plants throughout the world, employees name robots and sometimes even give them nameplates. Robots have been named after retired employees and foremen; in Japan, they are often given the names of rock-and-roll and
baseball stars. In one U.S. auto plant, because both were deemed unreliable,
employees named their robot after the supplier's salesman.

The process of naming a robot "humanizes" it, and this has concerned some
managers. On one hand, they see the humanizing effect as good because employees tend to feel more comfortable working with a robot with a name. On the other
hand, some company officials are concerned that the naming process could make
the robots too human, and this could eventually create employee relations problems. At least one major U.S. corporation has a corporate policy that robots are
not to be named. Ultimately, we think the answer to the naming issue is best left to
employees. If employees feel comfortable naming robots, management should
allow it.

* * *

REVIEW QUESTION

1 What are the "employee relations problems" that could result from the naming of robots
by employees?

CHAPTER 16

ORGANIZATIONAL COMMUNICATION

READING 57

Improving Face-to-Face Relationships

Edgar H. Schein*

The challenges of management in the 1980s are enormous, but they are fairly easy to identify. The great difficulties that we face lie not in deciding *what* our goals should be, but in determining *how* to achieve them. Our problems in this area are problems of *implementation: how* can we reach goals that are often perfectly clear but seemingly impossible to attain.

Several explanations of these problems readily come to mind:

- Large systems have become too complex to be understood.
- "Bureaucracy" makes it impossible to get anything done.
- Intergroup hostility paralyzes all constructive effort.
- Power politics undermine and subvert rational action.
- Irrationality and human resistance to change defeat even the wisest programs.

All of these explanations are true, but they are also incomplete. Sometimes they are used only as excuses for failure rather than as constructive analyses of our management problems. On the other hand, we *have* learned something about implementation in the last forty years or so, and what we have learned takes us back to one fundamental principle: societies, organizations, and families are *human* groups, and the face-to-face relationships among the members of these groups are a basic element of any social action. Whatever else we need in the way of systems, procedures, and mechanisms, the process of social action always starts with face-to-face relationships among people.

Face-to-face relationships can be thought of as the glue that holds organizations together, and such relationships are the links in the implementation chain. Therefore, we should take a fresh look at these relationships to see if we can articulate some of the skills which can make them more constructive, and thus enable us to move toward solving some of the pressing problems of the 1980s.

THE ELEMENTS OF FACE-TO-FACE RELATIONSHIPS

What does it take to build, maintain, improve, and, if need be, repair face-to-face relationships? I would like to discuss nine different elements, which are all closely interrelated yet distinct in important ways. These elements reflect motives and values, perceptual skills, and behavioral skills:

1 Self-insight and a sense of one's own identity;

2 Cross-cultural sensitivity—the ability to decipher other people's values;

3 Cultural/moral humility—the ability to see one's own values as not necessarily better or worse than another's values;

4 A proactive problem-solving orientation—and the conviction that interpersonal and cross-cultural problems can be solved;

5 Personal flexibility—the ability to adopt different responses and approaches as needed by situational contingencies;

6 Negotiation skills—the ability to explore differences creatively, to locate some common ground, and to solve the problem;

7 Interpersonal and cross-cultural tact—the ability to solve problems with people without insulting them, demeaning them, or destroying their "face";

8 Repair strategies and skills—the ability to resurrect, to revitalize, and to rebuild damaged or broken face-to-face relationships;

9 Patience.

I would like to discuss each of these elements in turn, putting most of the attention on those which have been insufficiently attended to in prior analyses and on those which are especially relevant to repair strategies.

SELF-INSIGHT

One can hardly work out common goals with others if one does not know where one's own values and goals lie. Leaders and managers especially must know where they are going, and they must be able to articulate their own goals. Parents and spouses must make a valiant effort to lift to the surface what is often left implicit—their own life goals and targets—so that there can be genuine negotiation among family members in the different life stages.

Self-insight is a *competence*—the ability to see oneself accurately and to evaluate oneself fairly. Through feedback from others and through systematic self-study, we can improve our ability to see ourselves. As we increase in self-insight, we lay the foundations for self-acceptance, which is to some extent, a prerequisite for some of the other skills to be discussed.

CROSS-CULTURAL SENSITIVITY

It goes without saying that we cannot offer leadership if we do not have perspective on ourselves and on others, and we cannot gain such perspective if we continue to be ethnocentric—to notice and appreciate only our own culture and values. Cross-cultural issues are not limited to the dramatic differences which can be identified in how different countries operate. Many of the most harmful cases of cultural misunderstanding occur right under our noses—with our spouses, friends, children, and subordinates—because norms, values, and behavioral codes vary widely within any country. American managers often tell tales of woe of trying to transfer people from the deep South to Manhattan, or from an urban center to a rural plant site.

A costly misunderstanding occurred in the small town where we used to spend our summers. The local wood-turning mill employed both men and women from the community, and the pay scales had developed historically around the status system in the town. A new manager who had experience in a progressive urban mill noticed that some of the skilled women operators were grossly underpaid in relation to their male counterparts. He set about to rationalize the pay structure to reflect actual skill levels. This action led to wives bringing home bigger paychecks, which neither they nor their husbands could accept in terms of the status system in the town. The dissatisfaction and turmoil that resulted from upsetting the social order was completely unanticipated by this manager.

Deciphering values, motives, aspirations, and basic assumptions across *occupational* and *social class lines* is particularly difficult. It is hard for the son of a successful middle-class businessman to understand the values and career aspirations of the son of an immigrant or an unskilled worker. It is hard for the general manager to understand the values and career aspirations of the technically oriented person and vice versa. It is hard for people in the different functional areas of a business to decipher each other's values and aspirations.[1]

Cultural Differences between Countries

When we go to countries where a different language is being spoken and where the culture is obviously different, we do wake up to the need to sharpen our deciphering skills. But even then we have a strong tendency to look for similarities and to rationalize that "people are people" and "business is business" no matter where it is conducted. My own tendency to ignore differences was brought home to me during a visit to Australia, which is superficially and historically similar to the U.S. It took me quite a while to discover that while Australians (like Americans) are achievement oriented, they also have the "tall poppy syndrome": one must not stand out above the crowd; one must accomplish things without seeming to work too hard at them; and one must not take too much personal credit for one's accomplishments. The son of a friend of mine told us how, after waiting all day for the perfect wave, he had finally succeeded in having a brilliant ride on his surfboard. When he hit the beach, he told his watching friends—as he knew he had to—"Boy that was a *lucky* one."

I kept hearing how complacent and security oriented the Australians were even when I was dealing with what seemed to be some pretty tough, aggressive managers. What one's true motives are and what is culturally acceptable as a legitimate explanation of one's motives are, of course, not necessarily the same. In comparing America and Australia, one sees a paradoxical reversal. In Australia, people claim to be mostly security oriented, though companies admitted they had many aggressive, ambitious, power-seeking managers working for them. In the U.S., the popular image is that most people are ambitious and want to climb right to the top of the organization—though I encounter a growing number of allegedly ambitious managers who admit in private that they are not motivated to continue the "rat race," that they would like early retirement, or that they are considering another career altogether. Both public images reflect cultural norms, yet both are to some degree a misrepresentation of the actual state of affairs. The public selves we wear—the way we are supposed to present ourselves to others—is a strongly ingrained set of cultural values in its own right, and tact prevents us from puncturing the illusions which cultures teach us to project.

"Face Work"

Erving Goffman has written articulately about what he calls "face work"—the behavior of people in a social situation which is designed to help everyone maintain the self which they choose to project in that particular situation.[2] Selves are forever constructed, and the audience for any given performance is culturally bound to uphold as much as possible the identities which the actors claim. At the minimum, we nod and say "uh huh" when someone is talking to us, or we try to laugh politely at a joke that is not really funny, or we ignore embarrassing incidents. If our boss tells us through his actions or demeanor that he believes himself to be very competent in handling a given meeting, we rarely challenge this claim even though we may privately believe that he will totally mismanage it. The skill in this situation is our ability to compensate for his incompetence or to repair what damage may have been done. But we do not destroy his face.

The Reciprocity of Relationships

One of the most interesting features of the cultural norms of face-to face interactions is their symmetric, reciprocal, exchange nature. We sometimes get into difficulty because we do not know how to complete an interaction. When someone in a strange country offers you an object in his house because you have admired it, are you supposed to take it and reciprocate at some future time when the visitor is in your home, or is it appropriate to refuse? The whole question of when and how to say yes and no is fraught with difficulty if we are talking across cultures or subcultures. And, as many businessmen have found out, how to interpret a yes or a no is even more difficult.

   The ability to detect the subtleties of how others perceive situations and of what the values of others are requires both formal training and practical experience. Learning a new language would seem to be a prerequisite since so much of every culture is encoded into the language. Many people pride themselves on their extensive travel, even making lists of how many countries they have been in, without ever encountering or deciphering any of the cultures of those countries; they do not learn the languages and therefore miss the important nuances of what is going on. On the other hand, I have heard repeatedly from multinational companies that one of the best prescriptions for success in an overseas assignment is to take time to learn the local language.

CULTURAL/MORAL HUMILITY

Beyond self-insight and the ability to understand others, we need something which we might call cultural/moral *humility*. Can we not only sense the values of other people but, more importantly, positively appreciate them? Can we see our own culture and values only as *different,* not necessarily as *better?* Our tendency to think of things as "funny" or "odd" is a good diagnostic here. I have often been shown or told about funny things people do in other countries. An American visitor to the mainland of China found it very amusing that some Chinese farmers were so proud of owning tractors which were, in fact, useless; the tractors could not turn on the tight terraces and they did not have attachable plows to pull. The fact that a Chinese farmer did not even know the function of the pin to which the plow attaches struck this American as very funny and weird. It never occurred to him that his own utilitarian, pragmatic values might not be the only relevant ones in this situation.

A few years ago, a group of American students teased one of their German peers about his heel-clicking, head-nodding, hand-shaking formality. After some months of being teased, he stopped them one day with the statement, "When I go to work in the morning, I go to my boss's office, click my heels, bow my head, shake his hand, and then tell him the truth." The teasing stopped.

Many American managers lack cultural humility. We are more pragmatic than other people, and if we encounter people less pragmatic, we view *them* as odd rather than wonder about the oddity of our being so pragmatic. We don't consider our own culture as funny, odd, and in need of explanation, yet *it is our culture which is probably in a statistical sense the most different from all other cultures.* Let me give a couple of examples:

1 Our mercantile attitude—embodied in our marketing skills and our efforts to sell anything to anybody—strikes people in other parts of the world as being rather crass and superficial. I have encountered managers in other countries who have real reservations about making products which they consider have no intrinsic value, and who have even greater reservations about using advertising skills to create markets for such products.

2 Our attitude towards efficiency—attempting to reduce all costs for the sake of higher profit margins, even if those costs are people's jobs—is clearly out of line with the value systems in some other countries. Yet we take the importance of efficiency for granted. We do not think of people as capital investments and we find it hard to comprehend systems of guaranteed lifetime employment.

My point is not to dissect the value system of the U.S. but rather to identify a strong tendency I have seen in managers all over the world (Americans and non-Americans alike) to be ethnocentric—to assume that one's own values are the best, and that one is excused from having to know what others think and value, or at least from having to take very seriously what others think and value. Such an absence of cultural humility can be a dangerous weakness when we are attempting face-to-face negotiations or problem solving. This point is important whenever we deal with people whose values are different from our own, whether these people are within our society or are from other countries.

PROACTIVE PROBLEM-SOLVING ORIENTATION

Solving face-to-face problems, especially where difficult cross-cultural under-standing and humility are required, presupposes a faith that problems *can* be solved if one works at them and an assumption that active problem solving will produce positive results. Communication and understanding are difficult to achieve, but if one does not even try, then there is no possibility for achievement.

A proactive orientation is itself to some degree a cultural characteristic. When Americans take the "can do" attitude, how do we determine when we are coming on too strongly, or when we are actually intruding in private lifespace in our eagerness to establish constructive face-to-face relationships in order to solve problems. The anthropologist Edward Hall has given us many excellent examples of how conducting business in different cultural contexts must be delicately handled, lest we invade people's territory and unwittingly destroy the possibility of better relationships.[3]

What I mean by a "proactive orientation" is a *motivation* to work on problems, not necessarily a high level of overt *activity*. We must base our actual course of action on genuine cultural understanding and not simply on a desire to act. As in the case of international diplomacy, we should always be ready to negotiate. No matter how bad the situation is between management and employees in a company or industry, each party should always be ready to sit down and try again to talk face-to-face.

PERSONAL FLEXIBILITY

It does us little good to sense situations accurately if we cannot take advantage of what we perceive. I know people who can tell you exactly what is going on but who cannot alter their own behavior to adjust to what they know to be the realities. One of the reasons why experiential learning methods—such as sensitivity train-ing or transactional analysis workshops—have been so successful is that they allow experimentation on the part of the participants to enlarge their repertory of face-to-face behavior. Role playing is perhaps the prototype of such behavioral train-ing and is clearly a necessary component of face-to-face skill development.[4]

NEGOTIATION SKILLS

Much has been written about the process of negotiation and the skills needed to be an effective negotiator. To a considerable degree, what has been said reflects the same themes that I am focusing on here. Negotiation requires great sensitivity, humility, self-insight, motivation to solve the problem, and behavioral flexibility. Part of the sensitivity required is the ability to decipher others' values. Another part is the ability to elicit information from others and to judge the validity of that information. Face-to-face relationships are not always benign, not always comfortable, not always safe, and not always open, yet they are always crucial to problem solving. Especially in situations where there initially is conflict, we need the ability to maintain relationships so that negotiations can continue, to decipher messages when deliberate concealment is attempted, to convince and to persuade, to bluff when necessary, and to figure out what the other will do in response to our own moves.

As we know, negotiations can become so dangerous and threatening to one's face that we have to resort to neutral third parties as catalysts, go-betweens, message carriers, and the like. Often what is most needed is to explain the values and goals of each principal to the other. Principals often lack the skills to reveal themselves to each other without making themselves seem either too vulnerable or too threatening.[5]

One of my Australian manager friends speculated that a lack of verbal articulation skills seriously hampers negotiation in his country. He noticed that in many labor-management confrontations in Australia each side would blurt out bluntly, and with some pride at their own ability to be so open, exactly what their *final* demands were. When these demands proved to be incompatible, an impasse occurred. The situation then deteriorated to name calling and to seeing the other side as being stubborn and exploitative. This manager speculated that the educational system was partly responsible for this situation in that written English is heavily emphasized in school while spoken English is hardly attended to at all. He thought of Australians as being quite inarticulate, on the average, and therefore at a real disadvantage in face-to-face negotiations.

The important point is to recognize that openness is not an absolute value in face-to-face relationships. For some purposes, it is better not to reveal exactly where one stands. One of the ways that relationships become more intimate is through successive minimal self-revelations which constitute interpersonal tests of acceptance: if you accept this much of me, then perhaps I can run the risk of revealing a bit more of myself. Total openness may be safe and charming when total acceptance is guaranteed, but it can become highly dangerous when goals are not compatible, and acceptance is therefore not guaranteed at all.[6]

INTERPERSONAL AND CROSS-CULTURAL TACT

Negotiation requires great tact. The tactfulness I refer to here is the *behavioral* manifestation of the cultural humility discussed above. If we don't feel humble in the face of others' values, we will certainly offend them. On the other hand, if we feel that there is genuinely room for different values in this world, then we have the basis for showing in our speech and behavior an adequate level of respect for others.

REPAIR STRATEGIES AND SKILLS

The repair strategies and repair skills needed to fix broken or spoiled relationships, careers, lives, negotiations, and other interpersonal or intergroup situations are probably the most important yet least understood of face-to-face skills.

As the world becomes more complex and more intercultural, there will be more communication breakdowns, diplomatic disasters, losses of confidence and trust, hurt feelings between individuals and groups, hostilities, wars, and other forms of social pathology and disorder. It will not help us to resign ourselves to such situations, to lament our cruel fate, or to merely explain why something happened: what *will* be helpful is our attempting to repair these situations.

The concept of "repair strategies" was brought to my attention by Jacqueline Goodnow, a cognitive social psychologist who now teaches in Australia. She has been struck by the Australian tendency to "knock" things rather than solve problems. I often heard the phrase in Australia that "we are a nation of knockers," which means that when things go wrong there is a tendency to blame government, unions, management, multinationals, OPEC, or any other handy group rather than to figure out how to repair the situation.

The Perception of New Elements

Repair strategies presume and require not only constructive motivation but also *the ability to see new elements in the situation which one may not have noticed before.* The new elements may be in *oneself;* one may discover that one has been unfair or selfish, or lacking insight concerning the consequences of one's own behavior or concerning one's true motives. In this instance repair may begin with apology.

One may also discover new things in the *other people* in the situation; *they may have changed in significant ways.* One of the most damaging things we do in our face-to-face relationships is to freeze our assumptions about ourselves and others. Our stereotype of the other person can become a straight jacket or a self-fulfilling prophecy. McGregor gave us the best example of this years ago in noting that if we assume people are lazy we will begin to treat them as if they *are* lazy, which will eventually train them to *be* lazy.[7] The energy and creativity which they might have applied to their jobs then gets channeled either into other situations or into angry attempts to defeat the organization.

We want and need predictability in our relationships, but that very need often prevents us from repairing damaged relationships. It may be psychologically easier to see the worker as lazy and hostile because we can then predict his or her behavior and can know exactly how to respond. To renegotiate the relationship, to permit some participation, or to admit that we may have been wrong in our assessment is to make ourselves psychologically vulnerable. We then enter a period in the relationship that may be less predictable.

As in the case of negotiation, we may need the help of third parties—counselors, therapists, consultants, or other helpers—to get through the period of vulnerability and instability. Often the motivation to repair is there but the skill is not—in the sense that neither party has self-insight, the capacity to hear the values or goals of the other, the articulateness to negotiate without further destruction of face, or the emotional strength or self-confidence to make concessions to reach at least a common ground of understanding.

Taking the Other's Perspective

Sociologists taught us long ago that in childhood the very process of becoming social is a process of learning to take the role of the other. We could not really understand each other at all—even though we live in the same culture and speak the same language—without the ability to put ourselves in the other person's shoes. We could not develop judgments, standards, and morals without the ability to see our own behavior from the standpoint of others, which gradually becomes abstracted into what sociologists call the "generalized other," or what we sometimes label as our "reference group." Guilt and shame, the products of one's internalized conscience, can be thought of as the accumulated empathy of a decade of growing up. As adults we have the capacity to see ourselves from others' perspectives and this capacity should help us to develop repair strategies. Why is it, then, that so often we end up in complete disagreement, convinced that the only thing the other party really wants is to gain a selfish advantage at our expense?

One factor certainly is our need to maintain our position and our pride. Having suffered an affront, a loss of face, or a loss of advantage sometime in the past, we feel the only safe thing to do is to protect ourselves from any repetition of such an unpleasant event. We may, in addition, recognize that our own interest and that of the other party are genuinely in conflict. If we are in a zero-sum game, we may not be able to afford too much sympathy for our opponent. In such an instance, a repair strategy should call for the ability to locate some superordinate goals, where goal conflict is not intrinsic, and to build a new set of interactions around such superordinate goals. Skillful diplomats, negotiators, and statesmen build their entire careers around the development of such repair strategies. They create one repair strategy after another as the people they deal with destroy one relationship after another.

Ordinary day-to-day relations with families, between managers and subordinates, and between groups in organizations are forever in danger of breaking down. We must be prepared to diagnose the situation when breakdown occurs and to have the skills to repair it, if repair is needed. Let me give two examples of what is involved.

REPAIR STRATEGIES IN MIDLIFE

Much of the research on midlife is beginning to point to the presence of two very broad phases, each lasting a decade or more.[8] In the first phase, which lasts roughly from age twenty-five to age forty, the family in a sense colludes with the primary career occupant to build a successful career. The primary career occupant, his or her spouse or partner, and the children all learn that our occupational structure requires that one go to school and then put in an intensive decade or so building one's career (and one's organizational membership if the career is pursued within an organization). The support by the family may be silent and stoic. The children are kept out of the career builder's hair while he or she is busy. The spouse or partner—gladly or resentfully—makes sacrifices and actively develops a viable ancillary support role as homemaker and as mother and father combined.

But something else is going on during these years. The homemaker is in a terminal career and knows it; at some point the children will all be off to school, the house will have had all the attention it needs, and being the ancillary spouse may not be a full enough life. The spouse builds up expectations that at some point "it will be my turn; I have helped you to build your career and now I want something in return—something for myself." As these feelings grow and are articulated, as teenage children begin to say "Why are you working so hard? What's it all about anyway?", and as the career occupant begins to reexamine his or her career, a new phase begins. In this phase, there may be a need for repair strategies, renegotiation of the family contract, and reassessment of who wants what and how it is best achieved. People discover either that their relationships are already damaged and need to be repaired or that they *will* be damaged if no preventive maintenance is undertaken.

Cross-Cultural Sensitivity within the Family

It should be noted that each family member has, in a sense, been living in a different subculture and that cross-cultural understanding and humility will therefore become very important. The career occupant will have to understand and respect the serious requirements of the spouse and the young adult children. The spouse and children will have to understand and respect the serious requirements of the world of work and organizations with which the career occupant grapples. This will tax each member's self-insight, commitment to the family, sensitivity, and perspective.

The moral humility issue is central here because the cause of a damaged relationship is often a devaluing of each other's goals and aspirations. The career occupant looks down on what may be regarded as the trivial or threatening values of the next generation; he or she cannot really appreciate why the homemaker spouse should have an issue about self-identity, the need to feel important and worthwhile in a society in which worth is defined almost exclusively by paid work and career involvement. The spouse (and most likely the children) find it easy to devalue organizational goals, to identify organizational careers with exploitation of the poor, marginal product quality, questionable business ethics, overworked people who are eventually cast off by cruel employers, and so on. If midlife family relationships are damaged by such feelings, then how can they be repaired?

The Interplay of Face-to-Face Skills

Each party in the relationship must first achieve some self-insight, some sense of one's own commitments so that defensiveness and denial can be reduced. We cannot hear others if we cannot accept ourselves. Next we need the kind of cross-cultural sensitivity I have been talking about, the relaxed, open ability to hear others' values with empathy and perspective. Once we can hear each other, we can begin to seek the common ground, the goals or aspirations around which some common activities can be designed; we can begin to renegotiate the relationships to make it possible for the desirable activities to happen. If, in hearing each other, we find a genuine lack of common ground, we can negotiate a reduced level of intimacy in the relationship yet maintain a high degree of mutual acceptance of what each other cares about; this can lead to nondestructive separations, more limited interactions with children, or both.

LABOR-MANAGEMENT RELATIONS

My second example has to do with face-to-face skills and repair strategies in labor-management situations. I am struck by the degree to which these situations seem to turn into intergroup struggles—struggles among unions, managements, and government bodies or political parties. Once the conflicts have escalated to the intergroup level, it is easy to give up one's proactive problem-solving orientation and to resign oneself to the idea that the problem is essentially unsolvable. Yet when one looks at successful enterprises—those which have managed to maintain harmony between management and employees—one realizes that the key to this harmony is a high degree of mutual trust, active listening, appropriate levels of participation, and consistently constructive face-to-face communications.

An example will highlight what I mean. A plant manager told me that he had spent many years developing a constructive relationship with his employees, in spite of the fact that they belonged to a strong national union which periodically calls for national strikes. One year his employees refused to strike. They were told by the national union that it would get all the suppliers of the plant to refuse to deliver, thus effectively shutting the plant down. Under these conditions, the manager and the employees got together and agreed that the employees should go out on strike, but everyone knew that it was not over local issues. The manager did not hold it against his subordinates that they had gone out on strike.

Intergroup trust, reinforced by open face-to-face communications on relevant issues, was strong enough to keep this plant functioning well even in a larger context that make periodic strikes inevitable. What we can learn from this is that constructive face-to-face relationships are necessary even though they may not be sufficient. Solving a problem at the national level will probably be useless if there continue to be destructive low-trust relationships within the enterprise.

DISENGAGING THE CRITICAL MIND

Achieving trust in a labor-management situation that has developed into a hostile intergroup conflict over a period of decades seems like a tall order. One prerequisite to working out the problem at the group level will be, as I have argued, the reestablishment of constructive face-to-face relationships. This will only be possible if both managers and workers find a way to see each other in less stereotypic ways. There is a need here to introduce in the interpersonal arena what Zen, gestalt training, encounter groups, and other training programs have emphasized—relaxing the active critical mind enough to let our eyes and ears see and hear what is really out there rather than what we *expect* to see and hear. Just as the person who is learning to draw must suspend what he or she knows intellectually about what things should look like, and, instead, must learn to see what is really out there, so the person concerned about repairing human relationships must first see now what he or she expects or knows should be there, but what is actually there.[9]

I don't think it is accidental that Americans are so preoccupied with sensitivity training, Zen meditation, inner tennis, and most recently, right-side brain functions.[10] What all of these programs and approaches have in common is a focus on learning how to perceive oneself, others, and the environment realistically, which apparently requires a certain relaxation of our active critical functions and a deliberate disengaging of our analytical selves. We cannot improve face-to-face relationships if we cannot perceive accurately. And accurate seeing and hearing is for many of us a lost skill that we must somehow regain. The place to begin practicing this skill is in our families and in our immediate superior-subordinate and peer relations.

If we cannot see ourselves and others in this relaxed, uncritical way, then we cannot develop perspective, humility, or tact, and we run the danger of acting on incorrect data. On the other hand, if we can really learn to see each other, and if we can combine more accurate perception with the ninth element in my list—patience—then we have some chance of improving and repairing face-to-face relationships.

> Even though you try to put people under some control, it is impossible. You cannot do it. The best way to control people is to encourage them to be mischievous. Then they will be in control in its wider sense. To give your sheep or cow a large, spacious meadow is the way to control him. So it is with people: first let them do what they want, and watch them. This is the best policy. To ignore them is not good; that is the worst policy. The second worst is trying to control them. The best one is to watch them, just to watch them, without trying to control them. The same way works for yourself as well. [S. Suzuki, *Zen Mind, Beginner's Mind.*][11]

REFERENCES

1 See P. R. Lawrence and J. W. Lorsch, *Organization and Environment* (Boston: Division of Research, Harvard Business School, 1967).

2 See E. Goffman, *Interaction Ritual* (Chicago: Aldine, 1967).

3 See E. Hall, *Beyond Culture* (Garden City, NY: Anchor, 1977).

4 See: E. H. Schein, *Organizational Psychology*, 3rd ed. (Englewood Cliffs, NJ: Prentice-Hall, 1980), chs. 9 and 13; T. A. Harris, *I'm OK—You're OK* (New York: Avon, 1967); E. Polster and M. Polster, *Gestalt Therapy Integrated* (New York: Bruner/Mazel, 1973).

5 See R. E. Walton, *Interpersonal Peacemaking: Confrontations and Third-Party Consultation* (Reading, MA: Addison-Wesley, 1969).

6 See. W. Bennis, J. Van Maanen, E. H. Schein, and F. I. Steele, *Essays in Interpersonal Dynamics* (Homewood, IL: Dorsey, 1979).

7 See D. McGregor, *The Human Side of Enterprise* (New York: McGraw-Hill, 1960).

8 See F. Bartolomé and P. A. L. Evans, *Must Success Cost So Much?* (London: Grant McIntyre, 1980); E. H. Schein, *Career Dynamics* (Reading, MA: Addison-Wesley, 1978); C. B. Derr, ed., *Work, Family, and the Career* (New York: Praeger, 1980).

9 See B. Edwards, *Drawing on the Right Side of the Brain* (Los Angeles: J. P. Tarcher, 1979); F. Frank, *The Zen of Seeing* (New York: Vintage, 1973).

10 See R. E. Ornstein, *The Psychology of Consciousness* (San Francisco: W. H. Freeman, 1972).

11 See S. Suzuki, *Zen Mind, Beginner's Mind* (New York: Weatherhill, 1977), p. 32.

REVIEW QUESTIONS

1 Schein contends that many elements are necessary for effective relationships, such as tact, patience, humility, and flexibility. How can a person acquire or develop such characteristics?

2 Rate yourself on each of the nine different elements presented in the reading. What are your greatest strengths and weaknesses, as you perceive them?

3 The reading concludes with a quote on control of people. How does this relate to Schein's major themes?

READING 58

Improving Productivity through Objective Feedback: A Review of the Evidence

Richard E. Kopelman*

A considerable body of literature provides evidence of the effectiveness of objective feedback as a technology for improving productivity. This article reviews the results of twenty-seven studies that report on the effects of objective feedback on either job performance (eighteen studies) or work behavior (nine studies). More specifically, results are examined in terms of: (a) the magnitude of impact, (b) cost effectiveness, and (c) the reliability and durability of the effect. After reviewing the empirical evidence, the article examines several explanations of why objective feedback is a technique that virtually always works. Finally, suggestions are offered regarding the practical steps an organization might take to implement an objective feedback system.

*From *National Productivity Review*, Winter 1982–83, pp. 43–55. Reprinted with permission.

OBJECTIVE FEEDBACK: THE EFFECTIVENESS EVIDENCE

Some indicators of job performance and work behavior are relatively objective, e.g., units of output, attendance, forms completed; others are relatively subjective, e.g., an individual's leadership skill, initiative, sense of responsibility. Importantly, the concept of productivity *requires* that job performance or work behavior be measured in terms of objective indicators. Subjective judgments cannot be incorporated into a ratio of outputs divided by inputs: for instance, it does not make sense to talk about rated leadership "points" per hour worked. Yet the distinction between objective and subjective criteria is one of degree, not kind. Measured output implies judgment about quality; and even attendance implies that the individual is both physically and mentally at work. Nevertheless, it is widely recognized that relatively objective indicators are preferable to relatively subjective ones. They allow computation of productivity ratios, and they provide more accurate information.

In recent years there has been an accelerating increase in research on the impact of objective feedback on job performance and work behavior. Of the twenty-seven studies known to this author, one was published prior to 1975, four between 1975 and 1977, and twenty-two between 1978 and 1980. Of these studies, eighteen focused on such end-result criteria as job performance or productivity (e.g., output per hour or percent defective), and nine focused on intermediate behavioral criteria (e.g., frequency of hand washing by kitchen workers or frequency of smiling at customers by restaurant employees).

Feedback, Job Performance, and Productivity

Table 1 summarizes the results of the eighteen studies that examined the effects of objective feedback on various indicators of job performance or productivity. The sample populations were highly diverse, including such blue-collar workers as truck drivers, sewing machine operators, and auto mechanics and such white-collar workers as payroll clerks, mental health technicians, and salespeople.

Three primary methods of providing feedback were employed: privately communicated individual feedback, publicly communicated individual feedback, and publicly communicated group feedback. Most studies used either (a) public group feedback alone, or (b) private individual and public group feedback combined.

Typically, feedback was used in conjunction with other interventions such as goal setting, social reinforcers (praise, recognition, encouragement), training, token reinforcers (e.g. pen and pencil sets, coffee and doughnuts), certificates, commendation letters, and preferred task assignments.

The effects of feedback were examined over study periods ranging from eight weeks to four years, the median time period being thirty weeks. In all eighteen studies, objective performance indicators increased after the provision of feedback. Increases ranged from 6 percent to 125 percent; the median result was an increase of 53 percent.

However, the 53 percent figure does not indicate that productivity was on the average increased by 53 percent. This is because some of the objective perfor-

TABLE 1
EFFECTS OF FEEDBACK ON JOB PERFORMANCE

Year	Sample	Type of feedback[a]	Other interventions[b]	Impact on job performance	Comments
1973[1]	sales, shipping	Pvt. I G	GS, P, R	150% increase in frequency of time meeting customer service standard; 110% increase in frequency of full use of containers; over 4 years	annualized savings of roughly $1 million
1975[2]	43 die-casting operators	Pvt. I G	P, E	production up 6.1% over 36 weeks	annualized savings of $77,000
1976[3]	4 groups of 113 blue-collar, unionized service workers	Pvt. I	GS, P	7.9% improvement in cost performance; 13.6% improvement in safety; 11.6% increase in service; over 3 months	best results were obtained in the group to which all interventions were applied
1977[4]	8 mental health technicians	Pub. I G		120% increase in group therapy sessions; 150% increase in one-on-one therapy sessions; 70% increase in daily routine activities; over 8 weeks	decrease in both staff complaints and patient complaints
1978[5]	58 plant managers; 92 truck drivers	Pvt. I (to both plant managers and truck drivers)	TR	43.9% decrease in truck turnaround time over 29 weeks	12% increase in total shipping productivity
1978[6]	32 nonunionized industrial workers at PPG Industries	Pvt. I G	P, E	8.7% increase in productivity over 4 months	productivity was higher with both forms of feedback than with G alone

(Continued)

TABLE 1 (Continued)

Year	Sample	Type of feedback[a]	Other interventions[b]	Impact on job performance	Comments
1978[7]	doffers in a textile yarn mill	Pvt. I G	GS, P, TR	reduced the incidence of high bobbins (which caused tangles in thread) by 74.6% over 8 weeks	when feedback was discontinued, the incidence of high bobbins increased by 64%
1978[8]	1 draftsman in an engineering firm	Pvt. I		72.2% increase in hours worked over 11 weeks	marked improvement in punctuality
1978[9]	4 textile machine operators at PPG Industries	Pvt. I	GS, P	7.8% increase in output over an average period of 32 weeks	annualized savings of $3,500; improved relationships between operators and foreman
1978[10]	195 truck drivers for textile company	Pvt. I Pub. I G	R, TR	5.1% increase in miles per gallon; 56.7% increase in use of company-owned fuel terminals; over 2 years	described as a "very substantial" dollar savings
1978[11]	23 inspectors at Eastman Kodak	Pvt. I G	GS, P	30% increase in productivity over 40 weeks	annualized savings of $105,000; increased contact between workers and supervisor; job seen as more interesting
1978[12]	6 repair shop workers	G	GS	20% increase in productivity over 22 weeks	annualized savings of $57,200
1979[13]	approx. 150 sewing machine operators in a garment factory	G	GS	62% reduction in defective garments ("seconds") over 12 months	pay satisfaction declined
1979[14]	approx. 12 workers in a federal agency personnel department	Pvt. I	GS, P, PWA, T, CL	69.7% average improvement in 11 output measures over 7 months	9 of 11 performance indicators improved, 1 was unchanged, and 1 showed a decline

1979[15]	clerical employees in payroll office of a large city personnel department	Pvt. I G		37.6% decrease in average backlog of work over 8 weeks	of 18 categories of work, backlogs decreased in 17 categories, 1 was unchanged
1980[16]	3 sales correspondents in an industrial products company	Pvt I	more complete sales information from salesmen	67% reduction in price quotation turnaround time over roughly 3 years	contributed to a 45% increase in sales and a 78% increase in profit over 4 years
1980[17]	back-office employees in Marine Midland Bank trust department	Pvt. I G	P, R, and group problem solving	71.9% reduction in outstanding daily accounts receivable (increasing cash flow)	assuming 15% cost of money, the annualized savings were $440,350
1980[18]	all employees in 16 departments of a large state hospital	Pvt. G G		83% increase in staff treatment programs and client hours with private group feedback over 15–23 weeks; 163% increase in the same criteria with public group feedback over 38 weeks	an increase in work-related conversations among all levels of employees

mance indicators focused only on a component aspect of output, such as truck turnaround time or the incidence of high bobbins. Ten studies did, however, employ comprehensive measures of performance, and in these studies feedback yielded a median productivity increase of 16 percent. This finding closely corresponds to the observation made by Milne and Doyle that feedback interventions alone produce an increase in productivity of 14 percent.

Six of the eighteen studies reported data on annualized dollar savings resulting from the feedback intervention. Savings ranged from $3,500 to $1 million, with the median result being an annual savings of $91,000. In large part, though, the total annualized dollar savings were a function of the number of employees involved in the interaction. Therefore, a more meaningful indicator of the financial impact of objective feedback is the annualized savings per employee involved. On this basis, annualized savings ranged from $500 per employee (at Emery Air Freight, with some 2,000 employees) to $9,533 (6 repair shop workers), the median savings being $3,178.

Feedback and Work Behavior

Table 2 summarizes the results of nine studies that examined the effects of objective feedback on work behavior. The results were uniformly positive and were obtained over treatment periods that ranged in duration from one week to fourteen months, the median time period being eight weeks. Increases in desired work behaviors, or decreases in undesired work behaviors, ranged from 41 percent to 429 percent, the median result being an improvement of 78 percent.

Of course, an improvement in a particular work behavior, e.g., the frequency of hand washing in the preparation of food, typically does not reflect a comparable increase in either job performance or productivity. Work behavior is an antecedent of job performance, which in turn is an antecedent of the ultimate quantity of output produced. Not surprisingly, therefore, there is a diminishing relationship between objective feedback and work behavior, job performance, and productivity, respectively. So while feedback improved work behavior by 78 percent, it raised job performance indicators by 53 percent and productivity by 16 percent, as we have already noted.

Advantages of Feedback

There are six distinct advantages of a feedback intervention. First, a feedback system often can be based on data already being generated. Hence, feedback is unobtrusive, requiring little change in ongoing procedures.

Second, and related to the first advantage, a feedback intervention is relatively simple to implement and requires little investment in time or money. Indeed, the initial outlay associated with the development of a feedback intervention is often less than $1,000; and, as noted previously, the median financial savings has averaged $91,000 per year.

TABLE 2
EFFECTS OF FEEDBACK ON WORK BEHAVIOR

Year	Sample	Type of feedback[a]	Other interventions[b]	Impact on work behavior	Comments
1976[19]	30 telephone reservation clerks for Aer Lingus	Pvt. I G	GS	66.5% reduction in un-desired verbal behaviors; 84.4% increase in desired verbal behaviors; overall effect was a 77.9% improvement; after 3 months	clerks had a positive reaction to the program
1978[20]	80 employees in a mental health organization	public posting of replies to suggestions offered		222.7% increase in the number of suggestions offered over 32 weeks	98% of employees said the program should be continued
1978[21]	6 therapists at a health service center	Pvt I G	T, P, R	429% increase in the percentage of graphs (of client behavior) completed over 8½ weeks	individual feedback was superior in impact to group feedback; individual plus group feedback was superior to individual feedback
1978[22]	supervisors and staff at 30 university laboratories	Pvt. G (sent to supervisor)	P	45.4% reduction in observed frequency of hazards over 7 to 14 months	feedback was adopted as a permanent part of a new safety system
1979[23]	all salespersons in 5 departments of a department store	G	T, R	95% increase in the percentage of customers approached by salespeople; service behavior score rose by 4%; over 5 to 11 weeks	

(Continued)

TABLE 2 (Continued)

Year	Sample	Type of feedback[a]	Other interventions[b]	Impact on work behavior	Comments
1979[24]	all workers in a fast-food snack bar	G		94% reduction in employee theft over a 1 to 4 week period	
1980[25]	55 employees in a city's vehicle maintenance department	G	T, GS	41.4% improvement in behavioral safety scores over 34 to 36 weeks	83% decrease in the number of lost-time accidents; employees had a favorable reaction to the program
1980[26]	11 front-line employees in a fast-food restaurant	Pvt I	T, P, R	58% increase in friendliness behavior (smiling) over a 1½ to 10 week period	
1980[27]	9 kitchen workers in a large university cafeteria	Pvt. I	T	203.7% increase in the frequency of hand washing over 3 weeks	in comparison, training alone increased the frequency of hand washing by only 21.7%

[a]Pvt. I = private individual; G = public group.
[b]GS = goal setting; T = training; P = praise; R = social recognition.

Third, the use of feedback is a natural (although not always welcome) means of control. It does not require use of contrived events, such as a lottery; on the contrary, it typically requires only minor changes in day-to-day routines.

Fourth, the effects of objective feedback are evident rapidly. Indeed, positive results are often achieved within twenty-four hours. In contrast, job redesign and participation interventions typically take 1½ to 3 years to take hold; and substantial changes in managerial practices (e.g., from System 1 to System 4) take 3 to 7 years.

Fifth, objective feedback can be implemented in virtually all work settings, including those where there are few alternative ways to improve productivity. Public agencies and not-for-profit organizations may find it difficult, if not impossible, to employ financial incentives or to redesign jobs. However, the provision of objective feedback should encounter fewer problems than other interventions.

Sixth, the use of feedback generally enhances the effects of other productivity improvement techniques. Describing the use of training alone compared to training combined with feedback, Komaki, Heinzmann, and Lawson[25] [Superior numbers refer to studies listed at the end of the article] have written:

> When employees receive training in the form of a slide presentation, verbal explanations, and written rules, performance improved slightly. It was not until feedback was provided along with continued training that performance significantly improved.

More specifically, they found that training alone yielded an improvement of 24.7 percent, whereas training and feedback yielded an improvement of 41.4 percent.

An even more dramatic illustration of the "enhancement effect" of feedback is provided by the research of Geller, Eason, Phillips, and Pierson.[27] Training alone improved sanitation practices—specifically hand washing behavior—among kitchen workers by 21.7 percent. Training combined with feedback led to an increase in (required) hand washing of 203.1 percent.

Two additional findings concerning feedback might be mentioned. First, it has been found that feedback helps to raise satisfaction and motivation more on nonstimulating jobs than stimulating jobs. Second, there is evidence that individual feedback has a greater impact on performance than does group feedback.

WHY FEEDBACK WORKS

There are two primary reasons why feedback increases productivity: (1) it enhances the desire to perform well, i.e., it functions as a motivator; and (2) it cues learned responses or serves to develop new responses, i.e., it functions in an instructional capacity.

How Feedback Motivates

Four explanations have been advanced as to why feedback motivates increased productivity. Although these explanations are actually interrelated, each is discussed separately for the sake of clarity.

1. *Feedback corrects misconceptions.* People often have somewhat distorted perceptions of their own work behaviors. The provision of objective feedback

calls attention to these misperceptions and may motivate corrective action.

A dramatic example of this mechanism is provided by the Emery Air Freight intervention conducted by Edward J. Feeney.[1]

> Executives at Emery were convinced that containers were being used about 90 percent of the times they could be used. Measurement of the actual usage—a measurement made by the same managers whose guesses had averaged 90 percent—showed that the actual usage was 45 percent, or half the estimate.

Subsequently, Emery Air Freight initiated a motivational program consisting of (a) goal setting, (b) performance measurement and feedback, and (c) positive reinforcement (praise, recognition). The net result was that the container usage rate rose from 45 percent to 95 percent. Also, the motivational program raised customer service so that the standard was met more than 90 percent of the time, compared to the prior level of 30 to 40 percent. Edward J. Feeney, the person responsible for designing and implementing the motivational program at Emery, noted that feedback was the critical variable in explaining the success of the program. In his words, "Most managers genuinely think that operations in their bailiwick are doing well; a performance audit that proves they're not comes as a real and unpleasant surprise."

Another illustration of the effect of objective feedback in eliminating misperceptions is provided by the case of the telephone reservation clerks at Aer Lingus.[19] The clerks were provided with profiles of their verbal behaviors obtained from unobtrusive work samples of twenty telephone calls per clerk. The feedback caused one telephone clerk to comment:

> When asked previously whether I used the customer's name I would have said—and believed—'Of course, we were trained to do that.' I was really surprised when I saw objective evidence on how little I was actually doing it.

As a result of the monitoring and feedback program, use of the customer's name by the thirty clerks rose by 87.5 percent. The frequency of interruptions by the telephone clerks dropped by 100 percent.

To the extent that feedback is objective, valid, and, hence, incontrovertible, it offers the possibility of informing an individual about his or her false self-perceptions. Certainly, the use of such feedback has been found to motivate improved job performance; presumably, it also has led to more accurate self-perceptions.

2. *Feedback creates internal consequences.* In the absence of performance feedback, it is unlikely that employees will have either positive or negative feelings about themselves as a result of their job performance. The provision of feedback, however, allows employees to experience positive (or negative) feelings about themselves—a psychological state called internal work motivation. Several examples of the motivational impact of performance feedback are to be found in the literature.

After the introduction of objective performance measurement and feedback among cash management clerks at Marine Midland, the average level of cash balances was reduced by 72 percent.[17] Supervisors offered the following comments. "The areas are completely aware of cash flow now; everyone gives 100 percent to the program. There seems to be that extra effort on the part of people to get more involved in cash flows. . . . People are now trying to solve problems before they occur. People are looking to help out other individuals rather than just saying 'that's not my job.' I can say as a supervisor that it has a big impact on my own feelings toward the people who work for me. I feel a sense of accomplishment. . . ."

One week after the introduction of a performance measurement and feedback system in the emergency room of a large hospital in Manhattan, the proportion of completed reports submitted by emergency-room clerks rose from 67 percent to 95 percent. The casewriter observed that,"The clerks for their part were experiencing increased job satisfaction. As one clerk put it, 'I used to go home evenings wondering what I had done . . . now I look at my feedback report and can see what I have accomplished.'"

In short, objective performance feedback allows the individual employee to be able to "keep score"; improvements or declines in the individual's score may potentially be a source of satisfaction or dissatisfaction. Yet, it should be noted that knowledge of results is a necessary but not sufficient condition for internal work motivation. Other relevant factors include the meaningfulness and responsibility for results that the job incumbent sees in his work and the individual's desire to grow and achieve.

3. *Feedback may entail social consequences.* In situations where objective performance feedback is provided (a) by an employee's supervisor, or (b) by public posting of data, the individual (or work group) will typically experience social consequences, which in turn have been found to increase performance in a wide variety of work settings. For example, among 195 experienced truck drivers, letters of commendation were used to provide private recognition, and the posting at each terminal of the names of drivers who achieved six miles per gallon provided public recognition. These two forms of social reinforcers, plus token tangible rewards, reduced energy consumption substantially for two years and increased drivers' job satisfaction.[10]

In a mental health setting, staff suggestions and comments were publicly posted, and responses (feedback) were posted as well. Although all suggestions or comments were publicly posted, anonymity was assured if desired; participants did not have to sign their names. The net result was that 1.8 suggestions were generated per employee per year, considerably greater than the national average rate of 0.8 in federal government agencies and .4 in private industry, where sizable cash awards are frequently offered.[20]

The use of recognition in improving performance does not require that performance feedback be uniformly positive. An interesting illustration of this point comes from the world of professional sports. Dave Anderson of the *New York Times* provides the following anecdote concerning Frank Robinson's first year as manager of baseball's Cleveland Indians.

> Buddy Bell, now with the Texas Rangers, was the Indian third baseman then. Buddy Bell was even-tempered, quiet, a hard worker, the organizer of the team's Fellowship of Christian Athletes Services. But midway through Frank Robinson's first season, Buddy

Bell confronted him. "I can't play for you," Buddy Bell told him. "You ignore me. You don't pat me on the back when I'm going good. You don't chew me out when I'm going bad. . . ." Apparently . . . Frank Robinson responded to this criticism. By the end of that season . . Buddy Bell confronted Frank Robinson again. "I just want you to know," he said, "that I enjoyed playing for you."

In a more practical vein, it has been found that the feedback of objective performance data can improve both productivity and the supervisor-employee relationship.[2] The supervisors of forty-three machine operators emphasized positive feedback (praise and favorable recognition) and adopted a constructive, problem-solving stance regarding undesirable behavior. Consequently, lines of communication opened up, trust increased, and interpersonal relations improved.

Thus, across such diverse groups as truck drivers, hospital employees, and machine operators, it is evident that recognition via performance feedback is an important motivator of improved work performance.

4. *Feedback creates external consequences.* The process of measuring and feeding back objective performance data tends to generate a heightened sense of evaluation consequences. As a result, individuals strive to "look good" to gain whatever rewards might result from managerial approval and to avoid "looking bad" and the accompanying adverse consequences resulting from managerial disapproval.

In his book, *Feedback and Organization Development*, Nadler has written: "One way in which data collection regenerates energy is through implied sanctions or rewards. The fact that an activity is measured through data collection sends a message that some potentially powerful individual or group feels that the activity being measured is an important one." Thus, the process of measurement and feedback represents a two-edged sword: there is the threat of punishers or relative deprivation on the one hand and the possibility of rewards on the other.

Reviewing the research literature, there is some evidence indicating that the implied threat/promise of punishment or reward is an important reason for the motivational effect of objective performance feedback.

In the case of the draftsman who monitored the time he spent working, the measurement and feedback intervention led to a 72 percent increase in hours worked.[8] The authors wrote: "The fact that the subject's behavior changed so dramatically with the onset of self-monitoring lends plausibility to the interpretation that the behavior changes were the result of perceived aversive consequences for failure to meet acceptable levels of performance.

As has been suggested by Donald Law of Arthur Young & Company, the absence of performance measurement implies that management finds any level of performance to be acceptable. However, upon the institution of performance measurement and feedback, the implicit message would seem to be that management is interested in how proficient each individual (or work group) is. More specifically, the message that is conveyed by measurement/feedback actions—not merely by words—is that inefficient workers will be treated less favorably than others, possibly penalized or even terminated. Further, because measurement and feedback are absolutely essential to the operation of a merit reward system, these actions raise the possibility that management will be responsive to high levels of proficiency, i.e., that meritorious contributors will in fact be recognized and rewarded.

How Feedback Instructs

The second primary reason why feedback increases productivity is that it serves in an instructional capacity, i.e., it directs or cues behavior. Objective performance feedback can provide information pertinent to (a) the specific kinds of activities that should be performed, (b) the levels of proficiency that should be achieved in each of these activities, and (c) the individual's current level of proficiency in these activities. Interestingly, this information addresses three of the (four) questions that Virgil Rowland, in his book *Evaluating and Improving Managerial Performance*, found managers most wanted to have answered: What are my real job responsibilities?; What standards apply to these areas of responsibility?; and, At what level am I now performing? Clearly, the first two questions directly relate to the instructional role of feedback; the third question relates more to its motivational role.

Lawrence Miller, in his book *Behavior Management*, asserts that feedback will improve job performance to the extent that it pinpoints specific, observable tasks or activities. In his words, "A typical reaction to substandard performance is to assume there is a problem in the employee's motivation. . . . Often, however, a more fruitful approach is to assume there is a problem in clarity of performance expectations and timely, objective feedback of results to the employee."

Research by Roland Tharp and Ronald Gallimore, in an article in *Psychology Today* (January 1976), is also pertinent to the instructional/correctional capability of feedback. They studied the verbal behaviors of John Wooden, the highly successful UCLA basketball coach, in talking to his team during fifteen practice sessions. Tharp and Gallimore found that at least 75 percent of Wooden's comments contained informational content. Further, most of his comments were specific statements of what to do or how to do it rather than motivational/positive reinforcing communications. Indeed, Wooden was more than five times as likely to inform than he was to praise or reprimand only.

Not only can feedback inform people about the activities they should be performing, it can also be used to provide information about standards of proficiency. This latter type of information is very important. For example, according to Jewell Westerman, a vice president at Hendrick & Company, a management consulting firm, "people who are measured know what's expected of them." Before going to work for Hendrick & Company, Westerman worked on productivity measurement at Travelers Insurance Company. Westerman found that white-collar workers often had "piles of work in front of them, but they didn't know if they were supposed to get it all out the same day. They needed feedback" and information about work standards. Indeed, insurance companies, such as Travelers, have pioneereed in the area of work measurement for white-collar employees.

IMPLEMENTATION OF A PERFORMANCE MEASUREMENT AND FEEDBACK SYSTEM

In a 1980 survey, nearly 46,000 employees of forty large companies responded to questions about their interest in seventeen organization/job-related subjects, including job advancement opportunities and the organization's community involvement. Interest in the issue of productivity improvement ranked second, trailing only the "organization's future plans."

Potential Pitfalls

Apparently, employees today *say* they are very interested in productivity improvement, but to date they have not been particularly eager to adopt performance measurement as a method of improving productivity.

A number of researchers have reported on this reluctance. Lawrence Miller has observed that some employees and managers are apprehensive that work measurement and evaluation will not provide a fair assessment of their work. It has also been reported that white-collar workers frequently are insulted by claims that their work, like that of blue-collar workers, can be measured and graded. Furthermore, Marvin Mundel, a consultant, has found that scientists and engineers argue that since their regular work is constantly interrupted by emergency assignments, time standards cannot be applied to them. (In fact, Mundel observes, estimated time standards pertain to time spent working on a given assignment, not to the time that transpires before an assignment is completed.)

Perhaps the situation is analogous to the case of extrinsic incentives: people work harder if they are paid for performance, but they prefer to be paid for time. Unfortunately, desired outcomes such as increased productivity or higher pay often come at the price of increased effort—in short, there is no free lunch.

Preconditions

Of course, some organizations are more receptive to a measurement program than are others. Irving Siegel, in his *Company Productivity: Measurement for Improvement*, has identified three favorable preconditions for a measurement program: (1) good rapport between labor and management (i.e., high trust); (2) acceptance of analysis and interpretation as necessary complements of measurement; and (3) a prior history of measurement.

But with or without these preconditions, there are a number of concrete steps organizations can take to facilitate the implementation of a performance measurement and feedback system.

Practical Steps

1 Obtain Visible Top Management Support   Management consultants and practitioners repeatedly stress that a performance measurement system requires effort and commitment from top management. In this vein, Gary P. Latham and Kenneth N. Wexley have written in *Increasing Productivity through Performance Appraisal* that "such support is essential as an umbrella under which new norms and expectations can flourish without the constant pressures to revert to the more comfortable and known ways of operating. Active senior management support is necessary for insuring a high level of commitment by middle managers for the system."

2 Set Up Mechanisms for Insuring Middle Management/Supervisory Commitment   According to Latham and Wexley, "A key reason for the failure of a performance appraisal system/process is lack of middle management support once the system has been implemented. Middle managers can easily sabotage a human resource program. Thus, middle managers must be rewarded for participating in and supporting the various components of the appraisal process." Of course, the same applies to the implementation of objective feedback.

In addition to using rewards and punishments, another mechanism for increasing support is early training and exposure to the program. There is evidence that when supervisors are trained to use a new system before lower-level personnel, program implementation is better than when supervisors are trained after lower-level personnel.

3 Encourage a High Level of Employee Participation   Evidence from various settings supports the finding that the involvement and participation of employees is vital for the successful design and implementation of a measurement program. With professional white-collar employees, it is especially important that participation occur, and early on. Carl Thor, a vice-president at the American Productivity Center, offers the following insight. "One mistake people get into is they adopt a productivity banner, and then dust off their stopwatches and start measuring. But these . . . high level white-collar personnel are college graduates and they aren't going to put up with it." He suggests that employees work with the measurers in determining the correct measures and then in going over the results.

4 Begin with Successes   The measurement program should be initiated in areas of the organization where there is a good chance of achieving positive results—"winners." With demonstrated successes, the credibility of the program increases, facilitating expansion to more complex and recalcitrant segments of the organization.

5 Build a Critical Mass   Unless a critical mass is attained, the program is unlikely to be sustained. Accordingly, the measurement program must be diffused throughout a significant part of the organization.

6 Establish a Task Force   In order to build a critical mass, the instrument for the design and implementation of the performance measurement system ought to be an ad hoc group of high-level employees. The task force, steering committee, or council should be chartered to represent top management in the development of a system within prescribed guidelines.

7 Use the Communications Network   From the very beginning, the task force should advertise its constructive intent. It should establish communications with a labor union and use in-house media to assure lower management and the operating staff that no revolutionary "new order" lies ahead. Additionally, the task force might designate liaison people throughout the organization, conduct briefings and demonstrations, and send out announcements.

8 Set Up a Trial Period   After a "debugging" period, performance measurement should be undertaken on a trial basis. To indicate the trial nature of the first installation, the system should explicitly be labeled as "first generation," suggesting that changes will occur.

9 Prepare an Instruction Manual and Offer Recommendations   Before the task force is disbanded, an instruction manual should be written for users. The manual should describe (a) the general nature of the system (i.e., the structure, data sources, and purposes), and (b) the measurement process per se (i.e., procedures, periodicity, forms, reports, and staffing). Also, the task force should report on early results and offer recommendations.

10 Implement Review System   Line managers should be responsible for reporting results of the program periodically. Having line managers do the reporting provides recognition and perhaps a feeling of accomplishment; it may also increase their sense of psychological ownership and commitment. Further, reviews should be addressed to high-level administrators (e.g., the vice-presidents of operations and human resources).

CONCLUSION

A review of twenty-seven empirical studies indicates that objective feedback does not *usually* work—it virtually *always* works. In all cases, results were positive. On the average: work behaviors improved 78 percent; job performance indicators increased by 53 percent; and overall outputs, i.e., productivity, increased by 16 percent. These uniformly positive results occurred across diverse occupational groups and in various work settings. Moreover, there was little evidence that the effects diminished over time.

Why does objective feedback work? There are two reasons: it both energizes and directs work behavior. What kinds of organizations can profitably apply objective feedback? All kinds. And finally, how can organizations implement such an intervention? The key steps include obtaining managerial support, encouraging employee participation, achieving initial successes, and diffusing the intervention throughout the organization.

NOTES

1 "At Emery Air Freight: Positive Reinforcement Boosts Performance," in Henry L. Tosi and W. Clay Hamner, (eds.), *Organizational Behavior and Management: A Contingency Approach* (Chicago: St. Clair Press, 1974), pp. 113–122. This article originally appeared in *Organizational Dynamics*, Winter 1973.

2 Everett E. Adam, Jr., "Behavior Modification in Quality Control," *Academy of Management Journal* 18(4):662–79, 1975.

3 Jay S. Kim and W. Clay Hamner, "Effect of Performance Feedback and Goal Setting on Productivity and Satisfaction in an Organizational Setting," *Journal of Applied Psychology* 61(1):48–57, 1976.

4 Robert Kreitner, William E. Reif, and Marvin Morris, "Measuring the Impact of Feedback on the Performance of Mental Health Technicians," *Journal of Organizational Behavior Management* 1(1):105–09, 1977.

5 Alex Runnion, Twila Johnson, and John McWhorter, "The Effects of Feedback and Reinforcement on Truck Turnaround Time in Materials Transportation," *Journal of Organizational Behavior Management* 1(2):110–17, 1978.

6 Gerald D. Emmert, "Measuring the Impact of Group Performance Feedback Versus Individual Performance Feedback in an Industrial Setting," *Journal of Organizational Behavior Management* 1(2):134–41, 1978.

7 Michael McCarthy, "Decreasing the Incidence of 'High Bobbins' in a Textile Spinning Department through a Group Feedback Procedure," *Journal of Organizational Behavior Management* 1(2):150–54, 1978.

8 P. A. Lamal and A. Benfield, "The Effect of Self-Monitoring on Job Tardiness and Percentage of Time Spent Working," *Journal of Organizational Behavior Management* 1(2):142–49, 1978.

9 H. Wayne Dick, "Increasing the Productivity of the Day Relief Textile Machine Operator," *Journal of Organizational Behavior Management* 2(1):45–57, 1978.

10 Alex Runnion, Jesse O. Watson, and John McWhorter, "Energy Savings in Interstate Transportation through Feedback and Reinforcement," *Journal of Organizational Behavior Management* 1(3):180–91, 1978.

11 L. Eldridge, S. Lemasters, and B. Szypot, "A Performance Feedback Intervention to Reduce Waste: Performance Data and Participant Responses," *Journal of Organizational Behavior Management* 1(4):258–66, 1978.

12 Albert Stoerzinger, James M. Johnston, Kim Pisor, and Craig Monroe, "Implementation and Evaluation of a Feedback System for Employees in a Salvage Operation," *Journal of Organizational Behavior Management* 1(4):268–80, 1978.

13 James L. Koch, "Effects of Goal Specificity and Performance Feedback to Work Groups on Peer Leadership, Performance, and Attitudes," *Human Relations* 32(10):819–40, 1979.

14 Craig E. Schneier and Robert Pernick, "Increasing Public Sector Productivity through Organization Behavior Modification: A Successful Application," paper presented at the 39th National Meeting of the Academy of Management (Atlanta), 1979, pp. 1–15.

15 Richard E. Kopelman, unpublished data, 1979.

16 Lucien Rhodes, "It Pays to be on Time," *Inc.*, June 1980, pp. 59−64.

17 John K. Milne and Stephen X. Doyle, "Rx for Ailing Bank Trust Departments," *The Bankers Magazine* 163(1):54−57, January/February 1980.

18 Donald M. Prue, Jon E. Krapfl, James C. Noah, Sherry Cannon, and Roger F. Maley, "Managing the Treatment Activities of State Hospital Staff," *Journal of Organizational Behavior Management* 2(3):165−81, 1980.

19 Stephen A. Allen, "Aer Lingus—Irish (b)," (Boston: *Intercollegiate Case Clearing House*, 1976), case #9-477-640, pp. 1−20.

20 O. Robert Quilitch, "Using a Simple Feedback Procedure to Reinforce the Submission of Written Suggestions by Mental Health Employees," *Journal of Organizational Behavior Management* 1(2):155−63, 1978.

21 Gerald L. Shook, C. Merle Johnson, and William F. Uhlman, "The Effect of Response Effort Reduction, Group and Individual Feedback, and Reinforcement on Staff Performance," *Journal of Organizational Behavior Management* 1(3):206−15, 1978.

22 Beth Sulzer-Azaroff, "Behavioral Ecology and Accident Prevention," *Journal of Organizational Behavior Management* 2(1):11−44, 1978.

23 Robert L. Collins, Judi Komaki, and Stephen Temlock, "Behavioral Definition and Improvement of Customer Service in Retail Merchandising," paper presented at the 87th Annual Meeting of the American Psychological Association (New York), 1979, pp. 1−12.

24 Patrick McNees, Sharon W. Gilliam, John F. Schnelle, and Todd Risley, "Controlling Employee Theft through Time and Product Identification," *Journal of Organizational Behavior Management* 2(2):113−19, 1979.

25 Judi Komaki, Arlene T. Heinzmann, and Loralie Lawson, "Effect of Training and Feedback: Component Analysis of a Behavioral Safety Program," *Journal of Applied Psychology* 65(3):261−70, 1980.

26 Judi Komaki, Milton R. Blood, and Donna Holder, "Fostering Friendliness in a Fast Food Franchise," *Journal of Organizational Behavior Management* 2(3):151−64, 1980.

27 E. Scott Geller, Serena L. Eason, Jean A. Phillips, and Merle D. Pierson, "Interventions to Improve Sanitation During Food Preparation," *Journal of Organizational Behavior Management* 2(3):229−40, 1980.

REVIEW QUESTIONS

1 In your own words, explain why feedback systems often have a positive impact on work behavior and job performance.

2 Many employees complain that their supervisors don't give them sufficient feedback. Suggest several reasons why this might be true.

3 Review the reading on O.B. Mod. In what ways is Kopelman's 10-step program for feedback similar or different?

READING 59

Feedback-Seeking Behavior

Susan J. Ashford
L. L. Cummings*

*   *   *

From the above arguments, it is clear that individuals respond to the costs inherent in their work setting. Individuals do not frequently ask for feedback because that behavior seems fraught with potential costs. These costs include potential embarrassment and the possibility that their asking may be misinterpreted to mean they feel uncertain of their own abilities. It is not surprising that, in such a situation, an individual will go to "great lengths" to find out how well he or she is doing without indicating a desire to know through directly asking others. An overreliance on a monitoring strategy, however, has certain predictable consequences. Information is often interpreted in line with the individual's expectations and goals. Monitoring individuals may interpret cues and develop a feedback impression different from the actual assessments of others. Many self-esteem theorists, for example, would argue that individuals of low self-esteem would overly attend to negative cues and miss many positive evaluations of their behavior (cf. Jacobs, Berscheid, & Walster, 1971; Shrauger & Lund, 1975). Such a tendency may explain why some subordinates, to the bewilderment of their supervisors, have low aspiration levels and lack confidence in their own competence. It is likely that these subordinates rely on monitoring as an FSB[†] strategy and have biases in the inference and meaning generation processes. The result is a biased impression of their own ability.

Conversely, some research shows that individuals tend to seek confirmatory feedback (Swann & Read, 1980). Individuals believing in their abilities may seek out confirmatory cues from their information. Thus, the overinflated views some employees have may result from an overreliance on a monitoring FSB strategy.

These arguments suggest that it may benefit both individuals and organizations to not only give subordinates more feedback as the current literature suggests but also to promote the use of inquiry as a FSB strategy. Such a promotion can be best achieved by attempting to reduce some of the risk and effort costs involved in this strategy. Managers can play a major role in manipulating the "shared meaning" of

*From Susan J. Ashford and L. L. Cummings, "Feedback as an Individual Resource: Personal Strategies of Creating Information," *Organizational Behavior and Human Performance*, December 1983, pp. 392–393. Reprinted with permission.
    [†]*Editor's note:* FSB stands for Feedback-Seeking Behavior.

this act. Rather than a sign of weakness and uncertainty, asking for feedback could come to represent a confident desire to understand one's strengths and weaknesses. Opening up this channel of feedback will allow employees to obtain more accurate appraisals of their work at the times when such appraisals are most valuable.

* * *

REVIEW QUESTION

1 Develop a list of the pros and cons for an employee to engage in feedback-seeking behavior.

CHAPTER 17

STRESS, BURNOUT, AND COUNSELING

READING 60

Employee Claims for Damages Add to the High Cost of Job Stress

John M. Ivancevich
Michael T. Matteson*

Item: *On the morning of January 31, 1979, Roger left for work early, as usual, and drove into the city to his office. Instead of putting in his customary long day, however, he left the office abruptly during the morning. He drove home, closed the garage door, and remained seated in his automobile with the windows down and the engine running. The autopsy report listed carbon monoxide as the cause of death, but Roger's widow doesn't agree. She has filed a $6 million lawsuit, claiming that Roger's job caused his death. She claims the employer (1) failed to respond to his repeated complaints about overwork and (2) displayed a callous and conscious disregard for his mental health.*

Item: *The Michigan Supreme Court granted lifetime workers' compensation to a General Motors Corporation parts inspector who was considered to be a "compulsive perfectionist." He suffered mental strain when assembly line workers kept installing parts labeled defective.*

Item: *An Atlanta air traffic controller is claiming stress from a fatal plane crash caused him to become insane and kill his wife. The controller was in control of an airplane when it ran into a hail storm and lost power over Georgia. The plane finally crash landed on a highway. Sixty-one of 81 people on board died.*

These items, which are both real and important, indicate that employees are now taking legal action against their employers with stress-related claims. In these and similar cases, employees have charged that occupational stress has been damaging and dangerous. Previously, court decisions generally concluded that individuals disabled as a result of a stimulus like workplace stress encountered problems because of "gradual wear-and-tear," and thus were not able to claim compensable personal injuries under the law. However, recently more and more courts have indicated in some cases that an employer is legally liable for an employee's mental illness. Because of the judicial trend to look seriously at employee-initiated lawsuits, organizations are now being forced to take some form of action to deal more effectively with the onslaught of stress-related claims.

The manager is in the forefront of any organizational response to the increase in these claims. The regular contact, evaluative responsibilities, personal familiarity, and overall knowledge of the manager provides a unique potential for observation and intervention of employee stress. If managers are unable or unwilling to recognize stress symptoms then they are increasing the possibility of subsequent legal action. Managerial ability to assess stress symptoms before they manifest themselves in the form of illness, reduced performance or even suicide is now almost an obligation and responsibility as more and more employers find themselves facing their employees in court.

Today many employers are being asked by the courts whether they took any type of action to identify stress and/or help employees who were allegedly under stress. In most cases, the response indicates that no systematic effort on the employer's part had been undertaken. On the other hand, some employers respond that they have introduced training programs designed to improve managers' ability to assess stress symptoms. One purpose of the programs is to be better able to aid employees in coping with occupational stress. Another benefit of the training is that employers can show the court that they are taking some positive action to deal with occupational stress.

Reactions to Occupational Stress

A common reaction to stress is anxiety. This may occur during the period of stress or sometime after. In addition to anxiety, specific fears of things or events related to the stress, such as fear of a new performance appraisal system, may occur. After such a stressful event, the individual may become and remain depressed for a considerable period. Depending on the individual and the situation, this depression may be intense or mild and be accompanied by complaints and guilt. Stress may also leave the individual more vulnerable to minor stressors and initiators, for instance, in the aftermath of losing a desired promotion, an employee may fly off the handle when a co-worker asks for assistance. Perhaps the most serious damage done by stress-induced irritability, however, is that we often think minor irritations are the cause of the anger rather than recognizing them as the triggers that set it off.

Cognitive Reactions   Under stress, individuals sometimes find it difficult to concentrate or to think clearly. An employee who must complete a major report may write everything up, but fail to schedule a secretary to type it on time. This effect of stress on concentration can lead to inefficiency. After the stress is over, individuals may have unpleasant recollections of the event intrude in their thoughts, sometimes repeatedly.

Physiological Reactions   Stress sets off an automatic physiological reaction through the sympathetic nervous system that prepares the body for "flight" or "fight." Blood is diverted from the skin and digestive system to crucial skeletal muscles; heart rate, blood pressure, and respiratory rate climb to better supply the body with oxygen; adrenaline is released; muscles are tensed; and so on. While these reactions were probably adaptive for our ancestors to fight the elements and saber-toothed tigers they are not well suited for organizational life today. People can fight or run from very few of the workplace stressors. When stress is intense and especially when it is chronic, overarousal can result in a variety of problems including migraine headaches, muscle aches, sleeplessness, trembling, muscle tics, and urinary and bowel dysfunction. Of course, whether these bodily reactions will occur, and the seriousness of them if they do occur, depends on the severity and duration of the stress and on the nature of the individual.

Other Reactions   Reactions may also occur in other behavioral dimensions. For example, it is not unusual to find a highly stressed good performer turn into a mediocre or poor performer. There may also be changes in motor (pacing or hand wringing), verbal (stuttering, rapid speech), or self-care (bathing, grooming) activities.

In cases of very severe reaction, the stress even may bring about a period of "irrational," "bizarre,"—even schizophrenic-like—behavior. Whether there is a severe reaction depends upon the individual and the intensity and duration of the stress event.

The stress response displayed by an employee may entail one or more of the reaction categories. Each of us has our own personal reaction system. The specific reaction will depend largely on a number of situational, organizational, and personal factors.

Managerial Consideration

A number of factors can help managers account for differences in their employees' reaction to stress. *Four* important ones are:

Intensity and Duration of Stress   In general, the more intense or prolonged the stress event, the more serious the reaction. Loss of a desired promotion is more likely to produce serious stress reactions than running out of typing paper.

Presence of Other Stress   Each source of workplace stress is likely to produce its own reactions in the individual as well as make the individual more vulnerable to other stress. Many studies have shown a link between illness and the number of stress events in a person's life. Research also indicates that stress events have a cumulative effect.

Prior Experience   Stress reactions are generally more intense when the employee has had no prior experience with the particular or similar stressor. An individual, for example, might be less threatened by a performance review if she has had previous experience with the review process.

Individual Characteristics   Various individual characteristics have been identified as being associated with stress reactions. Research suggests that individuals who are young, female, white, Protestant, from lower socioeconomic levels, and living alone tend to experience stronger reactions to stress than do others. While there is some disagreement among the experts regarding which individual characteristics are important, all agree that such differences play an important role.

The problem of managing stress is so pervasive that managerial practitioners need to be aware of reactions not only in terms of affective, cognitive, and other responses, but also need to consider the role that situation, organizational, and personal factors play.

The Manager's Role

One of a manager's most important functions in helping employees deal with stress is to recognize stress-related problems. Typically most managers would be hard pressed to recognize internally initiated physiological reactions or signs of stress. Thus, recognition of stress symptoms must typically focus on affective, cognitive, and other reactions, some of which were just discussed above.

Subtle warning signs of being stressed are what managers need to be trained to recognize. While not able or qualified to make a psychiatric diagnosis, managers, however, can be trained to identify warning signs of stress related problems (see the box below).

It is important to emphasize that simply because an employee exhibits a few of these signs in no way means that a stress problem exists. Occasionally, each of us experiences a few of these symptoms at one time or another. However, an increase in the number of warning signs a person displays, coupled with a growing frequency and intensity, can point to a stress problem. If the manager can recognize stress symptoms with even a moderate degree of accuracy, then he or she has already played an invaluable role in helping the person and the organization manage stress.

STRESS WARNING SIGNS

- A decreased quality and/or quantity of work.
- Loss of sense of humor.
- Working late or more obsessively than usual.
- Unusual or long-lasting fatigue.
- Difficulty making decisions.
- Making the safe choices, taking no risks at all.
- Anger, hostility, or outbursts of temper.
- Excessive or irrational mistrust of co-workers.
- Constant harping on failures and obsessive rumination.
- Hypochondria.
- Missing appointments or deadlines.
- Vague, disconnected speech or writing patterns.
- Sudden increase in accidents.
- Sudden increase in making careless errors.
- Difficulty communicating and getting along with others.
- Apathy.
- Sudden reversals of usual behavior: aloofness in normally friendly person; a careful worker becomes careless; shy worker becomes gregarious and vice versa; tendency of team player to want to go it alone; a casual worker becomes obsessively compulsive.

Identifying Stress Symptoms

Training managers in stress symptom identification can be an important step in coping with the increase in stress-illness lawsuits. Before outlining a specific stress identification program, let us first examine a few preliminary procedures that can be used by managers to start pinpointing stress symptoms.

What does the manager need to know in identifying stress symptoms? First, of course, the problem(s) or stressors must be identified. Is it a specific job, structural, career related, supervisory style stressor? The manager's recognition of the problem requires other information as well. How does the individual characteristically behave and perform? Are there now noticeable changes? What are the excesses and deficits shown by the employee? What kind of environmental work demands are typically placed on the employee?

The diverse and often conflicting bits of information about the employee's behavior, action tendencies, work environment demands, and so on must be systematically teased out by the manager. A manager trained in stress symptom identification would ask a set of questions:

- What are the stress symptoms that I observe? Have these symptoms been observed before? When? For how long?
- What has happened around work that could trigger off a severe stress reaction? Is this what the employee is stressed about?
- Have I been a stress carrier contributing to the employee's problems? How sure am I?
- Is there a possible medical (physical) problem? How sure am I?
- Does this employee have a long-standing personality problem that was noted long before these symptoms occurred?
- Has the employee effectively coped with stress in the past? How?
- Are there resources available (work, counseling, co-worker support, managerial support) to help reduce the symptoms?

After asking and answering these questions the manager should have a general explanation for what he or she considered to be stress symptoms. The key is not only asking but answering these probing questions. To answer the questions the manager needs to acquire a realistic picture of the individual in interaction with the environment. After all, the objective of the question and answer process is to work toward the creation of a better fit between the individual and organization by finding compatible stress levels.

Three procedures generally considered appropriate for managers to acquire a realistic picture are face-to-face interaction, observation, and self-report surveys. The manager that is knowledgeable about stress symptoms is able to discuss various objectively defined stressors that might be the reason behind the stress symptoms. Deadlines, noise, extremes of heat and cold, machine pacing, piece-work pay systems, transfer of job, change in shift pattern, and increase in number of job activities are examples of objectively defined stressors. The managers, because of knowledge about these stressors, can ask questions about them and listen to the employee's answers. Of course, answers may not be accurate. Also the answer may indicate that subjectively defined stressors (for example, role conflict, responsibility for people, pay inequity, underutilization of abilities) are implicated in the stress signs. However, since the manager is the most familiar with and has regular contact with the employee, he or she is in the best position to ask and talk about stressors and stress symptoms.

Direct observation of the employee's stress symptoms is another important method of acquiring a realistic picture of the individual-environment interaction. Managers can be trained to make direct observations to find out more about the stress symptoms, their duration, and their cause. A trained manager can make detailed observations periodically at work. These observations could include concise notations in a stress symptom log or diary. To facilitate these observations, rating scales can be used to enable the manager to indicate not only the presence or absence of stress symptoms, but also their number, duration, and severity.

A review of the attributes of self-report measurement suggests that this modality of assessing symptoms has both desirable and undesirable characteristics. An important positive property of self-report inventories concerns their economy. A self-report stress symptoms scale can be easily administered and scored; it can also be cost-efficient and brief. Probably the most compelling characteristic of the self-report method has to do with the fact that data derived arises from the individual experiencing the symptoms in question—the employee. All other observers are limited to reporting apparent versions of the individual's symptoms based upon the interpretation of face-to-face interactions or observations.

The self-report method does have some liabilities. For example, individuals do not always describe accurately experiences and behaviors. Many individuals have a response bias. That is, they give socially desirable answers or are defensive when asked personal questions. Thus, although the self-report method is useful, it should be used with other methods such as face-to-face interaction and observation.

A Training Program

The trend toward an increasing number of stress-illness lawsuits has encouraged some organizations to increase managerial proficiency in the identification of stress symptoms. A well designed, formal, structured training program can be an effective way to improve such proficiency. A growing number of organizations have experienced firsthand the benefits of providing some type of stress management training; similarly, stress identification training can be an equally effective training experience. The objectives of such programs are to improve knowledge, awareness, and symptom identification skills.

An example of a typical program is referred to as stress symptoms training (SST). This program is a seven hour, five module block of training for supervisors and managers. The objectives of the SST program are to:

- *Explain* the current judicial trend in stress-illness lawsuits.

• *Describe* stress reactions in terms of affective, cognitive, biological, and other responses.
• *Identify* factors that account for individual differences in employee responses to stress.
• *Outline* the manager's role in recognizing stress symptoms and what these symptoms are.
• *Learn* how to conduct face-to-face interaction, observation, and self-report procedures to acquire knowledge about stress symptoms.

The topics covered, training technologies used, and the anticipated results are briefly presented in the table adjacent. The SST program is designed to provide managers with an integrated and coherent plan for identifying stress symptoms. Once stress symptoms have been spotted an appropriate managerial response can be initiated. By taking stress symptoms as a focal point in managing stress, actions for correcting problems become more obvious to managers.

Although the SST program is designed for identifying symptoms in subordinates, it is also insightful for managers undergoing the training. They acquire knowledge about themselves and their own symptoms. Furthermore, skills in using and interpreting information acquired through various observation methods are learned in the SST program training experience. These skills can prove useful in coping with corporate liability for employee occupational health.

Many now realize that to effectively deal with stress in the workplace, we have to look to managers as the first line of prevention. Employee occupational health is an issue that is now beginning to transcend only concerns about productivity. Indeed, the illnesses created by stress and nourished by inadequate work environment stressors are a significant cause for managerial concern and alarm, particularly since we are witnessing a rapid acceleration in employee use of the courts to sue employers for stress-related illnesses.

Organizations now more than ever before must take—or be forced to take—decisive action to help employees deal effectively with job-related stress. If any employee shows signs of workplace stress that—correctly or not—he or she attributes to the job, a responsible employer would try to at least alleviate the work-related source. Accepting this type of responsibility is becoming a matter of legal obligation rather than an option that employers can accept or reject. Preparation through increased knowledge and training appear to be cost beneficial and socially responsible steps that employers need seriously to consider.

REVIEW QUESTIONS

1 Have you ever experienced stress? What were the causes? What were the symptoms?
2 "Employers should be held financially accountable for the impact of stress on employees." Discuss the pros and cons of this statement.
3 Examine the list of stress warning signs in the reading. Which of those are rather easy to identify in an employee? Which are rather difficult?

STRESS SYMPTOM TRAINING

Topic covered (modules)	Technology used	Time allocated	Anticipated results
Stress illness claims and compensation patterns	Lecture, case, and handouts on landmark cases.	1.5 hours	An improved understanding of the law, recent court decisions, and the future.
Stress reactions	Lecture, film, discussion, transparencies, handouts.	1 hour	An awareness of the mind-body interaction in terms of stress reactions.
Moderators: individual differences	Lecture, self-analysis, discussion, case studies.	1 hour	Knowledge about individual differences and their role in the stress-stress reaction linkage.
Managers' roles	Lecture, case vignette exercises, case analysis of critical incidents, group discussion.	1 hour	Learning to recognize various types of symptoms.
Observation skills	Lecture, case vignettes, role plays, critical incidents, diary development, self-report scale analysis (use of the stress diagnostic survey).	2.5 hours	Learning about and how to use face-to-face interaction, observation, and self-report scales.

READING 61

Executives under Fire: The Burnout Syndrome

Morley D. Glicken
Katherine Janka*

Worker burnout is suddenly a major concern in American industry and govern-ment. It may seem ironic at a time of layoffs, early retirement incentives, and other payroll cut measures, but the psychological condition of workers is a signifi-cant issue. Decreased productivity, shoddy work, high turnover, industrial sabo-tage, and high-level theft are compelling reasons to examine the causes and potential treatment of worker burnout. Because burnout at managerial levels is likely to affect workers at lower levels, this article considers burnout at the executive and managerial levels.

What Is Burnout?

There is little agreement on the definition or the cause of burnout. Many research-ers liken burnout to stress or see it as a reaction to job dissatisfaction or low morale. In our view, burnout is a unique adaptation to a variety of work-related and other factors, a clinically observable condition related to but often different from job dissatisfaction or stress.

Burnout, in our experience, is a type of existential crisis in which work is no longer a meaningful function. Burned-out workers may evidence high levels of apathy, depression, and lethargy—or they may not. The unifying factor is that such individuals no longer view their jobs as meaningful or important. Rather, work has become tedious, redundant, and insignificant. Whatever the cause, the act of work itself no longer satisfies the intrinsic needs of the executive. Burned-out executives feel either little enthusiasm for their work or an all-encompassing fatigue, which may show itself in the form of boredom, depression, and a powerful sense of alienation.

Burned-out executives may superficially appear to function adequately, but a careful look at their work-related behavior suggests that quality, quantity, creativ-ity, enthusiasm, and true contribution to the organization are in jeopardy. Often, burned-out executives demonstrate a combination of the following predictable behaviors: a tendency to blame others in the organization for their burnout, to complain bitterly about aspects of work which in the past were not areas of concern, to miss work because of nonspecific and increasingly prevalent illness, to daydream or sleep on the job, to be the last to come to work and the first to leave,

*Reprinted from *California Management Review*, vol. XXIV, no. 3, pp. 67–72, by permission of the Regents. © 1982 by the Regents of the University of California.

to bicker with coworkers or appear uncooperative, and to become increasingly isolated from others. Burned-out executives typically voice feelings that their present job does not seem suited to their needs and that outside pressures, such as financial need or parental manipulation, have forced them to work in fields unrelated to their real interests. It is not unusual for executives experiencing burnout to share with others fantasies about work in a totally different field or a desire to quit work and travel.

The Cause of Burnout

Executive burnout is a complex psycho-social state which may have a variety of causes. In our experience, it often stems from the following conditions.

Work Overstimulation   Overwork is commonly considered a major cause of burnout. We believe that overwork is seldom a cause of burnout if organization objectives are clear and a commitment to those objectives exists. However, when work takes place in a chaotic, unstable environment which encourages confusion about current duties and future directions, burnout is a likely result. Executives who feel that they are increasingly "putting out fires" are most likely to experience burnout as a result of overstimulation. Work as a reaction to crises, rather than a drive toward clear goals, often results in a sense of hopelessness, dejection, and immobilization.

Work Understimulation   When work continually fails to challenge and there seems little opportunity for future excitement, burnout is a distinct possibility. Executives frequently need a sense of challenge related to new problems and complex solutions. When work begins to lose its ability to stimulate and settles into a predictable routine, the probability of burnout is significantly increased.

Personal Problems   Times of extreme personal crisis and stress often affect an executive's productivity. It is not unusual for executives experiencing personal problems to feel less excitement about work than before or to experience the incapacitating emotional drain such personal problems may create. In fact, executives with a predisposition to burnout may be strongly affected by problems unrelated to work, having neither the internal mechanisms nor experience to resolve personal difficulties without spillover to the work place.

Job Mismatch   Often, executives choose jobs because of such extrinsic rewards as high salaries, status, and power, rewards which may initially heighten self-esteem. However, decisions to choose extrinsic rewards over intrinsic rewards frequently result in considerable unhappiness. Extrinsic rewards usually have limited ability to motivate executives and, in time, the lack of genuine gratification from work may lead to burnout. Other examples of mismatch are differences in personal and organizational values, in need and allowance for autonomy, and in need and allowance for use of special competencies.

Low Organizational Productivity   An executive may have excellent mental health, work satisfaction, and organizational commitment. If, however, the organization's objectives are not being met and the result is low productivity and reduced quality, burnout is possible. This is particularly the case when executives believe that they have limited ability to solve organizational problems and that outside factors, such as governmental regulations or labor strife, are primary reasons for low organizational achievement. Burnout may also occur in those organizations in which proper bureaucratic postures are more important than measurable productivity.

Treatment and Prevention

Executive burnout can often be treated, and even prevented, within the organizational framework. In fact, it is the potential for remediation that distinguishes the burned-out executive from the "burned-up" executive. The burned-out individual is smoldering in place, riddled with stress and dissatisfaction and responding with an ever-intensifying loss of energy and interest. The burned-up individual has progressed to such a degree of lethargy and immobilization that he or she is generally destined for a radical event, such as mental or physical illness, sudden resignation, or involuntary termination.

Unfortunately, in the absence of either organizational assistance or individual competence for self-help, many executives facing burnout inaccurately diagnose themselves as burned up. They determine that it is too late to regenerate the vitality and enjoyment they once experienced in their work, but they stick with it for a while anyway, not so much in hope as in indecisiveness about the next step. While "hanging in there," they rarely attempt positive remedies. Instead they let the symptoms of burnout spill over to families and friends.

When this state becomes sufficiently intolerable, many executives call a halt by opting for a dramatic change just at the time when they may be least psychologically prepared to make reasoned personal decisions. The resultant actions include career change, early retirement, divorce, and geographic relocation, steps that often prove to be regrettable at worst and avoidable at best.

One thirty-six-year-old manager we spoke with had, a year earlier, dealt a radical blow to his own burnout symptoms. Plagued by stress on the job, financial worries, and personal problems, he submitted his resignation just as he was finally being considered for a promotion to a position he had always desired. He also sold his house, his car, and a small business he had owned on the side. After a year of travel and whittling away at savings, he stated, "I have had a lot of fun this year, but I still have no idea what I'll do when my money runs out—which will be soon. I don't really regret leaving, but I do fear that I may have to return to the same sort of job, life style, and problems."

The Organization's Role

For such individuals, early and deliberate attempts to search out causes and cures for burnout may provide more satisfactory solutions than those found in a traumatic downhill slide followed by radical change. While this argument is not meant to advocate the application of a band-aid when a tourniquet it needed, it does imply that organizations and individuals should seek ways to remedy burnout rather than simply respond to its symptoms. Without a considered effort to remedy burnout, organizations stand to lose top-level human resources, either by their departure or deficient performance, and individuals risk suffering continued stress and destructive coping mechanisms.

Two obvious areas in which organizations can take an active role in the fight against executive burnout are prevention and treatment. Preventative measures generally can be applied organizationwide, while treatment programs often must be tailored to each individual.

To prevent executive burnout and its negative impact on the organization and individuals, organizations can learn to recognize the potential for burnout before the fact. This requires an openness to critical self-examination and a resistance to rationalization of the sort that claims, "He just couldn't take the high performance standards we set around here anymore." The three elements that are crucial to the process of prevention are the recognition of early warning signals, the diagnosis of potential causes, and the development of prevention strategies.

Early Warning and Diagnosis

While early indications of burnout may be confused, sporadic, and short-lived, clinical signs to be noted with concern include:

- periods of sustained lethargy or lack of consistent productivity;
- preoccupation with non-work related issues;
- a deep, if superficially considered, concern about the meaning of one's life;
- a tendency to feel that changing one's job and living arrangement may improve one's happiness on the job;
- a tendency to change jobs often without evidence of upward job mobility and increased responsibility;
- the indication that an executive is a loner but that isolation causes the executive acute discomfort;
- evidence that at crucial periods an executive may create situations which inhibit the possibility of personal success;
- failure to analyze future directions and a tendency to be directionless or claim that no direction is the best direction; and
- recent traumatic personal experiences such as death of someone close, illness, or divorce.

The diagnostic element of prevention requires inquiry into the various factors of organizational life that may ultimately contribute to burnout. These may emanate from the organization and its policies and practices, from the nature of the work and the way in which it is accomplished, or from the personal characteristics of individual employees. It is likely, in fact, that all three of these areas harbor potential causes of burnout, especially in terms of possibilities for a mismatch between the individual, the work task, and the organizational structure and norms.

A diagnosis of the organization requires consideration of both the informal and formal interaction systems and how they are likely to agree with the values and needs of employees. A highly bureaucratic organization may be congruent with employees who have low growth needs and are satisfied with predictable and repetitive tasks. However, employees who are stimulated by more creative and complex tasks and the opportunity for growth may quickly burn out in such a setting.

Additional causes which may be generated by the organization itself are those which contribute to unstable work environments and career ambiguity. Organizations which undergo substantial internal change or financial uncertainty are likely to produce signs of burnout among executives who feel they are continually fighting against having the rug pulled out from under them. A major structural change, such as a shift from a purely hierarchical system to matrix management, leaves executives questioning their own competence and career futures.

For some individuals, especially those who have arrived at the executive suite by moving through the ranks, the nature of the work itself can cause burnout. Depending on an individual's personal orientation, the executive functions may produce a syndrome of overstimulation or understimulation. Such is the case with the successful scientist who is excited by laboratory research but later, as an executive, finds administrative tasks boring. Likewise, the overstimulation of seventy-hour work weeks, full calendars, travel, and major responsibilities creates awesome opportunities for burnout.

Any diagnosis of individuals largely concerns the fit between their personal characteristics and the characteristics of the job and the organization. It is important that some understanding of the type of people who comprise the executive ranks of an organization exist. Are they creative technicians or politically astute entrepreneurs? Are they professional managers or did they rise through the ranks? Do they enjoy change and challenge, or do they prefer stability and security? Are they stimulated by the work itself or by other factors, such as association with colleagues? Why are they working for this particular organization?

Prevention

The prevention strategies which may be undertaken by the organization include:

- seeking a fit between characteristics of the individual, complexity of the job, and type of organizational structure;
- developing programs which help individuals cope with the causes of stress that lead to burnout; and
- teaching and supporting self-diagnosis and individual adaptation strategies for addressing burnout symptoms.

Efforts to assure a fit of organization, task and individual are the most elusive of these three categories. Generally, they must rely on individual and organizational awareness of the need for such a fit and the qualities that contribute to it. Such awareness can be supported by studies and surveys of executives themselves, the way their work is performed, and their perceptions of the organization.

Career development programs have been particularly useful in helping individuals assess their own capacities and needs, as well as the characteristics of jobs and values of the organization. Such programs need to be supported by organizational practices which reward the contributions of all highly competent professionals and do not reinforce the notion that executive ladder climbing is the sole sign of achievement. Experiments with dual career ladders, offering both technical and managerial rungs, provide some indication that organizations are seeking new strategies in this area, but they need to be carefully structured and monitored so that one ladder does not become a dumping ground for those who cannot make it on the other.

Additionally, organizations need to increase efforts to assure that the right person is selected for each job and to encourage change (without the stigma of retreat) when that does not occur. The use of assessment centers and rotational assignments allows companies to determine executive potential. However, they should be combined with candid feedback to individuals involved and efforts to encourage prospective executives to examine their own personal adaptability to the various functions required.

The organization must be flexible enough to accommodate various perspectives and values concerning executive work. For example, some executives may work twelve-hour days and never burn out, while others who are just as effective may need more time away from the office. Some may seek solitude, while others may thrive on conferences and negotiations with others. The organization that values and rewards only one type of executive may find it is contributing to the burnout of valuable resources. While job redesign efforts have centered on the functions of lower- and middle-level employees, they can be equally germane to enriching the work lives of top managers.

In a study of techniques used by workers to combat burnout, Christina Maslach found that sanctioned "time-outs" were "critically important for professionals."[1] Time-outs were defined as not merely short breaks, such as coffee breaks or rest periods, but opportunities in which the professional could choose other, less stressful work. Such findings indicate the usefulness of sabbaticals and mitigate against pay for accrued leave time which might discourage employees from taking vacations.

Company programs that help employees deal with stress-producing problems which affect work performance are growing in popularity but are generally utilized below the executive ranks. The employee assistance programs may be staffed by in-house counselors who help employees with legal, financial, family, alcohol, drug, and other problems, and who can guide employees to additional outside resources.

Top executives are typically reluctant to avail themselves of such programs, either because they do not want to admit that they have problems or because they do not want to identify with that segment of the work force comprising the major users of the programs. An alternative is to set apart special programs for executives, using a separate staff counselor or consultants and counselors from outside the organization. The probability of success of such a program can be greatly enhanced through initial orientation and training that breaks down reluctance to admit problems and through surveys of executives to determine what needs should be addressed by the program.

In the long run, it is the responsibility of each individual to recognize the signals of burnout and devise a personal strategy for dealing with his or her unique situation. Organizations, however, may help by providing information and education which help executives understand burnout and identify personal strategies to prevent it. Additionally, such support clearly signals that the organization is committed to assisting its top-level people and does not consider human needs a sign of failure.

We have found that programs which seek to assist burned-out workers, individually or in groups, work best when supported by consultation aimed at helping the organization develop positive support programs, such as career counseling, employee assistance programs, and educational strategies.

Treatment

In the process of treating a variety of workers who identified burnout symptoms as primary indicators of work-related pathology, we have developed an approach to treatment which suggests potential for counselors and therapists treating burnout. We call the approach Career Enhancement Therapy (CET). CET is designed to help burned-out workers achieve the following behavioral objectives:

- evaluate and understand the cause of burnout both at the obvious and the complex levels;
- determine changes, both personal and organizational, necessary to return to normal work-related functioning;
- develop sensitivity to the signs of burnout to help a worker cope more successfully with similar future episodes; and
- develop skills in discussing feelings and emotions which need to be processed with others so that burnout is less likely to occur in the future.

We have found that therapy is most effective when offered to a group of approximately twelve to fifteen executives. The approach, with its goal of helping executives design new strategies for coping with burnout, depends upon the ability of group members to develop a climate which encourages spontaneous and helpful interaction. It depends further upon the willingness of executives, who often lack introspection and self-awareness, to risk themselves by moving into a form of self and group evaluation which may be a unique and sometimes bewildering experience.

Our usual approach is to spend initial meetings with group members discussing the causes of burnout, techniques useful in changing burned-out behavior, and an explanation of the treatment used to help individuals in the group learn to change their behavior.

Burned-out executives are often unable to discuss the personal nature of their burnout and instead intellectualize or rationalize the causes. Our experience to date suggests that positive change generally does not occur until group members begin to look carefully at their own behavior, share it with others, establish awareness of the complexities of the behavior, and learn the often giddy and reinforcing skill of practicing new approaches to a problem initially recommended by others in the group. CET is very behavioral in the sense of attempting to establish new patterns of work-related behavior which may, in time, reduce or eliminate burnout. Sensitivity, insight, and awareness, while often important elements of treatment, are quite secondary to functional changes in behavior. Burned-out executives should, as a result of treatment, function at a more productive and less stressful level. They should be able to achieve prescribed goals which modify their painful behavior. If successful, treatment should lead to measurable improvements in an executive's work-related functioning.

After considerable experimentation, we found that CET is most effective when it is offered in a small group of twelve to fifteen executives in a two-day, eight-hour-a-day treatment session. The initial two-day session is followed up by six monthly four-hour group meetings to check on improvement and to offer the support and encouragement necessary for continued change.

Career Enhancement Therapy is, of course, not meant to be an intensive form of psychotherapy, and workers experiencing severe personal trauma, which may need a specific regimen of psychotherapy, are discouraged from group participation.

Summary: Out of the Frying Pan?

The foregoing discussion has delineated individual and organizational roles in addressing the problem of executive burnout. The individual and the organization both have a stake in assuring the health, productivity, and satisfaction of top-level executives. When these factors are jeopardized by debilitating burnout, both share responsibility for positive action.

REFERENCES

1 Christina Maslach, "Burn Out," *Human Behavior* (September 1976).

REVIEW QUESTIONS

1 Study the meaning of executive burnout. How does this differ from the definition of stress in the previous reading?

2 Review the Pierce reading on job design. What factors in the job could be manipulated to reduce the probability of executive burnout?

3 According to the authors, burnout is "suddenly a major concern." Why is burnout such a recent phenomenon?

READING 62

Counseling in Industry: A Selected Review of the Literature

Peter C. Cairo*

During the past decade there has been an increasing recognition in industry of the importance of providing help for employees with personal problems. Several recent surveys have attempted to document the extent to which industry is providing assistance for problems such as alcoholism, mental disorders, drug abuse, and various situational crises (American Society for Personnel Administration and The Bureau of National Affairs, 1978; Follman, 1978; Ralston, 1977). There has been similar involvement in the creation of programs for facilitating employees' career development (Griffith, 1980; Morgan, Hall, and Martier, 1979; Walker and Gutteridge, 1979) and easing the transition from work into retirement (Corporate Committee for Retirement Planning, 1980; Siegel and Rives, 1978). Many businesses consider the provision of these services a part of their corporate responsibility. Others acknowledge that personal problems or career dissatisfaction can adversely affect job performance and possibly overall company effectiveness. The purpose of this paper is to summarize what is known about (a) the extent to which personal and career counseling programs and services exist within industry and (b) the effectiveness of various counseling programs in dealing with specific employee problems or concerns.

The review is divided into three major sections. The first will describe various programs and research involving counseling for personal problems. This will be followed by a summary of efforts by industry to provide various forms of career counseling and guidance. Finally, the last section will offer several conclusions about the current state of counseling in industry and discuss some implications for future research and evaluation.

PERSONAL COUNSELING

Personal counseling in industry generally refers to employers' efforts to help troubled employees with problems that have a direct or an indirect effect on their job performance. Typically these employees are identified when they exhibit substandard performance due to problems such as alcoholism, mental disorders, and stress or situational crises involving marital relationships, financial matters, legal difficulties, etc. Employee services can take many forms—the establishment of direct in-house services, procedures for making referrals to community agencies, contracts for services with outside consultants, or direct provision of

*From *Personnel Psychology*, Spring 1983, pp. 1–18. Reprinted with permission.

services or referrals by trained supervisory personnel. The approach taken by an organization is determined by a number of factors such as available resources, number of employees, the extent to which services are available in the community, and the organization's policy regarding its own responsibility for helping troubled employees.

Personal problems can generally be categorized as either chronic or situational. The former include alcoholism, drug abuse, and mental disorders and normally require the help of professionals trained in clinical treatment methods, e.g., psychiatrists, clinical psychologists, and psychiatric social workers. Crises involving marital, legal, financial, and family matters are generally considered situational. From the standpoint of service delivery, however, this distinction is not always clear. Most of the programs described below provide services for employees with both types of problems. These services may entail referral to other professionals in-house or in the community, but the point is that there appears to be a growing trend in industry to provide comprehensive services for all types of personal problems (Follman, 1978). This trend has also made it difficult to summarize the extent of industry's involvement in the treatment of any one problem or type of problem. The one possible exception is programs created specifically to deal with the problem of alcoholism, a longstanding concern in industry. Treatment for alcoholism is perhaps the most common type of service made available by industry. It is also a problem about which much has been written. Consequently, this section will begin by briefly summarizing what is known about the extent and effectiveness of alcoholism programs in industry, and will be followed by a review of programs which offer counseling for other types of personal problems or include alcoholism treatment only as one of a number of counseling services provided.

Alcoholism Treatment Programs

The problem of alcoholism has an enormous impact on industry. Estimates of its cost in dollars range from $5 billion to $12 billion annually (Filipowitz, 1979; Follman, 1978; Ralston, 1977) taking into account the effects of absenteeism, tardiness, accidents, turnover, substandard job performance, and the expense of providing treatment and benefits to employees with an alcohol problem. Pell and D'Alonzo (1970) report that the disability rate for alcoholism is 13 days per year as compared to 5.8 days per year for non-alcoholics. Furthermore, it has been estimated that between 5% and 10% of the work force have a drinking problem which adversely affects their job performance (Perkins, 1978; Ralston, 1977).

Although the problem of alcoholism is widespread, it is difficult to determine precisely how many treatment programs exist. Gibson (1978) reports that the number of programs for alcoholics had risen from 50 in 1950 to 2400 in 1977. Follman's (1978) estimate, based on figures provided by the National Institute of Alcohol Abuse and Alcoholism, is more conservative. He indicates that approximately 1200 places of employment have established alcohol control programs.

While in neither case was the method for arriving at these figures described in detail, both authors agreed that the number of programs has grown rapidly over the past decade and that this trend is likely to continue.

Most alcoholism treatment programs use the same criterion for determining success: a return to work with no recurrence of the problem which prompted the action (e.g., chronic absenteeism, tardiness, etc). However, the period of time over which an employee's subsequent performance is examined varies from company to company as does the type of alcohol control program being implemented. Ralston (1977) conducted a survey of the 50 largest U.S. companies to determine the extent and type of alcohol control programs. Thirty-five companies responded, of which 25 had formal programs. Only eleven companies reported specific evaluation of their treatment program. All eleven used satisfactory performance over a specific period of time, normally one to two years, as the criterion for measuring success. Reported recovery rates ranged from 50% to 90%. A separate study by Carson (1976) claimed that a divisional level program at General Electric was 75% effective using a similar criterion. Using the criterion of two years post-treatment without a recurrence of poor job performance, a 70% success rate was achieved with 250 employees at the Kemper Insurance Companies who were treated over a three year period during the mid-1970's (Lavino, 1978). It must be kept in mind that these results are not comparable since there were differences in the length of time over which post-treatment job performance was examined. This problem is further complicated by the failure of these studies to describe the type of alcohol control program used for treatment. Nevertheless, these figures are consistent with Follman's (1978) review which reported recovery rates of 60% to 80% in what he described as well-conceived alcoholism control programs in industry. The following section describes several programs which were created to help employees with other types of personal problems, besides alcoholism.

Personal Counseling Programs

Only one known study has attempted to determine the extent to which personal counseling programs exist in industry. A joint survey was conducted by the American Society for Personnel Administration and the Bureau of National Affairs (1978) to determine which companies dealt with employees' personal problems. "Problem" was defined as alcoholism, prescription drug abuse, marijuana abuse, hard drug addiction, emotional illness requiring psychiatric treatment, and personal crisis situations. Questionnaires were mailed to a random sample of ASPA members. The total number of questionnaires distributed was not reported, but 65 members were said to have responded. More than one-third of those who did respond represented small companies (those with 500 or fewer employees). One-half of the companies reported offering some form of in-house counseling for personal crises and alcoholism. However, in-house counseling was frequently described as informal, in most cases consisting only of a discussion between supervisor and employee before the employee was referred to an outside agency. The conclusions drawn by the authors of this survey are open to question because of the absence of important information about the way it was conducted and the failure to report more detailed results. Nevertheless, it does appear that, at least among the companies reporting, what is typically labelled "counseling" is little more than a brief consultation leading to referral outside the company. The adequacy of this approach is dubious, particularly in view of the respondents' own impressions of their programs' effectiveness. Each respondent was asked to rate, on a four point scale ranging from poor to excellent, the effectiveness of their method of dealing with employee problems. The vast majority rated their approach poor (28%) or only fair (62%).

The absence of research on the effectiveness of personal counseling programs in industry was mentioned above. It is particularly disappointing to find so little in the way of evaluation in view of the growing interest in creating new programs and expanding existing ones. One exception is a study conducted by Weiner, Akabas, and Sommer (1973). With the support and assistance of the clothing industry in New York City, the Amalgamated Clothing Workers of America developed a mental health care component as part of an existing health services clinic. An evaluation of the project was conducted over a three year period during the mid-1960's. During that time 718 workers were referred, of whom 442 were evaluated and provided with services for various mental health problems. While still on the job, but receiving services from the clinic, these workers were compared to a random sample of 5% of the work force in the same industry and matched to control for variables which might affect the outcome, such as age, sex, work experience, etc. The criterion variable used for comparison of the two groups was quarterly earnings. Since all workers were paid by the number of pieces they produced, this was considered a reasonable indicator of their effectiveness on the job. One of this study's significant findings was that there were no differences between the earnings of those workers in treatment and their match peer group doing comparable work. Specific descriptions of both service providers and the range and type of services available at the clinic, however, were not reported.

The programs summarized in the remainder of this section have been included, despite weaknesses or lack of detailed descriptions of their evaluation designs, for two reasons. First, they were the only other programs identified which made any effort to evaluate effectiveness. Second, they offer examples of different approaches to providing counseling, namely, in-house counseling, referral to community resources, contracting with outside counseling agencies, and training employees to perform specific counseling functions.

Weissman (1975) described the development of the United States Steel South Works Counseling Center. Three social workers provided both referral services and in-house counseling for approximately 500 employees and/or family members who used services during the program's first four months. The only effort to evaluate effectiveness involved gathering self-report data from employees who had used the services. A questionnaire was sent to a random sample of one-half of the center's first 160 cases. Sixty-one (76%) individuals responded, of whom 80%

reported that the situation or problem presented at the center had improved and 74% indicated that they had received the kind of treatment they wanted. Neither the type of problem for which the respondent had sought help nor the service provided was reported. Moreover, no other outcomes were evaluated.

The Kennecott Copper Corporation's INSIGHT program relies exclusively on community resources as referrals for employees with personal problems. In addition to providing a description of this program Skidmore, Balsam, and Jones (1974) reported that separate studies had found "dramatic" improvement in employees exhibiting chronic absenteeism who received help through INSIGHT. In one study, 77% of a group of 83 employees who received counseling through the program were reported to have improved their attendance significantly. In a separate study of 150 male employees, attendance improved by an average of 52%, weekly indemnity costs decreased by 74.6%, and hospital, medical, and surgical costs for these employees dropped by 55.4%.

A different approach for providing personal counseling services to employees was used by the Norton Company of Massachusetts (Marshall, 1976). Rather than provide in-house counseling or formal referral services, "counselors" were selected from among the work force to serve as liaisons between workers in the plant and the personnel department. Their function, despite being referred to as counselors, was primarily helping supervisors to provide information on personnel practices and policies. The program was reported to have succeeded in reducing turnover and absenteeism, but no specific studies were described or cited.

For many small companies the cost of providing in-house counseling or perhaps even comprehensive referral services is sometimes prohibitive. Some of these companies have responded to this problem by contracting for services with a specific agency which provides counseling. Family Counseling of Greater New Haven provided services to both Olin Corporation and Southern Connecticut Gas Company (Brooks, 1975; Reardon, 1976). Workers who exhibited substandard job performance were referred for counseling if their supervisors were unable to handle the problem. No data concerning the effectiveness of the services were reported.

Related Research

In addition to identifying the results of program evaluations, this survey was intended to summarize other research directly related to personal counseling in industry, for example, studies comparing the outcome of various counseling methods or examining the critical characteristics of professionals providing counseling. Only one relevant study has been identified. Burnaska (1976) reported the results of a study to determine the effects of behavior modeling training on managers' behaviors and employees' perceptions. This study was judged to be relevant since one of the objectives of training was to enhance managers' counseling and discussion skills. The experimental group was composed of 62 middle level managers who had received the behavior modeling training. The control group consisted of 62 middle level managers who had not received training. Each subject's behavior was rated by trained judges in each of three simulated situations. Ratings were based on specific, operationally defined behaviors which were central to the objectives of the training. All subjects were tested immediately following the experimental group's training and again four months later. In addition, questionnaires were distributed to managers' employees to assess perceived improvement. The results of this study indicated that subjects in the experimental group performed significantly better than those in the control group. It was also found that performance after four months was better than just after training. This rather surprising finding was explained by suggesting that the opportunity to practice the skills taught in training led to significant improvement. Finally, few significant changes were found to have occurred in employees' perceptions of their managers despite the improvement in skills.

It is obvious that a great need exists for more and better studies of personal counseling in industry. The extent to which services are available is still relatively unclear. While there does appear to have been an increase in personal counseling services in recent years, additional investigations are required to get a more complete and accurate picture of their availability. Likewise relatively little is known about the effectiveness of various programs. In many companies counseling appears to be viewed as an "extra" service to employees, and efforts to evaluate effectiveness would make programs prohibitive in cost. With the exception of some alcoholism treatment programs, which seem to have achieved a fairly high level of success, few well-conceived evaluations have been conducted. Many programs use substandard job performance as both an indicator of possible personal problems and as a stimulus for recommending counseling. This is not a simple criterion to measure, but is probably more observable and relevant than behavior external to the work setting. Consequently, this would seem to provide at least one obvious criterion for evaluating the effectiveness of counseling, as evidenced by alcoholism treatment programs where a successful outcome was defined as an employee returning to the job without exhibiting the difficulty which led to treatment. While other methodological considerations would have to be taken into account, this criterion could be employed more widely and systematically in other studies.

CAREER COUNSELING AND GUIDANCE

A variety of methods have been employed by industry for promoting the career development of employees. Some take the form of information services designed to increase awareness of job opportunities in the company. Others provide support for continuing education through tuition aid programs or make available in-house training opportunities for enhancing career-relevant skills. Still others take the form of personal interactions with trained professionals who instruct, guide, and advise employees on planning their careers. However, not all of these career interventions fall within the domain of this review since the specific focus here is on counseling.

In order to help delineate the scope of this part of the review, Herr and Cramer's (1979) definition of career counseling was followed. They define career counseling as a "largely verbal process in which a counselor and counselee(s) are in dynamic interaction and in which the counselor employs a repertoire of diverse behaviors to bring about self-understanding and action in the form of good decision-making in the counselee, who has responsibility for his or her own actions" (p. 274). This definition was used as a guide for identifying and discussing the types of career interventions which seemed most appropriate to include. For example, programs which were restricted to training or providing financial assistance for continuing education were not considered. Only those programs and services which were devoted entirely to career counseling or which provided counseling among several other forms of career assistance were included.

Existing Services in Industry

Griffith (1980) conducted a survey of the career development services provided by the Fortune 500 companies. Questionnaires were mailed to each company's vice-president in charge of personnel. Twenty-three percent of the companies contacted responded. Owing to the low response rate, it is unclear to what extent the results of this study are representative of industry as a whole. It was found, however, that approximately 30% of the respondents offered counseling to facilitate career exploration and planning; 43% provided job separation (i.e., outplacement) counseling; and 56% had some form of retirement planning program. These services were usually provided under the direction of the personnel department, and in most cases development, implementation, and supervision of career guidance services were assigned to one individual who also had other job responsibilities.

Walker and Gutteridge (1979) conducted a survey of career planning practices in industry. Questionnaires were sent to 1,117 companies. The 225 companies which responded represented a wide variety of industries (e.g., manufacturing, banking, retail services, health care, etc.) of various sizes (i.e., from companies with sales or budgets under $50 million to companies with sales or budgets over $1 billion). While the responding companies indicated wide support for the concept of career planning, there appeared to be a wide gap between what was desired and the reality of actual practices. The two most prevalent types of career planning assistance available to employees were informal counseling by personnel staff and/or supervisors and disseminating information about related services such as educational assistance, equal employment opportunity programs, affirmative action, etc. Most companies reported viewing career planning as a serious need, not simply a fad, and an important part of overall employee development. Yet the results of the survey led the authors to conclude that for most companies career planning remains a largely informal, experimental, and fragmented activity.

The only other survey of career development practices in industry was reported by Morgan, Hall, and Martier (1979). They conducted a telephone survey of 56 companies in the Chicago area, including manufacturers, distributors, banks, retail companies, and insurance companies of from 130 to 125,000 employees. Numerous career activities were identified, among them career counseling, career pathing, career information systems, training, and programs for special groups. However, no data were presented identifying in which activities specific companies were engaged.

These surveys would suggest that the existence of career counseling and guidance services is relatively common in industry. Yet a thorough review of the professional literature yielded much the same result as in the case of personal counseling. Very few detailed program descriptions were identified and virtually all of these failed to describe any attempt to evaluate program effectiveness. The literature is replete with articles of the "how-to-do-it" variety, prescriptive models for implementing various forms of career assistance. Other articles offered program descriptions which were incomplete and superficial.

Only one report was identified which described an effort to evaluate, to some degree, the impact of a career counseling program on its employees. Hanson (1981) described on-going career activities at the Lawrence Livermore Laboratories, where employees are offered a combination of career development workshops, manuals, and professional counseling. The workshops encourage employees to engage in a number of self-awareness exercises and to identify what are described as job-motivated skills (i.e., those activities which an individual performs well and enjoys performing). The objectives of counseling are to help the employee synthesize the workshop experiences, to look for patterns, to define specific career goals, and to examine present qualifications and required training. Participants' self-reports indicated an increased awareness of choices in career decisions, of factors related to decision-making, and acceptance of personal responsibility for managing their own careers. Supervisor ratings elicited six months after the conclusion of the program revealed that at least half of the participants showed improvement in the quality and quantity of their work, their morale, and their ability to communicate effectively with their peers and supervisors. Additional data collected six months following the completion of the program indicated that a large number of participants were found to have engaged in a variety of career-related behaviors such as enrolling in courses, workshops, or self-development programs and pursuing new avocational activities. Finally, based on pretest-posttest differences on a measure of career adjustment, participants were found to have improved significantly their perceptions of being in control of actions related to their careers. Statistically significant differences were not found for increases in the accomplishment of specific career-related tasks and goals or increase in job involvement.

Related Research

As is the case with specific program evaluations, research on other topics related to career counseling is scarce. Super and Hall (1978) point out, "in view of the great number of training activities in industry specifically devoted to career planning, it is disappointing that there is so little published research on their effectiveness" (p. 360).

One exception is a study of methods for increasing self-development activities through career planning which was conducted by Miller, Blass, and Mihal (Note 1). Four hundred and fifty research and development employees from two major laboratories engaged in a variety of career planning efforts such as forecasting, goal-setting, action-planning, and group discussions. Follow-up data were then gathered from personal files to identify the extent and type of self-development activities in which the subjects engaged. Additional data were obtained from interviews and questionnaires. The results indicated that career planning enhanced the likelihood of certain self-development activities, but only for personnel at lower levels. Self-analysis and action-planning were found useful at higher levels; no effect of career planning on middle level personnel was observed.

In another related study, Thornton (1978) examined the differential effects of career planning on individuals who differed with respect to the belief that behavior is controlled by the individual and not by external events (internal vs. external locus of control). The subjects of this study were 95 secretaries working in companies throughout the Rocky Mountain Region. All subjects participated in a six-hour workshop consisting of small group discussions and specific career planning activities. A modified measure of internal/external locus of control was administered at the beginning of the workshop. Four months after the workshop a questionnaire inquiring about specific career behaviors was sent to all subjects of whom 66% returned them with completed responses. A content analysis of subject responses was conducted to determine the type and number of actions taken in three areas: identifying current strengths and developmental needs, exploring potential opportunities, and specifying and implementing means of attaining career goals. A median-split on the internal/external locus of control dimension scores was used to divide the original sample into two equal-sized groups. Results of the study showed that internals engaged in more career activities related to exploring opportunities and specifying and implementing means of attaining career goals. There was no difference between the two groups in the extent to which they engaged in activities related to identifying strengths and developmental needs. While there were certain limitations to this study, such as the absence of clear evidence that it was actually the workshop that affected the outcome and uncertainty as to the extent of career progress achieved by engaging in these activities, it is the only study found which has attempted to establish a relationship between differential effects of a career planning activity and a specific personality trait for employees working in a business setting.

It should also be pointed out that although there appear to be few studies of career counseling in industry, there is a large body of literature on career interventions investigated with populations outside of business and industry. The information which has been accumulated over the years on various forms of career assistance, including career counseling, group treatments, instructional materials, and occupational information, is considerable and has recently been summarized by Oliver (1979) and Holland, Magoon, and Spokane (1981).

Pre-Retirement Counseling

One form of career assistance which has received considerable attention during the last few years is pre-retirement counseling owing, in part, to the elimination of mandatory retirement at age 65. Several recent surveys of the Fortune 500 companies indicated that pre-retirement programs which consisted of more than a brief discussion of pension and social security benefits were already in place or were nearly ready to implement (The Corporate Committee for Retirement Planning, 1980; Siegel and Rives, 1978). The availability of these services in smaller companies in the rest of the industry was impossible to determine.

In contrast to other forms of counseling in industry which have been discussed thus far, a review of relevant literature revealed several reports of pre-retirement program evaluations. O'Rourke and Friedman (1972) in a counseling program for small plant managers, found no differences among two treatment groups and one control group on either attitude toward retirement or acquisition of relevant retirement information. Boyack and Tiberi (Note 2) compared three approaches to pre-retirement planning: group counseling; an information-media approach involving videotape cassette programs, booklets, and informal discussion; and lectures on relevant topics. The group counseling and lecture-discussion approaches were found to be most effective in improving attitudes. The latter also proved to be better than the other two approaches in helping participants acquire information. Glamser and DeJong (1975) found that individuals participating in a group discussion which focused on a variety of relevant topics had greater knowledge of retirement issues and had engaged in more preparatory activities than those who received an individual briefing about retirement benefits.

Several problems are revealed by a review of the pre-retirement counseling literature. First, it is difficult to determine precisely the extent to which services are available in industry and how comprehensive they are. While several surveys have been conducted, the generally low response rates raise doubts about their representativeness. And since most surveys drew responses only from the largest American corporations, the extent to which pre-retirement counseling services exist in smaller companies is unknown.

A second problem concerns the relationship between programs' objectives and their methods of achieving them. On the basis of the criteria used to assess effectiveness, pre-retirement counseling programs are typically concerned with two outcomes: (a) increasing knowledge about retirement issues and (b) improving attitudes toward retirement. However, program treatments are not always compatible with these intended outcomes. Kasschau (1974), in a review of pre-retirement planning programs, concluded that most programs claim to affect attitude toward retirement, but end up increasing knowledge about retirement issues without influencing attitudes. She distinguishes between the planning and counseling functions of pre-retirement programs, the former being primarily informational and the latter attitudinal. The implication is that counseling is not effective in influencing attitudes. However, this conclusion seems premature in view of the fact that most of the studies which examined the effects of the counseling function on attitudes involved their subjects in what must be considered weak interventions, sometimes only a brief session with an untrained member of a personnel department. The only study which did report significant positive changes in attitudes engaged subjects in a much more intensive group counseling experience. This issue is further complicated by the increasing amount of evidence suggesting that attitudes toward retirement are not as negative as some program developers and researchers have presumed. Several studies revealed "ceiling effects," explaining the absence of significant changes by pointing out that the level of pretest scores left little room for measurable improvement. Clearly, more investigations are required in order to determine the effectiveness of counseling interventions on retirement attitudes including the development of more sophisticated measures with broader range. Similarly, greater effort should be invested in determining the needs of the target population before they are involved in any pre-retirement planning program.

DISCUSSION

The purpose of this paper was to summarize what is known about counseling in industry. Two questions provided a focus for the review of literature: (1) To what extent do personal and career counseling services exist in industry? and (2) How effective are they in helping employees with various problems and concerns? Perhaps the most significant finding to emerge is that there are very few published studies which shed any light on these questions. Despite the increasing number of companies which appear to have instituted some form of counseling to assist employees with personal problems or career development, the vast majority of the numerous publications identified for consideration were judged to be inappropriate for this review. Most were brief articles recommending a type of counseling approach or method of dealing with employee problems which had been neither implemented nor evaluated. Other articles provided only superficial descriptions of existing programs, again without including information regarding evaluation. Very few publications were identified which either reported the results of efforts to evaluate a program's effectiveness or described other related research. In part this dearth of literature may have to do with the fact that many companies have little if any interest in publishing detailed program descriptions or evaluation results even if they are available. Another, perhaps more significant reason, is a willingness to accept a program on the basis of its good intentions rather than its demonstrated impact on employees.

Even those studies which were cited frequently in the literature had serious methodological and conceptual shortcomings, similar to those which typically emerge from other reviews of counseling research. These include: the frequent absence of a control group with which to compare the effects of a treatment group, absence of any detail about the characteristics of the subjects, lack of differentiation among the types of problems employees present, the absence of information about relevant characteristics of the counselors (e.g., professional background, education, training, etc.), excessive reliance on self-ratings as outcome measures, and, finally, ambiguity regarding programs' goals and objectives.

Consequently, to offer any conclusions on the basis of these fragmentary findings is hazardous at best. The only conclusion which can be drawn is that much remains to be done. What follows, then, are several observations about the information revealed by this survey and its implications for future research and evaluation.

1. Perhaps the most fundamental concern to emerge from this review is related to the great differences among the studies reported in what is referred to as "counseling." The term has been used to describe everything from a brief discussion with a supervisor to a series of regular sessions with a trained professional intended to resolve a marital crisis or career dilemma. There is little clarity as to exactly what kind of counseling actually exists in industry. Future studies of counseling must be more precise in describing the nature, content, and duration of the intervention which is being evaluated. At the same time there are a wide variety of interventions which can justifiably be termed counseling. What must be avoided is the tendency to treat widely divergent counseling forms as though they were the same.

2. The objectives of counseling and the criteria used to determine its effectiveness also require specification, particularly if any meaningful evaluation is to occur. Program evaluations have typically used some aspect of job performance as a criterion, for example, the elimination of a performance problem thought to be a result of personal difficulties. However, this has been possible only in supervisor-initiated programs in which substandard job performance is observed by a supervisor who then refers the employee for counseling. In programs which encourage and facilitate self-referrals, there may be no evidence of substandard job performance. Such situations necessitate criteria other than improved functioning on the job for evaluating counseling outcomes. Important considerations concerning the use of job performance as the criterion have consistently been overlooked or neglected by program evaluators. The first is that return to a satisfactory level of performance on the job does not necessarily imply that an employee's problem has been eliminated and the improvement may not only be temporary, it may also manifest itself in other ways in other settings. In the studies reviewed, the longest period of time over which performance was monitored was two years, which is probably long enough to determine the long-term and enduring effects of counseling. In most studies, however, the period of time allowed to elapse between treatment and evaluation is much shorter, and needs to be extended.

3. More studies comparing different counseling interventions or comparing counseling to other helping strategies and to no intervention should be conducted with subjects randomly assigned to groups. The only area in which such comparative studies have occurred is pre-retirement counseling where structured, quasi-instructional techniques have sometimes been compared to more open-ended

interactional methods. Similar efforts in other areas could have considerable value, particularly with regard to various career assistance programs where untested methods and techniques have proliferated.

4. Surveys of counseling services in industry have focused attention primarily on the nation's largest companies. While the results suggest that there has been an increase in the availability of counseling services in recent years, more precise and detailed information is needed before any firm conclusions can be reached. For example, if a better understanding of the extent of counseling services in industry is to be achieved, future investigations will need to include a more varied and representative cross-section of American companies. In addition, the scope of future studies needs to be expanded to include information on such aspects of service delivery as the background and training of counselors, the extent to which internal versus external counseling resources are used, the interface between companies and referral sources, and the administrative arrangements between various departments (e.g. personnel, medical, training, etc.) for service delivery.

5. Another question which must be asked is why many practitioner-oriented magazines, in contrast to professional research journals, are dominated by articles which either provide superficial descriptions of unevaluated programs or purport to offer "how-to-do-it" suggestions. Most of this literature is probably well-intentioned, but if counseling in industry is to endure beyond its recent surge in popularity some serious efforts at examining its impact must be undertaken. The responsibility for this lies both with those professionals who design and implement counseling programs and with practitioner-oriented magazines which provide information on the state of the art. Program developers in industry must assume a greater responsibility for evaluating the impact of their efforts. Admittedly this may be a complicated and even costly obligation. But the consequences of ignoring these efforts would be serious. How will it ever be possible to justify the existence of any program if there is no evidence of even modest impact? At the same time it would seem reasonable to argue that practitioner-oriented magazines have an obligation to impose higher standards for determining what type of manuscripts should be published. While it is not being argued that all descriptive or prescriptive articles should be omitted from the literature, the utility of publishing such articles must be viewed more critically.

Finally, the need for more rigorous and carefully conceived evalutions of counseling programs in industry is clear. Such efforts should ultimately become an integral part of every organization's program planning process. Just as the unexamined life, according to Aristotle, may not be worth living, so too may an unexamined intervention or program not be worth having. Clearly more is needed than blind faith and good intentions.

REFERENCE NOTES

1 Miller, J. A., Blass, B. M., and Mihal, W. L. *An experiment to test methods of increasing self-development activities among research and development personnel.* (Publ. TR-43). New York: University of Rochester, Management Resource Center, 1973.

2 Boyack, V. L. and Tiberi, M. A. *A study of pre-retirement education.* Paper presented at a meeting of the Gerontological Society, Louisville, Kentucky, October 1975.

REFERENCES

The American Society for Personnel Administration and The Bureau of National Affairs, Counseling policies and programs for employees with problems. *Bulletin to Management*, March 23, 1978, pp. 1–10.

Brooks, P. R. Industry-agency program for employee counseling. *Social Casework*, 1975, 56, 404–410.

Burnaska, R. F. The effects of behavioral modeling training upon managers' behaviors and employees' perceptions. *Personnel Psychology*, 1976, 29, 329–335.

Carson, J. H. Helping industry get rid of its hangover. *Industry Week*, 1976, 190, 44–49.

The Corporate Committee for Retirement Planning. Retirement preparation: Growing corporate involvement. *Aging and Work*, 1980, 3, 1–13.

Filipowitz, C. A. The troubled employee: Whose responsibility? *The Personnel Administrator*, 1979, 24, 17–20; 22–23; 33.

Follman, J. F., Jr. *Helping the troubled employee.* New York: AMACOM, 1978.

Gibson, W. D. They're bringing problem drinkers out of the closet. *Chemical Week*, 1978, 123, 85–91.

Glamser, F. D. and DeJong, G. F. The efficacy of pre-retirement preparation programs for industrial workers. *Journal of Gerontology*, 1975, 39, 595–600.

Griffith, A. R. A survey of career development in corporations. *Personnel and Guidance Journal*, 1980, 58, 537–542.

Hanson, M. C. Career counseling in organizations. In Montross, D. H., and Shinkman, C. J. *Career development in the 80's.* Springfield, Illinois: Charles C. Thomas, 1981.

Herr, E. L. and Cramer, S. H. *Career guidance through the life span.* Boston: Little, Brown, 1979.

Holland, J. L., Magoon, T. M., and Spokane, A. R. Counseling psychology: Career interventions, research and theory. *Annual Review of Psychology*, 1981, 32, 279– 305.

Kasschau, P. Re-evaluating the need for retirement preparation programs. *Industrial Gerontology*, 1974, 1, 42–59.

Lavino, J. J., Jr. Personal assistance programs. *The Personnel Administrator*, 1978, 23, 35–36.

Marshall, P. B. Employee counselors: Opening new lines of communication. *The Personnel Administrator*, 1976, 21, 44–48.

Morgan, M. A., Hall, D. T., and Martier, A. Career development strategies in industry— where are we and where should we be? *Personnel*, March–April 1979, pp. 13–30.

Oliver, L. W. Outcome measurement in career counseling research. *Journal of Counseling Psychology*, 1979, 26, 217–226.

O'Rourke, J. F. and Friedman, H. L. An inter-union pre-retirement training program: Results and commentary, *Industrial Gerontology*, Spring 1972, pp. 49–64.

Pell, S. and D'Alonzo, C. A. Sickness absenteeism of alcoholics. *The Journal of Occupational Medicine*, 1970, 12, 198 210.

Perkins, G. Alcoholism in the workplace. *Management World*, 1978, 1, 7–8; 10.

Ralston, A. Employee alcoholism: Response of the largest industrials. *The Personnel Administrator*, 1977, 6, 50–56.

Reardon, R. W. Help for the troubled worker in a small company. *Personnel*, 1976, 53, 50–54.

Skidmore, R. A., Balsam, D., and Jones, O. F. Social work practices in industry. *Social Work*, 1974, 3, 280−286.

Siegel, S. R. and Rives, J. M. Characteristics of existing and planned pre-retirement programs. *Aging and Work*, 1978, 2, 93−99.

Super, D. E. and Hall, D. T. Career development: Exploration and planning. *Annual Review of Psychology*, 1978, 29, 333−372.

Thornton, G. C. Differential effects of career planning of internals and externals. *Personnel Psychology*, 1978, 31, 471−476.

Walker, J. W. and Gutteridge, T. G. *Career planning practices*. New York: AMACOM, 1979.

Weiner, H. J., Akabas, S. H., and Sommer, J. J. *Mental health care in the world of work*. New York: Associated Press, 1973.

Weissman, A. A social service strategy in industry. *Social Work*, 1975, 5, 401−403.

REVIEW QUESTIONS

1. The author notes that a number of organizations have formal counseling programs (for alcoholism, career guidance, etc.). What is the first-line supervisor's role in personal counseling?

2 Relating this article to the previous two, what is the role of counseling in preventing, diminishing, or treating stress and burnout?

3 What responsibilities do employers have to provide counseling for employees on problems that do not affect job performance?

CHAPTER 18

LABOR RELATIONS AND CONFLICT RESOLUTION

READING 63

Prerequisites to Labor-Management Cooperation

Sar A. Levitan
Clifford M. Johnson*

* * *

If managers wish to ease conflict with labor, they must view workers more as equal partners than as silent followers. Genuine cooperation requires that labor contribute to the perception and definition of problems as well as to their solution. It requires a fair exchange of responsibilities and benefits, so that both sides share the fruits of cooperation equitably. Above all, it requires an environment of mutual trust and respect, which can develop only when labor and management believe that they are on an equal footing.

By initiating open dialogue with labor leaders, well-intentioned managers can begin to make progress toward genuine cooperation. Workers can gain equal standing with employers only by organizing and speaking with a single voice. Managers must therefore recognize unions as legitimate vehicles for the expression of workers' concerns and crucial to their sense of dignity.

* * *

REVIEW QUESTION

1 Reflect on the state of labor relations today. Are the ingredients for genuine cooperation present?

READING 64

Collective Bargaining— Pressures for Change

Thomas A. Kochan
Robert B. McKersie*

Based on preliminary evidence from our current research, we believe that the U.S. system of industrial relations is undergoing a fundamental change. While the most visible examples of change lie in wage, fringe benefit, work practice, and employment security concessions and tradeoffs negotiated in 1981, 1982, and 1983, other significant changes are occurring more quietly regarding employers, unions, and, to some extent, government agencies. One can reach a better understanding of these changes and their long-run implications if the focus of industrial relations were broadened to include an analysis of the basic business strategies of the firm and their effects on workers and their union representatives.

In other words, we should go beyond the traditional focus at which collective bargaining formally occurs and examine changes taking place at the highest levels of strategic decision making within firms and unions. In turn we should relate these strategies to the results of collective bargaining, and then analyze the significant changes occurring in the workplace.

Just as industrial relations has always been influenced by economic pressures, the changes occurring within firms and unions are partly a product of such pressures that have been building up through the 1970s and that are just now coming together in ways that call for a new orientation of the industrial relations system. These changes, however, are not occurring universally across organizations or collective bargaining relationships. Nor is a single pattern emerging. Instead, the variety of choices being made by employers, labor organizations, and the government may produce an even wider diversity of practices and results than was the case in previous years.

Pressures for Change

The 1970s was a decade in which the economic pressures for change in the unionized sector of the American economy were gradually building. However, negotiators did not respond accordingly. Instead, the approach developed in the post-World War period of the growth and evolution of collective bargaining continued to dictate the behavior of industrial relations professionals and the overall results of collective bargaining. Consequently, during the 1970s a gap

*Reprinted from "Collective Bargaining—Pressures for Change," by Thomas A. Kochan and Robert B. McKersie, *Sloan Management Review*, Summer 1983, pp. 59–65, by permission of the publisher. Copyright © 1983 by the Sloan Management Review Association. All rights reserved.

developed between internal practices in industrial relations and external economic pressures.

For example, the key economic development of the 1970s was the combination of increased competitive pressures on unionized industries and rapid and persistent rates of inflation. The sources of these pressures, including increased international competition, the rise of domestic nonunion competition, and more recently, the deregulation of key sectors of the economy, varied from industry to industry.

These pressures today have been accelerated by the force of the current recession. As a result of the inflationary pressures of the seventies and the expansion of cost-of-living escalators in collective bargaining agreements, the differentials in compensation costs between domestic union firms and their domestic nonunion and foreign competitors have increased. Thus the economic pressures along with the cyclical pressures of the 1980–82 recession may help to explain some of the current changes within firms.

Other Factors Leading to Changes in Collective Bargaining

Environmental Pressures   While economic pressures were building, pressure for changes in collective bargaining was also coming from other environmental factors. Jobs moved from the strongholds of unionism in the North to the Sun Belt. Technological changes and improvements in transportation made it more attractive for some firms to establish new smaller plants in rural and low-labor-cost regions of the country, rather than to reinvest in existing facilities. Shifts in both supply and demand for labor produced higher rates of growth in occupations outside of the traditional blue-collar base of union membership. Finally, the swing toward conservatism in the political climate of the country along with the economic pressures placed added pressure on the collective bargaining system.

Human Resource Management Policies   The U.S. industrial relations system's response to these pressures was not manifested within the collective bargaining system, however. Instead, American management chose to take a relatively status quo or a gradual adjustment approach to collective bargaining, while at the same time, it took steps to contain the expansion of trade unions or to avoid unionism altogether in the growth sectors of the economy. Indeed, the development of sophisticated nonunion human resource management policies and strategies may turn out to be the most important development in the American industrial relations system of the last two decades.

While no aggregate quantitative data are yet available for comparing the characteristics of the union and nonunion sectors of the economy, it is clear that unions are largely the result of mass organizing drives in manufacturing, transportation, mining, utilities, and communications industries that took place from 1930 to 1950. These industries are now the mature or declining sectors of the American economy. Even though some of them continue to grow, a higher percentage of new entrants and new establishments opened by existing firms operate without a union. Consequently, union members are currently concentrated in older industries, older firms, and older plants of firms that are partially unionized. Thus, we now have a bi-modal distribution of union and nonunion establishments.

While we traditionally tend to think that nonunion organizations follow the wage, fringe benefit, and personnel practices of unionized firms, the current period indicates that just the opposite is happening; that is, the innovations developed in human resource management in the nonunion sector are now being experimented with in unionized firms.

Two examples illustrate this point. The first involves strategies for promoting employment continuity. By emphasizing broad-banded job classifications and descriptions, transfer, retraining and attrition programs, and sophisticated human resource planning, many large nonunion companies have been able to manage their internal labor market so that few if any workers are separated involuntarily. Correspondingly, within the unionized sector, the realization that the practice of "parking the labor force outside the door" when demand falls off has been costly and has fostered an atmosphere of insecurity and instability. Consequently, the decision by Ford Motor and the UAW to experiment with the concept of employment guarantees is an important example of what may be a new trend in the unionized sector.

The second example is that of communication programs. In the absence of unions, management has been able to communicate directly with workers, usually using first-line supervisors as the delivery point for information about the future of the business. Until recently, companies with collective bargaining agreements found it difficult to do any extensive communication on a direct basis with employees. Some of the reluctance can be traced back to the era of collective bargaining history referred to as "Boulwarism," when General Electric and several other companies followed the practice of communicating directly with their workers in an effort to convince them of the fairness and rightness of management's position during contract negotiations. When this approach was declared an unfair labor practice by the NLRB a certain "chilling" of communication took place within unionized plants.

More recently, however, the sophisticated communication techniques that have been developed in nonunion firms have been applied more and more to unionized establishments. The need for more communication has been stimulated by concession bargaining and by a realization on the part of companies that worker expectations are often far out of touch with the competitive realities faced by those organizations. More and more unionized companies are realizing that they must find ways to communicate effectively with *both* union leaders and rank and file workers.

CHANGES IN MANAGEMENTS' INDUSTRIAL RELATIONS STRATEGIES

We can further expand on the current changes under way in the industrial relations system in selected unionized firms by examining developments in the management of industrial relations at the corporate, collective bargaining, and workplace levels.

Changes at the Corporate Level

During the past twenty years many labor relations professionals within unionized corporations have become increasingly isolated, conservative, and less influential. Because labor relations managers were primarily concerned with maintaining stable and peaceful union-management relations, they neither made aggressive attempts to change work practices or to change significantly wage and fringe benefit formulas or patterns. Nor did they readily accept the need to introduce direct strategies for involving workers and unions in efforts to improve the quality of working life and productivity. Thus they remained focused on the traditional collective bargaining activities and responsibilities.

Meanwhile, the growth of government regulations, the increase in the demand for managers, professionals, and technical employees along with the increasing interest in union avoidance among top executives led to the development of a new set of human resource management specialists who were more conversant with different types of planning, behavioral science-based innovations in work organization and personnel systems, and organizational change techniques that now form the foundation for nonunion human resources management systems. Thus, human resource specialists have gained power and influence, while traditional labor relations specialists have lost power. This new orientation has laid the foundation for the current change taking place in many firms in industrial relations.

The Nature of the Transformation The role of industrial relations within many companies is undergoing a transformation as companies search for new strategies that link their industrial relations performance to the larger business strategies of the firm and efforts to help reduce labor costs, increase productivity, and enhance the commitment and participation of individual workers. The changing role of industrial relations professionals can be seen in several ways. For example, the economic crisis facing many companies has highlighted the link between overall business policy and strategy and industrial relations and collective bargaining. Industrial relations professionals have traditionally been isolated from most decisions regarding investment in different businesses or plants. New demands for concessions from unions, however, coupled with countervailing demands for greater information-sharing on the part of unions, are drawing a closer link between investment (and other basic business decisions) and the industrial relations function. In this way, industrial relations and human resource management professionals are being called upon to engage in more long-term planning and strategic analysis of alternatives for reducing labor costs and increasing productivity. Indeed, the drive for productivity improvement and labor cost control is forcing corporations to forge a closer link between operating or line managers and the labor relations and personnel specialists.

Thus, strategic planning and analysis techniques are being introduced more directly into the industrial relations function than they have been in prior years.

Also, a wider group of managers is participating more in the planning and the development of strategy for contract negotiations than has been the case in the past.

The tremendous amount of publicity given to worker participation and involvement in Japan and in many nonunion companies has caught the attention of many top executives outside of the industrial relations function. This has led to an increase in corporate efforts to develop new patterns of employee communication and involvement in the workplace. Again, the skills and techniques required to implement this strategy require active cooperation between organizational development and traditional industrial relations specialists.

Changes in Collective Bargaining

The major changes occurring in collective bargaining can be easily summarized. Recent data from the Bureau of Labor Statistics (BLS) indicate that the rate of increase in major collective bargaining agreements in 1982 was 3.6 percent compared with an average of 9.8 percent for calendar year 1981. Furthermore, 43 percent of the workers covered under contracts negotiated during 1982 provided for no wage increase in the first year, and 35 percent provided for no wage increase over the term of the agreement.

Any average settlement figure misses important variations that always occur. In fact, in 1982 we experienced a larger than normal dispersion in settlement rates. While certain industries negotiated wage freezes, deferrals, or wage cuts, other industries under less intensive pressures settled at levels only marginally lower than settlements in earlier years. For example, if the auto and trucking settlements are eliminated from the BLS figures on major settlements for the first six months of 1982, the employees covered under the remaining agreements settled for approximately 7.8 percent.

Another indication of a major departure from previous trends can be seen in the number of *early* contract negotiations, such as in the auto, trucking, and steel industries. Perhaps even more significantly, 1982 appears to have brought about a renewal of *plant specific* bargaining concerning work practices, particularly over the scope of job definitions and classifications, rules governing the movement of people across jobs through bidding and posting procedures and bumping rights, and general plant practices that affect the flexibility and use of human resources and payment for time not worked. These all represent efforts to gain control over manufacturing costs, reduce compensation differentials with nonunion competitors, and achieve greater flexibility in the allocation of human resources.

Changes in the Workplace

Finally, a significant increase in the attention paid to the degree of involvement, commitment, and participation of individual workers and work groups in task-related decisions has resulted from both corporate strategy efforts reviewed above and efforts to bring about changes in work rules and practices at the plant level through collective bargaining. Indeed, while a number of quality of working life (QWL) efforts were started in the late 1960s and early 1970s, most of them deemphasized productivity issues and separated QWL efforts from the collective bargaining process.

However, in the current round, employee participation efforts are addressing more directly issues affecting work organization and productivity and, in some instances, are fostering innovations that are at variance with the provisions traditionally found in bargaining agreements. For example, as QWL programs grapple with operating problems, they are bound to confront issues involving the scope of jobs and provisions for moving workers across jobs. This leads to questions concerning the role of seniority, the compensation and job evaluation systems, and the promotion, transfer, and bumping rights of different workers. What appears to be of highest priority to managers today is to achieve the type of broadbanded jobs and higher degrees of flexibility in the assignment and utilization of people that are associated with the newer forms of work organization in many innovative nonunion firms. How employee involvement programs and the dictates of contracts and collective bargaining sort out their differences remains to be seen.

Labor Movement Strategies

Our analysis to this point has focused on changes in industrial relations resulting from the more proactive behavior on the part of employers. Union leaders are, however, also facing a number of strategic choices that will influence their future roles in the U.S. industrial relations system. Some of the issues facing unions at the three levels (corporate, collective bargaining, workplace) can be seen in a number of recent developments. These developments represent a testing and gradual movement by U.S. unions toward a greater involvement at the strategic level of business decision making.

Traditionally, the main point of contact for unions in industrial relations has been at the middle point, namely at the level at which unions negotiate collective bargaining agreements with individual firms. Presently, however, considerable thought and experimentation are given to greater union involvement at levels both below and above the level of contract negotiations.

At the lowest level of industrial relations (i.e., the relationship between individuals, work groups, and supervisors), unions are currently being challenged by the quality of working life and other employer efforts to involve more fully workers in the ongoing processes of the organizations. These efforts entail a "mixed bag" of risks and opportunities for local unions. Union leaders can play important roles in setting the stage, designing, and administering participation programs, thereby attempting to integrate them into their representational role at the workplace. On the other hand, over time, these efforts are likely to build a higher worker commitment to the firm, challenge existing work rules, and fashion new work organization arrangements. If this occurs, local unions no doubt will find it necessary to modify their traditional roles at the workplace and adjust to the increased flexibility and variation in practices that eventually result from greater worker involvement.

At the highest level of strategic decision making where employers make basic investment and resource deployment decisions, the emerging picture for the role of the union is one of experimentation. While U.S. unions have historically been reluctant to follow the European models of formal representation of unions on boards of directors, there is now more open discussion within the American labor movement concerning the advantages and limitations of representing job security and financial interests of the unions at the strategic level of the enterprise. Still, however, there is only a very limited number of actual cases (most notable at Chrysler and Pan Am) where unions are represented on company boards. Nevertheless, there is considerable movement in some sectors toward a unique "American" style of union influence in decision making.

Some U.S. union leaders are being brought into management councils for briefings and discussions about the directions of the business and the implications for the union's membership base. An increasing number of unions are now receiving information about the financial performance, maintenance programs, and investment plans for specific plants.

Internal Contradictions in American Industrial Relations

Yet despite the examples cited above where unions and employers are searching for a coherent or internally consistent way of relating to each other at all three levels of their relationship, the predominant pattern found in U.S. firms is one of internal contradiction. For example, many of the companies that have experienced significant diversification and growth during the sixties and seventies now find themselves following a very aggressive and sophisticated strategy of union avoidance at the corporate level and specifically for their new plants. Thus the broad corporate strategies decided at the highest level of the firm contain adversarial elements, while these same firms may seek to overcome antagonistic relationships at the plant level.

While only a few unions have been able to exert enough pressure to force these diversified firms to abandon their union avoidance strategies, many older plants are negotiating concessions and fostering employee involvement and labor-management cooperation. It is difficult, however, to see how long cooperation can last at the plant and workplace levels in face of a union avoidance strategy at the corporate level.

Conversely, in several companies that are more highly unionized and have accepted the reality that new facilities are likely to be unionized, there is greater recognition of and agreement among top management and union officials on key strategic issues and on the need for labor cost moderation. However, the level of conflict and distrust at the plant level between workers and plant management still remains quite high. Thus, in some relationships there exists a higher level of accommodation between the representatives of the company and the union than among workers, union leaders, and management representatives at the workplace.

Still other patterns are emerging. While in general the American labor movement has been quite reluctant to embrace the quality of working life and other forms of direct employee participation and involvement programs, there appears to be a number of union leaders who are becoming more vocal in their support of these employee participation efforts. Indeed, one can now say that there are key leaders within (at least) the following unions that advocate union participation in QWL and are actively responsible for facilitating expansion of such efforts: the United Automobile Workers, the United Steelworkers, the Communication Workers of America, the Amalgamated Clothing and Textile Workers, the International Union of Electrical Workers, and the Newspaper Guild.

While none of these unions has formally adopted policies that endorse worker participation programs, nor have they made them a part of their formal agenda for the future, a significant degree of experimentation is occurring within these unions. On the other hand, there remains a large number of skeptics within leadership ranks at all levels of the labor movement. Consequently, we clearly are in a testing stage, and how the labor leaders sort out and interpret such experimentations will have an important bearing on the role local unions will play at the workplace in the future.

Summary

The current changes in industrial relations at the three levels make this an extremely critical period for the future of the American industrial relations system. The strategic choices that managers and union leaders make will help determine whether the unionized sector of the labor force will expand or contract in future years. One way to interpret what is going on is that the unionized industrial relations system is now searching for a strategy to compete with the practices that have developed in the most innovative of the nonunion human resource management systems. At the same time, the American labor movement and American management continue to spar over the broad strategic and ideological issues concerning the acceptance of labor unions as legitimate institutions in society and within specific companies and organizations.

If companies and unions do not reach an agreement soon, there may be a much more direct and significant political and economic confrontation concerning the future of the American labor movement and the appropriate procedures to ensure that workers will participate in the determination and administration of terms and conditions of employment.

The implications for both practitioners and researchers are far-reaching. We need to look at the changes occurring in industrial relations in their totality, rather than to separate the study of collective bargaining from the study of work organization and employee participation at the workplace or from the study of business strategy and corporate structure. Essentially, what is needed is the following: new ways of studying industrial relations; new theoretical frameworks for assessing the performance of industrial relations systems at the workplace; new definitions of the roles of industrial relations professionals; and new forums for discussion of the design of industrial relations systems within specific companies and in our nation as a whole.

REVIEW QUESTIONS

1 Review the pressures for change that the authors contend resulted in substantial collective bargaining changes. Are these pressures still dominant today? If not, have they been replaced by others?
2 Study the readings in Chapter 9 on participative management. To what degree have those programs helped to "ensure that workers will participate in the determination and administration of terms and conditions of employment"?
3 Relate this article to the previous one by Levitan and Johnson. Are the authors' themes relatively consistent or divergent?

READING 65

Some Benefits of Interpersonal Conflict

Richard E. Walton*

*   *   *

The premise of this volume is *not* that interpersonal conflict in organizations is necessarily bad or destructive, and that third parties must inevitably try to eliminate it or reduce it. In many instances, interpersonal differences, competition, rivalry, and other forms of conflict have a positive value for the participants and contribute to the effectiveness of the social system in which they occur. Thus, a moderate level of interpersonal conflict may have the following constructive consequences: First, it may increase the motivation and energy available to do tasks required by the social system. Second, conflict may increase the innovativeness of individuals and the system because of the greater diversity of the viewpoints and a heightened sense of necessity. Third, each person may develop increased understanding of his own position, because the conflict forces him to articulate his views and to bring forth all supporting arguments. Fourth, each party may achieve greater awareness of his own identity. Fifth, interpersonal conflict may be a means for managing the participants' own internal conflicts.

*   *   *

REVIEW QUESTION

1 Walton describes some surprisingly positive potential benefits of conflict. What could a manager do to increase the likelihood of their emergence?

READING 66

Managing Conflict in Today's Organizations

Gordon L. Lippitt*

One of the key elements in modern management is the realization that conflict management and resolution has become an increasingly important competency of organizational managers.

The American Management Association recently sponsored a survey of managerial interests in conflict management. The respondents in the survey included 116 chief executive officers, 76 vice presidents and 66 middle managers. Their responses strongly suggest that conflict is a topic of growing importance:[1]

• They spend about 24 percent of their time dealing with conflict;
• Their conflict-management ability has become more important over the past ten years;
• They rate conflict management as a topic of equal or slightly higher importance than planning, communication, motivation and decision making;
• Their interests in the sources of conflict emphasize psychological factors, such as misunderstanding, communication failure, personality clashes and value differences;
• They feel the conflict level in their organization is about right—not too low or too high.

These executives and managers also revealed what they considered to be the principle causes of conflict within organizations: misunderstanding (communication failure), personality clashes, value and goal differences, substandard performance, differences over method, responsibility issues, lack of cooperation, authority issues, frustration and irritability, competition for limited resources and noncompliance with rules and policies.

Nevertheless corporate executives and managers devote 24 percent of their working time to conflict management. School and hospital administrators, mayors and city managers consider this quite low. In these and similar fields, conflict resolution commands nearly 49 percent of the attention of such officials. The causes of conflict usually are the same as those cited above, but in a different rank order.

*From *Training and Development Journal*, July 1982, pp. 67–74. Reprinted with permission.

It is obvious that one relevant management development activity should include helping managers *manage conflict*—the reality that conflict should sometimes be encouraged, tolerated and creatively channeled into effective problem-solving. Managers should know the causes of conflict, ways to diagnose the type of conflict and methods to cope with differences.

CONFLICT—AN EVERYDAY FARE

Fighting, hostility and controversy, all of which can be called conflict, are nearly everyday fare for individuals and groups, although they are not always evident. Too often, emotional effort and involvement goes largely unrewarded because people move in restrictive rather than constructive channels. Also, conflict releases energy at every level of human affairs—energy that can produce positive, constructive results. Two things should be recognized here: conflict is an absolutely predictable social phenomenon, and it should be channeled to useful purposes. Both of these facts lie at the heart of effective management. The goal of organizational leadership is not to eliminate conflict, but to use it—to turn the released energy to good advantage.

Conflict is almost always caused by unlike points of view. Because we do not learn exactly alike, and because we therefore see and value things differently, we vary in our beliefs. Because conflict, large or small, is inevitable, the extreme result at either end is an undesirably abrasive situation or dialogue that is creatively productive.

Most leaders look upon conflict as a negative experience. This is the key to the problem. We should take pains to see that conflict is a creative and positive occurrence; otherwise, we must recognize the destructive nature of conflict carried too far, too long. It:

- Diverts energy from the real task;
- Destroys morale;
- Polarizes individuals and groups;
- Deepens differences;
- Obstructs cooperative action;
- Produces irresponsible behavior;
- Creates suspicion and distrust;
- Decreases productivity.

But the list of positive and creative values inherent in conflict is equally long. Conflict:

- Opens up an issue in a confronting manner;
- Develops clarification of an issue;
- Improves problem-solving quality;
- Increases involvement;
- Provides more spontaneity in communication;
- Initiates growth;
- Strengthens a relationship when creatively resolved;
- Helps increase productivity.

Parties to conflict, for the most part, find themselves in one (or more) of four areas of disagreement: *facts* (the present situation or problem), *methods* (the best way to achieve our goals), *goals* (how we want things to be) and *values* (long-term goals and qualities we support). Generally, it is easiest to resolve differences over facts and most difficult to settle differences over values.

Conflict is a state of real difference between two or more persons where overt behavior is characterized by differing perceptions toward goals that, in turn, create tension and disagreement and tend to polarize those involved. Conflict is of increasing importance to management. Many reasons for this exist, including the growing scarcity of natural resources; the complexity and increasing interdependence of relationships between individuals, groups, organizations and nations; the values and lifestyle pluralism that characterize people of all ages, sexes and races; and the rising expectations and psychology of entitlement reflected in the motivation of employees, managers, owners, customers and all others who interact with the organization.[2]

CONFLICT RESOLUTION

In a study of the constructive use of conflict, in which 57 managers were interviewed, five principal methods of interpersonal conflict resolution were identified:

- *Withdrawal:* retreating from an actual or potential conflict situation;
- *Smoothing:* emphasizing areas of agreement and deemphasizing areas of difference over conflictual areas;
- *Compromising:* searching for solutions that bring some degree of satisfaction to the conflicting parties;
- *Forcing:* exerting one's viewpoint at the potential expense of another—often open competition and a win-lose situation;
- *Confrontation:* addressing a disagreement directly and in a problem-solving mode—the affected parties work through their disagreement.

It is important to depersonalize conflict by ensuring that the disputants do not judge each other and to focus the conflict on the basic issues by concentrating disagreement on facts. Progress in this direction, however slight, is usually self-continuing and tends to reduce wholesale indictment to retail packaging. This limits conflict to manageable areas that are more likely to be subject to negotiation, accommodation or compromise. When people are introduced to what they recognize as fact, they tend to become more objective. Unsupported opinion and implication generally cause an opposite effect. The leader, as a rule, should look at the issues coldly and at the people involved warmly.

Leadership in resolving organizational conflict creatively also requires empathy and equality, but not neutrality. The neutrality position is damaging because, by nature, it recognizes nothing. Empathy, on the other hand, means that leadership recognizes both the plight and the ideas of both sides in conflict, without necessarily agreeing totally with either. Equality means that neither of the conflicting parties will be made to feel inferior, for the alternative is greater jealousy and heightened competition.

Finally, adopting an attitude of one side winning and the other side losing is like pouring gasoline on a fire. On the other hand, the provisional try—honest fact-finding (all the facts), exhaustive exploration (both parties working together) and meaningful problem-solving (with a lot of "what if we try this. . . ?")—pries open the door to constructive creativity.

These are, of course, fundamental rules. The experienced leader knows that they do not always work as they should. It is necessary to contend with counterforces between those who passively refuse to engage in conflict and those who deliberately develop conflict as a battleground for hatreds and greeds, as well as those who view conflict as a healthy challenge for betterment. Nevertheless, management of human conflict is an objective of organizational renewal.

A helpful way to comprehend two particular styles of conflict management—that of assertiveness and cooperativeness—is illustrated in Figure 1. Each style has both positive and negative factors:[3]

FIGURE 1
Conflict-management styles. [*Adapted from Kenneth Thomas' "Conflict and Conflict Management" in M. Dunnette (ed.),* The Handbook of Industrial and Organizational Psychology, *Chicago: Rand McNally College Publishing Company, 1976, p. 900.*]

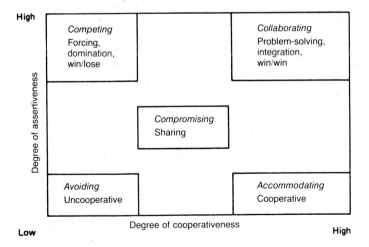

Competitor. A competing style is high on assertiveness and low on cooperativeness. This style is power-oriented and approaches conflict in terms of a win-lose strategy. On the negative side, a competitor may suppress, intimidate or coerce the other parties into conflict.

On the positive side, a competing style may be necessary when a quick, decisive action is required, or when important but unpopular courses of action may be taken. In addition, competing may be required when "you know you're right" on an issue. An avoiding style, however, can make sense when a conflict situation has relatively minor implications for managerial effectiveness, when there appears to be little chance for a person to "win" and when the benefits of confronting a conflict situation are overshadowed by the potential damage of confrontation.

Accommodator. The accommodating style is low in assertiveness and high in cooperativeness. A person who uses an accommodating style as the primary approach to conflict management may be showing too little concern for personal goals. Such a lack of concern may lead to lack of influence and recognition. It means that conflicts are resolved without each party to the conflict presenting his or her view in a forceful and meaningful way.

Like the other conflict management styles, however, the accommodating style has its uses. It is useful when a conflict issue is more important to the other person; when another style's disadvantages outweigh those of the accommodating style; when maintaining harmony is important; when it is advantageous to allow the other person to experience winning; and when an accommodating style on an issue may make the other person more receptive on another, more important issue.

Compromiser. To some people, the word "compromise" suggests weakness and lack of commitment to a position. A compromiser may be thought of as a person who puts expediency above principle or who seeks short-term solutions at the expense of long-term objectives. A compromising style results in each conflict participant sharing in some degree of winning and losing.

It is important, however, to recognize the potential value of compromise. Compromise is a common and practical approach to conflict management because it often fits the realities of organizational life. This "fit" occurs when a conflict is not important enough to either party to warrant the time and psychological investment in one of the more assertive modes of conflict management. In addition, compromise may be the only practical way of handling a conflict situation in which two equally strong and persuasive parties attempt to work out a solution.

Avoider. At first glance, an avoiding style may appear to have no value as a mode of managing conflict. An avoiding style may reflect a failure to address important issues and a tendency to remain neutral when there is a need to take a position. An avoider may also exhibit detachment from conflict and a readiness to comply or conform, based on indifference.

Collaborator. Given the two dimensions of cooperativeness and assertiveness shown in Figure 1, the collaborating style is high on both dimensions. How is it possible to be both assertive about personal goals and cooperative about others' goals? It is possible only if the parties to a conflict recast it as a problem-solving situation. A problem-solving approach requires the following conditions:

- There is an attempt to depersonalize the conflict. That is, the parties to the conflict channel their energies to solving the problem rather than defeating each other.
- The goals, opinions, attitudes and feelings of all parties are accepted as legitimate concerns, and all parties play a constructive role.
- The parties realize that a conflict issue can make a constructive contribution to the quality of human relationships if the issue is worked through in a supportive and trusting climate in which opinions and differences are freely aired.

By developing an awareness of conflict elements and the conditions that foster them, you can maintain a low-conflict setting with your associates. Some of the factors in the work setting that predispose individuals to engage in unnecessary conflict are:[4]

- Poorly defined jobs, tasks, responsibilities and ranges of authority.
- Prior history of conflict between two or more people or groups.
- Interdepartmental relationships that frequently place members at cross purposes; traditional adversary relationships such as sales versus engineering, production versus quality assurance, nursing versus administration or district office versus regional headquarters.
- Unreasonable levels of pressure and pace in the organization.
- Severe economic downturn that jeopardizes the job security of organization members.
- Overly competitive climate fostered by top management and managers at various levels.
- Favoritism shown by managers to one or two employees.
- Punitive or threatening style of treatment by a unit manager, leading to escapist behavior, such as blaming others and shifting responsibility.
- Unclear or arbitrary standards for advancement and promotion in the organization; inconsistent patterns of rewarding accomplishment; overly secretive and competitive organizational politics.
- Great confusion or uncertainty about upcoming major changes or upheavals in the organization; inability of employees to define their future roles and interactions.

By anticipating it, an effective manager tries to lessen the chance of open conflict. It can be observed that the evolution of open conflict passes through five distinct stages:[5]

- *Anticipation*. A change is to be made and problems are forecast.
- Conscious but unexpressed *difference*. Rumors are out, but there is no confirmation. People do not like what they hear.
- *Discussion*. Information is presented. Questions are asked. Sides of the questions become open.

• Open *dispute.* The principals in the situation confront the sides of the argument. Differing opinions become clear.
• Open *conflict.* The conflict sharpens up, with forces mobilizing behind each side of the argument.

A good general approach to minimizing and resolving conflicts consists of the following three basic steps:[6]

• Establish and maintain a low-conflict, low-stress climate, with cooperation as the norm.
• Isolate each significant conflict to a single, specific task issue or family of issues. Don't accept personality clashes, but insist that the protagonists focus on a concrete issue and its rational elements.
• Help the protagonists apply a rational problem-solving model or procedure to the issue; go for a workable compromise.

One aspect of management differences is also the management of agreement. Frequently, an organization does not confront and openly deal with how people might feel about an issue, problem or situation.

MANAGEMENT OF AGREEMENT

The essence of conflict management through confrontation, negotiation and collaboration is to come to agreement. In many cases, however, a condition of agreement may already exist—unrecognized, unspoken, unrealized. It has been well hypothesized that members of groups and organizations—as individuals— may be in agreement as to the nature of a situation or problem, but that no one individual has seen fit to present his or her agreement:

> Organizations frequently take actions in contradiction to what they really want to do and therefore defeat the very purposes they are trying to achieve. This also deals with a major corollary of the paradox, which is that the inability to manage agreement is a major source of organization dysfunction.[7]

Frequently, people in organizations know how to cope with a problem, but they do not share this knowledge with those in positions of authority or leadership—evidence of an unwillingness to communicate openly. As a result, all too often, invalid or inaccurate information leads to action that is contrary to the best interest of the organization. Members of the organization experience frustration, anger, irritation and dissatisfaction—whereupon the cycle repeats itself. Jerry Harvey identifies six reasons why this occurs:[8]

• *Action anxiety.* People tend to be anxious about acting in accordance with their beliefs.
• *Negative fantasies.* If we openly and positively correct a wrong, we may create new problems.
• *Real risk.* The reality of life whenever we confront others; it might affect job security and one's role.

• *Fear of separation.* If a person "opens up," it might threaten his or her acceptance in the group.

• *Fear of conflict* (real or artificial). Real conflict occurs when people have real differences. Artificial conflict, on the other hand, occurs when people agree on the actions they want to take and then do the opposite. The resulting anger, frustration and blaming behavior, generally termed "conflict" is not based on real differences. It stems from the protective reactions that occur when a decision that no one originally believed in or was committed to goes sour. As a paradox within a paradox, such conflict is symptomatic of agreement.

• *Group think.* A conforming pattern of group action that resists innovation, creativity and deviation.

All this brings us once again to the conclusion that the management of agreement is a matter of confrontation, search and coping. Confrontation has been called a process of interpersonal relating in which the behavior, the presence or the mere existence of one person makes a difference in the behavior of another because they openly "face up" to the situation in which they are involved.

To be productive, this process relies on all the individuals involved communicating honestly and with integrity; but even so it generally tends to be inversely related to the intensity of domination which the involved individuals bring to bear. The highest levels of confrontation are found in human interaction in which conflict, threat and domination—and hence the psychological necessity for defense—are negligible. Conflict, of course, is a kind of interacting, and little interacting takes place that is totally void of conflict, domination or attempts to influence. "Direct confrontation of relevant situations in an organization is essential. If we do not confront one another we keep the trouble within ourselves and we stay in trouble."[9]

All concerned must look for an understanding of the position taken by the other person or group. Each person must do this in his or her own way, communicating clearly and avoiding judgmental behavior to help establish a relationship of trust. If each person's autonomy and independence is to be preserved, there must be a minimal attempt by someone to control someone else. A problem-solving, goal-oriented, continuously experimental approach must be adopted, and there must be considerable flexibility with respect to the acceptance or rejection of the ideas of others.

Contrasted to the questions of attitude and procedure, coping brings us to the action in managing conflict and agreement. To cope requires an appropriate response to the situation, issue, problem or relationship that has been confronted. Appropriateness may be in the "eye of the beholder," but in the context of organization renewal, appropriate management of conflict or agreement is related to solving the problem in such a way that the person involved learns from the process; the human subsystems are strengthened by the coping; the organization is aided in its growth; and in some minor or major way, the resolution or solution contributes to the environmental forces affecting the organization.

The importance of managing conflict and agreement has been presented not because they are negative forces, but rather because they are positive aspects of human system renewal:

> Diversity of orientation and differences in point of view—"fruitful friction"—are essential if one seeks creative and effective organizations. Differences, of course, can result in irreconcilable, costly conflict unless the interaction-influence network and the problem-solving processes or organizations channel the differences to productive and not destructive ends. There is need to develop more sophisticated social institutions and organizations that have the capacity to deal constructively with the conflicts caused by change or by diversity.[10]

If the conflict situation is in the healthy zone, skills and techniques for successful management can be learned and applied effectively. If the conflict situation is in the unhealthy zone, a different set of analytic skills and insights is needed. This is more complex and often a longer process. It is important to know the unhealthy conflict can be managed as successfully as healthy conflict if there is clear understanding of its nature and the factors underlying it.

The management of conflict has assumed greater importance among managers. It should be an essential part of the management development process. Human resource development planners should initiate skill training opportunities for supervisors, managers and technical specialists in effective conflict resolution to allow for more effective problem-solving and planning.

REFERENCES

1 Thomas, K. W. & Schmidt, W. H. A survey of managerial interests with respect to conflict. *Academy of Management Journal*, 1976, *19*(2), 315–318.

2 Albanese, R. *Managing: Toward accountability for performance* (rev.). Homewood, Ill.: Richard D. Irwin, Inc., 1978, pp. 421–422.

3 Thomas, K. W. Conflict and conflict management. In M. D. Dunnette (Ed.), *The handbook of industrial and organizational psychology*. Chicago: Rand McNally College Publishing Company, 1976, p. 900.

4 Albrecht, K. *Stress and the manager.* Englewood Cliffs, N.J.: Prentice-Hall, Inc., 1979, pp. 273–274.

5 Rumley, J. *The management of difference.* Washington, D. C.: Development Publications, 1977.

6 Albrecht, K. *Stress and the manager.* p. 274.

7 Harvey, J. B. The abilene paradox: The management of agreement. *Organizational Dynamics*, 1974, *3*(1), 66.

8 *Ibid.,* p. 75.

9 Davis, S. A. An organic problem-solving method of organizational change. *Journal of Applied Behavioral Science*, 1967, *3*(1), 13.

10 Likert, R. & Likert, J. G. *New ways of managing conflict.* New York: McGraw-Hill, 1976, p. 23.

REVIEW QUESTIONS

1 How can you reconcile the apparent conflict between the fact that executives spend *one-quarter* of their time dealing with conflict and their feeling that the level of conflict is just about right?

2 Review the five conflict management styles. Which one(s) do you typically use the most frequently? What have been the usual consequences?

3 Interview about six other students, asking them to state three typical products of conflict. Classify each response as positive or negative. What proportion falls into each category? What does this tell you?

CHAPTER 19

SOCIAL ISSUES

READING 67

Alcoholism: A Productivity Hangover

Richard J. Tersine
James Hazeldine*

Only in the last decade have organizations begun to deal with an old problem that adversely affects productivity—the alcoholic employee. Many organizations have found ways to help the employee and reverse the effects of alcoholism on productivity. This is a look at such efforts.

It is estimated that about three-fourths of the adult population in the United States consume alcohol and that fourteen out of fifteen have no particular continuing problem with its use. But at least 5 percent of the labor force suffers from alcoholism, the percentage tending to be constant everywhere on the organizational ladder. The average alcoholic has between twelve and sixteen years of service with a company before termination and is between 35 and 45 years old. As alcoholics are approaching the middle stage of their disease, they are also reaching what should be their most productive years with their organizations. If the progression of the disease is not halted, the toll on the employee and on productivity rises dramatically.

MEASURING PRODUCTIVITY LOSS

A 1971 study indicated that alcoholism affects productivity in several ways:

- overtime costs due to absenteeism,
- administrative costs,
- weekly indemnity claims (more than average employees),
- life and health insurance costs,
- lessening of quantity and quality of work.[1]

The company under study had 1,700 employees of which 143 had a drinking problem. After narrowing the study group to 100 problem drinkers, the company concluded that the average cost per alcoholic employee was $1,006.50.

Most productivity loss figures have been based on demographic studies of the "typical" alcoholic employee. The National Council on Alcoholism has reported that the alcoholic employee is absent three times as often as the average employee, is involved in four to six times as many off-the-job accidents and two to four times as many on-the-job accidents, and makes sickness and accident benefits claims that are three times greater than those of the average employee.[2] Individ-

---

*From *Business Horizons*, November–December 1982, pp. 68–72. Reprinted with permission.
[1]S. T. Pritchett and L. Finely, "Problem Drinking and the Risk Management Function," *Risk Management*, October 1975: 17–18.
[2]S. E. Kaden, "Compassion or Cover-up: The Alcoholic Employee," *Personnel Journal*, July 1980: 357.

ual industry figures on alcoholic employee performance are even more alarming. Firestone reports that their alcoholic employees are absent from the job sixteen times more often than the nonalcoholic, have two and one-half times as many absences of eight days or more, receive three times more in sickness benefits, have an accident rate 3.6 times higher, and file five times as many compensation claims.[3]

The National Council on Alcoholism asserts that, for an individual company, the losses due to alcoholism might be estimated as being 3 percent of the total company payroll, *plus* increased health insurance premiums, increased workmen's compensation payments, and the more intangible consequences associated with turnover of personnel, lowered morale, and the loss of key employees. These intangible costs include the loss of experienced employees, job friction, lower morale, waste of supervisory time, bad decisions, and damaged customer and public relations. In one auto assembly plant, out of 746 grievances filed during one year, 363, or 48.6 percent, were alcohol related.[4]

JOB PERFORMANCE

Alcoholism is a progressive disease that manifests itself in stages of behaviors on and off the job. Dr. Selden Bacon, Director of the Center of Alcohol Studies at Rutgers University, in conjunction with the Kemper Insurance Company, has identified a progression of behavioral deviations that are common to most alcoholics.

1 Drinks more frequently than peers.
2 Goes beyond allowed license for drinking behavior.
3 Experiences blackouts or temporary amnesia.
4 Drinks more rapidly than others.
5 Sneaks drinks.
6 Loses control as to time/place/amount of drinking.
7 Hides liquor supply.
8 Drinks to overcome hangover effect.
9 Tries new patterns of drinking as to time/place/amounts/type of drinks.
10 Tries geographical cures—seeking out new locations or different drinking groups.
11 Becomes a loner in drinking.
12 Develops an elaborate system of lies/alibis/rationalizations to cover up or explain drinking.
13 Develops personality and behavior changes.
14 Experiences extended binges, physical tremors, hallucinations, deliria, rejection of social reality.

These patterns appear gradually but with increasing frequency and intensity

[3]"Business's Multibillion-Dollar Hangover," *Nation's Business*, May 1977: 66.
[4]Kaden: 357.

over a period of years until eventually they are all present. Behaviors 1 through 3 are considered to be the early stages of the disease, 4 through 10 the middle stages, and 11 through 14 the final stages of development. It is in the middle stages that the employee's drinking appears to affect job performance significantly.

Another study details common behavioral patterns of the alcoholic worker.

"Frequent episodes of unexplained absences with disappearances from the job during working hours."

"Habitually arrives late for work and leaves early. Lunch breaks stretch well into the afternoon (or worse yet, the employee fails to return to work after lunch). Excuses are highly suspect."

"Meetings, deadlines and important dates are missed. Job details go unattended. Procrastination increases and reliability decreases."

"Contact with coworkers, and especially superiors, is minimal. Exhibits antisocial behavior. Blames others for performance shortfalls."

"Judgmental errors and dulled decision-making skills result in sporadic, unpredictable performance and inferior work quality."

"For the industrial worker, accidents increase as concern for safety decreases."[5]

LEGAL ISSUES

In addition to production loss and poor work performance, employers must also be concerned about legal issues which have arisen concerning the alcoholic employee. The Vocational Rehabilitation Act of 1973, which prohibits employment discrimination by federal contractors or subcontractors against employable, handicapped workers, has been extended to include alcoholics and drug addicts. Alcoholics and drug addicts must receive the same rights as other handicapped workers who cannot be discriminated against in federally sponsored employment, education, and services. In addition, on July 5, 1977, the Department of Labor told employers who are recipients of federal contracts and subcontracts in excess of $2,500 to take affirmative action and hire alcoholics and drug addicts qualified and able to perform work. Employers are also prohibited from screening out alcoholics and drug addicts through pre-employment medical examinations.[6]

The law also implies that reasons for terminating an employee must be restricted solely to job performance.

"Our government spends a considerable amount of money each year to rehabilitate alcoholics and drug abusers, to help them again become employable, productive citizens. It would be incongruous to turn around and deny them protection under the antidiscrimination law."[7]

Business now may find itself in a "Catch-22" dilemma. Persons cannot be screened out of the hiring process because they are alcoholics, and firms cannot

---

[5]F. E. Kuzmits and H. E. Hammons, "Rehabilitating the Troubled Employee," *Personnel Journal*, April 1981: 238.

[6]J. Dolan, "Reducing Risks Through Employee Assistance Programs," *Risk Management*, October 1978: 66.

[7]Dolan: 66.

fire alcoholics based on any factor besides job performance. Brent E. Zepke has reviewed statutory and common law regarding the intoxicated employee and states:

"In addition, once an individual is hired, arbitrators have held that an employer has a duty to try and assist the employee who has problems with intoxication and not merely discharge him. Thus it is possible that an employer may have the multiple duty to hire a known drunkard or drug user, to protect the employee from his own acts, to protect fellow employees from his acts, and not to discharge the employee until treatment efforts fail."[8]

Courts and statutes have determined that employers are responsible for the safety of employees and the public. If the alcoholic employee hurts another employee or member of the public, the employer is liable if the alcoholic employee had not been ordered off the premises and the employer had knowledge that the employee was intoxicated.

Because alcoholism has come to be classified as a disease, health insurance has in the last decade begun to cover treatment of alcoholics. J. F. Follman, former vice president of the Health Insurance Association, reported that 17 of the top health insurance companies now will cover loss of income resulting from alcoholism if the illness is treated. Follman noted that such coverage has been made a requirement for group health insurance contracts by a number of states. The AFL-CIO found in a recent study of forty-six health and welfare insurance plans that thirty-seven provide some such benefits. While there are still some variations in coverage, the trend is overwhelmingly in the direction of recognition of alcoholism as a disease by those who provide insurance coverage.[9]

EMPLOYEE ASSISTANCE PROGRAMS

Prior to 1940 no companies were actively involved in alcoholism treatment programs. DuPont and Eastman-Kodak were the first companies to implement the rudiments of an alcohol treatment program for their employees. The late 1950s and early 1960s saw the beginning of employee assistance programs to aid troubled employees. By the late 1960s the clients using these programs were primarily alcoholic employees. In 1968 over 200 companies provided alcoholism referral programs or implemented fully staffed alcoholism treatment programs. By 1972 the number of these business-sponsored programs grew to 1,000, and today there are over 3,500.[10]

Companies used to play the ostrich in dealing with their alcoholic employees. This approach was best described by James M. Roche, former Chairman of the Board for the General Motors Corporation.

[8]B. E. Zepke, "Employer Liability for Intoxicated Employees," *Supervisory Management*, July 1977: 38.

[9]"What Industry Is Doing About 10 Million Alcoholic Workers," *U.S. News and World Report*, January 12, 1976: 67.

[10]"Ways Employers Can Help Drinkers, Drug Addicts," *U. S. News and World Report*, August 27, 1979: 62.

"Unfortunately, many companies still have an unwritten policy. It goes something like this: 'This company will pay a high economic premium in lost time and accidents to conceal alcoholism from the attention of labor and management. When alcoholism reaches the stage where it can no longer be concealed, the employee will be fired.'"[11]

Now companies look differently at the problem. Again, James Roche.

"Even without counting the costs to society in general, or the costs and suffering of the alcoholic's family, or the horrible loss of his own health and happiness, business and industry have a tremendous stake in the alcohol program. A program to help alcoholic employees is just plain good business."[12]

Thomas A. Murphy, James Roche's successor at General Motors believes employee assistance programs are economically desirable. He recently stated that for every dollar spent for treatment of employees in their program, more than two dollars was being returned within a period of three years.

There is now general recognition of the value of workplace programs for identifying and steering alcoholics in treatment. Most businesses accomplish this with the carrot versus stick approach. Keeping his or her job seems to be the single most important reason for an alcoholic to actively seek treatment; this threat appears to outweigh even the possibility of losing family and friends.

Government and business are now coming together to work on this problem. In 1970, the National Institute on Alcohol Abuse and Alcoholism (NIAAA) was established by the federal government to serve as a national clearing house on alcoholism treatment services. Two years later the Occupational Programs Branch of the NIAAA was implemented with a primary focus on assisting companies with alcoholism recovery programs and referral services. The labor unions have also played a large part in the creation of these programs, the United Auto Workers being the foremost advocate.

Most of the industrial programs start with a firm commitment by top management through the entire network of corporate communications (such as a letter from the president, posters, supervisor-employee meetings, letters to employee homes). Most programs stress that the problem drinker who seeks help will not jeopardize his or her job, that in-patient treatment will be covered by medical insurance, and that no record of any such actions will appear on the personnel file.

The next step is training the supervisors. In a series of several one- or two-hour training sessions conducted by professionals, they learn to be alert to evidence of deteriorating job performance. This involves breaking through the denial system of the alcoholic and the tendency for supervisory personnel to shield the alcoholic from detection. Joseph J. Walker points out the problem with doing otherwise:

"The supervisor who takes a bleeding-heart approach is setting himself up for a 'con job.' It is this writer's belief that a business-like, problem-solving, rational approach will be more effective in most instances. There should be at least as

---

[11]J. M. Roche, "Alcoholism, The Disease in Industry," *Vital Speeches of the Day*, December 1, 1972: 120.
[12]Roche: 120.

much emphasis on firmness as there is on fairness. The supervisor who looks the other way or covers up for the substance abusers is his own and the substance abuser's worst enemy."[13]

In companies where alcoholic recovery or treatment programs work best, regular performance evaluation and merit ranking systems have become the diagnostic tool of supervisors. They usually then refer the alcoholic employee to a particular individual within the company who serves as a program coordinator or employee assistance administrator. Regular employees of the company who are recovered alcoholics often staff this position.

One of the primary functions of this person is to have a side range of information as to the various professional and paraprofessional agencies and systems in the community to which the employee can be referred for help. Liaison is maintained between the program coordinator and the various helping agencies as to service available, and this information is publicized so that employees may also avail themselves of such services on their own, in addition to having such services available by referral from supervisors. In all cases confidentiality is maintained, and no company personnel receive any information about the professional contact unless the employee gives explicit permission for such information to be released.

Although exact numbers are difficult to come by, the best available data indicates that approximately 10 percent of any work force tend to use such information and referral services; somewhat less than half of these are sent by their supervisors. This would vary, of course, among companies. Alcoholism and alcohol-related problems tend to account for about half of such referrals, with personal, marital, family, financial-legal, and other problems making up the difference.

Smaller companies which do not have enough employees to warrant a program of their own often subscribe for such services with a local, public, or private community agency or unite in a consortium with other companies to set up a program.

Once an employee, either through a supervisor or on his or her own, makes contact with an outside agency for a professional diagnosis, the worker is then steered to the most appropriate helping agency. For later-stage alcoholics, the first step is usually a period of detoxification as an inpatient for about three days. The next step is follow-up. Some alcohol treatment centers have a twenty-eight day program which includes detoxification and then a comprehensive therapy and rehabilitation program which involves working with family members as well as the employee and setting up a network of continuing support, including AA. During that time a continuing recovery plan is formulated and the employee is provided with a continuous counseling program. Most problems, however, can be dealt with on a strictly out-patient basis, and medical insurance usually covers some or all of the treatment costs.

The success rates for companies using alcoholism recovery treatment programs are phenomenal. Most studies indicate a success rate of 50 to 85 percent, compared

---

[13]J. J. Walker, "Supervising the Alcoholic," *Supervisory Management*, November 1978: 31.

with 20 to 40 percent in social service agencies. The primary factors which account for the difference are (1) threat of job loss, (2) early identification, and (3) ease of follow-up through the working environment.

Two companies have done an excellent job of evaluating their programs. General Motors reports the following results during the first year after program entry:

- 40 percent reduction in lost time,
- sickness and accident benefits reduced by 60 percent,
- grievances cut by as much as 50 percent,
- disciplinary actions cut by 50 percent,
- on-the-job accidents reduced by 50 percent.

General Motors operates a corporate-wide alcoholism program in conjunction with the U.A.W.

Firestone, which has been operating alcoholism recovery programs for over a decade, has a recovery rate of 80 to 85 percent. Firestone used to terminate 95 percent of its identifiable alcoholics; now it estimates that it retains over 80 percent of them. This is remarkable, considering that 5 to 10 percent of Firestone's work force are alcoholics. At the program's inception, all participants were mandatorily referred by their supervisor and 95 percent had been warned that their jobs were in jeopardy. Now over 35 percent of the referrals are voluntary and only 2 percent of all referrals are involved in job discipline.

Pritchett and Finley have estimated that for every dollar a business spends on alcoholism programs it will save $10 in increased productivity, lower turnover, and lower absenteeism. The Great Northern Railway Company claims a 52 percent decrease in absenteeism and a 78 percent decrease in grievances among employees participating in the program.

The National Institute on Alcohol Abuse and Alcoholism reports that companies who have a penetration rate (program involvement) of 2.5 percent of the work force are probably operating a viable program that is reaching most of the problem drinkers. Of some concern is the lower figure for alcoholic women participating in recovery programs. Studies have shown that people are less sympathetic to a female alcoholic than to a male alcoholic.

Employee assistance programs are becoming more prevalent in business and are having a positive effect on productivity. Even more encouraging is the fact that these programs are more effective than traditional social service agency approaches in working with the alcoholic. More technical research should be performed in this area to increase knowledge of accomplishments and what works as well as to provide a framework for establishing new programs.

REVIEW QUESTIONS

1 Summarize the law that is relevant to employees who are alcoholics.
2 What are the major characteristics of employee assistance programs?
3 From a societal standpoint, why should organizations play a role in identifying and treating alcoholics?

READING 68

Mental Distress: Possible Implications for the Future

Mitchell S. Novit*

One of the more notable trends of recent years is concern for the emotional well-being of the organization's work force. Programs such as job enrichment and improving the quality of work life reflect a growing awareness that the organization's productivity and long-term prosperity are heavily dependent upon employee dedication and commitment. The proliferation of articles, books and seminars on stress management is another example of this concern. Thus programs to deal with employee attitudes and feelings are receiving high priority in more and more organizations.

But accompanying attempts to improve the psychological climate of the workplace has been a development which represents a counter trend. This is the extent to which employees, aided by both statutes and the common law, are finding ways through the courts to hold their employers legally liable for pyschological and mental distress said to be job and work related. Because no one law or major Supreme Court decision has created this liability, it has been occurring gradually with little fanfare and perhaps without attracting a great deal of attention.

This is unfortunate, because it is an area that needs watching. Not only is there a potential financial burden, but the problems in measuring, assessing and controlling something as intangible as emotional distress make its management unusually challenging. This discussion will show the three primary areas of the law where this development is taking place, each of which will be examined in turn:

• Mental injury resulting from work stresses and related factors for which the employer is liable under programs of workers' compensation.
• Compensation beyond "make-whole" remedies for mental anguish resulting from the employer's violation of certain anti-discrimination statutes.
• Emotional distress from intentional acts by the employer designed to humiliate and degrade; are compensated for by financial damages secured in suits under the common law doctrine of torts.

WORKERS' COMPENSATION AND MENTAL INJURY

Programs of workers' compensation, by which the worker is financially compensated for work-related injuries and occupationally caused illnesses, have been around since the beginning of this century. While many features of these programs have resulted in litigation based on differing interpretations as to the kinds of

*From *Personnel Administrator*, August 1982, pp. 47–53. Copyright 1982 by The American Society for Personnel Administration, Alexandria, Va.

injuries and illnesses which are compensable, a long accepted premise of workers' compensation has been that any injury or illness had to have some kind of physical or organic manifestation.

What has been happening more and more in recent years, however, is that workers have been putting in claims for something that might be called mental injury which has no discernible physical manifestation, at least not in the way this has traditionally been defined.[1] And the courts, particularly in certain states, have shown an increasing tendency to uphold such claims. (Workers' compensation programs are established by state law and are enforced by state boards and commissions, with state courts having power of review.)

As is true of the mental health field in general, definitions and categorizations in this area are difficult to make with precision. Thus the leading authority on workers' compensation has classified claims for mental conditions into three categories, though it should be noted that in actual cases the distinctions are not nearly so clear as the categories might suggest: 1. a mental stimulus resulting in a physical injury; 2. a physical trauma or stimulus resulting in a mental injury; and 3. a mental stimulus resulting in a mental injury.[2]

Over the years workers' compensation referees and boards, as well as the courts, have been willing to grant compensation for the first type, such as a 1922 Michigan case where a worker allowed a piece of machinery to slip and strike a coworker whom he thought he had killed.[3] He became highly anxious, went into a state of delirium and eventually died. His estate was awarded benefits on the basis that a work related shock had caused his physical injury (death).

The second type also has not created exceptional difficulties, such as when a head injury results in such anxiety that a person is unable to continue working. The physical evidence of the injury has made it possible to sustain the claim of a mental condition, even though the anxiety itself cannot be observed but must be inferred from what the claimant reports.

It is the third type that has created the most problems, and for which the courts are showing an increasing willingness to grant compensation. One of the early cases in this area was decided in 1955.[4] An ironworker was working on a scaffold when it gave way and a coworker plunged to his death. The ironworker was saved when he was caught in a cable. He developed a condition which made it impossible for him to resume work without becoming terrified and highly anxious, a condition diagnosed by his treating pyschiatrist as a form of neurosis. The Texas Supreme Court reversed the appeals court in upholding this as a compensable claim, clearly charting new directions for workers' compensation law at the time.

Similar cases have been increasing in recent years, not all of them being decided for the claimants, but enough are to suggest these cases may become commonplace.[5] An example is a 1980 Oregon case where a claimant alleged that job stress resulting from poor working conditions, having to perform two jobs and a personality conflict with a supervisor, led to anxiety and depression such that she was unable to continue working.[6] The Oregon Court of Appeals upheld both the referee and the Workers' Compensation Board in affirming this as a legitimate claim for benefits.

It is probable that such decisions may be more the exception than the rule in most states. But, the Oregon court made a point that suggests why more jurisdictions may be following its lead. It noted that the courts have traditionally been reluctant to recognize claims of this type because they would open a "Pandora's box" of potentially illegitimate claims. But the court emphasized that the possibility of illegitimate claims should not be a reason for denying compensation to legitimate claimants who became mentally disabled as a result of their work. Given our society's increasing sophistication regarding mental problems and the growing tendency to use the courts for redress of an ever-expanding list of perceived wrongs, it is not hard to see why these cases will increase.

ANTIDISCRIMINATION LEGISLATION AND MENTAL DISTRESS

In providing remedies for the victims of discrimination, there has never been serious question that the various discrimination statutes are to provide equitable or "make-whole" relief. This means the individual discriminated against should be made the same as before discrimination. Such things as a job offer, reinstatement, back pay and attorney fees fall into this category. The question of whether or not victims of discrimination should also receive compensatory and even punitive damages for pain and suffering has been much more difficult to resolve. This is best understood by looking individually at the major discrimination laws.

Title VII

Remedies for discrimination under Title VII of the 1964 Civil Rights Act are spelled out in Section 706 (g): The court may enjoin the respondent from engaging in such unlawful employment practice and order such affirmative action as may be appropriate, which may include, but is not limited to, reinstatement or hiring of employees with or without back pay . . . or any other equitable relief as the court deems appropriate."

It is the phrase "other equitable relief" which presumably could give the courts authority to assess compensatory and punitive damages. And for many years the U.S. district courts were quite inconsistent on this issue, some providing relief and some not. But gradually, as cases began reaching the circuit or appellate courts, the decisions became more consistent, affirming that it was not Congress's intent to provide damages for pain and suffering under Title VII. Since the U.S. Supreme Court has refused review of this issue, the circuit court rulings stand.

From the employer's perspective this is a favorable interpretation. But this has not meant that employers are immune from liability for pain and suffering claimed by victims of discrimination. The reason for this is found in two laws enacted shortly after the end of the Civil War.

Civil Rights Acts of 1866 and 1871

The Civil Rights Act of 1866, Section 1981, prohibits employment discrimination based on race, color and national origin. The Civil Rights Act of 1871, Section 1983, enforces certain constitutional rights, including the Fourteenth Amendment which provides for "equal protection of the laws." Thus the sweeping language of the 1871 Act includes the categories of Section 1981—race, color, and national origin—and adds religion, sex and age.

It may be a source of confusion as to why, with Title VII on the books, an individual would bring suit under these statutes. There are many reasons, but a primary one is that these laws permit recovery for damages that are not permitted under Title VII. A recent book written for those thinking of filing a discrimination suit, entitled *Sue Your Boss—Rights and Remedies for Employment Discrimination* (see review on page 9, March 1982 *Personnel Administrator*), is quite blatant in making this point: "The 1871 Act is important . . . because it permits individuals to win substantial monetary remedies above and beyond back pay. In fact, because of the availability of such monetary remedies as actual damages, compensatory damages and punitive damages, the 1871 Act often is used in conjunction with other laws to increase the overall remedies available . . ."[7] Similar words are used in discussing the 1866 Act, though it is more limited since it does not include sex, religion and age.

In order to obtain remedies under both Title VII and the 1866 and 1871 measures, it is not necessary to bring sequential suits since plaintiffs can simultaneously file charges under more than one statute. As attorneys and employees become increasingly familiar with the additional remedies available under the older statutes, it is likely they will be used more frequently.

The discrimination law, which has caused the most difficulties regarding damages for emotional distress, is the Age Discrimination in Employment Act. Section 7 (b) of the act provides in part that: "In any action brought to enforce this Act the court shall have jurisdiction to grant such legal or equitable relief as may be appropriate to effectuate the purposes of this Act . . ."

Because the Act provides for "legal relief" in addition to the equitable relief of Title VII, and because the Act is enforced under provisions related to enforcement of the Fair Labor Standards Act, the courts have had more than the usual difficulty in determining whether the law provides for compensatory damages.

A leading case in this area is *Rogers v Exxon Research and Engineering Company*, first decided in 1975.[8] A scientist for the company since 1938, Dr. Dilworth T. Rogers was involuntarily retired in 1969. He filed suit under the Age Discrimination Act and his estate continued the case when he died prior to trial. The company was found guilty of age discrimination and was assessed $30,000 in out-of-pocket damages and additional damages of $750,000 for Dr. Rogers' "pain and suffering," subsequently reduced to $200,000 by the trial judge.

The company appealed and the U.S. Third Circuit Court of Appeals in 1977 overturned the pain and suffering award contending that compensatory damages were not permitted under the Act.[9] Since the ruling, two other circuit courts have rendered similar decisions.[10]

However, since the Supreme Court has refused further review of these cases, these decisions are only binding upon the district courts in these three circuits. Some district courts in other circuits have continued to award compensatory damages in age discrimination cases. Thus, until the Supreme Court issues a definitive ruling, or until all the circuit courts have reached parallel conclusions as in Title VII cases, the issue of compensatory damages in age discrimination cases is likely to remain in a state of some uncertainty.

Equal Pay Act

The primary remedy under the Equal Pay Act of 1963 is equitable relief, the victim receiving the proper wage plus back pay to compensate for the time during which the improper differential existed. The Act does not permit compensatory damages for pain and suffering, but it does provide for double back pay at the court's discretion in cases of willful and wanton discrimination.

INTENTIONAL INFLICTION OF EMOTIONAL DISTRESS

Employees can also obtain damage awards through lawsuits charging the employer with inflicting distress by intentional or reckless acts designed to degrade and humiliate. This is covered under the common law doctrine of torts.

Personal injury is also being claimed in a lawsuit of the type under discussion, not for physical harm, but rather for injury of a mental or emotional nature. The charge is that the employer caused severe mental anguish and distress by extreme and outrageous conduct. For this reason it is often referred to as the tort of outrage.[11] It is not an easy charge to sustain and it must involve conduct truly outrageous, so far beyond the bounds of normal decency that a reasonable person would find it offensive and distressful in the extreme. Simply having hurt pride or feelings is not nearly enough to support a claim.

Numerous cases are on record charging the employer with intentional infliction of emotional distress.[12] The majority of cases have been dismissed because the facts would not support going to trial or have been won by defendant-employers when trials occurred. Nonetheless, there are cases on record where plaintiffs have won at least the right to have their cases heard.

One case which illustrates what is involved in cases of this type is *Alcorn v Anbro Engineering, Inc.,* decided in California in 1970.[13] In this case a black employee informed the company's white field superintendent that in his role as shop steward he had advised another employee not to drive a certain truck. The manager flew into a rage, cursed the employee using racial epithets of a vicious, derogatory and stereotyped nature and fired him on the spot.

Using the grievance-arbitration procedures in the collective bargaining agreement, the employee was reinstated in his job. He also brought suit against the employer for intentional infliction of emotional distress, alleging he was ill for several weeks after the incident, was unable to work and sustained shock, nausea and insomnia. He further alleged that the conduct was "intentional and malicious and done for the purpose of causing . . . humiliation, mental anguish and emotional and physical distress."

The trial judge dismissed the case on the basis that the facts did not support a cause of action because there was not physical injury. The California Supreme

Court reversed and returned the case for trial, noting the physical consequences of shock or other disturbances to the nervous system are sufficient to satisfy the requirement that some kind of physical injury has been suffered. The court went further in stating: "Moreover, the courts of this state have also acknowledged the right to recover damages for emotional distress alone, without consequent physical injuries, in cases involving extreme and outrageous intentional invasions of one's mental and emotional tranquility." The case was presumably settled out of court.

A similar case was decided in the state of Washington in 1977.[14] A Mexican-American, David Contreras, employed by Crown Zellerbach during the fall and winter of 1973, was falsely accused of stealing and discharged in January 1974. In addition to actions for discrimination, Contreras also brought a separate suit against the company for compensatory damages under tort law. He alleged that during his employment he was subjected to continuous humiliation and embarassment by reason of racial jokes, slurs and comments made by agents (managers) of the company and by employees who he claimed were not controlled by their supervisors. He further alleged that statements made by the company's managers and employees concerning his firing made it difficult for him to find work.

The trial court dismissed the charges saying there was no precedent in the state for the tort of outrage. But the Supreme Court of Washington reversed and returned the case for trial, noting the particular vulnerability of persons with varying ethnic backgrounds and that in today's social climate racial epithets which were once part of common usage may be something much more than "mere insulting language." This case too was apparently settled out of court.

As indicated, the majority of such cases have resulted in verdicts favorable to the defendant organizations and not the plaintiff employees. Nonetheless, once precedent has been established in a few cases, it provides a foundation for the judiciary to build upon as other cases are brought for litigation. Thus the tort of outrage is somewhat of a novelty at present, but it is one which organizations should keep an eye on.

CONCLUSION

This analysis shows the ways in which employees are more and more holding their employers liable for mental and emotional problems that are said to be work related. This may be somewhat ironic, since so much effort has been expended in recent years to make the working environment less dehumanizing and more congruent with higher level needs, thus presumably reducing the incidence of mental stress that workers feel. It would be both overstatement and overdramatization to say that the problem is a critical one at this time; nonetheless, today's developing trend can easily become the crisis of tomorrow.

REFERENCES

1 Wood, Norman J., "Workmen's compensation and mental injury," *Labor Law Journal*, October, 1977, pp. 641–644.
2 Larson, Arthur, *Workmen's Compensation Law* (New York: Matthew Bender & Co.), Sections 42.20 and 42.24, periodically updated and supplemented.
3 *Klein v Len H. Darling Co.*, 187 N.W. 400 (1922).
4 *Baily v American General Insurance Company*, 279 S.W. 2d 315 (1955).
5 "On-the-job stress leads many workers to file—and win—compensation awards." *The Wall Street Journal*, Sept. 17. 1980.
6 *James v State Accident Insurance Fund*, 605 P. 2d 1368 (1980).
7 Larson, Richard E., *Sue Your Boss—Rights & Remedies for Employment Discrimination* (New York: Farrar, Straus & Giroux), 1981, p. 173.
8 *Rogers v Exxon Research and Engineering Co.*, 404 F. Supp. 324 (1975).
9 *Rogers v Exxon Research and Engineering Co.*, 550 F. 2d 834 (1977).
10 Commerce Clearing House, Inc., 17 *EPD (Employment Practices Decisions)*, ¶8394, at 6006.
11 *Restatement (Second) of Torts*, 46.
12 Smith, Joel E., "Liability of employer, supervisor or manager for intentionally or recklessly causing employee emotional distress," 86 ALR *(American Law Reports)* 3rd 454.
13 *Alcorn v Anbro Engineering, Inc.*, 468 P. 2d 216 (1970).
14 *Contreras v Crown Zellerbach Corporation*, 565 P. 2d 1173 (1977).

REVIEW QUESTIONS

1 Explain briefly how the Civil Rights and Equal Pay acts are relevant to employee suits for mental distress caused by the job.
2 Why might employees perceive that their employers have *intentionally* inflicted emotional distress on them?
3 Given the increasing possibility of legal action by employees, what advice can you give employers for minimizing the likelihood of a suit based on mental distress?

CHAPTER 20

INTERNATIONAL ISSUES

READING 69

Japanese and American Management: Theory Z and Beyond

George W. England*

INTRODUCTION

Professor William Ouchi of UCLA has recently written a thought-provoking book about management, *Theory Z: How American Business Can Meet the Japanese Challenge*. The book is being widely read and undoubtedly will influence a large number of practicing managers and a considerable number of management scholars and researchers. The Theory Z approach to management quite simply suggests that *involved workers* are the key to increased productivity. Involved workers in large Japanese organizations result from an internally consistent set of norms, practices, and behaviors which are grounded in trust and interpersonal intimacy. Japanese organizations foster lifetime employment, slow evaluation and promotion, non-specialized career paths, implicit control mechanisms, collective decision making, collective responsibility, and holistic concern in internally consistent ways which produce worker involvement and thus higher productivity. This is the Japanese way according to Ouchi and it is the Theory Z way in which some American organizations seem to operate.

Serious consideration of Ouchi's work gives rise to a pair of related questions of considerable significance: 1) Is it likely that Theory Z management will become the accepted norm in American companies to the extent it has in Japan? 2) What are the important lessons we can learn from Japanese management? Addressing these 2 questions will be the primary purpose of this paper. To do so, however, one needs to review several studies that bear on these questions.

Although there is a wide variety of well-known studies available which focus on different aspects of Japanese work and organizational life [Abegglen 1958, 1973; Adams 1969; Cole 1971, 1979; Dore 1973; Drucker 1971; Hanami 1979; Hattori 1978; Hazama 1978; Kahn and Pepper 1979; Levine 1958, 1965; Lockwood 1954; Mannari 1974; Marsh and Mannari 1971, 1972, 1976; Okochi 1973; Pascale 1978; Pascale and Athos 1981; Tsurumi 1976; Vogel 1963, 1979; Whitehill and Takezawa 1968; Yang 1977; and Yoshino 1968, 1971, 1975], this paper will use only those that provide rather direct empirical comparisons between Japan and the United States and that are relevant to the issues just raised.

COMPARISON OF MANAGERS

In *Managerial Thinking* [1966], Haire, Ghiselli, and Porter studied leadership, the role of the manager in his culture, and motive satisfaction among 3600 managers

*From *Journal of International Business Studies*, Fall 1983, pp. 131–142. Reprinted with permission.

in 14 countries around the world including Japan and the United States. One general result was that Japanese managers, unlike other managers, did not fit into clusters of similar countries. There was a Nordic cluster (Denmark, Germany, Norway, Sweden); a Latin Cluster (Belgium, France, Italy, Spain); an Anglo-American cluster (England, U.S.); a developing countries cluster (Argentina, Chile, India); and there was Japan. Japanese managers are different from managers in all other countries studied; they stand alone.

Also, Japanese managers were found to embrace reciprocal participative attitudes and values to a greater extent than did any other country's managers and specifically more than did American managers. (See Table 1.)

Finally, Japanese managers saw their positions and roles as much more self-actualizing than did their American counterparts. (See Table 2.)

Thus Haire, Ghiselli, and Porter show that Japanese managers are quite different from other managers generally and from American managers specifically. Japanese managers (when compared to American managers) are more apt to embrace reciprocal participative attitudes and values and to perceive higher levels of self-actualization flowing from their positions and roles. These attributes of Japanese managers are partial elements of the internally consistent management framework which permits Theory Z management to work in Japan.

A study of the personal and organizational values held by over 1300 managers in Japan and the United States throws further light on these issues [England 1975]. The study found that Japanese managers as a group have more homogeneous values than do managers in the U.S., Australia, India, or Korea [p. 42].

Japanese managers, more than American managers, have internalized organizational goals concerning high productivity, organizational growth, and organizational stability. The behavioral relevance of personal goals of achievement and

TABLE 1
JAPANESE-AMERICAN PARTICIPATION
SCALE COMPARISONS

- In a work situation, if the subordinates cannot influence me, I lose some of my influence on them.
- Group goal setting offers advantages that cannot be obtained by individual goal setting.
  (5-point, Strongly Disagree—Strongly Agree Scale)

	Data	
Group	Mean raw scores	Standard scores across all countries (m = 0, sd = 1)
Japanese managers	3.98	.44
American managers	3.56	.02
All managers	3.54	0.00

Source: Haire, Ghiselli, and Porter [1966], p. 22.

TABLE 2
JAPANESE-AMERICAN SELF-ACTUALIZATION
SCALE COMPARISONS

- The opportunity for personal growth and development in my management position.
- The feeling of self-fulfillment a person gets from being in my management position (that is, the feeling of being able to use one's own unique capabilities, realizing one's own potentialities).
- The feeling of worthwhile accomplishment in my management position.
  (7-point, minimum amount—maximum amount)

	Data	
Group	Mean raw scores	Standard scores across all countries (m = 0, sd = 1)
Japanese managers	5.54	.44
American managers	4.96	−.09
All managers	5.05	0.00

Source: Haire, Ghiselli, and Porter [1966], p. 81.

creativity is higher for Japanese managers while the behavioral relevance of job satisfaction and individuality is higher for American managers. (See Table 3.)

The studies of value systems of managers in these 5 countries suggest that Japanese managers have a homogeneous value system and that both organizational and personal acheivement goals are more behaviorally relevant than for American managers. Again, these value attributes of Japanese managers are part of the reason why Theory Z management works in Japan. They are values that foster the successful application of Theory Z as the Japanese model of management.

TABLE 3
BEHAVIORAL RELEVANCE SCORES OF SELECTED
ORGANIZATIONAL GOAL AND PERSONAL GOAL
CONCEPTS FOR JAPANESE AND
AMERICAN MANAGERS

	Japanese managers	American managers
Organizational goal concept		
High productivity	79	63
Organizational growth	72	50
Organizational stability	58	41
Personal goal concept		
Achievement	77	63
Creativity	73	53
Job satisfaction	34	51
Individuality	23	33

Source: England [1975], pp. 30–32.

COMPARISON OF WORKERS

When one moves from the managerial arena to that of nonmanagers or workers, the most helpful research is the 20-year effort of Shin-ichi Takezawa and Arthur Whitehill. In 1960, these researchers studied and compared industrial relations systems between Japan and the United States and employee attitudes and beliefs among approximately 2000 production workers in the 2 countries [Whitehill and Takezawa 1968]. In 1976, they repeated major parts of the study among approximately 1200 workers from the same companies in the 2 countries [Takezawa and Whitehill 1981]. These studies provide a unique view of differences and similarities between workers in 2 countries as well as an indication of change between the 2 countries over a 16-year span of time. Thus both cross-sectional and longitudinal comparisons are possible. For the present purposes, the comparisons of countries and time periods in the areas of organizational involvement, acceptance of management policies and practices, and work effort values are most revealing. [Data for Tables 4–8 are from Takezawa and Whitehill 1981, pp. 200–219.]

Tables 4 and 5 show that Japanese workers place their company in a far more central life role than do American workers, and that this difference is increasing rather than decreasing.

TABLE 4
ORGANIZATIONAL INVOLVEMENT

I think of my company as:	1 the central concern in my life and of greater importance than my personal life;	2 a part of my life at least equal in importance to my personal life;	3 a place for me to work with management, during work hours, to accomplish mutual goals;	4 strictly a place to work and entirely separate from my personal life.

Figures are in percentages

		1	2	3	4
1	Japan 1960	11	54	27	8
2	Japan 1976	9	64	15	12

		1	2	3	4
3	U.S. 1960	2	27	52	19
4	U.S. 1976	1	20	42	37

		1	2	3	4
5	Japan 1960 Young	7	62	20	11
6	Japan 1976 Young	8	66	12	14

		1	2	3	4
7	U.S. 1960 Young	2	30	49	19
8	U.S. 1976 Young		18	35	47

(1 = 0)

TABLE 5
ORGANIZATIONAL COMMITMENT

	1	2	3	4
If you expect that your company will experience a prolonged decline in business, and if you can get a job with a more prosperous company, would you:	stay with the company and share whatever the future may bring because you have confidence in management;	stay with the company provided management pledges to try to keep you employed though perhaps at reduced pay;	stay with the company provided management pledges to try to keep you employed and not reduce your pay;	leave the company and take the job with the more prosperous company.

Figures are in percentages

		1	2	3	4
1	Japan 1960	46	10	41	3
2	Japan 1976	38	12	45	5

		1	2	3	4
3	U.S. 1960	41	7	29	23
4	U.S. 1976	26	8	30	36

		1	2	3	4
5	Japan 1960 Young	30	14	52	4
6	Japan 1976 Young	33	11	49	7

		1	2	3	4
7	U.S. 1960 Young	30	7	31	32
8	U.S. 1976 Young	14	7	32	47

Tables 6 and 7 show that Japanese workers have greater trust and acceptance of management decisions concerning application of practices and policies than do American workers.

Table 8 shows that Japanese workers value working at high levels of capacity and assisting other workers to a greater extent than do American workers, and that this difference is increasing over time.

All of these results suggest that there are fundamental and continuing differences between Japanese and American workers.

High levels of work effort and commitment; organizational involvement; and cooperation, acceptance, and trust in management policies and practices—all are the norm for Japanese workers; they are not for American workers. These Japanese worker norms and expectations are consistent with and supportive of the successful application of Theory Z in Japan. Takezawa and Whitehill [1981, p. 197] conclude:

Japanese improvements during the 1960–76 period seem best accountable, then, as a result of the continuous deliberate efforts by all parties in the total socioeconomic process, particularly in the area of industrial relations. Japanese management, unions, government, workers, and citizens apparently have come to share broader mutual goals,

TABLE 6
MERIT RATING PRACTICES

	1	2	3	4
Regarding the practice of comparing workers through merit rating, I am:	willing to be compared according to a procedure set at management's discretion;	willing to be compared provided it is on the basis of procedures long-established and widely recognized in other companies;	willing to be compared provided the procedure is set with the participation of the union;	unwilling to be compared through merit rating.

Figures are in percentages

		1	2	3	4
1	Japan 1960	6	11	57	26
2	Japan 1976	35	8	43	14
3	U.S. 1960	12	36	39	13
4	U.S. 1976	11	23	44	22
5	Japan 1960 Young	5	11	46	38
6	Japan 1976 Young	34	8	42	16
7	U.S. 1960 Young	16	27	41	16
8	U.S. 1976 Young	8	23	43	26

TABLE 7
DISCIPLINE PRACTICES

	1	2	3	4
Regarding rules and disciplinary penalties established by management, I would:	accept such rules and penalties, and regard violators as undesirable co-workers;	accept such rules and penalties, but show no ill feelings against co-workers who violate them;	reluctantly accept such rules and penalties, but speak against them and give moral support to co-workers who violate them;	evade such rules and penalties whenever possible in an attempt to control management's authority over worker behavior.

Figures are in percentages

		1	2	3	4
1	Japan 1960	72	8	5	15
2	Japan 1976	69	23	5	3
3	U.S. 1960	41	31	8	20
4	U.S. 1976	43	40	9	8

(Continued)

TABLE 7 *(Continued)*

		1	2	3	4
5	Japan 1960 Young	67	10	6	17
6	Japan 1976 Young	64	26	6	4

		1	2	3	4
7	U.S. 1960 Young	41	36	7	16
8	U.S. 1976 Young	33	49	9	9

TABLE 8
WORK EFFORT AND CAPACITY

I think it is most desirable for my co-workers to:	1 work at maximum capacity, without endangering their health, helping others when their own tasks are completed;	2 work at whatever level is necessary to perform their own jobs well;	3 work at whatever level is set by older members of their work group as being a normal day's output;	4 work at the minimum level necessary to keep their jobs, since this will spread the work among more employees.

Figures are in percentages   (4 = 0)

		1	2	3	4
1	Japan 1960	28	67		5
2	Japan 1976	49	47		4

(4 = 0)

		1	2	3	4
3	U.S. 1960	8	79	3	10
4	U.S. 1976	16	75	5	4

		1	2	3	4
5	Japan 1960 Young	17	79	3	1
6	Japan 1976 Young	47	49		4

(4 = 0)

		1	2	3	4
7	U.S. 1960 Young	9	77	2	12
8	U.S. 1976 Young	15	77	4	4

for the attainment of which the parties apparently are prepared to work better together in a spirit of cooperation. Obviously, at the time of our 1976 study, Japan was reaping substantial reward for such efforts.

COMPARISON OF SOCIETIES

At a more general and societal level, Geert Hofstede has recently developed 4 societal value dimensions on which nations differ considerably. His work, *Culture's Consequences: International Differences in Work-Related Values,* is a useful blend of conceptual, historical, methodological, and empirical concerns in studying work values of over 75,000 individuals in 66 countries. It deserves study by scholars in our field. The 4 societal dimensions developed by Hofstede from this massive data bank are:

Power Distance Index—a societal measure of inequality in organizations which has stabilized and is both functional and generally accepted.

Uncertainty Avoidance Index—A societal measure of the extent to which levels of perceived stress are dealt with by uncertainty-reducing mechanisms of rules orientation and employment stability.

Individualism-Collectivism Index—A measure of the relationship between the individual and the collectivity which prevails in a given society. This is essentially a measure of the extent to which concepts of self are perceived in individual terms or in collective terms.

Masculinity-Femininity Index—An index measuring the extent to which a society endorses work goals that are more commonly viewed as masculine (assertiveness versus nurturance, or earnings and advancement versus interpersonal goals and comfort).

Hofstede found that 40 countries differ greatly on these 4 major dimensions at the level of countries. Our immediate interest is in terms of Japanese and American comparisons. The dimensions on which Japan and the United States differ most are Uncertainty Avoidance and Individuality. The Japanese people score high on Uncertainty Avoidance and low on Individuality. (See Table 9.) These scores suggest that the Japanese people endorse social norms whereby uncertainty is reduced through systems of rules leading to stability. Additionally, the Japanese tend to view themselves in collective terms rather than in individual terms. These are elements of Japanese social norms which are very consistent with Theory Z management as described by Ouchi [1981]. Americans score in the opposite direction: high on Individuality and low on Uncertainty Avoidance, hardly consistent with Theory Z management practices.

CONCLUSIONS AND IMPLICATIONS

These real differences between Japan and the United States in general social values and norms and in manager and worker belief systems concerning work

TABLE 9
COMPARISON OF JAPANESE AND AMERICAN SCORES ON FOUR SOCIETAL DIMENSIONS

	Dimension Scores				
Dimensions	Japan	U.S.	Mean across all countries	SD across countries	Range across countries
Power distance	54	40	52	20	11−94
Uncertainty avoidance	92	46	64	24	8−112
Individuality	46	91	50	25	13−91
Masculinity	95	62	50	20	5−95

raise serious questions about widespread transferability of Theory Z management to the United States. In Japan, Theory Z practices are consistent with the general social norms and are generally supported by the actions of labor organizations and governmental bodies. In a word, they form a highly consistent and integrated theoretical framework whose application works well in the Japanese setting.

Will Theory Z management become the norm in the United States? Over the past 20 years, adversarial relations between government and business, and between labor organizations and business, have become sharper and less supportive of Theory Z applications. American management has not found an internally consistent framework of management practices that develops long-term employee involvement, and our productivity suffers from this. Thus, the first question is answered in the negative. Theory Z management is not likely to become the accepted norm in American companies to the extent that it has in Japan, based on the preceding analysis.

The second question stimulated by work on Theory Z (Ouchi [1981] and others) is: what can we learn from Japanese management systems and practices? While analysts might correctly focus on separate aspects of Japanese management and say we should learn this or that, it is the view of the present author that the overall cohesiveness and high level of internal and external consistency in the Japanese system are what merit our examination. From the Japanese we can learn the potential value of developing a management system that is internally consistent, that fits societal norms and expectations, and that obtains support from the major institutional actors in the world of work. This is the major conceptual or theoretical lesson we can learn from the Japanese.

If the above analysis is basically correct, it suggests an altered research paradigm for American management scholars to follow. Rather than continuing the current research paradigm of discovering empirically which elements of management philosophy and processes lead to which elements of management or enterprise effectiveness in this country or in several countries, as pioneered by Negandhi and Prasad [1979], scholars could pose a different question. What management philosophy and set of management processes would be sufficiently consistent internally, consistent with American societal norms and expectations, and supported by major institutional actors such as government and labor unions? This is a conceptual question to be first addressed through logical analysis and later tested by empirical study. Obviously, the usefulness of the paradigm is based on the premises that internal consistency in management systems and congruence between management system and general social norms will make a difference. Partial support for these notions can be found in the research and writing of Leavitt [1962, 1965], Khandwalla [1973], Child [1977], Lorsch and Morse [1974] and Galbraith and Nathanson [1978]. These premises do seem supportable, and they are what the Japanese management experience teaches. American management theorists might lead the field of American management if they focused sufficient energy and scholarship on this revised paradigm. We focus too much on the efficacy of individual processes, elements, and practices, and far too little on their internal consistency and supportive integration. This Japanese lesson is not new, but it is worthy of serious consideration.

REFERENCES

Abegglen, J. C. *The Japanese Factory*, New York: The Free Press, 1958.
_____. *Management and Worker: The Japanese Solution*. Tokyo: Kodansha International, 1973.
Adams, T. M. F. *The World of Japanese Business*. Tokyo: Kodansha, 1969.
Child, J. *Organization: A Guide for Managers and Administrators*. New York: Harper and Row, 1977.
Cole, R. E. *Japanese Blue Collar, The Changing Tradition*. Berkeley: University of California Press, 1971.
_____. *Worker Mobility and Participation: A Comparative Study of Japan and the U.S.* Berkeley: University of California Press, 1979.
Dore, R. *British Factory—Japanese Factory: The Origins of National Diversity in Industrial Relations*. Berkeley: University of California Press, 1973.
Drucker, P. "What Can We Learn from Japanese Managers." *Harvard Business Review*, March/April 1971, pp. 110–112.
England, G. W. *The Manager and His Values: An International Perspective*. Cambridge: Ballinger, 1975.
Galbraith, J. R., and Nathanson, D. A. *Strategy Implementation: The Role of Structure and Process*. New York: West Publishing Co., 1978.
Haire, M.; Ghiselli, E. E.; and Porter, L. W. *Managerial Thinking: An International Study*. New York: Wiley, 1966.
Hanami, T. *Labor Relations in Japan Today*. Tokyo: Kodansha International., 1979.
Hattori, I. "A Proposition on Efficient Decision-Making in the Japanese Corporation." *Columbia Journal of World Business*, Summer 1978, pp. 7–15.
Hazama, H. "Characteristics of Japanese Style Management." *Japanese Economic Studies*, Spring/Summer 1978, pp. 110–173.
Hofstede, G. *Culture's Consequences: International Differences in Work-Related Values*. Beverly Hills: Sage, 1980.
Kahn, H., and Pepper, T. *The Japanese Challenge*. New York: Crowell, 1979.
Khandwalla, P. N. "Viable and Effective Organizational Designs of Firms." *Academy of Management Journal*, September 1973, pp. 481–495.
Leavitt, H. "Unknown Organizations." *Harvard Business Review*, July–August 1962.
_____. "Applied Organizational Change in Industry." In *The Handbook of Organizations*, edited by James March. Chicago: Rand-McNally, 1965.
Levine, S. B. *Industrial Relations in Postwar Japan*. Urbana: University of Illinois, 1958.
_____. "Labor Markets and Collective Bargaining in Japan." In *The State and Economic Enterprise in Japan*, W. Lockwood, ed. Princeton: Princeton University Press, 1965, pp. 633–638.
Lockwood, W. W. *Economic Development of Japan*. Princeton: Princeton University Press, 1954.
Lorsch, J., and Morse, J. *Organizations and Their Members*. New York: Harper and Row Publishers, 1974.
Mannari, H. *The Japanese Business Leaders*. Tokyo: University of Tokyo Press, 1974.
Marsh, R. M., and Mannari, H. "Lifetime Commitment in Japan: Roles, Norms, and Values." *American Journal of Sociology*, March 1971, pp. 795–812.
_____. "A New Look at 'Lifetime Commitment' in Japanese Industry." *Economic Development and Cultural Change*, July 1972, pp. 611–630.
_____. *Modernization and the Japanese Factory*. Princeton: Princeton University Press, 1976.

Negandhi, A. R., and Prasad, S. B. *Comparative Management.* New York: Appleton-Century-Crofts, 1971.

Okochi, K., et al., eds. *Workers and Employers in Japan.* Tokyo: University of Tokyo Press, 1973.

Ouchi, W. *Theory Z: How American Business Can Meet the Japanese Challenge.* Reading, MA: Addison-Wesley, 1981.

Pascale, R. T. "Communication and Decision Making across Cultures: Japanese and American Comparisons." *Administrative Science Quarterly,* March 1978, pp. 91–110.

——, and Athos, A. G. *The Art of Japanese Management: Applications for American Executives.* New York: Simon & Schuster, 1981.

Takezawa, S., and Whitehill, A. M. *Work Ways: Japan and America.* Tokyo: Japan Institute of Labour, 1981.

Tsurumi, Y. *The Japanese are Coming.* New York: Ballinger, 1976.

Vogel, E. F. *Japan's New Middle Class.* Berkeley and Los Angeles: University of California Press, 1963.

——. *Japan as Number One.* Cambridge: Harvard University Press, 1979.

Whitehill, A. M., and Takezawa, S. *The Other Worker: A Comparative Study of Industrial Relations in the United States and Japan.* Hawaii: East-West Center Press, 1968.

Yang, C. Y. "Management Styles: American vis-a-vis Japanese." *Columbia Journal of World Business,* Fall 1977, pp. 23–32.

Yoshino, M. Y. *Japan's Management System.* Cambridge: MIT Press, 1968.

——. *The Japanese Marketing System: Adaptations and Innovations.* Cambridge: MIT Press, 1971.

——. *Marketing in Japan: A Management Guide.* New York: Praeger, 1975.

REVIEW QUESTIONS

1 What is Theory Z? How does it relate to the readings on participative management?

2 What conclusions did this study reach about belief systems of U.S. workers as a foundation for the transfer of Theory Z management?

READING 70

Can We Adopt the Japanese Methods of Human Resources Management?

Kae H. Chung
Margaret Ann Gray*

Japan is a small island, about the size of California, with few natural resources and yet it has emerged as the third most powerful industrial nation, after the United States and the Soviet Union. Despite the oil crisis in the 1970s, which hurt the Japanese more severely than others, Japan has demonstrated remarkable eco-

*From *Personnel Administrator,* May 1982, pp. 41–46ff. Copyright 1982 by The American Society for Personnel Administration, Alexandria, Va.

nomic growth. Its productivity grew an average of eight percent annually in the last decade, while that of American industries grew less than two percent. The United States is still ahead of Japan in gross national production per employed person. When the agricultural sector is excluded from the productivity index, however, the Japanese show a higher productivity than Americans. A *Fortune* magazine survey indicates that most American and Japanese executives believe that Japan is now stronger in overall industrial competitiveness than the United States and that Japan is continuously gaining an even greater edge. (*Fortune*, August 10, 1981.)

Until recently most American executives were unruffled by such an adverse development. But as American consumers turn their backs on American-manufactured products in favor of foreign-made goods, especially those of Japan, American managers become concerned. Robert B. Reich of the Federal Trade Commission indicated that, in the early part of 1980, foreign goods purchased by Americans amounted to 28 percent of new automobiles sold, 30 percent of athletic and sporting goods, 34 percent of microwave ovens, 90 percent of motorcycles and almost 100 percent of video-cassette recorders. The list grows longer as days go by, expanding into calculators, cameras, bicycles, footwear, radial tires, steel, digital watches and others.

Experts Cite Management Techniques

American responses to the adverse development are understandably complex and confusing. Some managers may argue that the Japanese success is primarily due to the supportive government policy, low cost financing and friendly unions rather than due to any particular managerial practice. These observers blame the U.S. decline in productivity growth on excessive governmental regulations, anti-business tax laws and unfriendly unions. Many experts such as William Abernathy, Robert Hays, William Ouchi, Richard Pascale and Ezra Vogel, acknowledge the importance of these factors, yet cite the Japanese managerial practices as the key to Japan's success. Similarly, these observers imply that poor managerial practices in the United States (*e.g.,* short-term profit-orientation, market driven behavior and employee exploitation) have caused a low level of capital investment and adversary relationships with government and unions.

Granting that the Japanese managerial practices are a key to Japan's success, a lingering question still remains unanswered. Can or should Americans emulate the Japanese experience as a way of reviving the American competitiveness? A growing number of scholars and practitioners, including William Ouchi and Ezra Vogel, feel that what the Japanese are doing is "good management," meeting the needs of both the employees and their organization and consequently they assert that such good management should be used universally. Contrary to this view of management, a number of scholars and practitioners question the applicability of the Japanese practices in this country. For example, Robert Cole and Edgar Schein argue that the Japanese managerial practices are so unique that they cannot be successfully transplanted in the United States unless they are substantially modified to reflect cultural, economical, social, and political reality. They maintain that such managerial practices as paternalism, seniority systems, lifetime employment, and participative management can be successfully utilized in the Japanese culture because it is characterized by racial homogeneity, uniform education, cooperation and collectivism. In contrast, American culture is characterized by heterogeneity, diverse education, individualism and competitiveness. Because of these cultural differences, the importation of Japanese managerial practices would not produce the same positive outcomes—high institutional loyalty and productivity—that the Japanese experience does. Tino Puri and Issac Shapiro further argue that we should not adopt the Japanese management systems because their emphasis on collectivism and group harmony would destroy American individualism, creativity and entrepreneurial spirit.

This article seeks to 1) understand the characteristics of Japanese human resources management and 2) see if we can adopt them in the United States. To this end, the article reviews the distinctive characteristics of the Japanese managerial practices, studies their cultural and philosophical backgrounds and discusses the adoptability of the Japanese practices in the United States.

HRM Japanese Style

What are the essential characteristics of Japanese human resources management? Are they different from that of American companies? Although not all Japanese or American companies have the same managerial characteristics, there are some practices that differentiate the Japanese from American companies. For example, William Ouchi pointed out that many Japanese companies practice lifetime employment, slow performance appraisal, non-specialized career paths, informal controls, collective decision-making, collective responsibility and wholistic concern. American companies practice just the opposite of these.

Long-Term Employment   In Japan, this term can be transformed to "permanent employment," particularly in the large firms. These companies hire new people once a year and retain them, barring the most severe infractions, until their retirement. In times of prosperity, these firms may hire individuals who know they are temporary employees or may subcontract some work. When encountered with economic difficulties, the companies may take such steps as reducing salaries or bonuses proportionately for all employees, releasing temporary workers and reassigning the permanent ones accordingly or reducing working hours. This no-layoff, no-firing policy greatly increases the loyalty between the individual and the firm. It enables the company to provide larger amounts of personal support, welfare benefits, belongingness and training which eventually yields economic returns to the business. Likewise, it allows the employees to build long-term relationships based on trust, to understand that the company's attainment of such relationships will benefit them and to readily accept such changes as new labor-saving devices which people without the benefit of permanent employment may see as a threat to their own jobs.

Slow Promotion and Evaluation   Seniority is a major factor in salary increases. There are low differentials in pay and status to workers of a given age group, particularly during the first several years of employment. This practice attaches value to the individual rather than to the job or title. Japanese employees know that they will work together for a lifetime and that the corporation will provide recognition later, hence, they learn to work together for mutual benefit. Furthermore, to accentuate awareness, there are frequent informal interactions allowing senior observations. Also evaluations rank loyalty, zeal and cooperation ahead of actual performance and knowledge; rewards make more of a psychological impact than a financial one. Because of the concept of permanent employment, Japanese workers may not anticipate immediate recognition. In addition, a bonus amounting to as much as five month's salary is tied to the performance of the entire firm at the end of the year.

Non-Specialized Careers   Permanent employment also makes it realistic for workers to rotate throughout the company. This lengthy continual training practice enables persons to learn different aspects of the business and establish a comradeship with many people. When individuals are in a more permanent position, they are generalists and thus able to consider the consequences of any action in terms of how it affects the superordinate goals of the entire organization; they also have established a network of people with whom they can work to meet these goals.

Collective Decision-Making   The Japanese word *nemawaski* means root binding; it is the term used to characterize the type of decision-making that takes place in business. Everyone has a sense of running the firm because virtually nothing gets done until all the people involved agree. The Japanese assume that differences can be resolved not by adversary means or by one side achieving a final victory, but by gathering as much information as possible from as many sources as possible. As a result, all parties are well-informed, everyone has time to adjust to the emerging decision and all are committed to the determination once a consensus is reached. This can be a lengthy procedure, but because of the ultimate commitment, implementation takes relatively little time.

Quality Circles Emerge

An example of this type of decision-making can be shown on a smaller scale by examining the quality control circles that have grown out of Japanese management. After the war, the Japanese recognized that the quality of their products would have to increase before they became a leader in the international market. Quality is not just a function of the finished product; it also includes such factors as the time to produce, prompt delivery, billing accuracy and followup repair and maintenance. Cost reductions in any of these areas may lead to increased productivity.

With this knowledge, the Union of Japanese Scientists and Engineers invited Edwards Deming to come to Japan for a series of lectures about quality control. Deming stressed the importance of placing quality control in the hands of middle management. The Japanese adapted his ideas to their country and gave this responsibility to the people on the shop floor. The result was the QC circle.

A quality circle is a relatively autonomous unit of approximately eight workers and one senior worker. In Japan participation is voluntary, but it is estimated that one in eight workers takes part in circles. The group is trained in problem solving including elementary statistical methods. The circles are not created as a response to a specific problem. They meet regularly and are able to find answers which reduce defects and scrap, decrease rework and down time and also improve working conditions and enhance self-development. These people are a better utilized, creative resource for the organization and even if the solutions are no better than those found by technical personnel, the workers are more highly motivated to carry out the results due to their own personal involvement.

Individual Responsibility   While such concepts as consensus decision-making and quality control circles place a great deal of emphasis on group responsibility, the individual also has certain obligations. The chief responsibility is that of loyalty of the group due to the long-term commitment between the firm and the individual. Duties include continual development of skills, improvement of quality control, maintenance of social harmony, service to the firm and interaction with its members outside of the normal working day. The Japanese systems will not function without such individual commitment to their organizations.

Implicit, Informal Control   While explicit measures are often necessary in the operation of many firms, the Japanese place more emphasis on implicit and informal controls. These controls focus on long-term developmental potential of employees rather than short-term performance. Since the employees are committed to each other on a long-term basis, they are less concerned with short-term benefits. The fact that the Japanese spend a great deal of time developing relations enables group norms to become an important source of implicit control. The control is further possible because of the undifferentiated pay and status system; small differences in treatment by those in authority are greatly noticed and have great psychological significance.

Wholistic Concern for Employees   Because employees are envisioned as resources for the firm, the growth of the whole person, rather than merely his or her job skills, is emphasized. One way the company displays its concern is through its substantial benefits and programs. Long-term employment allows individuals to develop multiple bonds through play and community involvement as well as through work. The result is personal growth through intimacy, trust and understanding.

Managerial Culture and Philosophy

Can we adopt the Japanese managerial systems in the United States? The answer is mixed. Experts William Ouchi, Richard Pascale and Steven Wheelwright argue that several well-managed companies such as IBM, General Electric, Hewlett-Packard, Lilly Company and Westinghouse have been using or are adopting something similar to the Japanese managerial practices of lifetime employment, participative decision-making, quality control circles and *clannish* management style. Despite this optimistic note, a prevailing feeling among some management scholars such as Cole and Schein is that the Japanese managerial practices are the outgrowth of Japan's unique cultural heritage, thus rendering these practices unadoptable in the United States.

Japanese Managerial Philosophies

What are the Japanese managerial philosophies that stimulated the use of human resources management in Japan? There are three managerial philosophies that may have positively impacted the use of humanistic approach to management. The first philosophy is the Japanese perception of the role of business enterprises in their society. As Peter Drucker and Ezra Vogel explain, the Japanese tend to view a business firm as a human community which serves the needs of its members including the employees, managers and the general public. Profits are important to the Japanese managers, but the bottom line performance becomes secondary to other functions such as meeting employees' needs and providing employment opportunities. This philosophy allows the Japanese managers to be sensitive to the needs of their employees and to develop a sense of common purpose among the members regardless of their ranks. In contrast, American managers tend to view their organizations as economic entities which serve the profit motives of their stockholders. In this view, meeting the needs of the employees and the public becomes secondary to the profit motive. The resulting difference is that American managers tend to be exploitative.

The second managerial philosophy concerns the way Japanese view their employees. Ouchi argues that Japanese managers see their employees as valuable resources who can make a major difference in organizational performance. Managers view employees to be as intelligent and responsible as they are. Because of these *Theory Y* assumptions about human beings, managers rely on workers for solving organizational problems and for producing high quality products and services. This view is in contrast with *Theory X* assumptions of human nature which view employees to be lazy, irresponsible and unintelligent. This philosophy prevents many American managers from utilizing the talents of workers in solving organizational problems.

Finally, Japanese managers tend to view groups as superior to individuals in solving their operational problems. This group philosophy is that most tasks in contemporary organizations require cooperation of their members. Few decisions of any consequence arise from individual effort. Most happen as a result of collective effort. It may take time to produce cooperative effort, but it pays off in prompt implementation. In contrast, American managers tend to have faith in individual effort, creativity and initiative. Collectivism usually means to them a loss of individual freedom and motivation. American decision-makers, however, must pay the price for slow implementation since many people resist change if they have had no input in the planning stages.

Japanese Cultural Backgrounds

What caused the differences in managerial philosophies between Americans and Japanese managers? Experts on Japanese management offer the following explanations. First, Cole asserts that the Confucian doctrine of human goodness, filial piety and altruism taught people to be well-educated, disciplined, committed to their organizations and compelled to help others. The pursuit of pleasure is viewed as moral decay and a person seeking this pleasure is considered to be a public enemy. This doctrine encouraged businessmen to be more altruistic and thereby they gained the public's respect. According to Pascale, Zen Buddhism also may have influenced the Japanese to be more harmonious in group settings. Rather than seeking individual competition and disharmony, Zen Buddhism taught them to search for harmonious living with others. In contrast, the Western culture has its root in Judeo-Christian heritage and the capitalistic doctrine. Cole points out that the Christian concept of original sin places an emphasis on the fundamental weakness of human beings and the capitalistic doctrine motivates people to pursue self-interests.

Japanese Are Savers

Second, Peter Drucker has argued that the difference in industrial structure, especially the method by which industrial firms raise capital, has influenced the way the Japanese view the role of these organizations. The lack of individualized capital formation has caused Japanese firms to rely on banks as the primary sources of financing. The Japanese save about 20 percent of their incomes, providing a major source of capital. With less pressure from stockholders and the capital market, they are able to pursue goals other than the short-term oriented profit goal. In contrast United States managers' performance is measured by their success in generating profits.

Third, Ouchi argues that the homogeneity in Japanese society encourages managers to view their employees as not very different from themselves. This egalitarianism in Japanese industry helps managers to treat their employers in a more humanistic way. Opportunities are given to employees equal to that which they have received. In contrast, Cole states that the heterogeneity in American society serves as an impetus for differentiating largely white Anglo-Saxon Protestant managerial groups from working classes, composed of diverse religious, ethnic and other social groups. This differentiation might hinder the use of human resources management tools in the United States, since it could foster an elitist attitude on the part of managers.

Fourth, Japan is an old nation which has a long history of paternalistic arrangements between employers and employees and between superiors and subordinates. The paternalistic relations known as the *"oyabu-kobun system"* govern the relationships between superiors and subordinates in industrial organizations. Persons of authority assume the responsibility of guiding and mentoring their subordinates as if they were foster parents and conversely the subordinates behave faithfully and hold personal loyalty toward their superiors. George DeVos maintains that the feudal-familial relationships foster mentoring relationships between superiors and their subordinates. By contrast, the United States is a relatively young nation, settling in a new sparsely populated land, encouraging people to be self-reliant and individualistic. This historical circumstance reinforces the cultural values expressed in individualistic pursuits of happiness, wealth and success. Although mentoring exists in American firms, it is not as widespread as it is in Japan.

Finally, the difference in natural endowment has caused differences in managerial philosophy. As indicated earlier, Japan is a small island, with few natural resources, but with a population of more than 100 million, half that of the United States population. This limited natural endowment indirectly forces the Japanese to pursue business strategies that promise the attainment of common goals— survival, high employment and international market expansion. According to Drucker, this kind of survival mentality has been the major force behind Japan's success. In contrast, the United States has been a land of plentiful natural resources and vast frontier. Although American managers are becoming increasingly aware of the problem of limited resources, many of their decisions are still made on an assumption that resources are plentiful.

Adoptability of Japanese Practices

What are the implications of these cultural and philosophical differences in adopting Japanese managerial practices in the United States? One's managerial practices are the reflection of his or her managerial philosophies which in turn are the reflection of culture. If American managers want to adopt the Japanese managerial practices, they need to adopt the Japanese managerial philosophies and cultural mores. This requirement will make the adoption of Japanese practices extremely difficult. It is not likely that American firms will restructure their methods of obtaining funds; it is unlikely that lifetime employment with slow promotion will be accepted by American managers; it is unlikely that labor-management relations will see the degree of compatibility they have in Japan and it is unlikely that homogeneity in employment could be achieved or would be allowed. In fact some Japanese companies with plants in the United States (for example, Matsushita's Quasar plant in Chicago) have not adopted their managerial practices in the United States because they are aware of the cultural differences. Furthermore, those companies which have adopted the Japanese systems, (e.g. Sanyo's San Diego plant and Honda plant in Ohio) are experiencing labor problems leading toward unionization.

Ironically, the basic ideas of the Japanese human resources management were originated by Westerners, mostly Americans. For example, the concept of stable employment was advocated by Max Weber in his famous theory of bureaucracy. The ideas of organizational family, employee participation, group management, and job enrichment were advocated by such American scholars as Chris Argyris, Peter Drucker, Fred Herzberg, Rensis Likert and Douglas McGregor. The Japanese borrowed such concepts and adapted them to their culture. Although these ideas were originated by Americans, they have not had the same impact on managerial practices in this country. Strong emphasis on individualism and competition, along with the United States' history of labor-management relations, which is full of mistrust, has probably hindered a widespread use of human resources management in this country. Walter Nord and Wickham Skinner point out that human resources management is more honored than practiced in American firms.

Does this mean that it is impossible or unadvisable to adopt the Japanese systems in this country? It all depends. The following points are germane when one considers an adoption of the Japanese managerial systems. First, firms in relatively stable and dominant industrial positions are more likely to or may more easily adopt the Japanese managerial systems than those in weak and unstable positions. Strong companies are less vulnerable to environmental constraints and can develop an internal organizational climate compatible to the Japanese management style. They can provide their employees with lifetime employment and make major investments in employee training. It is no surprise for IBM and General Electric to adopt such a managerial philosophy. A struggling company is less likely to look beyond current operational results, let alone long-term developmental goals. The irony, of course, is that the stable and dominant firms may not see the need for change.

Second, not all Japanese managerial practices are culturally-bound and non-transferable. Many of the technically-oriented programs such as quality control and plant maintenance can be easily transferred without much resistance. This is a reason many American companies, including General Motors, Champion Spark Plugs, RCA and Westinghouse have adopted quality control programs. Even among the culturally-bound managerial practices, some are more adoptable than others. For example, American managers seem to be receptive to the idea of long-term employment but not the practice of slow promotion with an emphasis on seniority. Many managers, especially those who feel that they are capable, seem to prefer a reward system based on performance rather than seniority.

Third, the Japanese managerial practices which stress consensual decision-making and group harmony are not all that desirable for industries pursuing aggressive and risky ventures. The Japanese systems are good at managing the nuts and bolts of manufacturing activities, but the emphasis on group harmony and consensus can easily smother creative thinking and innovative behavior. When technological innovation is the key to organizational survival, the American way of managing people, stressing creative ideas and individualistic performance, can be more advantageous than the Japanese approach.

Finally, if a company chooses to adopt the Japanese managerial system, it has to prepare the foundation on which the newly adopted system can stand. It involves careful selection of people who can function effectively under the new system, major investment in employee training on a continuous basis, decentralization of operational decisions and sharing its benefits with the employees. It also requires the development of a partnership attitude between management and unions. It is indeed a time-consuming process, requiring much dedication and subtlety on the part of management. Unless one is willing to change the whole philosophy of managing people, one would be better off by not altering the existing system of management.

REFERENCES

1 Cole, Robert E., "Learning from the Japanese: prospects and pitfalls," *Management Review,* September 1980, pp. 22–42.
2 De Vos, George A., "Apprenticeship and paternalism." in E. F. Vogel (ed.), *Modern Japanese Organization and Decision Making.* Berkeley, CA: University of California Press, 1975, pp. 210–227.
3 Drucker, Peter F., "Behind Japan's success," *Harvard Business Review,* January–February 1981, pp. 83–90.
4 Drucker, Peter F., "Economic realities and enterprise strategy," in E. F. Vogel, (ed.), *Modern Japanese Organization And Decision Making.* Berkeley, CA: University of California Press, 1975, pp. 228–250.
5 Hatvany, Nina, and Pucik, Vladimir, "Japanese management practices and productivity," *Organizational Dynamics,* Spring 1981, pp. 5–21.
6 Hayes, Robert H., "Why Japanese factories work," *Harvard Business Review,* July–August 1981, pp. 57–66.
7 Juran, J. M., "International significance of the QC circle movement," *Quality Progress,* November 1980, pp. 18–22.
8 Nord, Walter, and Durand, Douglas, "What is wrong with the human resources approach to management?" *Organizational Dynamics,* Winter 1978, pp. 13–25.
9 Ouchi, William, *Theory Z,* Reading, MA: Addison-Wesley Publishing Company, 1981.
10 Puri, Tino, and Bhide, Amar, "Crucial weakness of Japan, Inc.," *Wall Street Journal,* June 8, 1981, p. 18.
11 Schein, Edgar H., "Does Japanese management style have a message for American managers?" *Sloan Management Review,* Fall 1981, pp. 55–68.
12 Shapiro, Isaac, "Second thoughts about Japan," *The Wall Street Journal,* June 5, 1981.
13 Skinner, Wickham, "Big hat, no cattle: managing human resources," *Harvard Business Review,* September–October 1981, pp. 106–114.
14 Vogel, Ezra F., *Japan as Number One,* Cambridge, MA: Harvard University Press, 1979.
15 Wheelwright, Steven C., "Japan—where operations really are strategic," *Harvard Business Review,* July–August 1981, pp. 67–74.

REVIEW QUESTIONS

1 What caused the differences in managerial philosophies between Americans and Japanese managers?

2 In what ways do Chung and Gray agree and disagree with the conclusions of England in the previous reading?

3 Read the last sentence in this article, and then review the Douglas McGregor selection (Reading 2). How likely is it that U.S. managers will change their whole philosophy of managing people?

CHAPTER 21

EMERGING
ORGANIZATIONAL
BEHAVIOR

READING 71

The Changing Leader-Follower Relationships of the 1980s

Ronald Lippitt*

Many analysts agree that our world of the 1980s is going through more technological and human relationship transitions and transformations, at a more rapid rate, than we have ever experienced. I shall identify several of these trends of change that seem to have particular relevance for the relationships between leaders and followers, examining some of the changing role requirements and competency challenges for leaders and followers and for their interactions.

EMERGING CONTEXTS FOR NEW LEADERSHIP AND FOLLOWERSHIP

I believe the six trends identified below will greatly affect changes in leader and follower roles and represent very significant challenges for leaders and followers in all types of social contexts—communities, human service organizations, business enterprises, government departments, and social action groups.

The Double Bind of Maintaining Quality with Reduced Resources

Most committed leaders today are experiencing a difficult double bind. Clients need and expect better services, and followers expect more vigorous response to their needs. The more sophisticated and sensitive leaders are, the more they feel a gap between "what ought to be" and "what is," between "meeting goals" and "getting by." The threat of strikes, the loss of competitive advantage, the alienation of employees, are all indications of the necessity of improving the effectiveness and quality of leadership.

But, in the light of these demands on leaders, the message that "smaller can be beautiful" is not very compatible or congenial. Budget cuts clearly mean reductions in quantity and quality of personnel and of program and production resources. Standards of leadership achievement and competence are threatened. Leaders hear puzzling messages about critical functions being entrusted to untrained personnel. Followers feel threatened and unappreciated.

Leaders are under pressure to improve quality in the face of reduced resources. Followers are under pressure to be accountable and loyal in the face of job insecurity and reduced resources.

Expectations of Shared Power and Responsibility

A major trend of the postindustrial society is what has been referred to as the "flattening of the organization chart," meaning a wider delegation of responsibil-

*From Ronald Lippitt, "The Changing Leader-Follower Relationships of the 1980s," *Journal of Applied Behavioral Science*, August 1982, pp. 395–403. Copyright © 1982 by JAI Press Inc. All rights reserved. Reprinted with permission.

ity and power. Leaders expect more initiative and risk-taking on the part of those who have been dependent followers. Along with decentralization of decision-making responsibility and authority goes a complementary trend of centralization of accountability for the quality of output and organizational functioning. Many new, centralized leadership functions emerge, e.g., coordination, communication linkage, and quality control. These shifts in leader and follower functions add up to great stress for both groups. Leaders feel uncertainty and fear loss of control, and followers feel challenge but avoid the risks of new tasks for which they lack skill and support.

Interdependence, Collaboration, and Communication

One of the consequences of decentralized organizational functioning is the increase in interdependence and the need for collaboration between the managers and supervisors in the different units of the system. But the traditions of sibling rivalry and protected turf are so strong that a new emphasis on collaboration and interdependence is very difficult to develop. Frank communication and feedback between centralized and decentralized leadership are hard to achieve. The great increase in innovation that accompanies decentralized initiative causes an important problem of adequately disseminating the new practices through the organization or community or company. The new leader-follower pattern of the 1980s requires a tremendous awareness of interdependence, new values and skills of collaboration, and greater openness of communication (cf. Benne, Bradford, Gibb, & Lippitt, 1975; and Bennis, Benne & Chin, 1969).

More People Required for Problem Solving

The futurist, Esfandiary (1978), has pointed out that with each succeeding decade, the problems to be solved in the world have become more complex, requiring an understanding of more different variables and factors to find creative solutions. The average number of persons involved in creating significant inventions and innovations in the decade of 1900–1910 was two, while in the 1970s the average number of people was 12. Many leaders are, therefore, developing resource and skill banks to record and store the variety of skills and knowledge of each member of the organization so that the right people can be put together to tackle any new problem or task. This growing trend of problem solving through temporary task forces is requiring more flexible leaders, and it requires followers with greater tolerance and acceptance of persons from different backgrounds and orientations.

Integrating Technological and Human Resources

Becoming comfortable with the computer has become a new leadership challenge. "Computer persons" are more and more frequently part of problem-solving teams. Sometimes it seems hard to diagnose whether computers are leaders or followers. Clearly, it is a struggle to discover how the computers, and their programmers, can be collaborators rather than controllers or underutilized servants. Many older leaders are feeling very threatened by their followers' computer competencies, and frequently followers use their access to the computer as a support system for confronting leadership with demands for change.

Reorientation, Renewal, and New Competency Development

Changeability is a requirement for the leaders and followers of the 1980s and for the systems of which they are a part. This requires a proactive, rather than a defensive, reactive posture, toward the pressures and opportunities for change. It requires an acceptance and understanding of universal ambivalence, in all of us, about putting energy and risk into change efforts. It requires the acceptance of the continuing role of learner, of commitment to a renewal process for self, the investment in and support of continuing training programs for followers, and research and development as a major organizational priority.

I believe that with each succeeding year of the 1980s, these six trends will become more obvious and more crucial as challenges for leaders and followers in all sectors of the society.

LEADERSHIP CHALLENGES AND TASKS

For most leaders and followers, the most difficult challenge in the 1980s is the necessity to root out years of socialization into three traditional orientations of our culture. One of these is the model of the vertical dimension of authority and dependency, of superordinate and subordinate, of decision maker and implementer, of master and servant (cf. Greenleaf, 1977). A second ingrained assumption is that "doing it by yourself" is a sign of strength. Change from pride in independence and autonomy to pride in interdependence and mutual help is one of the toughest challenges and one of the most necessary. The third difficult confrontation is dropping the assumption that competition is a necessary motivation to achieve. This idea blocks seeking help, sharing resources, and pooling complementary abilities—all requirements for survival, growth, and development in the decades ahead (cf. White & Lippitt, 1960).

I shall briefly define what I see as some of the challenges and competency requirements for leaders on the cutting edge of the 1980s.

Attitudes and Skills of Proactive Response to Change

The natural, first reactions to resource reduction and cutback demands are to defend, to be equitable by cutting everybody by the same amount, to eliminate research and development and the other mechanisms for growth, to sacrifice the most vulnerable personnel (e.g., internal trainers and external consultants), and to permit the obsolescence of technical and material resources. The reactive temptation is to become more authoritative at a time when more democratic participation is more crucial than ever.

Other leaders in similar situations manifest what I would describe as proactive responses, such as re-examining priorities; exploring, exchanging, and sharing of resources with others; searching for alternative sources of support; scanning for innovative, new models of service and production that require less use of resources; restructuring roles and reorganizing operations to maximize use of human and technical resources; mobilizing volunteer time and energy.

Avoiding the reactive, defensive posture of response to confrontation and resource reduction is one of the most critical challenges for all leaders.

Mobilizing Resources for the Self

Giving up authority and taking on more responsibility are both sources of stress for the leader and the follower. The skillful mobilizing of resources for the self, and from the self, are the keys to reducing these stresses. These skills include learning how to ask peers for consultation, to use them for support, and to form coalitions for action, the utilization of followers to brainstorm creative problem solutions, to provide guiding data about their own needs and corrective ideas for one's own role. A second challenge is to mobilize the resources from within oneself. This requires developing the special skills of listening to one's own internal dialogue between positive and negative feelings, supports for risk-taking and supports for caution, and reflecting on different alternatives for action. Listening to and utilizing these resources requires a reflective attitude and use of time, a crucial necessity for every successful leader.

Achieving a Balance of Decentralization and Centralization

Moving decision making and responsibility closer to the action is a basic gain in leadership potential, if there is also centralization of planning for and providing the learning required to support the decentralized leadership personnel in achieving quality performance.

Getting more persons and competencies involved in leadership functions is great if there is centralized, systematic coordination and integration of their initiative and decisions. Using the experience and ideas of grass-roots followers is a great gain if there is centralized initiative to include other perspectives and to introduce quality assurance procedures.

These are some of the challenges of balancing centralized leadership functions and decentralized follower responsibilities. In the current enthusiasm for shared power and decentralization, there is a serious trap in neglecting the complementary, supportive central functions that require very different types of leadership competencies.

Achieving a Balance of Task Work Focus and Process Work Focus

The "laboratory movement" that has surrounded the seminars, publications (this journal is one), and workshops of the National Training Laboratories (NTL Institute) has taught much about the processes of group productivity. (See the article by Blake and Mouton earlier in this issue for an excellent example.) Probably the most significant contribution of the NTL laboratory movement has been the discovery that if groups that are engaged in production and problem-solving tasks will also focus on their process of interacting with each other, they will achieve significant improvements in productivity. In many committees, staffs, and task forces, it has become a regular part of their work to have brief "stop sessions" where they share data about "how things are going" and what could be done to improve the utilization of each member and increase productivity or problem-solving effectiveness. Leaders must be ready to take the risk of this type of intervention and to display candor in seeking and responding to feedback in such process reviews.

Diverse-Person Team Building

Getting persons with very different backgrounds, specialties, and disciplines to work together effectively is a great leadership challenge of the 1980s. Who should be put together for what and for how long? Leaders of any size group or system need to have some procedure for identifying, recording, and storing the skills, competencies, and training of the personnel they lead.

The even more difficult challenge is getting people to work together. Rather typically, the assumption is that differences are a source of problems and conflicts. The effective leader must understand that differences are great resources if they are used effectively. This means using techniques of process review to assess the effectiveness of task work and of problems of cooperation among team members, developing the concept of "creative compromise" or finding win-win approaches to problem solving, and using nonevaluative brainstorming by the group before turning to critical evaluation (cf. Schindler-Rainman & Lippitt, 1975; Lindaman & Lippitt, 1979).

Teaming People and Technology

The leader must help the machine-oriented and the person-oriented task members understand and appreciate each other. This involves setting up procedures for teaching each other, for cooperative simulation projects and understanding and accepting some of the typical cross-generational, cross-racial, and cross-cultural differences. Co-leadership of teams and projects by a younger, technically sophisticated person and an older worker more experienced in the human side of the enterprise is one useful strategy.

Leaders Have Neighbors and Outsiders as Potential Resources

There is a temptation in a world of reduced resources to define boundaries and emphasize territoriality, but a creative leadership role requires the opposite posture. A leader must share and exchange resources, including successful practices that are helping the group or organization to survive, grow, and profit in the changing environment. Such an orientation to securing resources and being a resource to other leaders and systems requires a special attention to documentation and evaluation. Sharing requires a much more systematic orientation toward what we do and how we do it and how well it works. Another temptation is to withdraw connections with and use of outside sources of consultation, critique, and review. The need for resources is even greater, and the competent leader is always improving her or his techniques of utilizing external resources.

FOLLOWERSHIP CHALLENGES AND TASKS

Followers, like leaders, must adapt their attitudes, roles, and skills to help meet the challenges of the 1980s and the decades ahead. Our major unused human resource is the very large proportion of followers who use the group and organization as a way to hide from actively taking responsibility and who use their alienation and apathy as a basis for functioning at a low level of energy and initiative. There is just as much need for a revolution of membership commitment and competence as for leadership development. Here are a few of the challenges for improving membership competence in the challenging years ahead.

A Proactive versus a Reactive Membership Stance

Most members are aware of a number of discrepancies between "the way things ought to be" and "the way things are." These are usually perceived as failures or inadequacies both of the group and of the leadership in meeting their needs. The defensive, reactive response to these discrepancies is either a withdrawal from participation and commitment or attacking and confronting the leadership that is blamed for the situation. Both of these reactions increase the pain and frustration in the situation and push the leadership into a circular pattern of negative response. Becoming positively active and collaborative in response to a negatively evaluated situation or leader is one of the key responsibilities of membership because members have the power to shape the leadership, to support the initiatives of the leadership, and to make the situation better both for themselves and for the group.

Rehearsal and Membership Skill Development

In my work with many groups of members on "influencing upward," we typically find that we start with assumptions about rejection and resistance of our influence efforts by the leadership. As we work on the specific skills of presenting needs, concerns, recommendations, and other feedback to leaders, it becomes obvious that "the assumption of no results" is a self-fulfilling prophecy of either "chip on the shoulder aggressiveness" or self-depreciating behavior. I have helped many members discover that rehearsal, or simulation, is crucial in discovering these negative postures and developing a repertoire of creative alternatives and strategies in becoming effective influencers of leaders. We have discovered again and again that leaders will listen to, respond positively, and welcome offers of collaboration when members have carefully developed the skills of presentation and effective communication. It is true that many leaders need to be helped to listen, but it is even more true that most members need to be helped to be positive and appropriately assertive in their efforts to express their needs and interests.

Reversing Our Sibling Rivalry

Kenneth Benne has said we only imported two-thirds of the French Revolution. We brought over *liberté* and *egalité*, but not *fraternité*. Instead, we installed sibling rivalry as the pattern of relationship between peers. Peer members vie with each other for the attention of and from the leaders, for status in the group, and for various special advantages. Member behaviors, in successful organizations, are more and more expressing the positive values of teamwork and the assumption that there can be win-win results from mutual collaboration.

As more members find it necessary to work with persons who are more and more different from themselves, the challenge of "bridging the empathy gap" becomes increasingly important, and the development of teams of those with complementary skills, who are very different from each other, provides a challenge and a source of greater creativity and productivity.

Balancing Self-Satisfaction and Contribution to Others

One of the themes of the 1970s and of the personal growth movement was "do your own thing." This reinforced the values of autonomy and self-sufficiency that are increasingly a weakness in dealing with a world of increasing interdependence. A strength of the personal growth movement has been the focus on self-development and self-caring, which became for many participants a narcissistic focus on self and a devaluing of commitment to others. In the 1980s, the trend is already reversing. The theme of concern for others and commitment to social values is growing stronger with each passing year. Membership in the 1980s must balance and integrate the two values and commitments.

Avoiding Role-Boundedness

One of the emphases for leadership in the 1980s is the increasing responsibility for using the resources of members more fully and avoiding the disuse and neglect of important skills and competencies. This implies for members a readiness to be flexible in what they are asked to do and what they are challenged to do. While there is a continuing condensation and reorganization of organizational structures and roles, members must be ready to seek and respond to challenge and opportunities for re-education, for training and new skills, for new tasks, and for relating to new leaders.

I believe these five trends are illustrative of the challenges to followership in the 1980s.

CONSEQUENCES FOR LEADER-FOLLOWER
RELATIONSHIP DEVELOPMENT

These challenges for new leadership and followership patterns have implications for the development of new patterns of relationship. One interesting discovery has been that, many times, leadership training is dysfunctional in that it puts an emphasis on strengthening the role of leadership without also focusing on strengthening the skills and competencies of members. Therefore, many programs are focusing on training the group as a group to function effectively together, and helping the group members develop the norms and expectations for supporting the leadership function. There is an increasing emphasis on helping the members develop a support system for clarifying and expressing their own membership needs and also for their supporting leadership in effectively representing them upward in the system (cf. Schindler-Rainman & Lippitt, 1975).

Another important development in leader-follower relationships is the development of two-way, shared evaluation and joint progress celebration of achievements in moving toward the goals of the group. The members and leaders of the effective groups of the 1980s will not only have achieved approaches to win-win problem solving solutions in conflict, as contrasted to polarizing, adversarial negotiation, but they will have gained skill in deciding when and how to utilize third party help in resolving differences.

Perhaps one of the most important gains in leader-member working relationships is the steady movement on the part of many groups toward utilizing techniques of process review to share data about their productivity, the blocks to communication and effective interaction, and the ways in which they can improve their working relationships and their productivity. The examples from Japan of quality circle discussions are one illustration of a growing commitment in many organizations and systems to focus on the ways in which leaders and followers can collaborate to achieve and improve quality of work life and quality of production.

In conclusion, I think that the emerging pattern of leader-follower relationships will have a tremendous payoff in the reduction of the waste of human energy and the mobilization and development of contributing talent. It will also be the basis for the creation of much new human energy that will result from the challenge and disequilibrium that results from the freedom to initiate risk-taking innovations and to respond to the support and security of interpersonal teaming and respect for the value of human differences.

Two types of skill training may become more important than the traditional "leadership training" courses. One trend, which is already emerging, is the training for "influencing upward." These workshops are focusing on training "followers"—i.e., those at lower levels in bureaucracies—to become more active and effective in communicating and influencing upward in their systems. They must work through all the psychological blocks of their assumptions that those above will always say "no" or will disapprove of initiatives toward change. By role-playing rehearsals they discover the self-fulfilling consequences of timidity and "chip-on-the-shoulder" postures.

The second trend will be toward training groups as groups to function productively rather than training just the leaders. There is evidence that training the leaders alone may increase the psychological distance between leaders and members and does not help the members learn how to utilize their leadership effectively and define expectations for leadership performance.

Clearly, both of these trends are leading toward shared accountability and power and toward shared responsibility for the quality of interaction between those in leader and follower roles.

REFERENCES

Benne, K., Bradford, L., Gibb, J., & Lippitt, R. (Eds.). *The laboratory method of changing and learning.* Palo Alto, Calif.: Science and Behavior Books, 1975.

Bennis, W., Benne, K., & Chin, R. (Eds.). *The planning of change.* New York: Holt, Rinehart, & Winston, 1969.

Greenleaf, R. *Servant leadership.* New York: Paulist Press, 1977.

Esfandiary, F. M. *Optimism one.* New York: Popular Library, 1978.

Lindaman, E., & Lippitt, R. *Choosing the future you prefer.* Washington, D.C.: Development Publications, 1979.

Schindler-Rainman, E., & Lippitt, R. *Taking your meetings out of the doldrums.* San Diego, Calif.: University Associates, 1975.

White, R. K., & Lippitt, R. *Autocracy and democracy.* New York: Harper & Row, 1960.

REVIEW QUESTIONS

1 Summarize Lippitt's views on how leader-follower relationships will change in the late 1980s.
2 Explain the difference between a proactive and reactive membership stance.
3 To what degree do you feel Lippitt is predicting actual trends in leadership, not just advocating his views of what would be desirable? Explain.

READING 72

A Case for the Relational Manager

Harold J. Leavitt
Jean Lipman-Blumen*

Both the changing world and our own common sense indicate that the relational side of U.S. organizations needs shoring up. Although direct observers of the management scene have been sending similar messages for a long time, their case is even stronger in today's world.

*From *Organizational Dynamics*, Summer 1980, pp. 27–32. © 1980 by AMACOM, a division of American Management Associations. All rights reserved. Reprinted with permission.

We seem continually to rediscover the truism that people really do need people; that communal hunger, however social scientists may label it, is deep, primitive, and important. Fritz Roethlisberger observed that need way back in the 1920s and described it lucidly:

> These (informal) relations of interconnectedness among persons . . . I call the strong, close, and warm relationships. They make the cheese more binding. The hierarchical ones in contrast are weak, distant, and cold. I do not draw these conclusions from any logic, but from observing the behavior of the persons in the systems we studied. . . .
>
> Whenever and wherever it was possible [employees] generated [these informal relationships] like crazy. In many cases they found them so satisfying that they often did all sorts of nonlogical things (that is, things that run counter to their economic interests) in order to belong to the small, warm, and cozy groups which these relations generated.
>
> The two kinds of relations were in sharp contrast. Among members of hierarchical relations, there were very few interactions, few close friends, and seldom any small, warm, cozy groups. There was sometimes "respect," but quite often distrust, apprehension, and suspicion.
>
> It was an unconscious battle between the logic of management and the sentiments of workers.

Here, we shall approach these same issues, but from a different perspective: the perspective of recent research on *achieving styles*. We also shall put forward some modest how-to-do-it suggestions for those managers who may decide they want to edge their organizations toward a more relational posture.

ACHIEVING STYLES AND THE MANAGING PROCESS

Our approach starts by dividing achieving styles into two major categories: *direct* and *relational. Direct* styles are get-it-done, task-oriented styles. Direct types of people do it themselves, organize and compete to win it—no matter what the "it" happens to be. *Relational* styles, in contrast, always involve intervening relationships with other people. Relational managers help, support, and back up other people—often getting their kicks from contributing to the success of others, or from a true sense of belonging.

Trying to convince tough-minded managers that they ought to become less direct and more relational may be like trying to convince them to give up their private offices. Most of us around organizations give a perfunctory nod to the notion that we ought to run a happy ship, but the bottom line is our unit's measurable, observable performance.

While the ideal image of the American manager may vary, one thing it never includes is a large dose of self-effacing altruism. The usual images of the effective manager are much more macho than that: the tough competitor, or the power-oriented director of other people's lives, or the logical, steel-minded decision maker, or the shaker and mover.

We do not (repeat, not) assert that relational behavior is necessarily the road to executive success in most U.S. organizations at this time. The direct models are still the ones that make it almost everywhere. Data from contemporary research indicate that people who now get to the top in management are strongly power-motivated. They do not typically show strong needs for affiliation—for those close, cozy groups that Fritz J. Roethlisberger observed.

But the organizational world is not fixed; it is slowly changing. So it seems quite possible that researchers will "discover" some years from now that successful managers are more relational than they had believed and less competitive or power-oriented. That does not seem an unreasonable possibility, particularly if we use a reverse example from the past: People with relational styles fare pretty well as elementary school teachers in 1980. Is that because of the nature of the profession or the nature of the contemporary educational environment? Would the same have been true in an earlier era when we believed that sparing the rod would spoil the child? Wouldn't people with greater power and control needs have been more consonant with that educational milieu?

Some relevant questions we have been worrying about include these:

• How much is the maintenance of the direct "macho" model of the executive an archaic rearguard action clung to by organizations that either don't recognize or don't know how to deal with changing realities?

• Do competitive, power-driven people now succeed because of the inherent nature of organized work, or because that's the way we set up our organizations in the old days and changing now is very painful?

• Does the direct, competitive, power image of the executive at least partly reflect the old organization's effort to attract people like itself from the shrinking population of young people who still share those standards?

Sterling Livingston points out one of the oddities surrounding this issue:

> One of the least rational acts of business organizations is that of hiring managers who have a high need to exercise authority, and then teaching them that authoritative methods are wrong and that they should be consultative or participative. It is a serious mistake to teach managers that they should adopt styles that are artificial and inconsistent with their unique personalities. Yet this is precisely what a large number of business organizations are doing; and it explains, in part, why their management development programs are not effective.

This quotation agrees with our observation of what happens. But we would interpret it a little differently from the way Livingston does. If it's that hard to teach consultation and participation to people with a high need to exercise authority, let's not throw out consultation and participation. Let's start hiring more flexible people who *can* be taught.

RELATIONAL MANAGEMENT AND THE CHANGING WORLD

Before moving to our model of achieving styles, we need to elaborate on the assertion that times are indeed changing in a direction calling for more *relational* managerial styles.

Consider the following findings and current trends:

1. Despite the widespread macho mythology about competitiveness in the executive suite, Janet Spence and Robert L. Helmreich, in work closely related to

ours, point out that competitiveness does not seem to be the key to success. Other, more "intrinsic" styles that they call "work" (preference for getting on with the work) and "mastery" (an interest in mastering skills and the like) seem to play a far bigger role.

2. *Young people are shifting their values and interests (not radically, but incrementally) away from careers as their central life focus and toward a concern about general "lifestyle."* Some of what that means is an interest in long weekends, sailboats, and a temperate climate. It also seems to mean a wish for a more pleasant and challenging work environment.

What's new in all this is the slow but steady increase, over the last decade, in the extent to which young managers emphasize those wants.

3. *The hunger for warm, affectionate relationships appears to be growing in the United States.* Many of the traditional institutions that provided people with a sense of membership and community have been declining. And faith in them has been declining more rapidly. The psychological and social vacuum left by their decline may be one reason that young people (and perhaps old people, too) seem to be trying to build new kinds of highly relational institutions. In the early 1970s, we saw a rash of such rebuilding attempts: communes, encounter groups, refurbished old religious movements, and newly invented cults. Almost all of these "experiments" carried with them a search for group, familial, or communal bonds.

4. *American managers now tend to see Japanese organizations as competent and innovative, not as industrial copycats.* Most scholars who have tried to pinpoint the key difference between Japanese and American management styles emphasize the *relational* quality of Japanese organizations. Japanese managers seem to build stronger social bonds among their employees. They invest more in company-related social activities. They are far less individually competitive (at least overtly) within their organizations. The Japanese organizational system rewards managers primarily for developing subordinates and emotionally supporting their supervisors; American firms, by contrast, more often reward employees for their own individual performances.

5. *Firms using strongly relational styles often are successful in the United States.* Recent studies of American companies, derived from earlier observations of Japanese organizations, suggest the advantages, including the cost effectiveness, of a relational milieu. The research indicates that even within the same industry, many companies with "relational" cultures seem to work at least as effectively as more internally competitive firms even when judged by the usual financial and economic criteria.

6. *Women are moving into management.* Women's entry into the executive suite initially was interpreted by some managers as a government-imposed hardship. But many managers recognize that an important advantage has accrued to organizations that have brought women into their managerial ranks. These organizations now have access to a large number of people in our society who traditionally have been trained to a very high level of relational orientation and skill.

7. *Divorce between the individual and the organization is becoming more difficult.* Selection and promotion procedures increasingly are coming under public

scrutiny. Partly in response to the Freedom of Information Act, managers are confronting demands for opening their personnel evaluation files, for laying bare their previously well-guarded personnel decisions. As the difficulty of justifying their hiring and firing practices increases, managers begin to place greater emphasis on "getting along" with their staffs. Like their European and Japanese counterparts, American companies increasingly find themselves compelled to create satisfactory ways to live with the collection of people who are currently there. Even forced retirement no longer can guarantee the departure of unwanted workers. Paradoxically, while divorce between husband and wife becomes easier, divorce between company and employee is becoming much more difficult.

8. *More and more, the tasks of contemporary organizations (particularly in high technology industries) require teamwork.* The industrial engineer and the computer have not obviated the need for committees, task forces, or project teams. Indeed, high technology seems just the nutritional medium in which committees grow. Teamwork becomes a term with much more immediate organizational meaning than it ever had before. And effective teamwork requires both competent individuals and a collaborative spirit. Buying collections of individual stars does not necessarily produce great team performance unless those stars can be bonded together with some strong relational glue.

9. *Where growth has slowed, the direct/competitive model is less functional.* The traditional reward of quick promotion for the aggressive young executive begins to dry up as growth rates decelerate. Satisfactory alternative rewards are hard to find, particularly for those preselected to view the world competitively. Since opportunities for relational rewards are largely independent of organizational growth, more relational people might very well create many of their own rewards, even in a levelled-off organization.

COUNTERRELATIONAL FORCES

While such forces drive toward relational organizations, one can also argue that sometimes these, plus other strong forces, appear to be driving in the opposite direction. Increased government regulation requires more impersonal, nonrelational lockstepped uniformity of rewards and control procedures. And innovations in informational technology point toward a console-to-console world without much need for human interaction.

But if such depersonalizing forces are growing, doesn't that only increase the relevance of the relational issue? One reason for government's expanding intrusion into management is the belief (true or not) that human beings are not always treated humanely in contemporary organizations. Paradoxically, by imposing rules and regulations, government may only be exacerbating that problem. And the informational innovations we can expect—like the automated office—also seem likely to intensify the relational problems of organizations. This argument assumes that human beings will continue to be the basic units in organizations and that they will still need and seek human interaction.

Taken together, the changes we are viewing seem to dictate a prescription for incremental, modest, but real shifts toward more relational strategies.

*   *   *

REVIEW QUESTIONS

1 Why do the authors predict that relational management will become more important?
2 How does relational management compare with Likert's concept of supportiveness?

EXERCISES

Labor Force Values*

OBJECTIVES

1 To identify the work values and attitudes of new entrants to the labor force
2 To explore the managerial implications of diverse employee values

ADVANCE PREPARATION

1 Read the related readings in Chapter 3
2 Read the Introduction
3 Complete Steps 1 and 2

INTRODUCTION

Television commentator Chet Huntley once remarked that "the degree of igno-rance concerning economics in this country is incredible. . . ." Is there a basis for such a remark? And are younger persons (high school graduates) especially guilty of such ignorance? If the problem is primarily a lack of knowledge, perhaps the problem can be solved quite readily through basic economic education.

However, if the problem is one of negative attitudes toward work among workers and the public, a more complex picture emerges. One challenge is for the managers of such employees to be aware of these attitudes or, as the title of this section implies, to better understand people in organizations. Substantial evi-dence suggests that most people are a product of the environment in which they were raised. In other words, a major social, political, or economic factor in our early lives may have had a strong impact on our present values. Examples include the Great Depression, World War II, television, and the Vietnam conflict. In particular, many people now believe that the "work ethic" has become unpopu-lar, thus accounting for the United States' slower growth in productivity in recent years compared with other countries.

The challenge for the managers of today is to become familiar with the work values of their employees and then examine the impact of such knowledge in the motivational strategies used to elicit productive behaviors. This exercise focuses attention on a sampling of relevant economic issues.

*Source: Louis B. Tagliaferri, "Understanding and Motivating the Changing Work Force," *Train-ing and Development Journal*, June 1975, pp. 18–22.

Step 1

Answer each of the following questions:

1 Do you believe that, nationwide, employers could give employees a 10 percent-an-hour raise, now, *without any effect on profits*?   Yes___No ___

2 Do you believe that employers generally benefit from increased productivity *at the expense of workers*?   Yes___No ___

3 What do you believe is the average net corporate profit rate (as a percentage of sales)?   ___%

4 Do you believe that you can increase your standard of living by producing more on the job?   Yes___No ___

5 Do you believe:

   a that hard work no longer pays off?   Yes___No ___

   b that it is immoral to ask workers to work up to their capacities?   Yes___No ___

   c that you (will) feel negatively about being supervised?   Yes___No ___

   d that the government should control major industries?   Yes___No ___

   e in the value of profits?   Yes___No ___

6 Do you basically have confidence in the actions of major U.S. companies?   Yes___No ___

7 Do you prefer to work for a business organization?   Yes___No ___

Step 2

Provide your best estimate of the responses obtained from recent (mid-70s) nationwide surveys. In other words, what data do you believe were reported in response to the following questions? Record your estimates in the "Individual estimate" column.

	Individual estimate	Group mean	Group range	Actual data
1 What percent of the present work force believe that their employers could give them a 10 percent-per-hour raise, NOW, *without any effect on profits*?	___	___	___	___
2 What percent of workers believe that their employers benefit from increased productivity *at the expense of workers*?	___	___	___	___
3 What do U.S. citizens believe average net corporate profits (as a percentage of sales) are?	___	___	___	___
4 What percent of employees believe that they should produce more to increase their standard of living?	___	___	___	___

5 What percent of incoming workers to the labor force:

  a believe that hard work no longer pays off?   _____   _____   _____   _____

  b believe that it is immoral to ask workers to work up to their capacities?   _____   _____   _____   _____

  c feel negatively about being supervised?   _____   _____   _____   _____

  d feel that government should control major industries?   _____   _____   _____   _____

  e do not believe in profits?   _____   _____   _____   _____

6 What percent of the following groups of American people expressed confidence in major U.S. companies?

  a in 1966?   _____   _____   _____   _____

  b in 1972?   _____   _____   _____   _____

  c in 1972, young people, ages 18–20?   _____   _____   _____   _____

7 What percent of graduating high school seniors stated that they would prefer *not* to work for business organizations?   _____   _____   _____   _____

Step 3

The group leader will now accumulate Step 2 data from the class, allowing you to estimate an approximate group mean response, as well as the range of estimates for each item.

Step 4

The group leader will now report to the class the actual results from a series of surveys. (1 = 66%, 2 = 80%, 3 = 28%, 4 = 24%, 5a = 69%, 5b = 62%, 5c = 64%, 5d = 55%, 5e = 61%, 6a = 55%, 6b = 27%, 6c = 15%, 7 = 70%.)

DISCUSSION QUESTIONS

1 Were your perceptions of the survey responses relatively accurate/inaccurate? Why?

2 Was the class's perception (group mean) of the survey responses relatively accurate/inaccurate? Why?

3 Was there a wide or narrow range of individual estimates? Why?

4 Compare your responses (Step 1) with the actual data (Step 4). Are they similar/different? Explain.

5 Groups of organizational managers who have completed this exercise are typically shocked at the actual data. Why? What is the impact of their holding inaccurate perceptions of the values and attitudes of their present/prospective employees?

6 Develop strategies designed to:
  a educate new employees in the facts (e.g., the meaning of profits, or profit rates)

  b sensitize managers to the actual attitudes of new employees on these and other topics

EXERCISE 2

Managerial Responsibility

OBJECTIVES

1 To examine the employee's feelings of responsibility toward the work organization

2 To explore the relationship between personal behavior and job expectations

ADVANCE PREPARATION

1 Study the related readings in Chapters 3 and 19

2 Read the Introduction

3 Complete Steps 1 and 2

INTRODUCTION

New employees are socialized by the work environment to act in organizationally acceptable ways. This is accomplished through several means: corporate policy documents, informal briefings and orientations, the models provided by key supervisors and executives, and the informal word from other employees.

New employees are challenged to merge these normative inputs with their own value systems that define what is right and wrong. In the absence of clear policy guidelines, employees may often procrastinate confronting numerous issues of ethics and responsibility until they are forced to do so. At that time, the minimal forethought involved may easily result in a crisis-oriented decision that lacks rationality or careful consideration of the consequences.

In an era in which some employees are becoming disenchanted with the work ethic and alienated from their jobs, it is particularly important to make conscious decisions about job involvement. This exercise allows the students to evaluate their personal attitudes toward a number of job-related behaviors and share this rationale with other group members.

Step 1

Examine the items in the Managerial Responsibility Form on pages 513–514. Each item describes a behavior that may or may not be related to job performance. Indicate with an "X" for each statement the degree to which you believe that it would describe *your own* behavior on your job.

Step 2

Compute your personal Managerial Responsibility Index in this manner. Total the number of "Disagree" responses (= D). Total the number of "Somewhat Agree/Somewhat Disagree" responses (= S). Compute as follows:

$$MRI = \frac{23 - D - .5S}{23}$$

Report your Index score to the instructor so that she or he may prepare a distribution showing the range of individual scores.

Step 3

Your instructor may now compute a Managerial Responsibility Index for each of the items (if time allows). This may be done easily by asking for a show of hands indicating the number of "Disagree," then "Somewhat Agree/Somewhat Disagree" responses to each of the twenty-three items (record the total on the form). Compute the class's overall Managerial Responsibility Index for each item as follows:

$$MRI = \frac{N - D - .5S}{N}$$

where N = the total number of students responding

DISCUSSION QUESTIONS

1 How close was the similarity among class members with regard to their individual Managerial Responsibility Index scores? Why are there differences?

2 With regard to the class's overall MRI scores for the twenty-three items, which items received high scores (close to 1.00) and which received the lowest scores (closer to 0)? What does this mean?

3 How does a new employee go about finding out what factors the organization (or your boss) deems most important in defining acceptable employee behavior?

MANAGERIAL RESPONSIBILITY FORM

Behaviors	Disagree	My feelings (check one) Somewhat agree/ somewhat disagree	Agree
1 Not to engage in theft of organization property, no matter how small	———	———	———
2 To return to work promptly after all established work breaks	———	———	———
3 To tell management whenever I observe another employee breaking a rule	———	———	———
4 To respect all confidences associated with organization position	———	———	———
5 To depart work no earlier than the established time	———	———	———
6 To refrain from any actions on the job which could harm the reputation of the organization even though they would not break the organization's rules	———	———	———
7 To make known personal ideas or methods that could benefit the organization regardless of whether I am compensated for those ideas	———	———	———
8 To safeguard information that might be beneficial to competitors	———	———	———
9 To safeguard my own health and the health of my fellow employees	———	———	———
10 To prepare for greater responsibility	———	———	———
11 To refrain from any actions off the job which could harm the reputation of the organization	———	———	———
12 To work for only one employer at a time	———	———	———
13 To speak favorably of the organization and its management to outsiders	———	———	———
14 To be active in groups and clubs which promote the general interests of business	———	———	———
15 To hold the goals of the organization above personal non-work goals which affect the job	———	———	———
16 To work at home on my own time if necessary to finish a job	———	———	———

17 To avoid the kind of careless actions, either on or off the job, that could compromise or weaken the competitive position of the organization   _____   _____   _____

18 To study information related to the job on my own time   _____   _____   _____

19 To purchase my organization's products or services rather than those of my competitors   _____   _____   _____

20 To ensure that my family's conduct reflects favorably on the organization   _____   _____   _____

21 To vote for issues and individuals which support the interests of the business community   _____   _____   _____

22 To get enough rest and sleep necessary for effective performance on the job   _____   _____   _____

23 Not to drink alcoholic beverages immediately before or anytime during the working day   _____   _____   _____

Source: Reprinted from John P. Loveland and Jack L. Mendelson, "Employee Responsibility: A Key Goal for Managers," *Human Resource Management*, vol. 13, no. 1, Spring 1974, pp. 32–36, Graduate School of Business Administration, University of Michigan, Ann Arbor. Used with permission.

EXERCISE 3

Expectancy Theory

OBJECTIVES

1 To clarify the major elements of the expectancy theory of motivation
2 To explore reasons why it might, and might not, work in practice

ADVANCE PREPARATION

1 Study the related readings in Chapter 4
2 Read the Introduction
3 Obtain a source of money (up to $4.20), a set of child's building blocks, and some blindfolds
4 Complete Step 1

INTRODUCTION

Expectancy theory is one approach that attempts to explain human motivation. It is based on the premise that employees choose to release energy at work as a function of two factors: valence and expectancy. Valence (V) is the degree to which a reward is preferred, liked, or desired. Expectancy (E) is the probability that a person's performance will lead to a reward. High motivation (M) is believed to result when an employee values a reward and expects that performance will bring about rewards, or $M = V \cdot E$.

This theory seems intuitively logical to many people. However, it may prove difficult to measure and (affect) the variables in practice. Furthermore, a manager faced with the task of computing the probable motivation of ten to fifteen subordinates would face a difficult task. The following exercise will demonstrate some of these problems.

Step 1

Four possible combinations of high and low (or uncertain) levels of valence and expectancy are shown below in Table 1. Rate the predicted effect of each combination in terms of their probable motivation. (A = high, B = moderate, C = low.)

Step 2

Four volunteers from class should be randomly assigned to each of the four possible combinations as shown below. Their task will be to stack twenty blocks vertically within one minute while using their nondominant hand only. Their possible reward will be 5 cents or $1, and their expectancy will be manipulated as high or low by blindfolding the "low" group. Complete the series of four trials as described, and observe the actual level of performance, recording the data as successful or unsuccessful in the far right column.

TABLE 1
PREDICTED MOTIVATION

Situation	Valence	Expectancy	Probable motivation
1	High	High	_____
2	High	Low	_____
3	Low	High	_____
4	Low	Low	_____

TABLE 2
OBSERVED MOTIVATION

Situation	Valence	Expectancy	Performance (motivation)
1	High ($1)	High (visual)	_____
2	High ($1)	Low (blindfolded)	_____
3	Low ($.05)	High (visual)	_____
4	Low ($.05)	Low (blindfolded)	_____

Step 3

Members of the class should now share their predicted motivation ratings for the four categories from Table 1. Note the frequency distribution of these predictions. Compare.

DISCUSSION QUESTIONS

1 Which situation resulted in the highest motivation? The lowest? Did these conform to your predictions?

2 Why might there be a discrepancy between the predicted results (Table 1) and the actual (Table 2)?

3 What factors would make it difficult in practice to use the expectancy theory to predict or affect motivation?

4 How might you go about gathering the information necessary in expectancy theory to better predict an employee's motivation?

EXERCISE 4

Behavior Modification

OBJECTIVES

1 To demonstrate the potential of behavior modification for changing behavior
2 To raise issues regarding the application of such procedures

ADVANCE PREPARATION

1 Study the related readings in Chapter 4
2 Read the Introduction

INTRODUCTION

Behavior modification is any systematic attempt to change behavior through the manipulation of rewards and punishments contingent upon the behavior. Following the premise that most behavior is a function of its consequences, a manager might attempt to increase an employee's responses by providing positive effects or decrease a certain behavior by administering negative consequences. Reinforcers and punishers are operationally defined by their demonstrated ability to change behavior. These are administered on a schedule, which might be continuous or partial. If it is partial, the consequences might be used on fixed or variable, ratio or interval bases. In general, continuous reinforcement is often most potent early, followed by variable ratio schedules.

Problems in behavior modification include precisely specifying the behavior to be changed, developing a measure of the frequency of the behavior, defining what will truly act as reinforcement (or punishment), and administration according to the defined schedule.

Step 1

Divide into small groups (four or five persons). Develop a plan for changing some element of your instructor's behavior (or that of a fellow student). Prepare a report to the class that focuses on:

a the behavior to be changed
b the measurement process
c the reinforcer
d the schedule of reinforcement
e the problems anticipated

Step 2

If possible, implement the behavior modification plan for a brief period of time. Describe the results, as compared with your expectations. Present both reports (before and after) to the class.

DISCUSSION QUESTIONS

1 Why were you (not) able to induce a change in behavior?

2 What flaws were in your plan?

3 What other factors prevented your plan from being as effective as you had hoped?

4 What are the ethical factors involved in trying to change someone else's behavior?

EXERCISE 5

Strokes

OBJECTIVES

1 To demonstrate the different combinations of positive and negative, conditional and unconditional strokes
2 To illustrate the fact that each person's need for strokes, and practice of stroking others, is different

ADVANCE PREPARATION

1 Study the related readings in Chapter 4
2 Read the Introduction
3 Working individually, complete steps 1, 2, and 3

INTRODUCTION

A stroke is any form of recognition that one person gives to (receives from) another person. Strokes may be physical (touch) or psychological (words), and therefore help satisfy either biological or emotional needs.

Everyone has a need for strokes. It is important to recognize that there are several different types of strokes, there are many sources (e.g., boss, friend, self), and the perceived value of strokes may vary from very small to very large.

Four important types of strokes are defined here. Positive strokes are those that make a person feel good when they are received. They contribute to a feeling of well-being, or OK-ness. Negative strokes do not feel good when they are received (they hurt us). They tend to detract from our self-image, and make us feel NOT OK.

Conditional strokes are only given subject to a prerequisite behavior (e.g., "*if* you do this, *then* I will stroke you"). The stroke is dependent upon the earlier activity. Unconditional strokes are words or behaviors or rewards that are offered freely, with no strings attached. They are earned simply by *being* someone or something.

Since strokes vary in their potency, it is helpful to think of them in units of one. Therefore, a glance from a stranger may be a one-unit stroke; a warm and extended gaze from a close friend may be a seven-unit stroke; a paycheck may be a forty-unit stroke.

Step 1

Consider all the strokes you receive on a typical day. How many *total* units of strokes do you believe you receive? _____ How many do you feel you *need*? _____ How many units of strokes do you believe that you *give* each day? _____

Step 2

Examine the chart below. The objective is to estimate the proportion of the total strokes you *receive* that fall into each of the four categories of combinations. You may either fill in the four boxes (A, B, C, D) directly so that they total 100 percent of your strokes received, or you may follow this procedure:

Estimate the proportion of positive versus negative strokes received (e.g., 65/35), and record those numbers in boxes E and F. (They must total 100 percent.) Then estimate the proportion of conditional versus unconditional strokes received (e.g., 20/80), and record those numbers in boxes G and H. (They must total 100 percent.) Now multiply the intersecting rows and columns to obtain an estimate of the four combinations (e.g., $E \times G = A$, $E \times H = B$, $F \times G = C$, and $F \times H = D$).

COMBINATIONS OF STROKES RECEIVED FROM OTHERS

	Conditional	Unconditional	Total
Positive	A	B	E
Negative	C	D	F
Total	G	H	

Step 3

Similarly, examine the chart below. The objective is to estimate the proportion of the total strokes you *give* that fall into each of the four categories of combinations. Use the same procedure as in Step 2 to accomplish this.

COMBINATIONS OF STROKES GIVEN TO OTHERS

	Conditional	Unconditional	Total
Positive	A	B	E
Negative	C	D	F
Total	G	H	

Step 4

Report your data to the class (or in small groups). Examine the range of scores. Explore the reasons for similarities and differences.

DISCUSSION QUESTIONS

1 Why do our perceived needs for strokes vary among individuals?

2 Why does our practice of giving strokes to others vary?

3 Assuming that there is an imbalance between the strokes given versus received, or needed versus received, what are the implications?

4 Are the four categories of strokes meaningful—in other words, can you tell when you have received (given) each of the four types?

5 What is the dominant pattern of strokes received from others? Is this a favorable mix?

6 What is the dominant pattern of strokes given to others? Is this a desirable mix?

7 What personal plan do you have for revising your stroke-giving, or stroke-receiving, behavior?

Job Satisfaction Analysis

OBJECTIVES

1 To demonstrate individual differences in job satisfaction
2 To explore the relationship between satisfaction and productivity
3 To illustrate the potential uses and abuses of satisfaction information

ADVANCE PREPARATION

1 Read the Introduction
2 Study the related readings in Chapters 2, 4, 5 (especially), 11, and 16

INTRODUCTION

Job satisfaction is a set of favorable or unfavorable attitudes with which employees view their work. It expresses the amount of agreement between an employee's expectations from a job and the rewards that the job actually provides. This satisfaction level is dynamic, meaning that it can change over time (sometimes quickly).

Job satisfaction has many different elements, and is not simply the sum of its parts (because its components may interact with each other). It also has a complex relationship to employee performance. Contrary to popular belief, performance level may actually lead to employee satisfaction, rather than the other way around. Job dissatisfaction often is a predictor of absenteeism, turnover, theft, and other negative employee behaviors. Consequently, it is important that managers understand the idea of satisfaction, and monitor and use the information in the workplace.

Step 1

Working individually, analyze the incident below, using the discussion questions as a guide.

As the manager of a small group of workers, you have just received the results of a confidential survey of job satisfaction which was taken by an independent consulting firm at your request. The replies were coded in such a way that the employees' names were identifiable to you after the questionnaires were collected and tabulated. The results indicate the rating each of your employees gave the job

	Employees					
Satisfaction area	A	B	C	D	E	F
Communication	2	5	3	7	9	2
Pay	9	6	2	1	8	8
Supervisory relations	6	5	3	5	9	5
Recognition	4	4	1	4	7	1
Employee benefits	9	4	4	2	8	9
Peer relations	5	5	4	6	8	7
Cafeteria	3	4	1	4	6	5
Job security	7	6	3	7	9	7
Growth & advancement	6	5	2	7	8	2
Working conditions	7	5	5	8	9	5
Productivity rating:	9	5	3	3	7	6

satisfaction area on a 9-point scale (9 = highest, 1 = lowest satisfaction). You have also filled in your assessment of each employee's work performance over the last six months, using the same 9-point scale to indicate the level of their productivity.

Step 2

Divide the class into seven groups. Designate one group as the managers, and the other six as employee groups A, B, C, D, E, and F. Assign one person from the managerial group to each employee group, and identify one employee in each group to act the role of the respective employee in the survey above. Then have each pair role-play the interaction between the manager and that employee, who has been called into the manager's office to "discuss what might be bothering you." When the role playing is complete, have observers from each group report what took place, and any suggestions for alternative handling of the interaction.

DISCUSSION QUESTIONS

1 What can you conclude about the overall level of job satisfaction from the data provided?

2 What can you conclude about the job satisfaction level of each employee?

3 What can you conclude about each of the ten specific areas of job satisfaction?

4 What conclusions can you reach regarding the apparent relationship between satisfaction and productivity among your six employees?

5 Is there any ethical problem involved in violating the promised anonymity of the employees' responses to the questionnaire?

EXERCISE 7

Quality of Work Life

OBJECTIVES

1 To stimulate students to consider the meaning of the phrase "quality of work life"
2 To initiate discussions relative to the creation and measurement of quality of work life

ADVANCE PREPARATION

1 Read the related readings in Chapter 10
2 Read the Introduction

INTRODUCTION

Employees, managers, and behavioral scientists have become increasingly concerned about the quality of work life (QWL) in organizations. Although there has long been concern about wages, hours, conditions of work, and job security, the QWL concept extends far beyond these factors. The defining components of contemporary QWL programs are the degree to which employees perceive that they are allowed to influence their work environment and receive awards commensurate with their contributions.

Organizations are now seeking to implement a variety of QWL-improvement programs and measure their impact. Some companies justify expenditures on QWL on the basis of direct improvements in productivity; others are content with the increased job satisfaction which may result from such programs.

Some experts contend that previous QWL experiments suggest these considerations: management must have organizational competence and technical expertise; the union (if present) must be strong; management should initiate QWL discussions; top management and union officials must both explicitly support the QWL programs; supervisors must also have a say in the process (and understand it); the objectives must be carefully evaluated and communicated; the program should be voluntary; a master plan should be prepared; misunderstandings should be resolved on the spot; and QWL programs should be viewed as dynamic and ongoing.

Step 1

Form small discussion groups (four to five persons). Address the question "What factors would create an organization with a really high quality of work life?" List all the ideas generated by the group.

Step 2

Working individually, complete the survey instrument (Figure 1) by checking the five items that are *most* important in your definition of QWL (column A), then the five items that are *least* important (column C), and finally the other six items of moderate importance (column B).

Step 3

Form groups again and quickly share your evaluations with one another so that you may check the degree of common perceptions. (Your instructor may also wish to obtain a quick show of hands from the entire class for the most important factors.)

DISCUSSION QUESTIONS

1 Has your definition/understanding of QWL changed as a result of this brief exercise? In what way?

FIGURE 1
ASSESSING THE FACTORS IN QUALITY OF WORK LIFE

Factors	A Most important (5)	B Moderately important (6)	C Least important (5)
1 *Employee commitment:* feelings of loyalty; a commitment to and concern for the future of the organization			
2 *Absence of developing apathy:* a measure of employee concern and ambition regarding their work			
3 *On-the-job development and utilization:* opportunity for the employee to learn and apply skills and abilities in a meaningful and challenging way			
4 *Employee involvement and influence:* the extent to which employees feel involved in decision making			
5 *Advancement based on merit:* the extent to which management is interested in the progress of individuals and rewards people on the basis of ability, performance, and experience			
6 *Career goal progress:* making progress in the achievement of career objectives and the belief that there are opportunities for further progress			
7 *Relations with supervisor:* the working relationship with one's supervisor as reflected in fairness, honesty, and mutual respect			
8 *Work group relations:* the way employees in a work group provide mutual support and encouragement			
9 *Respect for the individual:* the feeling of being treated as an adult, with respect and dignity			
10 *Confidence in management:* belief that management is aware of and concerned about employee problems and interests			
11 *Physical working environment:* conditions affecting employees' health, comfort, and convenience			
12 *Economic well-being:* receiving adequate financial rewards and having income protection			
13 *Employee state of mind:* whether the employee feels upset or depressed while at work			
14 *Absence of undue job stress:* the relative absence of excessive work demands and pressures which might interfere with doing the job well			
15 *Impact on personal life:* the spillover effect of the job on employees' personal lives			
16 *Union-management relations:* the extent to which the union and management recognize mutual goals and are working together			

Source: Reprinted by permission of the publisher from "Measuring the Quality of Worklife in General Motors . . . An Interview with Howard C. Carlson," *Personnel,* vol. 55, no. 6, November-December 1978, pp. 24–25. ' 1978 by AMACOM, a division of American Management Associations. All rights reserved.

2 How close was the agreement between your preliminary (brainstormed) list of QWL factors and the sixteen in the individual exercise? Explain.

3 Why did you select the five factors you did as most/least significant? How closely did your selection match that of other class members? What implications does this definitional problem have for real-world programs?

4 How would you go about measuring the QWL in an organization?

EXERCISE 8

Organizational Characteristics

OBJECTIVES

1 To demonstrate the differences between organic and mechanistic systems
2 To explore preferences for working under alternative organization structures

ADVANCE PREPARATION

1 Study the related reading in Chapter 12
2 Read the Introduction
3 Complete Step 1

INTRODUCTION

Organizations differ in the ways in which they are structured. In many cases, these differences exist as a conscious response to the nature of their environment, technology, and problems, as well as the personal preferences of their executives. Organizations that are fundamentally different in structure may yet be highly effective if they are congruent with their task environment. Furthermore, various units of a firm may be organized quite differently depending upon whether they are sales-oriented, production-oriented, or research-oriented.

Two extreme types of structures are called organic and mechanistic. Organic systems are most appropriate for firms or units with dynamic environments, where flexible structures are required. Mechanistic systems are more appropriate in stable environments, where the predictability of uniform procedures and policies leads to greater efficiency. Since neither form is ideal for all circumstances, tomorrow's managers must develop their structures on a contingency basis.

Step 1

Examine each of the organizational characteristics listed below. Indicate on each scale the degree to which you would prefer to work in an organization with that feature.

Step 2

Add up your total points from the ten items. Note that high scores (e.g., 40 to 50 points) indicate a strong preference for an organic system, while low scores (e.g. 10 to 20 points) imply that you would feel more comfortable in the traditional, mechanistic system.

Span of control	(Wide)	5 4 3 2 1	(Narrow)
Time span over which employees can commit resources	(Long)	5 4 3 2 1	(Short)
Degree of centralization in decision making	(Low)	5 4 3 2 1	(High)
Quantity of formal rules	(Low)	5 4 3 2 1	(High)
Basis of authority	(Knowledge)	5 4 3 2 1	(Position)
Specificity of job goals	(Low)	5 4 3 2 1	(High)
Opportunity to interact with persons in other units	(High)	5 4 3 2 1	(Low)
Range of compensation between jobs	(High)	5 3 3 2 1	(Low)
Number of levels of authority	(Low)	5 4 3 2 1	(High)
Purpose and content of communications	(Advice & Information)	5 4 3 2 1	(Instructions & Decisions)

Step 3

Share your score with the rest of the class, and note the distribution of scores as well as the mean (or median).

Step 4

Meeting in small groups, assess which items received the clearest endorsement for either organic or mechanistic systems, and which items received mixed responses. Explore the reasons for these similarities and differences.

DISCUSSION QUESTIONS

1 Which organizational system is preferred the most? Why?

2 What problems will result from a conflict between a new employee's expectations of a system and the actual characteristics of a system?

3 What examples of "pure" organic and mechanistic systems can you provide? What evidence is available to you that allows you to label them as one or the other?

4 Which system do you believe would be more motivational to the contemporary work force? Which needs might each system best satisfy?

EXERCISE 9

Formal and Informal Organizations

OBJECTIVES

1 To assess students' perceptions of the formal and the informal organizations
2 To differentiate between the components of the formal and the informal organizations

ADVANCE PREPARATION

1 Study the related readings in Chapter 14
2 Read the Introduction
3 Complete Step 1

INTRODUCTION

There has been a long debate in the organizational literature as to whether the formal or the informal organization plays a more important role in determining motivational climate and organizational effectiveness. Unfortunately, most writers have reflected a distinct and unsupported bias in their views, regardless of whether they are "classical" or "behaviorally oriented" scholars.

The importance of the issue revolves around the assumptions underlying organizational structure and managerial behavior. In other words, our belief that one system of variables or the other holds the key to organizational effectiveness tends to be self-fulfilling in that we may reject valid evidence to the contrary. It is especially important that students of organizational behavior reflect carefully on this issue during a time when they might be overly impressed by the content of a course or the views of their instructor.

This exercise is designed to assess your views of the formal and the informal organizations. It should also provide you with one perspective on the major ingredients of each system so that you may better grasp the complexity of the concepts involved.

Step 1

Working individually, complete Figures 1, 2, and 3. Score yourself on each upon completion of the entire set by applying the key at the bottom of each form.

FIGURE 1

Directions: Assess each of the following sixteen items as to the degree that it elicits a favorable (good) or unfavorable (bad) response in you. Place an "X" on each line in one of the blank spaces to indicate the strength of your feelings (e.g., 7 or 1 means very good or very bad, 6 or 2 means quite good or quite bad, 5 or 3 means only slightly good or slightly bad, and 4 means neutral between good and bad). Check all items.

Items	**Bad** 1	2	3	4	5	6	**Good** 7
1 Authority							
2 Job descriptions							
3 Voluntary teamwork							
4 Performance appraisal							
5 Chain of command							
6 Clique							
7 Personal influence							
8 Policies							
9 Coworker evaluation							
10 Social interaction							
11 Controls							
12 Group cohesion							
13 Organizational objectives							
14 Social group membership							
15 Grapevine							
16 Supervisor							

Key: F.O.E. score: Add responses to items 1, 2, 4, 5, 8, 11, 13, and 16 = _____
I.O.P. score: Add responses to items 3, 6, 7, 9, 12, 14, and 15 = _____

FIGURE 2

Directions: Assess each of the following sixteen items as to the degree that it elicits a strong or weak response in you. Place an "X" on each line in one of the blank spaces to indicate the strength of your feelings (e.g., 7 or 1 means very strong or very weak, 6 or 2 means quite strong or quite weak, 5 or 3 means only slightly strong or slightly weak, and 4 means neutral between strong and weak). Check all sixteen items.

Items	Weak 1	2	3	4	5	6	Strong 7
1 Authority							
2 Job descriptions							
3 Voluntary teamwork							
4 Performance appraisal							
5 Chain of command							
6 Clique							
7 Personal influence							
8 Policies							
9 Coworker evaluation							
10 Social interaction							
11 Controls							
12 Group cohesion							
13 Organizational objectives							
14 Social group membership							
15 Grapevine							
16 Supervisor							

Key: F.O.P. score: Add responses to items 1, 2, 4, 5, 8, 11, 13, and 16 = _____
I.O.P. score: Add responses to items 3, 6, 7, 9, 12, 14, and 15 = _____

FIGURE 3

Directions: Read the following list of terms:

1 Check the formal column if the term is related primarily to the formal organization.
2 Check the informal column if the term is related primarily to the informal organization.

Formal	Informal	Terms	Formal	Informal	Terms
_____	_____	**1** Authority	_____	_____	**9** Coworker evaluation
_____	_____	**2** Job Descriptions	_____	_____	**10** Social interaction
_____	_____	**3** Voluntary teamwork	_____	_____	**11** Controls
_____	_____	**4** Performance appraisal	_____	_____	**12** Group cohesion
_____	_____	**5** Chain of command	_____	_____	**13** Organizational objectives
_____	_____	**6** Clique	_____	_____	**14** Social group membership
_____	_____	**7** Personal influence	_____	_____	**15** Grapevine
_____	_____	**8** Policies	_____	_____	**16** Supervisor

Key: D.S.C. score: Give yourself one point each if you checked "formal" for items 1, 2, 4, 5, 8, 11, 13, and 16; "informal" for items 3, 6, 7, 9, 12, 14, and 15. (Perfect D.S.C. score = 16.)

Step 2

Report your five scores to the instructor for tabulation and computation of mean responses as follows:

Student	F.O.E.	I.O.E.	F.O.P.	I.O.P.	D.S.C.
1	——	——	——	——	——
2	——	——	——	——	——
3	——	——	——	——	——
4	——	——	——	——	——
5	——	——	——	——	——
6	——	——	——	——	——
7	——	——	——	——	——
8	——	——	——	——	——
9	——	——	——	——	——
10	——	——	——	——	——
11	——	——	——	——	——
12	——	——	——	——	——
13	——	——	——	——	——
14	——	——	——	——	——
15	——	——	——	——	——
16	——	——	——	——	——
17	——	——	——	——	——
18	——	——	——	——	——
19	——	——	——	——	——
20	——	——	——	——	——
21	——	——	——	——	——
22	——	——	——	——	——
23	——	——	——	——	——
24	——	——	——	——	——
25	——	——	——	——	——
Mean	——	——	——	——	——

Interpretation of Scores

F.O.E. is Formal Organization Evaluative score, an indicator of the perceived value and benefits of the formal organization for satisfying individual needs.

I.O.E. is Informal Evaluative score, an indicator of the perceived value and benefit of the informal organization for satisfying individual needs.

F.O.P. is Formal Organization Potency score, an indicator of the perceived dominance, pervasiveness, and influence of the formal organization in affecting individual behavior.

I.O.P. is Informal Organization Potency score, an indicator of the perceived dominance, pervasiveness, and influence of the informal organization in affecting individual behavior.

D.S.C. is Differentiating Systems Characteristics score, a measure of the accuracy with which the respondent correctly identified the eight formal organization characteristics and the eight informal organization characteristics.

DISCUSSION QUESTIONS

1 Examine the range of D.S.C. scores in the class, and the overall mean. Why were some persons less than 100 percent accurate? Which items were most frequently misclassified? Why is an understanding of the components of the formal and the informal organizations fundamental to our ability to use them to create effective organizations?

2 Compare your F.O.E. and I.O.E. scores (and those of the class's average). Which was highest? Why? What does this imply about the perceived *usefulness* of each system?

3 Compare your F.O.P. and I.O.P. scores (and those of the class's average). Which was highest? Why? What does this imply about the perceived *strength* of each system?

Note: For your information, a previous study reported data showing that employees believe the formal organization to be significantly stronger (more influential) than the informal; it was also perceived to be more pervasive and dominant than the informal. On the evaluative dimension, respondents perceived that the formal organization was more valuable in satisfying their needs. (See W. E. Reif, R. M. Monczka, and J.W. Newstrom, "Perceptions of the Formal and the Informal Organizations: Objective Measurement through the Semantic Differential Technique," *Academy of Management Journal*, vol. 16, no. 3, September 1973, pp. 389–403.)

EXERCISE 10

Group Decision Making by Consensus

OBJECTIVES

1 To compare the effectiveness of individual versus group decision making
2 To identify the process of achieving group consensus

ADVANCE PREPARATION

1 Read the related readings in Chapter 14
2 Read the Introduction
3 Complete Step 1, working individually

INTRODUCTION

Groups (committees) are used extensively in organizations for investigating problems, performing tasks, and making decisions. Unfortunately, nearly everyone has had a bad experience at some time with regard to groups, a fact that leads to unjust criticism of group effectiveness. Therefore, it is important to be aware of the pros and cons of using groups and to know the circumstances or conditions under which groups are most appropriately used.

On the positive side, groups can draw upon the great wealth of experience and expertise of their members; they can often generate diverse approaches to problems; they can produce a large number of solutions of high quality; they readily accept the decision and feel responsible for it; and the intragroup competitive pressure helps other members to contribute actively and perform well. On the other hand, the strong pressure toward uniformity can lead to unquestioned decisions (group think); some members become more concerned with their own egos than with the group's task; and some members may be either too passive or too domineering in the discussion.

In general, groups work best on those tasks where their feelings and emotions will affect the implementation of the decision, or on those problems to which various members can fruitfully apply logic, facts, or intuition to create a solution. Therefore, one of the most important managerial skills is to properly choose the types of problems appropriate for groups.

Step 1

Examine the list of occupations on the next page. Evaluate each of them on the basis of the amount of occupational prestige you think each one has. In the first column, rank order them from 1 to 15 (1 = highest, 15 = lowest) according to your estimate of their general status in the population today.

WORKSHEET

Occupations	Individual ranking	Group ranking	Key	Individual accuracy	Group accuracy
Accountant	————	————	——	————	————
Farmer	————	————	——	————	————
Flight attendant	————	————	——	————	————
Gas station attendant	————	————	——	————	————
High school teacher	————	————	——	————	————
Janitor	————	————	——	————	————
Lawyer	————	————	——	————	————
Member of clergy	————	————	——	————	————
Migrant worker	————	————	——	————	————
Model	————	————	——	————	————
Nurse	————	————	——	————	————
Plumber	————	————	——	————	————
Police officer	————	————	——	————	————
Taxi driver	————	————	——	————	————
University professor	————	————	——	————	————

Step 2

Form into small discussion groups (three to five persons). Physically arrange yourselves so that you can comfortably see and interact with each other. Proceed to develop a consensus rank order (column 2) from 1 to 15 and enter those numbers in the second column.

Step 3

You may now examine the actual rankings as generated by sociologist Donald Tieman (UCLA) from his data. Enter these data in the "Key" column.

OCCUPATIONAL PRESTIGE KEY

Occupations	Key
Accountant	3
Farmer	8
Flight attendant	7
Gas station attendant	13
High school teacher	4

Janitor	14
Lawyer	2
Member of clergy	5
Migrant worker	15
Model	10
Nurse	6
Plumber	11
Police officer	9
Taxi driver	12
University professor	1

Step 4

Calculate your group's mean "Individual Accuracy" score by computing the *absolute difference* (ignoring pluses and minuses) between your individual answers and the key, and adding them up. Share your personal accuracy score with the other group members and compute a mean individual accuracy score for your group.

Step 5

Calculate the "Group Accuracy" score by computing the *absolute difference* between the consensus ranking and the key, and adding up the fifteen difference scores (ignoring pluses and minuses) to obtain a total.

Step 6

Compare the "Individual Accuracy" and "Group Accuracy" scores. Which is better (lower)? If the group score is lower, explain why the discussion process apparently improved the decision's quality. If the group score is the same or worse, examine why the group did not make the best use of its resources.

Step 7

Compare your results with those of other groups. Was there a consistent pattern? How can you explain the differences observed?

DISCUSSION QUESTIONS

1 What factors caused the groups generally to show improvement over the average of the individual scores (if they did)? What factors might have prevented them from improving?

2 Develop a set of guidelines which, if followed, would assist groups in attaining consensus faster or easier. What does consensus mean to you?

3 What things did your group and its members do well to facilitate its decision process? What did they do poorly? Discuss these factors within your group.

EXERCISE 11

Interpersonal Relationships: Feedback and Disclosure

OBJECTIVES

1 To explore the importance of feedback and disclosure in relationships between superiors and subordinates
2 To identify the forces that contribute to, and inhibit, feedback and disclosure behaviors
3 To create operational examples of interpersonal feedback and disclosure

ADVANCE PREPARATION

1 Study the related readings in Chapters 6 and 16
2 Read the Introduction
3 Complete Step 1, working individually

INTRODUCTION

Effective interpersonal relationships require that both parties understand themselves, are observant of others, and help each other grow through the reciprocal exchange of useful information. Four processes in particular are believed to contribute to greater openness and personal growth: provision of feedback, solicitation of feedback, self-disclosure, and the facilitation of another's self-

Note: This exercise was adapted from Stephen R. Rubenfeld and John W. Newstrom, "The Assessment of Feedback and Disclosure in Interpersonal Relations: An Experiential Exercise," *Developments in Business Simulation & Experiential Exercises*, ABSEL, vol. 11, 1984, pp. 209–212. Used with permission of the authors.

disclosure. In work situations, these four processes or roles are played to greater or lesser degrees by both parties to a relationship, such as a superior and subordinate, or two peers.

New employees may not place sufficient emphasis on the value of developing positive relationships with others, and this lack of concern may contribute to initial adjustment problems. A preferred alternative is to consider in advance the relative importance of these interpersonal factors, determine what prevents their full use, and develop action strategies for implementing them.

Step 1

Examine the eight items in Figure 1. Examine each item carefully, and then rate it on a scale of 1 to 7 according to the importance you would place upon it in a work relationship with your immediate superior.

Step 2

Share your ratings for each of the items with the rest of the class. Note the frequency distribution of the ratings given by the class to each item, and then compute a class average for each.

Step 3

Meeting in small groups, discuss why there were differences in the average importance ratings across the eight processes. You may also wish to explore the reasons why some students rated an individual item relatively high or low in comparison with other students. Then compute the averages of the four "disclosure" item means, and the four "feedback" item means, to see if there is a difference across the two underlying dimensions.

FIGURE 1

Please rate each dimension according to its importance to the formation and continuation of a successful relationship in the work setting that you would have with your SUPERIOR (your boss, supervisor, or manager). Write the appropriate scale number on the line to the right of each dimension.

1	2	3	4	5	6	7
Very unimportant						Very important

MY SUPERIOR'S PROVISION OF FEEDBACK: My Superior provides me with his or her reactions to my behaviors, concerns, values, and attitudes. _____

MY SELF-DISCLOSURE: I reveal to my Superior how I feel about myself, and openly share my emotions, concerns, values, and attitudes with that person. _____

(Continued)

FIGURE 1 *(Continued)*

MY SUPERIOR'S SOLICITATION OF FEEDBACK FROM ME: My Superior actively encourages me to provide him or her with my reactions to his or her behaviors, concerns, values, and attitudes, and my Superior is receptive to my feedback.   _____

MY SUPERIOR'S FACILITATION OF MY SELF-DISCLOSURE: My Superior actively encourages me to reveal my feelings about myself, my emotions, concerns, values, and attitudes, and my Superior is receptive to these disclosures.   _____

MY FACILITATION OF MY SUPERIOR'S SELF-DISCLOSURE: I actively encourage my Superior to reveal his or her feelings, emotions, concerns, values, and attitudes, and I am receptive to those disclosures.   _____

MY SOLICITATION OF FEEDBACK FROM MY SUPERIOR: I actively encourage my Superior to provide me with his or her reactions to my behaviors, concerns, values, and attitudes, and I am receptive to that feedback.   _____

MY SUPERIOR'S SELF-DISCLOSURE: My Superior reveals how he or she feels about himself or herself, and openly shares his or her emotions, concerns, values and attitudes with me.   _____

MY PROVISION OF FEEDBACK TO MY SUPERIOR: I provide my Superior with my reactions to his or her behaviors, concerns, values, and attitudes.   _____

DISCUSSION QUESTIONS

1 How frequently do you think each of the eight processes are actually practiced in work organizations?

a What forces would encourage two people in a superior-subordinate relationship to increase their use of each of the eight behaviors?

b What forces discourage the use of the eight behaviors?

2 Provide some concrete illustrations of how each of the eight processes would sound if they were practiced between two parties (e.g., "How did I do on that project?" for the individual's solicitation of feedback).

EXERCISE 12

Assessment of Type A Behavior

OBJECTIVES

1 To explore the impact of stress on personal health
2 To identify the self-imposed causes of stress
3 To develop methods for reduction of stress

ADVANCE PREPARATION

1 Read the Introduction
2 Study the related readings in Chapter 17
3 Complete Step 1, working individually

INTRODUCTION

Stress is an inevitable part of work, and of life. It may have either positive consequences (e.g., creativity, effort, accuracy) or a negative impact (e.g., lack of concentration, frustration, or chemical dependency). Stress may arise as a product of the job, self, boss, or firm. Examples here include the underutilization of one's abilities, conflicting role demands, and heavy work pressures. Stress is sometimes imposed by the life environment around people (e.g., the frequency and size of personal crises in their lives). Other stress is created by people themselves, through adopting unattainable goals, or defining work as lacking relevance, or through an interwoven set of behaviors.

Two such sets of behaviors, labeled Type A and Type B, have been identified by Drs. Meyer Friedman and Ray H. Rosenman in *Type A Behavior and Your Heart* (New York: Alfred A. Knopf, Inc., 1974). They suggest that the product of Type A behavior is greater risk of heart problems, whereas a Type B person can be equally productive but is much less likely to suffer the consequences of a premature heart attack. The problem is to find a job that does not place unrealistic behavioral demands on us to act in ways that are inconsistent with our basic desires.

Step 1

Examine the thirteen items on the assessment form. Evaluate yourself in comparison with each of the criteria listed there. Circle the number that most closely indicates your honest assessment of the degree to which you typically display that behavior (5 = high degree, 1 = low degree). Total the scores from the thirteen items.

	Low degree			High degree	
1 Vocal explosiveness: habitually accentuating key words even when no real need exists	1	2	3	4	5
2 Perpetual motion: always moving, walking, eating rapidly	1	2	3	4	5
3 Impatience: belief that most events (such as others' speech) take place too slowly; undue irritation at poor drivers, waiting in lines, performing repetitious duties	1	2	3	4	5
4 Polyphasic activity: striving to think about or do two or more things simultaneously	1	2	3	4	5
5 Singular interests: difficulty in refraining from guiding a conversation to subject of extreme interest to you; pretending to listen if unsuccessful at accomplishing goal	1	2	3	4	5
6 Relaxation guilt: feeling guilty when you do absolutely nothing for hours or days	1	2	3	4	5
7 Environmental observation: failure to observe/recall important objects encountered in various environments (office, home, store)	1	2	3	4	5
8 Materialism: preoccupation with things worth *having* to the exclusion of becoming the things worth *being*	1	2	3	4	5
9 Time urgency: attempting to schedule more and more in less and less time, with fewer allowances for unforeseen contingencies	1	2	3	4	5
10 Aggressiveness: meeting another Type A person arouses you to challenge him or her	1	2	3	4	5
11 Gestures: extensive use of dramatic and habitual gestures such as clenching fist, pounding fist into palm, clenching jaw, or grinding teeth	1	2	3	4	5
12 Self-sufficiency: belief that your success has been due to your ability to get things done faster than your colleagues	1	2	3	4	5
13 Numbers: finding yourself committed to evaluating your own (and other's) activities in terms of numbers	1	2	3	4	5

Step 2

Report your score to the instructor so that the entire distribution of scores can be displayed visually. Examine the range of scores and the mean (or median). Are the scores widely or narrowly distributed? Are they generally high (39 or above) or low?

Step 3

Form small discussion groups (four to five persons). Select a business executive or political figure that most students can identify. Quickly develop a consensus assessment of that person's perceived behavior along each of the thirteen dimensions, and total the scores. Briefly report your conclusions to the entire class.

DISCUSSION QUESTIONS

1 What would it be like to work for a person (or organization) who exhibits most of the thirteen behaviors of a Type A person? Is it likely that subordinates would be expected to behave in the same way?

2 It has been suggested that Type A people have difficulty recognizing their own behavior. How comfortable do you feel with your self-assessment? Would your close friends perceive you the same way?

3 Why would Type A persons behave this way? How could Type A persons change if they recognized the physical danger they might cause themselves?

EXERCISE 13

Coping with Work Stress

OBJECTIVES

1 To provide an opportunity for self-assessment of job-related coping behaviors
2 To stimulate students to develop a balanced response to stress

ADVANCE PREPARATION

1 Study the related readings in Chapter 17
2 Read the Introduction
3 Complete Steps 1 and 2

INTRODUCTION

Workaholics—individuals whose work has become so dominant that it interferes with other dimensions of a normal life—have become the subjects of psychological research, as well as social criticism. This behavior involves committing great amounts of time and energy to work in the belief that it will lead to desired organizational rewards (e.g., promotion). However, when work truly becomes all-encompassing, it may produce undesirable side effects in one's personal life or physical/psychological health.

Dr. Alan McClean has suggested that an ideally successful person can adapt to a challenging work environment and yet be productive without extraordinary negative side effects. He describes five characteristics of such persons:

1 They know themselves at all levels, accept their strengths and weaknesses, and capitalize on their important skills.
2 They develop numerous interests away from work.
3 They vary their responses to stressful situations and learn to bounce back quickly.
4 They acknowledge and accept differences among people.
5 They remain active and productive at work, as well as at home in the community.

This exercise will allow you to gain some initial insights into your own propensity to become a workaholic.

Step 1

Complete the Coping Checklist on pages 546–547.

Step 2

Score yourself, using the key at the bottom of the checklist.

Step 3

Report your scores on each of the five scales to the instructor so that the array of scores might be seen and a class mean computed for each.

Step 4

Examine your own higher scale scores (especially those above 12). Develop a personal plan of action for improving on those dimensions.

Step 5

Meeting briefly in small groups, share with the other members your most useful ideas for "how to change yourself."

DISCUSSION QUESTIONS

1 Do you consider yourself a workaholic? Was your general self-perception supported by your Coping Checklist scores? If not, why?

2 Which scales had the highest class mean? Is there a logical explanation for this result?

3 What were some of the more creative ideas expressed for helping people become more effective copers?

COPING CHECKLIST

Directions: Read each of the following twenty statements. Assess the extent to which each statement describes the way you are now (or will probably be on a future job). Circle the appropriate number in each line.

	Very true	Quite true	Somewhat true	Not very true	Not at all true
1 I roll with the punches when problems come up.	1	2	3	4	5
2 I spend almost all of my time thinking about my work.	5	4	3	2	1
3 I treat other people as individuals and care about their feelings.	1	2	3	4	5
4 I recognize and accept my own limitations and assets.	1	2	3	4	5
5 There are quite a few people I could describe as "good friends."	1	2	3	4	5
6 I enjoy using my skills and abilities both on and off the job.	1	2	3	4	5
7 I get bored easily.	5	4	3	2	1
8 I enjoy talking with people who have different ways of thinking about the world.	1	2	3	4	5
9 Often in my job I bite off more than I can chew.	5	4	3	2	1
10 I'm usually very active on weekends with projects or recreation.	1	2	3	4	5
11 I prefer working with people who are very much like me.	5	4	3	2	1
12 I work primarily because I have to survive, not because I enjoy what I do.	5	4	3	2	1
13 I believe I have a realistic picture of my personal strengths and weaknesses.	1	2	3	4	5

14 Often I get into arguments with people who don't think my way. 5 4 3 2 1

15 Often I have trouble getting much done on my job. 5 4 3 2 1

16 I'm interested in a lot of different topics. 1 2 3 4 5

17 I get upset when things don't go my way. 5 4 3 2 1

18 Often I'm not sure how I stand on a controversial topic. 5 4 3 2 1

19 I'm usually able to find a way around anything that blocks me from an important goal. 1 2 3 4 5

20 I often disagree with my boss or others at work. 5 4 3 2 1

Scoring directions: Add together the numbers you circled for the four questions contained in each of the five coping scales listed below.

Coping scale	Add together your responses to these questions	Your score (write in)
Knows self	4, 9, 13, 18	_____
Many interests	2, 5, 7, 16	_____
Variety of reactions	1, 11, 17, 19	_____
Accepts other's values	3, 8, 14, 20	_____
Active and productive	6, 10, 12, 15	_____
		Total score
		_____

*Source: Alan A. McClean, "Is Work All You Do or Prize?" Scene Magazine, November 1979, pp. 83–86. Used with permission.

| | Coping Scale | | | | |
Student	Knows self	Many interests	Variety of reactions	Accepts other's values	Active and productive
1	____	____	____	____	____
2	____	____	____	____	____
3	____	____	____	____	____
4	____	____	____	____	____
5	____	____	____	____	____
6	____	____	____	____	____
7	____	____	____	____	____
8	____	____	____	____	____
9	____	____	____	____	____
10	____	____	____	____	____
11	____	____	____	____	____
12	____	____	____	____	____
13	____	____	____	____	____
14	____	____	____	____	____
15	____	____	____	____	____
16	____	____	____	____	____
17	____	____	____	____	____
18	____	____	____	____	____
19	____	____	____	____	____
20	____	____	____	____	____
21	____	____	____	____	____
22	____	____	____	____	____
23	____	____	____	____	____
24	____	____	____	____	____
25	____	____	____	____	____
Mean	____	____	____	____	____

EXERCISE 14

Interpersonal Conflict

OBJECTIVES

1 To demonstrate the impact of various approaches to conflict
2 To explore some of the common strategies in interpersonal negotiation

ADVANCE PREPARATION

1 Study the related readings in Chapter 18
2 Read the Introduction

INTRODUCTION

There are four major approaches to conflict:

Win-Win—in which each party believes there is a mutually satisfactory solution
Win-Lose—in which one party tries to take advantage of the other
Lose-Win—in which one party tries to lose the struggle (for whatever reasons)
Lose-Lose—in which each party believes that it will be worse off after the resolution takes place

Each of these approaches may be practiced (and observed) in a variety of different contexts. Generally, of course, the most productive approach is the win-win strategy, in which a problem-solving perspective is applied and both parties come out "winners."

There are also several common bargaining tactics in interpersonal negotiations such as:

1 Failure to disclose key information (e.g., weaknesses)
2 Bluffing regarding one's position
3 Threatened or actual walkouts from the discussion
4 Threats of the negative consequences of the other's actions
5 Stretching of the truth
6 Using real or arbitrary deadlines to force a decision
7 Using subterfuge to gain useful information
8 Constructive confrontation, leveling, or problem solving, in which both parties jointly and openly explore the situation for potentially acceptable decisions.

The utility of each of these should be carefully evaluated in advance before their use, to assure that they fit your value system, are appropriate for the task, and show promise of being effective.

Step 1

Divide the class into two-person groups. Each pair should then divide the roles between them, taking either that of Ed Smith or Ray Nelson. Study only your assigned role.

Step 2

At the instructor's signal, engage in role playing within your teams, continuing the conversation until there is a resolution (or obvious lack thereof) between you.

Step 3

Be prepared to report to the instructor:

a whether a deal was made
b if so, the price negotiated
c the strategy used (intended and actual) by each party

Role for Ed Smith

You are a new-car salesperson for the Jones Buick Company in a small town in Arizona. It is the last day of the month and you are one car short of your sales quota of nine cars for the month. If you reach that quota, you get a nice bonus check for $300 in addition to the regular commissions earned during the month. You have sold eight cars this month and get a $200 commission for each. You really would like that bonus check since you and your family leave on a two-week vacation tomorrow and otherwise you may have to cut it short for lack of funds.

You noticed a man (who is dressed like a tourist) currently looking at a new Buick in the showroom, and you are wondering if he is just browsing around or if he might be serious about a new car. He is looking at a car listing at a total price of $8300, which costs the company about $6500, plus the usual minimum of $200 profit and your standard commission of $200. (These latter figures are usually kept confidential to prevent customers from driving too hard a bargain.) You feel that you could sell that car for as low as $6900, but the boss has made several remarks lately about some possible layoffs if the salespeople continue to "give his cars away for a song."

There is only one other new-car dealer in town, and he sells a lower-priced make. Naturally he can give much better deals on his cars, but you are convinced that Buicks have much more to offer in the way of quality.

It is now 4:30 P.M., less than half an hour before closing time. Not a single customer has been around all day so far. You still have a hunch that the man is a tourist, and wonder how serious he is about a car.

Role for Ray Nelson

You and your wife were on your way home from a vacation in Las Vegas when you had the misfortune of having your car catch fire as you approached the outskirts of a small town in Arizona. The car was totally destroyed, but the local insurance adjuster immediately reimbursed you for the full market value of the vehicle—$6800. Since you must leave for home in New York City no later than tomorrow morning, you must buy a new car and get delivery on it today. You intend to pay cash for it since you have the insurance check, and a spare total of $1500 in traveler's checks, and consequently you hope to get the best deal possible.

The car you want is a new Buick sedan just like the one you are looking at, which has the necessary options of power brakes, power steering, air conditioning, automatic transmission, and a radio. Actually this car would be just like your old one, only one year newer.

The sticker on the window tells you that the total price of this car is $8300, including all accessories and taxes. You heard a rumor once that new cars cost the dealer only about 80 percent of the list price, and you tend to believe that that is probably true. You realize that dealers must make *some* profit on their car sales, however, and in addition the salesperson must get a commission for selling the car.

You are perfectly willing to pay a "fair" price for the car, but also hope to make a deal that will save you as much money as possible. As the salesperson approaches you, you mentally review your problems:

1 You *must* have a new car today to get back to New York on time.

2 The only other new-car dealer in town sells a lower-priced make, and your wife told you this morning that under no conditions would she be caught dead in one of those "junk heaps."

3 The better financial deal you can get, the more money you can save toward that much-needed addition to your house this fall.

4 The auto salesroom closes in less than half an hour.

Note: As you browsed around the new-car showroom, you noticed a chart on the manager's wall indicating that one of the salespeople, Ed Smith, was just one car away from reaching his monthly sales quota of nine cars. It is now the last day of the month. You also saw the vacation schedule for the salespeople through the office window: Ed Smith is leaving on a two-week vacation tomorrow.

DISCUSSION QUESTIONS

1 What approach was most clearly taken by each of the role players (win-win, win-lose, etc.)?

2 What approach was most effective?

3 What negotiating skills and strategies were used to obtain the ultimate solution in each case?

4 What suggestions would you have for participants who find themselves in future situations requiring interpersonal negotiations?

INDEXES

AUTHOR INDEX

SUBJECT INDEX